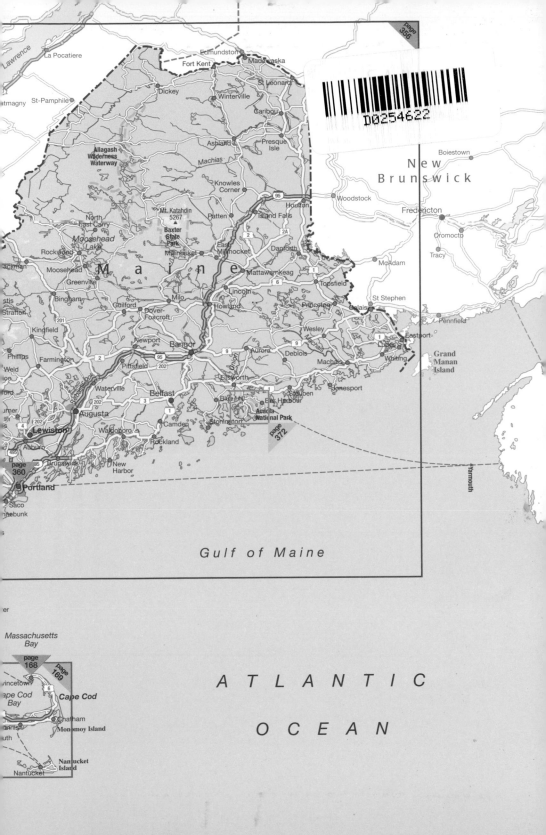

INSIGHT GUIDES

NEW ENGLAND

APA PUBLICATIONS L

Part of the Langenscheidt Publishing Group

INSIGHT GUIDE
NEW ENGLAND

Editorial

Project Editor
Astrid deRidder
Series Manager
Rachel Lawrence
Design
Ian Spick
Map Production
Original cartography Mapping Ideas, updated by Apa Cartography Department
Production
Linton Donaldson

Distribution

UK
Dorling Kindersley Ltd
A Penguin Group company
80 Strand, London, WC2R 0RL
customerservice@dk.com

United States
Ingram Publisher Services
1 Ingram Boulevard, PO Box 3006,
La Vergne, TN 37086-1986
customer.service@ingrampublisher
services.com

Australia
Universal Publishers
PO Box 307
St Leonards NSW 1590
sales@universalpublishers.com.au

New Zealand
Brown Knows Publications
11 Artesia Close, Shamrock Park
Auckland, New Zealand 2016
sales@brownknows.co.nz

Worldwide
**Apa Publications GmbH & Co.
Verlag KG (Singapore branch)**
7030 Ang Mo Kio Avenue 5
08-65 Northstar @ AMK
Singapore 569880
apasin@singnet.com.sg

Printing

CTPS-China

CONTACTING THE EDITORS
We would appreciate it if readers
would alert us to errors or out-
dated information by writing to:
**Insight Guides, PO Box 7910,
London SE1 1WE, England.**
insight@apaguide.co.uk

www.insightguides.com

ABOUT THIS BOOK

The first Insight Guide pioneered the use of creative full-color photography in travel guides in 1970. Since then, we have expanded our range to cater to our readers' need not only for reliable information about their chosen destination but also for a real understanding of the culture and workings of that destination. Now, when the internet can supply inexhaustible (but not always reliable) facts, our books marry text and pictures to provide those much more elusive qualities: knowledge and discernment.

How to use this book

Insight Guide: New England is structured to convey an understanding of the region and its people as well as to guide readers through its attractions:

◆ The **Features** section, indicated by a pink bar at the top of each page, covers the natural and cultural history of the region, together with illuminating essays on the maritime history, architectural traditions, and outdoor adventures to be found in New England.

◆ The main **Places** section, indicated by a blue bar, is a complete guide to all the sights and areas worth visiting. Places of special interest are coordinated by number with the maps. A list of recommended restaurants is included at the end of each chapter.

◆ The **Travel Tips** listings section, with a yellow bar, provides full information on transportation, hotels, activities from culture and shopping to sports, and an A–Z section of essential practical information. An easy-to-find contents list for Travel Tips is printed on the back flap, which also serves as a bookmark.

The contributors

This thoroughly updated edition was managed by **Astrid deRidder**, a Commissioning Editor at Insight whose earlier works include guides to US destinations such as Colorado, Arizona, and Florida.

The text was copyedited by **Wade Newbern**, who left Memphis long ago for New York City, but his musical heart is still in Tennessee. He runs his own jazz group, Newbern & Co; plays keyboards for Chinese pop bands, touring regionally and internationally; and teaches piano and voice to both seniors and whippersnappers. As a copy editor, Wade truly savors correcting things; consequently, he has few friends. He's looking to correct this.

Nothing stands still, even in such a traditional region as New England, and for this edition of one of Insight Guide's classic titles the text has been thoroughly updated by **Fran Severn**, who collects suitcases and carry-ons the way other women collect shoes. She has written about a school for butlers in London, worked on a cattle ranch in New Mexico, ridden camels in Morocco, and gotten lost in the back streets of Jerusalem. A private pilot, she has flown across the US and Canada. Fran has written more than 200 articles for publications as varied as *Delta Sky* and *Western Horseman*, is a contributing writer to the on-line travel publication Striped Pot, and blogs for *Chesapeake Life Magazine*. She currently lives on Maryland's Eastern Shore with her husband, dog, and three horses. Fran was assisted in her writing by **Nicholas Pino**, whose detailed research is greatly appreciated.

Much of the eye-catching photography in this book is the work of **Kindra Clineff**, whose work encompasses national magazine shoots and major advertising campaigns, at home and abroad. She cultivates a perennial garden and keeps bees at her historic 17th-century home in Massachusetts.

Many other photographs come from **Richard**, **Abraham**, and **Daniella Nowitz**. Richard, who lives in Maryland, has worked around the world for Insight Guides since the 1980s and his two children are now accomplished photographers in their own right. Richard has photographed for many travel destinations, including recent editions of Insight Guides to Colorado and Florida.

The text was proofread by **John King**; **Penny Phenix** indexed the book.

Map Legend

— · —	International Boundary
— — — —	State Boundary
— · —	National Park/Reserve
— — — —	Ferry Route
Ⓜ	Subway
✈ ✈	Airport: International/Regional
🚌	Bus Station
✉	Post Office
❶	Tourist Information
∴	Archaeological Site
✝ ✝ ✝	Church/Ruins
☪	Mosque
🏰 🏰	Castle/Ruins
∩	Cave
𝟏	Statue/Monument
★	Place of Interest
⚑	Beach
⟟	Lighthouse

The main places of interest in the Places section are coordinated by number with a full-colour map (eg ❶), and a symbol at the top of every right-hand page tells you where to find the map.

Contents

Maps

Travel Tips

Inside front cover:
New England.
Inside back cover:
Boston subway.

THE BEST OF NEW ENGLAND: TOP ATTRACTIONS

The region's dramatic past is imaginatively re-created, while the land and sea provide a wide range of outdoor recreations

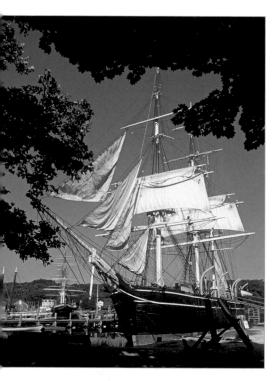

△ **New England cuisine.** Lobsters, maple syrup, and organic produce create New England's culinary delights.
See page 79

△ **Mystic Seaport, Connecticut.** An old whaling port, with vessels such as the *Charles W. Morgan*.
See page 269

▽ **Fall foliage.** Leaf-peepers seek out the best spots to marvel at spectacular hues of red, yellow and orange.
See page 164

△ **Cape Cod National Seashore.** More than 40 miles (65km) of secluded beaches, vast stretches of sand dunes, crashing surf, and swimming in the bracing Atlantic.
See page 172

△ **Freedom Trail, Boston, Massachusetts.** Follow the 2.5-mile (4km) red-brick path linking the major Revolutionary War sites. *See page 138*

△ **Shelburne Museum, Vermont.** Peerless collection of Americana, including the *Ticonderoga*. *See page 304*

◁ **White Mountains, New Hampshire.** A vast tract of rugged peaks, hiking trails and ski slopes, and a unique cog railway. *See page 338*

▽ **Acadia National Park, Maine.** The famed rock-bound coast of Maine preserved in a rugged 41,000-acre (16,500-hectare) parkland. *See page 371*

△ **Philip Johnson's Glass House** The architectural innovator created a new way of considering buildings. *See page 261*

▽ **Newport, Rhode Island.** Extravagant mansions that are monuments to America's Gilded Age. *See page 242*

THE BEST OF NEW ENGLAND: EDITOR'S CHOICE

The sights worth seeing, finding the best hiking and skiing, unique attractions ... here, at a glance, are our recommendations, plus a few tips even the locals may not know

TOP HISTORIC SITES

Freedom Trail, Boston. Follow the red-brick path that links Boston's most important Revolutionary War sites, including the Old State House, Paul Revere's Home, the Old North Church, and the 1797 frigate *Constitution*, alias "Old Ironsides." *See page 138*

Lowell National Historical Park, MA. With many of its massive textile mills still intact, the city's core is now a National Historical Park.

Tour downtown by canal boat or trolley, and visit a mill where power looms still turn out cloth. *See page 150*

Salem Maritime National Historic Site, MA. In the cradle of America's first mercantile fortunes, an old waterfront quarter contains an 1819 Custom House, the home of a merchant prince, and the replica of a 1797 sailing ship. *See page 144*

Minute Man National Historical Park, MA. The events of April 18 and 19, 1775, are brought to life on Lexington Green, where Minutemen and British soldiers first exchanged fire, and at Concord's North Bridge, where Revolutionary hostilities began in earnest. *See page 151*

Coolidge State Historic Site, VT. The preserved birthplace of President Calvin Coolidge isn't just a single home, but all of Plymouth Notch village. You can visit the house where Coolidge took the oath of office by kerosene lamp on learning of President Harding's death. *See page 290*

BEST PARKS

Baxter State Park, ME. This wilderness tract deep in Maine's interior is crowned with Mt Katahdin, the northern terminus of the Appalachian Trail. This is the place to look for moose, black bears ... and supreme solitude. *See page 377*

Acadia National Park, ME. Nowhere is the famed "rock-bound coast of

Maine" better exemplified – and better preserved – than in this rugged parkland. *See page 371*

Kent Falls State Park, CT. Fall Brook cascades down a series of waterfalls as it tumbles its way to the Housatonic River. The park has moderate hiking trails with spectacular views. *See page 254*

ABOVE: the Minute Man memorial.
LEFT: Salem's waterfront.

FINEST MUSEUMS

Museum of Fine Arts, Boston. One of the world's great museums, whose collections include some of the best Impressionist paintings outside Paris. *See page 125*

Shelburne Museum, VT. This matchless collection of Americana, folk and fine art, and vernacular New England architecture features the restored 1906 Lake Champlain steamer *Ticonderoga*. *See page 304*.

Isabella Stewart Gardner Museum, Boston. A Venetian palazzo with fine art, antique furniture, and a flower-filled interior courtyard. *See page 126*

Massachusetts Museum of Contemporary Art, North Adams, MA. One of the world's premier venues for the arts of our times. Soaring galleries for visual arts; theaters for dance, music, and film. *See page 217*

Springfield Museums, Springfield, MA. Wonderful gathering of four museums of art and history, plus the Dr Seuss Memorial Sculpture Garden, clustered around a park-like quadrangle. *See page 203*

LEFT: the Museum of Fine Arts in Boston.
ABOVE: Boston's Museum of Science.

BEST FOR FAMILIES

Mystic Seaport, CT. In this re-creation of a 19th-century waterfront community, shops and chandleries line the narrow streets and the *Charles W. Morgan*, the last surviving American whaling vessel to sail under canvas, rests at wharfside. *See page 269*

The "Big E," MA. There are state and county fairs all over New England, but the biggest is the region-wide Eastern States Exposition in West Springfield. Animal exhibits and judging, amusement rides, and big-name acts fill the 175-acre (71-hectare) grounds for 17 days in September. *See page 204*

Ben & Jerry's Factory Tour, VT. The tour tells the story of how two unlikely entrepreneurs created the famous ice cream, revealing the alchemy behind flavors such as Cherry Garcia and Phish Food. *See page 294*

ECHO Lake Aquarium and Science Center, Burlington, VT. An all-day adventure that goes far beyond other science centers with its range of explorations from under Lake Champlain, to Native American life, to seeing what you look like as a frog. *See page 303*

McAuliffe-Shepard Discovery Center, Concord, NH. Named for New Hampshire's space pioneers, Christa McAuliffe and Alan Shepard, it's a hands-on day of space discovery. *See page 330*

RECOMMENDED HIKES

Appalachian Trail. Linking every state except Rhode Island, the Georgia-to-Maine Appalachian Trail's northernmost portion offers opportunities for day or overnight hiking. *See page 312*

The Long Trail. Vermont's rugged trail, which partly overlaps the Appalachian, scales the Green Mountain peaks. *See page 294*

Block Island, RI. Called "one of the 12 best unspoiled areas in the Western Hemisphere," the heritage trail crosses the island's rolling green hills and ends at the dramatic Mohegan Bluffs overlooking the Atlantic. *See page 238*

LEFT: hiking along the Appalachian Trail.

TOP COLLEGE TOWNS

Cambridge, MA. Home to Harvard and the Massachusetts Institute of Technology (MIT), both have specialized museums, with Harvard's Fogg Museum (art) and Peabody Museum of Archaeology and Ethnology among the region's finest. Harvard Square bustles with shops, bookstores, restaurants, and clubs; Central Square, near MIT, offers inexpensive eateries and eclectic shops. *See page 128*

Hanover, NH. Here is one of the region's loveliest town greens, surrounded by the stately buildings of Dartmouth College. The school's Hood Museum of Art and Baker Memorial Library are cultural highlights. *See page 334*

Burlington, VT. The architectural treasures of the University of Vermont dominate the hilltop above the state's largest city. Church Street Marketplace is lined with boutiques, bars, and restaurants, and the waterfront sparkles with marinas, a natural history museum, and a bike path. *See page 302*

New Haven, CT. This is home to some of America's most spectacular collegiate Gothic architecture, on the campus of Yale University. Yale's impressive array of museums includes a center for British art, a rare book and manuscript library, a museum of natural history, and even a collection of musical instruments. *See page 263*

Worcester, MA. Home to 10 colleges, universities, and graduate schools, it also boasts the Worcester Art Museum, a museum of armor housed in a medieval setting, and an indoor-outdoor natural history museum with a treetop trail, and is the northern terminus of the Blackstone River Bikeway, which runs from Worcester to Providence, RI. *See page 198*

ABOVE: the Biological Sciences Building at Harvard.

FINEST HISTORIC HOUSES

Gillette Castle, CT. A medieval stone mansion on a site overlooking the Connecticut River in East Haddam. *See page 257*

Salem, MA. The homes preserved by the Peabody Essex Museum and Salem Maritime National Historic Site represent the pinnacle of the austerely beautiful Federal style of architecture. *See page 143*

Longfellow House, Cambridge, MA. This spacious Georgian mansion was George Washington's headquarters early in the Revolution and was later the home of Henry Wadsworth Longfellow. *See page 133*

Portsmouth, NH. A treasure trove of Georgian and Federal architecture, including the one-time home of naval hero John Paul Jones. *See page 324*

Newport Cottages, RI. The greatest monuments to America's Gilded Age are the extravagant mansions along Bellevue Avenue. The Breakers, Rosecliff, The Elms, and other monuments to untaxed riches were, amazingly, used for only a few weeks in summer. *See page 242*

LEFT: the Beechwood Mansion in Newport.

ABOVE: Cape Cod National Seashore.

BEST BEACHES

Block Island, RI. It's worth the ferry ride to enjoy these uncrowded strands – remote Mohegan Bluffs, calm State Beach, and Surfers Beach. *See page 238*

Plum Island, MA. Parking is limited, so there are never towel-to-towel crowds. A bonus: the island is one of the East's premier birding destinations. *See page 148*

Cape Cod National Seashore. Options for sunning and (brisk) swimming range from easy-to-reach Nauset in the south to the dune-circled Province Lands and Pilgrim Heights beaches in Provincetown and Truro. *See page 172*

Hammonasset State Beach, CT. The gentle, generally warm waters of Long Island Sound wash this broad, superbly maintained beach that has plenty of parking, and changing facilities. *See page 265*

TOP SKI AREAS

Stowe, VT. Some trails, including the famous "Front Four" on Mt Mansfield, date from the 1930s. The resort boasts spectacular terrain, aerial gondolas, and superb lodging. *See page 295*

Killington, VT. New England's biggest ski area has 200 trails and nearly three dozen lifts. The resort is a study in superlatives – steepest mogul run, a 3,140ft (955-meter) vertical drop, and a 10-mile downhill trail. *See page 290*

Jay Peak, VT. The most reliable snow cover and a variety of trails: harrowing steeps, long cruising runs, and even a slow skiing zone. *See page 299*

Sugarloaf, ME. Plenty of intermediate runs, but nearly half the trails are black diamonds. Glade action is terrific. *See page 380*

Sunday River, ME. Offers great grooming, high-speed quad lifts, and a double-diamond mogul run as foil to its more forgiving cruisers. *See page 381*

LEFT: snowboarding at Sunday River Ski Resort.

YANKEE COUNTRY

Old World traditions blended with New World experiences have melded together to create a region with unique character

No region in America has a longer or more impressive history than New England. Archeologists say the first "New Englanders" were living here as early as 9000 BC, and the Vikings stopped by briefly in AD 1000. But for most people, New England's history begins with the arrival of the Pilgrims in 1620. In the next 200 tumultuous years, it saw the faltering steps of tenuous settlements become the firm strides of healthy colonies and the creation of an education system unmatched in the other colonies or Mother England. Those led to the desire for self-determination that was so strong, it led to a revolution that created a new country and a new form of government.

The symbols of that history are all around: Plymouth Rock, Lexington, and the Old North Church; the whaling ports of New Bedford and Mystic, the fishing fleets of Maine. The literary world stretches from Mark Twain's Hartford home to Walden Pond and Robert Frost's Vermont cottage. And historic names: Adams (Sam and both Johns, and don't forget Abigail), Ethan Allen, and Nathan Hale.

While other areas respect their history, when a conflict arises between preservation and development the "practicality" of abandoning the old often wins. Not so much in New England, where there's an appreciation that the "old" is what gives the current world its value. Every town has its historical society, protecting its past and telling its story. It relishes the stereotypes that charm visitors: vivid autumn leaves, patchwork quilts of farms, trim colonial towns, sailboats on its bays, crashing waves against the coast, lighthouses sending their beams of safety into a fog-shrouded night.

But while rooted in the past, New Englanders reach for the future. Its cities are testaments to reuse and renewal; its schools are magnets for innovation and intellectual achievement; its cultural venues pride themselves on their creative visions in music, dance, and theater.

Though small in size compared to the rest of the country, New England offers a vast range of experiences for visitors to enjoy.

PRECEDING PAGES: Tunrbidge, VT; the Museum of Fine Arts in Boston. **LEFT:** the past on sale at Brimfield Antiques Show. **ABOVE, FROM LEFT:** Hartwell Tavern, Concord, Massachusetts; exhibit in First Harrison Gray Otis House, Boston.

THE LAY OF THE LAND

The Pilgrims believed in a stern, unforgiving God, so perhaps they were not surprised to find themselves in a stern, unforgiving land

Rocky, infertile soil; treacherous coastline; short, unreliable growing seasons; long, harsh winters. You wonder if the *Mayflower* would have had any passengers if they'd known what awaited them. What was it like – this "new" England that the Pilgrims envisioned as the location of their new home?

New England encompasses 66,672 sq miles (172,680 sq km) and consists of the Commonwealth of Massachusetts and the states of Connecticut, Rhode Island, Vermont, New Hampshire, and Maine. It is bounded by Canada to the north, the Atlantic Ocean to the east, Long Island Sound to the south, and New York State to the west. Moving inland from the coastal lowlands in the south and east, the terrain gradually rises to forested hills and culminates in the weatherbeaten peaks of the Appalachian system, represented by the White Mountains to the north and the Green and Taconic mountains and Berkshire Hills to the west.

Pangaea

The familiar New England landscape was formed by glaciers about 20,000 years ago, but what is now the North American continent started long before that. About 225 million years ago, the earth had just one giant land mass, called Pangaea, which was surrounded by one massive ocean. Through the constant shifting of the ocean floor – plate tectonics – Pangaea began to split apart and drift across the ocean to form the continents that we recognize today. How long Pangaea existed before it started to tear itself apart is unclear, but the granite gneiss and schist peaks

of New Hampshire – like Mt Monadnock – are about 400 million years old, and the granite found in eastern Massachusetts is even older – by about another 200 million years. That "Dedham" granite is found in only one other place – western Africa. Vermont's marble splits the difference. Geologists peg that at about 500 million years old.

The glacial effect

The modern landscape of New England was created in the last ice age by its glaciers. About 18,000 years ago, the Laurentide ice cap was 2 miles (3km) thick in some places, and stretched as far south as Pennsylvania. As the massive sheet of ice was forced south by its own bulk and gravity, it pushed everything in front of it – rock, soil,

LEFT: a model of the *Mayflower* in Plymouth, MA.
RIGHT: the colors of fall melt into the blue hills.

and sediment – like a geological bulldozer. If you picture the side of the road after a snowplow has come through, you get an idea of what happened. The rocks and debris scraped up from the road surface at the bottom of the pile of snow are like what the glacier pushed along. And just as that debris is left when the snow melts, the rocks, soil, and sediment from the glacier remained as hills and valleys. Those were dry land on a vast landscape, but it did not stay that way for long. The glaciers did not "retreat" as much as melt, and the water began filling the empty spaces and causing more changes in the land as it coursed through and created the landscape.

rapidly melting ice as it ran underneath the land created landforms that look something like solid waves. Called "drumlins," they're the Boston Harbor Islands and Bunker Hill. New Hampshire's "notches" – Franconia, Pinkham, and Crawford – are U-shaped valleys gouged by glacial movement. A "cirque" has nothing to do with the acrobats of Cirque du Soleil; it does come from French, however. It means an amphitheater-shaped basin with steep walls, usually found at the head of a glacially formed valley. Tuckerman Ravine is an example.

As the glaciers melted, the sea levels rose and played their own role in creating the landscape.

Geologists have names for everything the glaciers created: "glacial moraines" are the hills of rubble and soil left behind as the glaciers retreated. When the melting water rose around them, the moraines became Cape Cod, Nantucket, and Block Island. Up in Maine, meltwater running along the ground that was under the ice created the finger-like spits of land north and east of Casco Bay – "eskers" – of the Boothbays and Bailey Island. Henry David Thoreau's Walden Pond is a glacial "kettle pond." Those are the holes left when a chunk of ice breaks off from a parent glacier, is surrounded by sediment and rocks, and then melts. Elsewhere, some geologists think the wave action of floodwaters of

Originally, fresh water filled the low areas of the moraines, like Block Island and Long Island sounds and Narragansett Bay. But the sea levels rose by as much as 400 feet (12m) and breached the moraines, filling them with salt water. Elsewhere, the weight of the glaciers pushed down the land in many places, which meant that seawater came far inland. Originally, Lake Champlain was an inland saltwater sea because the St Lawrence River connected it to the Atlantic. As the glacial debris closed off the ocean's access, the Champlain Sea drained and became the much smaller, freshwater Lake Champlain, but evidence of its former life remains, like the skeleton of a whale found encased in a 10,000-year-old layer of clay near Burlington.

The most famous and easily recognizable glacial landscape feature is "glacial erratics." The famous stone fences lining the pastures of Vermont are made of these – rocks transported and deposited by glaciers from distant geologic formations. The farmers – then and now – wrestling them from the ground undoubtedly thought (and think) of them as something other than merely "erratic."

As the glaciers melted 10,000 years ago, plants and animals suitable for cold climates appeared – caribou, grasses, the trees that would become sugar maples and pine. This was tundra, the same soil and climate found in Alaska and northern

were a hunter-gatherer society, which practiced what we'd call today sustainable living – taking what was needed and no more and making sure there was enough left for it to regrow or repopulate. They believed in being part of a balance of nature, not that they were to dominate and tame it. It was a concept as alien to Puritan thinking as dressing in buckskins and using bear grease as a hair conditioner.

The Puritans didn't care that the treacherous shoals off the coast of Maine or the tricky navigation around Cape Cod were the results of eons of geologic activity or that the soil so hard to cultivate was barren because of the

Canada. The first humans showed up at about the same time. The earth was warming, and it was gradually creating a climate hospitable for plants to grow and animals and humans to thrive.

The Pilgrims' arrival

By the time the *Mayflower* landed, the region was covered with dense forests filled with game; the rivers provided both drinking water and fish, but they were also the transportation routes and the location for most villages. The Indians did practice some agriculture, but they

ABOVE, FROM LEFT: sunlight filters through the fall foliage on a Vermont backroad; the Portland Head Lighthouse in South Portland, Maine.

scouring action of blocks of ice. They needed to build shelters and plant crops if they hoped to survive. From a psychological perspective, their no-nonsense practicality and conviction that life is supposed to be difficult probably prepared them for the rigors, disappointments, and tragedies they faced. It's as though each obstacle to be overcome hardened them to the next. You have to wonder if they would have remained so stern and so obstinate for so long if they'd made landfall in the Chesapeake, where the 1634 Catholic colony thrived almost immediately, or if they had arrived in May and not November and had a chance to plant a few crops and gather enough food to sustain them over the winter.

Clearing the land was their first priority; without that, there would be no land to cultivate, no way to plant crops. Trees were cut down, rocks laboriously dug from the ground and dragged from fields. Only the flat terrain near Lake Champlain was fertile, open farmland, but it was decades before there was any significant settlement there.

There was plenty of game to be had; the written records tell of groups of men leaving the settlement to go "fowling" and of hunting deer. There's no mention of moose; the behemoth wasn't found in the areas the Pilgrims first settled – Massachusetts, Rhode Island, and Connecticut. One wonders what they would have made of them. What they did have were catamounts – mountain lions. They were a real threat as they could attack people, although the animals more usually went after livestock. But within a century, the cats were gone, victims of the changes the settlers were causing to the land.

The clear-cutting of the forest and establishment of agriculture had a profound effect on the region's ecological balance that no one would have understood. The colonists viewed the forests as both an impediment and a commodity; the trees needed to be cleared, but the wood built their houses and ships and was

THE FIRST ENVIRONMENTALIST

Born in Woodstock VT in 1801, George Perkins Marsh is considered the first environmentalist. Growing up, he witnessed the effects of farming and logging practices. Later, he developed a theory that the actions of humans had a direct effect on the environment. The great civilizations of the Mediterranean, he suggested, had collapsed because of environmental degradation initiated by human activity. Until that time, common wisdom held that all changes were the result of natural phenomena. His 1864 book, *Man and Nature*, explored the interdependence between the natural and man-made worlds.

transported to a Europe which had denuded its vast forests centuries before. They believed that the resource was limitless, so they went about harvesting it with the industriousness that typified everything about their lives. In the first 150 years of colonization, nearly half of Vermont's 6 million acres (2.4 million hectares) of forest had been cut down. The practice set off a disastrous ecological chain of events. In a land where topsoil was already scarce, clear-cutting led to soil erosion as the land had no protection from the effects of rainfall, snowmelt, or wind which made it even more difficult to farm the already challenging land. With their natural habitats, breeding areas, and food sources depleted or eliminated, wildlife declined or migrated

The Pilgrims experienced harsh weather in their first year in New England, including severe rain and snow; although the reports sent back to England focused on the positive rather than dwelling on the harsh conditions.

elsewhere, upsetting the balance between prey and predator. That was further exacerbated by the settlers themselves killing wolves, mountain lions, and other predators. Forage for wild creatures became annoying weeds; damaging insects which had been held in check could

to give areas time to refresh themselves – not unlike modern ideas of crop rotation. The rivers were vital transportation, although in the earliest years, colonists cut crude roadways through the forests, since canoes could never carry the supplies and equipment needed to build houses and farms. They became a valuable resource in the Industrial Revolution, when the swiftly flowing water powered the machinery that powered the region's economic growth. That came at a cost as, once again, the resource was viewed as a commodity and was used to dispose of industrial waste as well as transport industrial production.

overpopulate when the birds which ate them flew away to find new nesting areas.

Logging

Like the Indians, the settlers built along what historians call "lines of least resistance," places where it was easiest to find suitable living conditions. Those were along waterways, but while the Algonquin, Abenaki, and other native groups deliberately kept their populations small – splitting into new groups when one village became too large – and migrated as seasons changed and

ABOVE, FROM LEFT: George Perkins Marsh; storing up firewood for the long winter nights; a rainbow peaks above a New Hampshire valley.

Vermont, to its credit, recognized the damage that had been done. It began a reforestation program in the 1920s. Today, much of the state looks as it did three centuries ago. Grassroots and state-level programs clean up the waterways. Development is challenged to prove that it won't cause more environmental damage than create economic benefits. In Maine, there are efforts to establish a national park which would protect the vast forests from development and over-logging, although it's not universally supported. It seems that the cycle has come full-circle; efforts to restore the forest, land, and water are being pursued with the same energy the Pilgrims and industrial magnates used to exploit them.

DECISIVE DATES

9000 BC
Earliest evidence of human activity in New England, at Shawville VT.

AD 1000
The Viking Leif Erikson discovers Vinland the Good, the location of which remains unknown.

14th–15th centuries
The Algonquin Indians arrive.

1524
Explorer Giovanni da Verrazano travels as far north as Narragansett Bay.

1609
Samuel de Champlain is the first European to visit the lake later named for him.

1620
The Plymouth Company finances a group of 66 Puritans to establish a permanent settlement in North America.

1630
The Massachusetts Bay Colony is founded by John Winthrop with the settlement of Boston.

1636
Harvard College is established. Reverend Roger Williams is banished from the Massachusetts Bay Colony and founds Providence RI.

1692
Salem witch trials: 400 stand accused of sorcery and other crimes. Of those found guilty, 20 are executed.

1764
The Revenue Act, imposed by Britain, taxes sugar, and wine.

1765
The Stamp Act taxes commercial and legal documents, newspapers, and playing cards.

1767
The Townshend Acts place harsh duties on paper, glass, and tea. Two regiments of British troops land at Boston to impose order.

1773
Sixty men (disguised as Mohawk Indians) dump tea over the railings of three ships in Boston Harbor in protest against taxes on tea.

1774
Britain retaliates against the Boston Tea Party by closing Boston Harbor. The First Continental Congress convenes at Philadelphia.

1775
Britain and the colonists engage at Lexington in the first battle of the Revolution.

1776
George Washington drives the British from Boston. On July 4, the Declaration of Independence is adopted.

1789
The first cotton mill begins operating in Pawtucket RI.

1800
Poor conditions at Pawtucket lead workers to strike, in the nation's first industrial action.

1831
The abolitionist William Lloyd Garrison founds the weekly *Liberator* newspaper.

1833
New England's first steam railroad opens between Boston and Lowell MA.

1845
Henry David Thoreau builds his cabin at Walden Pond.

1845–50
More than 1,000 Irish immigrants fleeing from the Potato Famine at home arrive in Boston each month.

1852
Uncle Tom's Cabin, by Harriet Beecher Stowe, encourages the abolitionist movement.

ABOVE, FROM LEFT: Viking longboats arrived from Norway around AD 1000; the view from Beacon Hill; Giovanni de Verrazano; the pilgrims meet the Indians; the battle of Bunker Hill, 1775.

1854
The Boston Public Library becomes the world's first free municipal library.

1876
Boston's Museum of Fine Arts opens.

1886
Great Barrington MA pioneers the use of street lights.

1891
Basketball is invented in Springfield MA.

1923
Vermont's Calvin Coolidge becomes US president when Warren Harding dies in office.

1929
The Wall Street crash and the resultant Great Depression hits New England hard. Its manufacturing industry, begins a long decline.

1944
A conference at Bretton Woods NH creates the framework for a postwar world monetary system.

1954
The first nuclear submarine, the USS *Nautilus*, is launched at Groton CT.

1960
Massachusetts Senator John F. Kennedy is elected US president.

1992
The Mashantucket Pequot Indians open the controversial but very profitable Foxwoods Casino in Mashantucket CT. It is soon followed by the Mohegan Sun casino.

1997
Sebastian Junger's best-selling book *The Perfect Storm* tells the story of a doomed Gloucester trawler. Hollywood films it in 2000.

2000
Vermont advances gay rights by passing a civil union bill. Four years later, Massachusetts recognizes gay marriages. By 2012, only Maine still does not recognize same-sex marriages or civil unions.

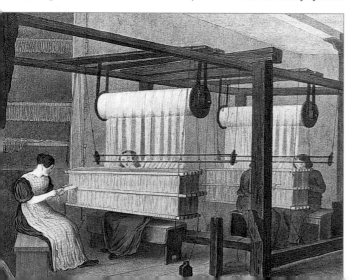

2007
Massachusetts elects its first African-American governor, Deval Patrick.

2008
Film star Paul Newman dies at Westport CT. Barack Obama wins all six states in the November election.

2002
Controversy rages over aesthetics vs. renewable energy as giant windmills for electrical generation are proposed for Vermont ridgetops and Nantucket Sound.

2005
Completion of America's biggest-ever public works project, the "Big Dig," which moved Boston's Central Artery underground and added a third harbor tunnel.

2009
Senator Edward Kennedy dies of brain cancer. In the special election to fill his seat, Republican Scott Brown wins in an upset victory.

2003
New Hampshire's iconic rock formation, The Old Man of the Mountain, collapses.

2006
Massachusetts passes a health care reform act which mandates that nearly every citizen obtain health insurance.

2011
Hurricane Irene causes massive flooding and destruction, particularly in Vermont.

2004
Boston's Red Sox, based at Fenway Park, take the World Series baseball crown for the first time in 86 years. They win again in 2007.

ABOVE, FROM LEFT: the perils of whaling; Boston in 1853 – a detail from a John White Allen Scott painting; Boston's Fenway Park; textiles boom in the 1800's; Massachusetts senator Jack Kennedy's campaign buttons, 1960.

BEGINNINGS

The first people arrived in the region around 12,000 BC, but it was the landing of the Pilgrim Fathers in 1620 that changed the face of America

Although, as the name suggests, it was the English who sowed the seeds of New England's fortune, they were not the first to gaze on these northern shores. Anthropologists generally agree that the first pilgrims reached North America overland from Asia via the then-frozen Bering Straits, arriving on the continent between 12,000 and 25,000 years ago.

The oldest fossil finds of human activity in New England, uncovered in Shawville VT and Wapunucket MA, date respectively to 9000 and 4000 BC and include a variety of spear points, knives, pendants, and ancient house floors. These early settlers were to witness the landing of the Vikings in AD 1000, the first documented European visitors to North America. Initially, the Vikings got on well with the Indians, cordially trading Viking cloth for local furs. But soon hostilities broke out, and the Vikings abandoned the New World.

The Algonquins

The Algonquins seeped into the New England forests probably sometime during the 14th or 15th century. They did not come in droves; by 1600, no more than 25,000 Indians populated New England, fewer than one for every 2 sq miles (5 sq km). Nor did this population comprise a unified culture: the Algonquins broke down into at least 10 tribal divisions. Some tribes had no more than 200 or 300 members.

Far from being the nomads of later characterizations, the Algonquins were agricultural and semi-sedentary. Tribal communities moved with the seasons, following established routes restricted to particular tribal domains. In the winter they occupied the sheltered valleys of the interior, in the warmer months the fertile coastal areas.

HOW ALGONQUIN SOCIETY WORKED

Politics and state affairs were left in the charge of the sachem, a hereditary chief who commanded each tribe. The powwows, or medicine men, gained considerable political might as the vicars of Indian religion; they combined healing with religion through mystical rites, and held powerful positions in the tribe.

In no sense did the Algonquins comprise a united nation. Unlike their Iroquois neighbors to the west, no council, senate, or chief-of-chiefs disciplined the Algonquian tribes toward unified action. This lack of unity gave the European settlers an advantage.

But the Indians had to toil year-round to feed and clothe themselves. With an excellent understanding of agricultural techniques, they grew crops such as beans, pumpkins, and tobacco, but relied most heavily on maize, the Indian corn. Meat and fish sufficiently balanced the vegetable fare. Plentiful moose and beaver, turkey and goose, lobsters and clams, salmon and bass, along with other delectables, made for a varied menu.

Path to settlement

The early European explorers were not mere adventurers, but determined fortune-hunters seeking an easier passage to the Orient and its

America's northern shores (at Labrador, historians believe), Cabot was blessed with a huge royal pension of £20 a year after his 1497 expedition. It was a good bargain for the Crown, considering that England based its claim to all America east of the Rockies and north of Florida on the extent of Cabot's exploration.

For most of the 16th century, Spanish conquistadors dominated the New World, where they profitably exploited resource-rich Central and South America. After Cabot's venture, the less inviting and accessible north was largely neglected and the Northwest Passage remained a merchant's dream.

treasures. When the Genoese sailor Cristoforo Colombo (Latinized as Christopher Columbus) was trying to finance his expedition, he spoke of riches and trade. So when he returned with news of an undiscovered continent, but without the gold and spices he promised, he was ridiculed and disgraced.

Columbus' countryman Giovanni Caboto (John Cabot), searching for the Northwest Passage to the East, received slightly better treatment from his patron, Henry VII of England. The first European since the Norse to visit

ABOVE, FROM LEFT: early contacts with the local tribes were generally peaceful; artwork depicting an Indian ritual ceremony of worship.

The English take over

In the closing decades of the 16th century, Elizabeth I's England eclipsed Spain as master of the seas. Recognizing conquest and colonization as a path to power, the late-starting English were to take over from the conquistadors as pioneers of the New World.

In 1583, equipped with a royal charter to discover "remote heathen and barbarious land not actually possessed by any Christian prince or people … and to have, hold, occupy and enjoy" such territories, Sir Humphrey Gilbert was the first Englishman to attempt the settlement of North America. Sailing from Plymouth with his flagship *Delight* and three other vessels, Gilbert intended to establish a trading post at

"Algonquin" is the French word for the tribe. It's thought to be a mispronunciation of elehgumoqik, the Algonquin word for allies. The Algonquin identify themselves as the Anishnabe, which means "original people."

the mouth of the Penobscot River. But after reasserting English control of Newfoundland, he sailed south to disaster: three out of the four ships sank and Gilbert himself died.

The first years of the 17th century saw a renewed interest in exploration. In 1606,

James I granted charters for two new ventures, the Virginia Companies of London and Plymouth, giving the latter rights to found a colony somewhere between North Carolina and Nova Scotia. Loaded with the usual arms and foodstuffs, some livestock, and trinkets to trade with the Indians, the first band of 100 adventurers built Fort St George on Parker's Island in Maine. There they wintered but, finding no evidence of precious metals, and the weather "extreme unseasonable and frosty," the group left the following spring.

Recognizing the need to plan more carefully, the Plymouth Company next commissioned the experienced surveyor John Smith to take a critical look at the region's potential for settlement and profit. Smith is credited as the first to give the region its name of "New England."

Answering a higher call

The explorers of the 16th century were driven by the profit motive. Since they discovered neither the coveted Northwest Passage nor gold and diamonds, they couldn't discern the promise of the New World. Decades of work produced no more than a few crude maps and travelogues.

Renaissance Europe did not foster religious tolerance. Dissent was treason, and heretics mounted the same scaffolds as did traitors. To the Puritans, devotees of more extreme Protestant beliefs than their Church of England (Anglican) countrymen, the symbols of papal domination – jeweled miters, elaborate rituals, and power-hungry bishops – were the devil's work, from which the Anglican establishment had not sufficiently distanced itself. Even more

THE CRUSADE TO CONVERT THE ALGONQUINS

Although the Puritans owed much to the Algonquins for their cooperation in the early days of settlement, and although they professed no racial prejudice against the Indians (one contemporary theory held that they were descended from a lost tribe of Israel), the Puritans soon assumed the task of converting their newfound neighbors from their heathen ways. The Bible was translated into the Algonquian language. The Reverend John Eliot set up a string of "Praying Towns" of Christian Algonquins. During the 1660s and early 1670s, these communities may have accounted for as many as one-fifth of all New England Indians. But the Puritans were looking for more than

religious fellow-travelers; they sought to create nothing less than a breed of neo-Englishmen.

As the historian Alden T. Vaughan concluded, the Indians would have had to "forsake their theology, their language, their political and economic structures, their habitations and clothing, their social mores, their customs of work and play" – in short, commit cultural suicide – to satisfy the Puritans. Several Algonquins were sent to Harvard to receive ministerial training, but only one, Caleb Cheeshahteaumuck, graduated. His portrait was hung in Harvard in 2010. *Caleb's Crossing* by Geraldine Brooks, a novel based on his life, was published in 2011.

disturbing to the Puritans was the persecution they suffered under James I in his attempts to impose religious conformity.

A group of Puritans from Lincolnshire struck a deal with the Plymouth Company to finance a settlement in the unpopulated north of America. For the Plymouth Company, it was a chance to at least recoup its so-far-wasted investment in the region. If the colony succeeded, the company might actually turn a profit. For the Puritans, it was an opportunity to escape persecution and a corrupt environment and create their idealized society in an unsullied location. In 1620, 66 of these pilgrims left from Plymouth on the 180-ton *Mayflower*, carrying everything they needed to start and maintain a self-sufficient community. The trip itself was no luxury cruise, and after more than two months at sea the travelers "were not a little joyful" to sight Cape Cod on November 11. Deciding that the sandy cape lacked fresh water and arable land, the group dispatched Captain Myles Standish (nicknamed "Captain Shrimp" because of his height) to find a more fertile site. In mid-December, the Pilgrims disembarked at Plymouth Rock.

The first winter was a miserable ordeal, testing fully the hardened Puritan will. Scurvy, pneumonia, and other infections killed more than half of the settlers, including Governor John Carver. At any one time, no more than six or seven remained in good health. But spring brought better times, notably the signing of a treaty of friendship with the local Indians, one of whom, Squanto, had been temporarily abducted to England by an earlier expedition and now acted as ambassador, recommending mutual cooperation.

Heavenly aspirations

Acknowledging the contribution of the local people, the Pilgrims hosted a feast of celebration nearing the first anniversary of their arrival. In a three-day harvest celebration, similar to those they knew in England and Holland, both natives and newcomers enjoyed a meal of venison, lobster, clams, and fruits. A few weeks later, 35 freedom-seekers, well stocked with provisions, joined the *Mayflower* survivors, and by

the spring of 1624, Plymouth was a thriving village of more than 30 cottages.

In 1628 another group of Puritans, led by Thomas Dudley, Thomas Leverett, and John Winthrop, obtained a royal charter as the Company of the Massachusetts Bay in New England. The next summer, 350 hopefuls arrived at Salem, followed by another 1,500 in 1630. Not only more numerous than the Plymouth Pilgrims but also better financed, the Massachusetts Bay Company founded the town of Boston that year on the Shawmut Peninsula – a neck of land whose only prior English inhabitant had been the scholarly

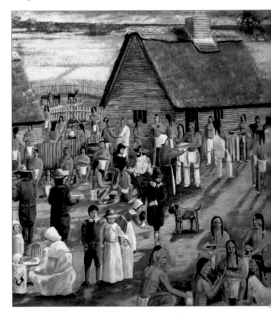

hermit William Blaxton, who promptly removed himself to Rhode Island. As Charles I and Archbishop William Laud tightened the screws of persecution back home, the Massachusetts Bay Colony grew quickly despite primitive conditions.

Growth was not limited to the area of the first landings on the Massachusetts shore. The reverends Thomas Hooker and Samuel Stone, along with former Bay governor John Haynes, left Cambridge for Connecticut, where they settled the towns of Hartford, Wethersfield, and Windsor. Two Londoners, Theophilus Eaton and John Davenport, soon after established themselves at New Haven. The Plymouth Colony had been operating a trading post on Maine's

ABOVE, FROM LEFT: eight-year-old Anne Pollard, the first girl to set foot in Boston (1630); settlers mingle with Indians at Plimoth Plantation.

Kennebec River since 1627. The New World's first real estate developers, John Mason and Sir Ferdinando Gorges, tried to capitalize on their vast property grants in New Hampshire and Maine, but these ambitious ventures were humbled by the region's daunting inhospitability.

Elsewhere, groups of New Englanders helped expand the frontiers outside the region. Puritan communities transplanted to New York, North Carolina, and Georgia maintained ties with their old homes. One such group, from Westmorland CT, continued to send representatives to the Connecticut Assembly long after moving to Pennsylvania.

The founding of Providence

In the early years of Massachusetts Bay, the Reverend Roger Williams took it upon himself to condemn the shackles of imposed religion, preaching from his pulpit in Salem that "forced worship stinks in God's nostrils." His compatriots in the General Court banished him from the colony in 1636.

But Williams did not return to England. He turned instead to Canonicus and Miantonomi, the two Narragansett leaders he had befriended in the course of studying the Indian population. The chieftains saw fit to grant him, gratis, a large tract on the Pawtuxet River. Here, Williams founded Providence. Fellow exiles joined him over the next few years – Anne Hutchinson (who later died in an Indian attack on her final home on Long Island Sound) and William Coddington on nearby Aquidneck Island, and Samuel Gorton in Warwick.

Though the new settlement grew slowly – from fewer than 20 families in 1638 to no more than 1,000 individuals three decades later – the Providence and Rhode Island plantations proved an unholy thorn in Massachusetts' underbelly. No kind words here. The unholy partisan rhetoric make Parliamentary and Congressional sniping sound like tributes to Mother Teresa. Hutchinson, with her "very voluble tongue," lambasted her former parish with "Call it whore and strumpet not a Church of Christ," while back in Massachusetts, the ordinarily restrained Cotton Mather continually insulted the colony as the "fag end of creation," "the sewer of New England," and, ever so cleverly, "Rogue's Island."

But Rhode Island lived up to its intent, and religious freedom was guaranteed by a 1663 royal charter. It welcomed New England's first Jewish émigrés in 1662, along with scores of Quakers and French Huguenots.

Violence breaks out

Missionary zeal alienated many of the Indians, but it was empire-building that led to bloodshed. At first, there was plenty of room for the Indians and settlers to coexist peacefully. About a third of the Algonquin inhabitants had fallen victim to a great plague in the early 1600s, which may have been illnesses brought by the first explorers and against which the Indians had no immunity, leaving their lands underpopulated when the *Mayflower* landed. But, as the ambitious English settlements expanded and pushed south, friction between the two peoples was the inevitable result.

In 1636 war erupted with the Pequots (a fearsome tribe whose name means "destroyer" in Algonquian), and battles at Fort Mystic and Fairfield CT, saw several hundred lives lost on both sides. It was King Philip's War (1675–76), however, that marked the demise of Indian society in most of New England. The Nipmuc, Narragansett, and Wampanoag forces, nominally led by Philip (whose real name was Metacomet), suffered from chronic tribal disu-

Mary Rowlandson was captured by the Narragansett Indians during King Philip's War (1675–76) and held for eleven weeks. Her book, A Narrative of the Capture and Restoration of Mrs. Mary Rowlandson, was a best seller.

philosophical disagreements, and the worldly temptations of material gain and power. While religion still played an important role in setting the tone of discussions and decision, political power would be the rallying call of a new era.

nity and were outnumbered by at least five to one. At the "Great Swamp Fight" near present-day South Kingston RI, 2,000 Narragansetts were slain (many of them women and children trapped in burning wigwams) in one of the fiercest battles ever fought on New England soil. The Indian will was broken; for them, the war had been a holocaust.

For the settlers, their initial ascetic zeal and belief that they could create an unchallenged theocracy had been tempered by the realities of life in a rugged wilderness, internal

ABOVE, FROM LEFT: Roger Williams believed in fair dealings with the local people; King Philip's War, a vicious conflict in 1675-76.

ORGANIZING THE NEW WORLD

Some 2,000 immigrants arrived each year between 1630 and 1637, and new communities such as Ipswich, Dorchester, Concord, Dedham, and Watertown sprang up. In 1636, the Puritan clergy established Harvard College to train future ministers. The Great and General Court – to this day the name of the Massachusetts legislature – was formed to manage administrative and judicial affairs, a governor and deputy governor being indirectly chosen by the colony's freeholders. At the town level, landowners convened to discuss problems – a practical arrangement since the average town included no more than 200 or 300 families.

BIRTH OF A NATION

Lexington Green's "shot heard round the world" in 1775 heralded the start of the American Revolution and the struggle for independence

The colonies of New England had, for the most part, been left to their own devices from the first landing at Plymouth. Suffering serious political turmoil in the early 17th century, highlighted by the beheading of Charles I, England had little time to attend to the governing of dissident settlers 3,000 miles from London. The Puritans gladly filled the vacuum and took on the responsibilities of de facto autonomy.

Puritan values

Even before reaching their destination, the Pilgrims signed the famous Mayflower Compact, creating a government "to enact, constitute, and frame such just and equal Laws, Ordinances, Acts, Constitutions, and offices, from time to time, as shall be thought most meet and convenient for the general good." John Winthrop and his followers carried with them their royal charter when they sailed to Massachusetts, and in 1631 the freemen of the new colony gave an oath of fidelity not to the king but to the Bay Company and its officers. The settlers agreed that if England tried to impose its own governor on them, "we ought not to accept him, but defend our lawful possessions."

Fifty-five years later, they were given the chance. In 1686, James II unilaterally revoked the northern colonies' sacred charters and consolidated English holdings from Maine to New Jersey into a vast Dominion of New England in America. The monarch justified his decision as a security measure, a benevolent protection from the French and Indians. The Puritans were not convinced. They scorned the king's first envoy, Joseph Dudley, an avid Anglican, as having "as many virtues as can consist with so great a thirst for honor and power." They branded his successor, Edmund Andros, "the greatest tyrant who ever ruled in this country."

A strong cue from England itself moved New England to action and revolt. At the "Glorious Revolution" of early 1689, William and Mary, in cahoots with Parliament, seized the throne from James II. New England spontaneously erupted; Andros and his cronies were dragged from state house to jail cell. The old powers of self-government were largely restored, along with a certain mutual respect between Crown and colonies.

A later English king, George III, presided over the loss of Britain's New World empire. Initial attempts by London to raise taxes in New England were successfully resisted. But in 1767 Britain's prime minister, Charles Townshend, boasted: "I dare tax America." Parliament passed the Townshend Acts, imposing duties on such imports as paper, glass, and tea. Two regiments of British troops landed at Boston to put some muscle behind the waning control of Governor Thomas Hutchinson.

The Boston Massacre

The Redcoats were not well received. On the night of March 5, 1770, a crowd of several hundred rowdy Bostonians gathered to taunt a lone "lobster-back" standing guard outside the customs house on King Street (present-day State Street). When shouts turned to stones and snow-

gesture given that tea then was as important as a Starbuck's latté is now.

American addicts turned to smuggled Dutch blends or to "Liberty Tea," a nasty brew made from sage, currant, or plantain leaves. The British responded by subsidizing their brand and, in September 1773, flooded the market with about half a million pounds of their product, with shipments to ports all along the eastern seaboard. It didn't work.

Boston emerged once again as the focus of resistance. The Massachusetts Committee of Correspondence, an unofficial legislature, and the Sons of Liberty, a fast-growing secret

balls, seven Redcoats came to aid the sentry. One fired into the melee without orders, others followed, and, after the smoke had cleared, three colonists lay dead (including a black man named Crispus Attucks) and two were mortally wounded. The American revolt had its first martyrs, and the growing anti-British element in New England had a field day with the incident.

Tempers cooled briefly. Parliament struck down the Townshend Acts – all except one, that is. To assert the king's authority, and to try to raise at least some revenue, Britain maintained the tax on East Indian tea, a not insignificant

society at the forefront of revolutionary activism, demanded that Governor Hutchinson send home the tea-laden *Dartmouth*.

When he refused, the protesters' reaction was swift and calculatedly theatrical. On December 16, 60 men (among them Sam Adams and John Hancock), disguised as Mohawk Indians, descended on the *Dartmouth* and two sister ships. Boston Harbor was turned into a teapot as they dumped 342 crates over the railings. The Boston Tea Party, as it came to be called, was a display of profound disrespect to Parliament and the king. Parliament responded with the "Coercive" Acts. Most infamously, the Boston Port Act sealed off the city by naval blockade. The First Continental Congress convened

ABOVE, FROM LEFT: patriot Paul Revere's famous ride; the Boston Massacre of March 5, 1770.

angrily in Philadelphia on September 5, 1774. Revolution was at hand.

A shot heard round the world

An uneasy stalemate prevailed until the spring of 1775. British garrisons controlled only the major towns. The countryside became virtually unpoliceable. New Englanders stockpiled arms and ammunition to prepare for the inevitable conflict.

In early April 1775, London instructed Boston commander General Thomas Gage to quash seditious activities in rural Massachusetts, where a Provincial Congress had assumed de facto governmental control. Late on April 18, Gage dispatched

a contingent of 700 soldiers to destroy a makeshift arms depot in Concord, 20 miles (32km) west of Boston. At Lexington, 70 citizen soldiers, the original Minutemen (those who could be summoned for duty at a minute's notice), lay in wait for the British, having been forewarned by the daring

Paul Revere's famous ride ended when he was stopped by a British patrol just west of Lexington. Luckily, two men riding with him, William Dawes and Dr Samuel Prescott, were able to escape and warn the Minutemen.

THE BATTLE OF BUNKER HILL

The Battle of Bunker Hill broke out in June 1775 on the Charlestown Peninsula, across the Charles River from Boston. To consolidate control of overland access to the port city, Continental Army general Artemas Ward ordered the fortification of Bunker's Hill (as it was then known), although it was actually on adjoining Breed's Hill that the Americans dug in.

The British could not allow such a build-up if they were to entertain even the faintest hope of holding Boston. On June 17, Redcoats scaled Breed's slopes twice but were rebuffed. In a desperate third attempt they succeeded, but only because the colonial force had exhausted its supply of ammunition. It was for

this reason, and not out of bravery, that Colonel William Prescott issued his famous command: "Don't fire until you see the whites of their eyes, men."

Bunker Hill was a costly victory for the Crown, which suffered more than 1,000 casualties. Optimism, seen in remarks like General John Burgoyne's "We'll soon find elbow room," was reduced to the doubting reflections of another British officer, "This victory has cost us very dear indeed... Nor do I see that we enjoy one solid benefit in return, or are likely to reap from it any one advantage whatever." Less than a year later, under siege by George Washington, General Gage evacuated his troops to Halifax.

early-morning rides from Boston of patriots Paul Revere and William Dawes.

The two forces met on the town common. A musket was fired. Minutes later, eight Americans lay dead. The British continued on to Concord, where the colonial militia triggered, in Ralph Waldo Emerson's words, "the shot heard round the world." The Minutemen made up for their lack of numbers by employing unconventional guerrilla tactics, harassing the enemy with crack sniper fire. By nightfall they had killed 273 British soldiers.

As the British retreated to Boston, officers lost control of their men, who began ransacking

was adopted by the Continental Congress. Of the signatories, 14 came from the charter states of Massachusetts, Connecticut, New Hampshire, and Rhode Island. Except for Newport RI, not taken from the British until October 1779, New England had achieved its independence.

After the Treaty of Paris ended the Revolutionary War in 1783, the magnates of New England's prosperous cities turned to protect their newly established interests as the 13 independent colonies hammered out an integrated union. Concerned that a centralized federal government would prove as insensitive to local sentiment as had the Crown, revolution-

homes and taverns, attacking those they found inside. "The devastation committed by the British troops on their retreat," reported one sensationalized and exaggerated account, "is almost beyond description, such as plundering and burning of dwelling houses and other buildings, driving into the street women in childbed, killing old men in their houses unarmed."

Independence is declared

The war's first year did not go well for Britain and on July 4, 1776, the Declaration of Independence

ABOVE, FROM LEFT: *First News of the Battle of Lexington* by William Tylee Renney (1813–57); soldiers at the Battle of Bunker's Hill, 1775.

ary heroes Sam Adams and John Hancock gave only grudging support to the Constitution. Rhode Island, in more than a dozen votes between 1787 and 1789, voted it down and ratified it only after the Bill of Rights was added.

The industrial age

New England's leaders became increasingly reactionary as they guarded their economic interests. In Massachusetts, poor hill farmers rose against the state government in Shays' Rebellion of 1786, demonstrating that genuine equality remained a dream. In 1812, fearing the loss of a thriving maritime trade, New England firmly opposed renewed and greater conflict with Great Britain.

But the first two decades of the 19th century showed how vulnerable maritime trade was to the whims of international politics. The Napoleonic Wars, President Thomas Jefferson's Embargo Acts, and the War of 1812 severely hampered New England's chase after an honest, apolitical dollar. Recognizing that it is best not to put all one's commercial eggs in one flimsy basket, its merchants turned to the herald of a new industrial age.

The machine age

In the fall of 1789, a teenage Samuel Slater sailed from England to New York disguised as

a common laborer, defying British laws forbidding the emigration of skilled mechanics. For seven years he had apprenticed to Jedediah Strutt, a partner of the famed innovator Richard Arkwright, and knew the specifications of Arkwright's factory-sized cotton-spinning machine.

In America, the reduction of raw cotton was still being done by laborers working in their own homes on individual looms. An early attempt at consolidating the process, a mill at Beverly MA, had been a failure owing to the crudeness of its machinery. Arkwright's device, already proven across the Atlantic, was the answer, so Quaker financier Moses Brown engaged Slater to come to Providence and put his knowledge to use. Together, they built America's first successful cotton mill on the Blackstone River at Pawtucket.

With underpaid workers kept at the grind for 70 hours a week, Pawtucket became the site of the nation's first strike in 1800. It was left to Bostonian Francis Cabot Lowell (from the family that would later produce a Harvard president, a celebrated astronomer, and three poets) to take a more enlightened approach.

During a two-year visit to England, Lowell became an avid industrial tourist and, on his return to Massachusetts, he was determined to duplicate British weaving feats. Putting up $10,000 of his own money, he collected another $90,000 from the so-called "Boston Associates" – the families of Lawrence, Cabot, Eliot, Higginson, and others – to establish a small mill (with a power loom and 1,700 spindles) at Waltham.

HOW BOSTON BECAME THE ATHENS OF AMERICA

Colonial New Englanders enriched their intellectual life by founding such pioneer colleges as Harvard, Yale, Dartmouth, and Brown. As the 19th century progressed, and with the interest on their old China Trade money compounded tremendously via investment in the new manufacturing technologies, Boston's first families sponsored a new round of institutions that would lend weight to the city's position as "the Athens of America."

The Handel and Haydn Society dates from 1815, the New England Conservatory of Music from 1867, and the Boston Symphony Orchestra – founded and supported for 40 years by the arch-Brahmin Major Henry Lee Higginson – from 1881. The BSO is the parent organization of the less classically oriented Boston Pops, and makes its summer home at the renowned Tanglewood music festival. Boston's magnificent Museum of Fine Arts (1876) evolved from a collection room in the Boston Athenaeum – itself a great New England Institution, founded in 1807 and still one of America's premier privately owned libraries.

Governor John Winthrop believed strongly in aristocratic rule. He wrote: "A democracy is, among civil nations, accounted the meanest and worst of all forms of government."

A "commercial utopia"

Lowell died in 1817, but his plans were realized by his associates under the aegis of the Merrimack Manufacturing Company. In 1820, the mill was moved to a tract on the Merrimack River, just above the village of Chelmsford.

The Merrimack Company took care of its people. Though grievously overworked by modern standards, "mill girls" enjoyed clean, safe dormitory housing and opportunities for cultural enrichment. New England's first company town was, in the words of the English novelist Anthony Trollope, "the realization of commercial utopia." Soon the efficient new factory

More than 100 new towns were established in New Hampshire in the 15 years preceding the Revolution; between 1790 and 1800, the populations of Vermont and Maine nearly doubled.

On the craggy hillsides, the pioneers set up small farms, built their own houses and barns, and raised wheat, corn, pigs, and cattle to fill the dinner table. These rugged families prided themselves on being almost completely self-sufficient; in fact, it used to be said of upcountry farms that all they needed to import were nails and salt. This was a new frontier, New England's frontier.

But this frontier's potential was limited by nature. The climate was inhospitable: in

system – if not its early paternalism – would spread up the Merrimack River to Lawrence MA and ultimately to the vast Amoskeag mills at Manchester NH, destined to become the greatest producer of cotton cloth on earth.

Life on the frontier

Not everybody shared in the boom. During the second half of the 18th century, the northern areas of New England had enjoyed a dramatic infusion of people, as land began to grow scarce in the densely populated coastal areas.

ABOVE, FROM LEFT: the USS Constitution takes on the British Navy in 1812; Boston's Old State House, around 1801.

WHY THE STAMP ACT WAS HATED

Needing to cover the cost of keeping troops in the colonies, Britain's parliament passed a Revenue Act in 1764 taxing on sugar, silk, and wines. The Stamp Act followed a year later, requiring that all commercial and legal documents, newspapers, and playing cards be taxed. The measure was fiercely assailed. Stamp distributors were hanged in effigy and ridiculed at mock trials. Liberty was buried in symbolic funerals. New Englanders, who had no say in electing British parliamentarians, argued that there should be no taxation without representation. Britain's prime minister, William Pitt, responded by repealing the Stamp Act in 1766.

1816, for instance, a June snowfall resulted in total crop failure. Agricultural machinery could not plow the irregular farmland. As for those famous New England stone walls, they were in actuality a practical by-product of what many disillusioned farmers called the region's prime produce: rocks. Property consolidation was difficult, as families jealously guarded original claims; small-scale production could not compete with more efficient new suppliers elsewhere in the United States and around the world. As far as agriculture was concerned, northern New England had seen its zenith by 1850.

After that, a slow, sapping decline attacked upland vitality. By the turn of the century, population growth had leveled and agricultural production dived. More than half of New Hampshire's farmland lay abandoned. Cheese production in Maine, New Hampshire, and Vermont fell by 95 percent between 1849 and 1919. The California Gold Rush of 1849 drew young men from the farms. The Civil War took away even more, with veterans often heading west to seek their fortunes rather than returning to their fathers' stony acres. And girls went to the Massachusetts mills.

Athenaeums for all

Boston had become established as the center of cultural activities. Elsewhere, Salem's Peabody Essex Museum was founded, in part as a repository of curiosities brought home by the city's far-faring merchant captains. In Hartford, the Wadsworth Athenaeum was founded as an art museum in 1842 by local businessman Daniel Wadsworth ("atheneum" or "athenaeum" was a cultural catch-all title in the 19th century). New England was a leader in the concept of libraries being in the public domain. In 1854, the Boston Public Library became the world's first free municipal library. Cradle of the Revolution, pioneer in commerce and industry, and now America's cultural capital – New England had shown its leadership in one realm after another. But as the 20th century approached, it would have to face a challenge not of invention, but re-invention.

LEFT: one of an outstanding collection of 19th-century figureheads in Salem's Peabody Museum.

TRADING IN TEA, RUM, SPICES, AND SLAVES

When not calling comrades to religious or political barricades, the colonial New Englander attended to the more practical pursuit of commerce: it was both out of the seas and on the seas that New England's money was made. Codfish provided a lucrative export to Catholic Europe, while whaling provided oil for lighting and lubricants.

New England was at the pivot of the profitable Triangle Trade: in harbors like Newport, a fleet of 350 ships unloaded West Indian molasses and reloaded the ships with tuns of rum. From there, the rum was transported to Africa, where it was traded for kidnapped slaves who were shipped to the West Indies and, in turn, traded for

molasses. It was a cyclical venture that brought much profit to the New Englanders, and untold suffering to the trafficked slaves.

New England shipyards gained world fame for crafting swift, easily managed ocean-going vessels, a tradition launched even before Pilgrim settlement with the 1607 construction of the *Virginia* in the short-lived Popham colony in Maine.

Although disrupted by the Revolution, maritime trade bounced back quickly, mining the riches of China and India so coveted by the early American explorers. In 1792, Boston's *Columbia* threaded the Straits of Magellan en route to Canton to trade for tea, spices, silk, and opium.

The Shakers

These disciplined people were famous for their unique way of life, their manner of worship, and their influential craftsmanship

The founder of the United Society of Believers in Christ's Second Appearing was Ann Lee, born in 1736 in Manchester, England. An illiterate factory worker, she was a woman of deep convictions at a time of religious persecution. Ann Lee became the spiritual leader of a group of dissidents from the Anglican Church often called the "Shaking Quakers" because of the movements they made as the Holy Spirit took hold of them and purged their sins. They became known as the Shakers, and their cultural contributions to furniture design and music have lasted through the centuries.

Persecuted and sent to jail, she had a vision that she had a mission to teach a new way of life, one where men and women were equal, free from lust, greed, and violence, with their lives governed by material and spiritual simplicity. She was convinced that only through celibacy could men and women further Christ's kingdom on earth.

After a second vision, she and eight followers set sail for New York in 1770. It was not until the 1780s, however, that converts were attracted in great numbers. Mother Ann died in 1783, soon after a proselytizing tour of New England and before the full flowering of Shakerism. At its peak in the 1840s, more than 6,000 members lived in 19 communities.

The Shakers, officially known as the United Society of Believers in Christ's Second Appearing, aimed for perfection in life. Devoted to orderliness and simplicity, they were also dedicated to such progressive notions as sexual equality (facilities for men and women were identical and jobs were shared on a rotation), and they welcomed technological advances that might improve the quality of their work.

The Shakers ran model farms and, as keen gardeners, were the first to packet and sell seeds; they also marketed medicinal herbs. They sold their meticulously crafted baskets, boxes, chairs, and textiles. By blending discipline, business acumen, ingenuity, and superb craftsmanship, they achieved prosperity, both spiritual and financial.

Celibacy, a key principle, made it difficult for communities to renew themselves, but their ranks were swelled by converts, and many orphans were adopted from the city. Numbers dwindled after the mid-1800s, though, and today just a handful of "Believers" remain, mostly in Sabbathday Lake ME. The Shaker ideals of simplicity and practicality live on, however, in a legacy of architecture, furniture, and arts and crafts.

There are modern Shaker furniture stores, but to find an original Shaker piece is rare, and can be quite costly.

The villages at Canterbury NH and Hancock MA are preserved as museums, where visitors watch craftsmen make baskets, boxes, and chairs in the Shaker manner. In the Dwelling Houses tourists can see the efficient kitchens, including the wall pegs on which chairs and utensils were hung, and the built-in cupboards designed so that no dust could accumulate on top or underneath.

The Shakers were one of the first societies to have gender equality, which was institutionalized in the 1780s, long before the concept became common elsewhere.

RIGHT: history preserved at Hancock Shaker Village. the Shaker dance, an integral part of worship and an alternative to the tremblings of early believers.

EVOLUTION AND REINVENTION

When jobs and political influence left the region, New England responded by developing new opportunities and addressing emerging economic and environmental concerns

By the beginning of the modern era, New England had come to represent America's achievements and ideals – or, conversely, it could be said that America was New England writ large. But no one looking at the American social and economic landscape in 1900 could doubt that the nation's energy and drive now found their sources in other places – in the dynamo of New York, in the raw busy cities of the Midwest, and even in upstart California.

The changes began with the vanishing of the ethnic and religious homogeneity which had

> *"The political condition of Rhode Island is notorious, acknowledged and it is shameful,"* wrote influential journalist Lincoln Steffens. *"Rhode Island is a State for sale and cheap."*

aided the old political consensus. Uprooted by the Potato Famine of 1845–50, the Irish sailed to the land of opportunity, arriving in Boston at a rate of more than 1,000 a month. Immigrants from Quebec and throughout Europe followed: Catholics, Jews, and Orthodox Christians upset Protestant homogeneity. The influx touched every corner of New England; the waves of immigration meant that "New Englanders" had adopted, not inherited, the American flag.

Electoral corruption

In the wake of this human shock wave, an anti-immigrant backlash erupted among the established citizenry, whose forebears had ironically fought so hard to achieve democracy and equal rights. The doors of society were shut to even the most successful of the new arrivals, and their children and grandchildren. In the 1850s, openly racist legislatures controlled Massachusetts, Rhode Island, Connecticut, and New Hampshire. Anti-immigrant organizations, such as the American Protective Association and the Immigrant Restriction League, attracted substantial memberships in their efforts to limit the electoral power of the new arrivals.

Their efforts failed. No matter how unfamiliar the immigrants were with the workings of democracy when they arrived, they soon learned the power of political organization

– particularly the Irish. In 1881, John Breen, born in Tipperary, became the first Irish-born politician to take high office when he was elected as mayor of Lawrence MA. His triumph launched the Irish not only into political influence but also to political domination of Massachusetts and Rhode Island politics. Hugh O'Brien, a journalist, won the mayoral election in Boston three years later, and Patrick Andrew Collin won a congressional seat in Washington. By the turn of the century, all levels of government were being run by what was, after all, the majority of the population.

Jobs and capital migrate

Days of industrial glory passed as industrial jobs migrated south, where wages were 20–50 percent lower than in New England. The South also remained relatively free of labor unions, a distinct advantage to employers with bitter memories of the strikes that shut down textile mills in Lawrence MA in 1912 and at the Amoskeag mills in Manchester NH in 1922.

The bulldozers move in

By the 1950s, it was clear that the economic malaise was not confined to factories; New England's cities and towns were also showing

But with newfound responsibility came insidious corruption. In Rhode Island, Providence was run by a political machine that openly paid between $2 and $30 per vote, depending on the candidate. Even astute leaders were often as corrupt as they were effective. James Michael Curley, major of Boston for five terms and governor of Massachusetts for one, improved the economic conditions of his less-privileged constituents. But he doled out jobs and money to community leaders who made sure voting in their neighborhoods went his way.

ABOVE, FROM LEFT: Mayor James Curley, a legend in Boston; a busy Boston wharf in the late 19th century.

Poverty was endemic. In 1930, only 81 out of 5,030 apartments in Boston's North End had refrigerators. Only one in two had bathrooms.

their age. One remedy was renovation. Boston led the way by establishing a redevelopment authority. Without sacrificing the charm of its venerable Beacon Hill and Back Bay neighborhoods, the Massachusetts capital set about remaking its downtown into a new landscape of modern civic structures, office buildings, and apartments. Providence RI is considered the example of how to do it right; the revitalized downtown Riverwalk is a magnet for recreation, shopping, dining, and festivals like WaterFire. Yet in keeping with the sorry tradition, the mayor who supervised the resurrection – Buddy Cianci – was convicted of corruption.

Other cities followed suit, with greater and lesser degrees of success; from Portland ME to Rutland VT, noble old train stations and civic buildings came crashing down, with the wrecker's ball tearing all too freely into the downtown streets of Victorian-era buildings around them. Often, the result was a bland city center of sterile office plazas and suburban-style malls. The smaller and more

economically disadvantaged cities usually came out best in the long run: places like Newburyport MA and New London CT inadvertently saved their old downtowns by neglecting them until restoration and adaptive reuse had become popular.

Urban renewal would have been simply window dressing without a revival of the regional economy. Salvation would have to come through exploitation of New England's particular resources. But what were they? They certainly weren't oil, gas, or minerals. Just about the only thing of value taken from New England ground was the granite and marble and marble stone from the quarries of Vermont. Manufacturing hadn't disappeared altogether, either; the Bath Iron Works in Maine still built ships for the Navy, and there were still specialty textile, footwear, and machinery factories scattered throughout the six states. But these were hardly growth industries. When New England searched for the key to future prosperity, it looked to its most protean and dependable resource of all: its people.

More precisely, it looked to people and to education, one of the oldest New England pursuits. When it became clear that the high technology and financial service sectors would become prime drivers of the American economy, New England was ready. The concentration of colleges and universities in the Boston area provided a splendid resource at the dawn of the computer age. Schools already known for their liberal arts programs expanded into the new world of technology.

THE GREAT DEPRESSION TAKES ITS TOLL

New England was hard hit by the Depression. Unemployment in factory towns left idle a quarter of the total labor pool. Even the mighty Amoskeag mills in New Hampshire finally closed their doors in 1935.

In Boston it cramped even upper-class lifestyles, but the worst hardships were suffered in the already squalid working-class quarters. Here, wages halved, and unemployment was almost 40 percent after the 1929 Wall Street crash. By the end of 1935, nearly a quarter of Manchester's families were receiving public welfare.

Like the rest of the country, New England was rescued from the Depression by America's involvement in World War II. Shipyards hummed in Bath ME and Quincy MA. In Hartford, Springfield, and even Island Pond VT workers assembled machinery and weaponry for the Allied armies.

But the resurging economy slumped again after V-E and V-J Day. Peace came to a New England that still hadn't solved its core economic difficulties – the migration of jobs to states where labor was cheaper, the aging of the manufacturing infrastructure, and a location that was at the outer corner of America's transportation network, instead of at its center.

The problems of the early- to mid-20th century were endemic in New England, and New Englanders were forced to come up with creative solutions, taking advantage of the region's natural bounty.

MIT with its emphasis on research and innovation and Worcester Polytechnic Institute with its focus on practical application became leaders in evolving engineering and computer sciences.

By the 1970s, Route 128 – the beltway surrounding Boston and its inner suburbs – was touted on official road signs as "America's Technology Highway." Raytheon and Microsoft, among others, plugged in here. Massachusetts General Hospital and other medical institutions conduct research, often in conjunction with MIT's biotechnology labs and Harvard's medical school.

the mid-1980s and again in the late 1990s, and both hit the ground hard when the economy crashed in the 2000s. But while the cities are suffering severely, diversification is easing the effects regionwide. New England has not suffered as much as other regions of the country from the steep decline in housing values that accompanied the mortgage crisis of 2007 and 2008 – in large part, most analysts believe, because real estate prices in the six states simply hadn't gone along for as wild a ride during the boom that preceded the bust. There weren't many places here where developers had overbuilt, flooding the market.

A need for new directions

High technology gave a boost to the burgeoning financial services industry. Boston became an investment banking capital, and the center of the mutual-fund business. John Hancock, Fidelity, Putnam, and MFS all headquartered here. In Hartford, two dozen insurance companies, dominated by titans such as Aetna, call the Connecticut capital home.

High technology and finance have been at the core of the boom-and-bust cycle of the past quarter-century. Both industries flew high in

ABOVE, FROM LEFT: looms stand still in a busy textile mill; Boston City Hall, built in the 1960s, was much criticized for its architectural style of New Brutalism.

The diversification of the region's economy ranges from "electronic cottages," in which individuals run publishing, consulting, and other businesses from their homes, to the traditional pursuits of farming, logging, and fishing.

Life hasn't been easy for people involved in those primary industries. Dairy farmers, mostly centered in Vermont, have seen their ranks dwindle as expenses spiral and milk prices stagnate. The forest products industry struggles against foreign competition and high energy costs; throughout northern New Hampshire and Maine, paper mills – once reliable bluecollar employers – have closed, while the vast tracts of woodlands owned by their parent companies increasingly have been sold, to face

Wind power is being used in places as diverse as ski resorts in Vermont and wastewater treatment facilities in Massachusetts, but many opponents say they mar the mountain views so vital to New England's tourist economy.

the possibility of subdivision and vacation-home development.

Alarmed by this threat to the integrity and wildness of the "Great North Woods" that ranges from northern Maine to New York State, activists have proposed – and, in the

northeastern corner of Vermont, have accomplished – government purchase and protection of large swaths of forest. There has even been lobbying for the establishment of a national park that would take in much of the Maine woods, although many local residents – and both Maine senators – are wary of government intrusion and regulation.

Along the Atlantic coast, fishing fleets have seen the depletion of the cod stocks and lobster population, and are struggling to stay afloat in the face of high fuel costs and permit fees and restrictions of the size of their catch. That same price spiral applies to

ELECTION IMPORTANCE

"Independent" is the operative political word in New England, regardless of the conventional political labels worn by its leaders. This independent streak reveals deep divisions over many issues.

New Englanders have long led the way in protecting the environment, but every economic slump makes jobs vs. development regulations an issue in state elections. Education is a time-honored priority, but tempers flare over financing schools via property taxes vs. broad-based levies. Vermont bucked the trend in many states by recognizing same-sex civil unions; now only Maine still refuses

to recognize such relationships or same-sex marriage.

While strongly supporting the military, particularly troops in Afghanistan and Iraq and their families, the majority of the region's citizens staunchly opposed the Iraq War. At town meetings in 2008, two Vermont municipalities actually voted to indict President George Bush and Vice-President Dick Cheney for war crimes if they set foot within their jurisdictions. Few Vermonters are surprised by the fact that theirs is the only state in the Union that George W. Bush never visited while in office.

heating and transportation, in a region more heavily dependent on oil for heat than any other in the United States. As for the third great consumer of energy, electrical generation, New Englanders are eager to innovate in a "green" direction, but argue as to which technologies to embrace. Controversy swirls around proposals to erect giant windmills in Nantucket Sound, where they would be visible from Cape Cod shores, and on ridgelines in northern Vermont, which might spoil famous views. Dozens of grassroots and more formally organized groups work to address the problems locally and network to develop

Plenty to argue about

Argument and controversy, of course, have long been bread and butter to New Englanders. Budget issues are always hot topics, even when the economy is booming. With the economic crisis hitting municipal and personal pocketbooks, passionate, often bitter, debates rage over how to balance the books – if that's even possible – while still providing essential services. The arguments revolve around the definition of "essential." On both the state and local levels, many expenditures are mandated by law – in some areas, as much as 80 percent of the budget is required to be spent on mandated programs

a consensus and action plans to solve them on a regional level.

Once again, the region's educational institutions are playing a major role in addressing the ecological issues. With student bodies facing a future shaped by how the problems are solved, there's been a growth in courses of study which concentrate on ecological concerns. Scientific programs in everything from marine biology to forest management and sustainable agricultural practices are routinely offered at many schools, as are new fields like environmental economics.

ABOVE, FROM LEFT: lobsterman at Penobscot Bay, Maine; Boston's modern waterfront.

and allocations, like Medicare (government-sponsored healthcare for senior citizens) and various welfare programs. That leaves little flexibility or cash to fund education, libraries, infrastructure maintenance, social programs, police and fire departments, or recreation. Each affected group makes a strong argument that budget-balancing should come at the expense of someone else. About the only common ground is the conviction that raising taxes to raise revenue is unacceptable. The polarization of political parties on the national level largely angers voters "back home." Most polls show that the voters want to see compromise and action on national issues, even as they often resist yielding on anything at their local level.

NEW ENGLAND'S PEOPLE

It's easy to describe New Englanders by stereotype – stern Puritans, revolutionary patriots, aristocratic Bostonians, taciturn farmers, crusty fishermen, beefy Irish cops – but none of these people are that one-dimensional

N ew Englanders often think of themselves as a nation within a nation. They are as likely to identify themselves with the region as with their individual state. In 1798, Yale's president, Timothy Dwight, said New Englanders were distinguished by their "love of science and learning, love of liberty, morality, piety, and unusual spirit of enquiry." That's as true now as it was then.

Demographics

Nearly 15 million people call New England home. One-quarter of them are under the age of 18; 15 percent are over 65. Of these, the majority are Caucasian (84 percent), far outnumbering the next largest groups – Hispanic, African-American, and Asian-American – with a combined population of about 12 percent. Native Americans and Oceanic peoples largely complete the head-count. Nearly 2 percent describe themselves as multi-racial. Massachusetts has the largest population: 6.5 million residents; Vermont has only 625,000.

Three-quarters of the population lives in Massachusetts, Connecticut, and Rhode Island. Most of them reside in metropolitan Boston and along the stretch of I–95 corridor from Massachusetts through Connecticut toward New York. Southern Connecticut's fortunes are so tied to those of New York that some demographers remove the state from many surveys of New England and use it as a source of information about New York.

Because of that urban concentration in a relatively small area, New England overall has the highest population density in the country, belying the image of an area of bucolic landscapes, vast tracts of mountain wilderness, and isolated fishing villages. It's just one of the juxtapositions of the many facets of the region.

Original people

When the Pilgrims arrived they were met by members of the Wampanoag tribe. Before the arrival of the Europeans, there were an estimated 250,000 people of the Algonquian tribes scattered through New England. But the first explorers brought more than an avaricious interest in exploring, settling, and exploiting the New World; they also brought diseases against which the Native Americans had no immunity. The

PRECEDING PAGES: decorative buoys in Cape Cod.
LEFT: recreating the Puritan heritage. RIGHT: a man dressed as a Wampanoag Indian at Plimoth Plantation.

plagues wiped out as much as 90 percent of the population. Today, there are an estimated 40,000 American Indians in the region. A minority live on nine reservations; most live in the general community, with varying degrees of success. Decades of subtle and overt discrimination are being replaced by a new sense of tribal identity and pride. The nations are fighting legal battles to regain land either taken outright by settlers or through violations of treaties.

Settlers

Of the European-originated population, English dominance has been superseded by those of Irish,

French/French Canadian, and Italian descent. The centers of population break down along ethnic lines. Boston has a large Irish and Italian population which is more numerous now than those who trace their lineage to the city's British roots. Rhode Island has strong Italian connections, but Providence boasts a large Portuguese neighborhood. Northern Vermont and New Hampshire have a strong French influence due to its proximity to Quebec. But there's also a French accent in central Massachusetts, stemming from the Industrial Revolution when large numbers of French Canadians migrated south to work in the factories.

Spiritually, the Pilgrims would be displeased, at best, by the region's religious affiliations. Given the influx of Irish, Italian, Portuguese, and Hispanic immigrants, it's no surprise that 36 percent of New Englanders are Catholic, with another 32 percent identifying themselves as Christian. But 22 percent claim no religious affiliation of any kind, one of the highest levels in the country. So much for the Puritans' determination to create a theocracy in which pleasing God – particularly the non-Papist God – was fundamental.

Patriotism

It's a small wonder that the spark of independence was fanned into flame here. The nature of New England fostered self-reliance and a distrust of authority. Those were the driving motivations of the Pilgrims' self-imposed exile, after all. Once here, they found no land of milk and honey, but a wilderness that further tested their resolve.

Fiercely proud of their history as founders of the nation (dismissing Spanish explorers in 16th-century Florida and the 1607 Jamestown Colony in Virginia) and as the Cradle of Liberty and the Revolution (Franklin, Jefferson, and Washington are appreciated for their contributions, but New Englanders will aver that Samuel Adams, Ethan Allen, and Captain John Parker at the Battle of Lexington set the stage for the others' success), New Englanders are almost obsessively patriotic. Patriots Day – the observance of the Battles of Lexington and Concord – is a state holiday in Massachusetts, and the week surrounding the 4th of July is a citywide festival in Boston. The first Independence Day parade was in Bristol RI in 1785. The town still displays the nation's colors everywhere – including on the main road through town, where the center line is painted red, white, and blue. They point with pride to Maine's Bath Iron Works and Electric Boat Company in Groton CT – both of which produce vessels for the US Navy – the Naval War College in Newport, and the US Coast Guard Academy in New London. When the USS *Constitution* sails around Boston Harbor every 4th of July, many of those watching from shore and on the private boats escorting her are misty-eyed.

Presidential hopefuls ignore New England in general and New Hampshire in particular at their peril. New Hampshire's election primary, coming at the beginning of the official campaign season, is vital for contenders. A loss in New Hampshire usually means an end to the presidential dream, while a victory is a major boost to the campaign. The state bookends its importance in the presidential saga by being the first to open its polls on election day when the 30-odd registered voters of Dixville Notch cast their ballots at midnight. (In the primaries, the Dixville voters have chosen the eventual Republican candidate in every election since 1968; it's a bit spotty on the Democratic side, and the general election results are accurately predictive no more than half the time.)

Common personality traits

It's impossible to separate the New England mindset from the land and the climate. The region's personality was cast in years of digging rocks out of pastures, felling trees in the wilderness, and fighting ocean waves. It was hard to transport goods and supplies then; it's still not always convenient now. And no one has ever claimed to meet a rich or lazy fisherman or farmer. As a result, rural New Englanders – be they Vermont dairy farmers, Maine fishermen, or New Hampshire loggers – all share a certain fundamental sense of practicality and frugality. "Use it up, wear it out, make it do, do without" is a phrase often used to sum up the philosophy of New Englanders to material goods.

Small towns are often accused of being cool to outsiders, particularly "flatlanders" moving in from anywhere – particularly anywhere outside New England. The joke is that it takes at least 20 years of living in a town before you're

no longer called "the new folks." It's not hostility, but another instance of practicality, this time merging with experience. New England doesn't grant its residents the leisure time to sip tea on a veranda and "visit" as they might in the South. There are always chores to be done: livestock to feed and water; fishing gear to repair; the chain saw to tune up; and the ever-present need to collect firewood. Towns are insular, and their people have come to know and rely on one another. Outsiders are kept at a distance until they prove themselves as a part of the community. In the meantime, their motivations, ideas, and attitudes are watched and weighed.

Tensions arise when they propose ideas that are interpreted as changing the structure and functions of the community that attracted the newcomers in the first place.

There's a level of community involvement in government that's not seen elsewhere. At annual town meetings, residents publicly debate and decide issues like the town budget, local ordinances, and canine leash laws. Everyone has his or her say, and the debates are generally conducted in an atmosphere of respect. While attendance has slipped over the decades, with some places seeing only a quarter of the residents showing up and others choosing to establish a more representative system, the town meeting is still a valued institution.

ABOVE, FROM LEFT: visitors to Applefest, Vermont's biggest apple festival and craft show, held in October; students at Harvard University, Cambridge.

Urban centers

The urban centers of Boston, Providence, and southern Connecticut share, enjoy, and endure the same elements – major cultural and entertainment venues, traffic congestion and pollution, and more employment opportunities. They are as homogeneous as any cluster of cities can be, for reasons that reflect their history. Insulated from the rest of the country and seeing few new arrivals, they remained the enclaves of those who founded them for two centuries. Then came the waves of immigrants, starting with the Irish. Each group tried to re-establish a sense of what they left behind by

SANCTUARY CITIES

As in many other areas of the country, immigration – particularly the arrival of undocumented immigrants – is a highly controversial issue. Federal law and the Department of Homeland Security both require local governments to cooperate with immigration enforcement policies, but some places object to the requirements, either for humanitarian or economic reasons. Maine limits state employees' ability to report the presence of illegal aliens, while Vermont maintains a bias-free policy in providing state services. Several municipalities in New England act as sanctuary cities, with police and municipal offices providing services without verifying immigration status.

living in the same neighborhood, going to the same schools and churches, developing a common shopping area. In every practical way, those neighborhoods are as much small towns as any place in the Berkshires or central Maine. The impact of the immigrants on the social and political establishment was another revolution, as they applied the same drive which led them to leave their old homes to gaining political and social power in their new one – not unlike the Pilgrims.

Conservative image, modern ideas

The image of the dour, fundamentalist Puritans gives the region a reputation for conservative attitudes, but in practice it usually takes a liberal stand. Upon reflection, that's not unexpected; the Puritans were liberals in their own way, and the region's history is, after all, one of revolutionary ideas put into practice. A line from the play *1776* has Rhode Islander Stephen Hopkins admonishing the delegates to the Continental Congress that "there's no idea so dangerous that it can't be talked about."

Vermont was one of the first states to recognize civil unions and same-sex marriages. By 2012, Maine was the only New England state still prohibiting such relationships. Massachusetts enacted a universal health law in 2006 which, while controversial, provides health care to nearly all of its residents. New England's first casinos opened on Indian tribal lands in Massachusetts, and the region is a national leader in tackling environmental issues.

Impact of tourism

Inconvenient to the rest of the nation, far from transportation routes, with few manufacturing jobs, and few resources to export, New Englanders seek ways to achieve economic viability. Taking advantage of the wealth of universities and medical facilities, it is positioning itself as a leader in research and high-tech fields, areas that pay well and need less infrastructure to support. Tourism was a natural field to develop. Residents often spend their vacation time within the region, which keeps tax revenue and spending dollars in the local coffers.

ABOVE, FROM LEFT: doller bills are pinned to a statue of San Gennaro at Boston's annual Little Italy street festival; protests have a long history in New England.

The impact of tourism in New England is significant. It is now the largest industry in Maine, generating $10 billion in sales and responsible for 28 percent of the state's sales tax and 17 percent of its jobs. In Vermont, it creates 23 percent of the jobs in the state, and over $335 million in business tax revenue. And it's a $14.4-billion industry in Massachusetts, generating over $3.4 billion as year annually in wages.

Most areas are well able to handle the visitors; there may be a lot of them, but they are either spread out or drawn to magnet areas that are able to handle the numbers. Peak times like fall foliage and very popular destinations like Martha's Vineyard or and the Kennebunks in the summer are sometimes victims of their own success.

It's ironic that the forbidding land and conditions that so nearly defeated the Puritans were the very things that are the foundations for New Englanders' success: a tough spirit willing to take on challenges and adapt to change, a measure of common sense in deciding how to live, an appreciation of the beauty of the elements, and the willingness to rely on one another. While New England is a region of many differences, these are the traits its people share in common.

ETHNIC FESTIVALS

Almost every weekend, you can hear the music, see the traditional costumes, shop for crafts, and taste the flavors of cultures the original Pilgrims never imagined. Some of the more interesting are: the La Kermesse Festival, the largest Franco-American festival in the US, held every June in Biddeford ME; (www.lakermessefestival.com); the Cape Verdean Independence Day celebration in Providence; (www.ricapeverdeaenheritage.com); the Southeast Asian Water Festival, which honors the spirits and spirituality of water, held on the third Saturday in August in Lowell MA; (www.lowellwaterfestival.org); and the largest Portuguese festival in New England, the Feast of the Blessed Sacrament in late July in New Bedford MA.

(www.portuguesefest.com). One of the largest West Indian communities holds its Caribbean Festival in Hartford CT in June (www.cayasco.org). The Abenaki, French trappers, and English settlers never imagined the foods served at the Green Mountain Chew Chew festival in Burlington VT in June. In addition to cultural performances, it features food from Vietnam, China, Pakistan, Afghanistan, Mexico, and the Middle East. Rhode Island celebrates the diversity of its population with a multi-cultural celebration on the State House lawn in August with crafts, dances, music, and food from African-American, Bolivian, German, Guatemalan, Indian, Irish, Laotian, and Puerto Rican groups (www.preservation.ri.gov).

THE BOUNTIFUL SEA

Even though the codfish has yielded to the computer as the most important element in New England's economy, the sea still plays a central role in coastal life

The first generation of Europeans in America all had the same "baptism by sea": a two-month voyage across the stormy North Atlantic. Most of the settlers who came were landlubbers; many had never seen the ocean before. But shipbuilding was one of the first enterprises the early colonists undertook. Ships maintained the connection to the homeland and provided an income from trade. The vast virgin forests of the New World supplied materials for their construction. One hundred years after the Pilgrims stepped onto Plymouth Rock, New England's coastal shipyards were launching a ship a day. With labor and lumber costs so much cheaper than those in England, American-made ships dominated the market.

For the early settlers, the sea brought news from home, fresh legions of colonists, and ships involved in the Triangle Trade (the transport of slaves, molasses, and rum between ports in Africa, the Caribbean, and New England). Early on, fishing was seen as a prime source of the region's prosperity. Codfish nourished not just New Englanders, but also colonists in Mid-Atlantic and Southern towns. One of the first important acts of the Great and General Court of Massachusetts was to set standards for the regulation and encouragement of the fishing industry.

The whaling boom

Lamps were fired by vegetable and animal oils; candles were made from animal tallow. The light was dim and the lamps were smoky until someone made the discovery that blubber from

LEFT: in the harbor at Stonington, Connecticut.
RIGHT: Boston harbor in the late 19th century.

a beached whale could be rendered and the oil extracted would provide a clearer, brighter light.

Whales beached themselves frequently on the New England shores, and whaling began as a shore activity. Teams of townsfolk gathered whenever they saw a whale, tethering it to a stake to prevent the tide taking it out to sea. The blubber was cut away, rendered in the kettles of a "tryworks" set up on the beach and transformed into a high-quality oil which could be burned in the town's lamps or traded. Soon such business became an industry.

Watery highways

In colonial times, overland routes were expensive to build and maintain, so coastal freighters and passenger boats regularly sailed from

Boston to New York and Philadelphia. The more enterprising captains headed south, where they unloaded their cod at Philadelphia or Annapolis and took on corn and flour, beans, and barrels of pork, which could be sold at a great profit at home.

Though a boon to New England's maritime economy, the coastal trade, like fishing and whaling, was not an easy way to make a living. Every trip between Boston and ports to the south involved a voyage around Cape Cod, and the weather that had so discouraged the Pilgrims was a constant threat. Ships and men were regularly lost to the ravages of the sea.

Though fishing and the coastal trade helped New England employ its people and pay its bills, the region was not a rich one. Because it always imported more goods than it exported, ways had to be found to reduce the trade deficit.

Merchants and sea captains decided that, if they couldn't produce goods from their rocky soil, at least they could transport the goods produced by others. New England merchant vessels undertook long and arduous voyages to Europe, Africa, and the Orient. And it was not only the cargoes that were put up for sale: the ships themselves were frequently on the auctioning block, bringing added revenue to their builders back home.

LIT BY WHALE OIL

The demand for whale oil became so great that fishermen, hoping to get rich from its sale, began to pursue whales along the shore, thus initiating New England's whaling industry. The trade took a great leap forward in 1712, when Captain Christopher Hussey of Nantucket was blown off course into deep water and accidentally bagged the first sperm whale. Although it had teeth in lieu of coveted baleen – bony upper jaw slats useful as stays for collars and corsets – the spermaceti oil proved far superior to that of the already endangered "right" whale (so called because it was the right one to pursue). Nantucket whalers came to specialize in the pursuit of this purer, lighter, and more profitable oil.

Whalers out of Nantucket and New Bedford pursued their mammoth quarry for months, even years, as far as the Pacific, until their holds were filled with barrels of the oil that would fire the nation's lamps and illumine the capitals of Europe. The whaling ships themselves served as complete processing plants.

Until 1859, when petroleum was discovered in Pennsylvania and distillers began producing kerosene, the sea was the world's great proven oil reserve. For a closer look at this fascinating chapter in maritime history, see the last surviving whaler, the *Charles W. Morgan*, tied up at Mystic Seaport in Connecticut, or visit the whaling museums in Nantucket or New Bedford.

Trade was good to the region. While the pioneer towns of inland America were primitive and rough, New England seaports took on the polish of wealth and culture. Fortunes made at sea were translated into fine mansions and patronage of the arts. From the profits of their voyages, captains brought home art treasures, luxury goods, and curiosities from exotic destinations. The Peabody Essex Museum of Salem is filled with the wealth that came to New England on returning merchant ships.

Clocks, shoes, and ice

As time went by, the new republic developed industries that produced goods for trade. Connecticut's household utensils, machines, clocks, pistols, and rifles, plus shoes and cloth from Rhode Island and Massachusetts, ultimately made their way around the world.

Perhaps the most ingenious export of all was ice. Cut from ponds, rivers, and lakes, ice was packed in sawdust, loaded into fast clipper ships and sent off to Cuba, South America, and beyond. The rulers of the British Raj in India sipped drinks cooled by ice from New England. In exchange for a commodity that was free for the cutting, New Englanders brought back spices, fine porcelain, silks, and other items.

The taming of the sea

The War of 1812 sent New England's maritime commerce into depression, but by the mid-19th century its seaports returned to glory during the brief heyday of the clipper ship. "Never, in these United States, has the brain of man conceived, or the hand of man fashioned, so perfect a thing as the clipper ship," wrote the great Massachusetts historian Samuel Eliot Morison.

But the clippers' days were numbered, as were those of the larger, bulkier schooners carrying up to six masts, built to transport coal and other heavy loads that clippers, with their small holds, could never profitably carry. Neither clipper nor schooner could go anywhere when the wind failed – but the new steamships could travel even in a dead calm, and even keep to schedule. They could work their way around Cape Cod, ignoring the winds that had caused

so much trouble since Pilgrim times. Steam also powered the new railroads that linked the Atlantic and Pacific coasts, putting the ships that had sailed all the way around South America to reach California out of business.

Safer waves

Today, the sea is still a major source of income – and at a much lower price in lives lost to storms. A century ago whole families, even most of a town, might be lost to a single ferocious storm. There are still tragedies at sea, but radar, radio, and stricter safety precautions help prevent many accidents.

Still a working sea

By the 1970s, New England fishermen, working from their small boats, were competing with large trawlers from Europe and Japan. In 1976, the US imposed new regulations prohibiting the foreign vessels from coming within 200 miles of the US coastline. Initially, that appeared to be a good thing, but the fleet soon expanded exponentially and it became clear that the fishery was collapsing. Despite angry disagreements from the fishermen, regulations were imposed limiting the catch. These were largely ignored and rarely enforced, however. By 1989, the population of groundfish – cod, flounder, redfish, and other bottom dwellers – had dropped 65 percent. Tighter regulations

ABOVE, FROM LEFT: whalers sometimes pursued their quarry for months; Elias Hasket Derby (1739-99) was the owner of the *Grand Turk*, the first New England vessel to trade directly with China.

were established, aimed at better management of resources.

Today, the fishing fleet has largely consolidated. There are fewer ships and they are limited as to how many days they can fish and the size of their catch. There is less over-fishing and smaller hauls, but revenues are higher. But there are also fewer fishermen, and those who are on the water are aging. The average age of a fisherman in Massachusetts is 58; the number of young men seeking to make their living at sea is shrinking. The cost of a boat is upwards of $200,000; fuel is expensive; maintenance costs are high; permits are costly; income is spotty.

Woods Hole

Woods Hole is the world's largest non-profit ocean research, engineering, and education organization. It's dedicated to research and higher education at the frontiers of ocean science. For many years, this facility on the western shore of Cape Cod was considered a source of interesting, if arcane, information. With increased concern about ocean pollution, fishery health, and global warming, its research is now widely reported. It supports four "ocean institutes" which encompass areas of concern for the public, other scientists, and policymakers: Coastal Oceans; Deep Ocean Exploration; Oceans and Climate Change; and Ocean Life.

Many fear that the future of fishing lies in the hands of large corporate trawlers, which will destroy the economies of small fishing villages which depend on their large fleet of small boats.

And for the lobster? The population was in steep decline in the 1980s, and then seemed to revive strongly. It's now shrinking, or so say the regulators. The lobstermen disagree, saying they see signs of a growing population. A proposed five-year moratorium on lobstering from Cape Cod to North Carolina has been proposed.

There's one success story in the saga – scallops. When the 6,600-sq-mile (17,000-sq-km) George's Bank fishery was closed as a result of the cod limitations, the population of the bivalve increased dramatically. The fishery is now run on a rotating schedule, with some areas closed every year while others are harvested. It's become an example of a successful sustainable fishery. But it appears unlikely to win support from fishermen or lobstermen to try it elsewhere.

Cruising the coast

In previous centuries, a New Englander either went to sea to earn a living, or remained a landlubber. But now New England's seacoast has become a major playground, and the variety of maritime sports seems limitless. As in so many other realms, the world of work has become the world of play, and places once associated solely with danger and hardship are visited just for fun.

Forty miles (64km) of Cape Cod's sandy beaches have been set aside as the Cape Cod National Seashore, one of the great tourist attractions of New England. The beaches of Connecticut, Rhode Island, New Hampshire, and Maine attract visitors. Reliable ferries carry vacationers to Nantucket, Martha's Vineyard, Block Island, and the outer islands along the Maine coast. Tourists stroll among the handsome sea captains' houses, and explore the world of the seafaring men who built them.

Perhaps the clearest indication of the taming of the sea is this: the perilous voyage undertaken by the Pilgrims in 1620 is now done for sport. Transatlantic yacht racing began in 1866 when the *Henrietta* raced the *Vesta* to England. In 1851, the schooner

ABOVE, FROM LEFT: "widow's walks" were built on top of sea-facing houses so that sailors' wives could watch for their husbands' return; a cruiseship navigates the rocky shore with the help of a lighthouse.

America won the Royal Yacht Squadron Cup, and the America's Cup became the great event of yachting, with the first race held in Newport in 1870. The beauty and science of yacht design and racing is pursued passionately in Newport and in dozens of other ports along the coast.

New England's waters are particularly suited to yachting: Cape Cod Bay has provided calm sailing ever since the days of the Pilgrims. With the cutting of the Cape Cod Canal and the establishment of the Intra-coastal Waterway, coastal cruising has been made safer and more enjoyable than ever before.

Boaters along the coast will often see the colorful bobbing floats that mark the location of the fish-baited traps on the bottom; each captain has his own float design.

The whalers that sailed out of New Bedford and Nantucket are long gone. Yet boats from a dozen ports still head out each day in search of whales, but now it's tourists' cameras, not harpoons, that are aimed at them. It's strange that the leviathans that once made New England "oil-rich" should still be helping its economy.

LIFE-SAVING STATIONS

The waters off the New England coast were (and still are) treacherous. Many ships and crews came to grief when they ran aground or were caught in fierce storms. In 1784, the Humane Society of the Commonwealth of Massachusetts was created to help ships in distress. Huts were built along the beach to provide shelter for shipwreck survivors. Those were followed by the use of whaleboats which were rowed out to ships by 10-man crews. Those aids were only near major ports, leaving the rest of the coast still unprotected.

In 1878, Maine native Sumner Kimball organized the US Life-Saving Service. He established a chain of life-saving houses along both coasts and the Great Lakes. These provided the first large-scale, round-the-clock lookout and rescue service. The life of the crews was strenuous. Sumner wanted physically fit fishermen who knew the idiosyncrasies of the local coastline. Their main piece of equipment was the surfboat, a 1,000-pound (455kg) boat which they would hoist onto a wheeled cart. Every day, they would rehearse dragging it along the shore and across the beach and launching it in the surf. At night, two men would patrol the beach, looking and listening for any signs of a ship in trouble. When help was needed, the crews would launch the surfboats, usually in heavy seas, high winds, and driving rain. The Life-Saving Service merged with other agencies to become the U.S. Coast Guard in 1915.

THE PURITAN TRADITION

H. L. Mencken once quipped that a Puritan is someone tormented by the fact that somebody, somewhere, is having fun; but the strength of character that the original settlers showed has molded the region

The Puritans did more than settle New England; they created it. Yet today people laud their optimism and courage in deciding to risk everything for their ideals, while criticizing the methods they used to achieve them. "Puritanism" is a pejorative term denoting an excess of zeal in pursuing rigid ideas of morality and law. Nor is this a 21st-century judgment: in 1917 Mencken further dismissed Puritanism as "all that's unattractive about American culture, compounded over time by evangelism, moralism from political demagogues, and relentless money-grubbing."

Certainly, the creed was not a cozy one. Out of the Calvinistic doctrines regarding humanity's inherent evil and the predestination of the soul grew a society that was stern and uncompromising. Even at its best, the Puritans' dogma was a hard one, an ultimate faith that required everyone – from the most prominent minister to the humblest child – to strain toward an ineffable God.

Arthur Miller's celebrated play The Crucible, based on the Salem witch trials, was written in 1953, at the height of McCarthyism. During that era, people were accused of supporting Communism, usually without any evidence.

Puritans argued that humans, in their fallen state, could never know God and could thus never truly know the state of their own souls. Salvation came not through human action, but through God's mysterious grace. Abject though we human creatures may be, we must always examine our conscience, always repent our inevitable sin, always attempt to lead a just life, and always know that no matter how sincere and devout our efforts, they will probably fall short.

Spiritual values

The Puritans' difficult faith stood them in good stead, but it found little room for gentleness or pleasure. Regarding discipline and hard work as spiritual values, these early settlers labored long for the greater glory of God – while incidentally accumulating considerable wealth and building prosperous communities. Puritans came to identify worldly success with godliness, rewards bestowed by God as signs of His approval.

In America, as in England, class distinctions were important. But the Puritans, eschewing such worldly signs of status as expensive clothes and fancy carriages, had to devise other more subtle ways of indicating social class. Thus, the title "Master" was reserved exclusively for educated men.

The search for perfection

Education was essential to the Puritans'vision of what their new society in America was to be. Most of the settlers were well educated; four officers of the Massachusetts Bay Colony – John Winthrop, Sir Richard Saltonstall, Isaac Johnson, and John Humphrey – had attended Cambridge University. For them, the journey to the New

was destined to develop an impressive school system. As early as 1635, Boston voted a declaration that "our brother, Mr Philemon Pormont shall be intreated to become scholemaster for teaching and nourtering of children with us."

Pormont established Boston Latin School, the country's first secondary school and still one of Boston's finest high schools. Massachusetts Bay Colony officials chartered the institution that was to become Harvard College in 1636.

The witch hunts

In the mid-1600s, when the fever for witch-killing blew across the North Atlantic from Europe,

World was more than an adventure to a new frontier, it was a chance to transport their old society in purified form to a new land. Discontented in a country where they were persecuted for their religious practices, they came to America to build an ideal society, their "city on a hill." These men knew that unless they provided for the education of clergymen, they might quickly lose sight of the New (and perfect) England.

A society in which education established one's credentials before God and the world

ABOVE, FROM LEFT: John Winthrop, the Puritan leader who aimed to build an ideal society; the idealized *First Thanksgiving* (1914) by Jennie Augusta Brownscombe.

WHERE DEMOCRACY MATTERS

Town meetings were central to the social and political structures of the Puritans. Unlike a representative governing body, these were public gatherings during which all local matters were discussed and decided. A serious attempt was made to introduce a high degree of participation and this principle is still pursued. Town meetings can be displays of democracy in its purest form; all town issues are on the agenda and they are decided after debates, which are often long and lively, usually respectful but sometimes acrimonious. It often takes several sessions to reach consensus on many matters, particularly budgetary ones.

the colonies of Rhode Island, Connecticut, and Massachusetts joined the pack with decrees of death. Non-conformity – which threatened the carefully constructed society – was now equated with devil worship. Connecticut quickly seized and executed nine victims. Bostonians hanged Margaret Jones of Charlestown on a bright June day in 1648, and for an encore on Boston Common they hanged the beautiful and cultured Anne Hibbins, widow of the colony's former representative to England.

Against that lunatic background, the fanatical Rev. Cotton Mather sensed a great opportunity for self-promotion and professional success. He

was already the colony's most highly acclaimed clergyman. He was learned and brilliant, and he was also ambitious. He longed to succeed his father, the Rev. Increase Mather, as the president of Harvard. He decided it would boost his reputation and enhance his career if he could identify assorted witches and promote their executions. So he went to work and soon focused on a witch-suspect named Goodwife Glover, the mother of a North End laundress. With Mather's help, poor Mrs Glover quickly wound up in the noose of a Boston Common gallows rope.

The most notorious expression of religious hysteria emerged in the Salem witch trials of 1692, which the playwright Arthur Miller described as "one of the strangest and most awful chapters in human history." The trials grew from the feverish imaginations of adolescent girls who became swept up in tales of voodoo and mysticism as told to them by Tituba, a slavewoman from Barbados. All too eager to discover depravity in someone else, the Puritans sat in eager judgment on the accused. Unrelenting in their desire to purge their world of evil and in their arrogant belief in their own righteousness, they sent 20 innocent people to their death.

Cradle of reformation

As if to live down the small-mindedness of their predecessors and to return to their original ideals of creating a just society, the New England philosophers and legislators of the 19th century stood in the very vanguard of political reform. Having abolished slavery themselves by the end of the 18th century (but not before accumulating

THE TRANSCENDENTALISTS WHO PURSUED UTOPIA

The gradual liberalization of New England's churches and colleges in the 18th century gave way to a true intellectual flowering in the 19th century. Flushed with the success of the Revolutionary War and the founding of a nation that was growing prosperous from the lucrative China trade, the Puritan temperament was ready for an overhaul, perhaps even a transformation.

Many New Englanders were embracing the doctrines of Unitarianism, which taught that God was a single rather than tripartite entity, and rejected such old Calvinist mainstays as predestination and the innate baseness of the human personality. Henry Ware, who founded the Harvard Divinity School in 1819, was a Unitarian, as was the great

Boston pastor William Ellery Channing. Unitarianism's liberal cast of thought prepared the ground for the sweet optimism of Transcendentalism, a mystical philosophy which argued the existence of an Oversoul unifying all creation, and which preached the primacy of insight over reason and the inherent goodness of humankind.

The movement spawned several experiments in living, the best known being Henry David Thoreau'sThoreau's solitary retreat on Walden Pond, and short-lived communal farms at Brook Farm in Concord and Fruitlands in Harvard MA. Led by Ralph Waldo Emerson, the movement attracted some of the brightest minds of the day. Today, at transcendentalists.com, its ideas inhabit the internet.

great fortunes by providing the ships and transporting the rum and molasses which were all part of the Triangle Trade), high-minded New Englanders dedicated themselves to nationwide abolition. William Lloyd Garrison founded his weekly newspaper *The Liberator* in Boston in 1831 (not all shared his views at that time: he was nearly killed by a Boston mob in 1835) and persisted until 1865, when the 13th amendment was finally passed. Joining him in the struggle were writers such as Harriet Beecher Stowe, who delivered one of the abolitionist movement's most effective tracts in the form of her best-selling 1852 novel, *Uncle Tom's Cabin*.

After the Civil War, New England's reformists turned their attention to the labor abuses brought on by the Industrial Revolution and to the role of women in society. Susan B. Anthony turned her attention to women's rights from her home in Massachusetts. The first women's college to open in the US was Vassar Female College, founded in Poughkeepsie NY in 1861. By 1879, four outstanding colleges for women had been established in Massachusetts: Smith, Wellesley, Mount Holyoke, and Radcliffe.

Despite this growing willingness to entertain change – reinforced by decades of stability and prosperity – remnants of the Puritan strain persisted. For the most part, New England remained a deeply moral, and occasionally moralistic, society. At their worst, New Englanders suppressed books they deemed offensive to public taste, and considered theater – and, worse yet, actors – a pernicious influence on impressionable minds.

The demon drink

Blue laws, first introduced in Connecticut in 1781 to control public and private conduct, especially on the Sabbath, enjoyed regular revivals in the 19th and 20th centuries. Alcohol was frequently seen as a destructive influence, although Increase Mather wrote, "Drink is in itself a good creature of God, and to be received with thankfulness, but the abuse of drink is from Satan." To this day you cannot buy alcohol in Connecticut on Sundays, except in restaurants. In Massachusetts, would-be imbibers must wait until noon to purchase alcohol on

Sundays, and large retail stores may not open on Thanksgiving and Christmas. Maine does not allow car dealerships to operate on Sunday.

What, then, is the true Puritan legacy? It's easy to grumble about arcane liquor laws, or to see the cold hand of Puritanism in each new dictum about what we should and shouldn't eat. But New England wasn't going to get settled by people out to have fun; the soil and the climate would not have cooperated. On the credit side, Puritan legal principles helped craft the Constitution, with its emphasis on the supremacy of law. Reinforced by the determination of immigrants who arrived in New

England from the antebellum days onward, the fabled "Puritan work ethic" and a conviction in the ability to achieve self-determination is as much of part of New England as Thanksgiving.

As for the Puritan sense of rectitude and moral improvement, it survives today in activist movements – strong in New England – dedicated to social change and promoting environment-friendly policies. With the exception of Maine, same-sex unions are legal; Massachusetts has established health benefits for nearly all citizens; groups throughout the region work on immigration issues. The Puritans' zeal to create a perfect society lives on in what has become one of the country's most progressive regions.

ABOVE, FROM LEFT: the influential Puritan minister and educator, Rev. Increase Mather (1639–1723); Salem Witch Trials, 1692.

TRAINING NEW ENGLAND'S MINDS

The Puritans recognized that education was vital to their survival; that appreciation has made New England a magnet for the best in higher education

New England is the cradle of American education. Although justly recognized as the home for many of the most respected and influential colleges and universities, learning at all levels has always been important.

In an age when literacy was largely a luxury, the reformers who created the first settlements in New England firmly believed that every church member – every citizen, in other words – should be able to read Scripture. By 1639, Boston and the communities of Charlestown and Dorchester had hired schoolmasters. Boston Latin School was established in 1635; in 1642 education was decreed as compulsory for all males. By 1672, every colony except Rhode Island had compulsory elementary education.

The curriculum centered around the incorporation of Calvinist doctrine in every aspect of life. The first textbook was *The New England Primer*, which taught reading through rote memorization. A typical passage for the young scholars read, "In Adam's fall/We sinned all," a far cry from the innocent "See Dick. See Dick Run" readers of later years.

The birth of the Ivy League

References to New England's Ivy League schools are so pervasive that it is sometimes tiresome. Yet the schools had a profound effect on the early years of colonization, and their influence is equally profound nearly four centuries later.

In 1636, the Great and General Court of Massachusetts Bay had appropriated the sum of £400 for "a schoale or colledge," which was established the following year at New Town,

LEFT: Yale University campus, New Haven, CT.
RIGHT: a fencing lesson at Yale in the early 20th century.

across the Charles River from Boston. The first class assembled two years later.

In that same year of 1638, a young minister in nearby Charlestown died of consumption. Rev. John Harvard left his library of 400 books and half of his estate to the new college, which would thereafter bear his name.

Yale's beginnings

In Connecticut, a group of 10 clergymen met in 1701 to found an institution called the "Collegiate School." Their impetus was in part a reaction against the perceived liberalization of the Harvard curriculum. It, too, benefited from a philanthropic gesture from an immensely wealthy, Boston-born ex-governor of the East India Company. His name

was Elihu Yale, and so generous were his donations to New Haven's fledgling school that it was
named in his honor in 1718.

New England's third-oldest college was the fruit
of a growing ecumenical spirit. It isn't surprising
that a representative of the relatively new Baptist
sect should have chosen to establish a college in
Rhode Island, a colony devoted from its infancy
to religious freedom. Rev. James Manning secured
a charter for a "College of Rhode Island" in 1764,
which included Baptists, Congregationalists, and
Episcopalians. Established on College Hill in
Providence by 1770, the college counted among
its 1783 class Nicholas Brown Jr, son of one of

hectares). The school, Dartmouth College,
received its royal charter in 1769.

The prep schools

Several "preparatory" boarding schools were
established where sons could receive a better

> "I am obliged to confess I should sooner live in a
> society governed by the first two thousand names
> in the Boston telephone directory than in a society
> governed by the two thousand faculty members of
> Harvard University." William F. Buckley

the four Brown brothers who dominated Rhode
Island commerce in that era. Nicholas Jr would
give his alma mater some $160,000 over his life-
time. Hence the institution's new name, from
1804 onward – Brown University.

One of the more unlikely locations for
a college in the 18th century was the New
Hampshire wilderness. In the 1760s, one Rev.
Eleazar Wheelock was looking for a place to
relocate a Christian school for Indians, which
he had established in Connecticut. Having
secured a pledge of £11,000 and the patronage of the Earl of Dartmouth, Wheelock's next
step was to find a community that wanted
the school. The most eager candidate was tiny
Hanover NH, which offered 3,000 acres (1,200

education than locally. Phillips Andover (1778),
Phillips Exeter (1781), and Deerfield Academy
(1797) served as feeders for the Ivy League
schools. They went co-ed in the 1970s and are still
elite and elitist in their student body and mission.

Education for women

Girls did not get much of the same consid-
eration in education. While they were usually
taught to read – because they needed to study
the Scriptures, too – they were not taught to
write. Activities requiring that talent were the
purview of men. Other areas of study were
deemed completely unsuitable for women. It
was not uncommon for women who could read
a contract to sign it with an "X."

In the 1800s, this began to change as women were seen as an important influence in building a society of strong, moral leaders. In 1825, Boston opened the first high school for women. That was followed by the establishment of Mount Holyoke Female Seminary in 1837 by Mary Lyon. Born in remote Buckland MA in 1797, she was unusual in that she attended school regularly until she was 13. The women were taught English, math, history, and geography. Her inspirational words, "Go where no one else will go, do what no one else will do," remain the school's philosophy. Notable graduates include Emily Dickinson; former Obama Deputy Chief of Staff

few schools in the areas where they lived. The white colonists distrusted and discriminated against the Indians, setting up a pattern of displacement and poverty that still exists among the Algonquin and Abenaki people.

School segregation

It was an equally grim situation for African-Americans. In 1800, Prince Hall began teaching black students in his Boston home, after the state legislature refused to extend public education to African-Americans. When abolitionists opened Noyes Academy in Canaan NH, a mob tore the building down and fired cannons at the

Mona Sutphen, and Dulcy Singer, executive producer of *Sesame Street*.

Native Americans at Dartmouth

While education was advancing for women, other groups were ignored. Although Dartmouth was founded with the express purpose of educating Native American males and incorporating them into "civilized" society, the effort largely failed. Few Indians arrived, and only one graduated. Many tribal members were not interested in assimilation, and, even if they were, there were

ABOVE, FROM LEFT: serious study at Boston Public Library; on display at the Hart Nautical Museum, MIT Campus, Cambridge, MA.

"In New York," said Mark Twain, "they ask how much money a man has; in Philadelphia, what family he's from; in Boston, how much he knows."

homes where the students were living. In 1849, Benjamin Roberts sued the City of Boston for the right of his daughter to attend high school. He lost the case, and it became the precedent which created the "separate but equal" concept of school segregation. In Canterbury CT, Prudence Crandall's decision to admit a black woman to her Female Boarding School in 1833 led to violent demonstrations and her arrest. The school was attacked by a mob following her acquittal, and she moved away. Even in more modern times, school busing – transporting children to schools in order to achieve racial balance – was met with rioting in Boston.

Ironically, many of the most vocal opponents of the busing program were descendants of Irish immigrants, who were not welcome in public schools when they arrived. The Irish established a system of parish schools (parochial schools) to provide elementary and secondary education, which became a mainstay of Catholic education.

How Harvard Made its Mark

Although it was technically not a religious but a civic institution, Harvard College served primarily to train ministers throughout the 17th century – a century which saw only 465 documented graduates. Harvard's greatest strides were taken during the four-decade presidency of Charles William Eliot (1869–1909), who introduced the elective system, modernized the teaching of law and medicine, and created a graduate school of arts and sciences. Born into an old Boston family himself, Eliot did more than any Harvard educator to elevate the university beyond its onetime status as a school largely attended by the local Brahmin class.

The Little Ivies

New England is peppered with the campuses of the "Little Ivies" – schools which rival their better-known counterparts in excellence. The list of is long, with Bowdoin in Maine, Middlebury in Vermont, Wesleyan in Connecticut, and Amherst and Williams in Massachusetts the best known. The "Seven Sisters" are schools that were established when women were not admitted to other colleges. Mt. Holyoke Mount Holyoke is one; the others in New England are Smith and Wellesley. Radcliffe was another, but has since been absorbed by Harvard and no longer exists as an independent entity.

The 19th century also saw the rise of the great public universities; each New England state supports one, with the University of Vermont (1791) occupying an unusual semi-private status. The Jesuit institutions Boston College and College of the Holy Cross (Massachusetts) and Fairfield University (Connecticut) are among the leaders in church-sponsored higher education.

Town vs. gown

Most of the colleges are in small towns, which reflect both the atmosphere of intellectual pursuits of the college and the youthful exuberance of their students. "Town–gown" issues arise over off-campus housing, loud parties and drinking, and parking congestion in residential areas near the schools. The towns are well aware of the positive economic impact the schools play in their community; the schools are aware of the need to maintain good relations with their non-collegiate neighbors. Compromises and conflict are constants in the communities. Most towns have only one school to consider. Some cities have several. Worcester MA is home to nine colleges; Providence RI to six.

Specialty schools and programs

While New England's liberal arts schools are justly famous, the region also excels in the number of schools with specific concentrations.

Massachusetts Institute of Technology (MIT)) enrolled its first students in 1865. MIT occupies an expansive campus along the Charles River in Cambridge. The Institute's graduates have been instrumental in making Boston a hub of the computer and other high-technology industries, an eastern counterpart to California's Silicon Valley. In nearby Worcester, Worcester Polytechnic Institute also opened in 1865. Its unique program sees students working on real-world projects from their first semester. Their incoming freshman student profile is actually better than that of MIT's entering class.

At the New England Conservatory of Music, students concentrate on orchestral music, voice, and composition. Berklee College of Music in Boston is the largest college of contemporary music in the world. Focusing on jazz and rock, it also offers courses in reggae and bluegrass. The New England Culinary Institute in Montpelier

ABOVE, FROM LEFT: interior view of a new, modern science building on the campus of the University of Massachusetts-Amherst; Harvard University's Graduation Day.

VT and Johnson and Wales University in Boston graduate highly trained chefs. Chester College in New Hampshire has a focus on creative writing as well as fine arts. Rhode Island School of Design and in Providence RI, the School of the Museum of Fine Arts in Boston, and Lyme Academy College of Fine Arts in Old Lyme, CT are all renowned for their visual arts programs.

The funding predicament

Even in an era when public education largely fits a national rather than a regional mold, one strong aspect of the old colonial legacy robustly survives: a passionate grassroots involvement in education

issues. Of the six New England states, only Rhode Island fails to make the Top Ten list of the best primary and middle schools in the nation.

In the recent past, Vermont and New Hampshire have grappled with the problem of school funding, with courts ruling that reliance upon local property taxes is unfair to children in towns with meager tax bases, and that revenue-sharing systems must be initiated. Even in more populous and urban Massachusetts, where professional educators are more likely to insulate citizens from education policy decisions, there have been heated public discussions over issues such as teacher competency tests, and the question of English-only instruction actually reached the ballot box in 2002.

LITERARY UTOPIA

From Cotton Mather to Emily Dickinson and Robert Parker, New England writers have chronicled and commented on the region's people from Puritan times to modern day

The Massachusetts Bay Colony was barely 10 years old when its first printing press turned out a new edition of the Book of Psalms. The 1640 *Bay Psalm Book* represented not only the beginning of American printing, but, as it was a fresh translation, of American literature as well. Along with Scriptures and sermons, 17th-century New England writers favored histories and biographies extolling the Puritan experiment.

The religious strain in early New England writing was the only approved context. The Puritan ethos had no room for a worldly focus. Even the poignant poems of Anne Bradstreet, which reflect on her life and family, are filled with religious imagery. (There are those who read into her works frustration and dissatisfaction with Puritan attitudes.)

The sacred and the secular

The literary oratory of the Puritan preachers was as frightening as any Stephen King novel. Increase

PIONEERING POETS

New England produced two poets of merit in the 17th century. Anne Bradstreet, who arrived with the first settlers of Boston in 1630, collected her early work in The Tenth Muse Lately Sprung Up in America (1650). She found inspiration in her own life experiences. Edward Taylor, a Massachusetts pastor, was the finest 17th-century American poet. His religious meditations have been compared to the English metaphysical poetry of his era; and his observations on commonplace subjects, as in "To a Spider Catching A Fly," reveal a talent for observation that transcend their purpose as religious metaphor.

Mather's *An Essay for the Recording of Illustrious Providences* (1684) tells of the Devil tormenting Massachusetts villagers, and credits a Connecticut River flood as "an awful intimation of Divine displeasure." His son, Cotton Mather, was author of more than 400 works and a dogged chronicler of supernatural manifestations. His 1689 *Memorable Providences, Relating to Witchcrafts and Possessions* helped set the stage for the 1692 Salem witch hysteria. And staunchly orthodox Reverend Jonathan Edwards' 1741 sermon "Sinners in the Hands of an Angry God" must have made his congregation's blood run cold.

But it was also an era in which secular concerns became a part of the colonial life of letters. In Boston, James Franklin (brother of

Benjamin) published one of New England's first successful newspapers, the *New England Courant*, beginning in 1721. Isaiah Thomas began publishing his *Massachusetts Spy* in 1770, airing revolutionary sentiments.

The early Federal period was the age of the "Connecticut Wits," a coterie noted for their fondness for formal Augustan poetry. Among them were lawyers John Trumbull and Joel Barlow, and longtime Yale president Timothy Dwight. The best remembered of their works is Barlow's *The Hasty Pudding*, a mock-heroic tribute to the simple cornmeal concoction that still appears on New England menus as "Indian Pudding."

The Transcendentalists

That era began with the 1836 publication of an essay called *Nature*, by Ralph Waldo Emerson, a young clergyman from Concord MA. Emerson, a Unitarian, found in that denomination's liberal humanism a cornerstone for the philosophy of Transcendentalism, which emphasized the unity of the individual soul with the rest of creation and with the divine. Its principles suffuse Emerson's poetry and essays such as *Self-Reliance*, as well as the work of Bronson Alcott (father of *Little Women* author Louisa May Alcott), Margaret Fuller, and Jones Very.

Although he made his fame in New York City as a newspaper editor, Massachusetts-born William Cullen Bryant was still a New Englander when, in 1811, he wrote the first draft of his poem *Thanatopsis* at the age of 17. *Thanatopsis* (Greek for "a view of death") is noteworthy not only for reflecting the new romantic feeling in English poetry, but for presaging the influential role that nature would play in the Transcendentalist movement of the coming decades.

ABOVE, FROM LEFT: Cotton Mather, author of more than 400 works; an 1875 literary portrait in Boston includes Oliver Wendell Holmes, John Greenleaf Whittier, Ralph Waldo Emerson, John Lothrop Motley, Nathaniel Hawthorne, and Henry Wadsworth Longfellow.

The essay Civil Disobedience posits that individuals must not allow governments or actions to overrule their conscience. The essay influenced Mohandas Gandhi and Martin Luther King Jr.

Emerson owned land just outside Concord, on Walden Pond. Here, his friend Henry David Thoreau built a cabin and spent two years living the life of rustic simplicity and contemplation which he chronicled in *Walden* (1854). Thoreau coupled the Transcendentalists' near-mystical sense of the oneness of man and nature with a naturalist's eye for observation and the fierce independence of conscience that blazes in his seminal essay *Civil Disobedience*.

Fireside entertainment

New Englanders brought the Puritan's moral rectitude to the greatest national drama of their day, the struggle over slavery. The abolitionist movement had deep roots in New England, home of William Lloyd Garrison and his uncompromising newspaper *The Liberator*, and *Uncle Tom's Cabin* (1852) author Harriet Beecher Stowe. William Wells Brown, an escaped slave, wrote *Clotel*, which deals with the destructive effects of slavery on slave and mulatto families. It is considered the first novel written by an African-American. John Greenleaf Whittier, a Quaker poet devoted to the cause, is today remembered less as an abolitionist than as one of the "fireside poets" of the post-Civil War years. Working in genres such as the pastoral (Whittier's 1866 *Snow-Bound*) and historical narrative (Henry Wadsworth Longfellow's *Evangeline* and *The Song of Hiawatha*), these created a common popular literature, often read aloud at the fireside.

One of the finest New England poets lived a secluded life in Amherst MA, far from literary salons. Emily Dickinson had a gem-cutter's way with language, crafting nearly 1,800 short lyric poems in which sharp observation of the material world was a prism for the timeless and universal. She shunned publication, and the first volume of her work didn't appear until 1890 – four years after her death.

The two New England giants of American literature in the mid-19th century defy any association with a school or movement of their day. Nathaniel Hawthorne had an early flirtation with Transcendentalism and radical communalism (his *The Blithedale Romance* is based in part on the Brook Farm commune is Massachusetts), but he was far too independent a figure to fit comfortably into Concord, where he spent part of his early career. Hawthorne mined the annals and mores of Puritan New England for the themes of guilt and consequence that inform *The Scarlet Letter* (1850) and *The House of the Seven Gables* (1851). His short stories, many deeply allegorical, are often set in a mythic Puritan past.

NATHANIEL HAWTHORNE

The descendant of Salem Puritans, Hawthorne (1804–64) grew up with a family legend of a Judge Hawthorne, who, as a magistrate at the witchcraft trials, was cursed by a woman he convicted. Hawthorne would later use this story in *The House of the Seven Gables*.

In fact, much of Hawthorne's darkly romantic work was drawn from real life. In the 1836 tale, "The Minister's Black Veil," the protagonist explains: "If I hide my face for sorrow, there is cause enough, and if I cover it for secret sin, what mortal might not do the same." Hawthorne was no doubt familiar with the story of the Rev. Joseph Moody of York ME, who, after accidentally shooting and killing a friend on a hunting trip, became morbidly frightened of having his friend's family and fiancée look upon him, and therefore covered his face with a black handkerchief.

"Young Goodman Brown," one of Hawthorne's greatest tales, also draws on his Salem heritage. In what may be a dream, Brown, wandering in the dark forest, comes upon the Devil, who leads him to a clearing where villagers are engaged in Devil-worship; among the congregation is Faith, Goodman's wife. In this tale, Hawthorne depicts a world sunk in evil: if Goodman Brown's vision is true, the Devil rules; if not, and if Goodman has imagined innocent people in Satan's service, he reveals, like the Salem Puritans, the depth of his own corruption.

Herman Melville was born in New York City, but spent much of his working life in New England. His masterpiece, *Moby Dick*, employs the New England settings of New Bedford and Nantucket, both important whaling ports in the 19th century.

Regional focus

The post-Civil War era saw the rise of the Regional movement in American literature, represented in New England by figures such as Sarah Orne Jewett, a novelist of coastal Maine, and Rowland Robinson, a Vermonter with a sharp ear for the dialect of upcountry Yankees and French-

happily set down roots in the region: Samuel Langhorne Clemens, better known as Mark Twain, built a sprawling mansion in Hartford CT and transported a representative native of the state to medieval England in *A Connecticut Yankee in King Arthur's Court*.

Modern trends

By 1900, New England had ceased to be the most socially and economically vigorous part of the United States, but it still provided fertile ground for writers. Edward Arlington Robinson (1869–1935) drew upon characters of his native small-town Maine to create incisive

Canadian immigrants. William Dean Howells, who edited *The Atlantic Monthly*, made Boston the setting of *A Modern Instance* (1882) and *The Rise of Silas Lapham* (1885), both of which deal with men on the make in a city flush with prosperity.

Henry James (1843–1916) set many of his short stories in Boston's upper-class society, which also provided the milieu for *The Europeans* (1878) and for *The Bostonians* (1886), his satire on the city's radical and reformist circles.

It was an age that saw one writer who belonged to a world far from New England

ABOVE, FROM LEFT: statue of Nathaniel Hawthorne in his native Salem; the enduring image of Moby-Dick; the author Herman Melville.

portraits of often darkly conflicted individuals. Robert Frost (1874–1963), born in California of an old New England family but a resident of rural Vermont and New Hampshire for much of his life, created a universal language out of dry, economical Yankee speech. Edith Wharton was the first woman to win the Pulitzer Prize for fiction in 1920 for *The Age of Innocence*.

In the theater, Eugene O'Neill (1888–1953), brought up partly in Connecticut and associated as a young man with the Provincetown Players on Cape Cod, offered the bleak *Desire Under the Elms* and the uncharacteristically comic *Ah, Wilderness*, both with New England settings.

Local fiction in the 20th century ranged from John P. Marquand's skewering appraisal of the Boston Brahmin class run to ground in *The Late George Apley* (1937) to philosopher George Santayana's darker analysis of a similar scion of the old order in *The Last Puritan* (1936). John Cheever may have moved from his native Massachusetts to New York, but his morally struggling suburbanites traded heavily in the old New England themes of guilt and redemption. John Updike, a New Englander by choice, presented the quandaries of his characters in early novels and stories set in the suburbs of Boston. And, far from the middle class of Cheever and Updike, Jack Kerouac set several autobiographical novels in the French-Canadian quarter of his native Lowell MA.

Today's top writers

With its scores of colleges and universities, and its many writers' workshops, the region has attracted authors not necessarily rooted in the region and its traditional concerns. Jhumpa Lahiri, London-born but Rhode Island–raised and educated, uses Boston as a setting for some of her short stories which explore conflicts and confusion of Indians adjusting to new cultures in her 1999 book *Interpreter of Maladies*, for which she garnered a Pulitzer Prize. Even a small state like Vermont

HERMAN MELVILLE

At the age of 20, Melville set sail on a packet to Liverpool in England, and two years later, in 1841, traveled to the South Seas on the whaler *Acushnet*. Although he later jumped ship to join the US Navy, it was to be a life-changing voyage, for it provided him with his first successful books, *Typee or a Peep at Polynesian Life* (1846) and *Omoo: A Narrative of Adventures in the South Seas* (1847).

He married Elizabeth Shaw, whose father was chief justice of Massachusetts, and they had four children. He continued to write sea stories, mostly because he needed to earn money, but he was inspired by the dark genius of Nathaniel Hawthorne to attempt the epic narrative that became *Moby-Dick; or, The Whale* (1851). This masterpiece, written while he was living in Pittsfield MA, draws upon the character of Yankee whalers Melville met during his own time in the "fishery," but the tale of Captain Ahab's relentless pursuit of the whale that had bitten off his leg assumes allegorical overtones as the crew of the Pequod are carried to their doom by Ahab's monomania.

Like much of his work, Moby-Dick was better received in England than in America. After a breakdown, Melville visited Hawthorne in Liverpool, where Hawthorne was serving as American consul. Later he worked as a customs officer in New York harbor. He died in 1891, his work largely forgotten.

In recent years, some critics have perceived homoerotic overtones in works such as *Pierre* and *Billy Budd*.

can boast internationally recognized names such as Julia Alvarez, Jamaica Kincaid, and David Mamet. Boston lawyer George V. Higgins gave us the rough side of his city's life and language via *The Friends of Eddie Coyle* (1972). Dennis Lahane does much the same with *Mystic River* (2001) and *Gone, Baby, Gone* (1998). In *Empire Falls* (2001) Richard Russo serves up his characters in the matrix of a decaying Maine mill town. John Irving, who lives in Vermont, made the quirks of New Englanders part of *The Hotel New Hampshire* (1981) and *The Cider House Rules* (1985). Another Vermont resident, Jodi Picoult, places many of her 18 novels in New England.

Carter's *New England White* (2007) and Philip Roth's *The Human Stain* (2001), both dealing with the complexities of race on campus, and Donna Tartt's *The Secret History* (1992), about a murder committed by precocious classicists at a bucolic Vermont college.

In the realm of literate popular reading, Robert B. Parker's Spenser detective novels have a vivid Boston setting. And, up in Bangor, in a big Victorian house behind an iron fence festooned with bats and spiderwebs, lives a native son who uses nondescript Maine settings while scaring his readers out of their wits. His name is Stephen King.

Howard Frank Mosher, also a Vermonter, lovingly portrays the vanishing world of the backcountry yeomen and eccentrics of the state's remote Northeast Kingdom in *Where the Rivers Flow North* (1978) and *On Kingdom Mountain* (2007). Another Vermont author, Chris Bohjalian, has set moral dilemmas in small towns in novels such as *Midwives* (1996) and *The Law of Similars* (1998).

New England academia has provided the setting for works such as Yale professor Stephen L.

ABOVE, FROM LEFT: Mark Twain, professional wit and master storyteller; John Irving with the Oscar he won for adapting his novel *The Cider House Rules* for Hollywood; Stephen King, pictured with motorcycle, in 1986.

STEPHEN KING'S MAINE

Stephen King has done for Maine what Charles Dickens did for Victorian London, and fans of the prolific writer have fun trying to identify the real-life locations that turn up, thinly disguised, in his creepy tales. Indeed, there's a nascent Stephen King Trail, taking in Kezar Lake, near Lovell (Dark Score Lake in *Bag of Bones*), Bridgton (setting for *The Mist* and *The Body*), Hampden (*Carrie*), Orrington (*Pet Sematary*), Long Lake (*The Shining*), and Durham (*Salem's Lot*). King, born in 1947, has a summer lodge near Lovell and an old lumber baron's mansion near Bangor (a town disguised as Derry in *It*). To locate the mansion, look for a locked gate decorated with a bronze vampire.

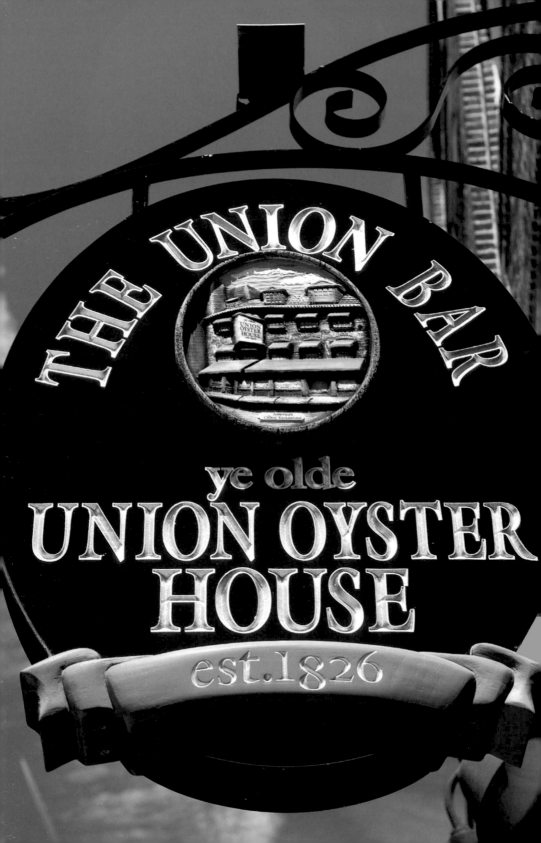

LOBSTERS AND LOCAVORES

A new generation of chefs with fresh ideas and a novel appreciation for locally sourced ingredients is whetting appetites from the Maine coast to the Berkshire Mountains

I f it weren't for codfish, New England might never have been settled. It was the abundant cod that initially lured English fishermen, and eventually settlers, to this land. New arrivals quickly learned to appreciate oysters, clams, and the many types of fish that swam in the offshore waters. The unforgiving land was hard to till, but the Indians taught them how to cultivate corn and wheat and which plants and berries were edible. All healthy, to be sure, but not exciting. Even when the maritime trade brought in spices and ingredients from around the world, New England had a reputation for dull food.

That's changing as creative chefs – like groundbreaker Lydia Shire (often considered the first of the truly inventive New England chefs) at Scampo or Gordon Hamerley at his self-named bistro, both in Boston; Matthew Varga at Gracie's in Providence; or Doug Mack at Mary's in distant Bristol VT – with a passion for fresh, local, organic ingredients find surprisingly fertile ground in New England's rocky soil.

Harvest from the sea

The sea is where the new New England cuisine started and it still provides the primary offering on most menus. The Pilgrims wouldn't have known what to make of our mania for lobster. They considered the crustaceans fit only for pig food, or bait; well into the 1800s, boatloads of lobsters sold for pennies, and prisoners rioted at the prospect of yet another lobster dinner. But lobster has gone upscale. While creative preparations abound, menus retain traditional boiled lobsters, lobster ravioli, lobster macaroni

and cheese, and "lobster rolls" – toasted hot dog buns filled with chunks of lobster meat, tossed with celery and mayonnaise or melted butter.

New England's fabled clam chowder got its name from the French settlers of Canada, who simmered their soups in a *chaudière* (cauldron). Such long, slow cooking is needed to render large hard-shell quahogs (pronounced "ko-hogs") palatable. Small and medium-size clams – cherrystones and littlenecks – are delectable served raw on the half-shell. Soft-shell, longneck clams – commonly known as "steamers" – are a favored repast all along the coast, dipped first in their own broth (to wash off the grit), then melted butter. Clam shacks fire up their fry-o-lators to prepare another

---

LEFT: sign for The Union Oyster House, Boston.
RIGHT: Cape Cod is world-renowned for its oysters.

favorite: clams batter-coated or simply rolled in cornmeal and fried.

Clambakes were once a New England tradition, especially on Cape Cod. The customary procedure was to dig a pit on the beach, line it with stones, build a driftwood fire, cover the hot stones with seaweed, add clams and their accompaniments (typically, lobsters, potatoes, corn on the cob), and then top it all off with more seaweed, a sailcloth tarp, and plenty of sand, leaving the whole to bake for about an hour. Most restaurants these days dispense with clambake per se, and just serve what's called a "shore dinner" – steamed.

Oysters are a popular dish in New England, and have been from the very beginning. As early as 1601, Samuel de Champlain had singled out the area now known as Wellfleet, on Cape Cod, for its exceptional beds. To this day, Wellfleet and Cotuit, on Cape Cod, are world-renowned for their oysters.

Fillet of young cod, haddock, striped bass, and bluefish still grace traditional menus, although exposure to European traditions has introduced two relatively new seafood treats: mussels, long ignored by New England restaurants, are now very nearly ubiquitous, while scallops are finding favor in the kitchen.

NEW ENGLAND'S BREWERY SCENE

New England was at the forefront of the microbrew revolution, which began in the early 1990s. Starting in garages and basements, the fledgling brewmasters found appreciative audiences and quickly expanded their offerings and the availability of their product. While some limit their production strictly to brewing beer, many others operate brewpubs, sometimes only serving their own beers; others offering other regional brews as well as some from across the country and the world.

Vermont has more microbreweries (meaning a very small output) per capita than any other state. Its most popular labels include Otter Creek, Long Trail, Magic Hat, Catamount, Rock Art, Trout River, and Wolaver's

(organic). New Hampshire holds its annual brewfest of beers from throughout New England every June in Lincoln. Redhook, Smuttynose, and Shipyard are all "craft brewers," which generally and informally means their output is fairly large and is distributed throughout New England and often beyond. It also means that if you like it, you can probably find it wherever you travel.

Although Boston sports bars like The Fours on Canal Street or Mike's on Davis Square sell a lot of the national brands, like Budweiser and Coors, it's no longer unusual for someone who drifts in to watch a BoSox game on the big screen to have a critical conversation with the bartender about the "hoppiness" of what's on tap.

Favorites from the hearth

Not all New England culinary standards come from the sea. New Englanders ate pot roasts, potpies, and stews – the sort of things people living a demanding physical life needed to keep themselves going. They're still found on the menus of traditional restaurants specializing in "comfort food."

Boston has its famous baked beans, more commonly found in northern Maine and New Hampshire. For dessert, try Indian pudding, based on cornmeal and molasses; you'll soon notice that Vermonters will add maple syrup to almost anything. Blueberries ripen in early

Once thought too cold for planting vineyards, New England now has several wineries. Experts say it's a sign of global warming – that once-frigid New England is developing a climate favorable for growing grapes.

economy), and reducing the environmental impact of transporting foods over long distances. Pick-your-own farms and farm stands proliferate throughout the region from early summer to early autumn, as fruits and vegetables come into season.

summer, and cranberries star in fall festivals from Plymouth to Nantucket.

Locavores and local sourcing

Despite its relatively short growing season, New England has become a center for the "locavore" movement. Advocates obtain most, if not all, of their foods locally. They promote the value of eating foods grown without chemicals (whether pesticides or fertilizers), supporting local farmers (which supports the local

ABOVE, FROM LEFT: serving Boston's theater district since 1868; Boston's Cheers Bar, inspiration for the classic television series *Cheers* (1982–93).

Artisan cheese-making is all the rage in upcountry New England, particularly in Vermont. Shelburne Farms and Grafton cheddars, Bayley Hazen and Green Mountain blue cheeses, and sheep's milk cheese from Willow Hill Farms and Three Shepherds of the Mad River Valley are all worth seeking out.

Chefs eagerly support the "locally sourced" concept, for many of the same reasons consumers like it. Many menus brag about their use of local ingredients. The "Vermont Fresh" program gives restaurants buying locally a decal to display, while Massachusetts "Culinary Cuisine" tourism initiative directs visitors to locavore-minded restaurants.

Discovering flavors

For decades, American palates accepted bland staples as de rigueur when dining out. Italian restaurants, steak houses, and Chinese takeaway were standard. Mexican restaurants with combo platters of burritos and refried beans were considered exotic. Aside from a few ethnic islands like the Portuguese enclaves in Providence, there was little to distinguish one town's cooking from another. The shift to an interest in flavorful dining coincided with the waves of immigrants arriving not just from Europe, but from Asia, Latin America, and the Caribbean. Japanese, Thai, and Vietnamese restaurants opened to serve the new communities, and the enticing aromas drew customers for whom chicken korma and lobster sautéed with ginger and scallions were a revelation. It didn't take long for the trend to extend to New England's ingredients.

Chefs transform traditional New England products into creative new "fusion" preparations. Adventurous eaters can have salad of Maine rock crab with lobster knuckles and fried taro, crispy squash risotto cakes, pumpkin ravioli with mussels marinière, lightly fried lobster with lemongrass and Thai basil, or seared scallops in cider sauce.

Taking it national

Some of the specialty foods made in New England are distributed nationally. In Connecticut, the late actor Paul Newman's "Newman's Own" brand of salad dressing, pasta sauces, popcorn, and cookies still donates its profits to charities. Vermont's maple syrup and Waterbury-based Ben and Jerry's Ice Cream are found in groceries nationwide. That may violate the tenets of the culinary environmentalists, but it's a boon to the region's economy and promises that a taste of New England can be had anywhere.

ABOVE: traditional atmosphere at the White Barn Inn at Kennebunkport.

Sweet Treats

These sweet New England treats will make you say "Whoopie" for Whoopie Pies and other tasty concoctions

It's official: in April 2011, Whoopie Pies became the Official Treat of the State of Maine. The "pie" is really two round, mound-shaped pieces of chocolate cake with a sweet, creamy filling sandwiched inside. Just the right size to fit in your hand, it's a caloric, teeth-decaying bit of happiness.

The whoopie pie's origins are obscure and the subject of some culinary controversy. Maine claims it as its own, although the Amish in Pennsylvania say it's one of their creations. Mainers suggest that the Amish moving up north to live Downeast brought it with them. It's never actually come to blows, but residents of each state are quick to claim the original recipe.

Maine's Official State Dessert, meanwhile, is the blueberry pie. Considering that Maine is the primary grower of blueberries in the country, it seems fair. The berry is often used in one of the region's other famous desserts: pandowdy (or pan dowdy, the spelling varies; it's also sometimes called grunt, cobbler, crumble, or buckle). It's a pie plate filled with apples or berries sweetened with maple syrup, honey, or molasses, with a crumbled crust baked on top. Blueberry pie is frequently served warm with vanilla ice cream on top, in a combination that wins hearts around the world.

New Englanders have a passionate love of ice cream. Although vanilla is almost always the favorite in polls, you should try Grape-Nuts ice cream. The crunchy cereal (which has neither grapes nor nuts) is mixed into the ice cream before it freezes. The United States leads the world in per capita ice cream consumption, and New Englanders are said to eat 14 pints more of the stuff every year than the average American.

Strawberry shortcake is also popular treat, but New Englanders make theirs with a biscuit, not shortcake. For overseas visitors, this can be a bit confusing, because a biscuit is a cross between a roll and a crumpet – a far cry from the traditional cookie. The basic concept of the strawberry shortcake has been expanded to include cakes, cookies, and even cartoon characters.

RIGHT: a whoopie pie makes for a tasty treat.

Perhaps the dessert with the most valid historical pedigree is Indian Pudding. Also called Hasty Pudding (although it doesn't take long to make), it was one of the first desserts the Pilgrims made. Used to creamy concoctions they left behind in England, they were thrilled when milch cows finally arrived in the New World. They blended milk with cornmeal, eggs, butter, cinnamon, ginger, and molasses and baked it. Boston Cream Pie (the State Dessert of Massachusetts) also has Colonial origins. The early colonists put cream filling between two cakes; in 1855, a chef at the Parker House Hotel in Boston added the chocolate icing and renamed it.

The sweetest of all New England ingredients is maple syrup. The Indians taught the Pilgrims how to tap the sap from maple trees and turn it into a thick, sweet syrup. Traditionally, buckets are hung from tubes drilled into trees, collected and drained by hand, with the sap being boiled for hours until it reaches the desired consistency. Modern methods reduce some of the labor, and you can visit "sugar shacks" in the spring to see how it's done. It takes about 40 gallons of sap to make one gallon of syrup, so that bottle of syrup can be quite valuable. Maple syrup is used in almost everything: maple syrup over pancakes, maple-cured sausage and bacon, maple ice cream, maple candy. It's even poured onto freshly fallen snow and eaten as a frozen confection.

BUILDING NEW ENGLAND

Shingles and clapboards, gables and steeples; New England's buildings reflect the beauty of its landscape and the practicality of its people

Tourists visiting the full inventory of historic homes in New England hear a lot of architectural terms – Palladian, neoclassical, Greek Revival, Federalist. If asked, only a few could define them and fewer could explain why they matter. But the buildings of New England say as much about the people and their history as the events that took place in and around them. If you can read New England's architecture, you come close to reading New England itself.

Puritan practicality

No original examples of the very first New England architecture remain. Those were the steep-gabled, one-room huts the Pilgrims shivered in during the winter of 1620–21. They understandably built something more substantial as soon as they could.

Their new homes were not built with an eye towards beauty, although there is something stirring and attractive in their stark simplicity. These "first period" houses are heavy and medieval and almost entirely without ornamentation. Simple oblong boxes, they were framed and filled with the waddle-and-daub that was left visible on half-timbered houses in England. That stemmed equally from the Puritan's disdain for worldly affectations and the sheer practicality of their situation. Faced with the rigors of simply surviving in the harsh New England environment, they did not have the time or inclination to spend on anything that was unnecessary. Clapboards provided a thin blanket of protection against winter's snow and cold. Combined with the steep roof and massive central chimney shared by rooms on both levels of the house, the early dwellings of the stern Pilgrims reflected their authoritative character. (Good examples of these are the 1640

Whipple House in Ipswich MA and the 1641 Wing Fort House in East Sandwich MA).

In many of the early homes, the upper floor extended slightly beyond the lower. This overhang mimicked the practical design of townhomes in English cities, where the lower floor entrance was set back from the busy, dirty, congested street. In the colonies, however, space was not at a premium and houses could be set back easily. Within a few years, that style was abandoned and both levels of the houses were flush with each other. (The 1683 Parson Capen House in Topsfield MA is an example of this design.)

17th-century public buildings – called meetinghouses – were equally without embellishment. The large rooms often served as both the town hall and center for worship, reflecting the early ties between church and state. While most houses of this period are gone, many of the meetinghouses remain. (The Old Ship Meetinghouse in Hingham MA is one.)

The Georgian style

As survival became more assured and their finances improved, the colonists began to indulge themselves by adding flourishes to their humble homes. In heavily Puritan-influenced areas, those were modest touches, justified by deciding the improvements were rewards from God for living a properly sacred life.

"Gingerbread" is the architectural term describing elaborate ornamentation, particularly hand-carved wooden latticework on verandas of houses built in the latter part of the 19th century.

Pre-Revolutionary architecture is called variously "Georgian," "Colonial," and "Palladian." Although there are subtle variations in the specifics, only a dedicated historian or obsessed amateur can tell the difference. These are the buildings you are likely to think of when you

At the turn of the 18th century, settlements were being established away from the original towns, and commerce was developing with other locations even farther afield. These drew the more adventurous spirits and those who chafed at the rigid religious principles which limited personal expression. Along the coast, where maritime trading and fishing were making their mark, money and exposure to influences from abroad combined to weaken the religious hold on taste and propriety and allow for displays of success in the form of impressive mansions.

ABOVE, FROM LEFT: the 1683 Capen House, Topsfield, Massachusetts; classic Georgian style in Deerfield Village.

imagine the homes of patriots in powdered wigs. The overall concept of the design is symmetry: Everything is in balance; the proportions are equal; the construction is solid. The buildings exude stability, serenity, elegance, and wealth. The style has a staying powder that has far outlasted its origins; "Colonial"-style homes are the most frequently built and most popular in the US real estate market.

The inspiration for the style came from the 16th-century Italian architect Andrea Palladio (hence the term "Palladian"). His designs were used extensively as London was rebuilt following the 1666 fire which reduced much of the city to ashes. It was only natural that what was popular in England would make its way to the colonies, where the people were eager to imitate the latest fashions of the Mother Country.

The term "Georgian" came into use a bit later. It refers to the time of the three English King Georges (1714–1820). Given the souring of relations between the colonies and the kings during that time frame, it wasn't a term used often by 17th-century realtors.

One distinguishing feature of a typical Colonial/Georgian/Palladian house was its size. Georgian homes, with wood-paneled walls and broad stairways, had larger rooms and more privacy. Four full rooms, both upstairs and down, were the norm. Two separate chimneys serviced

House and the 1760 Wentworth-Coolidge House. and the 1760 Wentworth-Coolidge House.

By the end of the Revolution, architectural tastes were changing. The new nation sought new expressions of its personality. Perhaps deliberately, perhaps subliminally, during the first decades of the new republic, it developed a distinctive architectural appearance.

The Federal style

Following the Revolution, optimism was palpable in harbors from Boston to Bath, Salem to New Bedford. Even inland, whaling, shipbuilding, and the expansion of trade around

the two, now larger, halves of the house. These two leaner towers added to exterior elegance and richness while leaving room for a deep hallway where the massive chimney had been.

Old Deerfield MA has several fine examples of Georgian houses which managed to survive the frequent raids by Native Americans during the early days of settlement. The 1733 Ashley House and 1743 Sheldon-Hawks House stand at the north end of Deerfield's main thoroughfare.

By mid-century, coastal ports were very profitable, as sea captains' and merchants' houses showed. Many of these were later remodeled, making it difficult to find a "purebred" house of the period. Portsmouth NH is blessed with two unsullied originals – the 1763 Moffatt-Ladd

the globe brought the influence of the sea to many New Englanders as the coastal merchants commanded the goods and natural resources of the whole region. Fine houses were built in towns far from the seaports by prospering local businessmen. But no country carpenter could rival the skills of Salem's Samuel McIntire or Boston's Charles Bulfinch. Their combined work represents the finest of the period. McIntire's inspiration was Robert Adam, the Scottish architect who raised the art of interior decoration to exquisite heights with his dainty stucco reliefs. Such detailing, along with freestanding curved stairways and delicate fireplace mantels, characterize Federal interior design. The structural design is a square, three-story building with chimneys on the outer walls and a portico over the entrance. McIntire introduced these elements in Salem.

The full impact of McIntire's work in Salem is best grasped on Chestnut Street, which in its entirety has been designated a National Historic Landmark. Up and down both sides of this majestic street are stunning Federal-style mansions, built in the early 1800s when the sea captains decided to move away a little from the noise and clutter of the port. (To see McIntire's interior artistry, tour the Gardner-Pingree House.)

Salem stands as a success in the often-heartbreaking saga of period buildings being

New England portfolio is the Massachusetts State House, standing atop Beacon Hill. (The claimant for the top spot in his showcase is the US Capitol in Washington DC). Majestic in scope and symbolism now, it was even more so in 1798 when it was surrounded by open land and dominated the city by its visibility from anywhere.

The neoclassical State House, very Palladian in inspiration, has been extended twice in two contradictory styles. The 1890 addition to the back of the building is a lumpish but highly mannered Baroque echo of its opposing side. The second addition in 1914 neutralized the first by blotting it out from view. The two mas-

discarded and destroyed in the face of newer architectural styles and community needs. Both there and in nearby Newburyport, preservation-minded private owners and community groups buy and restore the old buildings and lead efforts to rejuvenate historic town centers by putting them to new uses and promoting them as the historic landmarks they are.

Bulfinch's masterpieces

The Federalist era peaked with the work of Charles Bulfinch (1763–1844). The jewel of his

ABOVE, FROM LEFT: Federal style home in Newburyport; the Massachusetts State House, Back Bay brownstones.

sive marble wings serve as a neutral backdrop for the golden-domed Bulfinch original.

Bulfinch was in on the beginning of the Beacon Hill speculation, and the three homes he built for developer Harrison Gray Otis in 1796, 1802, and 1805 reflect the evolution of the Federal residential style. Several other Bulfinch-designed rowhouses grace Chestnut Street.

Greek grandeur

Along with covered bridges, the white steeples of village churches are a symbol of rural New England. Their design can be traced to Asher Benjamin, an influential force in New England architecture at the beginning of the 19th century. In his first architectural handbook, he rendered a steepled church which became the prototype for hundreds of buildings. Although the fundamental design has never changed, the detailing gives clues as to when a church was built.

In 1830, Benjamin encouraged New England to adopt the Greek Revival style, which was popular elsewhere. Identified by the grand size and use of massive columns, its most popular use is for civic buildings and institutions. In Boston, the Quincy Marketplace building and the 1828 Arcade in Providence RI are sterling examples of the style. (The Arcade, used most recently as an upscale shopping venue, has fallen on difficult financial times and is currently closed.)

Form vs. function

The beginning of the Industrial Age saw a shift in the principles of the region's architecture. Houses were primarily shelter; industrial buildings were sturdy and practical. By 1850, something had changed. Perhaps for no other reason than boredom with symmetry, scale, and four-square plans, architecture took off in a riot of historic revivals.

Gothic, Italianate, Renaissance, and Romanesque are among the eclectic labels attached to the late 19th-century designs. Descriptions are lengthy and confusing; visual examples provide a better frame of reference.

VILLAGE DESIGN

Just as houses reflect the New Englander character, so did the arrangement of their villages. The idea of a planned community is not unique to 20th-century developers. Early settlements were compact, practical affairs, with houses nestled around a village green, which was dominated by a church, demonstrating the supremacy of religious authority. The green served several purposes. It was a common grazing area for livestock; it was safer to let the animals graze there than to let them roam freely. It was a community gathering place, and criminal punishments like floggings and hangings were big draws.

The Connecticut capitol in Hartford is Gothic; so are the "gingerbread" cottages on Martha's Vineyard. Boston's Trinity Church is an outspoken example of Romanesque design (by Henry Hobson Richardson); Boston Public Library is Renaissance Revival as interpreted by McKim, Mead & White. For an immersion course in all the variations and applications, tour the summer "cottages" built by the elite on Newport. The mansions reflect everything from Italian Renaissance to Beaux Arts, Rococo to the Palace of Versailles. Far from being an evolutionary development growing out of New England's personality, these were imports reflecting mainstream American trends.

Influence of Philip Johnson

Architect Philip Johnson (1906–2005) pro-foundly influenced architectural styles and phi-losophy in the 20th century. His principles of clean lines with no applied decorations and vol-ume over mass inspired a generation of modern buildings, used extensively in inner-city urban-renewal projects – accused as often of being soulless and sterile as they are inspiring and ethereal. His first major work was his personal residence. The "Glass House" in New Canaan CT is the ultimate example of his concept. It uses the landscape to create the "walls" which set the visual and mental limitations of space. His

> Often considered the enfant terrible of modern architecture, Philip Johnson was instrumental in starting a revolution in American architecture by forcing designers to rethink their concepts of style, ornamentation, and use of space.

works in the region include the List Art Gallery in Providence RI and the Kline Science Center at Yale. (He graduated from rival Harvard.)

International input

Johnson's ideas as interpreted by both domes-tic and non-native architects play an important part in the look of 20th-century New England. Harvard University boasts the only LeCorbusier building in the United States (the Carpenter Center), and Walter Gropius built a model Bauhaus house in the Boston suburb of Lincoln. At MIT, Eero Saarinen designed the striking Kresge Auditorium and Chapel. I.M. Pei designed Boston's Hancock Tower, a cool glass 60-story rhomboid that reflects its surroundings and con-stantly changing cloudscapes above; other Pei projects in the city include an addition to the Boston Public Library which quotes the origi-nal's mass without copying its rich ornamenta-tion – a direct line between Johnson's ideas and practical application. Pei is also responsible for the Christian Science Center, centered on an oversize infinity pool.

More recently, British architect James Stirling chose a postmodernist–Egyptian motif

for Harvard's Sackler Museum of ancient, Islamic, and Asian art; and Japanese architect Tadao Ando took his inspiration from mid-century's austere International style in his 2008 Stone Hill Center at the Clark Institute in Williamstown MA. Like Ando, the New York firm of Diller Scofidio + Renfro places great emphasis on sleekly framed outdoor vistas in its 2006 Institute of Contemporary Art (ICA) on the Boston waterfront. With its top floor canti-levered over the harbor's edge, the ICA is, in the words of *Boston Globe* architecture critic Robert Campbell, "intensely involved with the sea." As, indeed, nearly all of New England once was.

ABOVE, FROM LEFT: Lowell's sturdy, practical industrial buildings; Boston's Trinity Church, built in 1872–77, contrasts with the 1970s John Hancock Tower.

CHARLES BULFINCH

Even in an age where success often came young, Charles Bulfinch (1763–1844) was exceptional. Often considered America's first professional archi-tect, he had his first major commission at the age of 25, when he designed the Hollis Street Church in Boston. His works are noted for their simplicity and balance, creating an aura of good taste and respect-ability. His most famous work in Boston is the Massachusetts State House (1798); Boston Common and University Hall at Harvard show his influence. His most important work is the US Capitol Building in Washington DC, although most people probably do not know who designed it.

SPORTS AND OUTDOOR ACTIVITIES

One of the biggest reasons to visit New England is to enjoy its great outdoors; you don't have to go far to get close to nature, and the possibilities for exploration are endless

Regardless of ability or interest, New England is the place to get outdoors and enjoy nature. You can explore on foot, by bicycle, or on back of a snowmobile. With a variety of activities in every kind of weather, make sure your trip to New England takes advantage of the great sports and outdoor activities.

Biking

Everywhere you go in New England, you see bicycles. Even in busy Boston, a new bike-rental program encourages people to pedal around town. It's certainly the most relaxing way to view the countryside. Forget the traffic: on a bike, you're able to really enjoy the scenery, stop when and where you want to look at a view or watch a moose grazing in a marsh by the roadside, park the bike for an impromptu stroll up the beach or splash in the ocean, pause at a covered bridge for pictures, pedal past stately sea captains' mansions and back roads where cows look up from their grazing to watch you roll by. It's particularly nice during fall foliage season; on a bike, you don't have to deal with the heavy traffic and can really slow down, take side roads on a moment's whim, and savor the views.

You can plan a trip to go inn-to-inn, staying somewhere different each night or use one town as a base and explore the area in a different direction every day. There are at least a half-dozen companies offering guided biking tours in New England. That's a good choice if you don't know the area and are not comfortable with making your own arrangements. Most of them concentrate on tours of three to six days on the Maine Coast and Acadia, Martha's Vineyard and Nantucket, or Rhode Island's coastline, all of which are easy rides, although some are more

challenging. One treks through the Berkshires, one along the Champlain Valley, and a more strenuous one bikes in the White Mountains. Their itineraries all include stops at museums and extra activities like kayak excursions. Several of them also offer self-guided tours, making all arrangements for accommodations and providing you with detailed maps and cue sheets. Bike trails – like the Blackstone River Bikeway which runs 48 miles from Providence RI to Worcester MA, or the Cape Cod National Seashore biking trails – are developed routes bikers can enjoy for a day or longer. Mountain bikers consider New England to have some of the best trails in the eastern US, particularly in the White Mountains and Maine. Many ski resorts (like Jiminy Peak) offer mountain biking during the summer, which is a great introduction to the sport. There are no organized tours, but several websites connect bikers. For tour companies, visit www.sosojourn.com, www.summerfeet.com, www.CTbiketours.com, www.bikethewhites.com, or www.bikeandthelike.com. If mountain biking is more your style, visit www.nemba.com or www.bustedspoke.com.

Camping

Camping means many things to many people. For the purists, it's pitching a tent along a mountain trail far from any human influence. For others, it's hooking up a motor coach with

"primitive" sites are just that: a clearing along a trail that might or might not have a portable toilet or pump for drinkable water nearby. Others accommodate RVs. The best resource for detailed information on campsites on national property is the *U.S. National Forest Campground Guide* (www.forestcamping.com), which lists complete details of every site, however humble and remote. Private campgrounds are equally diverse, some striving to create as "natural" an experience as they can, while others have pools, game rooms, and planned activities. Woodall's (www.woodalls.com) produces an excellent directory with detailed information about campgrounds,

air-conditioning and a flat-screen TV at an RV park with resort amenities. And there's a vast middle ground of "pop-up" campers, cabin stays, and "sleep in the back of your SUV" adventures. Most campers want some chance to get closer to the outdoors; campgrounds are usually in or near places for hiking or along beaches. Some are on the outskirts of tourist-popular areas – like the towns of Mystic or Shelburne – which give the best of both worlds. All of those options are met by state parks and national parks and forests, although what options are offered varies greatly, depending on the location. Some

with a strict ranking system. Backpackers, thru-hikers, and tent campers use resources like the Appalachian Mountain Club (www.outdoors.org) as a starting point for information. KOA campgrounds (www.koa.com) are particularly welcoming to tent campers; some of their facilities have on-site cabins, vintage trailers, yurts, and tepees for rent. *(For statewide campground listings, check Travel Tips: Activities at the back of the book.)*

Dog sledding, dog carting, and skijoring

There are few more thrilling ways to experience the backcountry than by being a passenger in a dog sled gliding over the snow, powered by a team of incredibly strong, deliriously happy

ABOVE, FROM LEFT: mountain biking on Killington Mountain, Vermont; camping in the backwoods of Maine.

huskies. Most people are happy with a ride, but if you want to imagine yourself in the Iditarod, consider a course in dog mushing. Lasting from one to three days, you learn all about the care and feeding of the dogs; how to harness and hitch the team; how to drive, steer, and – hopefully – how to stop. The longer courses usually involve overnight trips, staying at lodges. A lack of snow doesn't end the fun. Most places use wheeled carts in spring and summer and during fall foliage. The newest human–canine activity is skijoring, which is dog-assisted Nordic skiing. Human and dog are harnessed together and the dog helps pull the skier. The Vermont Outdoor

literally set your own pace and itinerary. Like the region itself, there are a nearly infinite number of possibilities: the scenic Cliff Walk in Newport; through the woods to a stunning waterfall in a state park in Massachusetts; learning to identify trees and birds on marked trails near towns in Vermont; scrambling up rockfalls on rugged trails in New Hampshire. During fall foliage, it's the overwhelming beauty of walking through a tunnel of brilliantly colored maple trees; in winter, the quiet serenity of snow-shrouded pines. Hike-it-yourselfers can be overloaded with the sheer number of trails anywhere there are hills – from the relatively gentle

Guide Association (www.voga.org) has a detailed directory of dog-sled operations. New England Dog Sledding (www.newenglanddogsledding.com), located on the Maine–New Hampshire border, has all sorts of packages and courses.

Geocaching

Consider it a high-tech scavenger hunt. Using a hand-held GPS, geocachers look for a "cache" at coordinates. It can be as large as a shoebox or as small as a matchbox. They log their finds on-line. It's a growing family, group, and individual sport.

Hiking

The other popular self-propelled way to explore New England is on foot. Like biking, you very

By far the most undemanding way to enjoy the water is with a "float trip." Sitting on an oversize inner tube, you drift down the river, letting the current set the pace. A second tube holds a cooler with sandwiches and drinks.

Berkshires and western Connecticut to the fierce passes in the White Mountains. Cape Cod and Block Island have their own rugged beauty that's best appreciated on foot. The most comprehensive website for trails, directions, and contacts is www.hikenewengland.com. The interactive site breaks everything down by region and difficulty. Most casual hikers are happy with day trips, but hiking vacations are a nice option if you aren't trying to cram in seeing all of New England in one week. Some use one inn as a base and take day trips, returning to the inn each night. Others are inn-to-inn, with hikers exploring new areas every day. Your luggage is moved for you; you carry a day pack with water and sunscreen. These are good if you don't know an area and don't want to make your own accommodations. Most are for casual or intermediate hikers (www. nehikingholidays.com), but a few are multiday, strenuous excursions (www.distantjourneys. com). Options are fewer if you are looking for a simple day trip. Northwoods Outfitters (www.

the ride is the first time they've touched a horse, much less ridden one, so the mounts are docile and well-trained. Rides rarely move faster than a walk and last between one and two hours. There are frequent stops to enjoy the scenery and take photos. Rides are particularly nice during fall foliage. Most stables are open from mid-May through October, but a few offer winter rides. Those are not to be missed. Some resorts have sleigh rides in the winter, which are pure magic. If you want an overnight experience, Berkshire Horseback Adventures (www.berk-shirehorseback.net) has an overnight camping trip which is suitable for beginners.

maineoutfitter.com), based in Greenville ME, has guided hikes lasting a few hours. One of the most popular is the wildlife tour that specifically looks for moose. In winter, they'll teach you how to snowshoe.

Horseback riding

Why should you do all the work going up the mountain? Let a sure-footed, well-trained horse do it for you and you just go along for the ride. Stables offering trail rides know that most people aren't experienced riders; for many people,

ABOVE, FROM LEFT: huskies pull a sled on winter snow; trail markers in Acadia National Park, Maine; ice fishing is a favorite pastime in winter.

Ice fishing

Truly obsessed anglers know that fishing doesn't end when the lakes freeze over; the fish are still waiting to be caught. They bundle up, pack a thermos of hot chocolate or coffee, slide a hut across the ice, auger through the ice, and drop a line. For those huddled around the hole sitting on wooden crates or folding chairs while jigging their lines, it's a bonding experience that will never be forgotten. It's also a lot of quirky fun. The Fly Rod Shop (www.flyrod-shop.com) in Stowe has half-day tours and free ice fishing clinics every Saturday morning from January through mid-March. Pickett Hill Guide Service (www.pickethillguideservice.com) in Bennington serves a full meal in a warm shanty;

Spikehorn Ridge Guides (www.spikehornridge. com) suggests a very early rise to enjoy the fragile beauty of the winter sunrise in Vermont as part of the ice-fishing experience.

Paddle sports

Traveling New England's inland waterways has always been done by paddle. Canoes carried the Abenaki and Algonquin, French trappers, and English explorers along Lake Champlain and the region's rivers. Many of those waterways are still as undisturbed now as they were then. Red-eyed, brilliantly spotted loon glide across your path; egrets stand in the grasses; you may

before descending to Lake Champlain and continuing into New York. Another famous trail is the Allagash River Waterway in Maine, which is protected as a national Wild and Scenic River. Overnight guided tours along this waterway run from two to eight days; Northwoods Outfitters (www.maineoutfitter.com) has complete

> Non-skiers find plenty to do at most ski resorts, which have almost all developed into one-stop destinations with spas, entertainment, and plenty of non-slope diversions.

spot the occasional moose in the swamp or eagle overhead. It's as far removed from the hustle and hassle of the "real world" as it gets. You can rent canoes and kayaks by the hour or day at lakes, rivers, and coastal areas. Many of the outfitters offer instruction and guided tours. The nature tours are especially fun, since birds and other wildlife are easier to spot and approach by canoe or kayak. If nature's not your thing, there are also tours that stop at wineries and ice cream stands.

There are several well-documented long-distance trails: the Northern Forest Canoe Trail (www.northernforestcanoetrail.com is an excellent resource) runs from the very northern tip of Maine along the US–Canada border (with a short stretch into Quebec; bring your passport)

packages for that trip and several others in Maine. All trips have dozens of photo opportunities, but the moose and wildlife overnight trip by New England Outdoor Center (www.neoc.com) is particularly designed to get you to the most scenic spots and promises plenty of moose sightings.

Stand-up paddling can be described as surfing with training wheels, although you provide the propulsion, not the waves. Standing, sitting, or kneeling on a very wide, very stable board, you use a modified kayak paddle to move. It takes about 10 minutes to learn and is an easy workout. Umiak Outdoor Outfitters (www. umiak.com) in Stowe VT has the equipment and location to try out this fast-growing, family-friendly, fitness-not-required sport. Rocky stretches of New England's rivers create some exciting white-water rafting. From gentle riffles to full-fledged, hold-your-breath-'til-it's-over rapids, rafting is a drenching, exhilarating adventure. New England Outdoor Center (www.neoc.com) has a full range of options from "soft adventure" trips that are ideal introductory afternoons to the "full river" experience, which is not for the faint-hearted.

Sea kayaking takes paddling into another dimension, since you're dealing with waves and tides and ocean currents. Most day trips stay close to shore and sheltered waters, making the paddling relatively easy. The best trips are around

On the water

With hundreds of miles of coastline dotted with fine harbors, sailing is a natural part of any vacation. With the snap of canvas as it fills with wind and the feel of the salt spray as you move almost effortlessly across the water you understand the lure of the sea that called men to the water and away from more mundane (although usually safer) lives ashore. Experienced sailors can rent vessels in Newport in Bristol RI or charter a boat with a crew (www.bareboatsailing.com; www.sailboatcharter.com). Sailing schools generally have three- to six-day courses, but there are a few with one-day instruction and sails. If you'd

Acadia National Park (www.acadiafun.com and www.mainekayak.com have all the options), where guided trips routinely spot harbor seals – who sometimes decide to swim alongside the paddlers – porpoises, osprey, and sea birds. The sunset cruises are especially nice, as the tempo of the day slows and the nesting birds swoop past you to settle in for the night. Overnight camping trips let you watch the stars as you lie on the beach on an uninhabited island or spend several days working up the coast on an inn-to-inn adventure.

ABOVE, FROM LEFT: sailing on the Charles River in Boston; a white water kayaker navigates the falls at rocky gorge in the Swift River near the Kancamagus Pass in New Hampshire.

rather someone else do all the water work, scenic cruises take you around Boston Harbor, close to lighthouses, to Connecticut's Thimble Islands, and along Lake Champlain. Seeing a whale breach the water is breathtaking. The power and beauty are unforgettable. Whale-watching trips sail daily from Boston, Gloucester, Nantucket, Portland, Provincetown, and Plymouth MA. Discover New England (www.discovernewengland.com) keeps an up-to-date list of the boats and their schedules.

Skiing

There aren't quite as many ski resorts as there are snowflakes in a blizzard, but it sometimes seems that way. Although a few try to keep the simple, rustic ambience of the first ski lodges, most are major resort destinations with a range of activities, not just downhill skiing but snowboarding, tubing, snowshoeing, and Nordic (cross-country) skiing. There are après-ski massages, spas, dining, dancing, indoor pools, retail shops; newly renovated Jay Peak even has an indoor water park. Towns like Stowe and Killington VT and North Conway NH thrive during the winter as the restaurants, shops, B&Bs, and bistros welcome the skiers. Although most ski resorts are in Vermont, New Hampshire, and Maine (Sugarloaf is the largest ski area east of the Rockies), western Massachusetts has sev-

eral respectable slopes. Most people stick to the groomed trails at ski centers; there's always a variety from "bunny trails" for the novices to triple black diamonds for those with great skill (or great bravado or both). Experienced skiers with winter survival skills try backcountry skiing. Pinkham Notch and Tuckerman Ravine are both popular areas for the sport. Great Glen Trails (www.greatglentrails.com), in Gorham NH, is a good place to connect with others heading for the wilderness on skis. Cross-country skiers looking for a challenge take on the Catamount Trail (www.catamounttrail.org), which runs the length of Vermont. *(For a list of ski resorts, check the Travel Tips: Activities section at the back of the book).*

Snowmobiling

Vermont has 5,000 miles (8,000km) of groomed trails for snowmobilers which lace through the mountains and valleys. Smuggler's Notch Snowmobile Tours (www.sterlingridgeresort.com) leads one- and two-hour trips; Vermont Outdoor Guides Association (www.voga.org) has a list of rental outlets. The Katahdin region in Maine has a reputation for some of the finest snowmobiling trails (www.neoc.com), while the northernmost woods of New Hampshire have trails that link with those in Vermont, Maine, and Canada (www.nhconnlakes.com).

Spectator sports

Boston is home to professional teams in sports, both well-known and rarely followed. The Red Sox, Celtics, and Bruins play baseball, basketball, and hockey, respectively. The New England Patriots are the National Football League team, based in Boston, but drawing from a regionwide fan base. Soccer has the New England Revolution and the Breakers, the women's professional soccer team. There are both outdoor and indoor lacrosse teams (the Cannons and the Blazers), softball (Riptides), women's football (the Militia), and World Team Tennis (the Lobsters).

Baseball's minor league has a charm of its own. In small towns from Pawtucket to Pittsfield, young players hone their skills and hope for their big break. Cape Cod has its own league, with 10 teams. Minor-league ball is a family night out; the small stadiums often have playgrounds and pre-game entertainment for kids.

College teams also have dedicated followers, although most New England schools are not powerhouses on the national level. The exceptions there are the University of Connecticut's Huskies, who consistently go to the NCAA men's and women's basketball playoffs. The men's team won in 2011, while the women had undefeated seasons in both 2009 and 2010. The University of Connecticut is also strong in soccer and baseball. The University of Vermont, meanwhile, also has strong basketball, hockey, and soccer programs. The Ivy League schools may be intellectual champions, but on the athletic field only Brown is notable, with lacrosse, football, hockey, and basketball teams of note.

LEFT: skiing in Stowe, Vermont. **RIGHT:** a baseball game at Fenway Park.

PLACES

A detailed guide to the six New England states,
with principal sites clearly cross-referenced by
number to the accompanying maps

Although America's Industrial Revolution started in New England, it's the region's flaming fall leaves and charming white-steepled churches that local tourist boards promote. Certainly, the six states are bursting with 300 years of historical sights and influence – considerably more than any other place in America. But they are also remarkably vital: attend a town meeting in one of the superficially sleepy rural communities and you'll find that the robust tradition of democracy bequeathed by the Founding Fathers lives on, making many a town manager's life little easier than the president's.

It is precisely this juxtaposition of past influence and present prestige that is so compelling. What's more, each state has retained a well-defined identity, teasing visitors into testing their preconceptions against 21st-century reality – Maine associated with solitude and contemplation; Massachusetts with bustle and culture; Vermont with beauty and peace; Connecticut with carefully kept, white clapboard homes; Rhode Island with its renowned sailing; and tranquil New Hampshire, whose bellwether presidential primary every four years encourages the pollsters to predict the political fortunes that are about to be won and lost.

A trip to New England can mean finding a priceless antique in an out-of-the-way backwoods store or dining in a sophisticated Boston bistro. It can mean rafting down a Maine river or skiing down a New Hampshire mountain, lounging on a Nantucket beach, or picnicking on the harbor in Newport RI. Yet the region is surprisingly compact.

State boundaries have more political significance than practical importance to the visitor. But, for convenience, each state is explored in depth in the following pages as a self-contained unit. Massachusetts, the most populous, has been divided into separate chapters: Boston, the areas surrounding Boston, Cape Cod and the islands of Martha's Vineyard and Nantucket, central Massachusetts, the Pioneer Valley, and the Berkshires.

PRECEDING PAGES: fall in the White Mountains, Hart's Location, Crawford Notch; a view over Boston at night. **LEFT:** Boston Light lighthouse, Little Brewster Island. **RIGHT:** scarecrows are dressed up to chase birds away from fields that are close to being harvested.

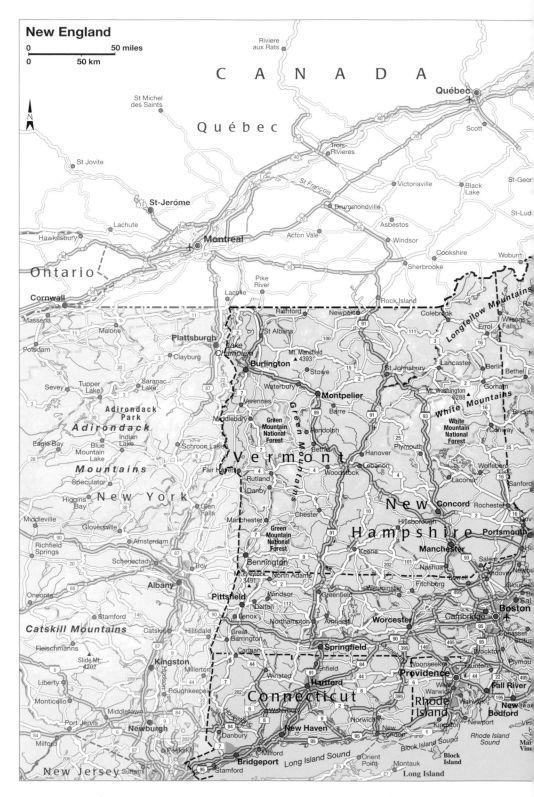

New England

0 _____ 50 miles
0 _____ 50 km

N

CANADA

Riviere
aux Rats

Québec

Québec

St Michel
des Saints

Scott

St Jovite

St François

Victoriaville

Black
Lake

St-Geor

St-Lud

St-Jeróme

Lachute

Trois-
Rivieres

Drummondville

Asbestos

Windsor

Cookshire

Woburn

Hawkesbury

Montreal

Acton Vale

Sherbrooke

Rock Island

St-Lud

Ontario

Cornwall

Massena

Potsdam

Malone

Clayburg

Plattsburgh

Lacolle

Pike
River

Richford

Newport

Colebrook

Longfellow Mountains

Ra

Wilsons
Falls

Errol

St Albans

100

Berlin

Bethel

Sevey

Tupper
Lake

Saranac
Lake

Lake
Champlain

Burlington

Mt. Mansfield
4393

Stowe

Montpelier

St Johnsbury

Lancaster

Mt Washington
6288

Gorham

Conway

Bridg

White Mountains

Waterbury

Verennes

Barre

Adirondack
Park

Adirondack

Indian
Lake

Middlebury

Green
Mountain
National
Forest

Randolph

Bethel

White
Mountain
National
Forest

Eagle Bay

Blue
Mountain
Lake

Schroon Lake

Hanover

Lebanon

Plymouth

Wolfeboro

Laconia

Sanfor

Mountains

Speculator

New York

Fair Haven

Vermont

Rutland

Danby

Woodstock

Concord

Rochester

Dov

Middleville

Higgins
Bay

Glen
Falls

Chester

New

Hillsborough

Portsmouth

Gloversville

Amsterdam

Manchester

Hampshire

Richfield
Springs

Schenectady

Troy

Bennington

Green
Mountain
National
Forest

Keene

Nashua

Salem

Andover

Newb

Manchester

Oneonta

Albany

Mt.Greylock
3491

North Adams

Windsor

Greenfield

Westminster

Fitchburg

Lowell

Glouces

Sal

Boston

Stamford

Catskill Mountains

Catskill

Hillsdale

Pittsfield

Dalton

Lenox

Northampton

Amherst

Worcester

Cambridge

Fleischmanns

Slide Mt.
4202

Great
Barrington

Springfield

Woonsocket

Brockton

Plymou

Kingston

Millerton

Canaan

Enfield

Hartford

Providence

Fall River

New
Bedford

Liberty

Poughkeepsie

Winsted

Rhode
Island

West
Warwick

Monticello

Middletown

Waterbury

New Haven

Norwich

Newport

Rhode Island
Sound

Mar

Port Jervis

Newburgh

Danbury

Connecticut

New London

Kingston

Block Island Sound

Milford

Peekskill

Bridgeport

Milford

Long Island Sound

Orient
Point

Montauk

Block
Island

New Jersey

Stamford

Long Island

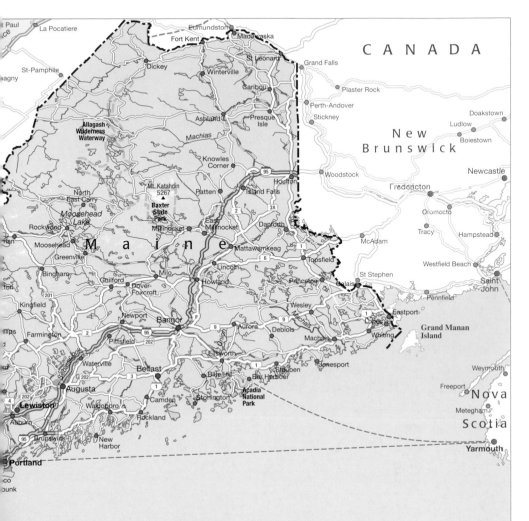

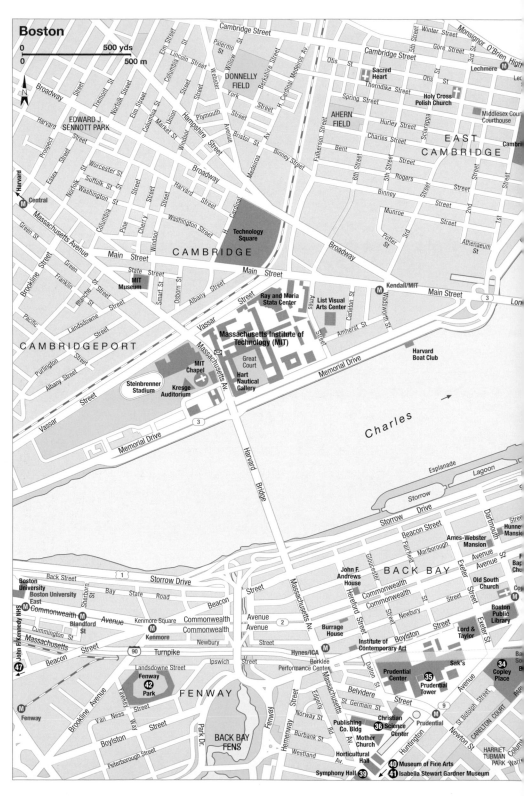

Boston

0   500 yds

0   500 m

N

DONNELLY FIELD

AHERN FIELD

Sacred Heart

Holy Cross Polish Church

Middlesex County Courthouse

EAST CAMBRIDGE

Lechmere

EDWARD J. SENNOTT PARK

Central

Technology Square

CAMBRIDGE

MIT Museum

Ray and Maria Stata Center

List Visual Arts Center

Kendall/MIT

Harvard Boat Club

Massachusetts Institute of Technology (MIT)

Great Court

Hart Nautical Gallery

CAMBRIDGEPORT

MIT Chapel

Steinbrenner Stadium

Kresge Auditorium

Memorial Drive

Charles

Esplanade

Lagoon

Storrow Drive

Storrow Drive

Beacon Street

Ames-Webster Mansion

Hunneman Mansion

BACK BAY

John F. Andrews House

Old South Church

Boston University

Boston University East

Commonwealth

Commonwealth

Kenmore Square

Boston Public Library

Burrage House

Lord & Taylor

Kenmore

Institute of Contemporary Art

Sak's

Copley Place ③④

Turnpike

Berklee Performance Center

Hynes/ICA

Prudential Center

Prudential Tower ③⑤

Fenway

Fenway Park ④②

FENWAY

Christian Science Center ③⑥

Publishing Co. Bldg

Mother Church

Horticultural Hall

BACK BAY FENS

Museum of Fine Arts ④⓪

Symphony Hall ③⑨

Isabella Stewart Gardner Museum ④①

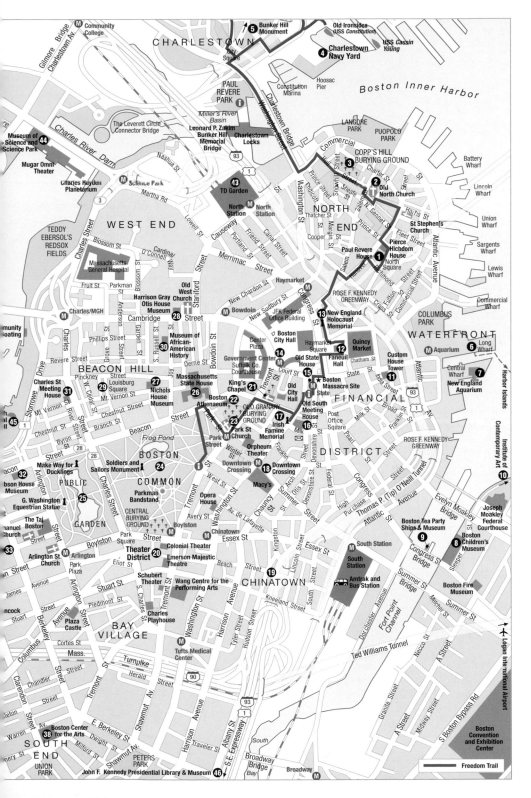

Freedom Trail

BOSTON

Boston has always taken itself seriously;
it does, after all, have Revolutionary history,
famed universities, vibrant arts, creative
cuisine, and the legendary Red Sox

The poet and essayist Ralph Waldo Emerson wrote: "This town of Boston has a history… It is not an accident, not a windmill, or a railroad station, or a crossroads town, but a seat of humanity, of men of principle, obeying sentiment and marching to it…" It might be fair to say that Boston does not have a history, but rather that it is history. New York may be more dynamic, Washington more imposing, and Seattle more gorgeously situated, but no city in America so nobly mingles its past with its present, or a history of tradition with a future of innovation.

A walking city

Despite urban development, Boston changes so abruptly in mood and nuance from one street to another that it cries out to be explored on foot. The city is charmingly, perversely bereft of a main drag, and its streets practice the old European vices of waywardness and digression. The visitor should, too.

Every day hundreds of visitors walk the red line on the sidewalk that marks the 2.5-mile (4km) **Freedom Trail**, a self-guided, or narrated, 90-minute tour (tel: 617-357 8300; www.freedomtrail.org) that takes in the major sites of the city's momentous Revolutionary history. Note that the Freedom Trail guided tour price

does not include admission to sites along the way. If you want to visit several locations, buy a combination, reduced-price admission ticket. There are several commercial tour operators who conduct guided tours along the Trail (and other Boston itineraries).

The North End

This picturesque neighborhood is Boston's original heart, and to walk its streets is to walk among legends. The Freedom Trail threads through the North End on its way between

Main attractions
THE FREEDOM TRAIL
NEW ENGLAND AQUARIUM
FANEUIL HALL AND QUINCY MARKETPLACE
OLD GRANARY BURYING GROUND
MUSEUM OF FINE ARTS
ISABELLA STEWART GARDNER MUSEUM
FENWAY PARK
MUSEUM OF SCIENCE

LEFT: high-rise buildings in Boston.
RIGHT: the old Acorn Street, Beacon Hill.

A Sicilian festival in North End garlands the Madonna with dollar bills.

BELOW: the USS *Constitution* in Charleston Navy Yard.

Boston Common and the Bunker Hill Monument in Charlestown.

The North End was the original nub at the end of the Shawmut Peninsula where the first settlers planted their town. Later, it became Boston's immigrant core: once Irish, then Jewish, and now Italian. Gentrification has homogenized this ancient quarter, but many older Italians remain – along with fragrant Italian grocery stores, bakeries, restaurants, and festivals.

A stroll through the North End can start at the **Paul Revere House ❶** (19 North Square; tel: 617-523 2338; mid-Apr–Oct: daily 9.30am–5.15pm, Nov–mid-Apr 9.30am–4.45pm; charge) in North Square. Built around 1680, it is the city's oldest building, and its period furnishings include some items owned by the Reveres. The age and architecture of the place are the main attractions; for Revere's exquisite work in silver, visit the Museum of Fine Arts. A new visitors' center and museum is under construction adjacent to the house.

From here, head north toward Hanover Street and the Revere Mall, with its equestrian statue of Revere.

(Ironically, Revere did not reach his destination on that fateful night. He was captured by the British a few miles from Concord. A fellow rider, William Dawes, spurred his horse over a stone wall and rode on to alert the Minutemen.) At the end of the tranquil, tree-shaded mall stands Boston's oldest church, the 1723 **Old North Church ❷** (193 Salem Street; tel: 617-523 6676; daily 10am–4pm, closed Jan–Feb Mon; donation. Guided tours on the hour weekends in June, daily July–Oct and week between Christmas and New Year's; charge), where beneath the graceful spire the sexton Robert Newman famously hung two lanterns on April 18, 1775, on the orders of Paul Revere, to signify to the citizens the British plan to move troops inland by boat rather than on foot. Inside, the stately pulpit and a bust of George Washington preside over the original box pews. The beauty of this space finds lovely accompaniment in the "royal peal" of its eight bells, one of which is inscribed, "We are the first ring of bells cast for the British Empire in North America, Anno 1774." Nearby,

between Hull and Charter streets, stand the weathered headstones of **Copp's Hill Burying Ground 3** (open daily 9am–5pm), where many early Bostonians are buried and where several gravestones bear evidence of British soldiers' musket practice.

Charlestown

Across Charlestown Bridge from the North End a famous bit of history lies at anchor in the **Charlestown Navy Yard 4**, which opened during the War of 1812 and functioned until 1974. The USS *Constitution* (1 Constitution Road; Charlestown; tel: 617-242 5585; Apr–Sept Tue–Sun 10am–6pm (October at dusk), Nov–Mar Thur–Sun 10am–4pm. Visitors over age 18 must have a valid photo ID and all bags will be inspected.), the venerable frigate known as "Old Ironsides" was built in 1797 and is the world's oldest commissioned vessel. It fought over 40 battles in the War of 1812 and won them all. Tours of the vessel, given by US Navy sailors every half hour, illustrate the cramped and dangerous world of a man o' war in the days of sail. On July 4, when the *Constitution* makes its annual turn-around cruise (no public allowed), there's a 21-gun salute; on July 5, the public is invited to a sunset parade.

Other sites in the Navy Yard include: The **USS *Constitution* Museum** (tel: 617-426 1812; www.ussconstitution museum.org; Nov–Mar daily 10am–5pm, Apr–Oct daily 9am–6pm; donation), which tells the ship's story through uniforms, weapons, paintings, and 1812-era objects, and the **Boston Marine Society** (tel: 617-242 0522; daily 9am–4pm), the oldest association of sea captains in the world, housed in the old octagonal Muster House, which contains a diverse collection of nautical art and artifacts. Of these three, children will most enjoy the Constitution Museum, with its interactive exhibits. Also in dock: the World War II destroyer USS *Cassin Young* (tel: 617-242 5601; same hours as USS *Constitution*; tours 11am, 2pm, 3pm, 4pm). Inside the Yard, stop for information at the Boston National Historical Park Visitors Center (tel: 617-242 5601; open daily 9am–5pm, until 6pm July–Aug).

The name's the same: Boston's trolley, trams, trains, and ferries are all known as the "T."

BELOW: Old North Church, Freedom Trail.

The Bunker Hill Monument as seen from Charlestown Marina.

The Freedom Trail continues to the **Bunker Hill Monument** ❺ (Monument Square; tel: 617-242 5689; daily 9am–4.30pm), a granite needle 221ft (67 meters) high, commemorating the battle. There are 294 steps to the top, where there's a panoramic view of the harbor and city. **The Bunker Hill Museum** across the street from the monument (43 Monument Square; daily 9am–5pm) has exhibits about the battle, the building of the monument, and the history of Charlestown. The **Charlestown Visitor Center** (55 Constitution Road; tel: 617-241 7575, daily 9.30am–4.30pm) has brochures and other information about the area.

The Waterfront

The eastern boundary of the North End is the Waterfront District. The great wharves of windjammer days remain, many now supporting apartments, shopping arcades, and upscale restaurants. At the center of it all is Columbus Park, part of a green space linking the Waterfront with the downtown area.

BELOW: the New England Aquarium.

Close to the Aquarium subway station, **Long Wharf** ❻, the hub of Boston's shipping industry in the 17th century, is now the starting point for harbor cruises and the high-speed harbor islands ferry. Or you can get harbor views for free by strolling along the walkway southwards to Rowes Wharf. This is a section of the 47-mile (76km) **HarborWalk** (www.boston-harborwalk.com), more than 38 miles (61km) of which have been completed. Connecting the water's edge to the city's open spaces, it stretches from Chelsea Creek to the Neponset River, passing through East Boston, Charlestown, the North End, downtown Boston, South Boston, and Dorchester.

The Aquarium

The **New England Aquarium** ❼ (1 Central Wharf; tel: 617-973-5206; July–Labor Day Sun–Thur 9am-6pm, Fri–Sat 9am–7pm, Sept–June Mon–Fri 9am–5pm, Sat–Sun 9am–6pm; charge; discount combination ticket to aquarium and IMAX Theater. Extremely popular; try to visit on a weekday at opening time). It has a gargantuan four-story, 200,000-gallon (900,000-liter) cylindrical tank in which sharks, sea turtles, moray eels, and other tropical species glide in never-ending circles in a simulated Caribbean coral reef. The tank is so large that it was built first and the rest of the aquarium was constructed around it. African penguins greet visitors as they arrive, and northern fur seals cavort in their open-air tank. The Aquarium operates three- to four-hour whale-watch cruises from early April through late October (additional charge), with researchers and naturalists on board, and its **Simons IMAX Theater** (tel: 866-815 4629) shows 3-D movies with digital sound on New England's largest screen.

Children's Museum

Follow HarborWalk southwards past Rowes Wharf and cross old Northern Avenue/Evelyn Moakley Bridge to

Museum Wharf, home of the **Boston Children's Museum** ❽ (308 Congress Street; tel: 617-426 6500; daily 10am–5pm, Fri until 9pm; charge). Housed in a renovated warehouse, it is a hands-on adventure, where children can climb a 3-D maze and visit an authentic Japanese house transplanted from Boston's sister city, Kyoto. New England's maritime traditions are reflected in hands-on boating exhibits and environmental exhibits. Like the Aquarium, the museum makes a good, if not centrally located, respite for kids getting "historied out" by Freedom Trail attractions.

Nearby, on Congress St Bridge, is the **Boston Tea Party Ships & Museum** ❾ (Congress Street; tel: 617-338 1773; www.bostonteaparty-ship.com; charge), due to reopen in late 2012 after a serious fire. Check the website for updates. It has full-size replicas of three 18th-century ships – *Beaver*, *Dartmouth*, and *Eleanor* – whose cargo of tea was thrown overboard on the chilly night of December 16, 1773, by 60 whooping patriots dressed as Mohawk Indians.

They were protesting Britain's having imposed taxes on such cargos without granting the colonists representation in Parliament.

Contemporary art

The four-story **Institute of Contemporary Art** ❿ (100 Northern Avenue; tel: 617-478 3100; Tue–Wed and Sat–Sun 10am-5pm, Thur–Fri until 9pm; charge) cantilevers starkly over the waterfront. The permanent collection features contemporary artists who've exhibited at the ICA. A comprehensive venue for the arts, it has exhibits, performances, indie films, speakers, and family activities. There's a free summer concert series on the piazza in the summer.

Just west of the New England Aquarium rises the 26-story **Custom House Tower** ⓫ (3 McKinley Square; tel: 617-310 6300), for many years Boston's tallest building. It's certainly the city's quaintest high-rise, with the *c.*1910 clock tower placed somewhat incongruously on the 1847 Greek Revival-style building. It's now a Marriott timeshare.

Samuel Adams statue, Faneuil Hall.

BELOW: Postal Inspector Anthony Comstock.

Banned in Boston

The phrase "banned in Boston" generally refers to something controversial, particularly if it has sexual content. In the late 19th and early 20th centuries, authorities could prevent books, plays, and movies from being seen or distributed in Boston. The practice, however, goes back to much earlier times.

In 1651, William Pynchon wrote "The Meritorious Price of Our Redemption," which was highly critical of the Puritans' religious views. The General Court, which effectively ruled Massachusetts as a theocracy, was not amused. It burned the book and "encouraged" Pynchon to return to England, which he did.

In the 1870s, along came Anthony Comstock. A postal inspector with moral views that made the Puritans look like Romans at an orgy, he engineered the passage of the Comstock Act, which prohibited the distribution of "obscene, lewd, or lascivious" material through the mail. Even anatomy textbooks destined for medical students were outlawed. After hearing Comstock speak, the Watch and Ward Society formed in Boston. For decades, it dictated the cultural scene in Boston. Many publishers and theatrical troupes publicized their "banning," to attract more readers or a larger audience. Not until the Supreme Court limited the ability of local authorities to regulate content in their jurisdiction did "banned in Boston" cease to be meaningful.

TIP

A discounted admission to the Old State House, the Old South Meeting House, and Paul Revere's House will save you money. You can purchase the combo ticket at any of the three sites or on-line at www.paulrevere house.org.

BELOW:
the Old State House.

Faneuil Hall

Close by is **Faneuil Hall** ⓬ (parking lot: 75 State Street; 617-523 1300; Mon–Sat 10am–9pm, Sun 11am–6pm), donated to Boston in 1742 by merchant Peter Faneuil to give the city a central marketplace and enlarged in 1805 by Charles Bulfinch. Patriot orators stirred the embers of the Revolution in the early 1770s here, earning the hall the name "Cradle of Liberty."

Facing it is the domed granite arcade called Quincy Market, built in 1826. In 1976, the complex was reborn as **Quincy Marketplace**, a 6.5-acre (2.63-hectare) complex of flower stalls, jewelry stores, pushcarts, restaurants, and shops. Several dozen food stands line the long hall of the central building, offering everything from freshly shucked oysters to French pastry. Jugglers, mimes, acrobats, and other street performers contribute to the festive atmosphere. On Thursdays, free outdoor concerts entertain from late afternoon through early evening.

The Rotunda of Faneuil Hall has photos and old signage showing the history of the hall. On the fourth floor, the museum of the Ancient and Honorable Artillery Company is open Mon–Fri 9am–3pm (tel: 617-523 1300). Two of Boston's landmark restaurants are also two of the oldest dining spots in the country: **Durgin Park**, in the marketplace, which opened its doors in 1827, and the **Union Oyster House** (41 Union Street; one block from Faneuil Hall), which started serving in 1826.

In Carmen Park on Congress Street six glass towers comprise the **New England Holocaust Memorial** ⓭. Six luminous towers, each 54ft (16 meters) tall, internally lit to shine at night, sit atop dark chambers from which smoke rises. The towers are etched with six million numbers, reminiscent of the numbers tattooed on the arms of the victims of the Nazis. Every Friday and Saturday fruit and vegetable vendors pack nearby **Haymarket Square's** outdoor marketplace to sell their wares.

Government Center

Looming just inland from Faneuil Hall is **Government Center** ⓮. Here, in the 1960s, the Boston Redevelopment Authority razed buildings and removed streets to create a huge open space – some 56 acres (23 hectares). The centerpiece of this plaza is a massive concrete **City Hall** in the cheerless brutalist style, described as an "Aztec temple on a brick desert." The plaza is used for outdoor concerts in the summer months, but it has never become the civic gathering place its creators envisioned.

To the southeast rise the banks and office towers along Franklin, Congress, Federal, State, and Broad streets. Soaring confidently from a primitive warren of jumbled byways, these behemoths constitute the hub of business.

Old State House

To the southwest lies downtown's retail heart, as well as some buildings illuminated brightly in history.

At the intersection of Washington and Court streets stands the **Old State**

House ⑮ (206 Washington Street; tel: 617-720 1713; daily 9am–5pm; charge), once the seat of British rule. It was here that cousins Sam and John Adams, James Otis, and John Hancock led the arguments against continued British rule over its North American colonies. The museum works hard to be more than yet another collection of colonial artifacts. The multimedia presentation on the Boston Massacre (which took place just outside) illustrates an early example of "media hype." There are lots of hands-on activities and a few historic artifacts, such as tea from the Boston Tea Party.

The handsome, gambrel-roofed brick building, currently unoccupied, at the corner of School and Washington streets was once the Old Corner Bookstore, a gathering spot for such writers and thinkers as Hawthorne, Emerson, and Thoreau.

Old South Meeting House

Continue down Washington Street to the **Old South Meeting House** ⑯ (310 Washington Street; tel: 617-482 6439; Apr–Oct daily 9:30am–5pm, Nov–Mar daily 10am–4pm; charge; discount combo ticket for Paul Revere House available), scene of scores of protest meetings denouncing British policy. From here on December 16, 1773, the 60 patriots set off to conduct the Boston Tea Party. A stunning state-of-the-art audio exhibit, "If these Walls Could Speak," sets the scene. It's the headquarters for the annual re-enactment of the Tea Party usually held the weekend closest to December 16.

Nearby, at Washington and School streets, the **Irish Famine Memorial** ⑰, a pair of sculptures by Robert Shure, commemorate the immigrants driven to America by the Potato Famine of the 1840s. Set in the round, with seating for passersby, one sculpture depicts a desperate family about to leave Ireland, and the other shows the three hopeful and determined immigrants arriving in Boston.

Downtown Crossing

A little farther to the south is the city's mercantile heart, the pedestrian-friendly **Downtown Crossing** ⑱. Roughly bordered by Boston Common, and Essex, Devonshire, and Court streets, it's filled with retail shops and restaurants, office buildings and hotels, student housing and residential space.

The Art Deco **New England Telephone Company** (185 Franklin Street) rises 298ft (91 meters) in the heart of the Financial District. A small display in the lobby shows the development of the telephone. Around the lobby, murals show the history of the phone, from its invention to linemen working in the field.

Chinatown

Continue on Washington Street to Beach Street into the heart of **Chinatown** ⑲. The Asian-American quarter has seen its population boom in recent years with the arrival of citizens from countries including Vietnam, Thailand, and Cambodia. The narrow, crowded streets are packed with tiny restaurants and shops selling

The New England Holocaust Memorial.

BELOW: the Irish Famine Memorial.

An intimation of mortality in the Old Granary Burying Ground. Three signers of the Declaration of Independence are buried here, as are five victims of the Boston Massacre.

BELOW:
steamed dumplings.

everything from back scratchers to thousand-year-old eggs, and is a wonderful place to wander for a few hours.

Theater District

The **Theater District** ❷⓪ runs along Washington and Tremont streets, then follows Boylston and Stuart streets almost to Back Bay. The performance season runs from early fall through late June, with some acts in July and August. More than a dozen performance venues are along this route, including the magnificently opulent **Opera House** (539 Washington Street; www.bostonoperahouse.com) and **Citi Performing Arts Center** (270 Tremont Street; www.citicenter.org), which encompasses the 1925 **Wang Center for the Performing Arts**, and the 1910 **Shubert Theater**.

Nearby Bay Village is a six-block neighborhood adjacent to Park Square and along Stuart Street whose homes are diminutive versions of those on Beacon Hill. The reason: many of the Hill's craftsmen and builders lived in the village and designed their homes in a similar fashion.

King's Chapel

Back on School Street, pass the **Old City Hall**, a grand affair now leased as office space, and turn right at Tremont Street to look into **King's Chapel** ❷① (64 Beacon Street; tel: 617-227 2155; services Wed 12.15pm and Sun 11am). The congregation was established in 1686 as the first Anglican church in Boston. Built in 1754 of Quincy granite, it retains its crisp white box pews. Paul Revere said the bell he cast for the church was "the sweetest I ever made." You can hear it on Sunday mornings. Its burial ground is Boston's oldest. Among those interred here are colonial governor John Winthrop, and Mary Chilton, the first woman to step off the *Mayflower* (summer: Mon, Thur–Sat 10am–4pm; winter: Sat 10am–4pm; donation).

On Tuesdays at 12.15pm the church hosts a 30- to 45-minute recital series featuring a variety of performers and repertoires from jazz to medieval. Admission is by donation. Crossing over Tremont Street, head left to the **Old Granary Burying Ground** (tel: 617-635 4505;

Eating in Chinatown

No visit to Chinatown would be complete without having lunch at one of its myriad restaurants, and the dim sum "palaces" – always good value – are among the most authentic. Waitresses push carts laden with appetizer-size dishes such as steamed buns, spare ribs, and, yes, chicken feet, through vast, cavernous rooms packed with tables. Diners point at the dishes they want, are charged for each (it's OK if you don't speak the language, because pointing is universal), and pay at the end of the meal. Most dishes are $2–$3, and patrons can dine heartily for $12–$15 each (a small tip is appreciated). Literally, dim sum means "touch your heart."

Favorite dim sum eateries include **Empire Garden** at 690 Washington Street, **China Pearl** at 9 Tyler Street, and **Dim Sum Café** at 10 Tyler Street.

daily 9am–5pm), founded in 1660, a pleasant glade where Peter Faneuil, John Hancock, Samuel Adams, Paul Revere, and the victims of the Boston Massacre are interred.

Boston Athenaeum

Overlooking the burial ground are the windows of a private library, the **Boston Athenaeum** ㉒ (10½ Beacon Street; tel: 617-227 0270; first floor and gallery: Mon, Wed 9am–8pm, Tue–Thur 9am–5pm, Sat 9am–4pm. Guided tours of the building, including floors otherwise off-limits to the public, Tue and Thur 3pm. Reservations required). There are reading rooms, marble busts, and prints and paintings, as well as books from George Washington's library. The Athenaeum is one of the best places to spot specimens of the species known as the Proper Bostonian, short of joining an exclusive Beacon Hill club.

A few more paces down Tremont Street, at one corner of the Boston Common, is Peter Banner's elegant 1809 **Park Street Church** ㉓ (1 Park Street; tel: 617-523 3383; open for tours mid-June–Aug Tue–Fri 9am–4pm Sat 9am–3pm). On July 4, 1829, William Lloyd Garrison made his first anti-slavery speech here, launching his far-reaching emancipation campaign.

Boston Common

Every American city has a great park, but only Boston can caim the oldest, the venerable **Boston Common** ㉔, a magical swath of lawn and trees and benches. Sitting in the sun-mottled shade, watching pigeons strut and children frolic around Frog Pond, out-of-towners can understand how Bostonians might mistake this spot for the very center of the world.

The land that was to become the Common originally belonged to Boston's first English settler, one Reverend William Blaxton, who had made his home in 1625 on the western slope of what is now known as Beacon Hill. His life was interrupted in 1630 by the arrival of a band of settlers led by Governor John Winthrop of the Massachusetts Bay Company. The new Bostonians were nobly determined, as Winthrop had

An 1869 bronze of George Washington presides over the Commonwealth Avenue entrance to the Public Garden.

BELOW: the Albert Gordon reading room at the Boston Athenaeum.

Pedal-powered (and wheelchair-accessible) swan boats, a tradition since 1877, can carry up to 20 people around the Public Garden's lagoon on a 15-minute cruise.

BELOW LEFT: stained glass in the 1798 building's State Hall.
BELOW RIGHT: the State House, built on land used as a cow pasture by John Hancock.

written, to "be a Citty upon a hill," and in 1634 he sold his land to the town for around $150 and fled farther into the wilderness.

The 45 acres (18 hectares) he left behind quickly became a versatile community utility. During the next 150 years, it was used for pasturing livestock, as a militia drilling ground, and as a convenient place to whip, pillory, or hang people. As a military post, the Common put up the Redcoats all through the Revolution.

Now the Common is "just" a park: glorious when the magnolias bloom or when snow at sunset evokes the impressionist paintings of Childe Hassam.

Public Garden

Just across Charles Street, the elegant **Public Garden** ㉕ strikes a more formal pose. These variegated trees, meandering paths, and ornate beds of flowers were once part of the fetid Back Bay marshes; but by 1867, the Garden had taken its present graceful shape, complete with weeping willows, a bridge for daydreamers, and a shallow 4-acre (1.6-hectare) pond.

In summer, swan boats (tel: 617-522 1966; www.swanboats.com; open mid-Apr–mid-Sept daily; charge) carry happy tourists across the placid waters of the garden's lagoon. At the Commonwealth Avenue entrance, an equestrian George Washington bronze by Thomas Ball presides, while a row of bronze ducks on the north side pays tribute to Robert McCloskey's classic 1941 children's picture book, *Make Way for Ducklings.* Real ducks, too, inhabit an island in the pond and paddle about to toddlers' delight.

Beacon Hill

Back up at the east end of the Common, the gold dome of the **State House** ㉖ (24 Beacon Street; tel: 617-727 3676; open weekdays; free tours 10am–3.30pm: reservations required) gleams atop Beacon Hill on land once owned by John Hancock. Completed in 1798, this peerless Federal-style design by Charles Bulfinch, with less successful but happily unobtrusive additions by several others, symbolizes the eminence of politics in Boston. The approach to the legislative

chambers passes through a series of splendid halls leading to the Senate Staircase Hall and the Hall of Flags, both symphonies of fin de siècle marble opulence.

One of the highlights is the House Chamber, a paneled hall under a two-stage dome. Great moments of Massachusetts' history decorate the walls in a series of Albert Herter paintings, while above circles a frieze carved with a roll-call of the state's superachievers. The portentous codfish known as the "Sacred Cod," a sleek, stiff carving in pine that commemorates Boston's great Federal-era fishing industry, was first hung in the Old State House. Without this old mascot, the house refuses to meet. Less recognized is the pine cone atop the gold dome. It symbolizes the importance of the logging industry to Boston in the 18th century. At the beginning of the 19th century, a large, steep three-peaked hill known as the Trimount dominated the area. In the 1780s, a primitive beacon atop one of the peaks warned ships against running aground. In 1795,

Bullfinch and partner Harrison Gray Otis leveled 60ft (18 meters) of the Trimount, using it to fill in part of the Charles River. The newly accessible land quickly became the idyllic gas-lit neighborhood of bow-fronted town houses now known as "The Hill." At first, everyone expected that the new residences of Beacon Hill would be urban estates along the lines of Bulfinch's freestanding No. 85 Mount Vernon Street (1800) – his second house for Otis – which is to this day one of Boston's most majestic houses (not open to the public). But the mansion plans were quickly scaled down to today's smaller blocks.

At No. 55 Mount Vernon Street is the 1804 Bulfinch-designed **Nichols House Museum** ㉗ (tel: 617-227 6993; Apr–Oct Tue–Sat 11am–4pm, Nov–Mar Thur–Sat 11am–4pm; tours on the half hour; charge). The former home of the philanthropist, suffragist, and landscape designer Rose Standish Nichols, it is a splendidly accurate portrayal of an early-19th-century Beacon Hill interior.

The first Harrison Gray Otis House. Otis (1765–1848) was a lawyer, senator, mayor of Boston, and a leader of America's first political party, the Federalists.

BELOW: 19th-century Beacon Hill life as seen in the Nichols House Museum.

BELOW: Charles Street Meeting House, where anti-slavery activists once preached.

Federal-era tastes

To get a sense of The Hill, walk west down Beacon Street from the State House. At Nos 39 and 40 stand twin 1818 Greek Revival mansions, one built for Daniel Parker, owner of the Parker House, Boston's oldest hotel. At Nos 42 and 43, the Somerset Club, built in 1819 as a mansion for prominent merchant David Sears, was bought by the most exclusive of Boston social clubs in 1872. At 45 Beacon Street is the third house designed by Bulfinch for Otis (1805).

The first (1796) **Harrison Gray Otis House Museum** ㉘ at 141 Cambridge Street, just outside Beacon Hill proper (tel: 617-994 5920; Wed–Sun 11am–4.30pm; tours on the hour; charge), is the last surviving mansion in what was Boston's most elite 18th-century neighborhood. It offers a glimpse into the elegant life of Boston's governing class immediately after the American Revolution.

Louisburg Square ㉙, developed between Pinckney and Mount Vernon streets around 1840, epitomizes the Beacon Hill style and its

urban delicacy. Created as a model for town house development, it has long been *the* address in Boston. Louisa May Alcott (1832–88), author of *Little Women*, once lived here.

Another charming example of Beacon Hill's spirit is at Nos 13, 15, and 17 Chestnut Street, one of America's most beautiful residential streets, where Bulfinch built for the daughters of his client Hepzibah Swan three exquisite town houses in a prim little row.

African-American history

During the 19th century much of Boston's free African-American population lived on the north side of Beacon Hill. The **Museum of African-American History** ㉚ (46 Joy Street; tel: 617-720 2991; Mon–Sat 10am–4pm; guided and self-guided tours; charge) encompasses two sites open to the public. The African Meeting House (8 Smith Court), dedicated in 1806, is the oldest black church building still standing in the United States. It was here that William Lloyd Garrison founded the New England Anti-Slavery Society in 1832. The Abiel Smith School (46 Joy Street) served as the country's first publicly funded grammar school for African-Americans from 1834 until 1855, when Boston's schools were integrated.

The museum also oversees a site on Nantucket and Boston's Black Heritage Trail with the assistance of the National Park Service.

Charles Street

On the west side of Beacon Hill, Charles Street, with its restaurant, coffee houses, bakeries, and boutiques, is a prime spot to stroll, shop, and snack.

The street's principal landmark is the **Charles Street Meeting House** ㉛ at the corner of Charles and Mount Vernon streets. Built for the Third Baptist Church in 1807, it later served as the home of the First African Methodist Episcopal Church and the Unitarian-Universalist

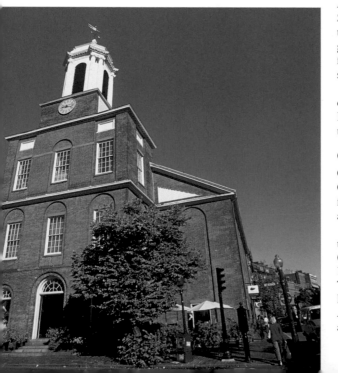

Church; over the years luminaries including Frederick Douglass and Sojourner Truth spoke here. It was converted into offices and retail space in the 1980s.

Wander off Charles onto the shady, peaceful streets that trail toward the Charles River or lead back up the hill. Many houses here are noteworthy for their former occupants. Polar explorer Admiral Richard E. Byrd (1888–1957) lived in Nos 7–9 Brimmer Street, while No. 44 in the same street was the lifelong home of the great historian Samuel Eliot Morison. The Victorian clergyman and philosopher William Ellery Channing lived at No. 83 Mount Vernon Street, next door to the second Otis mansion.

Back Bay

From Beacon Hill, it's an easy transition both in distance and architectural feeling to the handsome streets of Back Bay. Although it epitomizes "Old Boston," this neighborhood dates only to the 1850s filling of a noxious tidal mudflat declared, in 1849, "offensive and injurious" by the Board of Health.

The legislature's grand 1857 plan for Back Bay, influenced by Baron Haussmann's recent rebuilding of central Paris, called for long vistas down dignified blocks, and a wide boulevard with a French-style park down the middle. In 1858 the first load of fill arrived by train from Needham, 10 miles (16km) to the southwest. During the next 20 years, 600 acres (240 hectares) of dry land emerged from the muck that was Back Bay.

Back Bay's imposing rowhouses, now nearly all divided into condominiums or apartments, line **Commonwealth Avenue**, a verdant 32-acre (13-hectare) promenade shaded by mature elms, sweet gum, ash, and linden trees. (Starting near the Charles River and going right to left, the axial thoroughfares are Beacon Street, Marlborough Street, Commonwealth Avenue, Newbury Street, and Boylston Street.)

Head west to 137 Beacon Street, between Arlington and Berkeley (the cross-streets ascend in alphabetical order), to visit the **Gibson House Museum ㉛** (tel: 617-267 6338; Wed–Sun; guided tours only at 1pm, 2pm, and 3pm; charge). Built in 1859, the brick rowhouse has been left much as it was; it houses a museum whose furniture, paintings, books, clocks, and textiles recreate the feel of Back Bay living in its heyday, including the servants' "downstairs" world of kitchen and laundry.

In the block between Clarendon and Dartmouth, Commonwealth Avenue displays its most memorable structures. The romantic houses that march down this stretch perfectly justify the avenue's reputation as America's Champs-Élysées.

Along Newbury Street

Newbury and Boylston streets are the only part of the Back Bay zoned for commerce. **Newbury Street ㉝**, the "Rodeo Drive of the East," is lined with jewelers, day spas, restaurants, sidewalk cafés, designer boutiques,

The view from Top of the Hub restaurant, on the 52nd floor of the Prudential Tower. The adjoining Skywalk Observatory offers 360° views.

BELOW: open-air jazz on Newbury Street.

The Boston Public Library is visited by more than 2.25 million people each year.

and art galleries, including the venerable Vose Galleries of Boston at No. 238, which specializes in American painting from 1669 to 1940.

Copley Place

Copley Place ❸ (100 Huntington Avenue; tel: 617-369 5000) is a two-story megaplex occupying more than 9 acres (3.6 hectares) with two hotels, dozens of inviting restaurants, and all of the familiar retail stores: Neiman Marcus, Louis Vuitton, Barneys New York, Armani.

According to *Women's Wear Daily*, Prudential Center is one of the top five shopping centers for women in the country. With Saks Fifth Avenue and Lord & Taylor as anchor stores, who can argue? The south garden is an oasis where you can rest, recoup, and plan the rest of the shopping expedition. This is also the location for the Hynes Veterans Memorial Convention Center. The **Prudential Center** is connected to Copley Place by a "skyway" in Boston's original skyscraper, the 52-story **Prudential Tower** ❸ (800 Boylston Street). Its

50th-floor Skywalk Observatory (tel: 617-859 0648; open daily late Mar–Oct 10am–10pm, Nov–late Mar 10am–8pm; charge) provides an exhilarating, map-like, four-way view of the city. An "Acoustiguide" audio tour details points of interest far below. It's available in English, French Canadian, and Japanese. The Top of the Hub is an elegant, expensive spot to have lunch, or enjoy a cocktail and watch the sunset.

The Mother Church

In 1866, Mary Baker Eddy credited her rapid recovery from a serious accident to a glimpse of God's healing power. The religious movement that she founded in 1879 today has its world headquarters on 22 acres (9 hectares) immediately south of the Prudential Center on Huntington Avenue. The **Christian Science Center** ❸ (175 Huntington Avenue; tel: 617-450 2000; Sunday services at 10am, noon, and 7pm; testament meeting Wed at noon and 7.30pm) complex includes three older buildings – the Byzantine-Renaissance Mother Church (1894), the Italianate Mother Church Extension

The Brahmins

The fabled history of Boston, the Puritans' "City Upon a Hill," had a rather prosaic origin. The settlers were merely looking for good drinking water. When the final location was chosen, they believed that the site was divinely chosen. They also believed that the future success of the settlement depended on their acting in accordance to divine will. "The eies of all people are upon us," declared John Winthrop, their leader.

God must have approved, because the "Bible Commonwealth" grew quite quickly. By 1700, its fleet was the third-largest in the English-speaking world, and its population the largest in North America. Bostonians developed the self-confidence that is a hallmark of self-reliant and self-made people.

During the decades following the Revolution, Boston's maritime domination created a "codfish aristocracy" of fortunes netted from the sea. They were the "Boston Brahmins," a name borrowed from the Hindu priestly caste. Their fortunes nourished the center of America's intellectual and cultural life. Among these were the Boston

Public Library, the Boston Symphony Orchestra, the Massachusetts Institute of Technology, and Boston University. Harvard was already one of the world's great universities.

When the Irish Potato Famine struck in 1845, Boston was at the apogee of its gleaming social and cultural pre-eminence. Suddenly, thousands of impoverished Irish immigrants arrived, promptly constituting a new underclass. They were followed by Italians, Poles, and Russians. By 1900, Boston's population had swelled to more than half a million.

Once dominated by descendants of English colonists, the Puritan capital became a mostly Catholic metropolis. Newcomers and incumbents clashed, and Boston was divided into two distinct cultures. The established elite still maintained power even as it withdrew into its world of Back Bay addresses. But while the new citizens sweated in factories, they remade Boston – and its politics – in their own image: scrappy, practical, and anything but elite.

(1904), and the Publishing Society (1933) – as well as I.M. Pei's 1973 additions. (Tours daily except Mon. Hours vary greatly. Check website or call.)

In the publishing wing, the **Mapparium** (tel: 617-450 7000; Tue–Sun 10am–4pm; charge) is an extraordinary stained-glass walk-in representation of the globe. Visitors walk across a 30ft (9-meter) glass bridge to stand, literally in the center of the world. From there, they have a 3-D view of the world's nations as they were in 1935, the year the globe was built. A new presentation uses words, music, and LED lights to demonstrate how ideas travel through time and geography and influence the world. Another gives the background of the concept and construction of the Mapparium. The acoustics are disorienting, with whispers in one continent being clearly heard in another.

Copley Square

Follow Dartmouth Street to Boylston for one of the city's most stimulating displays of architecture: **Copley Square** ㊲. First, there's Charles McKim's 1895 **Boston Public Library** (700 Boylston Street; General information: tel: 617-536 5400; tour information: tel: 617-859 2379; free, one-hour art and architecture tours begin at the Dartmouth Street Lobby entrance Mon at 2.30pm, Tue 6pm, Fri–Sat 11am; self-guided brochures available). This Italian Palazzo masterpiece might well be the center of the Boston that claims to be the "Athens of America." With more than 6 million volumes and a vast, ornate reading room, it is one of the great libraries in the world. But it's more than a building of books. There's art everywhere – murals by Sargent and Puvis de Chavannes, statues by Saint-Gaudens and Daniel Chester French – and, at the center of a maze of stairs and passages, a peaceful inner courtyard. Philip Johnson's massive 1972 addition "quotes" the original structure in a vastly simplified modern vernacular.

Across the square stands H. H. Richardson's 1877 masterpiece, **Trinity Church** (206 Clarendon Street; tel: 617-536 0944; www.trinitychurchboston.org; free "Art and Architecture" tours after Sun 11.15am service; guided tours daily, hours vary, call for times; charge; self-guided tour daily, call for church opening hours; charge for self-guided brochure). This is a tour de force in Romanesque inventiveness and a striking medievalist contrast to the Public Library's classicism. Inside, what impresses is the wealth of murals, mosaics, carvings, and stained glass. This is Boston's most sumptuous interior space. Organ concerts (by donation) are held Fridays 12.15pm.

The John Hancock Tower

Above everything looms I.M. Pei & Partners' magnificent blue-green mirror, the **John Hancock Tower**, built in 1976. The Tower initially had a propensity in windy weather to lose the huge sheets of glass covering it; miraculously, no one was hurt when the glass fell. That problem was solved

The John Hancock Tower stands tall above the city of Boston.

BELOW: the Christian Science Center, surrounded by a reflecting pool.

after the tower was completed, when all 10,344 panes were replaced; the building also swayed in high winds and required more retrofitting to stiffen the building's core. The observation deck at the top of the building was closed after the terrorist attacks in New York and Washington, DC on September 11, 2001.

The South End

To the south and east of the Christian Science Center and Copley Square sprawls the South End, an ethnically diverse but much gentrified quarter of Victorian bowfront town houses. Particularly pleasing architecturally are the areas around Worcester Square, Rutland Street, and leafy Union Park Square, where it's evident that London – rather than Paris, as in the Back Bay – was the developers' inspiration.

On Sundays from May through late October from 10am to 4pm the parking lot at 540 Harrison Avenue is transformed into a European-style **open market** as local artists and growers display their wares. Look for unique handbags and jewelry, paintings, and antiques, plus fresh produce and baked goods.

The **Boston Center for the Arts** ❸❽ (539 Tremont Street; tel: 617-426 5000; www.bcaonline.org) is a lively performing and visual arts complex encompassing the **Mills Gallery** (Sun, Wed 12am–5pm, Thur–Sat 12am–9pm), which mounts five large-scale expositions each year, and four theaters which present more than 50 productions yearly.

Boston's greatest hall

From the South End, Huntington Avenue leads southwest past several of Boston's greatest institutions. At the northwest corner of Massachusetts Avenue stands the majestic gable-roofed **Symphony Hall** ❸❾ (301 Massachusetts Avenue; for tickets tel: 888-266 7575; 617-266 1200; www. bso.org; free tours offered, schedule erratic. Call 617-638 9390 for hours). The acoustically impeccable, beautifully appointed 1900 building is home to the renowned Boston Symphony Orchestra and, in summer and during the Christmas holidays, its less formal

BELOW: the altar of Trinity Church.

offshoot, the Boston Pops Orchestra. Tickets can be hard to come by. Two options are "rush tickets" – a limited number of tickets set aside for Tuesday and Thursday evening and Friday matinee and evening performances. They are deeply discounted, available a few hours before the show, and must be paid for in cash. Open rehearsals are also open to the public at discounted prices. Call for information.

The MFA

Continue down Huntington Avenue to reach the **Museum of Fine Arts** (MFA) ❹ (465 Huntington Avenue; tel: 617-267 9300; www.mfa.org; Sat–Tue 10am–4.45pm, Wed–Fri 10am–9.45pm; charge, ticket allows for free return visit within 10 days). You'll need two days – at least – to even begin to see, much less appreciate, everything that the museum has on display. Built in 1909 and repeatedly enlarged since then, this incredible museum is perhaps best known for its Impressionists – including the largest number of Monets outside France. A new wing houses 55 galleries devoted

to the Art of the Americas with pieces from pre-Columbian to the 20th century. The museum has the world's best collection of 19th-century American art. The finest collection of Egyptian Old Kingdom objects outside Cairo includes a statue of King Mycerinus, who built the Third Pyramid at Giza, and his queen Kha-merer-nebty II. There are gilded and painted mummy masks. Cyrus Edwin Dallin's elegantly poignant bronze Appeal to the Great Spirit is in the forecourt. Over 200 works by contemporary artists are on display in the seven galleries of the renovated I.M. Pei building (built in 1981). There are almost as many tours available as there are galleries. Free guided tours and gallery walks are included in the admission price. Each focuses on a specific theme. The schedule is available at the admission desk, but check the website or call ahead for advance planning. Tours are also available in French, Russian, and Spanish; again, call ahead to be sure a guide and the tour you want are available. A new outdoor walking tour of the building and surrounding

Museum of Fine Arts.

BELOW: a street map of the Rose Kennedy Greenway.

The Rose Kennedy Greenway

When the Big Dig buried the interstates that sliced through downtown Boston, it left a gaping hole in the cityscape. The solution was to create a mile-long chain of parks – The Rose Kennedy Greenway – built above the I-93 tunnel and reuniting neighborhoods long separated by the now-gone freeway. Named after the matriarch of the Kennedy clan, it reflects her love of Boston and of gardens. It takes about 30 minutes to hike the greenway, but the idea is to stroll, not powerwalk. Each of the five parks has its own personality, fountains, events, vendors, gardens, and artwork. The Conservancy which manages the Greenway hosts historical and horticultural tours. For details and a schedule, tel: 617-292 0020 or visit www.rosekennedy-greenway.org.

Feeding the hungry at Fenway Park.

BELOW: a baseball game at Fenway Park.

neighborhood is offered several times a week. Call for the schedule. Finally, a multimedia guide with details about 500 objects in the museum is available for do-it-yourself touring. The guide is available at the admission desk. There is a charge for the guide.

Mrs Jack's Palazzo

Close to the MFA, the **Isabella Stewart Gardner Museum** ❹ (280 The Fenway; tel: 617-566 1401; www.gardnermuseum.org; Tue–Sun, 11am–5pm; charge) is an exquisite 1903 neo-Venetian palazzo assembled by Boston's most flamboyant grande dame. The unstoppable "Mrs Jack" may have scandalized Brahmin Boston when she paraded two pet lions down Beacon Street, but she proved an astute patron of the arts.

During the 1890s, she set her sights on such masterpieces as Titian's *Rape of Europa*, Rembrandt's *Storm on the Sea of Galilee*, and Vermeer's *The Concert*. In 1896, when her collection was outgrowing her home, she commissioned her fantasy palace at the very edge of town. Today her eclectic collection constitutes one of the world's great small museums. A new wing opened in January 2012 which allows the museum to more properly handle the over 200,000 visitors each year. It includes a dedicated performance hall for the Sunday afternoon concert series. Other improvements include restoration of The Tapestry Room and improved lighting throughout the museum.

Fenway Park

North of the museums is another of Boston's shrines, **Fenway Park** ❷ (4 Yawkey Way; tel: 617-226 6666; http://boston.redsox.mlb.com). Built in 1912 and famously called a "lyrical bandbox" by novelist John Updike, the Red Sox's home field is the oldest ballpark in the major leagues. Behind-the-scenes 50-minute tours (tel: 617-226 6666; charge daily 9am–4pm on the hour. If there's a game, the last tour is 3.5 hours before game time).

The home of the Boston Celtics, who have been National Basketball Association champions 17 times, and the Bruins, Boston's National Hockey

League team, and the National Lacrosse League Blazers is the state-of-the-art **TD Garden** ㊸ (formerly Banknorth Garden; box office: tel: 617-624 1050; www.tdgarden.com) at 100 Legends Way near North Station.

The Charles River

Like many great cities, Boston lies in the embrace of a great river. Along Back Bay, the Charles River widens into a large basin, like a giant mirror held up to the city's profile. It was designed to do just that, by the civic-minded citizens who created the Charles River Dam in 1908.

The dam itself is home to Boston's **Museum of Science and Science Park** ㊹ (1 Science Park; tel: 617-723 2500; July 5–Labor Day Sat–Thur 9am–7pm, Fri 9am–9pm, Labor Day–July 4 Sat–Thur 9am–5pm, Fri 9am–9pm; charge. Additional charge for Omni/IMAX, butterfly garden, planetarium, 3-D cinema. Some combo tickets). Here, visitors can watch simulated lightning, become sleuths at CSI: the Experience, explore the potential of wind and solar power, design nanobots, and enjoy a wide variety of ever-changing hands-on exhibits and live animal and bird demonstrations. For reasonably inquisitive kids over 7, this temple of science and technology surpasses even the Children's Museum as a respite from history and art.

The Shell

The river's edge is one of the city's favorite places to stretch its legs. Roller skaters wired for sound, joggers, bike riders, and sunbathers all migrate here. So do the great crowds that turn out to hear the free concerts and watch movies under open summer skies at the **Hatch Memorial Shell** ㊺ (www.hatchshell.com). The Boston Pops' Fourth of July concert with fireworks is spectacular; get there very early and bring a blanket or chairs.

Every Wednesday evening from early July through early September the **Boston Landmarks Orchestra** (tel: 617-520 2200; www.landmarksorchestra.org) performs classical music at the Shell. It also puts on concerts for children and neighborhood concerts throughout the city.

Sunset over the Charles River.

BELOW LEFT: a bust of conductor Arthur Fiedler near the Hatch Shell.
BELOW RIGHT: bug-eyed attraction at the Museum of Science.

Exhibits in the John F. Kennedy Presidential Library and Museum.

BELOW: Zakim Bridge over Charles River.

JFK's legacy

A short subway ride away is a point of pilgrimage for many people, the **John F. Kennedy Presidential Library and Museum** ④⑥ (Columbia Point; tel: 617-514 1600 or 866-JFK 1960; www.jfklibrary.org; open daily 9am–5pm; charge; free parking; MBTA red line south to JFK/UMass and free shuttle bus marked "JFK"; GPS address: 220 Morrissey Boulevard, Boston). Set dramatically beside the ocean, the museum, dedicated to the life and legacy of JFK, makes excellent use of film, videos, and recreated settings (including the Oval Office) to evoke a masterful portrait of politics and society half a century ago. The building, designed by I.M. Pei, has a very large library and archive, and is surrounded by a 9.5-acre (3.8-hectare) park. A new exhibit is based on the 1964 interviews with Jacqueline Kennedy by historian Arthur Schlesinger, Jr which covers her memories of the early campaigns through the Cuban Missile Crisis and her role as First Lady, mother, and wife. Docent-led highlight tours and a presentation about *PT-109* are included in the admission. Museum brochures are available in Chinese, Korean, Italian, Russian, French, Portuguese, German, Spanish, and Japanese. To put JFK's life into historic perspective, look in on the **John F. Kennedy Historic Site** *(see page 133)*.

CAMBRIDGE

Literary critic Elizabeth Hardwick once described Boston and Cambridge as "two ends of the same moustache." Indeed, across the Charles lies a separate city that is absolutely inseparable from its companion metropolis.

Just across Harvard Bridge is the **Massachusetts Institute of Technology (MIT)** ④. Housed in solid neoclassical buildings with the trim logic of natural laws, MIT almost routinely produces Nobel laureates, new scientific advances, and White House science advisors.

The Finnish architect Eero Saarinen designed two of its highlights: the inward looking, cylindrical **MIT Chapel**, illuminated by light reflected from a moat, and the tent-like **Kresge Auditorium**, which rises from a

The Big Dig

The official name is the Central Artery/Tunnel Project, but to Bostonians, it's the Big Dig. The most ambitious highway project ever undertaken in the US, the project reconfigured the hugely complicated, congested, and confusing highway and interstate system in central Boston. The Big Dig moved the ground-level I-93, which sliced through downtown Boston, to a 3.5-mile (5.6km) tunnel, extended the I-90 to Logan International Airport, and built a new crossing over the Charles River – the Bunker Hill Memorial Bridge. Originally scheduled to be completed in 1998 for a cost of $2.8 billion, with cost overruns, design flaws, and construction delays, it was finally completed in December 2007 at a cost of $14.6 billion. Although expensive, there is no doubt that the Big Dig has improved car travel in and around Boston.

circular brick terrace, its roof apparently balanced by slender metal rods on three points. The school welcomes visitors. The **visitor center** (77 Massachusetts Avenue; tel: 617-253 4795) has maps and directions, and is the starting point for tours. Display labs across the campus demonstrate engineering phenomena, artificial intelligence, and computer science. The **Visual Arts Center** is a venue for temporary exhibits. The permanent collection is spread out across campus.

Exhibits at the **MIT Museum** (265 Massachusetts Avenue; tel: 617-253 5927; open daily 10am–5pm) explore inventions, ideas, and innovations in creative interactive exhibits, and include the world's largest holography collection. It's most suited for those above 12 years old. The **Hart Nautical Gallery** has ship models showing the development of 1,000 years of naval design. A new exhibit focuses on mechanical engineering, with displays about robotics, bioengineering, and ocean science.

Harvard Square ⑬, at the heart of Cambridge, is home to Harvard University and a playground of bookstores, coffeehouses, and shops to the west and north of the Yard. At its center is the international Out of Town News, housed in a historic kiosk and stocked with a mind-boggling array of national and international publications, and beside it, Dmitri Hadzi's gently humorous stone sculpture, *Omphalos*, suggesting that Harvard is, as its supporters have long held, the center (or navel) of the universe.

The venerable Harvard Cooperative Society ("Coop" for short) was founded in 1882 as an alternative to overpriced local shops; both the Harvard and the MIT stores are the best places to buy souvenirs from either school.

Harvard University

Standing proudly above the red-brick and green ivy are the spires of America's oldest institution of higher learning, **Harvard University**. Self-confident and backed by enormous wealth – its endowment exceeded $26 billion at last count – Harvard has been a world index of intellectual

TIP

MIT tours: Info Center open Mon–Fri at 77 Mass. Avenue; free 75- to 90-min tours at 11am and 3pm Mon–Fri from lobby of Building 7 during academic year (tel: 617-253 4795; www.mit. edu). Of course there is a mobile download walking tour; this is MIT, after all. Search for "MIT Mobile."

BELOW: a student dormitory at MIT in Cambridge, MA.

Boston by the Book

Boston's literary history is almost as long and storied as its Revolutionary one. Names like Emerson, Wadsworth, and Alcott are as well known as Adams, Revere, and Hancock

Touring Boston and its environs should include visiting the places made famous by the authors – both historic and contemporary. You can explore the places that shaped them and are the settings for their novels, locations of their memoirs, or inspirations for their poetry. You can drink at their characters' favorite bars, channel their energy by visiting their homes, and pay your respects at their graves.

The easiest way to get your literary bearings is with a walking tour. **Boston by Foot** (www.boston-byfoot.com; 617-367 2345) conducts two great literary-themed strolls escorted by knowledgeable, entertaining guides. The first focuses on the Victorian "Golden Age" of Hawthorne, Longfellow, and other names familiar from required reading in school. The guides' enthusiasm and chatty stories explain why these people were the mega-stars of

their time and why they matter now. The other tour covers the 20th century, with stops relating to the poets Robert Frost and Sylvia Plath, novelists Robin Cook and Frances Parkinson Keyes, and historians Samuel Eliot Morison and David McCullough. Even Julia Child gets into the mix.

If you'd rather edit your own itinerary, grab a copy of *Boston's Literary Trail* by Susan Wilson. Written with the cooperation of the **Boston Historical Collaborative** (which occasionally runs tours: http://bostonhistorycollaborative.org) it's a lively romp through Boston, Cambridge, and Concord, visiting places as well-known as Walden Pond and as obscure as the site of the original Parker House Hotel. (Charles Dickens lived in the original building and first performed *A Christmas Carol* there.) There's a lot of insider gossip which is as entertaining as any of the books they wrote.

No guidebook or tour can promise to point out sites associated with personally favorite writers, particularly the most contemporary ones. For that, you need to make notes, use a map , and do a little sleuthing. Fans of Robert Parker's Spencer series can sit on a bench in Boston's Public Park near the swan pond and the *Make Way for Ducklings* sculpture, just as the detective (and Parker) often did, then have a drink at the Bristol Lounge at the Four Seasons Hotel, Spencer's hangout. Dennis Lehane's troubled characters frequent any of the corner bars in South Boston. In Gloucester, the Crow's Nest Bar is where the crew of the *Andrea Gail* drank before the "perfect storm." Linda Greenlaw, mentioned in the book (she was the skipper of a nearby boat) can direct you to the Dry Dock Bar in Portland ME, the setting for *All Fishermen are Liars*. New Bedford is no longer home port for a whaling fleet, but the ghosts of the ships and crews are at the dockside museum there. More ghosts are in Salem, of course, the setting for Arthur Miller's famous play *The Crucible*, which relates the tales of the Salem witch trials of 1672.

True bibliophiles must make a pilgrimage to the **Brattle Bookstore** in Cambridge (9 West Street), one of the oldest and largest antiquarian bookstores in the country. And it's fitting to pause in front of the **Old Corner Bookstore** in Boston (Washington and School streets). Currently empty, it was once the gathering place for Victorian writers.

LEFT: a vacant lot on West Street, near Brattle's Bookstore, is used as a temporary shop to sell overstock or used books.

accomplishment almost since its 1636 founding. Eight American presidents graduated from Harvard, 41 Nobel laureates, 36 Pulitzer Prize winners, and heads of state of some two dozen countries.

The heart of the place is **Harvard Yard ©**, withdrawn tranquilly behind the walls that separate it from Harvard Square outside. Passing through the gate that proclaims "Enter to Grow in Wisdom," the visitor encounters a hallowed world of grass and trees, ghosts and venerable brick – a living, eminently walkable museum of American architecture from colonial times to the present.

Massachusetts Hall (1720), Harvard's oldest standing building, quartered Revolutionary troops, as well as housing a lecture hall, a famous drama workshop, and, since 1939, the offices of the university president. Nearby stands little **Holden Chapel** (1744), once described as "a solitary English daisy in a field of Yankee dandelions."

At the Yard's center stands Charles Bulfinch's **University Hall**, built of white granite in 1815. In front is Daniel Chester French's 1814 statue of John Harvard (1607–38), the young Puritan minister for whom the college was named after he left it half his estate and all his books. Since no likeness of John Harvard existed, French used a student as his model.

East of University Hall, three massive buildings set off the central green on which commencement is celebrated each June. These are H. H. Richardson's 1880 masterwork **Sever Hall**, with its subtle brick decorations; **Memorial Church** (1932), with its Doric columns; and the monumental **Widener Library**. Given by the mother of alumnus and bibliophile Harry Elkins Widener, who died on the *Titanic* in 1912, the library is the center of Harvard's network of 92 libraries, which together house over 12 million volumes, America's third-largest book collection.

To the east of the Yard stands the **Carpenter Center for the Visual Arts ①** (24 Quincy Street; tel: 617-495 3251; Main Gallery open Mon–Sat 10am–11pm; Sun 1pm–11pm; Sert Gallery, open Tue–Sun 1pm–5pm), a cubist, machine-like building built in 1963 that represents the only American work of the great French architect Le Corbusier. The five levels, a "synthesis of the arts," include the top-floor Sert Gallery exhibiting works by contemporary artists, and the Harvard Film Archive, which shows rare and experimental films (tel: 617-495 4700; www.ves.fas.harvard.edu).

For decades, Harvard has been home to three art museums: the **Fogg** (European and American art), the **Busch-Reisinger** (northern European art), and the **Arthur M. Sackler** (ancient, Islamic, and Oriental art). A major building project, the **Harvard Art Museums** building **③** (32 Quincy Street), will locate all three collections under one roof, while maintaining their individual identities. The project is scheduled for completion in 2013. In the meantime, selected works from

The MIT campus is an attractive addition to Cambridge.

BELOW: Harvard University campus.

The inauthentic 1814 statue of John Harvard.

BELOW: Harvard's Botanical Museum.

the Fogg and the Busch-Reisinger are on exhibit at the Sackler Museum (485 Broadway; tel: 617-495 9400; www.harvardartmuseums.org; open Tue–Sat 10am–5pm; charge).

A few blocks north on Oxford Street stands the **Harvard Museum of Natural History ⑤** (26 Oxford Street; tel: 617-495 3045; open daily 9am–5pm; charge), a huge complex housing several museums. A major draw is the **Botanical Museum,** recently renovated and expanded. Permanent galleries now include a multimedia exploration of New England forests, an African gallery concentrating on endangered species, a renovated Great Mammal Hall, and an exhibit on evolution research. The most enchanting and famous exhibit is "Glass Flowers," a collection of over 3,000 astoundingly accurate models of more than 830 plant species executed by Leopold Blaschka and his son Rudolph in 19th-century Dresden.

In the same building, the **Museum of Comparative Zoology** includes George Washington's stuffed pheasants as well as the world's oldest reptile eggs. Also on the site is the **Mineralogical and Geological Museum,** with over 5,000 samples of minerals, rocks, and meteorites (both daily 9am–5pm).

The **Peabody Museum of Archaeology and Ethnology ⑥** (170 Whitney Avenue; tel: 203-432 5050 or 617-432 8987; Mon–Sat 10am–5pm, Sun 12am–5pm; charge) is filled with fossils, dinosaurs, Native American cultural objects, and wonders from ancient Egypt. A free audio tour is available via wand or MP3 download. Guided highlight tours take place on weekends at 12.30pm.

Nearby, the University's collection of Near Eastern archaeological artifacts is housed in the **Semitic Museum ⑪** (6 Divinity Avenue; tel: 617-495 4631; open Mon–Fri 10am–4pm, Sat 1pm–4pm; donation). There are over 40,000 artifacts from Egypt, Israel, Syrian, Iraq, Jordan, and Tunisia, which the museum uses to illustrate Near Eastern history, culture, and archaeology.

Cambridge Common

On July 4, 1775, George Washington assumed command of the Continental Army on **Cambridge Common ❶**. A trio of cannons abandoned by the British when they left Boston in 1776 stand close to a bronze relief of Washington on horseback under an elm tree. On the south side of the Common, just across Garden Street, Christ Church (1761) was used as a barracks by patriots, and its organ pipes were made into bullets. Close by is an entrance to **Radcliffe Institute for Advanced Study ❶**, formerly Radcliffe College (www.radcliffe.edu), the women's college that merged with Harvard in 1975.

Longfellow's legacy

In the 18th century, Brattle Street was home to so many British loyalists that it was known as Tory Row. Its handsome homes include No. 90, designed by H. H. Richardson of Trinity Church fame, and No. 94, the

17th-century Henry Vassall House. Look out for the yellow clapboard Longfellow House at the **Longfellow House – Washington Headquarters National Historic Site** Ⓚ (105 Brattle Street; tel: 617-876 4491; www.nps.gov/long; June–Oct Wed–Sun; guided tours only at 10.30am, 11.30am, 1pm, 2pm, 3pm, 4pm; free). Ironically for its setting in the midst of British loyalists, this was the place where George Washington took command of the Continental Army in 1775 and which he used as his headquarters during the Siege of Boston in 1775–76. This was the idyllic wedding present given to the poet Henry Wadsworth Longfellow and his wife, Fanny, by her father in 1843.

Little has changed inside; Longfellow's library and furniture are here, including a chair made from the "spreading chestnut-tree," which stood at 56 Brattle Street and was immortalized in his poem *The Village Blacksmith*. Unhappily, Fanny was fatally burned in the house in 1861.

Periodically there are poetry readings, concerts, re-enactments, and other events. Check the website for schedules.

John F. Kennedy National Historic Site

The nation's 35th president was born at 83 Beals Street in Brookline, now the **John F. Kennedy National Historic Site** ㊼ (tel: 617-566 7937; open late May–late Sept Wed–Sun 9.30am–5pm; free), where his family lived from 1914 to 1920. In 1967 his mother, Rose Kennedy, returned to the house and restored it to the way she recalled it looked in 1917, the year of his birth. An unprepossessing house typical of turn-of-the-century homes in Boston's then-new "streetcar suburbs," the birthplace is surprisingly modest for a family later associated with its exclusive Hyannisport compound on Cape Cod – but then, even patriarch Joseph P. Kennedy had to start somewhere. Guided and self-guided tours are available. The self-guided tours can be accessed by cell phone (usage charges apply). They are translated into French, Spanish, German, and Japanese.

TIP

A Harvard Hot Ticket ($10), on sale at the Harvard Collections Store in Holyoke Center and at all museums except the Semitic Museum, covers admission to all six museums at the university.

How to Reach the Harbor Islands

Thirty-four islands, ranging from little more than piles of rock (The Graves) to 214-acre (87-hectare) Long Island, make up the **Boston Harbor Island National Recreation Area** (tel: 617-223 8666; www.bostonharborislands.org; the site has an excellent map), where visitors can camp, swim, hike, and bird-watch.

If you're already on location, the best place to get information is at the pavilion between Quincy Market and Long Wharf-North. There are also visitor centers on Spectacle and Georges islands.

For centuries, the islands have been used for civic punishment and isolation centers. They were used to incarcerate Native Americans during the Puritan era, as a holding area for Irish immigrants, as the site of a hospital and a prison, and as the location of harbor defense forts during times of conflict. In 1996 Congress decided to support local and state efforts to turn them into a recreational state park. They are now prime examples of environmental stewardship.

The **Boston Harbor Islands Partnership** (www.boston harborislands.org; tel: 617-223 8666) coordinates the management of the island park. It runs ferries from Long Wharf in Boston and from both Hingham and Quincy. It also operates a three-hour Lighthouse Tour, which includes a chance to climb (76 steps and two ladders) to the top of Boston Light. Those trips leave from Moakley Courthouse Dock and sell out quickly.

The high-speed **Harbor Express** (tel: 617-770 0040; www.harborexpress.com) runs from Boston's Long Wharf and the Hingham Shipyard to Georges and Spectacle islands. There are free shuttles between some of the islands. For those totally without sea legs, four of the islands are accessible by car: Deer Island from Winthrop; Nut, World's End, and Webb Memorial State Park from Quincy and Hingham. Access to these islands is restricted at times, and you'll have to check with the police station located on the causeway of the Squantum peninsula.

Some islands are accessible by private boat, but be sure to check the docking requirements with the harbour master before you travel.

RESTAURANTS AND BARS

Prices for a three-course dinner per person with a half-bottle of house wine:
$ = under $20
$$ = $20–45
$$$ = $45–60
$$$$ = over $60

Restaurants

Boston

Aquitaine
569 Tremont Street
Tel: 617-424 8577
http://aquitaineboston.com
$$–$$$
A lively French bistro and wine bar (although the "bar" is tiny) in trendy South End restaurant district.

Back Bay Social Club
867 Boylston Street
Tel: 617-247 3200
www.backbaysocialclub.com $$

The dark paneling and plush red booths give it a very retro-1940s feel and encourage socializing. New England culinary staples: pork tenderloin with sweet corn pudding, smoked rib eye, herb-roasted monkfish.

Barking Crab
88 Sleeper Street, at Northern Avenue
Tel: 617-426 2722
www.barkingcrab.com $–$$
Seaside clam shack transported to the city. Big, boisterous, busy. On the water. New England boil pots and lobster.

Basho Sushi
1338 Boylston Street
Tel: 617-262 1338
www.bashosushi.com $$
Not just sushi, but the full

range of Japanese cuisine. You can sit at the counter and watch the sushi chefs slice and dice, or prepare freshly skewered food by *robata* – a Japanese style of grilling.

Betty's Wok and Noodle
250 Huntington Avenue
Tel: 617-424 1950
www.bettyswokandnoodle. com $–$$
Asian-Latino inspired noodle and rice-based dishes and sake cocktails in a sophisticated "diner" across from Symphony Hall.

Deuxave
371 Commonwealth Avenue
Tel: 617-517 5915
http://deuxave.com $$–$$$
Very refined, contemporary setting for nouvelle continental French recipes with American ingredients.

East Ocean City
25 Beach Street
Tel: 617-542 2504
www.eastoceancity.com $–$$
More than 600 lbs of fresh-from-the-tanks seafood is served daily in a Chinatown eatery that encourages guests to order meals with an eye towards sharing.

Hamersley's Bistro
553 Tremont Street
Tel: 617-423 2700
www.hamersleysbistro.com $$$
Imaginative touches dress up sophisticated comfort food at one of the first res-taurants to open in what's now the hopping South End restaurant row. Hearty, rustic food.

House of Siam

542 Columbus Avenue
Tel: 617-267 1755
www.houseofsiamboston.com
$–$$
Generally considered Boston's best Thai experience. Unusually lengthy menu, with over 130 dishes, each one prepared and plated with attention.

Lala Rokh on Beacon Hill
97 Mount Vernon Street
Tel: 617-720 5511
www.lalarokh.com $$–$$$
The aromatic, subtly nuanced flavors of Persia (now northwest Iran) are showcased in this fine restaurant.

La Verdad Taqueria Mexicana
11 Lansdowne Street
Tel: 617-421 9595
www.laverdadtaqueria.com
$$
James Beard Award-winning chef Ken Oringer proves there's a lot more to Mexican cuisine than the burrito with choices like duck carnitas; achiote and citrus marinated slow-roasted pork; and lamb enchilada with mole, sweet potatoes, and hazelnuts.

L'Espalier
774 Boylston Street
Tel: 617-262 3023
www.lespalier.com $$$$
Boston's premier location for "special event" dinners. Ultra-chic and elegant, the options are a three-course prix-fixe dinner or a seven-course degustation (tast-ing) menu (there's a

vegetarian version).

Mamma Maria
3 North Square
Tel: 617-523 0077
www.mammamaria.com **$$$**
An elegant setting in a 19th-century rowhouse, this very classy, very upscale, very highly awarded restaurant serves traditional dishes from Tuscany. The menu changes daily, but look for things like truffle-scented veal rib chop, tuna putta-nesco-style, rabbit Tuscan-style.

Mooo
15 Beacon Street
Tel: 617-670 2515
www.mooorestaurant.com **$$–$$$**
A bounty of fine bovine dining in this modern steakhouse in the XV Beacon Hotel.

No Name Restaurant
17 Fish Pier
Tel: 617-338 7539
www.nonamerestaurant.com **$–$$**
When it opened in 1917, the restaurant was the place the fishermen came to eat after they unloaded their day's catch. It's still the place to come for the freshest catch of the day.

Paramount
44 Charles Street
Tel: 617-720 1152
www.paramountboston.com **$$**
A casual institution that's equally popular with students, executives, and folks just wanting a nice night out. Routinely selected as the "Best in Boston" by some survey in some category. Chicken picatta; ahi tuna tacos.

Toscano
47 Charles Street
Tel: 617-723 4090
www.toscanoboston.com **$$$–$$$$**
Newly redesigned to accent the Old World feel in the dining room while the kitchen continues to produce classic and classy Tuscan dishes, this long-time Beacon Hill favorite has attracted even more aficionados.

Scollay Square
21 Beacon Street
Tel: 617-742 4900
www.scollaysquare.com **$$**
A local neighborhood bistro-style spot conveniently near the Theatre District. "American Comfort Food," but your mom never made mac and cheese with lobster or prosciutto and truffle oil.

Sel de la Terre
774 Boylston Street
Tel: 617-266 8800
www.seldelaterre.com **$$$**
"From our farm to your fork" is the motto. The style is the country fare of Provence and southern France. Go à la carte or choose the five- or seven-course "Chef's Whim" tasting menu. The aroma of fresh breads wafting from the boulangerie is beyond tantalizing.

Sonsie
327 Newbury Street
Tel: 617-351 2500
www.sonsieboston.com **$$–$$$**
International fare in a trendy spot. In summer, the French doors open and it becomes a sidewalk café. In winter, the Euro-lounge with comfy chairs and sofas invites conversation.

Stella
1525 Washington Street
Tel: 617-247 7747
www.bostonstella.com **$–$$$**
The restaurant serves up good Italian fare nightly in a chic setting, and the kitchen stays open until 1.30am. The adjacent café is one of the hot spots for breakfast and lunch.

The Gallows
1395 Washington Street
Tel: 617-425 0200
www.thegallowsboston.com **$$**
A rather disturbing name (public hangings reportedly took place nearby) for a great pub in South Boston with a menu that encourages sharing. The menu changes weekly, but it focuses on hearty fare: Scotch eggs, Ploughman's Board, chicken liver pâté, Tuscan bread soup.

29 Newbury
29 Newbury Street
Tel: 617-536 0290

http://29newbury.com **$$–$$$**
Hip and popular bistro with a strategic sidewalk café for people watching.

Silvertone
69 Bromfield Street
Tel: 617-338 7887
www.silvertonedowntown.com **$$**
In the financial district, this simple, laid-back restaurant fixes what you'd fix at home if you were in the mood to cook: meat loaf, bistro-style chicken, pork chops. The bar is one of the most popular in town.

Sultan's Kitchen
116 State Street
Tel: 617-570 9009
www.sultans-kitchen.com **$$**
The new menu and revamped dining room continues to present the endless variety of fine Turkish and Eastern Mediterranean cuisine, considered one of the world's greatest cuisines.

Left: informal fast food at Faneuil Hall Marketplace.
Right: treats at Top of the Hub, Prudential Center.

Prices for a three-course dinner per person with a half-bottle of house wine:
$ = under $20
$$ = $20–45
$$$ = $45–60
$$$$ = over $60

Tremont 647
647 Tremont Street
Tel: 617-266 4600
www.tremont647.com
$$–$$$
A neighborhood restaurant and bar specializing in American "melting pot" cuisine. Taco Tuesday, with fillings like braised pork, roasted sweet potatoes, chicken chorizo. Consider the chef tastings ($$$–$$$$).

Union Oyster House
41 Union Street
Tel: 617-227 2750
www.unionoysterhouse.com **$$**
"America's Oldest Restaurant" (est. 1826) is said to have been a

favorite of Daniel Webster and John F. Kennedy. Steaks and seafood are served in atmospheric rooms with creaky floors, low ceilings, and wooden booths. A popular raw bar.

Cambridge

Atasca
50 Hampshire Street
Tel: 617-621 6991
www.atasca.com **$$**
Newly redecorated, this popular gathering place is still equally popular for meeting friends or sharing a romantic dinner for two. The new menu keeps favorites from the original, solid Portuguese fare while expanding and introducing new dishes.

Casablanca
40 Brattle Street
Tel: 617-876 0999
www.casablanca-restaurant.
com **$$**
Harvard Square's oldest

restaurant is almost as legendary as the movie after which it is named. The mural of scenes from the film is a tourist attraction in its own right.

Chez Henri
1 Shepard Street (off Massachusetts Avenue)
Tel: 617-354 8980
www.chezhenri.com **$$$**
Modern French fare with a Cuban accent in a snug bistro north of Harvard Square.

Cuchi Cuchi
795 Main Street
Tel: 617-864 2929
www.cuchicuchi.cc **$$–$$$**
Antique lighting, stained glass, and Victorian tiles set the mood at this "belle epoque" establishment that serves appetizer-size portions of dishes such as "swallowed clouds" (shrimp wantons) and "Cuban cigars" (beef short ribs in dough).

East by Northeast
1128 Cambridge Street
Tel: 617-876 0286
www.exnecambridge.com
$$
Asian fusion marriage of Chinese ingredients and cooking styles and the New England palate – dumplings stuffed with Vermont pork and Massachusetts cabbage.

Harvest
44 Brattle Street
Tel: 617-868 2255
www.harvestcambridge.com
$$–$$$
One of Harvard Square's most reliably innovative bistros celebrating the "modern New England table." In summer, be sure to grab a table in the delightful garden terrace.

Mr. Bartley's Burger Cottage
1246 Massachusetts Avenue
Tel: 617-354 6559
www.mrbartley.com **$**
For five decades this casual eatery with dorm room decor across from Harvard Square has served up burgers, sweet potato fries, and onion rings.

OM
92 Winthrop Street (Harvard Square)
Tel: 617-576 2800
www.omrestaurant.com **$$**
Raved over equally for its fantastic menu of foods inspired by Asia, Thailand, and Nepal, the quietly elegant upstairs dining room and chic, hip, and swanky downstairs lounge, and the fabulous Buddhist sculptures and artwork commissioned throughout.

Salts
798 Main Street
Tel: 617-876 8444
www.saltsrestaurant.com **$$$**
A cozy oasis of tranquility and elegance serving French-influenced American food. Much of the produce comes from the restaurant's own farm in New Hampshire. Roasted duck for two available nightly with advance notice. Chef's tasting menu available.

The Elephant Walk
2067 Massachusetts Avenue
Tel: 617-492 6900
www.elephantwalk.com **$$–$$$**
Cambodian and French dishes meet in a light and airy restaurant of wood and brick.

Charlestown

Navy Yard Bistro and Wine Bar
6th Street (in the Navy Yard)

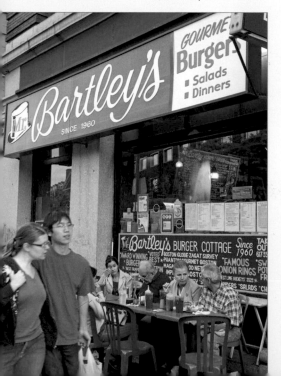

Tel: 617-242 0036
www.navyyardbistro.com **$$**
An open-kitchen atmosphere, indoor and outdoor dining, cozy bar, and menu that focuses on well-prepared basics with just enough innovation to be fun makes this a good spot for dinner after a day's sightseeing. Rib eyes and chops; daily vegetarian special, buttermilk fried oysters with Andouille sausage and Cajun rémoulade.

Tangierino
83 Main Street
Tel: 617-242 6009
www.tangierino.com **$$$**
Moroccan cuisine is a delicate fusion of North African, Spanish, and French ingredients and techniques; this is the place to savor it. Authentic belly dancing nightly; henna "tattoos" and tarot readings on the weekends.

Warren Tavern
2 Pleasant Street
Tel: 617-241 8142
www.warrentavern.com **$$**
After touring historic houses, stop off at the oldest tavern in Massachusetts. Just steps off the Freedom Trail, George Washington may not have slept here, but he certainly downed a pint or three with Paul Revere and other locals. Standard pub grub, well prepared.

Somerville

Bergamot
118 Beacon Street
Tel: 617-576 7700
www.bergamotrestaurant.com
$$–$$$
A big buzz as soon as it

opened for its Progressive American Cuisine, which combines local and international ingredients with very tasty results.

Redbones
55 Chester Street (off Elm Street)
Tel: 617-628 2200
www.redbones.com **$–$$**
Massive plates of barbecued ribs at one of the area's most popular spots. 24 microbrews on tap.

Sabur Restaurant
212 Holland Street
Tel: 617-776 7890
http://saburrestaurant.com
$$–$$$
Cuisine of Bosnia, Greece, Italy, North Africa, and the Balkans in a handsomely decorated establishment in Teele Square.

Bars
Boston

Beacon Hill Pub
147 Charles Street
Tel: 617-625 7100
One of the last of its type on the Hill: a neighborhood pub with reasonably priced beer.

The Burren
247 Elm Street
Rel: 617-776 6896
Comfortable Davis Square Irish pub draws locals, yuppies, and students for Guinness, fish and chips, and nightly traditional Irish music.

Game On
82 Lansdowne Street
Tel: 617-351 7001
In the shadow of Fenway Park and the next best thing to box seats, this sports bar has 90 screens. Bar classics such as quesadillas and pizza.

Red Hat Café
9 Bowdoin Street
Tel: 617-523 2175
One of Boston's oldest drinking places, in historic Scollay Square, has a bustling downstairs neighborhood bar, and an upstairs restaurant.

Sanctuary
189 State Street
Tel: 617-573 9333
Very young and lively; voted Boston's "sexiest" bar by local publications

Sunset Cantina
916 Commonwealth Avenue, Allston
Tel: 617-731 8646
Students from nearby Boston University pack in for a huge range of beers, margaritas, heroic portions of food, and 21 pool tables.

Cambridge

Bukowski's Tavern
1281 Cambridge Street
Tel: 617-497 7077

A cozy spot in Inman Square famous for its large selection of beers, sweet potato fries, and loud rock.

Grendel's Den
89 Winthrop Street
Tel: 617-491 1160
This landmark bar/restaurant has a huge selection of beers, and international dishes.

Noir
Charles Hotel, One Bennett Street
Tel: 617-661 8010
This very hip, upscale bar in Harvard Square uses dramatic lighting and old films projected on louvered screens to create a mood described as "decadent but sophisticated."

The Independent
75 Union Square
Tel: 617-440 6022
Newly renovated with a bigger dance floor. DJ or live music almost nightly. 32 draught beers, 60 bottles.

LEFT: a venerable venue on Massachusetts Avenue.
RIGHT: the Union Oyster House.

BOSTON'S FREEDOM TRAIL

Boston is rich in history and is small enough to navigate on foot. The Freedom Trail is a handy way for visitors to take in the most important sites of this historic city

The Freedom Trail, a 2.5-mile (4km) brick path linking 16 historic locations that all played a part in Boston's Colonial and Revolutionary history, was born in 1951. Aware that "Tourists were going berserk, bumbling around and frothing at the mouth because they couldn't find what they were looking for," newspaperman William Greenough Schofield suggested that the sites be linked in a numbered sequence. In 1974, part of the Trail became Boston's National Historical Park.

A leisurely pace

It's tempting to see the city by tour bus, sightseeing trolley, or the amphibious vehicles called "duck boats". All provide quick introductions to some of the major sites and help you get your bearings as to where things are in relation to each other. But by walking you can choose your own pace, decide what you really want to see, when to eat, or take time to explore that interesting-looking building around the corner that isn't on the tour guide's itinerary. Good walking shoes and a map are a necessity. (Free Freedom Trail maps are available at the National Park Visitor Center at 15 State Street next to the Old State House, or at the visitor center at the Boston Common on Tremont Street, near Park Street). The entire trail can be walked in one day, but it's much more satisfying to do it in a more leisurely fashion over two days.

ABOVE: in Boston's Veterans' Day parade, groups dress as Revolutionary War-period soldiers and march with flags from Boston Common to City Hall.

BELOW: King's Chapel Burying Ground became the town's first cemetery in 1630. A chapel joined it in 1689. Many colonists are buried here, including John Winthrop, the colony's governor; Hezekiah Usher, its first printer; and Mary Chilton, the first woman to step off the *Mayflower* in 1620.

LEFT: the idea for the Freedom Trail was conceived by local journalist William Schofield in 1951, as a pedestrian trail to link important local landmarks.

Above: the Freedom Trail is marked by a red line of paint or brick running from Boston Common to the Bunker Hill Monument in Charlestown.

PAUL REVERE RIDES AGAIN

Boston misses few opportunities to relive its stirring history. On March 5, Boston Massacre Day, the Charlestown Militia leads a parade from the Old State House to City Hall Plaza. Patriots' Day, on the third Monday in April, is the year's biggest one-day celebration. Paul Revere's and William Dawes' rides are re-enacted, this time with a state police escort. After a parade in Back Bay, the first two battles of the Revolution are staged with gusto at Lexington Green and Concord. June sees the Ancient and Honorable Artillery Company parade, and the Battle of Bunker Hill is re-enacted at the Monument following a parade from Charlestown. And on December 16, the Boston Tea Party of 1773 is re-enacted. For a condensed version of all of the above, Boston Harborfest is a nine-day festival that runs from late June through the July 4th weekend. There are British encampments on Boston Common, a replay of the Boston Tea Party, and the reading of the Declaration of Independence from the balcony of the Old State House. It culminates with the annual fireworks-enhanced outdoor concert by the Boston Pops.

RIGHT: the Freedom Trail is simple ground markers that note 16 significant historical sights, including graveyards, notable churches, and a historic naval frigate.

BELOW: Charles Bulfinch designed the magnificent red-brick and domed State House ("the hub of the solar system") when he was only 24. Guided tours are available.

AROUND BOSTON

The arc around Boston is filled with attractions and historical sites, where meadows are haunted with the echoes of musket fire and philosophers sought the meaning of life

There are a number of histori-cal sights that can be visited as day trips from the city. To the north of the city is the iconic sea-coast with its weathered villages and fishermen dominates. To the west are vivid reminders of the American Revolution, while south of the city is a region with a rich legacy that includes Pilgrims, presidents, and whalers.

NORTH OF BOSTON

Just a few miles north of Boston via Route 1 (Main Street/Saugus Exit) is the **Saugus Iron Works National Historic Site ❶** (244 Central Street; tel: 781-233 0050; Apr–Oct daily). The buildings have been recon-structed as they were in 1646, with a blast furnace and forge, ironworks house, and a restored 17th-century home. The site was established by John Winthrop Jr and, though ultimately unprofitable, launched America's ironworking industry. On summer weekends, there are iron-casting demonstrations.

Marblehead

Take Route 1A north to Route 114 to **Marblehead ❷**, founded as a fishing village in 1629. The narrow streets of the Historic District are lined with over 200 pre- and post-Revolutionary homes, many now chic B&Bs, shops, and galleries.

The **Marblehead Museum & Historical Society** (170 Washington Street; tel: 781-631 1768; June–Oct Tue–Sat, Nov-May Tue–Fri; fee) preserves the city's history; exhibits include a delightful collection of folk-art paintings by self-taught J.O.J. Frost, who first picked up a brush at age 70.

The original of Archibald Willard's painting *The Spirit of '76* (aka **Yankee Doodle**) is displayed in the Selectmen's Room of Abbot Hall (188

Main attractions
MARBLEHEAD
SALEM
GLOUCESTER
PARKER RIVER NATIONAL WILDLIFE REFUGE ROCKPORT
LEXINGTON AND CONCORD
WALDEN POND
PLYMOUTH
FALL RIVER

LEFT: Lowell's Boat shop, where America's oldest working boat builder plies his craft.
RIGHT: North Shore boathouse.

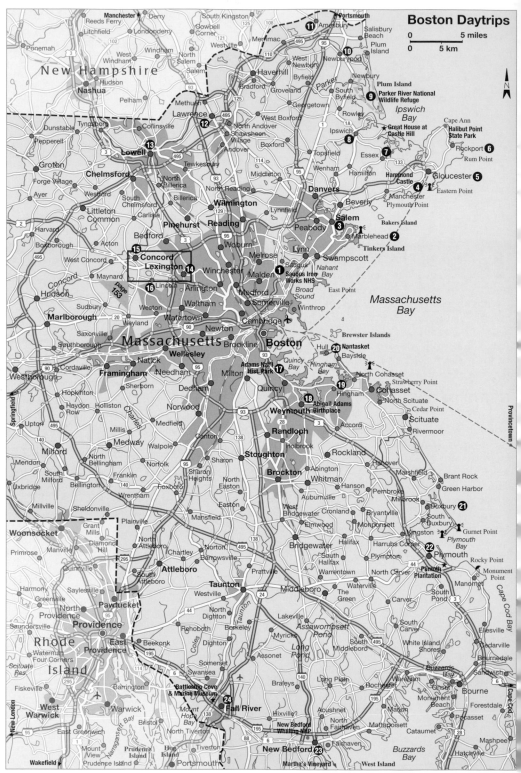

New Hampshire

Massachusetts

Rhode Island

Massachusetts Bay

Ipswich Bay

Cape Cod Bay

Buzzards Bay

Washington Street; tel: 781-631 0000; open weekdays).

Old Burial Hill, overlooking the harbor, is the final resting place for 600 soldiers of the Revolution.

Salem

Founded in 1626 as a seaport, **Salem's ❸** maritime history, cultural attractions, and colonial atmosphere rival any other town. A red line along th sidewalks marks the route linking the historic sites. Begin with a visit to **the National Park Service Regional Visitor Center ❹** (2 New Liberty Street; tel: 978-740 1650; open daily), which shows an excellent film detailing the area's history. Translations are available in French, German, Spanish, and Russian.

Most visitors will initially want to tour the scenes of the infamous witchcraft trials of 1692. When normalcy returned, the "witches" of Salem entered into fact and folklore which support a bewitchingly popular array of attractions. There's a sense of theme park in much of the town, with souvenir shops selling incense and potions,

psychic readers, even a bronze statue of Elizabeth Montgomery in her role as Samantha in *Bewitched*.

For all of the frivolity, the trials were a horrific time. Particularly moving is the **Salem Witch Trials Tercentenary Memorial ❸**. The paving stones and walls surrounding the stark granite court are incised with pleas of innocence from the accused. Adjoining is Charter Street Burying Point, the final resting place of witch trials Court Magistrate John Hawthorne.

The **Salem Witch Museum ❷** (19 Washington Square North; daily; fee), **Witch Dungeon Museum ❶** (16 Lynde Street; Apr–Nov daily; fee), **Witch History Museum ❺** (197 Essex Street; Apr–Nov daily; fee), and **Witch House ❻** (310 Essex Street; May–early Nov; fee), home of Judge Jonathan Corwin, all present historically accurate, although often sensationalized, versions of the events.

Nautical Salem

It's a shame that witch kitsch dominates, because the area has much else to recommend it. Salem owes its

A flower shop in Marblehead is a profusion of color.

BELOW: a statue outside the Salem Witch Museum.

TIP

It's easy enough to walk to all sites – both "witchy" and otherwise – but to get a comprehensive overview, hop on the Salem trolley (tel: 978-744 5469; www.salemtrolley.com) for an hour-long, historically accurate tour. It's not a flying broomstick, but you can also tour Salem via Segway (283 Derby Street; tel: 781-626-4000; www.witchcitysegway.com).

restored grandeur to its former prominence as a seaport.

Salem Maritime National Historic Site G (193 Derby Street; Jan–Oct daily) recreates Salem's rise as an important port. A short film explains how Salem opened up trade with the Orient, its role in the Triangle slave trade, and privateering. Visitors tour the Custom House, a public house, a goods store, and a merchant's mansion. The replica 1797 East Indiaman *Friendship* is magnificent. Admission to the site is free, but there is a charge for the ranger-led tours. You can also download an audio tour for MP3 players.

Commercial, but fun, the **New England Pirate Museum H** (274 Derby Street; tel: 978-741 2800; May–Oct daily, Apr and Nov weekends; fee. Combo tickets with Witch Dungeon and Witch History Museums available) brings to light a little-known piece of Salem history. In the 1690s, Capt. Kidd, Blackbeard, and other nefarious figures frequented the area. The museum displays recovered pirate loot; you'll also board a mock-up of a pirate ship.

Peabody Essex Museum

The **Peabody Essex Museum I** (161 Essex Street; tel: 978-745 9500; Tue–Sun; fee) began as a place for sea captains to show off the oddities and objects collected on their voyages. Its collections of Asian, maritime, and Oceanic art are extensive. The Yin Yu Tang house, a 200-year-old Chinese dwelling, was carefully dismantled and reconstructed in the museum's courtyard.

On Essex Street, the Museum preserves six houses that span two centuries of New England architecture; the McIntyre Historic District preserves Georgian and Federal-period houses designed or inspired by architect and master builder Samuel McIntire. The district offers a tour de force for anyone interested in both architecture and American cultural history: this is where, and how, the nation's first millionaires lived.

New England's oldest remaining 17th-century wooden mansion is the forbidding-looking 1668 **House of the Seven Gables J** (115 Derby Street; tel: 978-744

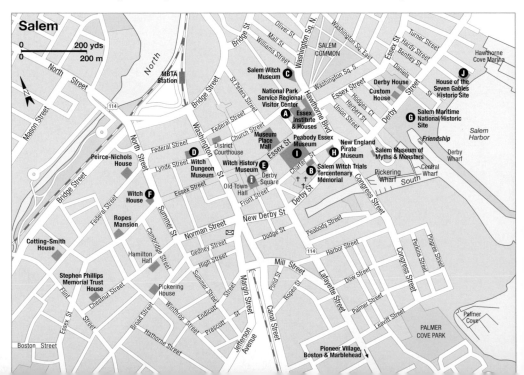

0991; daily; fee; tour booklets available in French, German, Spanish, Italian, and Brazilian Portuguese). The structure is famous for more than mere antiquity, having been the inspiration for the house in the classic 1851 novel by Salem native Nathaniel Hawthorne. The house in which Hawthorne was born has been moved next door, and visitors can tour both houses as well as the handsome colonial revival gardens.

South of town in Forest River Park, **Pioneer Village** (tel: 978-867 4767; mid-June–Oct daily; fee) is a re-created, living-history Puritan village which further helps explain the mindset of the Puritans.

Essex Scenic Byway

Cross the Danvers River on Route 1A to Beverly, to Route 127, the Essex Coastal Scenic Byway. The route hugs the rocky shoreline, passing through 13 coastal communities filled with New England ambience and over 8,000 buildings on the National Register of Historic Places.

Hammond Castle

Just before Gloucester stands **Hammond Castle ❹** (80 Hesperus Avenue; tel: 978-283 2080; Labor Day–Oct open weekends; www.hammondcastle.org; fee). This was the 1920s fantasy abode of the prolific inventor John Hays Hammond Jr – remote control via radio waves was his most important idea – who plundered Europe for elements to work into his dreamhouse, including a medieval village facade to overlook the indoor pool.

The entire castle was built around the monumental 8,200-pipe organ (the largest organ in a private home in the US) that Hammond designed – although he is not the Hammond of Hammond Organ fame. Check the museum's website for a schedule of organ concerts.

Gloucester

Approaching **Gloucester ❺** from either Route 127 or Route 133, you pass the **Gloucester Fishermen's Wives Memorial**. Overlooking the harbor, the statue of a fisherman's family looking out to sea is a fitting compliment

TIP

Each September Essex National Heritage Area (www.essexheritage.org) coordinates more than 150 free events from Amesbury to Rockport as part of its Trails & Sails weekend. Their schedule, along with the brochure, *Guide to the Great Outdoors*, can be downloaded from their website.

BELOW LEFT: Hawthorne's House of the Seven Gables.
BELOW RIGHT: Salem Maritime National Historic site includes the replica tall ship *Friendship*.

Salem's Witches

Behind the tawdry merchandising and overwrought re-enactments lies one of New England's darkest episodes of religious intolerance

Since its founding in 1626, the town (whose name derives, ironically, from *shalom*, the Hebrew word for peace) had never been a bastion of tolerance and goodwill: it was from Salem that Roger Williams, the founder of Rhode Island, had been exiled for preaching religious freedom.

The townspeople's rigid ways took a destructive turn when Tituba, a Barbados slave serving the household of Salem's minister, Samuel Parris, began regaling his daughter, Elizabeth, and niece, Abigail Williams, with vivid accounts of voodoo. Fascinated, Elizabeth and Abigail invited a handful of their friends to listen to Tituba's tales.

Meetings of such a nature, being strictly forbidden in Puritan Salem, held an illicit appeal that the girls must have found difficult to resist, but no doubt they also found their guilty pleasure difficult to live with, for all soon began to exhibit bizarre behavior: they would crawl on the floor, making choking sounds, and cry out that needles were piercing their

flesh. The town doctor was called in to examine the girls and, after medicine failed to cure them, he diagnosed them as victims of witchcraft.

The Rev. Mr Parris suggested that Tituba might be their tormentor, and the slave was charged with witchcraft. In confessing, under pain of torture, she gave a lurid account of how a tall man from Boston, accompanied by witches, had molested the girls.

Satan himself, she claimed, had ordered her to murder the girls, and other witches had beaten her for her refusal to comply; she merely tormented them, trying to abate her own pain. In her stories, she pointed a finger at two women unpopular in the village, Sarah Osborne and Sarah Good, who were charged with everything from bewitching cattle to using voodoo dolls.

Inflamed by the oratory of such self-promoting preachers as Cotton Mather, subsequent accusations spread like wildfire. Ultimately, 400 people ended up accused – many of them marginal members of society, whose lack of prosperity the Puritans took to mean a lack of godliness.

Imprisoned in cold, damp cells, several of the accused women died while awaiting trial. Of those found guilty in Salem, 19 were hanged and one man was pressed to death beneath a wooden plank piled with rocks. These executions took place between June and September, and the terror might have continued through the fall had Governor General Sir William Phips not returned from the north woods, where he had been fighting an alliance of French and Native Americans, and put a stop to the madness. In December 1692, he ordered all the suspects released – including his own wife.

ABOVE: the reality of a 1692 persecution – *The Ducking Stool*, by Charles Stanley Reinhart.
LEFT: kitsch toys boost the local economy.

to the famous Fishermen's Memorial (Route 127), the statue of a fisherman who grips the wheel and peers oceanward. The city's fishing fleet was immortalized in Sebastian Junger's 1997 bestselling novel and the subsequent movie *The Perfect Storm*. The bar where the movie was shot, the Crow's Nest, still looks much as it did during filming a decade ago.

The **Cape Ann Museum** (27 Pleasant Street; tel: 978-283 0455; Tue–Sun; fee) uses artwork to preserve and explore the history of Gloucester's mariners. **Maritime Gloucester** (28 Harbor Loop; tel: 978-281 0470; Memorial Day–mid-Oct daily; fee) immerses visitors in the realities of fishing with displays about fitting out schooners and an operating marine railway. Underwater cameras allow for a virtual visit to the Stellwagen Bank National Marine Sanctuary, New England's only maritime sanctuary. Visitors can take a cruise on the center's schooner *Ardelle*.

The visitor center (9 Hough Avenue; tel: 978-282 4101; www.gloucest erma.com) has information about whale-watching cruises. Pick up a walking/driving tour of the galleries of the Rocky Neck art colony just east of town.

Overlooking Gloucester harbor is the wonderfully over-the-top **Beauport/Sleeper-McCann House** (75 Eastern Point Boulevard; tel: 978-283 0800; June–mid-Oct Tue–Sat; fee). Henry Davis Sleeper was one of the first professional interior decorators. Work started on his house in 1907 and continued for 27 years. Each of the 40 rooms is thematic and fanciful: one bedroom is in chapel style, the belfry is rich in chinoiserie, and the book tower has wooden "damask" curtains salvaged from a hearse.

Rockport

Granite was shipped to ports around the world in the 19th century from **Rockport ❻**, a bustling former fishing village-turned-artists' colony and tourist attraction. The seagoers' cottages that crowded onto Bearskin Neck have become tourist-oriented shops. The red fishing shack on the harbor is known as Motif No. 1 because it is said to be more frequently

TIP

On the last Sunday in June, the fishermen of Gloucester participate in the Blessing of the Fleet. The unusual, Mission-style Our Lady of Good Voyage Church (142 Prospect Street; tel: 978-283 1490), overlooking the harbor, was built for the Portuguese community.

BELOW LEFT: the seafaring symbol on display at the Peabody Essex Museum in Salem.
BELOW RIGHT: a fisherman's shack at Rockport Harbour.

painted and sketched than any other building in America.

Signposted off Curtis Street on the edge of the village, the **Paper House** (52 Pigeon Hill Street; tel: 978-546 2629; spring–fall open daily; entrance fee) is an endearing oddity, built entirely of rolled-up newspaper reinforced with glue and varnish. Begun in 1924 by an inventor of office supplies, the project took 20 years, and includes a desk made of copies of the *Christian Science Monitor*.

Essex

Essex ❼ was a major shipbuilding center in the age of sail. The **Essex Shipbuilding Museum** (66 Main Street; tel: 978-768 7541; May–Oct Wed–Sun; fee) traces the region's rich boatbuilding history through thousands of photographs, documents, and shipbuilding tools. Two schooners – one authentic, the other a reproduction – share the dock. A burial ground full of interestingly designed 18th- and 19th-century gravestones is on the property. **Gogswell's Grant** (60 Spring Street; tel: 978-768 3632;

June–Oct Wed–Sun; fee) is a fabulous collection of American folk art fittingly displayed in an 18th-century farmhouse.

Ipswich

Continue on Route 133 into **Ipswich** ❽, which has more homes built between 1625 and 1725 than any other community in the country. The **Ipswich Museum** in the 1800 Heard House (54 South Main Street; tel: 978-356 2811; daily; fee) has artifacts of the town's 400-year history. Nearby, the 1640 **John Whipple House** (same hours) is a fine example of a Puritan homestead.

Parker River National Wildlife Refuge

On the way out to **Plum Island** along Water Street, the Massachusetts Audubon Society offers interpretive displays at their 54-acre (22-hectare) **Joppa Flats Education Center** (tel: 978-462 9888; open Tue–Sun and Mon holidays).

Just across the road, the **Parker River National Wildlife Refuge**

BELOW: Seaport Sailor Stan's Luncheonette. Detail by the Rocky Neck Artist Colony.

Rocky Neck Art Colony

A tiny spit of land less than 1 square mile (2.6 sq km) in size just outside Gloucester is the home of Rocky Neck Art Colony. The nation's longest continuously operating art colony, it has attracted realist painters, sculptors, and writers since the 1850s. Childe Hassan, Winslow Homer, Edward Hopper, and John Sloan all drew inspiration from the landscape and lighting. Many of their works hang in galleries and museums across the country and the world, bringing New England's landscapes, wildlife, and people to audiences far outside the region.

A walking tour visits 12 sites used by the artists. In most cases, both the vistas they saw and the buildings where they worked are unchanged (www.rockneckartcolony.org)

visitor center ❾ (978-465 5753; daily; entrance fee) offers interactive exhibits about the flora and fauna found in the 4,662-acre (1,887-hectare) refuge. There are ample opportunities for wildlife observation, paddling, and shellfishing. Depending on the season, the 6 miles (10km) of sand dunes and ocean beach yield a riot of false heather, dune grass, scrub pine, and beach plums. Geese, pheasants, rabbits, deer, woodchucks, turtles, and toads roam freely over the preserve. In March and October the skies are dark with migrating geese and ducks. From April through mid-August, large areas of the beach are roped off to permit the piping plovers – an endangered species of shorebirds – to nest and feed in peace.

Newburyport

Continue north to **Newburyport** ❿. The "Clipper City," once home to a magnificent merchant fleet and a thriving shipbuilding industry, has benefited from careful preservation.

The **Market Square** is a symphony of brick and bustle with fine shops and restaurants adjacent to a waterfront promenade and piers where whale-watching tours embark. Newburyport is the birthplace of the US Coast Guard. Exhibits at the **Custom House Maritime Museum** (25 Water Street, tel: 978-462 8681; mid-May–Dec Tue–Sun; fee) chronicle the history of the "Coasties" and the area's shipwrecks, as well as displaying maritime art.

The **Cushing House** (98 High Street; tel: 978-462 2681; June–Oct Tue–Sun; fee) belonged to Caleb Cushing (1800–79), a lawyer and diplomat who became America's first ambassador to China. Visitors to the 1808 house can view the exotic booty he brought back.

Amesbury

In nearby **Amesbury** ⓫, **Lowell's Boat Shop** (495 Main Street, tel: 978-834 0050; call for opening hours) is the oldest continuously operating boat shop in the US and birthplace of the fishing dory. It continues to make dories and skiffs much as it did when it first opened its doors in 1793.

TIP

Like any paradise, the Parker River National Wildlife Refuge has its bugbears – in this case, small, flying insects called greenhead flies, whose bite is very painful. They're most common from July through mid-August. Also, watch out for poison ivy and deer ticks carrying lyme disease.

BELOW: Plum Island in the Parker River National Wildlife Refuge.

Close by is the **Whittier Home** (86 Friend Street; tel: 978-388 1337; whittierhome.org; open May–Oct Tue–Sat; entrance fee). It was here that the "Quaker Poet" and abolitionist John Greenleaf Whittier (1807–92) lived as an adult. The house and furnishings have been preserved as they were during his life.

WEST OF BOSTON

Aside from Boston proper, this has probably the most historic real estate in the country. The colonial era ended and the Revolutionary era began here, but it also saw the birth of trade unions – another revolutionary idea – as part of the aptly named Industrial Revolution.

Lawrence

North of Boston on I–93 is **Lawrence** ⓬, one of the country' first planned industrial cities. More than 30 immigrant populations worked in the city's mills. Their story is ably recounted at **Lawrence Heritage State Park** (1 Jackson Street; tel: 978-794 1655; daily). Exhibits at the visitor center,

housed in a restored 1840 boarding house, recreate the living conditions of mill workers, and include a multimedia program about the Great Strike of 1912, also called the "Bread and Roses" strike.

The one-time model mill town of **Lowell** ⓭, southwest of Lawrence on I–495, is America's best brick-and-mortar chronicle of industrial history. The **Lowell National Historical Park** (246 Market Street; tel: 978-970 5000; daily; fee for some tours) incorporates sites throughout the city which illustrate the history of the Industrial Revolution. Sightseeing ferries ply the old canals and trolleys clang through the streets. At the **Boott Cotton Mills Museum** (115 John Street; daily; fee) authentic looms pound at full speed, while the typical boardinghouse for women workers who lived in appalling conditions is recreated in the Morgan Cultural Center (40 French Street; daily; fee). Exhibits at the vast **American Textile History Museum** (491 Dutton Street; tel: 978-441 0400; Wed–Sun; fee), housed in an 1860s

BELOW: the Boot Mill in Lowell National Park.

canal-front factory, include textile samples and trade catalogs.

Jack Kerouac, the Beat Generation icon, was born, raised, and buried here. The **Kerouac Memorial**, in Kerouac Park on Bridge Street, is a series of metal tablets displaying his most poignant quotes. The website www.lowellcelebrateskerouac.org is informative about his local links.

The artist James Abbott Whistler (1834–1903) spent the first three years of his life in what is now the **Whistler House Museum of Art** (243 Worthen Street; tel: 978-452 7641; open Wed–Sat; fee). The collection of 19th- and 20th-century New England representational arts includes his etchings.

It's appropriate that the center of the nation's textile industry is home to the **New England Quilt Museum** (18 Shattuck Street; tel: 802-452 4207; open Tue–Sat; fee). It recounts the history of American quiltmaking with more than 150 traditional and contemporary quilts.

Hop aboard *New Orleans #99*, the trolley that inspired playwright Tennessee Williams' *A Streetcar Named Desire* for a 2-mile (3km) ride at the **National Streetcar Museum** (25 Shattuck Street; tel: 978-458 5835; Sat–Sun; streetcar rides weekends May–Oct).

The shot heard round the world

On April 19, 1775, British regulars clashed in a battle with militia and Minutemen in **Lexington**  and **Concord** ⑮, and "the shot heard round the world" launched the eight-year War for Independence. The route of the British advance from Boston is designated the **Battle Road**.

Chronologically, a visit to the Lexington and Concord battle sites should go east to west. From Lowell, take Route 3 to exit 31. From Boston, all of the revolutionary sites can be reached via Route 2. The best place to start a visit to the area is at one of the visitor centers at the **Minute Man National Historical Park** (Headquarters 174 Liberty Street, Concord; tel: 978-369 6993; www.nps.gov/mima); **Minute Man Visitor Center** (270 N. Great Road, Lincoln; mid-Mar–Nov daily 9–4; closed

The iconic statue of John Parker on Battle Green, Lexington.

BELOW: guarding the approach to the mills, in Lawrence, MA.

The Bread and Roses Strike

In 1912, Lowell MA had dozens of textile factories operating around the clock. While the mill owners prospered, their workers dealt with low pay, hazardous working conditions, and deplorable living conditions. Nearly 40 percent of the workers died before age 25.

When a new law went into effect lowering the work week from 56 to 54 hours, employers cut the workers' wages by a similar percent. The workers – mostly immigrant women – walked away from their looms and took to the streets, demanding better pay and dignified treatment.

Their cause inspired poet James Oppenheim to write *Bread and Roses*, which included the lines "We come marching, marching in the beauty of the day; A million darkened kitchens, a thousand mill lofts gray… Our lives shall not be sweated from birth until life closes; Hearts starve as well as bodies; give us bread, but give us roses."

Within a month, 30,000 millworkers had joined the strike. The governor called out the militia which violently confronted the marching women. After 63 days, the owners and workers came to agreements. But the success was short-lived. The agreements were largely verbal, not written, and within a few years the working conditions and pay had deteriorated; employers thwarted efforts at union organizing; and a depression further undermined the gains.

WHERE

The **Battle Road Trail** is a 5-mile (8km) walking and biking trail which begins at the eastern boundary of the park in Lexington and ends at Meriam's Corner near Concord. It's more historically accurate than the highway which shares the name. The trail largely follows the road which existed in 1775, with a few detours through the fields and forests the Minutemen used.

Dec–mid-Mar); and the **Hartwell Tavern** (Route 2A, Lincoln; late May–late Oct daily), a restored, 18th-century home and tavern where park rangers in colonial attire offer 20-minute programs daily. The **North Bridge Visitor Center** (174 Liberty Street, Concord; daily) has an excellent multimedia presentation, *The Road to Revolution*, which explains the events for those who aren't steeped in American history and those Americans who didn't pay attention in history class.

Lexington

Most of the important Lexington sites are within a musket shot of each other. The **Lexington Visitor Center** **Ⓐ** (1875 Massachusetts Avenue, across from the green; tel: 781-862 1450; open daily) is a good place to get your bearings. Across the street is **Battle Green** **Ⓑ**, with the famous statue of Minuteman Captain John Parker. Seventy-seven militiamen faced 1,000 British regulars here. The remains of the eight Minutemen who died rest underneath the obelisk on the Green. **Buckman Tavern** **Ⓒ** (1 Bedford

Street; tel: 781-862 5598; mid-Apr–Oct daily; fee) was the place Captain Parker and his Minutemen sipped beer while waiting for the British.

The **Hancock-Clarke House** **Ⓓ** (36 Hancock Street; tel: 781-862 1703; June–Oct daily, Apr–May weekends; fee) was Paul Revere's destination. He was trying to warn John Hancock and Samuel Adams with news of the British advance. A mile outside town, **Munroe Tavern** **Ⓔ** (1332 Massachusetts Avenue; tel: 781-862 1703; June–Oct daily; fee) sheltered British Brigadier General Earl Percy and his troops during their retreat from Concord. A bit farther on, the **National Heritage Museum** **Ⓕ** (33 Marrett Road, Route 2A; tel: 781-861 6559; Wed–Sat) focuses on the history of American freemasonry and fraternalism, as well as the period surrounding the American Revolution.

Leaving Lexington on **Battle Road** (aka Route 2A and Massachusetts Avenue), you'll pass the **Ebenezer Fiske House Site Farmhouse** **Ⓖ**, where a historical marker explains

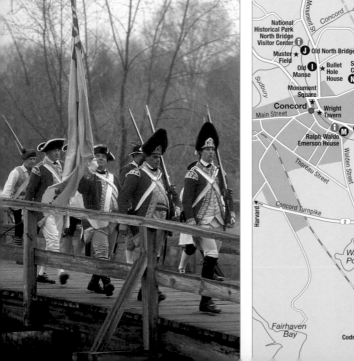

BELOW: a Patriots Day re-enactment on Concord's replica Old North Bridge.

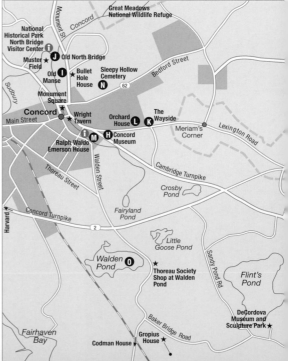

the course of the fierce fighting that broke out there. A section of the original road here is unpaved and closed to traffic, giving an idea of its original appearance.

Concord

Concord Museum ❶ (53 Cambridge Turnpike, Route 2A; tel: 978-369 9763; daily; fee) has excellent displays relating to Revolutionary Concord, including one of the two lanterns hung by Robert Newman in Old North Church in Boston. The town's literary legacy is also strongly covered. A gallery devoted to Concord's Henry David Thoreau (1817–62) has a superb collection of artifacts associated with the great author and naturalist, including furnishings from his cabin by Walden Pond.

The **Old Manse** ❶ (269 Monument Street; tel: 978-369 3909; mid-Apr–Oct daily; fee) was built by Minister William Emerson around 1770, and was used to shelter women and children during the battle. It became home to his grandson Ralph Waldo, who wrote *Nature* (1836) here, and

was rented for three years to Nathaniel Hawthorne.

At **Old North Bridge** ❶, rangers tell how the tide of the battle turned against the British here. Pass Daniel Chester French's *Minute Man* statue to reach the North Bridge Visitor Center.

Concord's literary associations

From 1845 to 1848 the writer Louisa May Alcott lived in **The Wayside** ❶ (455 Lexington Road, Route 2A; tel: 978-318 7863; guided tours Memorial Day–Oct; reservations required; fee). In 1852 it was bought by writer Nathaniel Hawthorne. He added the tower, but found it unsatisfactory for working in, and said he would happily see the house burn down.

From 1858 to 1877, the Alcott family lived at **Orchard House** ❶ (399 Lexington Road, Route 2A; tel: 978-369 4118; daily; fee), where Louisa May penned *Little Women* and *Little Men*. The house still has most of the family's furnishings and looks as it did when they lived here. There's an excellent orientation video and a

Buckman Tavern.

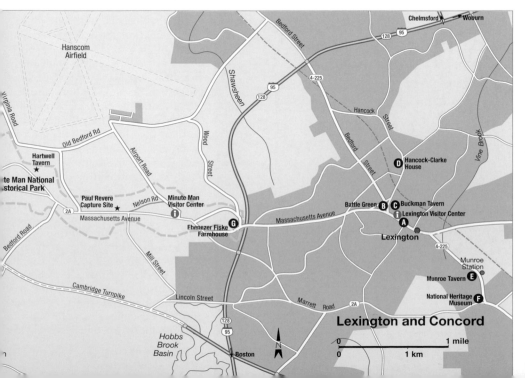

Lexington and Concord

Walden Pond is the birthplace of the conservatism movement.

BELOW: a statue of Thoreau outside a replica of his cabin at Walden Pond.

self-guided tour of Bronson's School of Philosophy, which functioned from 1880 to 1888.

Thoreau and Emerson

Philosopher and author Ralph Waldo Emerson lived most of his adult life nearby; his house, furnished as it was when he died in 1882, is preserved as the **Ralph Waldo Emerson House** (28 Cambridge Turnpike; tel: 978-369 2236; open mid-Apr–mid-Oct daily; fee).

Sleepy Hollow Cemetery (Bedford Street, Route 62) is the resting place of most of the Concord big names, among them Hawthorne, the Alcotts, Emerson, and Thoreau.

Walden Pond

South of Concord off Route 126, Thoreau spent 26 months in a one-room cbin (there's now a replica) by **Walden Pond** (tel: 978-369 3254; open year-round; parking fee) striving to be self-sufficient and recording the progress of nature, all of which he recounted in *Walden* (1854). A National Historic Landmark, the pond and surrounding land are now a state reservation.

Lincoln

Tiny, upscale **Lincoln** , just south of Lexington and Concord, has the superb **DeCordova Sculpture Park** (51 Sandy Pond Road; tel: 781-259 8355; Tue–Sun 10–5; fee). With around 75 large-scale contemporary outdoor American sculptures, the 35-acre (14-hectare) museum is the largest of its kind in New England. The house of the one-time estate, known as "The Castle," is now a museum of modern and contemporary American art. The café serves light lunches.

The **Gropius House** (68 Baker Bridge Road; June–Oct Wed–Sun; Nov–May weekends; fee) was built by the renowned 20th-century architect who helped launch the Bauhaus school in 1938 when he came to teach at the Harvard Graduate School of Design.

SOUTH OF BOSTON

The first settlers arrived in this part of the New Wold, hoping to establish a theocracy unfettered by outside influences. That drive for self-determination led a later resident, John Adams, to argue for establishment of an independent government for their descendants. The whalers and fishermen in New Bedford and Fall River continue that self-reliant life as they challenge the elements while earning their living from the sea.

From Boston, head south on I–93 to exit 12 and follow Route 3A to Quincy and the **Adams National Historical Park** (visitor center at 1250 Hancock Street; tel: 617-770 1175; houses open mid-Apr–mid-Nov daily, visitor center open year-round; fee). This was home to four generations of Adamses from 1720 to 1927. The site includes the birthplaces of America's first father-and-son presidential pair – John Adams (second president of the US) and his son, John Quincy Adams (the sixth) – and Peacefield, the

elegant home that John and his wife, Abigail, moved to in 1787.

High points of the tour are J.Q. Adams's library, with 14,000 volumes, and the formal garden, especially appealing when the daffodils bloom. Entrance to the buildings is by guided tour only, first-come, first-served: on weekends and holidays, waits of one to two hours are common.

Abigail Adams

The second first lady, John Adams's wife Abigail, was born at the **Abigail Adams Birthplace** ⓲ (180 Norton Street; tel: 781-335 4205; call for tour information) in **Weymouth** in 1744. The house, built in 1685 and once referred to as "The Mansion," has been restored to its mid-1700s appearance.

Hingham

Farther down the coast off routes 1 and 3A is **Hingham** ⓳, beautified by Frederick Law Olmsted, creator of Boston's "emerald necklace" of parks and New York's Central Park; his handiwork here is the bucolic **World's End Reservation** (250 Martin's Lane;

tel: 781-740 6665; open daily; fee), a 250-acre (100-hectare) harborside preserve with walking trails providing views of the Boston skyline and Hingham harbor.

Nantasket

Enclosing Hingham Bay and curving toward Boston like a beckoning finger is the sandy spit of **Nantasket** ⓴, a long-time summer playground of which only a carousel has survived redevelopment. The classic 1928 **Paragon Carousel** (205 Nantasket Avenue; tel: 781-925 0472; open Memorial Day–Labor Day daily; entrance fee) is a gem. An "adopt a horse" program helps fund the restoration of the 66 horses that prance to the music of a Wurlitzer organ.

The **Hull Lifesaving Museum** (1117 Nantasket Avenue; tel: 781-925 5433; open Mon, Wed, Fri, also weekends July–Oct; fee), in a restored 19th-century lifesaving station at the mouth of Boston Harbor, gives visitors a good idea of the heroic measures required when the lighthouse warnings failed to stave off disaster.

John Adams (1735–1826) served as ambassador to the Netherlands and Britain and became the second president of the United States. In helping to frame the Constitution, he ensured that rigorous checks and balances were included.

BELOW: Walden Pond.

One of the family homes in the Adams National Historic Park.

BELOW: a recreation of the *Mayflower* stands at attention in Plymouth.

Hands-on exhibits focus on storms, lighthouses, wrecks, and rescues. There are fabulous views of Boston Light (America's oldest operating lighthouse) and Graves lighthouse from the observation cupola.

At the end of the Hull Peninsula, the observation deck at the top of the water tower in **Fort Revere Park** (tel: 617-727 4468; Memorial Day–Labor Day; entrance fee) offers a panoramic view from Cape Ann to Provincetown. There's also a small military museum.

Duxbury

Just off gently meandering Route 3A to the south is **Duxbury** ㉑. It was settled in 1628 by Pilgrims, and they are well remembered here. A statue of Captain Myles Standish, *Mayflower* passenger and Plymouth colony leader, crowns a 125-step observation tower at the top of Captain's Hill in **Myles Standish Monument State Reservation** (Crescent Street; tel: 508-208 0676; open daily). Fellow *Mayflower* passengers John and Priscilla Alden lived at the finely preserved 1653 **Alden House** (105 Alden Street; tel: 781-934 9092; open June–Sept Wed–Sat; fee) and are buried, along with Myles, at the **Old Burying Ground** on Chestnut Street.

Wealthy shipbuilder/merchant Ezra Weston Jr., affectionately nicknamed King Caesar (New England's then-largest ship, *The Hope*, was constructed in his shipyard in 1841), built a stately Federal mansion in 1809 that today stands as a testament to his wealth and good taste. Highlights at the **King Caesar House** (120 King Caesar Road; tel: 781-934 6106; open July–Aug Wed–Sun pm, Sept Sat and Sun pm; entrance fee) include rare French scenic wallpaper and a variety of 19th-century furnishings.

Carl A. Weyerhaeuser, the grandson of the founder of the hugely successful lumber company, began collecting art with a discerning eye while a student at Harvard. Today the **Art Complex Museum** (189 Alden Street; tel: 781-934 6634; Wed–Sun; fee) houses his superb collection, including prints by Dürer; Shaker furniture; American paintings by artists such as Sargent, Cropsey, and

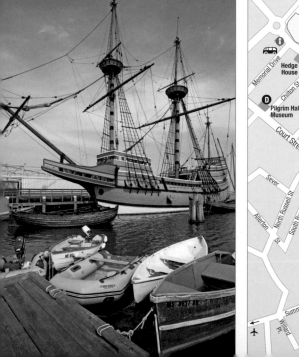

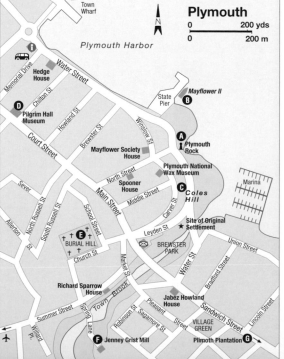

Bellows; and Asian art. A Japanese teahouse occasionally hosts traditional tea ceremonies.

Plymouth

Southward on Route 3 lies **Plymouth ㉒**, where the Pilgrims made landfall in 1620. **Plymouth Rock Ⓐ**, legendary 1620 landing place of the Pilgrims, enjoys a place of honor under an elaborate harborside portico which resembles Athens' Parthenon. The rock is… well, a rock, but even if taken with a grain of salt as the actual landfall, it's an interesting example of origin mythology.

A stone's throw from the monument is the *Mayflower II* Ⓑ (State Pier, Water Street; tel: 508-746 1622; open late Mar–Nov daily; fee). A replica of the original *Mayflower*, this was built in England and sailed to Plymouth in 1957. Actors on board the 104ft (32-meter) -long vessel portray the original passengers and field visitors' questions with accuracy and wit, vividly conveying the hardships that its 102 passengers endured on their 66-day voyage.

Across the road from the Rock is **Coles Hill Ⓒ**, where, during their first winter, the Pilgrims secretly buried their dead at night to hide the truth about their fast dwindling numbers from the Indians. **Pilgrim Hall Museum Ⓓ** (75 Court Street; tel: 508-746 1620; open Feb–Dec daily; fee) displays such relics as John Alden's halberd; Myles Standish's sword, razor, and Bible; and the cradle of Peregrine White, born aboard the *Mayflower*.

Farther east, beyond Main Street, is **Burial Hill Ⓔ**, with gravestones dating back to the colony's founding. "Under this stone rests the ashes of Willm Bradford, a zealous Puritan and sincere Christian, Governor of Plymouth Colony from April 1621–57 (the year he died, aged 69) except 5 years which he declined." The hill was the site of the Pilgrims' first meeting house, fort, and watchtower.

South of Burial Hill is the replica **Jenney Grist Mill Ⓕ** (tel: 508-747 4544; open Apr–Nov Thur–Tue; fee), where corn is still ground as it was by the Pilgrims in 1636. A costumed

Interpreting the past at Plimouth Plantation.

BELOW: the replica of the Jenney Grist Mill.

Plimouth Plantation.

BELOW: Battleship Cove in Fall River, CT.

guide gives 30-minute tours (reservations recommended).

Plimoth Plantation

South of town on Route 3, **Plimoth Plantation** (Warren Avenue; tel: 508-746 1622; mid-Mar–Nov daily; fee) is a painstaking reconstruction of the English settlement in 1627. Costumed re-enactors portray actual residents of the colony. Their homes are thatched huts; their crops and livestock true to the era. Their accented English is the historically accurate Jacobean dialect, which is unlike the modern American or British mode of speaking, although Shakespeare and Queen Elizabeth I would have recognized it. As they go about their daily chores, they engage visitors in conversations about religion, child-rearing, relations with local Indian tribes, and village gossip. They stay true to their "character," only answering questions within the knowledge base of a person in their era. Other topics are met with incomprehension.

At the Wampanoag village on the banks of the Eel River, members of the Wampanoag nation – not re-enactors – plant crops, gather food, make tools and personal items, and maintain their dwellings. Although they wear traditional clothing, they are not role-playing, and converse from a modern perspective (and in modern English) about their history and culture.

The café serves food inspired by Wampanoag and English Colonial ingredients (as well as more usual fare); and a display at the Visitors' Center concentrates on the Puritans' most famous social event, the 1621 Thanksgiving (and how it has developed into the annual celebration of over-indulgence and postprandial football). It's all self-guided and tickets are good for two days. There are a variety of combo packages.

New Bedford

From Plymouth, take Route 44 to I–495 and I–195 to **New Bedford** ㉓, onetime whaling capital and today the East Coast's busiest fishing port. The narrow cobblestone streets and historic buildings of the old quarter have been incorporated into the **New Bedford Whaling National Historical Park** (33 William Street; tel: 508-996 4095; open daily). A video explains the role of whaling in New Bedford's development. There's a Portuguese translation and devices for the hearing impaired. At weekends in July and August, park rangers conduct Underground Railroad tours of the city, relating the history of the escaped slaves who fled to New Bedford for freedom and jobs.

The park incorporates several sites which operate independently. The **New Bedford Whaling Museum** (18 Johnny Cake Hill; open May–Sept daily, Oct–Apr Tue–Sun; audio tour download for MP3 players) evokes the lifestyles of the whalers and fishermen, and has a huge collection of ship models – most memorably the *Lagoda*, a half-size replica of a 19th-century whaling vessel – plus a collection of

scrimshaw, intricately carved out of whalebone by the sailors on their long voyages.

Across from the museum is the **Seamen's Bethel** (open daily; donation) with the "Whaleman's Chapel" mentioned by Herman Melville in *Moby-Dick*. The 156ft (57-meter) Grand Banks fishing schooner *Ernestina*, launched in Essex in 1894, sailed to within 600 miles (966km) of the North Pole and then brought immigrants from Europe. She's now moored at the State Pier.

Taking up a full city block, the 1834 **Rotch-Jones-Duff House & Garden** (396 County Road; tel: 508-997 1401; open daily; fee) is a superb example of residential Greek Revival architecture. Originally built for a prominent whaling merchant, it chronicles life in New Bedford from 1834 to 1981. The gardens are equally magnificent, formally laid out with ornamental beds, graceful walkways, and an apiary garden.

Fall River

Nine miles (6km) west of New Bedford, **Fall River 24** is dominated by huge mills, reminders of the city's long-defunct cotton industry. The city's life is told at **Fall River Heritage State Park** overlooking Battleship Cove (Davol Street; tel: 508-675 5759; open daily). You can ride on a 1920 carousel (open late May–early Sept; fee), housed in a Victorian pavilion.

Battleship Cove (tel: 508-678 1100/800-533 3194 in New England; open daily; entrance fee) has the world's largest collection of historic naval ships. Among them are the submarine USS *Lionfish*, the 46,000-ton battleship USS *Massachusetts*, and the world's only restored pair of PT boats. The submarine and the battleship – "Big Mamie," a fighting veteran of World War II – can be visited.

Virtually adjacent, the **Marine Museum** (70 Water Street; tel: 508-674 3533; open Wed–Sun; entrance fee) traces the history of the Fall River Line from 1847 to 1937, and is packed with nautical paraphernalia, including a major display about the *Titanic*, and a new exhibit about the sinking of the liner *Andrea Doria*.

Anchors aweigh at Battleship Cove.

BELOW: wild turkeys.

Thanksgiving

While both Florida and Virginia claim that "Thanksgiving" was first celebrated in their territory, the holiday is inextricably linked to Massachusetts and the Pilgrims. Far from realizing they were starting a national tradition, they were merely partaking in a familiar European harvest celebration. They had a lot to be thankful for. Nearly half of the *Mayflower*'s passengers died during the first winter. Only help from the Wampanoags saved the rest. But the harvest of 1621 was a good one. The party lasted three days, with a menu that included venison, fish, lobster, clams, berries, watercress, dried fruit, and plums. The guest list included the 53 surviving Pilgrims and about 100 men from Chief Massasoyt's tribe. The next celebration was not held for several years, and by then relations between the two groups had soured.

Making Thanksgiving a national holiday was the obsession of Sara Josepha Hale. Starting in 1827, she organized support and lobbied endlessly to have a national day of thanksgiving. In 1863, she finally succeeded when Abraham Lincoln issued a proclamation naming the last Thursday of November as a day of thanksgiving. But that was a one-time thing. It wasn't a permanent national holiday until 1941, when Franklin Roosevelt signed the paperwork.

RESTAURANTS AND BARS

Prices for a three-course dinner per person with a half-bottle of house wine:
$ = under $20
$$ = $20–45
$$$ = $45–60
$$$$ = over $60

Restaurants
North of Boston

Amesbury
Ristorante Molise
1 Market Square
Tel: 978-388 4844
www.ristorantemolise.com
$$–$$$
Traditional entrées and antipasti in a high-ceilinged, beamed dining room with a very family feel.

Essex
Periwinkle Restaurant

74 Main Street
Tel: 978-768 6320
www.periwinklesrestaurant.
com **$$–$$$**
Fresh seafood well-prepared using traditional recipes in a upscale casual restaurant with the Essex River lapping just under the big windows.

Gloucester
Dog Bar
65 Main Street
Tel: 978-281 6565
www.dogbarcapeann.com
$–$$
A casual, neighborhood bar and restaurant with a limited, but well-done menu.
The Rudder
73 Rocky Neck Avenue
Tel: 978-283 7967

www.rudderrestaurant.com
$$–$$$
Waterfront dining in the Rocky Neck artists' colony.
Passports
110 Main Street
Tel: 978-281 3680
www.passportsrestaurant.
wordpress.com **$$**
Foods from around the world, including fresh fish dishes from the Adriatic, sushi from Japan, creative pastas. Rejoice; they now serve breakfast on the weekends.

Ipswich
Ithaki Mediterranean Cuisine
25 Hammatt Street
Tel: 978-356 0099
www.ithakicuisine.com **$$–$$$**
An oasis for homesick Greeks and discerning diners. Moussaka and baklava like Yia Yia (Grandmom) used to make. Completely renovated and expanded. New smaller-bite menu.
The Clam Box
246 High Street
Tel: 978-356 9707
www.ipswichma.com/
clambox **$–$$**
Serving fabulous fried clams and other native seafood for 60-plus years. Self-service either indoors or on the deck.

Marblehead
Le Bistro Café and Grille
1 Atlantic Avenue
Tel: 978-631 7457
www.marbleheadbistro.com **$$**

Very Mediterranean menu of lighter fare: kabobs, salads, shawarma in a cozy spot near the water.
The Landing
81 Front Street
Tel: 781-639 1266
www.thelandingrestaurant.
com **$$–$$$**
New England seafood in a cheerful dining room overlooking the harbor. Opt for the deck in nice weather.

Newburyport
Agave Mexican Bistro
50 State Street
Tel: 978-499 0428 **$$**
Yes, it is a bistro, but with Mexican-influenced decor and a totally Mexican menu, which concentrates on the cuisine that's far removed from the usual combination plates.
David's Tavern at Brown Square
11 Brown Square
Tel: 978-462 8077
www.davidstavern.com **$$**
Long-time local favorite with steaks, pizza, grilled seafood. Childcare (with meal) while you dine Thur–Sat.
Glenn's Restaurant & Cool Bar
Merrimack Street
Tel: 978-465 3811
www.glennsrestaurant.com
$$–$$$
Very hip, SoHo-feel spot adjacent to the waterfront. Menu changes almost daily. Jazz on Sunday night in the lounge.

LEFT: The Rudder in Rocky Neck.

The Grog
13 Middle Street
Tel: 978-465 8008
www.thegrog.com **$–$$**
For more than 30 years the city's premier rendezvous for burgers, seafood, chowder, and drinks in a laid-back atmosphere. Gluten-free menu.

Michael's Harborside
Tournament Wharf
Tel: 978-462 7785
www.michaelsharborside.com **$$**
A long-time riverfront favorite, with a varied menu including sandwiches, fresh fish, and baby-back ribs. Gluten-free menu. Live music upstairs at the tiki deck.

Rockport
The Lobster Pool
329 Granite Street
Tel: 978-546 7808
www.lobsterpoolrestaurant. com **$–$$**
For more than 60 years one of the area's best waterfront "in the rough" dining destinations. Among specials are the "no celery lobster rolls," chowders, and homemade pie. Self-service dining room. No tipping.

My Place by the Sea
68 Bearskin Neck
Tel: 978-546 9667
www.myplacebythesea.com **$$$**
On the tip of Bearskin Neck, a rocky promontory edging into the Atlantic, this is a beautiful, relaxing restaurant filled with flowers and soft light. Elegantly prepared seafood. Linger on a clear night to watch the moon rise.

7th Wave
7 Tuna Wharf
Tel: 978-546 5048

www.7thwaverockport.com **$$**
"New England Fusion," which means New England seafood with accents from Trinidad and Hawaii.

Salem
Grapevine
26 Congress Street
Tel: 978-745 9335
www.grapevinesalem.com **$$–$$$**
Upscale, elegant spot for Northern Italian fare sparked with occasional Spanish and Asian influences.

Red's Sandwich Shop
15 Central Street
Tel: 978-745 3527
www.redssandwichshop.com **$**
For more than 35 years this landmark spot has been popular for breakfasts, classics such as American chop suey, and homemade desserts.

Salem Beer Works
278 Derby Street
Tel: 978-745 2337
www.beerworks.net **$–$$**
Salem's contribution to microbreweries. Upscale bar food and fresh-brewed beers are served in a renovated warehouse building.

Capri Seaside Italian Grille
3 Central Avenue
Tel: 978-462 7543
www.capriseaside.com **$$**
The name says it all. Good, basic rustic Italian fare. Kids' menu. Wednesday night pasta specials are a good deal.

West of Boston

Concord
Liberty Restaurant at Concord Colonial Inn
48 Monument Square
Tel: 978-369 2372
www.concordscolonialinn.com **$$**

A new culinary team oversees the revamped menu and atmosphere in this historic inn on the town square. Decidedly unstuffy and relaxed, it is the perfect place to unwind after hours of heavy, historical sightseeing. Inviting menu of American casual fare with Spanish and Latin influences. Ask for the Red, White, and Blueberry salad.

La Provence
105 Thoreau Street
Tel: 978-371 7428
www.laprovence.us **$**
Good place for breakfast and to pick up lunch to go. A self-serve, informal bistro with French country foods. Carry out chicken salad to beef Bourguinon.

Main Streets Market & Cafe
42 Main Street
Tel: 978-369 9948
www. mainstreetsmarketandcafe. com **$–$$**
In a building that has been standing since the 1700s (it was used for storing ammunition during the Revolution), the Andersons have been running the restaurant for four generations.

Lawrence
Wichit
15 Union Street
Tel: 978-794 0199
www.wichitsandwich.com **$**
Dedicated to the idea that a good sandwich is a culinary sacrament, made with artisan breads, hand-made condiments, and organic ingredients. Build-your-own from a very long list of options or choose from an equally long list of hot and cold sandwiches. The

dessert sandwiches are worth the trip: carrot cake, Whoopie pies.

Lexington
Dabin
10 Muzzey Street
(off Mass Avenue)
Tel: 781-860 0171 **$$**
Japanese and Korean cuisine in an intimate setting. Sushi bar where you can watch while chefs work. Tempura and noodle dishes. Korean BBQ.

Lemon Grass
1710 Massachusetts Avenue
Tel: 781-862 3530
www.lemongrassmenu.com **$–$$**
A low-key Thai café in a Colonial storefront in the heart of town. Extensive, well-explained menu. They will adjust the heat to your liking. Traditional entrées and some fun takes on New England staples.

Lexx
1666 Massachusetts Avenue
Tel: 781-674 2990
www.lexx-restaurant.com **$$**
Rave reviews for its ambience and food from opening day. Old town tavern feel with a clean contemporary decor. Familiar foods with interesting touches: Yukon gold potato fries smothered in blue cheese alongside the grilled porterhouse is the very definition of decadence.

Lincoln
AKA Bistro
145 Lincoln Road
Tel: 781-259 9920 **$$–$$$**
One chef brought recipes from his native France, the other from Japan. The menu has classic French dishes, sashimi, and Asian-inspired

Prices for a three-course
dinner per person with a
half-bottle of house wine:
$ = under $20
$$ = $20–45
$$$ = $45–60
$$$$ = over $60

dishes. Outside dining in the
sculpture garden in summer.

Lowell

Cobblestones
91 Dutton Street
Tel: 978-970 2282
www.cobblestonesoflowell.
com **$$**
Housed in a 1859 board-
inghouse that was known
for its style and fine food,
the restaurant has lived up
to its history. Most of the
architectural detail
remains and is a perfect
complement to a menu of
fresh fish, prime beef, and
the "Lobster Palooza" list
of lobster done in an
amazing number of ways.

La Boniche
143 Merrimack Street
Tel: 978-458 9473
www.laboniche.com **$$–$$$**
An intimate French-style
bistro serving creative
Euro-fare in a landmark Art
Nouveau building. Pre-
theater dining and post-
curtain bar. Mid-week
prix-fixe menu is a good
deal.

The Olympia
453 Market Street
Tel: 978-452 8092
www.newolympia.com **$–$$**
Lowell's oldest restaurant,
a friendly, family-run
traditional Greek spot. Lots
of skewers and kabobs.

Natick

Casey's Diner
36 South Avenue
Tel: 508-655 3761 **$**
Established in 1805, this
tiny diner seats just 10 and
is legendary for its hot
dogs. There's a side

window for carry-out.
Maxwells 148
148 E. Central Street
Tel: 508-907 6262 **$$–$$$$**
A melting pot of cuisines
includes rib eye, gravlax,
Pho Max soup, and home-
made ricotta gnocchi with
Maine lobster.

Waltham

Naked Fish
455 Totten Pond Road
Tel: 781-684 0500
www.nakedfish.com **$$**
Upbeat, often busy, serving
seafood and meats with
Cuban and South
American recipes. Long list
of Cuban cocktails.

The Tuscan Grill
361 Moody Street
Tel: 781-891 5486
www.tuscangrillwaltham.com
$$–$$$
A new chef refreshed what
was an excellent menu of
northern Italian favorites.
Quaint setting designed to
look and feel like an outdoor Italian piazza.

Wellesley

Blue Ginger
583 Washington Street
Tel: 781-283 5790
www.ming.com/blueginger
$$$–$$$$
Celebrity chef Ming Tsai's
energy and enthusiasm for
food and joyful living car-
ries into his elegant restau-
rant. Recent expansion
added a chic lounge which
serves Asian tapas. Very
accommodating for cus-
tomers needing gluten-free
and other food allergy
preparation.

South of Boston

Fall River

Estoril

1577 Pleasant Street
Tel: 508-677 1200
www.estorilrestaurant.com
$$–$$$
Elegant, fine dining with a
Portuguese menu. The
lounge with deep leather
sofas is popular for after-
dinner liqueurs and
conversation.

Lepage's
439 Martine Street
Tel: 508-677 2180
www.lepagesseafood.com **$$**
Casual, friendly, family-run
seafood place that's been
serving the locals at its
waterfront location for over
two decades.

**Tabacaria Açoriana
Restaurant**
408 S. Main Street
Tel: 508-673 5890
www.tarestaurant.com **$$**
A casual, family-owned
Portuguese café with flavors
of Portugal and the Azores.

Hull

**Jake's Seafood
Restaurant & Market**
Steamboat Wharf, 50 George
Washington Boulevard
Tel: 781-925 1024
www.jakesseafoods.com **$–$$**
A large dining room over-
looking the water on
Nantasket Beach claims to
serve the best fried clams
on the South Shore.

New Bedford

Waterfront Grille
36 Homers Wharf
Tel: 508-997 7010 **$$**
It's so close to the pier
where the fishing fleet
docks, the catch could
jump from the boat into the
kitchen. The New Bedford
sea scallops are a delicacy
not always found
elsewhere.

Plimoth Plantation
Patuxet Café
Warren Avenue
Tel: 508-746 1622
www.plimoth.org **$**
You can wash down a venison burger or bowl of turkey and cranberry soup with a Mayflower Golden Ale, brewed by Boston Brewing Company to replicate beer consumed by the English in the 17th century.

Plymouth
Cabby Shack
38 Town Wharf
Tel: 508-746 5354
www.cabbyshack.com **$–$$**
A great outdoor deck on the upper level; family-friendly, with big menu of casual foods: pastas, burgers, wraps. The clam chowder in a bread bowl is so rich it should be taxed.

Isaac's Restaurant
114 Water Street
Tel: 508-830 0001
www.isaacsdining.com **$$–$$$**
Relaxed class overlooking the water and the Mayflower. Seafood, of course, but a good choice of pastas and meats , too.

Union Seafood
14 Union Street
Tel: 508-747 4503 **$$–$$$**
Comfortable seafood shack atmosphere serving New England seafood classics. New second-floor wraparound deck overlooks the marina.

Bars
North of Boston
Barking Dog Bar & Grill
21 Friend Street, Amesbury
Tel: 978-388 9537

Care for a carrot cake martini? How about coconut almond? If not a martini, order from the extensive beer and wine menus.

Crow's Nest
334 Main Street, Gloucester
Tel: 978-281 2965
The funky waterfront bar that Sebastian Junger made famous in his book (and the subsequent movie) The Perfect Storm looks just as it did in October 1991, when the crew of the Andrea Gail set out on their fateful voyage.

In a Pig's Eye
148 Derby Street, Salem
Tel: 978-741-4436
Live music every night but Tuesday. To make up for that, it's Mexican specials on the menu.

Park Lunch
181 Merrimac Street, Newburyport
Tel: 978-465 9817
With two large-screen TVs tuned to sports, this bar is in a very busy, very good, and very moderately priced establishment a short distance from downtown.

The Peddler's Daughter
45 Wingate Street, Haverhill
Tel: 978-372 9555
A dimly lit Irish pub with cold pints, and great fish 'n' chips wrapped in newspaper. Live music Thursday–Saturday nights. The menu offers classic bar fare and more creative fusion dishes.

Salem Beer Works
278 Derby Street, Salem
Tel: 978-741 7088
A place to quench your thirst with Boston microbrews.

West of Boston
The Claddagh Pub & Restaurant
399 Canal Street, Lawrence
Tel: 978-688 8337
A serious spot for darts, pool, and live bands.

J.J. Boomers
705 Pawtucket Boulevard (Route 113), Lowell
Karaoke, pool, and darts keep patrons happy when the Red Sox and Patriots aren't playing.

Village Forge
48 Monument Square in the Colonial Inn, Concord
Tel: 978-369 2373
The wide plank floors and ceiling beams attest to the tavern's past as a storeroom for supplies during the Revolution. It's now a pub with live music, trivia contests, and nightly entertainment.

Watch City Brewing Company
256 Moody Street,

Waltham
IPA, stouts, Belgian-style beers, and wheat beers all brewed on the premises.

South of Boston
The Fours
15 Cottage Avenue, Quincy
Sports bar with many, many televisions tuned to many, many games.

The Room at Water Street Café
Battleship Cove, Fall River
Live music, open jam nights, and large dance floor. Often crowded, always convivial.

Union Brewhouse
550 Washington Street, Weymouth
The "Home of the 99 Club" truly does have 99 kinds of bottled beer, as well as 17 drafts, along with broadcasts of local sports and an expanded pub menu served until midnight.

LEFT: Colonial Inn. **RIGHT:** the art of preparing oysters.

FALL FOLIAGE

A revered ritual of New England life is leaf-peeping – driving to see the green leaves of summer turn to the vivid oranges, yellows, and reds of fall

Droves of dedicated leaf-peepers come by the car- and busload every autumn. Time and place are everything when it comes to watching the fall colors change, and advance reservations at inns and restaurants are essential if you want to secure the best spots. In the far north of New England, leaves start turning mid-September, moving gradually farther south over the next few weeks. By the end of October, the show is pretty much over. Plan your travel accordingly, moving from north to south. New Hampshire and Vermont are most often linked with great foliage, but all six states have colorful fall vistas.

Virtually every ski resort transforms its lifts into "foliage" rides. Take a hike and surround yourself with the colors of the forest. An online fall foliage map which updates conditions regularly and suggests several driving routes is at www.discovernewengland.org.

Almost any highway route designated as "scenic" on a state map will yield bountiful leaf color. But while it may be fun to drive back roads in search of great fall color, Interstates often have the best foliage. In Maine, I–95 offers some great leaf-peeping in the 75-mile (120km) stretch from Augusta to Bangor. Similarly, in northeastern Connecticut, I–395 always puts on a fine leaf show. In Massachusetts, one of the best foliage drives is westward along the Mohawk Trail (Route 2, Greenfield to Williamstown). But it's virtually impossible not to see beautiful colors.

Foliage hot-lines: Connecticut, tel: 800 CTVISIT; Massachusetts, tel: 800-271 6277; New Hampshire, tel: 800-258 3608; Vermont, tel: 800-828 3239; Maine, tel: 888-624 6345 Rhode Island, tel: 800-556 2484.

ABOVE: day breaks on a sugar house and maple trees in the autumn countryside of Vermont. There are many historic wooden buildings and bridges that complement the fall colors.

BELOW: on the road from the scenic town of Millinocket to Baxter State Park in Maine, you'll have the opportunity to see the golden leaves of fall, and perhaps a few moose or white-tailed deer.

LEFT: the color of the fall leaves is largely determined by the quality of soil in which the plant grows. A plant with rich soil and many nutrients will remain slightly greenish, while a plant that is in poor soil will turn a bright and fiery red.

Above: leaf-peeping is a popular activity in New England, and a number of locales have set up special "leaf watching" websites to help track the changing colors, to make sure you get the best experience possible.

Peak Timing

As nature has one last fling before settling in for the long winter, the colors of autumn leaves are sometimes so vivid it seems they will shine in the dark.

By trying too hard to pinpoint the absolute peak of foliage, however, you risk missing the majesty of the leaf-changing phenomenon: If you're lucky enough to be in New England in October, you're sure to see peak foliage somewhere, because each tree changes its color according to an inner timetable that's affected by moisture, temperature, and the shorter days of fall.

Botanists call the color change "leaf senescence" – the process by which the green pigment chlorophyll is drawn back into the tree to nourish it. The tree is essentially turning off the system that carries nutrients to the leaves so that it can store the energy it needs to survive until spring. When chlorophyll is cut off, other pigments shine through. Brightest of all are red swamp maples and sumac. Aspen and birch turn yellow, sugar maples a peachy orange. Warm, sunny days and cool, crisp nights seem to be the recipe for the most spectacular colors.

Above: the Virginia Creeper *(Parthenocissus quinquefolia)* can turn a particular shade of crimson in the fall, and is frequently seen in gardens throughout New England.

Left: when the summer months gently dwindle into fall, New Englanders call it an "Indian Summer,"; it provides the opportunity to explore the great outdoors via the regions many accessible hiking and biking trails.

CAPE COD AND THE ISLANDS

This sandy summer playground has clam shacks, historic B&Bs, National Seashore beaches, and a lively arts scene, plus the islands of Martha's Vineyard and Nantucket

Bostonians consider Cape Cod their own private playground, but its fame has spread so far that it attracts international travelers. In high season, lodgings are filled to capacity, traffic on the Cape's few highways is heavy, and local merchants work hard to make the profits that will carry them through the virtually dormant winters. Even at the height of its summertime popularity, when the roads, restaurants, and beaches tend to be jammed, Cape Cod manages to preserve its wild charm and dramatic beauty.

Much of this quality is protected within the boundaries of the Cape Cod National Seashore, a vast 27,000-acre (11,000-hectare) nature reserve established by far-sighted legislators in 1961. Precisely because it has not been commercially exploited, this huge expanse of untouched dunes survives as one of the Cape's most alluring features.

Getting your bearings

Shaped like a flexed arm, it's important to note the nomenclature of the island. "Upper Cape" refers to the portion nearest the mainland; "Mid-Cape" is roughly from Barnstable County eastward to Chatham and Orleans, where the "arm" bends; "Lower Cape" is the "forearm" jutting northward to Eastham, Truro, and Provincetown.

Technically, Cape Cod is an island. The **Cape Cod Canal** was built by New York financier August Belmont in 1914 to eliminate the need for ships to round the Cape via the often stormy Atlantic. Belmont ran the canal as a private endeavor until 1928, when it was purchased by the US Government. The US Army Corps of Engineers supervised the building of the two bridges and improvements to the waterway: by 1940 it was the widest sea-level canal (there are no locks) in the world. Two 7-mile (11km) service roads

LEFT: fishing charters are readily available.

which parallel the canal are great for bicycling or hiking.

The **Cape Cod Canal Visitor Center** ❶ (60 Ed Moffitt Drive, Sandwich; tel: 508-896 9678: open May–mid-June Wed–Sun, mid-May–Oct daily), off Route 6A, recounts the history of the canal and the bridges. Park rangers conduct guided walks, bike hikes, and themed programs.

Choose a bridge

Expressways funnel traffic to the two access bridges over the canal. At the waterway's eastern end, Route 3 comes south from Boston and crosses the Sagamore Bridge to join Route 6, the Mid-Cape Highway.

The other span, the Bourne Bridge, is handy if you approach the Cape from the west. This is the crossing to use if you want to head south toward Falmouth and Woods Hole via Route 28. For those wishing to avoid the drive, there are summer ferries between Provincetown and Boston, Provincetown and Plymouth, and flights into Hyannis and Provincetown.

Which route?

Itineraries on the Upper and Mid-Cape offer a choice of speedy, feature-less highways or scenic, meandering roads. Those intent on reaching the Outer Cape in a hurry generally opt for Route 6, the four-lane, limited-access Mid-Cape Highway; those headed for Falmouth, Woods Hole, and points along Nantucket Sound can take the equally speedy Route 28.

To get a true sense of the Cape, however, take the prettier back roads. Roughly parallel to the Mid-Cape Highway, two-lane Route 6A starts in Sagamore and runs eastward along the bay through old towns full of graceful, historic houses and crafts and antiques shops.

The same can be said of Route 28A, hugging the shore en route to Falmouth. As Route 28 veers north-eastward from Falmouth to Chatham, it's marred by recurrent stretches of overdevelopment but, again, one has only to venture off the main road a bit to discover such towns as Osterville and Centerville, Harwich Port and Chatham itself.

TIP

A beach entrance fee is collected from late June through early September, and on weekends and holidays from Memorial Day through September. In 2011, vehicles were charged $15, bicyclists, motorcyclists, and pedestrians $3. Those fees could increase as governments seek new ways to generate revenue. If you're going to be visiting for an extended period, a $45 vehicle pass covers all beaches on the National Seashore for the season.

BELOW: the four-lane Sagamore Bridge over the Cape Cod Canal opened to traffic in 1935.

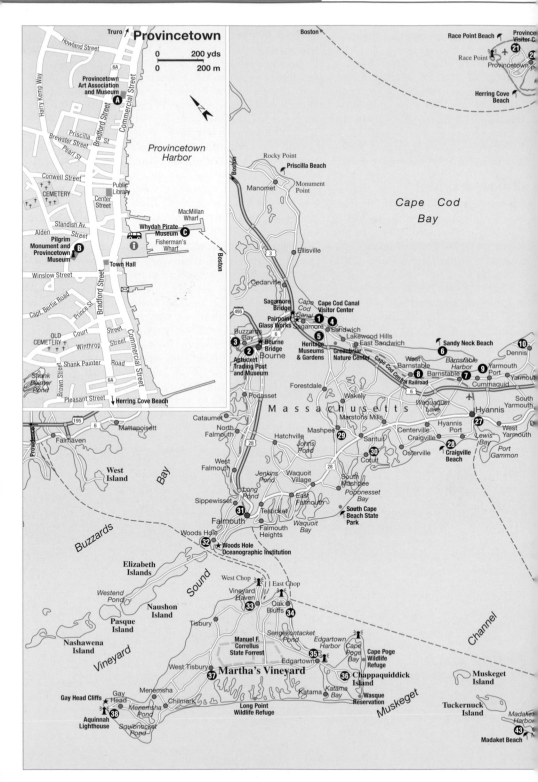

Provincetown

Truro

0   200 yds
0   200 m

Howland Street

Harry Kemp Way

6A

Commercial Street

Bradford Street

St

Priscilla

Brewster Street

Pearl St

A Provincetown
Art Association
and Museum

*Provincetown
Harbor*

Conwell Street

CEMETERY

Center
Street

Standish Av.
Street

Alden

Public
Library

MacMillan
Wharf

Pilgrim
Monument and
Provincetown
Museum **B**

Whydah Pirate
Museum **C**

Fisherman's
Wharf

Town Hall

Winslow Street

Capt. Bertie Road

Prince St

Bradford Street

OLD
CEMETERY

Court

Street

Winthrop   Street

Shank Painter   Road

Commercial Street

Shank
Painter
Pond

Brown Street

Pleasant Street

6A

Herring Cove Beach

Boston

Race Point Beach

Province
Visitor C

Race Point   **21**

Provincetown P

2

Herring Cove
Beach

Boston

Rocky Point

Priscilla Beach

Manomet

Monument
Point

*Cape Cod
Bay*

Ellisville

3

Cedarville

Sagamore
Bridge

*Cape
Cod
Canal*

Cape Cod Canal
Visitor Center

Pairpoint
Glass Works

Sandwich

Lakewood Hills

Sandy Neck Beach

10

1

Sagamore

4

5

East Sandwich

Dennis

495

Buzzards
Bay

Bourne
Bridge

Heritage
Museums
& Gardens

Greenbriar
Nature Center

West
Barnstable

*Barnstable
Harbor*

Yarmouth
Port

3

2

Bourne

6

9

Yarmouth

Aptucxet
Trading Post
and Museum

Cape Cod Central Railroad

8 Barnstable

7

Cummaquid

Forestdale

Wakely

*Wequaquet
Lake*

South
Yarmouth

M a s s a c h u s e t t s

Pocasset

Marstons Mills

Hyannis   **27**

West
Yarmouth

Catumet

Mashpee

Centerville

Hyannis
Port

North
Falmouth

28

Hatchville

29

Santuit

Craigville

*Lewis'
Bay*

*Johns
Pond*

Osterville

28 Craigville
Beach

*Port
Gammon*

West
Falmouth

*Jenkins
Pond*

Waquoit
Village

Cotuit

30

South
Mashpee

Sippewisset

*Long
Pond*

Teaticket

East
Falmouth

*Poponesset
Bay*

31   Falmouth

Falmouth
Heights

*Waquoit
Bay*

South Cape
Beach State
Park

Woods Hole

32   Woods Hole
Oceanographic Institution

Buzzards

195   6

Mattapoisett

Falhaven

West
Island

Provincetown

*Elizabeth
Islands*

Bay

Sound

West Chop

East Chop

Vineyard
Haven

Oak
Bluffs

33

34

Westend
Pond

*Naushon
Island*

Tisbury

Pasque
Island

*Sengekontacket
Pond*

Manuel F.
Correllus
State Forrest

Edgartown
Harbor

*Cape
Poge
Bay*

Cape Poge
Wildlife
Refuge

Channel

Nashawena
Island

Vineyard

West Tisbury

Martha's Vineyard

Edgartown

35

36 Chappaquiddick
Island

Muskeget
Island

Gay Head Cliffs

Gay
Head

Menemsha

Chilmark

*Menemsha
Pond*

Katama

*Katama
Bay*

Wasque
Reservation

Muskeget

Tuckernuck
Island

38

Aquinnah
Lighthouse

*Squibnocket
Pond*

Long Point
Wildlife Refuge

*Madaket
Harbor*

43

Madaket Beach

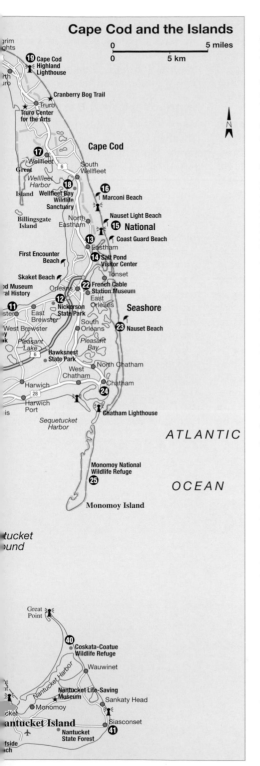

Cape Cod and the Islands

0   5 miles
0   5 km

N

Cape Cod

grim
ghts

⑲ Cape Cod
Highland
Lighthouse

rth
uro

Cranberry Bog Trail

Truro
Truro Center
for the Arts

⑰ Wellfleet
Great

South
Wellfleet

Wellfleet
Harbor ⑱

⑯

Island   Wellfleet Bay
Wildlife
Sanctuary

Marconi Beach

Billinggate
Island

North
Eastham

Nauset Light Beach

⑮ **National**

⑬

First Encounter
Beach

Eastham

⑭ Salt Pond
Visitor Center

Coast Guard Beach

Skaket Beach

Tonset

od Museum
al History

Orleans

⑫ ⑭ French Cable
Station Museum

⑪

ster

East
Brewster

Nickerson
State Park

East
Orleans

Seashore

West Brewster

South
Orleans

⑬ Nauset Beach

y
k

Pleasant
Lake

Pleasant
Bay

Hawksnest
State Park

North Chatham

Harwich

West
Chatham

Chatham

⑭

Harwich
Port

is

Chatham Lighthouse

Sequetucket
Harbor

ATLANTIC

Monomoy National
Wildlife Refuge ⑮

OCEAN

Monomoy Island

tucket
und

Great
Point

⑩ Coskata-Coatue
Wildlife Refuge

Wauwinet

Nantucket Life-Saving
Museum

Sankaty Head

Monomoy

cket

antucket Island

Siasconset

⑪

Nantucket
State Forest

fside
ch

Once Route 28 and Route 6 merge in Orleans, Route 6 north is pleasant all the way to Provincetown, if traffic-clogged in summer.

Attractions near the bridges

On the Cape side of the Sagamore Bridge, glass-blowers at the **Pairpoint Glass Works** (851 Sandwich Road; off Route 6A; tel: 800-899 0953; open daily) give demonstrations on weekdays.

West of the Bourne Bridge, on the mainland side near the canal, the Bourne Historical Society's **Aptucxet Trading Post and Museum** ❷ (Aptucxet Road, Bourne; tel: 508-759 9487; open Memorial Day–Columbus Day Tue–Sat; charge) is a replica of the first English-speaking trading post in North America, set up in 1627 to trade with the Wampanoag Indians, the Dutch in New York, and the Plymouth settlement.

Many of the houses along Sandwich Road and Keene Street in Bourne date to the 1800s. This includes the **Briggs-McDermott House**, restored to reflect the period of 1840 to 1910.

In nearby **Buzzards Bay** ❸ the **National Marine Life Center** (120 Main Street; tel: 508-743 9888; late May–early Sept daily, Labor Day–Columbus Day weekends; donation) rescues and rehabilitates stranded marine animals such as sea turtles, seals, dolphins, and terrapins.

The Bay Side: Sandwich to Brewster

This region gained a reputation for its glass after Boston merchant Deming Jarvis founded a glass factory in **Sandwich** ❹ in 1825. It thrived until competition from plants in the Midwest, and a strike by exploited workers, shut the enterprise down in 1888. Outstanding examples of their output are found in the **Sandwich Glass Museum** (129 Main Sreet; tel: 508-888 0251; open Apr–Dec daily, Feb–Mar Wed–Sun; charge), where there are demonstrations of the art of glass-blowing every hour.

Sandwich, the first town to be founded on the Cape, in 1637, is one of the prettiest and best-preserved. At its center stands the restored 1654 **Dexter Mill** (mid-May–early Sept daily; charge; stone-ground cornmeal available in summer) and the 1637 **Hoxie House** (Water Street; tel: 508-888 1173; open June–Sept daily; charge), a remarkably well-preserved saltbox reputed to be the Cape's oldest dwelling.

Peter Rabbit, Reddy Fox, Jimmy Skunk, and all of the other whimsical characters created by the author and naturalist Thornton Burgess

Glass blown at Sandwich Glass Museum & Glassworks.

BELOW: relaxing near Sandwich, the oldest town on Cape Cod.

(1874–1965) come to life at the **Thornton Burgess Museum** (4 Water Street; tel: 508-888 6870; open May–Oct daily; donation). Sometimes they come to life, literally, as summer storytelling sessions include the live animals featured in the stories.

Peter Rabbit's favorite briar patch – a 57-acre (23-hectare) conservation area – is adjacent to **Greenbriar Nature Center** (6 Discovery Hill Road; open Apr–Dec daily, Jan–Mar Tue–Sat; donation) in East Sandwich.

Heritage Museums & Gardens

For more glimpses into the American past, follow the signs – past a lovely historic cemetery overlooking Shawme Pond – to **Heritage Museums & Gardens ❺** (67 Grove Street; tel: 508-888 3300; open May–Oct daily; charge), a spacious complex of three museums of Americana that includes toys, military artifacts, folk art, and a working carousel (ride included in admission). A round stone barn (copied from the Shaker original in Hancock MA) houses an outstanding array of early cars. The grounds have the largest public garden in southern New England. In spring, they are awash in the vivid pinks and purples of flowering rhododendrons.

Sandy Neck and Barnstable

Motoring east along Route 6A, you'll pass the turnoff for the 6-mile (9km) **Sandy Neck Beach ❻** (tel: 508-362 8300; parking fee), which is a favored habitat of the diamondback terrapin and the endangered piping plover. Hikers and swimmers are welcome to explore, provided they don't disturb the birds' nesting sites.

Barnstable ❼ is also home to 4,000-acre (1,620-hectare) **Great Marsh**, the Cape's largest saltwater marsh. **Hyannis Whale Watcher Cruises** (tel: 800-287 0374) depart from Barnstable Harbor May through October.

Just up the hill from the harbor, the **Coast Guard Heritage Museum** (3353 Route 6A; tel: 508-362 8521; May–Oct Tue–Sat; charge) tells the story of the Lighthouse Service, Lightship Service, Lifesaving Service,

and Revenue Cutter Service – all predecessors of the Coast Guard.

In **West Barnstable ⑧**, **West Parish Meetinghouse** is an outstanding example of early colonial architecture and has a Paul Revere bell cast in 1806. When the congregation grew too large in 1723, the parishioners cut the building in half, pulled the north end away, and added 18 feet (5.5 meters) to the middle.

East of Barnstable, **Yarmouth Port ⑨** is a delightful village with fine old houses. The **Captain Bangs Hallett House** (Strawberry Lane; tel: 508-362 3021; open June–mid-Oct Thur–Sun; charge) is the only sea captain's house open to visitors on Cape Cod; it's arranged as though the captain had just returned from a voyage to China, with silk, porcelain, and lacquered treasures on display. The **Edward Gorey House** (8 Strawberry Lane; tel: 508-362 3909; open July–early Sept Wed–Sun, mid-Apr–June and Oct–Dec weekends; charge) exhibits possessions of the artist/illustrator who lived here and focuses on one of his lifetime passions: animal welfare. The 1889 **Hallett's Store** (139 Main Street; tel: 508-362 3362) claims to be the oldest soda fountain in America.

Cape Playhouse

In the town of **Dennis ⑩**, follow signs for the **Scargo Hill Tower**, a stone turret from which, on a clear day, you can see Cape Cod laid out like a map, with Provincetown visible at the northern tip. Dennis is home to America's oldest, and perhaps most outstanding, professional summer theater, **Cape Playhouse**.

On the playhouse grounds, the **Cape Cod Museum of Art** (tel: 508-385 4477; open end May–mid-Oct daily, Jan–May Thur–Sun, also Wed in Apr, Tue–Wed in May; charge) restricts its permanent collection to works by artists with regional associations, although temporary exhibits may showcase artists whose work influences or is influenced by the Cape.

East to Brewster

In **Brewster ⑪**, home to numerous fine old houses and inns, the **Stony Brook Mill** (Stony Brook Road, southwest off Route 6A) grinds cornmeal Saturdays from June to August; there's a small museum upstairs with a loom used for weaving demonstrations. Each spring, from mid-April to early May, schools of herring leap up a series of ladders to spawn in the freshwater pond behind the mill.

The **Cape Cod Museum of Natural History** (869 Main Street, Route 6A; tel: 508-896 3867; June–Sept daily, Feb–Mar Thur–Sun, Apr–May and Oct–Dec Wed–Sun; charge) explores 400 acres (162 hectares) of the local habitat through hands-on exhibits and nature trails.

Railroad magnate Roland Nickerson once owned 2,000 acres (800 hectares) of wooded land in Brewster, using them as a personal hunting and fishing preserve. In 1934 his widow donated most of this tract to the state; today **Nickerson State Park ⑫** (Route 6A; tel: 508-896 3491) is a popular spot for camping,

TIP

Performances take place mid-June–mid-Sept at **Cape Playhouse** (Dennis, Route 6A; tel: 877-385 3911). Independent films and simulcasts of live performances at the National Theater and Metropolitan Opera are screen at the adjoining **Cape Cinema** (tel: 508-385 2503; www.cape cinema.com). With leather armchairs and Art Deco frescoes by Rockwell Kent (1882–1971), the theater is a sensory treat.

BELOW: the Gulf Stream keeps the Cape's temperatures warmer for longer.

Scalloping at Wellfleet. Bay scallops are found in the low tide in eelgrass and tide pools.

BELOW: Cape Cod National Seashore.

swimming, picnicking, and walks. The 8-mile (13km) bicycle trail connects with the **Cape Cod Rail Trail**.

The Lower Cape: Eastham

Eastham ⑬, easily recognized by its 1793 windmill on the town green, has the **Swift-Daley House** (Route 6, next to post office; tel: 508-240 0871; open July–Aug Mon–Fri; donation), built in 1741 by a ship's carpenter and furnished with items from its long history; and, across from the Salt Pond Visitor Center, a **one-room schoolhouse** built in 1869 (tel: 508-2240 0871; open July–Aug Tue–Fri, Labor Day and Columbus Day weekends; donation).

For a side trip into Cape Cod's history, head west to **First Encounter Beach**. It's here that a Pilgrim scouting party out of Provincetown first encountered a band of Indians, who, wary after earlier encounters with kidnappers, attacked the Pilgrims and were rebuffed by gunfire. This uneasy meeting is one of the reasons why the Pilgrims pressed on to Plymouth. Today, the historic site is a peaceful town beach (which, like most, charges a parking fee in summer).

Cape Cod National Seashore

Established in 1961 when part-time Cape resident John F. Kennedy was president, **Cape Cod National Seashore** (headquarters: 99 Marconi Site Road, Wellfleet; tel: 508-771 2144; www.nps.gov/caco) extends from Eastham to Provincetown and protects 27,000 acres (10,930 hectares) of land, including 40 miles (65km) of pristine beaches, lighthouses, cranberry bogs, marshes, ponds, hiking and biking trails, and sand dunes.

The **Salt Pond Visitor Center** ⑭ (Route 6; tel: 508-255 3421; open daily) provides an excellent introduction to the area. Interpretive films and exhibits explain the ecology of the Cape, and a bicycle trail (bikes can be rented nearby) winds through pine forests and marshes to end at Coast Guard Beach, where, in 1928, writer-naturalist Henry Beston produced his classic book *The Outermost House*, chronicling a year spent living on the dunes. The 0.25-mile (0.4km) Buttonbrush Trail is a multisensory path with a guide rope and text panels in large type and Braille. Park

rangers offer numerous outdoor programs and guided tours, including a visit to the 1730 **Atwood Higgins House**, a typical early settler's home in nearby Wellfleet and the **Capt. Penniman House**, home to a whaling family.

Farther north is **Nauset Light Beach ⓯**, graced with an 1877, 48ft (15-meter) lighthouse which was rescued from an eroding cliff in nearby Eastham in 1996 and moved to its present site. Tours (tel: 508-240 2612; www.nausetlight.org; donation) are given Sundays from early May through October, and Wednesdays in July and August. Breeches buoy rescue demonstrations are held on Thursday evenings throughout the summer at the 1897 Old Harbor Life Saving Station on Race Point Beach.

At the Seashore's **Marconi Beach ⓰**, Guglielmo Marconi set up the first wireless station in the United States and transmitted the first transatlantic wireless message to Europe in 1903. **The Atlantic White Cedar Swamp Trail**, starting from the Marconi site, is especially beautiful.

Wellfleet

Famous for its oysters, **Wellfleet ⓱** is full of fine galleries and fun restaurants, and surrounded by inviting wildlife areas. Just south of town, off Route 6, the Audubon Society maintains the 1,100-acre (445-hectare) **Wellfleet Bay Wildlife Sanctuary ⓲** (tel: 508-349 2615; visitor center open Memorial Day–Columbus Day daily, Columbus Day–Memorial Day Tue–Sun; trails open daily; charge). Five miles (8km) of walking trails lead from the visitor center which has two 700-gallon aquariums, which introduce both salt marsh and fresh water habitats and residents.

Truro

Farther north, the landscape becomes ever more wild and barren. Scrubby vegetation gives way to desert-like sand dunes. This is **Truro**, whose light and scenery led realist painter Edward Hopper (1882–1967) to make his summer home here for 30 years.

East of Truro, the **Cranberry Bog Trail** accesses the natural habitat of the tiny red fruit that proved such a boon

BELOW: a drive-in theatre in Wellfleet, Cape Cod.

Wellfleet Drive-In

For a bit of social and cinematic nostalgia, spend one evening at the Wellfleet Drive-In. Built in 1957, it still shows a family-suitable double feature every night from late May through Labor Day. All of the elements are there: the mono-speakers you hang on your window (although the modern transmission with much better quality is available through your car's FM radio), the playground and mini-golf under the giant screen, the snack bar serving popcorn and hot dogs until the second feature starts, people setting up beach chairs and blankets in front of their vehicles. The drive-in is at 51 State Highway (Route 6) at the line between Wellfleet and Eastham. In one more nod to nostalgia, bring cash; they don't accept debit or credit cards.

TIP

On summer weekends, traffic jams in Provincetown can be frustrating. A good alternative is The Flex (tel: 800-352 7155; www.theflex.org), a bus that runs between Harwich and Provincetown. You can buy a one-way fare, day pass, or multiple-use pass. You flag the driver down along the route (except along Route 6).

BELOW: on the beach at Provincetown.

to Cape Cod agriculture. Another road east leads to **Highland Light**, towering over Head of the Meadow Beach, which is the local name for the **Cape Cod Highland Lighthouse** ⑲ (tel: 508-487 1121; open mid-May–mid-Oct daily; charge). Erected in 1857, it is the peninsula's oldest lighthouse. From May to October, there are nighttime tours during the full moon.

The **Highland House Museum** (Highland Light Road; tel: 508-487 3397; open late June–Sept Mon–Sat; charge) was built as a hotel in 1907. The museum offers an interesting look at the hardscrabble life of the Lower Cape before tourism, and even has a pirate's chest.

The **Truro Center for the Arts** (10 Meetinghouse Road; tel: 508-349 7511; www.castlehill.org) hosts a summer-long festival of craft workshops, concerts, and forums.

Provincetown

With its well-protected harbor, **Provincetown** ⑳ started out as a natural fishing port, settled by the Nauset Indians long before the Pilgrims

came along. So it remains to this day. Portuguese fishermen, many from the Azores, came here in the heyday of the whaling trade and stayed on for the good fishing. Their descendants still make up a sizable proportion of the town's year-round residents. (Some of them conduct whale-watching cruises from April through October. MacMillan and Fisherman's wharves are where the boats dock.)

The subtle beauties and serenity of the National Seashore contrast dramatically with the blatant development and frenetic energy along Commercial Street. Shops thrive on tourists buying fine art and T-shirts, swanky barware and saltwater taffy, jewelry and kitsch souvenirs. There are bistros and hot dog stands, delightful old inns and inexpensive guest houses, tacky shacks and beautiful landscaped captains' mansions. The town is proud of its fully open and integrated attitude, which has made it the Cape's pre-eminent destination for the gay and lesbian communities.

Led by painter Charles Hawthorne, who in 1899 founded the Cape Cod

School of Art, hordes of artists and writers flocked to Provincetown in the early decades of the 20th century, drawn partly by the area's stark beauty and largely by the cheap rents and food to be found here (thanks to the tourist boom they inspired, the latter are, of course, history).

Among the notables who passed through here, if only briefly, are dramatists Eugene O'Neill and Tennessee Williams and writers Sinclair Lewis, John Dos Passos, and Norman Mailer. A dozen or more illustrious painters, such as the abstract expressionist Robert Motherwell (1915–91), have left their mark. A number of galleries specialize in Provincetown art from the early 1900s onward.

The **Provincetown Art Association and Museum** Ⓐ, founded in 1914 (460 Commercial Street; tel: 508-487 1750; open Memorial Day–Sept daily, Oct–May Thur–Sun; charge) focuses on Provincetown and Cape Cod–inspired artists.

The lofty Italianate tower looming above the town is the **Pilgrim Monument** Ⓑ (High Pole Hill Road; tel: 508-487 1310; open Apr–Nov daily; charge). It was built in 1892 to commemorate the *Mayflower* Pilgrims' first landing in the New World; they spent five weeks here before moving on to Plymouth. The determined climber (252 steps) will be rewarded with a panoramic view of the town and the entire Cape. At the monument's foot is the **Provincetown Museum** (same opening times as monument), whose intriguing exhibits document the town's colorful history. One ticket admits visitors to both sites.

Spoils from the *Whydah*, a pirate ship that sank in 1717 and was discovered off Wellfleet in 1984, are displayed at the **Whydah Pirate Museum** Ⓒ on MacMillan Wharf (tel: 508-487 8899; open May–Oct daily; charge).

The very tip of Cape Cod – which is almost entirely within National Seashore boundaries – has a desolate beauty. The waters off **Race Point Beach** experiences experience rip tides, so it is more popular for sunbathing and off-road driving than swimming. **Herring Cove** is one of the Cape's most popular beaches; there's no

The Pilgrim Monument.

BELOW: the Provincetown Art Colony.

Provincetown's Art Colony

Bay and ocean, sand and sky, the Mediterranean-like light: the natural beauty of Provincetown at the tip of Cape Cod has attracted artists since the town was little more than a fishing pier.

The colony began in the late 1800s. Studios rented for as little as $50 a year, a boon to the "starving artists." In 1899, Impressionist painter Charles Webster Hawthorne opened the Cape Cod School of Arts. By 1916, the Provincetown Art Colony had matured, with more than 300 artists – many of them fleeing the war in Europe – attending six schools of art. The Bohemian atmosphere attracted poets, writers, and playwrights, leading the *Boston Globe* to dub Provincetown "the biggest art colony in the world." It was as renowned as the colonies in Taos NM and East Hampton on Long Island NY. The Great Depression and World War II weakened the colony, but it began to rebound in the 1950s. The community supported efforts to create affordable studio space (places were now renting for $1,500 for a season) and encourage artists to migrate to the area. Today, Provincetown has dozens of art galleries, many of which specialize in contemporary works by local painters, photographers, and sculptors such as Joel Meyerowitz, Paul Bowen, and Paul Resika.

In summer, visitors need to guard against overexposure to the sun, wind, and biting insects.

Below: Chatham's Old Godfrey Windmill, built in 1797 to grind corn, was moved to its present location in Chase Park in 1956.

undertow, which families appreciate. By custom, family activities are on the right hand of the beach, while the gay community relaxes on the left. It has the best sunsets on the Cape. Although officially forbidden, there are periodic reports of informal nude sunbathing in some of the more remote areas of the already remote sand dunes. For information, stop at the **Province Lands Visitor Center ㉑** (Race Point Road; tel: 508-487 1256; open mid-May–Oct daily), which has a good viewing platform. This is the best place to get information about the dune shacks of the **Peaked Hill Bars Historic District**: 18 tiny dwellings (inhabited: please respect privacy) scattered throughout the Province Lands. There is a lottery for rentals of these bare-bones lodgings, several of which were once inhabited by seclusion-seeking writers and artists.

The Sound: Chatham to Falmouth

Leaving Provincetown, turn left onto Route 28 at the junction with Route 6 to **Orleans**, called by its Indian name of Nauset until it was incorporated in 1797 and renamed for the Duke of Orleans (the future king of France), a recent visitor. Orleans has another "French connection" – it was the stateside terminus for a transatlantic telegraph cable to Brest in France.

The cable performed well from 1891 to 1959 before it become obsolete, and is now commemorated in the **French Cable Station Museum ㉒** (41 South Orleans Road; tel: 508-240 1735; open June and Sept Fri–Sun, July and Aug Thur–Sat; donation). There are displays of the equipment used to test, install, and repair the underwater telegraph cable, worth a look for "look-how-they-did-it-then" enthusiasts.

Turn onto Route 6A through East Orleans to Nauset Beach Road and **Nauset Beach** (parking fee) ㉓. Almost 10 miles (16km) long, this is one of the Cape's best stretches of coast, popular for bathing as well as surfcasting for stripers and bluefish. Facilities include a concession stand and public restrooms. Gentler **Skaket Beach** (parking fee) on the bay side is popular with those who prefer calmer waters.

Chatham

Cape Cod's southern shore, from Chatham to Falmouth, is a zone where the battle for – and against – commercialization has raged for decades. Some pockets of subdued gentility still reign just off the honky-tonk stretches.

Chatham ㉔ at Cape Cod's "elbow" is one of the aristocratic enclaves. The "Old Village" and Chatham Historic Business District are classy examples of how to blend historic and commercial interests. The Chatham Fish Pier is a perfect spot to watch the fishing fleet bring in the daily catch. Seals sometimes follow the boats. The Fisherman's Monument on the pier shows a stylized hand raising a fishing net. The **Chatham Railroad Muscum** (153 Depot Road; tel: 508-945 5199; mid-June–mid-Sept Tue–Sat; donation) is housed in the town's ornate but defunct Victorian railroad station. Rail buffs will

be interested in reminders of the days when passenger trains ran all the way to Provincetown. **Chatham Light** (tel: 508-430 0628; tours May–Dec Wed), an active Coast Guard station, overlooks South Beach. The Chatham Marconi Maritime Center (847 Orleans Road, also known as Route 28; tel: 508-945 8889; late June–Labor Day Tue–Sun, Labor Day–Columbus Day Fri–Sun; charge) was part of the transatlantic underwater cable and early aviation radio communications systems developed by Guglielmo Marconi. It has a lot of original equipment and memorabilia of that era.

Bird fanciers will want to make a visit to **Monomoy National Wildlife Refuge ㉕**, a 7,600-acre (3,100-hectare) preserve which is a stopping point for hundreds of species of birds traveling the Atlantic Flyway. Continue past Chatham Light to the refuge headquarters (Morris Island Road, Chatham; tel: 508-945 0594; refuge open daily; visitor center: Memorial Day–Labor Day Mon–Sat; other times as staff is available), where a 1,200-meter nature trail begins. But most of the refuge is accessible only by boat: Monomoy Island Ferry (tel: 508-945 5450; www.monomoyislandferry.com) offers transportation Apr–Oct, and also offers walking tours to Monomoy Lighthouse, as well as seal-watching tours. Reservations for all services are essential.

Harwich Port to Hyannis

Picturesque Harwich and Harwich Port are the last peaceful settlements east of the Cape's commercial belt. From West Harwich to Hyannis, Route 28 is lined with motels, restaurants, businesses, and amusements. It's a long stretch, where traffic usually crawls all summer, making it seem even longer.

Detour a short distance to visit **South Dennis ㉖**, nicknamed "Sea Captain's Village." Many of the handsome homes built by prosperous 19th-century sea captains are preserved in the Historic District.

Hyannis

Hyannis ㉗ is probably best known as the summer home of the Kennedy clan. In the old Town Hall, the highlight is the **John F. Kennedy Hyannis Museum** (397 Main Street; tel: 508-790 3077; www.jfkhyannis-museum.org; open mid-Apr–Oct daily, mid-Feb–Mar Thur–Sun, closed Jan–mid-Feb; charge). The museum displays photos and mementos of the president, who summered in adjoining Hyannis Port. Although the Kennedy compound is the object of many a pilgrimage, it is not open to the public and very little of it can be seen from the road. A small park dedicated to Kennedy's memory adjoins Veterans Beach, on Hyannis's harbor.

An "old-fashioned swashbuckling adventure" awaits kids and parents aboard the **Pirate Adventure on Sea Gyspy** (Ocean Street Docks; tel: 508-394 9100; www.capecodpirateadventures.com; mid-June–Labor Day, eight sailings daily; reservations essential; charge).

Alternatively, you can take to the rails aboard one of **Cape Cod**

Memorial at the John F. Kennedy Hyannis Museum. JFK once said "I always go to Hyannisport to be revived."

BELOW: playing at pirates.

The Cohoon Museum covers American art from pre-Revolutionary times to the present.

Central Railroad's excursions (252 Main Street; tel: 508-771 3800; www. capetrain.com). These include a scenic two-hour trip, an adults-only five-course dinner train, a Sunday brunch ride, and a family supper train.

More than 50 classic sports cars – mostly British, and all red – are on show in **Hyannis Port** on the grounds of the Simmons Homestead Inn (288 Scudder Avenue; tel: 508-778 4999; daily). Visitors can play with the more than two dozen felines that roam the grounds, or sample some of the 700 single malt Scotch whiskeys in the bar.

Craigville Beach

West of Hyannis, the tide of commercialism subsides occasionally to provide glimpses of Cape Cod's beauty. Make a southward detour for Centerville. Here, relatively warm-watered **Craigville Beach ㉘** (1050 Craigville Beach Road; tel: 508-790 6345; charge in summer) on Nantucket Sound, with lifeguards and bath houses, is one of the Cape's most popular.

Mashpee Indian Meetinghouse

Heading toward Falmouth, take a side trip north to **Mashpee ㉙**, located amid Wampanoag tribal lands which have been carved up by development. The **Old Indian Meetinghouse** (Meeting House Road at Route 28), the oldest church building on the Cape, built in 1684, and the burial ground next door, are well worth a look.

Cahoon Museum

The contemporary primitive and very charming paintings of American folk artists Ralph and Martha Cahoon are on show, along with 19th- and early-20th-century American marine art, in **Cotuit ㉚** at the **Cahoon Museum of American Art** (4676 Falmouth Road; tel: 508-428 7581; open Tue–Sun; closed Jan). The building is a 1775 farmhouse.

Falmouth

Falmouth ㉛ is a microcosm of Cape Cod life. The pretty town green, a Revolutionary militia training ground, is ringed by fine old houses,

BELOW:
the Cohoon Museum of American Art.

including several delightful B&Bs, and the Historical Society's **Museums on the Green** (Village Green; tel: 508-548 4857; open mid-June–mid-Oct Tue–Sat; charge). The two 18th-century houses contain an extensive display about the people and practices of whaling and the story of Katherine Lee Bates, who wrote *America the Beautiful*.

Falmouth Harbor is filled with pleasure craft; swimmers and windsurfers favor the beaches and guest houses of Victorian era Falmouth Heights overlooking Nantucket Sound. Spring, when thousands of daffodils and rhododendrons bloom, is the best time to visit the 6-acre (2.4-hectare) **Spohr's Gardens** (45 Fells Road; tel: 508-548 0623; daily; donation) overlooking a scenic oyster pond.

Woods Hole

One of the most pleasant activities in Falmouth is to rent a bicycle and follow the old railroad bed, now a bike path, down to **Woods Hole ㉜**. Most travelers come here merely to board the ferry for Martha's Vineyard, a 45-minute voyage away, but Woods Hole itself warrants a stopover. It is devoted almost exclusively to maritime activities and has several excellent seafood restaurants.

The world-famous **Woods Hole Oceanographic Institution** (15 School Street; tel: 508-289 2252; open May–Oct Mon–Sat, Nov–Dec Tue–Fri; donation) maintains a visitor center to describe its fascinating research with a mock-up of a deep water submersible and videos of exploration of the *Titanic*. Weekdays in July and August the institution offers free 75-minute tours of the dock area and restricted village facilities; reservations recommended. Visitors can tour the **Marine Biological Laboratory** and learn about using marine organisms in research (100 Water Street; tel: 508-289 7423; July–Aug Mon–Fri at 1pm and 2pm; note: children under the age of 5 cannot take the tour; reservations required). The visitor center (July–Aug daily; varying hours rest of the year; call) has interesting displays about the research if you can't make a tour.

The small but intriguing **Woods Hole Science Aquarium** (166 Water

TIP

The Shining Sea Bikeway is a 10.7-mile (17.2km) paved bikeway that stretches from Falmouth to Woods Hole. It's the only one of the many bike trails on Cape Cod that skirts the shoreline. The name comes from *America the Beautiful* which was penned by Katherine Lee Bates, a Falmouth native.

BELOW: a Wampanoag Indian.

Mashpee Wampanoags

If it weren't for the Mashpee Wampanoag tribe, the history of New England would have probably been a lot different. These were the people who greeted the Pilgrims, taught them the basics of farming in the new colony, and helped them survive the first harsh winter. Initially the two groups enjoyed a cordial relationship, but as the colony grew, things deteriorated; between land grabs, wars, diseases inadvertently introduced by the Europeans, assimilation, and migration, the once-powerful, independent Mashpee tribe dwindled to almost insignificant numbers. In 2007, their decades-long fight for federal recognition as a tribe succeeded, bringing with it opportunities for economic development and cultural renewal. One of the most important projects is reviving the native language. Ironically, the English settlers' determination to "civilize" the tribe plays a key role in this. Because they wanted legal documents proving all transactions with the tribe, the Wampanoag developed an alphabet and written language, the first tribe to do so. Tribal members, historians, and linguists are using those deeds, contracts, wills, letters, translated scriptures, inventories, and bills of sale to develop dictionaries and reconstruct grammar and usage. The tribe sponsors an annual three-day pow-wow over the 4th of July weekend which attracts dancers and drummers from tribes across the country (www.mashpeewampanoagtribe.com)

TIP

Parking in Woods Hole
is metered and can be
extremely hard to find.
During the summer a
trolley runs between
Falmouth (free parking)
and Woods Hole on the
half-hour (tel: 800-352
7155).

BELOW: boats in the
Cape Cod village of
Woods Hole, including
the Woods Hole
Oceanographic
Institute's *Knorr*
research vessel.

Street; tel: 508-495 2001; open
Memorial Day–Labor Day daily; call
for other times; donations) is home to
140 species of marine animals, mostly
from northeast and mid-Atlantic
waters. A highlight is the outdoor
seal pool, with Bumper – a blind seal
– and LuSeal.

Martha's Vineyard

Over the decades, Vineyard residents
have grown blasé about the celebrities
in their midst, and precisely because
of that laissez-faire attitude, the roster just keeps growing. The latest is
President Obama and his family, who
have spent summer vacations at the
Blue Heron Farm in Chilmark on the
southwest coast.

Like Cape Cod, Martha's Vineyard
is a geological remnant of the last
ice age. Two advancing lobes of a
glacier molded the triangular northern shoreline, then retreated, leaving
hilly moraines, low plains, and many-
fingered ponds. And Martha? She was
the daughter of Thomas Mayhew, who
bought a large tract of land in 1642,
including Nantucket Island, for £40.

(Mayhew named the nearby Elizabeth
Islands after another daughter.) The
"Vineyard" part of the name refers to
once-abundant wild grapes.

Vineyard Haven, Oak Bluffs, and
Edgartown, the three protected harbor
towns of the northeastern portion of
the island, have always been active and
prosperous, although the main order
of business is no longer shipping
and whaling, but tourism and summer homes. By contrast, the sparsely
populated "up-island" (that is, to the
west and south) towns of West Tisbury,
Chilmark, Menemsha, and Gay Head
remain determinedly rural.

It may come as a disappointment
to many visitors to find that, as a
rule, Martha's Vineyard's extensive
beaches are not accessible to outsiders but have been reserved for home-
owners; the major exception, beyond
the placid Joseph Sylvia State Beach
on the bay side, is South Beach,
fronting the rolling Atlantic south
of Edgartown; other public beaches
are Katama (good for surfing and
for strong swimmers), Moshpu, Oak
Bluffs, and Menemsha.

Vineyard Haven

Known until 1870 as Holmes Hole, **Vineyard Haven** ㉝ (the official name of the town is Tisbury, but everyone calls it by the name of its primary village) blossomed into a busy port during the 18th and 19th centuries, with both maritime businesses and farmers profiting from the constant movement of ships. Today, the homey **Black Dog Tavern** (Beach Street Extension; tel: 508-693 9223), with its offshoot bakery, store, and catalog business, enjoys a similar relationship with the legions of vacationers who arrive by ferry from Woods Hole.

Handsome houses grace Williams Street, a block off Main Street. The 1829 **Old Schoolhouse Museum** (110 Main Street; tel: 508-693 2729) was the island's first schoolhouse; the building was also once a carpentry shop and a church.

Covering a swath of more than 5,000 acres (2,000 hectares) in the middle of the island, **Manuel F. Correllus State Forest** (tel: 508-693 2540), site of one of the largest environmental restoration projects in the country, is laced with 15 miles (24km) of walking, bicycling, and bridle paths. Take Edgartown Road out of Vineyard Haven to Barnes Road, then turn right (south) to the forest entrance. The park was originally created in 1908 as a refuge for the heath hen, in an attempt to prevent the bird's extinction. Initially successful, a disastrous wildfire, severe winters, and arrival of predators accounted for the death of the remaining birds. A sculpture of the bird is installed in the forest.

Oak Bluffs

Religion tinged with tourism produced an unusual community in **Oak Bluffs** ㉞. The resort town has the largest marina on Martha's Vineyard, and boats at anchor bob at their moorings in front of gingerbread houses which face the water. It is also home to Martha's Vineyard Camp Meeting Association. In 1835, Edgartown

Methodists chose a secluded circle of oak trees here as a site for a camp meeting. Twenty years later, there were more than 320 tents at Wesleyan Grove, as it was named, and thousands of people gathered here each summer. Small houses soon replaced the tents – tiny gingerbread cottages that are a riot of color and jigsaw carving with all manner of turrets, spires, gables, and eaves. They were laid out along circular drives known as **Trinity Park**. At its center is the "tabernacle" where the congregation gathers, a wrought iron-and-wood shelter that's nearly as elaborate as the cottages, with two clerestories with glass windows and an octagonal cupola. The building is used for both revival and worship services (Sun 9.30am) and secular community events. In mid-August, the **Grand Illumination** recreates the camp's traditional closing-night ceremony when colorful Chinese lanterns are hung on the porches of the cottages and in the trees. Visitors can tour **Cottage Museum** (One (1 Trinity Park; open daily in summer; charge), an 1867 home which recreates life at the Campground in the 1800s. **Union**

TIP

There are numerous bike rental shops on the island, including **Martha's** (Vineyard Haven; tel: 508-693 6593; will deliver to any island location) and **Anderson's** (23 Circuit Avenue, Oak Bluffs; tel: 508-693 9346).

BELOW: the main street of Falmouth.

TIP

If your time on Martha's Vineyard is limited, consider taking a trolley tour. **MV Tours** (tel: 508-627 8687; www.mvtour.com) offers 2.5-hour narrated trips around the island, and includes a 30-minute stop at Gay Head Cliffs.

Chapel, built in 1870 as a non-sectarian place of worship (55 Narragansett Avenue; tel: 508-627 4440), is as remarkable for its unique octagonal design and dormer-studded cupola as for its acclaimed acoustics.

Flying Horses Carousel (15 Lake Street; tel: 508-693 9481; daily in summer; charge) is the oldest operating carousel in the country. Originally in Coney Island, it was moved to Oak Bluffs in 1884, and its horses have been giving rides ever since.

Many of the ever-expanding number of sites included in the island's **African-American Heritage Trail** (www.mvheritagetrail.org) are located in the area.

East Chop Lighthouse (East Chop Drive; tel: 508-627 4441; tours mid-June–mid-Sept Sun; charge) was erected in 1878 and nicknamed "the Chocolate Light" because of its brown color.

Edgartown

South of Oak Bluffs on Beach Road, **Edgartown** ㉟ is the oldest settlement on Martha's Vineyard.

The imposing Greek Revival **Old Whaling Church** of 1843 (89 Main Street; tel: 508-627 4440), with enormous pillars and a soaring tower, is a rare instance of monumental scale in Edgartown. The church is now the venue for concerts, a film series, and community events. Tucked behind the church is the **Vincent House Museum**, the oldest house on the island (1672), furnished to show four centuries of life in the town.

The **Martha's Vineyard Museum** (59 School Street; tel: 508-627 4441; open Mon–Sat; charge) records the island's unique history, culture, and traditions on a pretty campus with several old buildings containing agricultural and nautical equipment. The **Ross Fresnel Lens Building** houses a 19th-century first-order Fresnel lens; the **Francis Foster Maritime Gallery** exhibits logbooks, ship models, and other nautical treasures; and the 1845 **Captain Francis Pease House** has exhibits about the island's history, a Native American Gallery, a book shop, and local crafts.

The museum oversees **Edgartown Lighthouse** (open late June–Labor Day daily, Labor Day–Columbus Day weekends; tel: 508-627 4441; charge).

BELOW LEFT: Victorian architecture adds character to Oak Bluffs.
BELOW RIGHT: the shore at Chappaquiddick.

Chappaquiddick Island

A stone's throw away from Edgartown, across a narrow neck of the harbor, is **Chappaquiddick Island ㊱**. The island's native name means "The Separated Island," which it steadfastly remains. The Chappy Ferry (tel: 508-627-6965 for operating times and conditions; daily; charge) carries cars (three or four at a time) and clusters of pedestrians over the 200-yard crossing. The main attraction on "Chappy," several miles from the ferry landing, is the **Wasque** (pronounced *way-skwee*) **Reservation** (east end of Wasque Road; tel: 508-627 7689; open year-round; charge Memorial Day–mid-Oct), a 200-acre (80-hectare) preserve with walking trails, excellent bird-watching, and beach (be careful: there's a strong current).

Cape Poge Wildlife Refuge, at the island's eastern end, offers 6 miles (10km) of dunes, woods, salt marshes, ponds, tidal flats, a lighthouse, and beach. A variety of narrated tours (tel: 508-627 3599; www.the trustees.org) are offered, including a 1.5-hour lighthouse trip and a 2.5-hour overland exploration.

Up-island escape

Tiny **West Tisbury ㊲** is home to Alley's General Store (1041 State Road; tel: 508-693 0088; open daily), which opened in 1858 and still deals in "most everything." There's a lively farmer's market on Wednesday and Saturday mornings outside the 1859 **Grange Hall** (1067 State Road).

The popular agricultural fair (www.mvas.vineyard.net) held in town each August is a slice of old fashioned country fun, with fiddle and corn-shucking contests, horse pulls, and rides. The **Granary Gallery at the Red Barn** (636 Old County Road; tel: 508-693 0455) exhibits photographs by Margaret Bourke-White and Alfred Eisenstaedt, a summer regular. It carries works by a long list of contemporary artists.

Highlights of a visit to **Long Point Wildlife Refuge** (tel: 508-693 3678; open daily; charge mid-June–mid-Sept), part of a sand barrens ecosystem which exists in patches from New Jersey to Maine, include a lovely beach and an easy 2-mile (3km) nature trail. There are sheltered fresh and saltwater ponds, safe for exploring with kids.

Edgartown, an old whaling port first settled by the English in 1642.

BELOW:
the Cape Cod
Rail Trail.

The Cape Cod Rail Trail

In the Cape's early heyday, summertime visitors arrived by train. But, except for the excursion trains run between Hyannis and the Cape Cod Canal by the Cape Cod Central Railroad (www.capetrain.com; tel: 508-771 3800), rail travel has disappeared from the Cape. However, at least one section of roadbed has been put to a pleasure-making use: the Cape Cod Rail Trail is a 25-mile (40km) paved recreational path located mid-Cape and stretching from South Dennis through Nickerson State Park to Wellfleet. Ideal for bicycling, skating, walking, and jogging, it's an intimate, relaxing way to discover and enjoy the "real" Cape. Along the way, it passes through quaint villages, salt marshes, pine forests, and cranberry bogs. The most scenic sections are the National Seashore spur trails in Eastham and Wellfleet that terminate at the Atlantic Ocean. You can rent bicycles at a number of places along the way, including Barbara's Bike & Sport (tel: 508-760 4723 in Dennis and 508-896 7231 at the Park; www.barbsbkieshop.com) with locations at the State Park and in Dennis, Idle Times Bike Shop (tel: 508-255 8281 North Eastham; 508-240 1122 Orleans; www.idletimesbikes.com) at the trail in North Eastham and Orleans, and Little Capistrano Bike Shop (tel: 508-255 6515 Eastham, 508-349 2362 Wellfleet; www.littlecapistranobikeshop.com) with locations in Eastham and at the trailhead in Wellfleet.

Bringing a good catch to Menemsha, where Steven Spielberg's Jaws was filmed.

Chilmark to Gay Head

Of the parallel roads traveling from West Tisbury to Chilmark, Middle Road traverses the most rugged, interesting glacial terrain. At **Chilmark Center** is Beetlebung Corner, a stand of tupelo trees from which "beetles" (mallets) and "bungs" (wooden stoppers) were once made. The residents of Chilmark (incorporated in 1694) built their dwellings at a generous distance from one another, and the once-inexpensive property and evocative natural settings attracted an influx of artists such as Jackson Pollock.

Nearby **Menemsha** is a tiny fishing village on Vineyard Sound, famed for its appearance in Steven Spielberg's ever-popular 1975 movie *Jaws* and prized for its technicolor sunsets. Fishing charters operate from the harbor, which has a number of shops and restaurants.

One of the most spectacular natural sights on Martha's Vineyard is at its westernmost tip, looking out to the untamed sea. From Chilmark, follow the single hilly road that at several points offers breathtaking views of Menemsha Pond northward and Squibnocket Pond to the south.

At the end, **Gay Head Light** (aka **Aquinnah Light**) ❸ (tel: 508-627 4441; open mid-June–mid-Sept Tue–Sat; charge) marks the western terminus of the island and the location of the stunning, ancient geologic strata that compose the majestic **Gay Head cliffs**. Clays of many colors – from gray to pink to green – are most vibrant towards late afternoon and represent eons of geological activity: fossils found amid the ever-changing contours of this 150ft (46-meter) promontory have been dated back millions of years. For sailors returning from a voyage, this magnificently colored embankment was the first sign they were home, thus giving Gay Head its "gaiety."

Nantucket Island

An Indian word meaning "that faraway land," Nantucket Island isn't too far away for the thousands of people who visit each year by ferry and airplane. The winter population of 7,000 increases sevenfold when the

The Unpromising Peninsula that Became a Playground

Shaped like a bodybuilder's flexed arm, Cape Cod extends 31 miles (50km) eastward into the Atlantic Ocean, then another 31 miles to the north. Well forested up to about the "elbow," then increasingly reduced to scrub oak and pitch pine, this sandy peninsula is lined with more than 300 miles (500km) of beaches. The crook of the arm forms Cape Cod Bay, where the waters are placid and free of often treacherous ocean surf.

Lighthouses guide mariners plying the cold Atlantic waters. The lighthouses are frequently photographed symbols of the Cape. Some of the most popular include Nauset Light, Chatham Light, Nobska Light, and Race Point Light. Most are operated by the U.S. Coast Guard, although a few function under independent groups.

In 1602, Bartholomew Gosnold, a British mariner sailing by this long arm of sand, noted a great many codfish in the waters and added the name "Cape Cod" to his map. In 1620, the *Mayflower* pulled into the harbor of what is now Provincetown and, before debarking to explore, its passengers drew up the Mayflower Compact for self-government.

This early constitution grew into the government of the Commonwealth of Massachusetts.

Before the advent of modern transport, Cape Cod was a hardscrabble area peopled by the Wampanoag tribes, hardy Yankees, and industrious immigrants from the coasts and islands of Portugal. Since the land supported only subsistence farming, most people earned their living from the sea.

The first hordes of tourists arrived in the late 19th century, brought by steamship and railroad. Escaping the summer heat of Boston, Providence, and New York for the cool sea breezes along the shore, they found low prices, inexpensive real estate, and simple pleasures in abundance. Real estate is no longer a bargain, but the location is priceless.

With almost 600 miles of coastline and 60 public beaches, Cape Code is one of the best places to get out on the water. The greens are also popular destinations, with 27 public and 15 private golf courses on the island. The peak seasons are from late-May to early-September, but if you can travel in the spring or autumn there are usually deals to be found.

"summer people" take over the sidewalks of town.

In sharp contrast to Martha's Vineyard, Nantucket's mid-island moors and miles of beautiful, unspoiled beaches are open to visitors, most of whom use the preferred island mode of transportation: bikes (several shops stand ready to equip tourists near the ferry dock). The harbor town of Nantucket, centrally located on the north shore, is unquestionably the focal point of the island and its only commercial center.

Nantucket town

The town of **Nantucket ❸❾** is a gem of 18th- and 19th-century chitecture, from he dominant clapboard-and-shingle Quaker homes to the grandeur of the buildings lining **Upper Main Street**. Because the twists and turns can prove disorienting, it's best to tour with a street map (available from the bike shops, or in the free local newspapers distributed on the ferry).

As in whaling days, the waterfront is the focus of life in Nantucket town. Several wharves extend into the harbor, the most central of which – **Straight Wharf** – is an extension of Main Street. First built in 1723, rebuilt after an 1846 fire, and renovated in the late 1950s, it's now like a small village unto itself, surrounded by luxury yachts and sailboats, some of which are available for charter. (The untouched barrier beach of Coatue is an ideal destination.)

Old South Wharf has also been spruced up and rendered tourist-friendly with boutiques and cafés; it's possible – for a tidy sum – to rent tiny but picturesque wharfside cottages here.

Along Main Street up from Straight Wharf, a picturesque shopping district lines the gently rising cobblestone street. Although the 1-sq-mile (2.5-sq-km) **National Landmark Historic District** contains 800 pre-1850 buildings, the redbrick facades lining Main Street are relatively new. With its tree-lined, brick-paved sidewalks, Main Street is a hub of activity in summer, offering distractions from collectibles to edibles.

The 1805 Old Gaol, with its unassuming shingled facade, contained four barred cells, two with fireplaces. Most of its prisoners were allowed to go home each night, having no real chance of escaping from the island.

BELOW:
Gay Head Cliffs.

Nantucket's Harbour.

BELOW: Brant Point Lighthouse at Nantucket Harbor.

Nantucket is proud of its history, especially its grand old homes and museums. The **Nantucket Historical Association** (15 Broad Street; tel: 508-228 1894; charge) oversees more than a dozen properties on the island. Most are open daily from Memorial Day to mid-October. Among them are the **Whaling Museum** (13 Broad Street), housed in a former spermaceti candle factory, which commemorates Nantucket's seafaring days with impressive displays, including the skeleton of a 43ft (13-meter) sperm whale. If your only exposure to old-time whaling was via a high-school reading of *Moby-Dick*, the museum will bring the hardship and heroics of the "fishery" vividly to life.

The 1686 **Jethro Coffin House**, on the northwest edge of town on Sunset Hill Lane, is the oldest on the island. This plain saltbox design reflects the austere lifestyle led by the island's earliest settlers. Other attractions include the 1746 **Old Mill**, the oldest functioning mill in the country; the 1805 **Old Gaol**; and the 1838 **Quaker Meetinghouse**.

Climb up the tower of the **First Congregational Church** (50 Prospect Street; tel: 508-228 0950) for a spectacular view of the island; Sunday service is at 10am.

The three-story red-brick **Jared Coffin House** (tel: 508-228 2400/800-248 2405), at the corner of Centre and Broad streets, made its 1845 debut as the island's showiest dwelling; within two years it became a hotel, and today it remains one of the island's finest inns.

The family was so prolific that it accounted for half the island's population by the early 19th century, and two more Coffin residences stand at 75 and 78 Main Street, examples of the brick Federal style of architecture.

Farther up Main Street are the **"Three Bricks,"** architectural triplets built by wealthy whaler Joseph Starbuck for his three sons. Across the street, and worlds apart in style, stand the **"Two Greeks,"** Greek Revival mansions built for two Starbuck daughters. One, the **Hadwen House** (96 Main Street), showcases the affluent lifestyle of a wealthy whaling family.

Ralph Waldo Emerson gave the inaugural address at the 1847 Greek Revival **Nantucket Atheneum**, now a public library and cultural center, at the corner of Lower India Street.

The **Museum of African American History** (29 York Street; tel: 508-228 9833; www.afroamemuseum.org; July–Oct Tue–Sat; charge) maintains two historic sites documenting the history of the island's African-American community: The **African American Meeting House** and the **Florence Higginbotham House**. The Black Heritage Trail is a guided or self-guided tour of 10 sites illustrating the heritage of African-Americans living on Nantucket, particularly in the 19th century. The map is available at the museum or for download.

No. 99 Main Street, with its detailed and finely proportioned facade, is one of the handsomest wooden Federal-style buildings on Nantucket; it was built by forebears of Rowland Macy, who left the island to seek his fortune and founded a rather well-known namesake store.

Overlooking the harbor from **Brant Point** is one of America's oldest lighthouses. Visitors departing by sea often toss the traditional penny into the water off Brant Point to ensure that they'll return to the shores of Nantucket.

A few blocks out of town, the **Maria Mitchell Association** (4 Vestal Street; tel: 508-228 9198; mmo. org; mid-June–mid-Oct, most facilities open Mon–Sat; charge) honors the local savant who discovered a comet at the age of 29 in 1847, garnering international acclaim. She became the first woman admitted to the American Academy of Arts and Sciences, and America's first female college professor, teaching astronomy at Vassar. The Association oversees several facilities: the Natural Science Center, which focuses on the natural world of and around Nantucket Island; two observatories which offer public tours, programs,

and stargazing; Mitchell's home; and a seasonal aquarium at the harbor. Work is under way to bring all of the elements together in one building; most of the project should be completed by 2014.

The classic and unique arts of the island, including basket-making and scrimshaw, are displayed at **the Nantucket Lightship Basket Museum** (49 Union Street; tel: 508-228 1177; late May–early Oct Tue–Sat, call for off-season hours; charge).

Outside Nantucket town

"Nantucket! Take out your map and look at it," urged Herman Melville in *Moby-Dick*. An inspection of the map reveals an island with hamlets and hideaways sprinkled across its 14-mile (23km) length. Despite some mid-island development in recent decades, about one-third of the island is under protective stewardship. Although environmental restrictions limit activities on dunes and moors, much of the land can be explored. Wear long pants and use insect repellent; deer ticks carry Lyme disease.

TIP

The NRTA (tel: 508-228 7025; www.shuttle nantucket.com) runs buses from mid-May through Columbus Day, 7am–11.30pm, and offers service throughout the island, stopping at beaches, towns, and attractions. All-day passes are available.

BELOW: a sea view from the White Elephant Inn.

Nantucket's Stormy Past

The island's golden age didn't last long, but the handsome little town that whaling fortunes had built found new prosperity in tourism

In 1830 the whaling ship *Sarah* returned home to Nantucket Island, carrying 3,500 barrels of valuable whale oil after a voyage of nearly three years. On the island, stately mansions, decorated with silks and china from faraway lands, awaited the returning captains of such vessels. Schools, hotels, a library, and the commercial activity on Main Street were indications of a prosperous people.

There was no more glorious way for young men to seek their fortunes than aboard a whaling ship, but it was dangerous work. "For every drop of oil, a drop of blood," the whalemen's saying went.

Chasing the whales

Since its earliest days, Nantucket has been populated by determined and spirited people. The first colonists, who arrived in 1659, were emigrants who chafed at the Puritan severity of towns on the North Shore of Massachusetts. Taught "onshore" whaling by the Algonquins, they traveled out in open boats to chase

and harpoon whales sighted from land. By the beginning of the 18th century, offshore whaling had begun and with each generation of larger, more seaworthy craft, the whaling industry grew.

The Algonquins, however, lost out. Although they sailed on whaling boats, their way of life on the island was irreversibly changed by the colonists. By 1855, diseases (introduced to the country from Europe), alcohol, assimilation, and exile had taken the last of Nantucket's original residents.

Both the Revolutionary War and the War of 1812 battered Nantucket's whaling industry, but the islanders' tenacity brought it back to life. Nantucket ships again sailed throughout the world and brought back record quantities of oil. During this period the town acquired much of its urbanity, but the islanders' prosperity was short-lived: the Great Fire of 1846 razed the port, and in the 1850s kerosene replaced whale oil. Too heavily dependent on whaling, Nantucket was left in a permanent urban drydock.

Tourism arrives

From a peak of around 10,000, Nantucket's population dropped to 3,200 in 1875. Those who remained applied their ingenuity to a new venture, one that thrives today and continues to capitalize on the gifts of the sea. Tourism took off toward the end of the 19th century, as steamboats made the island more readily accessible. Land speculators built hotels and vacation homes, many of which now house the country's rich and famous.

Quaint Siasconset (pronounced "Sconset"), linked to the town by a narrow-gauge railroad built in 1884, was especially popular, drawing such luminaries as the popular actress Lillian Russell. The railroad is gone now – it was used for scrap metal during World War I – but tourism lives on.

ABOVE: offshore whaling began in the 170s.
LEFT: harvesting cranberries, the focus of a Nantucket festival that kicks off the harvesting season each October.

Stretching northeast from the town of Nantucket is a 6-mile (10km) inner harbor, protected from Nantucket Sound by **Coatue**, a thin spit of land with flat white beaches. This sweep of land, encompassing the 1,117-acre (453-hectare) **Coskata-Coatue Wildlife Refuge** ⓰ (pronounced *co-skate-uh coat-oo*; Wauwinet Road; tel: 508-228 5646), is accessible by boat or over-sand vehicle. The 16 miles (26km) of trails extend north to **Great Point**, where a lighthouse – a solar-powered 1986 replica of the 1818 original, swept away by a 1984 storm – warns boats away from the sand-bars of Nantucket Sound. Gray and harbor seals rest here after they have fed on fish provided by the riptide. The refuge and beaches are patrolled from April to October. The Trustees of Reservations, which administers the refuge, offers 2.5-hour naturalist-led excursions June to Columbus Day weekend. They depart daily at 9.30am and 1.30pm and are limited to eight persons: reservations are needed (tel: 508-228 6799).

The excellent **Nantucket Shipwreck and Life-Saving Museum** (158 Polpis Road; tel: 508-228 1885; open Memorial Day–Columbus Day daily; charge), en route to Great Point, presents fascinating exhibits, including artifacts from the Italian liner *Andrea Doria*, which sank not far from here in 1956.

Monomoy, the most populous settlement other than Nantucket town, affords spectacular views from its bluffs. From here, the Polpis Road leads across the rolling and delicate Nantucket Moors, which are carpeted with bayberry, beach plum, heather, and other lush vegetation – a lovely green and flowering pink in summer, brilliant red and gold in the fall.

Siasconset

Tourists discovered **Siasconset** ⓱ in 1848 when the first hotel opened in this easternmost town on Nantucket. By 1888, a clever entrepreneur had built a colony of fully equipped, fully furnished cottages, including a "spare room" on wheels, for vacationers. The Bluff Walk edges the ocean-facing side of the properties. Erosion from the unrelenting ocean waves is claiming the bluffs; each year, some of the dwellings tumble down the cliffs. The views are wonderful.

Nantucket's most popular beaches are located on the flat, windswept south shore, open to the cold, spirited waters of the Atlantic Ocean. At **Surfside Beach** ⓲, a colorful Victorian lifesaving station serves nowadays as the island's only youth hostel. Surfers favor the beach at Cisco, a bit more remote, at the end of Hummock Pond Road, while **Madaket Beach** ⓳, at the southwestern tip of Nantucket, is popular for swimming, fishing, and, especially, sunset-gazing.

The northern coast east of Madaket Harbor, heading back toward town, offers the gentle surf of **Dionis** and **Jetties** beaches. **Children's Beach**, tucked well inside the West Jetty near Steamship Wharf, is especially placid and enhanced by a playground.

The island has long attracted painters. The Artists Association of Nantucket, formed in 1945, has more than 500 members and runs a gallery.

BELOW: cranberries, cultivated in Cape Cod since 1816.

RESTAURANTS AND BARS

Prices for a three-course dinner per person with a half-bottle of house wine:
$ = under $20
$$ = $20–45
$$$ = $45–60
$$$$ = over $60

Restaurants
Cape Cod

Brewster

Chillingsworth
2449 Route 6A
Tel: 508-896 3640/800-430 3640
www.chillingsworth.com **$$$$**
The seven-course prix-fixe menu, a feast of classic French/American cuisine, is among the Cape's ultimate dining experiences. Lunch, dinner, and Sunday brunch are served in the

less formal Green House.

Brewster Fish House
2208 Main Street (Route 6A)
Tel: 508-896 7867 **$$$**
An unassuming cottage and former retail fish market has evolved into one of the Cape's most appreciated seafood restaurants. That's why the line of people waiting for a table is so patient.

Buzzards Bay

Mezza Luna
253 Main Street
Tel: 508-759 4667
www.mezzalunarestaurant. com **$$–$$$**
The Cubelli family opened the restaurant more than 70 years ago, so it's small wonder that you feel like family while you're there.

Dennis

Gina's by the Sea
134 Taunton Avenue
Tel: 508-385 3213
www.ginasbythesea.com **$$–$$$**
A break from all the seafood with lots of chicken and veal dishes at the popular Italian dining spot. No reservations; peak-time waits can be long.

The Red Pheasant
905 Route 6A
Tel: 508-385 2133
www.redpheasantinn.com **$$$**
This romantic spot in a historic barn has been a favorite for innovative New American cuisine for over 25 years. Upscale cuisine and classy versions of comfort foods.

Scargo Cafe
799 Route 6A
Tel: 508-385 8200
www.scargocafe.com **$$–$$$**
Wonderfully international menu and fresh takes on New England favorites.

Eastham

Woody's Eastham Lobster Pool
4360 Route 6
Tel: 508-255 9706
www.woodyeastham.com **$$**
Busy, bright, no-frills seasonal seafood place with seafood fried, baked, or broiled, lots of sandwiches and rolls.

Falmouth

Chapoquoit Grill
Route 28A
Tel: 508-540 7794

www.chapoquoitgrill.com **$$**
The locals call it "Chappy." Lots of pastas and pizza from a wood-fired brick oven.

Hyannis

Alberto's Ristorante
360 Main Street
Tel: 508-778 1770
www.albertos.net **$$$**
Classy Italian restaurant that boasts it introduced Northern Italian cuisine to the Cape, a fine addition for which they should be thanked.

The Black Cat Tavern
165 Ocean Avenue
Tel: 508-778 1233
www.blackcattavern.com **$$**
Recently renovated, the interior has a warm, nautical theme. The outdoor patio has a rarity – an awning! Enjoy the view of the water and ferry dock while under shade. Grilled meats and Greek chicken go along with seafood prepared with both traditional and unusual recipes.

Brazilian Grill Churrascaria
680 Main Street
Tel: 508-771 0109
www.braziliangrill-capecod. com **$$**
The south Brazilian tradition of rotisserie barbeque. Servers slice grilled beef, pork, chicken, and lamb from skewers brought tableside.

Island Merchant
302 Main Street
Tel: 508-771 1337
www.theislandmerchant.com

$$–$$$
Lively place serving regional seasonal cuisine with an island flair.

Sam Diego's Mexican Cookery & Bar
950 Iyannough Road (Route 132)
Tel: 508-771 6071
www.samdiegos.com **$$**
Southwest décor; Tex-Mex and excellent Mexican menu. Outdoor patio in season is perfect for sipping margaritas or a Dos Equis. Four indoor dining areas keep the place from feeling crowded.

The Original Gourmet Brunch
517 Main Street
Tel: 508-771 2558
www.gourmetbrunch.com **$–$$**
Late, lazy breakfasts are what vacations are all about. Over 100 omelets are on the menu, but there are also Belgian waffles, eggs Benedict, and a full luncheon menu.

Tugboats
21 Arlington Street
Tel: 508-775 6433
www.tugboatscapecod.com **$$**
Recently expanded, it now has three dining areas, an outdoor deck with shaded seating, and two bars. The lobster bisque/lobster roll special and a kids' menu make this harborfront spot popular with families.

Mashpee
Bleu
Mashpee Commons, 7 Market Street
Tel: 508-539 7907 **$$–$$$**
Chosen by one poll as the Best Bistro in Massachusetts. Classic French bistro cuisine done with flair. Inviting decor and friendly, efficient staff.

Bobby Byrne's
Mashpee Commons, Routes 28 & 151
Tel: 508-477 0600
www.bobbybyrnes.com **$$**
"An eating, drinking, and talking establishment" with a Celtic theme and feel and extensive menu of well-prepared pub grub.

Orleans
Captain Linnell House
137 Skaket Beach Road
Tel: 508-255 3400
www.linnell.com **$$$$**
One of the Cape's most revered and romantic restaurants, housed in a sea captain's elegant 1811 mansion on spacious grounds, this is the place for a very special occasion.

Mahoney's Atlantic
28 Main Street
Tel: 508-255 5505
www.mahoneysatlantic.com **$$$**
Classy, contemporary modern American cuisine. Blackened tuna "sashimi" as a starter or entrée.

Land Ho!
38 Main Street
Tel: 508-255 5165
www.land-ho.com **$$**
A genuine local hangout where the characters work hard to maintain their reputation. Good deli sandwiches along with the usual casual dining menu.

Pocasset
Bopha's Stir Crazy Restaurant
570 MacArthur Street
Tel: 508-564 6464
www.stircrazyrestaurant.com **$$**
Cambodian cuisine has elements of Chinese and Indian cooking, but with its own tastes. In a stereotypical Cape Cod house that's about as far from Asian architectural as you can get, Bopha Samms creates memorable meals in a happy, inviting ambience.

Provincetown
Cafe Edwige and Edwige at Night
333 Commercial Street
Tel: 508-487 2008 **$$–$$$**
In the morning, the café serves up big, good breakfasts – the sort you never get around to making for yourself. At night, it's creative American cuisine with Mediterranean, Middle Eastern, and Asian influences. Lots of special bar drinks, like ginger and fruit Cosmos.

Front Street
230 Commercial Street
Tel: 508-487 9715
www.frontstreetrestaurant.com **$$$–$$$$**
Mediterranean-American fusion food in an intimate dining room. Look for lobster cappuccino, tea-smoked duck, and Gorgonzola-stuffed rack of lamb.

Karoo Kafe
338 Commercial Street
Tel: 508-487 6630
www.karookafe.com **$$**
South African cuisine, a mélange of Dutch, African, Malay, and British seasonings and ingredients, stars here. Try Bobotie – about as authentic as it gets – the national dish of spiced minced meat with an egg-based topping.

The Mews Restaurant & Cafe
429 Commercial Street
Tel: 508-487 1500
www.mews.com **$$–$$$**
Very sophisticated menu, very well prepared and

LEFT: old-style soda fountain restaurant.
RIGHT: fresh lobster is a regularly on the menu in Cape Cod.

Prices for a three-course dinner per person with a half-bottle of house wine:
$ = under $20
$$ = $20–45
$$$ = $45–60
$$$$ = over $60

beautifully presented. Lovely setting (second-floor has better views) near the east end arts district.

Napi's
7 Freeman Street
Tel: 508-571 6274
www.napis-restaurant.com **$$**
A block off the main thoroughfare, it's a cozy, fun, locally famous spot, built and decorated with architectural salvage. Menu spans the world. Lunch is sandwiches and salads; dinner is far more extensive and interesting. Award-winning clam chowder.

Provincetown
Portuguese Bakery
299 Commercial Street

Tel: 508-487 1803 **$**
Baking fresh pastries, lunches, and breakfasts for at least 100 years (no one is entirely sure). Fried dough Malasadas are legendary, and the key lime and blueberry tarts are reaching that status. Meat turnovers and other savories are a nice lunch break from seafood.

Sandwich
Dunbar Tea Shop
1 Water Street (Route 130)
Tel: 508-833 2485
www.dunbarteashop.com **$**
A proper English tearoom housed in a 1740 carriage house serves afternoon tea, pastries, light lunches, and ports and sherries inside and on the garden patio.
Marshland Restaurant
Route 6A
Tel: 508-888 9824
www.marshlandrestaurant. com **$–$$**
Diner-feel with excellent

food. The stuffed quahogs and clam chowder have fans who drive in from the other side of the Cape to order them. Fabulous breakfasts that keep you going all day.

South Yarmouth
The Jerk Café
1319 A Route 28 (across from the Ambassador Suites Hotel)
Tel: 508-394 1944
www.thejerkcafe.com **$$**
Hey, mon! Real Jamaican jerk cooking: chicken, pork, beef, and shrimp done right. Laid-back Jamaican vibe.

Woods Hole
Shuckers World Famous Raw Bar and Café
91A Water Street
Tel: 508-540 3850
www.woodshole.com/ shuckers **$$**
The freshest of seafood, to be slurped dockside. The raw bar and lobster boil are particularly popular. Expect a wait during high season.

Yarmouth Port
Inaho
157 Route 6A
Tel: 508-362 5522
http://inahocapecod.com **$$$**
A superb Japanese restaurant, with the freshest sushi imaginable and presentations that are works of art.
Jack's Outback II
161 Main Street
Tel: 508-362 6690 **$**
No website, because they don't need to promote themselves; the regulars fill the place. Tourists who find the place are rewarded with great breakfasts. Cash only.

Cape Cod Islands
Edgartown
Atria

137 Main Street
Tel: 508-627 5850
www.atriamv.com **$$$–$$$$**
Sophisticated, elegant New England cuisine. Menu changes frequently to reflect availability of seasonal ingredients.
Chesca's
38 N. Water Street
Tel: 508-627 1234
www.chescasmv.com **$$–$$$**
Urban Italian and American menu in a comfortably upscale setting. Enjoy the front porch with its rocking chairs; you'll need them while you wait for a table.
L'Etoile
22 N. Water Street
Tel: 508-627 5187
www.letoile.net **$$$$**
Superlative French cuisine served in the elegant rooms of a whaling captain's mansion, the garden terrace, or new, stylish bar. Seasonal, regional foods, locally sourced.

Menemsha
Homeport
512 North Road
Tel: 508-645 2679
www.homeportmv.com **$$–$$$**
Overlooking the harbor and one of the best spots on the island for fresh fish: eat-in, on the lawn or on the deck. Walk-up raw bar. They also have "bike beach delivery" and call-ahead-for-pick-up service. BYOB; they provide ice buckets, misers, and glassware.

Oak Bluffs
Offshore Ale Company
30 Kennebec Avenue
Tel: 508-693 2626
www.offshoreale.com **$–$$**
Serious brewpub (with 10 beer lines) that's equally

serious about its food. Very casual, "peanuts on the floor" atmosphere. Wood-fired pizza selection includes all the traditional favorites, as well as roasted duck pizza and classic Roma finished with truffle oil.

Vineyard Haven
Black Dog Tavern and Bakery
Vineyard Haven Harbor
Tel: 508-693 9223
www.theblackdog.com **$–$$**
It's one of the island's most popular restaurants for good reason, serving fresh seafood, homemade breads and pastries, and offering a children's menu.

The Black Dog Café
508 State Road, 1 mile uép island west of Vineyard Haven
Tel: 508-696 8190
The café has a similar menu to the tavern. It's a good place for take-away meals for picnics.

Nantucket
Boarding House
12 Federal Street
Tel: 508-228 9622
www.boardinghouse nantucket.com **$$$**
Farm to table kitchen with a neighborhood bar: a good combination. The covered patio of this beach house is the perfect place to enjoy a weekend brunch, a casual dinner, afternoon drinks, and lots of people-watching.

Corazón del Mar
21 South Water Street
Tel: 508-228 0815 **$$$**
A little bit of Mexico in Nantucket. Latin and Mexican kitchen produces

tasty results with local seafood, a break from the usual treatment. Very Latin American ambience.

The Pearl
12 Federal Street
Tel: 508-228 9701
www.thepearlnantucket.com
$$$$
Ranked as one of the top seafood restaurants in all of New England. Very heavy Asian influences: seafood laska hot pot; lemongrass and cilantro beef BBQ. Signature salt and pepper wok-fried lobster.

Rope Walk
Straight Wharf
Tel: 508-228 8886
www.theropewalk.com **$$$**
New England seafood comfort food: clam chowdah, salmon Reuben, oyster po'boy, overlooking the harbor. Raw bar.

Brotherhood of Thieves
23 Broad Street
Tel: 508-228 2551
www.brotherhoodofthieves.
com **$$**
Great burgers, live music, and an appreciative crowd in an 1840 whaling bar.

Bars
Atlantic House
6 Masonic Place, Provincetown
The town's most famous gay bar – located in a 1798 tavern – is actually three bars: a dance club; a "Macho Bar" big on leather and Levi's; and the fire-placed Little Bar, a cozy hangout once frequented by Tennessee Williams.

The Beachcomber
1120 Cahoon Hollow Road,

Wellfleet
Tel: 508-349 6055
Watch the sunset while sipping a frozen Mudslide and feasting on a dozen oysters from the raw bar.

The Chicken Box
14 Daves Street, Nantucket
Tel: 508-228 9717
A local institution for more than 50 years, this hot spot serves up a fine menu of local and nationally-known jazz and blues bands.

Crown & Anchor Inn
247 Commercial Street, Provincetown
The complex's six bars offer something for most adventurous tastes, including the town's largest nightclub (Paramount), its only video bar (Wave), a cabaret venue, a poolside bar with heated pool, a piano bar, and a landmark, cruisy leather bar (The Vault).

The Lampost/Rare Duck
111 Circuit Avenue, Oak

Bluffs, Martha's Vineyard
A lively night spot with a split personality – upstairs features live bands and DJs with dancing (and more expensive drinks); the homier "basement" is the place to hear acoustic acts.

The Newes from America Pub
22 Kelley Street
Housed in a structure built in 1742, this is about as authentic a pub as it gets. A good list of regional microbrews is on tap, with the option of trying five of them in a "rack."

The Squealing Pig
335 Commercial Street, Provincetown
One of the straight bars in town, the Snug Pig features an extensive selection of beer, excellent fish and chips and lobster rolls, and decent jukebox selections for when the bands aren't playing.

LEFT: relaxing by the sea at Provincetown.
RIGHT: lobster at Union Oyster House.

COVERED BRIDGES

Masterpieces of folk technology, covered bridges were the creation of craftsmen who acted as designers, engineers, and builders

New Englanders didn't invent covered bridges – they have been built in Europe for centuries – but they did perfect their design and engineering. The roofs covering the wooden supports extended the life of the bridge by as much as 40 years. And just as today's highway signs warn, the roadways on bridges freeze before those on solid ground, so the covered road was safer in winter.

Yankee bridge builders devised systems of load-bearing that still stand up to traffic. The "kingpost" design uses diagonal braces leading from a central upright towards the opposite shores. The "queenpost" elaborates on this with two parallel uprights, allowing for a longer bridge.

Perhaps the most elegant approach was devised in the 19th century by Ithiel Town. The "Town Lattice" truss incorporates a pair of crisscrossed diagonal members, which opened out like an old-fashioned laundry rack and were made rigid with wooden pegs. The Cornish-Windsor Bridge, spanning the Connecticut River between Vermont and New Hampshire, is a Town Lattice type and is the second-longest covered bridge in the US (a longer Ohio bridge was completed in 2008).

BELOW: the Carleton Bridge in Swanzey, New Hampshire was built in 1789. Historians believe that it was constructed by local farmers, as the truss structure is similar to that used in barns in the area. The height and width of the bridge matches the dimensions of a small wagon of hay.

ABOVE: the grand-daddy of covered bridges, the Cornish-Windsor was the longest standing covered bridge in the US until 2008. The bridge spans the river that separates Vermont from New Hampshire and locals frequently argue about which state can claim the historic structure, but the state of Connecticut owns and maintains the bridge

ABOVE: locals believe that the architects of the Cilleyville Bridge had a disagreement, and one partner deliberately cut one set of timber supports shorter than the other, while structural engineers believe that the charming tilt is a result of the Town Lattice design.

ARCHITECTURAL TRAITS

The image of the barn-red, wooden bridge is a special icon in New England. The design was based in practicality: covered bridges survived the New England weather better than open ones. The roofs were high and the roadways wide so that fully loaded hay wagons could pass through without difficulty. The interior walls were covered with posters advertising everything from medicinal elixirs to religious revivals. And why are the bridges almost always painted red? The usual explanation is that it would trick skittish horses into thinking they were entering their familiar barn. Another – that red paint was available and protected the wood from the elements as effectively as any other coating – probably has just as much validity. The worst enemy of wooden covered bridges is vandalism, usually in the form of fire. Most recently, Hurricane Irene in August 2011 completely swept away bridges in Bartonsville VT and the Turkey Jim Bridge in New Hampshire and left another 13 damaged. But they are so well loved by their communities and aficionados that it's a rare occasion when a lost bridge isn't replaced. Within days of Irene, the Covered Bridge Society (www. coveredbridgesociety.org) was organizing surveys of the damage and lobbying for funding to repair and rebuild these historic treasures.

BOVE: the Groveton Bridge passes over the Ammonoosuc River ear Northumberland, New Hampshire. The bridge was built with a ddleford truss, and has several additional arches for support. ere is a water supply suspended beneath the bridge, which is ly accessible on foot.

BOVE: this tiny and romantic structure is the Kent lls covered bridge in Connecticut. Built in 1967 with a wn Lattice construction, this bridge has a length of ly 37ft (11 meters).

CENTRAL MASSACHUSETTS

Tucked between Boston and the western regions, the midsection of Massachusetts harkens back to an earlier era of agriculture and small-town industry

Main attractions
FRUITLANDS MUSEUM
BLACKSTONE RIVER VALLEY
WORCESTER
SOUTHWICK'S ZOO
OLD STURBRIDGE VILLAGE
QUABBIN RESERVOIR

West of Boston on Route 2 is the little town of Harvard. In the mid-19th century, idealistic self-improvement and social betterment advocates settled in the area. The **Fruitlands Museum ❶** (192 Prospect Hill Road; mid-Apr–mid-Nov Mon–Fri; charge), set in a rustic, wooded 210-acre (85-hectare) campus, chronicles those efforts as well as Native American and fine art traditions. Between 1914 and 1945 Clara Endicott Sears, who had been born into a privileged Boston Brahmin background, assembled an astonishing collection on the site. The result was one of America's first outdoor museums, now a National Register Historic District.

In 1843, Transcendentalist Amos Bronson Alcott, father of Louisa May Alcott (author of *Little Women*), left his Concord home to found an anti-materialist utopian community called Fruitlands, as one of the goals was to "live off the fruits of the land." Vegetarianism, asceticism, and a philosophical return to nature were their mandates, but the commune lasted barely six months. The Fruitlands Farmhouse details the community. The Shaker Office was built in 1794 at the now-defunct Shaker Community in Shirley MA. The building was moved to the Fruitlands where it displays ephemera about the Massachusetts Shakers. The Native American Gallery has cultural and archaeological materials from across the country. The Art Gallery concentrates on Hudson River landscapes and 19th-century portraits. Note that access to the buildings is via outdoor trails through uneven wooded terrain, so proper footwear is advised. There are 3.5 miles (5km) of nature trails on the property, giving fine views of the Nashua River valley.

LEFT: the past is preserved at the Fruitlands Museum in Harvard MA.

Wachusett State Reservation

For a bird's-eye view of the geographic center of the state, visit the **Wachusett State Reservation and Ski Area ②** (345 Mountain Road, off Route 140; tel: 978-464 2987; charge for some activities) in Princeton. The **visitor center** (open daily) atop the 2,006ft (649-meter) summit provides maps of the hiking trails, which are open year-round. This is the nearest ski and snowboard center to Boston, an hour to the east.

Blackstone River valley

Beginning in the mid-1800s, a swath of central Massachusetts extending from Worcester into Rhode Island was a bustling industrial center whose factories made everything from monkey wrenches to the whimsical Mr Potato Head toy. The **John H. Chafee Blackstone River Valley National Heritage Corridor** links 24 communities from Providence RI to Worcester MA which were the birthplace of America's Industrial Revolution.

A non-traditional national park, it's a living landscape whose people and their environs tell a fascinating story of early industrial America. There are visitor centers in Massachusetts at the 1,000-acre (400-hectare) River Bend Farm in Uxbridge and in Worcester at Broad Meadow Brook Wildlife Sanctuary and the Worcester Historical Museum.

The Blackstone River Greenway (formerly "Bikeway") will be a 48-mile (77km) off-road trail running parallel to the Blackstone River and using the canal towpath to connect 15 communities from Worcester MA to Providence RI. So far, about 5 miles (8km) in Millsbury and Worcester have been completed. Another 3.5 (5.5km) miles from Blackstone to Millville are under construction. In Rhode Island, about 12 miles (19km) are complete. For updates, check with www.cycleblackstone.com, which conducts tours of the greenway, and www.blackstonebikewaypatrol.org, which produces an excellent pocket guide to the Greenway (including ice-cream stands and restroom locations).

A statue at the Fruitlands Museum.

BELOW:
a ski school instructor at Wachusett Mountain.

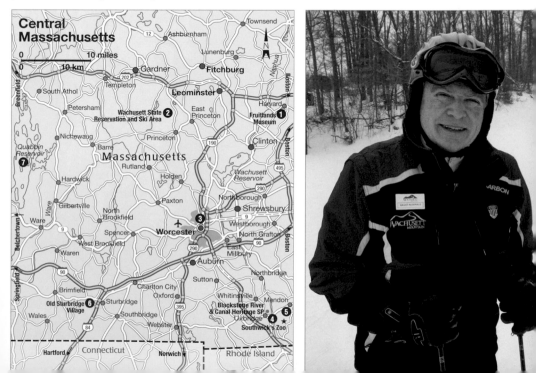

The Worcester Art Museum, which opened in 1898, contains 35,000 pieces.

BELOW: Higgins Armory Museum.

Worcester

About 15 miles (24km) south of Princeton on Route 3 is **Worcester** ❸, the state's second-largest city. This gritty industrial center spawned the country's first park, first wire-making company, first steam calliope, first carpet loom, first diner manufacturer, first Valentine, and (suitably enough) first birth-control pill, not to mention the beginnings of liquid-fuel rocketry, female suffrage, and the Free Soil Party, precursor of the Republican Party. Twelve colleges and universities are here, including Worcester Polytechnic Institute, whose alumni include rocket scientist Dr Robert Goddard.

Goddard was a Worcester native. A fine collection of his rocketry patents and other memorabilia is exhibited at the **Goddard Library** ❹ at Clark University (990 Main Street; tel: 508-793 7206; open daily). Other notable Worcesterites include composer Stephen Foster, socialist leader Emma Goldman, humorist Robert Benchley, and 1960s radical Abbie Hoffman.

Publisher Isaiah Thomas, a Son of Liberty who fled Boston in advance of the British Army in 1770 and continued to publish his rabble-rousing revolutionary newspaper, the *Massachusetts Spy*, was from Worcester. In 1812 he established the **American Antiquarian Society** ❸; its Worcester headquarters, at 185 Salisbury Street, is now a research library whose vast collection focuses on American history, literature, and culture from 1640 through 1876 (tel: 508-755 5221; one-hour tours Wed 3pm). Tours include an especially interesting visit to the document preservation laboratories.

The city is a trove of antiquarian delights. The **Worcester Historical Museum** ❸ (30 Elm Street; tel: 508-753 8278; open Tue–Sat; charge) traces the city's industrial and cultural history and maintains the splendid 1772 Georgian Salisbury Mansion (40 Highland Street; open for guided tours only Thur 1–8.30pm, Fri and Sat 1–4pm; charge). The museum is also a visitor center for the John H. Chafee Blackstone River Valley National Heritage Corridor (*see page 197*).

The **Higgins Armory Museum** ❸ (100 Barber Avenue; tel: 508-853 6015;

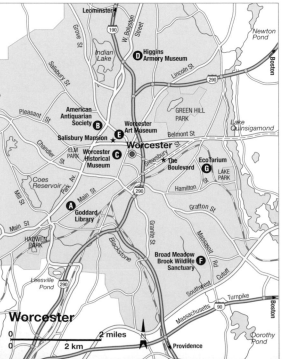

open Tue–Sat daily; charge) is the only museum in the Western Hemisphere solely dedicated to exhibiting arms and armor. Interactive exhibits encourage visitors to experience life in the Middle Ages (including trying on a suit of armor). Thirty-five suits of armor are displayed in a vast, two-story Medieval Great Hall. A new exhibit introduces the original "extreme sport" – jousting.

Ancient and traditional art

With more than 35,000 works of art, the **Worcester Art Museum** **E** (55 Salisbury Street; tel: 508-799 4406; open daily; charge except first Sat 10am–noon and for under 17s) is the second-largest in New England. Its sponsorship of excavations at Antioch, Syria, in the 1930s yielded a remarkable collection of 2nd-century AD Roman mosaics. Equally appealing is the extensive gallery of 17th-, 18th-, and 19th-century American art, including paintings by John Singleton Copley, Winslow Homer, and John Singer Sargent.

More than 78 species of butterfly make their home at the 400-acre (160-hectare) **Broad Meadow Brook Wildlife Sanctuary** **F** (414 Massasoit Road; tel: 508-753 6087; open daily; charge). Some of the nature trails are accessible for physically and visually impaired visitors. The visitor center has a floor-to-ceiling map of the Blackstone River watershed. It's also an information center for the John H. Chafee Blackstone River Valley National Heritage Corridor.

Two miles (3km) from downtown Worcester, you can walk through treetops, visit a digital planetarium, ride on a narrow-gauge railway, and see a polar bear at the **EcoTarium** **G** (222 Harrington Way; tel: 508-929 2700; open daily; charge). The unique indoor–outdoor center introduces visitors to the region's ecosystem and wildlife.

South to Rhode Island

South of Worcester on Route 122, tiny **Uxbridge** **4** is home to the **Blackstone River and Canal Heritage State Park** (287 Oak Street, off Route 122; tel: 508-278 6488; open daily) on **River Bend Farm**. Displays at the visitor center tell

A red-winged blackbird calling from the bulrushes.

BELOW: demonstrating how to raise a barn in Old Sturbridge Village.

the story of the area's canals; visitors can walk along restored sections of the towpath, and explore 1,000 acres (400 hectares) of natural area.

Wildlife from around the world is at **Southwick's Zoo** (2 Southwick Street, off Route 16; tel: 800-258 9182; mid-Apr–Oct daily; charge) in **Mendon** . The largest private zoo in New England has more than 100 animals – from white rhinos and Bengal tigers to Barbary sheep and prairie dogs.

Old Sturbridge Village

Off Route 20, **Old Sturbridge Village** , a recreated community of more than 40 period buildings scattered over 200 acres (80 hectares), offers a take on New England rural life between 1790 and 1840 (tel: 800-733 1830; www.osv.org; open daily; hours vary by season: call or check website; entrance fee includes 2 days' admission within 10 consecutive days).

Visitors are given illuminating explanations, couched in modern parlance, as the interpreters go about the daily business of farm and town life: cobbling shoes, making tin lanterns, and leading prayers. Depending on the season, they make soap, shear sheep, or laboriously build stone walls. Concepts of political freedom and discourse grew, in part, from the emergence of a free press, and the activities of the Isaiah Thomas Printing Office are designed to show how printed communication became an integral part of the new nation's growth.

Quabbin Reservoir

Lying northwest of Sturbridge amidst rolling hills that are especially beautiful in autumn is the huge **Quabbin Reservoir** (visitor center: Route 9, Belchertown; tel: 413-323 7221; open daily). One of the country's largest man-made public water supplies, it comprises 128 sq miles (331 sq km) of flooded valley that holds 412 billion gallons and supplies the drinking water to Greater Boston.

Four towns were flooded in 1939 to create this great body of water. Quabbin is prized as a place to fish, hike, canoe, and admire the bald eagles that breed here.

BELOW: Johnny Appleseed.

Johnny Appleseed

Born on a hardscrabble farm near Leominster, John Chapman became a legend as "Johnny Appleseed." The image of a barefoot man wearing ragged clothing with a tin pot on his head while randomly tossing apple seeds into the air is more accurate than most people might think. A follower of the Swedenborgian religion sect which believed that the more deprivations you endure in this life, the better your reward in the next, he did go barefoot – even in the winter, clothed himself in rags, and used a tin pot as a hat, drinking vessel, and cook pot. But his understanding of apple cultivation was as sophisticated as his personal living habits were crude. As Chapman traveled through Ohio, Indiana, and Illinois, he planted apple nurseries, constructed fences around them to keep out livestock, instructed caretakers on how to tend to the saplings, sold half-grown trees for replanting, and returned every few years to maintain the nurseries. He did not graft his trees, which is the only way to develop edible varieties. His fruit could only be used to press cider. As much a spiritual missionary as an environmental one, Chapman would preach to farmers in exchange for a place to sleep and a meal. He was almost Zen-like in his concern for animals; one story tells of him dousing a fire rather than seeing insects attracted to its light being burned by the flames. Much beloved for his gentle nature, eloquent sermons, and endearing eccentricities, he died in Fort Wayne, Indiana. A local family buried him in their family plot.

RESTAURANTS AND BARS

Prices for a three-course dinner per person with a half-bottle of house wine:
$ = under $20
$$ = $20–45
$$$ = $45–60
$$$$ = over $60

Restaurants

Devens

Devens Grill
4 Ryans Way (Route 2)
Tel: 978-862 0060 **$–$$**
Casual neighborhood place for the planned community of Devens.

Linwood

Brian's
91 Providence Road (Route 122)
Tel: 508-234 9256
www.briansrestaurant.com **$–$$**
Friendly, bright, family place with a big menu, everything from teriyaki chicken to meat loaf.

Mendon

Alicante Mediterranean Grille
84 Uxbridge Road
Tel: 508-634 8188
www.alicantema.com
$$–$$$
Fine Portuguese and Spanish preparation of beef, veal, and chicken in a restaurant with a lake view.

Sturbridge

Cedar Street Grille
12 Cedar Street
Tel: 508-347 5800 **$$–$$$**
An American bistro with a "small plates" menu designed for sharing and a

"robust" menu for full meals.
Publick House
295 Main Street
Tel: 508-347 3313 **$$$**
This gracious 1771 inn and tavern, once a stop for Boston–New York stagecoaches, serves New England fare with a contemporary flair.

The Whistling Swan
502 Main Street
Tel: 508-347 2321.
www.thewhistlingswan.com
$$–$$$
Both casual and fine dining entrées in a Greek-Revivial mansion. The stuffed cheeseburgers are fun, the Bouillabaise classic.

Worcester

Armsby Abbey
144 Main Street
Tel: 508-795 1012 **$$**
Slow food and good beer. Everything that omes out of the kitchen has been sourced locally and prepared without any shortcuts.
Coney Island Lunch
158 Southbridge Street
Tel: 508-753-4362 **$**
Folks have been flocking to this Art Deco shrine to the wiener since 1918: look for the neon sign – a 60ft (18.2-meter) -long hand holding a weiner.
111 Chop House
111 Shrewsbury Street
Tel: 508-799 4111
www.111chophouse.com **$$$**
Serious steaks and other

grilled meat for serious carnivores. Good wine list.
Viva Bene
144 Commercial Street
Tel: 508-799 9999
www.viva-bene.com **$–$$$**
The menu at this casual downtown Italian restaurant ranges from basic pizza and calzones to creative chicken and veal dishes.
Wholly Cannoli
490 Grafton Street
Tel: 508-753 0224 **$**
www.whollycannoli.com
The popular restaurant has a large selection of pizza, but patrons flock for the 20 flavors of cannoli.

Bars

Pioneer Brewing
195 Arnold Road, Fiskdale

Huge selection of hand-crafted beers, many big-screen TVs, live music.
Blackstone Tap
81 Water Street, Worcester
A classic sports bar with TVs, a pool table, and live entertainment.
The Boynton Restaurant & Spirits
117 Highlands Street, Worcester
Half-bar, half-restaurant, and always a popular hangout for students from nearby Worcester Polytech. Giant TVs broadcast sports; there are 51 beers on tap.
Dive Bar
34 Green Street, Worcester
No frills, just a small and simple place with a large selection of craft beers.

RIGHT: breakfast with waffles and maple syrup.

MASSACHUSETTS: THE PIONEER VALLEY

The Connecticut River passes through several counties in the western Massachusetts lowlands; in 1939 the area was dubbed "Pioneer Valley" in honor of the 17th-century settlers who tamed these wild lands

The Pioneer Valley may be named for the early settlers who faced rugged mountains, fierce weather, and determined resistance from the native population, but it can apply equally to the people who followed. Pioneers in sports invented basketball and volleyball here; pioneers in engineering manufactured the first automobile; pioneers in thought graduate from its 14 colleges and universities. It's a mix of bucolic rural towns and sophisticated culture, modern amusement parks and classic carousels, iconic Americana and remnants of Eastern European culture.

Springfield ❶, the Pioneer Valley's largest cy, was established as a trading post in 1636. Throughout its history Springfield has been a manufacturing hub: Indian motorcycles, Rolls-Royces, and Smith & Wesson revolvers have all been made here. But it was in 1892 that Dr James Naismith invented a game that would make possible the city's major attraction: the $103 million, interactive, state-of-the-art **Basketball Hall of Fame ❹** (1000 W. Columbus Avenue; tel: 413-781 6500; open daily; charge; three-day pass available). The 48,000-sq-ft (4,500-sq-meter), three-level facility fascinates the sport's aficionados: others may experience an information overload.

In 1779 George Washington chose Springfield as the site of one of the nation's first two arsenals. The **Springfield Armory National Historic Site ❸** (Armory Square; tel: 413-734 8551; open daily) now houses a museum featuring one of the world's largest historic firearms collections.

The **Springfield Museums at the Quadrangle ❻** (21 Edwards Street; tel: 413-263 6800 or 800-625 7738; open Tue–Sun, Welcome Center open daily; charge; one ticket covers all) oversees four museums clustered

Main attractions
SPRINGFIELD
HOLYOKE
SMITH COLLEGE MUSEUM OF ART
HADLEY FARM MUSEUM
AMHERST
EMILY DICKINSON MUSEUM
HISTORIC DEERFIELD

LEFT: Brimfield Antique Show in Worcester.
RIGHT: the Dr Seuss National Memorial Sculpture Garden.

BELOW: a collection of historic wooden planes at the Hadley Farm Museum.

around a common square. The **George Walter Vincent Smith Art Museum** features Asian decorative arts. The **Science Museum** contains a planetarium and plenty of hands-on exhibits. The **Michele and Donald D'Amour Museum of Fine Arts** has an impressively broad collection, from traditional themes to contemporary shows. The **Museum of Springfield** places the city's history in the larger context of America in the 18th and 19th centuries. (A fifth museum, the **Connecticut Valley Historical Museum**, is closed indefinitely for renovation and reinstallation.)

Sharing the Quad is the **Dr Seuss National Memorial Sculpture Garden**, a fanciful outdoor park with life-size bronze sculptures of characters created by the city's favorite son, the children's author and cartoonist Theodor Seuss Geisel (1904–91).

The 735-acre (300-hectare) **Forest Park ⓓ** (Sumner Avenue; open daily; charge) has a zoo (tel: 413-733 2251; open Apr–mid-Oct; charge) with more than 100 species, and a seasonal, child-size train tour.

The city's rich cultural life is headquartered in **Symphony Hall ⓔ** (1 Columbus Center; tel: 413-788 7033; www.symphonyhall.org), home of the Springfield Symphony Orchestra and CityStage Theater.

Follow State Street to Berkshire Avenue and then turn right on Main Street to the **Titanic Historical Society** (200 Main Street, Indian Orchard; tel: 413-543 4770; Mon–Sat; charge). Modest in size, its collection of artifacts from the legendary shipwreck is – well – titanic in scope. Mrs Astor's lifejacket, the bell from the ship which recovered most of the victims, the wireless message sent to the ship warning of icebergs which never reached the bridge are all displayed.

The "Big E"

Across the river, in **West Springfield ❷**, the Theater Project at the Majestic Theater (131 Elm Street; tel: 413-747 7797) mounts live performances.

Every September, prize livestock and top-name talents entertain the crowds for just over two weeks at the **Eastern States Exposition** (the "Big E"; tel:

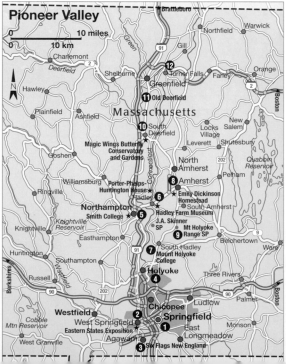

413-737 2443), New England's largest agricultural fair. The Storrowton Village Museum (tel: 413-205 5051; www.thebige.com; mid-June–early Oct; special programs at other times; charge), on the fairgrounds, is nine transplanted 18th- and early-19th-century buildings surrounding a traditional town green.

Six Flags

In nearby **Agawam**, **Six Flags New England** ❸ (tel: 413-786 9300; open weekends in spring and fall, daily in summer; charge) is New England's largest amusement park.

Holyoke

Head 8 miles (13km) north from Springfield on Route 5 or I–91 (exit 16) to **Holyoke** ❹, home to **Wisteriahurst Museum** (238 Cabot Street; tel: 413-322 5660; tours Sat–Mon; charge). The elegantly furnished mansion is a fine example of the Beaux Arts movement.

The visitor center at **Holyoke Heritage State Park** (221 Appleton Street; tel: 413-534 1723; open Tue–Sun) recounts the history of the city and its industrial heritage. Next to the center is a 1929 **merry-go-round** (July–Aug Tue–Sun).

Also in the park, the **Children's Museum** (444 Dwight Street; tel: 413-536 5437; open Wed–Sun; charge) has lots of hands-on activities. In the same building, the **Volleyball Hall of Fame** (tel: 413-536 0926; open Thur–Sun) immortalizes William G. Morgan, who invented the game at the Holyoke YMCA in 1895.

Northampton

Continue north alongside the Connecticut River to **Northapton** ❺. Surrounded by colleges – Amherst, Mount Holyoke, Hampshire, the University of Massachusetts, and Smith – Northampton's lively bistros, restaurants, and galleries reflect the youthful energy of the educationally elite. The area has attracted hundreds of artisans and artists, who showcase their wares at craft shops all over town.

Smith College Museum of Art (Elm Street, Route 9; tel: 413-585 2760; open Tue–Sun) focuses on

That sinking feeling at the Six Flags amusement park.

BELOW: exhibits at the Basketball Hall of Fame.

WHERE

Near Holyoke, detour to Mount Tom State Reservation (125 Reservation Road; tel: 413-534 1186) and amble along any of the 20 miles (30km) of trails. The views of the Connecticut River valley and the Berkshire Mountains are worth the work.

American art and French impressionists. It also houses an impressive collection of Asian and African pieces. The college's **Lyman Conservatory** (tel: 413-585 2742; open daily; donation) has an audio tour of the 1896 greenhouse. There's a brochure of the 127-acre (51-hectare) **arboretum and gardens**.

Calvin Coolidge (1872–1933), the governor of Massachusetts who became the 30th US president, began his law practice in Northampton. A collection of his papers is on exhibit in the **Coolidge Memorial Room** in the **Forbes Library** (20 West Street; tel: 413-587 1011; open Mon–Sat).

Hadley

To the east along Route 9, between Northampton and Amherst, is **Hadley** ❻, whose long history of farming from the 1700s forward is documented at the **Hadley Farm Museum** (Junction Routes 9 and 47; open daily mid-May–mid-Oct; charge).

The nearby **Porter-Phelps-Huntington Historic House Museum** (tel: 413-584 4699;130

River Drive; (130 River Drive; tel: 413-584 4699; www.pphmuseum.org; open May–Oct Sat–Wed; charge) is a Georgian-style house, built in 1752 and structurally unchanged since 1799.

The museum hosts concerts and lectures in the summer. Just off Route 47 in nearby **J.A. Skinner State Park** (tel: 413-586 0350), a road (open Apr–Nov) climbs to a viewpoint immortalized in Thomas Cole's 1830 painting, *The Oxbow*. The **Summit House**, a former 19th-century hotel, is undergoing renovation and should reopen in late 2012.

South on Route 116, in nearby **South Hadley, Mount Holyoke College** ❼ (tel: 413-538 2000) is America's oldest women's college. Its 400-acre (160-hectare) campus was the work of landscape architect Frederick Law Olmsted. Students run regular campus tours (www.mtholyoke.edu/adm/tours for details).

The *Lady Bea*, a 49-passenger boat with indoor seating and sundeck departs Brunelle's Marina for narrated scenic cruises on the Connecticut River (tel: 413-315 6342; www.brunelles.com; Memorial Day–early Oct Thur–Sun afternoons and evenings).

Amherst

Continue east on Route 9 to **Amherst** ❽, long a hotbed of intellectual vigor and social independence. Lexicographer Noah Webster lived here, as did a reclusive genius of American poetry.

Visitors to the **Emily Dickinson Musuem** can experience the spartan environment that housed a self-confined soul who poured her emotions solely into her poetry (280 Main Street; tel: 413-542-8161; open Mar–Dec Wed–Sun; charge). Guided tours of The Homestead where she lived most of her life, and The Evergreens, home of her brother, leave from the visitors center. An audio tour of the grounds is available. Just off the spacious central green, **Amherst College**'s stately fraternity

BELOW: cartoon classics at Six Flags.

houses flank a campus quadrangle that is a classic of early 19th-century institutional architecture. At the college's **Mead Art Museum** (tel: 413-542 2000; open Tue–Sun; free) more than 16,000 works include a superb collection of American art, Russian modernist paintings, and West African sculptures. More than 2,500 Japanese woodblock prints make this one of the major collections of *ukiyo-e* ("pictures of the floating world") in the country.

The skeleton of a woolly mammoth is the centerpiece at the **Beneski Museum of Natural History, Amherst College** (tel: 413-542 2000; open Tue–Sun; free), showcasing a trove of fossils and geological history.

South on Route 116, The **Eric Carle Museum of Picture Book Art** (125 W. (125 W. Bay Road; tel: 413-658 1100; www.carlemuseum.org; open Tue–Sun; charge) celebrates the first art most of us experience – the illustrations in children's picture books.

Yiddish spoken here

Hampshire College alumnus Aaron Lansky is the motivating force and director of the **National Yiddish Book Center** (tel: 413-256 4900; (1021 West Street, Hampshire College, Route 116; tel: 413-256 4900; open Mon–Fri, Sun; closed Sun in winter). This is a collection of more than a million Yiddish books housed in a wooden complex designed to resemble an Eastern European *shtetl* (village). It's a heroic exercise in the preservation of an imperiled language and the tradition it represents.

Encompassing a 7-mile (11km) ridge that stretches from Hadley to Belchertown, **Mount Holyoke Range State Park ❾** (Route 116; tel: 413-253 2883; visitor center open daily) offers some of the Pioneer Valley's best scenery.

South Deerfield

Backtrack to Route 5 (or hop on I–91) and head north to **South Deerfield ❿**. Here it's always Christmas in the Disneyesque Bavarian Village and

Santa's Workshop at "the world's largest candle store," **Yankee Candle Company** (Route 5; tel: 877-636 7707/413-665 2929; open daily). This is one of the area's major attractions for children, who have the chance to dip their own candles, colonial-style. Also, Chandler's Restaurant at Yankee Candle Company hosts a concert series through the summer and fall.

Less than 3 miles (5km) up Route 5 is **Magic Wings Butterfly Conservatory and Gardens** (tel: 413-665 2805; open daily; charge), where thousands of butterflies flutter about in an 18,400-sq-ft (1,710-sq-meter) indoor – and, in summer, outdoor – conservatory garden.

Historic Deerfield

Farther northwest, just off Route 5 is the well-preserved pioneer village of **Old Deerfield ⓫**. Along Main Street, 13 museum houses make up Historic Deerfield (Main Street; tel: 413-775 7132; open daily; charge).

Deerfield has a fascinating history that dates from its settlement in 1669. The Pocumtuck Indians, who farmed

Calvin Coolidge's reputation as a man of few words once prompted a matron at a society banquet to coax him: "Mr President, I have a wager with a friend that I can persuade you to say more than two words." His reply: "You lose."

BELOW: the Wistariahurst Museum, Holyoke, a Beaux Arts gem.

The 1730 Ashley House in Deerfield.

the fertile valley, were not pleased to see their land usurped, and massacred the entire population (by then 125 strong) in 1675. That deterred settlers, but the lure of the land was irresistible, and interlopers eventually won out, despite a French-instigated Indian raid in 1704 in which half the village was burned, 100 colonists carried off to captivity in Quebec, and 50 slaughtered.

Tomahawk marks can be seen on one sturdy wooden door, but the town's lurid history is not what attracts most visitors. The draw is an extraordinary architectural cache: the carefully restored Colonial and Federal structures along "The Street," Deerfield's mile-long main thoroughfare. The treasures inside the houses, representing decades of changing decorative styles, easily equal the exteriors.

Among the buildings open to the public are the **Ashley House** (1730), a former parson's home with intricately carved woodwork and antique furnishings; the **Asa Stebbins House** (1810) with early paintings, Chinese porcelain, and Federal and Chippendale furniture; and the **Hall Tavern** (1760), which serves as the information center. Deerfield doesn't offer the costumed interpreters and crafts demonstrations of a Sturbridge Village, but anyone enamored of the restrained elegance of colonial design will find it fascinating.

Memorial Hall Museum (Memorial Street; tel: 413-774 7476; open May–Oct daily; charge) houses a wonderful hodgepodge of folk art, Native American relics, and local lore. The **Channing Blake Meadow Walk** (May–Dec) passes by a working farm and through meadows to the Deerfield River.

The historic mill town of **Turner Falls** ⑫, north of Deerfield on Route 2, is an old mill town which is reinventing itself as an arts and outdoor recreation center. There are historic and geologic walking tours, the **Great Falls Discovery Center** (2 Avenue A; tel: 413-863 3221) housed in an old mill complex, and an ongoing calendar of community arts events and festivals.

The Man Who Created The Cat in the Hat

The Dr Seuss National Memorial Sculpture Garden is an enduring tribute to the winderful and whimsical characters created by the equally beloved Springfield native, Theodor Geisel.

Beloved characters such as Yertle the Turtle, the Grinch and his dog Max, Horton the Elephant, Thidwick the Big-Hearted Moose, and the Lorax are clustered in a corner of the Quadrangle green in Springfield. The Cat in the Hat is there, too, looking over the shoulder of a sculpture of Geisel at work at his drawing board.

The son of German immigrants who wanted him to become a college professor, Geisel attended Dartmouth College. He worked on the college newspaper, but when he was discovered drinking alcohol underage, he was forced to resign from his extra-curricular activites. To continue working for the college humor magazine, he wrote under the pseudonym Seuss. Geisel then entered Lincoln College at Oxford, intending to study for a Doctorate in Literature, before deciding that academia was not for him.

Working as a cartoonist, he designed advertisements and sold the occasional cartoon to *The Saturday Evening Post* and *Vanity Fair*. His first book, *And to Think that I Saw It on Mulberry Street*, was rejected 27 times before it found a publisher.

The Cat in the Hat was written on request, using words from a 225 "new reader" vocabulary list. He said his talent for rhyming came from his mother, who used to recite silly lists of rhyming words to him at bedtime, although it is also known that he used rhythmic inspiration from other encounters, including the pattern of noise from the ship's engine on a trans-Atlantic voyage.

Many of his books have Springfield locations. The streams of Horton's Jungle of Nool are those of Forest Park. Mulberry Street is a Springfield thoroughfare, and the police officers ride red motorcycles, the color of Springfield's famed Indian motorcycles. When Geisel died in 1991, he had sold over 200 million copies of his 44 books, which have been translated into 15 languages.

RESTAURANTS AND BARS

Prices for a three-course dinner per person with a half-bottle of house wine:
$ = under $20
$$ = $20–45
$$$ = $45–60
$$$$ = over $60

Restaurants

Amherst

Bistro 63 @ the Monkey Bar
63 N. Pleasant Street
Tel: 413-259 1600
www.bistro63.com **$$–$$$**
Contemporary atmosphere serving classic dishes and some worthwhile excursions to the rest of the world. The staff speaks French, Italian, and Spanish. Thur–Sat, the tables are removed and it becomes a local dance club.

Judie's
51 N. Pleasant Street
Tel: 413-253 3491
www.judiesrestaurant.com
$–$$
With a bright garden room, skylight eat-in bar, and dining at hand-painted tables, this place sends out vibes of happiness as irresistible as the giant and justly famous popovers that come with most meals. You can use them as the "bread" for most sandwiches.

Tabellas
28 Amity Street
Tel: 413-253 0220
www.tabellasrestaurant.com **$$**
Wonderful menu of foods sourced locally, all prepared to order by a kitchen that proves the "slow food," "ethical eating" concept can also mean a fine

dining experience. The wine list is nice, but order the West Country hard cider instead.

Deerfield

New Italian restaurant featuring Southern Italian and Mediterranean dishes. Pasta specials on Sundays.

Deerfield Inn
81 Old Main Street
Tel: 413-774 5587/800-926 3865
www.deerfieldinn.com **$$$**
Damage and flooding from Hurricane Irene in August 2011 has closed the restaurant and inn until the summer of 2012. Call for updates. The restaurant expects to reopen with its forward-thinking Continental menu.

Northampton

East Side Grill
19 Strong Street
Tel: 413-586 3347
www.eastsidegrill.com **$$**
Wildly popular Cajun influenced grill. he food may not convince you that New Orleans has come north, but the room is always bustling.

Mama Iguana's
274 Main Street
Tel: 413-732 6262
www.spoletorestaurants.com **$$**
Very lively party place (you can don a sombrero as you enter) with all of the usual Mexican favorites. Many, many Margarita variations. Next to the Basketball Hall of Fame.

Spoleto
50 Main Street
Tel: 413-586 6313
www.spoletorestaurants.com

$$–$$$
New and traditional Italian fare in a lively contemporary café. Whole wheat and gluten-free menu available.

South Deerfield

Alina's Ristorante
6 Elm Street, South Deerfield
Tel: 413-397 2190
www.myalinas.com **$$$$**

Chandler's Restaurant
Yankee Candle, Route 5
Tel: 413-665 1277
www.yankeecandle.com **$$$**
A surprising and welcome oasis in one of the area's largest tourist attractions, serving creative New England dishes, along with classic favorites such as prime rib. Excellent kids' menu.

Springfield

Chef Wayne's Big Mamou
63 Liberty Street
Tel: 413-732 1011
www.chefwaynes-bigmamou.com **$$**
Laissez les bon temps roulez! N'Awlins North! Highlights of the Cajun and Southern fare include fried oysters, crawfish quesadillas, and sweet potato pie. L & D Mon–Sat. There's a second location at 15 Main Street in Williamsburg (northwest of Northampton).

Student Prince and Fort Restaurant
8 Fort Street
Tel: 413-788 6628
www.studentprince.com
$$–$$$
This reliable downtown spot, popular since the 1940s, offers stout German cuisine

and an authentic beer-hall ambience.

Theordore's Booze, Blues & BBQ
201 Worthington Street
Tel.413-736 0000
www.theobbq.com **$$**
Slow-smoked ribs with hickory wood, chicken and sausage étouffé, wings with many choices of sauces, and some of the best blues music anywhere on weekends.

Bars

Moan & Dove
460 West Street, Amherst
Popular beer bar, well situated on Route 116 between Amherst and Hampshire colleges. Hard-to-find labels include Old Rasputin Imperial Stout and Avery Maharaja.

Northampton Brewery Bar & Grill
11 Brewster Court, Northampton
A venerable brewpub with an outdoor rooftop beer garden. Full menu.

Theodore's
201 Worthington Street, Springfield
"Blues, booze, and BBQ" are staples at this popular club which hosts local, regional, and national blues bands Friday and Saturday nights.

The Tunnel
Union Station Restaurant, 125A Pleasant Street, Northampton
It really is a renovated railroad tunnel, but a luxurious one, with plush couches and leather easy chairs in which to sip one of the bar's signature martinis or single-malt scotches.

MASSACHUSETTS: THE BERKSHIRES

Berkshire County encompasses valleys dotted with shimmering lakes, rolling farmlands and orchards, deep forests abundant with deer, and powerful rivers that cascade into waterfalls

Main attractions
BASH BISH FALLS STATE PARK
NORMAN ROCKWELL MUSEUM
ASHINTULLY GARDENS
TANGLEWOOD
HANCOCK SHAKER VILLAGE
MASS MoCA, NORTH ADAMS
SHELBURNE FALLS

Though less dramatic than the mountains of New Hampshire or Vermont, the Berkshire Hills were still formidable enough to insulate western Massachusetts from the rest of the state. The first settler didn't arrive until the relatively late date of 1725; the terrain, climate, and hostility of the tribes living in the area slowed the rate of development. The Industrial Revolution was a boon to the region, as its iron foundries smelted ore for factories and railroads and its marble graced the dome of the US Capitol.

In the late 1800s, the Berkshires' economic wave ebbed and it became a backwater region. During the Gay Nineties, the cool mountain breezes lured the Carnegies and Vanderbilts to build summer homes near Stockbridge and Lenox. Visitors today arrive for the renowned summer festivals, splendors of fall foliage, or fun of winter skiing.

Native Americans and early settlers used the Housatonic Valley from Connecticut to reach the Berkshires. Today's travelers can do the same, following US Highway 7 north along the Housatonic or by taking the Massachusetts Turnpike from the eastern part of the state.

The southern Berkshires

Just inside the Connecticut border on Route 7A is **Ashley Falls ❶**, a village surrounded by hayfields and dairy farms. The village was named for Colonel John Ashley (1709–1802), a prominent lawyer and Revolutionary War officer.

Off Route 7A, the **Colonel John Ashley House**, built in 1735, is the oldest structure in Berkshire County. It was here that the Sheffield Declaration protesting British tyranny and advocating for individual rights was drafted (published 1773). It has been restored as a colonial museum (Cooper Hill Road; tel: 413-229 8600; grounds open year-round; guided

SOUTH FACE FARM

LEFT: fall foliage in the Berkshires.

house tours Sat and Sun Memorial Day weekend–Columbus Day weekend; charge). Although the furnishings are not all true to the home's earliest period, it's worth a visit as an example of serenely proportioned early country Georgian architecture.

Sheffield to Great Barrington

Up the road is the 329-acre **Bartholomew's Cobble** (105 Weatogue Road; tel: 413-229 8600; open daily; charge), a natural rock garden with hiking trails that meander along the banks of the Housatonic. It contains more species of fern – at their most prolific in June – than any other area in the continental United States. There's a small natural history museum.

Guided three-hour canoe tours, led by expert naturalists, explore Bartholomew's Cobble and the river in the summer. Children 12 and older are welcome, and advance reservations are mandatory.

North on Route 7, **Sheffield** ❷, established in 1733, is the oldest town in Berkshire County. In 1994 the state's oldest covered bridge, just off Route 7, was destroyed by vandals. A new one (pedestrians only) replaced it a few years later.

The Berkshires' true beauty lies in its backroads and small villages. **Mill River** and **New Marlborough**, small communities that prospered in the heyday of the Industrial Revolution, are gems.

The drive north along Route 7 skirts the Housatonic River, passing Sheffield Pottery and several antiques shops.

Great Barrington ❸ offers an excellent base from which to explore the towns and villages of the southern Berkshires. Although it does not have the architectural treasures of towns farther north such as Stockbridge and Lenox, Great Barrington has long been a popular vacation destination for sophisticated New Yorkers, and upscale galleries, shops, and restaurants line the main and side streets.

Fans of singer Arlo Guthrie's **Alice's Restaurant** *Massacree* will want to see the **Guthrie Center** (4 Van Deusenville Road; tel: 413-528 1955), where Alice once lived. Built as a church in 1829, it is now an interfaith center.

Tom's Toys (297 Main Street; tel: 413-528 3330; www.tomstoys.com) is Santa's off-season warehouse. It's filled with toys, puzzles, games, dolls, and crafts – very few of which have commercial tie-ins.

Head west on Route 23 and south on Route 41 to the tiny hill hamlet of Mount Washington, in the state's southwestern corner. This smallest of Berkshires towns offers some of the finest fall-foliage viewing and the most dramatic natural waterfall in New England: at **Bash Bish Falls State Park** ❹ (Falls Road; tel: 413-528 0330), in Mount Washington State Forest, water plummets 80ft (24 meters) into a deep gorge.

Stockbridge

North of Great Barrington on Route 7 is **Monument Mountain** ❺, a craggy peak whose summit is a pleasant half-hour hike from the parking lot at its base. The mountain is a Berkshire literary landmark of considerable repute.

BELOW: kayaking on the Deerfield River.

The unmistakable aroma of vanilla extract permeates the air at the Charles H. Baldwin General Store in West Stockbridge (1 Center Street; tel: 413-232 7785). It comes from the heavy oak barrels near the door, where the extract ages for several weeks. The family has been producing the high-quality extract since 1888.

BELOW LEFT: the Mission House, Stockbridge. **BELOW RIGHT:** the Norman Rockwell Museum. **FAR RIGHT:** small potteries are scattered around the Berkshires.

The poet William Cullen Bryant sang its praises while practicing as a local attorney in the 1830s.

Stockbridge ❻ was incorporated as an Indian mission in 1739. Its first missionary was John Sargeant, a young tutor from Yale who lived among the Mohegan Indians for 16 years. He slept in their wigwams, shared their venison, and spoke their language while introducing them to the colonists' ways. Eventually, Sargeant helped them establish a town, build homes and cultivate the land. Some among the Mohegan tribe held public office, serving alongside whites in the town government. But as more colonists moved into the area, the tribes were slowly deprived of their land.

By 1783, the mission was history, and surviving Mohegans were forced to settle on the Oneida reservation in New York State. All that remains is the 1739 **Mission House**, now a museum on Stockbridge's Main Street (tel: 413-298 3239; open daily late May– mid-Oct; charge). It is furnished with a superb collection of 18th-century American furniture and decorative

arts and has a unique Colonial Revival garden. There's a small museum about the Mohegans behind the house.

If Stockbridge's Main Street looks familiar, it may be because its New England essence was captured on the canvases of that remarkable illustrator of American life, Norman Rockwell, who created more than 300 covers for the *Saturday Evening Post*. He kept a studio and made his home here for a quarter of a century, until his death in 1978. Located on Route 183 is the stunning **Norman Rockwell Museum** (9 Glendale Road, Route 183; tel: 413-298 4100; nrm.org; open daily; charge). Designed by Robert A.M. Stern, it showcases his work and even recreates his Stockbridge studio.

Naumkeag Museum and Gardens, a half-mile off Route 7 and Route 102 (Prospect Hill; tel: 413-298 3239; open Memorial Day weekend–Columbus Day daily; charge), is a 44-room, Norman-style mansion designed by Stanford White for Joseph Choate, the US ambassador to Great Britain, in 1899. It served as the summer home for three generations

of the family. The furniture and artworks are outstanding, as are the 8 acres (3.2 hectares) of terrace gardens and grounds.

Chesterwood, the meticulously preserved summer home of sculptor Daniel Chester French (1850–1931), is 3 miles (5km) west of Stockbridge (4 Williamsville Road, off Route 183; tel: 413-298 3579; open mid-May–mid-Oct daily; charge). It was here that he created his masterpiece, *The Seated Lincoln*, focal point of the Lincoln Memorial in Washington DC. Many of his pieces are on exhibit, and displays in the Barn Gallery document his outstanding career.

Tyringham

To the southeast, off Route 102, the tiny unspoiled village of **Tyringham** ❼ became an artists' colony in the early 20th century. **Ashintully Gardens** (Sodem Road; tel: 413-298 3329; mid-June–early Oct Wed and Sat pm; charge), a charming assemblage of fountains, ponds, and statuary, is all that remains of the magnificent estate of the Egyptologist

and politician Robb de Peyster Tytus (1875–1913), which was destroyed by fire. Recreating it was the 30-year project of composer John McLennan.

Bilbo Baggins would feel at home at **Santarella** (75 Main Road), the fairytale "gingerbread house" and studio of Sir Henry Hudson Kitson, sculptor of the *Minute Man* statue in Lexington. Although only open for functions, it is worth a drive-by.

Jacob's Pillow (358 George Carter Road; tel: 413-243 0745; www.jacobspillow.org; tickets go on sale in Feb), America's premier dance festival, is held every summer near **Becket** ❽. Over 50 dance troupes and performers, over 200 free performances, talks, events, and tours fill the schedule.

In the terraced grounds at Naumakeg, Steele's Blue Steps is a series of deep blue fountain pools flanked by four flights of stairs ascending a hillside and overhung by birch trees.

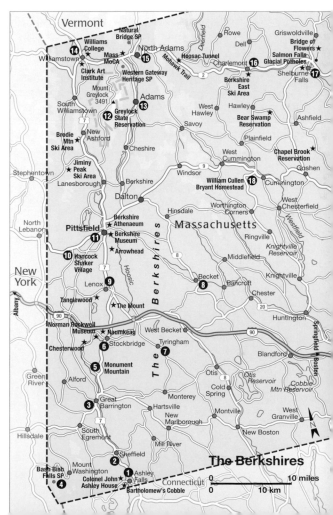

Lenox

Farther north, off Route 7, in **Lenox** 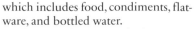, are novelist Edith Wharton's grand neoclassical 1902 mansion and magnificent formal gardens at **The Mount** (2 Plunkett Street; tel: 413-551 5111; open daily; charge). After a \$9 million restoration, they now look much as they did when she wrote *Ethan Frome*, *The House of Mirth*, and other works here.

Just out of town, **Tanglewood**, the 550-acre (220-hectare) summer home of the Boston Symphony Orchestra (297 West Street, Route 183; tel: 413-637 5165/888-266 1200; bso.org; open July–Aug; charge), has been a haven for performers, students, and music lovers since 1937. The BSO, the Boston Pops, and special guest artists also perform throughout the summer season in the 6,000-seat Music Shed, designed by architect Eero Saarinen. Tickets to Saturday morning rehearsals are offered at a reduced price.

There is a café and grille on the grounds, but picnicking is a huge part of the Tanglewood experience. The on-site Meals to Go offers several options, including the Picnic Tote for Two, which includes food, condiments, flatware, and bottled water.

Also in the grounds is a replica of the little red cottage where Nathaniel Hawthorne lived and wrote *The House of the Seven Gables* and *Tanglewood Tales*.

Continue on Route 183 past the entrance to Tanglewood to visit **Kripalu** (tel: 866-200 5203; www. kripalu.org), the country's largest center for yoga and holistic health. "Shadowbrook" was once the estate of Andrew Carnegie. Day passes – most generally available off-season and weekdays – include use of all facilities.

Hancock Shaker Village

"'Tis a gift to be simple," says the old Shaker hymn, and the **Hancock Shaker Village** ⑩ (tel: 413-443 0188; open mid-Apr–Oct; charge), on Route US 20, 3 miles (5km) west of Pittsfield, testifies to the virtues of simplicity.

The Shakers settled in Hancock in the late 1780s. The community prospered through farming, printing, selling garden seeds and herbs, and making their distinctively designed furnishings.

BELOW: a sculpture at A Chapel for Humanity.

A Chapel for Humanity

After visiting MASS MoCA, make a pilgrimage to 82 Summer Street and Eric Rudd's epic sculptural work, *A Chapel for Humanity*. Inside the 1893 building, last used as a Unitarian Church, 150 stylized human figures are grouped in the nave, positioned to evoke religious and social themes. Visitors follow pathways around and through the groupings, encouraged to reflect on the nature of mankind, relationships, and society.

Rudd started the work in 1991 and completed the body of it over the next decade. He has since added low-relief panels on the ceiling of another 250 figures observing the scene below them. The chapel (tel: 800-689 0978) is open Wednesday to Sunday in the summer, weekends in the fall.

Shakers lived in Hancock until the 1950s, when the community had dwindled to a few staunch survivors, celibacy and changing times having led to their decline. The 20 buildings in the village are open for self-guided tours.

Pittsfield

Returning to Route 7, continue north into **Pittsfield ⑪**, the Berkshire County seat and largest city (population 52,000). Herman Melville completed *Moby-Dick* (1851) while living at Arrowhead (off Route 7 at 780 Holmes Road; tel: 413-442 1793; open Memorial Day–Columbus Day; guided tours hourly; charge). He lived in the 1780 farmhouse from 1850 to 1863; the view of the distant hills, he claimed, reminded him of the rolling ocean as he labored at his masterpiece.

A room in the **Berkshire Athenaeum** (1 Wendell Avenue; tel: 413-449 9480; open Mon–Sat) exhibits photographs, documents and memorabilia of Melville.

Theater-lovers praise the **Barrington Stage Company** (30 Union Street, Pittsfield; tel: 413-236 8888; www.barringtonstageco.org). The company supports two stages, one which presents familiar and classic works, the other dedicated to new plays and a musical lab.

The **Berkshire Museum** (39 South Street; tel: 413-443 7171; daily; charge) presents an eclectic collection of natural science and history exhibits, ranging from a 143lbs (65kg) meteorite to shards of Babylonian cuneiform tablets. Its art collection is equally eclectic: it was the first gallery to exhibit Norman Rockwell, but it also showcased Andy Warhol and Robert Rauschenberg.

North to Williamstown

Off Route 7, just north of Lanesborough, turn right to **Greylock State Reservation ⑫** (tel: 413-499 4262; mass.gov/dcr/parks). Rising to 3,491ft (1,064 meters), Mt Greylock is the tallest peak in Massachusetts. At the top is a distinctive granite monument, the 92ft (28-meter) Veterans' Memorial Tower, commemorating the casualties of all America's wars.

From the top, the writer Nathaniel Hawthorne looked down upon

Food and music mix at Tanglewood.

BELOW: the Hancock Shaker Village.

The Veterans' Memorial Tower.

BELOW: music makers celebrate fall in the Berkshires.

Williamstown – "a white village and a steeple set like a daydream among the high mountain waves." The visitor center at the base of the mountain is open daily.

Route 7 continues north past the turnoff for **Jiminy Peak**, with the highest skiing mountain in the state.

Susan B. Anthony, the 19th-century social reformer, abolitionist, and suffragist, was born in **Adams** ⓭. Her birthplace has been restored as a museum (67 East Road; tel: 413-743 7121; Memorial Day–Columbus Day Thur–Mon, Columbus Day–Memorial Day Thur–Sat; charge) to her life and the history of the causes she espoused. The house itself was in excellent condition when the restoration began and much of it is original.

Williamstown

In the state's northwest corner, **Williamstown** ⓮, among the most beautiful of New England villages, is home to two excellent art museums. The **Williams College Museum of Art** (Main Street; tel: 413-597 2429; open Tue–Sat; Sun pm), under the auspices of **Williams College** (founded in 1793), houses more than 12,000 works from diverse eras and cultures, with a special emphasis on modern and contemporary art.

Just down the street is the exceptional **Sterling and Francine Clark Art Institute** (225 South Street; tel: 413-458 2303; open July–Aug daily, Sept–June Tue–Sun; charge June–Oct). Between 1918 and 1956, the Clarks amassed a superb private collection that included silver and porcelain, as well as European and American paintings, including works by Botticelli, Goya, Gainsborough, and Fragonard. The museum is best known, however, for its French Impressionist collection. There are additional galleries in the new Stone Hill Center, designed by Japanese minimalist architect Tadao Ando.

Along the Mohawk Trail

The **Mohawk Trail** (Route 2) winds for 63 miles (101km) eastward from Williamstown, across I–91 to Orange. The section from North Adams to Greenfield (I–91) is a designated

Summer Festivals in the Berkshires

Tanglewood is the best known of several Berkshires summer music and theatrical festivals, but cultural junkies can overdose on the number and variety of events. The South Mountain Concerts (tel: 413-442 2106; www.southmountainconerts.org), featuring chamber music by renowned performers on most Sunday afternoons at 3pm in September and October, take place south of Pittsfield, on Route 7. For Renaissance and Baroque music, head for the Aston Magna Festival (tel: 413-528 3595; www.astonmagna.org), at St James Church in Great Barrington and at the Clark Museum in Williamstown.

When the Jacob's Pillow Dance Festival was launched in the early 1930s in the hill town of Becket, southeast of Pittsfield on State 8, modern dance was in its infancy. Today, it's a national institution and hosts a 10-week summer program (tel: 413-243 9919; www.jacobspillow.org).

At the Berkshire Theater Festival (tel: 413-298 5576; www.berkshiretheater.org) in Stockbridge, the emphasis is on American classics. For fans of the Bard, there's Shakespeare & Co (tel: 413-637 1199; www.shakespeare.org) in Lenox, performing throughout the year. Film buffs attend the Berkshire International Film Festival (www.biff.slated.com) in Great Barrington every June for screenings of dozens of indie and international films.

scenic drive. An old Indian path-turned-roadway, it offers some of the most rugged and romantic scenery in the Berkshires. It is a popular leaf-peeping route in the fall.

Stop in **North Adams ⓯** to visit one of the state's best museums, the **Massachusetts Museum of Contemporary Art (MASS MoCA))** (Junction Route 2 and Marshall Street; tel: 413-664 4481; www.mass-moca.org; open Wed–Mon; charge). The vast, renovated 19th-century factory complex houses a fine collection of contemporary art, including some pieces so large they've not been exhibited before. The large space is also a performance arts center, presenting a year-round program of dance, cabaret, films, and avant-garde theatre. The Museum's **Kidspace** (open Sat–Sun noon–4pm) is a contemporary art gallery and workshop for the kids.

Western Gateway Heritage State Park (115 State Street, Building 4; tel: 413-663 6312; open daily), in a restored freight yard, chronicles the town's history, including the

building of the nearby 4.75-mile (7.6km) Hoosac railroad tunnel. An engineering marvel at the time, it was a deadly project. Two hundred men died during its construction.

Just north on Route 8, in **Natural Bridge State Park** (tel: 413-663 6392; open Memorial Day–Columbus Day daily; charge), a water-eroded bridge that was formed in the last ice age spans a vast chasm.

Charlemont

In **Charlemont ⓰**, the Mohawk Trail winds past *Hail to the Sunrise*, a stirring statue of a Mohawk warrior performing his morning thanksgiving ritual. It was erected in 1932 to commemorate the Native Americans who used the trail as a migration route back when it was a dirt road through the forest. A pool near the monument is lined with stones inscribed with messages from tribes and councils from across North America. Farther along, the **Berkshire East** ski area ski area has summer activities as well as winter skiing.

Crab   Apple   Whitewater (Route 2; tel: 800-553 7238; http://

In Hail to the Sunrise, a Mohawk Indian lifts his arms to the Great Spirit.

BELOW LEFT: fishing on the Deerfield River, best known for its trout.
BELOW: hiking in Greylock State Reservation.

The Bridge of Flowers at Shelburne Falls, tended by the local women's club.

BELOW: the potholes at Shelburne Falls.

crabapplewhitewater.com) offers half- and full-day rafting trips on the Deerfield and Millers rivers for all skill and courage levels.

Bridge of Flowers

In **Shelburne Falls** ⑰, turn onto Route 2A East to visit the one-of-a-kind Bridge of Flowers, a trolley bridge until 1928, now pedestrian-only, which displays more than 500 varieties of flowers, vines, and shrubs. When the flowers are in bloom, it's truly worth a stop. At the **Shelburne Falls Trolley Museum** (May–Oct Sat–Sun and holidays, July and August Mon; charge), climb aboard for a spin on an 1896 trolley car that used the bridge. The glacial-carved **Salmon Falls Glacial Potholes** at the base of Shelburne Falls are no longer accessible, but you can view them from an overlook which explains the curious derivation of these geologic oddities.

Head south on Route 112, passing by the **Bear Swamp Reservation**, a 285-acre (115-hectare) wilderness area with 3 miles (5km) of hiking trails, and **Chapel Brook Reservation**,

whose Pony Mountain is popular with technical climbers. Both are properties of the Trustees of Reservations (tel: 413-684 0148; thetrustees.org). The pools that form at the base of Chapel Falls are a delightful spot to cool off on a hot summer's day.

The Bryant Homestead

Turn west where routes 112 and 9 merge to **Cummington** and the **William Cullen Bryant Homestead** ⑱ (Bryant Road off Route 112; tel: 413-634 2244; House: July–Aug Sat; tours at 1 and 3pm; charge. Grounds: open daily; free). This was the boyhood home of Bryant (1794–1878), a widely published poet, editor/publisher of the *New York Evening Post*, and mentor to Walt Whitman. Bryant used the house as a summer retreat, converting it from Colonial style to Victorian. Today it is filled with objects he purchased while traveling overseas. There are footpaths and hiking trails round the property.

Continue west on Route 9 back to Pittsfield and Route 7, or east on Route 9 to Northampton and I–91.

Shelburne Falls' Potholes

Visitors to Shelburne Falls can view a fascinating geologic display in the form of potholes in the granite boulders at the base of Salmon Falls. About 50 near-perfect holes pockmark the rocks; the smallest is only 6 inches (15cm) diameter, while the largest is 39 feet (12 meters) in diameter. The "kettles" – to use their proper geologic name – were formed when stones were caught in the rushing waters of the falls at the end of the last ice age. The whirlpool effect caused trapped stones to slowly grind the circular indentations. Access to the boulders is prohibited, but you can get a good look at the rocks from an observation platform on Deerfield Avenue.

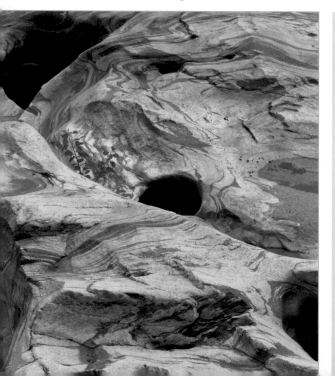

RESTAURANTS AND BARS

Prices for a three-course dinner per person with a half-bottle of house wine:
$ = under $20
$$ = $20–45
$$$ = $45 60
$$$$ = over $60

Restaurants

Great Barrington

Barrington Brewery
420 Stockbridge Road
Tel: 413-528 8282
www.barringtonbrewery.net
$$
At any time, they have at least eight ales and stouts brewed on-site on tap. They are also the first brewery in the east to use solar power to heat the water used in the brewing process and restaurant. Very casual dining area and menu, with an emphasis on comfort foods.

Route 7 Grill
999 Main Street
Tel: 413-528 3235
www.route7grill.com **$$**
Beef, pork, and chicken – all from local farms – smoked in-house over hickory wood. Outdoor patio in the shadow of June Mountain is the perfect place to appreciate that pulled pork platter.

Xicoh Mexican Restaurant
50 Stockbridge Road
Tel: 413-528 2002
www.xicohmexican.com **$$**
Just say "Shee-Ko." If you must, you can order the usual combo platters, but this is Mexican fine dining. They brag about their mole dishes, and they have fun applying Mexican treatment to non-standard ingredients: Shitake Chipotle, for instance.

Lenox

Blantyre
16 Blantyre Road (off Route 20)
Tel: 413-637 3556
www.blantyre.com **$$$$**
The place for the elegant, blow-out formal dinner, served in the paneled room of the Tudor mansion, with big bouquets on the tables, Oriental carpets on the floors, and antique sideboards along the walls. The five-course tasting menu (there's a vegetarian version) is worth considering. They can also prepare baskets for an unforgettable picnic. Reservations and jacket and tie required.

Firefly
71 Church Street
Tel: 413-637 2700
www.fireflylenox.com **$$$–$$$$**
New American bistro with a rather small menu. Upscale comfort food: vegetarian shepherd's pie, beef brisket. The prix-fixe menu with wine is a particularly good deal. Gluten-free options (including desserts). Reservations recommended.

Prime Italian Steakhouse & Bar
15 Franklin Street
Tel: 413-637 2998
www.primelenox.com
$$–$$$
Candlelight, reasonable prices, and fine service have made this a local favorite. Look for classic Italian dishes, along with savory beef offerings including a superb rib eye and braised short ribs.

Church Street Café
65 Church Street
Tel: 413-637 2745
www.churchstreetlenox.com
$$–$$$
Completely renovated using reclaimed woods for the flooring and tables and other recycled material and creating a spacious, airy atmosphere with clean lines and good energy. The menu is equally fresh, with many grilled items.

Sudbury

Longfellows Wayside Inn
72 Wayside Inn Road
Tel: 978-443 1776 **$$$**
In a 1716 tavern and inn, t's very atmospheric wth a menu that George and the rest of the Founding Fathers would enjoy – basics done with a bit of flare. New patio open for summer lunches.

West Stockbridge

Truc Orient Express
3 Harris Street
Tel: 413-232 4204
www.trucorientexpress.om
$–$$$
A handsome dining room, fne service, and creatively presented Vietnamese fare, with specialties such as Shaking Beef and Happy Pancake.

Bars

Barrington Brewery and Restaurant
Jennifer House Commons, Route 7, Great Barrington
Handcrafted beers made in a barn on the premises – Barrington Brown is a rich, English-style ale; also try stouts, lagers, IPAs, and seasonal specialties. Tasty pub menu, including an updated "plowman's lunch."

Brick House Pub
425 Park Street, Great Barrington
Popular local hangout with a broad selection of beers on tap. Locals swear by the burgers and wings.

Old Heritage Tavern
12 Housatonic Street, Lenox
An inexpensive, casual spot in an atmospheric 125-year-old building. Locals and the Tanglewood crowd belly up for expertly poured Guinness.

Pittsfield Brew Works
34 Depot Street, Pittsfield
The stouts and porters brewed on-site at this big, friendly establishment have an avid following. Inexpensive "pub grub" includes burgers and fried calamari.

The Purple Pub
8 Bank Street, Williamstown
Williams College students have hoisted their cold ones here since 1973. The baked-not-fried appetizers are served until midnight.

RHODE ISLAND

With Providence's cosmopolitan, collegiate, cultural energy; Newport's elegant opulence; and great stretches of ocean coast and inland countryside, the smallest state offers a long list of attractions

lthough the smallest state in the nation, Rhode Island always had a disproportionate influence in power, prosperity, and prestige. Free-thinking settlers inspired innovations in industry; vessels sailing from her ports brought wealth from fishing and trade; millionaires in the Gilded Age of the 19th century built stunning mansions on oceanside cliffs they called their summer "cottages."

Rhode Island's official founder was clergyman Roger Williams. Driven out of Salem in 1636 for preaching religious tolerance, Williams headed south to establish a settlement where all were free to practice their own faith. Traveling by canoe with a cadre of followers, he arrived at the head of Narragansett Bay and negotiated with the Wampanoag people for permission to start a settlement which he named Providence. In 1663, Charles II granted a charter to the rather wordily named Colony of Rhode Island and Providence Plantations – a name it still officially retains as a state. There's debate over where "Rhode Island" comes from. Explorer Giovanni da Verrazzano compared Aquidneck Island (the location of Newport) to the Greek isle of Rhodes. A less romantic, but more probable, claim may be by the practically minded Dutch explorer

Adriaen Block. He noted that the soil in the islands was reddish in colour or "Roode Eyland."

Soon many of the era's "outsiders" flocked to Rhode Island's shores. Quakers fleeing Puritan persecution made Newport their home, and as early as the 18th century, Jews from Portugal and Holland settled here. The first Baptist church, Quaker Meeting House, and Jewish synagogue in the colonies were all established in Rhode Island. In the ensuing centuries immigrants from Europe, the Mediterranean, China, and

Main attractions
WATERPLACE PARK AND RIVERWALK
RISD MUSEUM
BROWN UNIVERSITY
NEWPORT
OCEAN DRIVE
BLOCK ISLAND

PRECEDING PAGES: Snug Harbor, Block Island.
LEFT: the Elms, on Bellevue Avenue. RIGHT:
Newport's Second Beach.

TIP

La Gondola (tel: 401-421 8877; www.gondolari.com) offers a unique way to tour the river: in a genuine Venetian gondola. Private rides for parties from two to six people are offered evenings May–Oct, and the gondoliers provide cheese, ice buckets, glasses, and, of course, music.

Cape Verde followed. With a population in excess of 1 million crowded into its 1,214 sq miles (3,143 sq km), Rhode Island is a bustling, multicultural cross-section of New England life.

Revitalized Providence

Rhode Island's capital is wonderfully diverse. With five schools of higher education and a rejuvenated downtown, it hums with a creative vibe. It cherishes the outstanding 18th- and 19th-century architecture throughout its downtown and its appealingly diverse neighborhoods. It's also easily reached from Boston, a feasible day trip by car, train, or bus.

In its early days, **Providence ❶** struggled to survive. The hilly, rocky soil was not conducive to agriculture, and the same predisposition to dissent which attracted many settlers led to arguments over any form of community goals or government. Still, its deepwater port thrived. By the 1760s, Providence and Newport were the busiest seaports in the New World. In the years following the Civil War, the Industrial Revolution became the economic driving force for the region. As a major manufacturing center, Providence was dubbed "the cradle of American industry." But with the Great Depression and the textile industry's exodus to the south, Providence lost its industrial pre-eminence. Today it is rebounding as a center for finance, health care, healthcare, and higher education, while its designation as the state capital insures strong government employment. As one of the only two

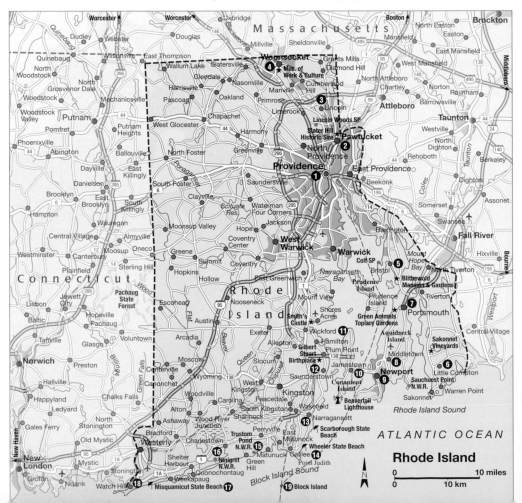

Rhode Island

0   10 miles

0   10 km

ATLANTIC OCEAN

deepwater harbors in New England, it remains one of the busiest ports in the North East. But like most other cities in the region, it struggles with unemployment and poverty. The city has lavished restorative attention on its downtown. Massive redevelopment removed railroad tracks and roadways that covered the Providence River; old buildings received facelifts and found new tenants; parks became clean, safe, popular gathering places. Providence is a city best seen on foot. The street system follows no discernable pattern and can be a challenge even with GPS. Many residents forego cars altogether and walk to their destination. It's a compact, lovely city in which to stroll. Like Rome, it was built on seven hills, the three best-known being College (officially, Prospect), Federal, and Constitution.

Center of town

Constitution Hill is impossible to miss because of the **State Capitol** Ⓐ that dominates its crest (Smith Street; tel: 401-222 3983; reserve ahead for tours Mon–Fri at 9am, 10am, 11am. Self-guided tour brochure available at entrance). Exhibits include an historic portrait of George Washington by Rhode Islander Gilbert Stuart.

Just across the way, **Providence Place** Ⓑ has more than 180 stores, restaurants, and leisure options, including the six-story **Feinstein IMAX** theater (tel: 401-270-4646) in an enclosed three-story shopping mall.

The 4-acre (1.6-hectare) **Waterplace Park and Riverwalk** Ⓒ are the stars of Providence's waterside renaissance. The long-neglected riverside was cleaned up, equipped with an Italian-inspired piazza, cobblestone walkways, and boat landings. The **WaterFire** nights draw thousands of spectators and participants to downtown.

Kennedy Plaza Ⓓ is the site for a wide-ranging schedule of free concerts, outdoor art exhibits, and a marketplace. In winter, there's an outdoor ice-skating rink that's twice the size of the one in Rockefeller Center.

The Mile of History

In historic East Side, **Benefit Street**, the "Mile of History," deserves walking from one end to the other. Originally it was a twisting dirt path that led to family graveyards. When a communal cemetery was created and ancestral remains moved there, the lane was widened and straightened "for the benefit of the people of Providence." It quickly became the haunt of the Provident elite. There are more than 200 restored 18th- and 19th-century buildings built by sea captains and merchants; many bear bronze plaques identifying their original owners and dates of construction. In the late 1960s and early 1970s the street was run down and nearly demolished as part of a renewal program; only the efforts of the Providence Preservation Society (www.ppsri.org) saved the day. Staff at the John Brown House Museum offer 90-minute walking tours (Tue–Sat at 11am mid-June–mid-Oct; charge).

In 1638 Roger Williams established the **Meeting House of the First Baptist Church in America** Ⓔ (75 North Main Street; tel: 401-454 3418; guided tours June–Oct

EAT

If you're hungry late at night, look for the Haven Brothers Diner. A true original rolling food cart, it rumbles into place on Dorrance Street about 4.30pm and feeds lobster rolls, burgers, and other hot-oil-reliant basics to an endlessly interesting collection of customers until 5am.

BELOW: a statue of Roger Williams in a public park stands guard over the city he founded, Providence.

TIP

Cindy Salvado leads three-hour culinary walking tours (tel: 401-934 2149; www.savoringrhodeisland.com) of Federal Hill which go behind the scenes at restaurants, butchers, and specialty Italian food shops. Watch ravioli being made, inhale lungsful of garlic, and sip some good Chianti.

Mon–Fri and after Sunday worship service; Nov–May, self-guided tours Mon–Fri; charge). Built in 1774–75, it seated 1,200 people, over one-third of the population of Providence at the time. It is a premier example of traditional New England architecture. You can hear the magnificent Foley-Baker organ during the 10am Sunday service.

Prospect Terrace ❻, on Congdon Street, is a tiny park that gives a fine view of the city. Roger Williams, the city's founder, is buried here. A statue of Williams stands on the bluff overlooking his city.

The bookstacks of **Providence Atheneum** ❼ (251 Benefit Street; tel: 401-421 6970; open daily) witnessed the demise of the courtship of Edgar Allan Poe and a local resident, Sarah Whitman (possibly the inspiration for "Annabel Lee"). While visiting the library, she learned he had broken his promise to stay sober. She broke their engagement, and they never saw each other again. The library is worth a visit for its collections of rare books, prints, and paintings.

Virtually opposite is the prestigious **Rhode Island School of Design (RISD) Museum** ❽ (224 Benefit Street; tel: 401-454 6500; open Tue–Sun; entrance fee except Sun 10am–1pm, third Thur of each month 5–9pm, and last Sat of month). It has paintings by 19th-century American masters and French Impressionists, a major Oriental collection, Egyptian and Ancient art, 20th-century American furniture, and decorative arts.

Brown University ❾ (College Hill) dominates this part of Providence. The independent, co-educational Ivy League establishment was founded as Rhode Island College in Warren in 1764, and moved to Providence in 1770. The name change came in 1804 in recognition of a $5,000 endowment from alumnus and Providence businessman Nicholas Brown. In 2010, it was recognized as "The Happiest College in the Country" for the student satisfaction in curriculum, cultural and campus life, community service opportunities, and athletics. Among the buildings of interest on the campus: the 1770 University Hall

BELOW: residents of Providence stop at a Portuguese market.

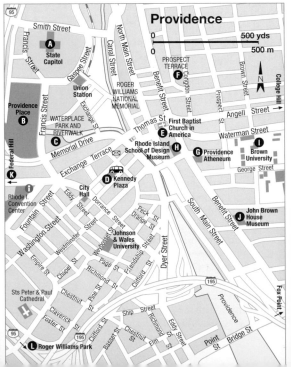

(on the Quadrangle), used as a barracks during the Revolutionary War; the 1904 Beaux Arts John Carter Brown Library (corner of George and Brown streets) with the largest collection of primary sources of pre-1825 Americana; and the Annmary Brown Memorial (21 Brown Street; open Mon–Fri) with European and American paintings from the 16th to the early 20th centuries.

The heart of the **College Hill** shopping area is Thayer Street, which borders the eastern edge of the Brown campus. It caters to collegiate clientele with interesting restaurants, bars, shops, and bookstores. "The most magnificent and elegant private mansion that I have ever seen on this continent," said John Quincy Adams of the 1786 **John Brown House Museum** ❶ (52 Power Street; tel: 401-273 7507; tours Tue–Sat; charge). Brown's life reflected the early years of the Republic. More than just viewing a collection of period furnishings, you learn about the genesis of the China tea trade, women's life and education, and Brown's participation in the slave

trade. The museum staff also gives tours of Benefit Street.

Federal Hill ❶, to the west of I–95, is Providence's "Little Italy." The sculpture of the pignola hanging from the arch across Atwells Avenue is one of the most recognizable landmarks in Providence. It is a traditional Italian symbol of welcome. Wander along Atwells Avenue and enjoy the aromas of crusty Italian breads, cheeses, herbs, and spices. DePasquale Plaza is lined with open-air cafés. It's a good stop for a meal and people-watching. In recent years, the area has added trendy boutiques and art galleries. South of Brown University and bordered by the Providence and Seekonk rivers, Fox Point is home to the city's Portuguese community. On holy days, celebrants parade with statues of the Virgin Mary while children dressed in their best suits and crinolines follow along. Early morning brings the tantalizing scent of Portuguese sweet bread wafting from small bakeries.

It's well worth a trek south on I–95 to exit 17 to see **Roger Williams Park** ❶ (Elmwood Avenue; tel: 401-785 9450), a 435-acre (176-hectare)

Marina on the Providence River. The river is 8 miles (13km) long and has a barrier near the city to guard it against tidal floods.

BELOW: WaterFire is a festival that takes place in the summer evenings on the Providence River.

WaterFire

WaterFire (www.waterfire.org for schedule of installations) is a unique expression of interactive installation art that graces Providence's riverfront on several nights throughout the year. More than 100 braziers in the river are lit at sunset, while torch-lit vessels drift down the river accompanied by sounds and music related to ritual, religious, and symbolic inspiration for the living artwork. Artist Barnaby Evans created the first WaterFire in 1994. A second in 1996 was so successful that a non-profit organization was created to support and fund future performances. The event draws thousands of people who are integral to the success of the living sculpture by their involvement with the music, the movement on and around the river, and their emotional response to the evening.

The resilient Rhode Island Red was originally bred in the 1830s in Adamsville, now part of Little Compton, where a monument to it was erected in 1925.

BELOW: the green at Brown University.

complex filled with ponds, specimen trees, and outdoor sculpture. The acclaimed **Zoo** (daily; charge) is home to nearly 1,000 animals, including some of the rarest, living in natural surroundings. The **Botanical Center** (Tue–Sun; charge) is the largest indoor display garden in New England. Outside, there is a wonderfully scented rose garden maze. The **Museum of Natural History and Planetarium** (daily; charge) concentrates heavily on items from Rhode Island, including fossils which pre-date the dinosaurs. For children, visit the **Carousel Village**, with a Victorian-style carousel and a barrier-free Hasbro playground.

Leave the park via the Montgomery Avenue exit, jog right on Narragansett, then turn left on Harborside. Foodies will salivate over the **Johnson and Wales Culinary Arts Museum** (315 Harborside Boulevard; tel: 401-598 2805; Tue–Sun; charge). It bubbles over with gastronomic exhibits from the Roman Empire to the present day, including over 60,000 cookbooks and collections donated by chefs and restaurateurs.

BLACKSTONE RIVER VALLEY

America's Industrial Revolution began in the Blackstone Valley. Called "America's hardest working river," the Blackstone runs for 46 miles (74km) from Worcester MA to Providence.

The **John H. Chafee Blackstone River Valley National Heritage Corridor** links 24 communities along the river. The **Blackstone Valley Visitor Center** (175 Main Street; tel: 401-724 2200; daily) in **Pawtucket ❷**, 5 miles (8km) northeast of Providence on I-95, has information on most of the sites along the route. There's a 20-minute orientation film about the rise and fall of the textile industry. The **Blackstone Valley Explorer** (tel: 401-724 2200; www.rivertourblackstone.com; May–Oct Sun afternoons; charge), a 40-passenger riverboat, departs from Central Falls for a 45-minute narrated tour of the river's industrialized past and efforts to restore its ecosystem.

Techniques of mechanized textile production were pioneered in 1793 by Moses Brown. The riverfront **Slater Mill Living History Museum**

(67 Roosevelt Avenue; tel: 401-725 8638; open Mar–Apr Sat–Sun, May–Oct Tue–Sun, Nov Sat–Sun; closed Jan–Feb; charge) offers a rare look into the earliest days of the Industrial Revolution, showing how textiles progressed from being handcrafts to a major industrial undertaking.

Lincoln

Seven miles (11km) to the northwest of Pawtucket, in **Lincoln ❸**, Lincoln Woods State Park (tel: 401-722 3033; daily) has one of the largest freshwater beaches in the area, plus hiking, kayaking, and fishing. There's a newly constructed covered bridge and trail rides. Blackstone River State Park (Lower River Road; tel: 401-723 7892) follows the course of the Blackstone Canal towpath. Adjacent to the path, the **Wilbur Kelly House Museum** (Lower River Road; tel: 401-333 0295; open Apr–Oct daily) narrates the history of the river and canal and how it was long used for transportation by Native Americans.

Twelve miles (19km) of the planned 48-mile (77km) **Blackstone River Bikeway** (tel: 401-333 0295; www.blackstonebikeway.org), which will eventually stretch from Providence to Worcester, are now completed between Lincoln and Cumberland. Blackstone Valley Outfitters (tel: 401-312 0369; www.bvori.com) in Lincoln rents bikes and kayaks.

Woonsocket

In **Woonsocket ❹** on the Massachusetts border, visit the **Museum of Work and Culture** (42 South Main Street, Market Square; tel: 401-769 9675; daily; charge). Interactive displays immerse visitors in the lives of the French Canadians who migrated from Quebec to work in the textile mills in the 1840s. In 1900, 60 percent of Woonsocket's population was French Canadian.

EAST BAY

Head east out of Providence on I–195 to Route 114 south (exit 7), which winds along the eastern shore of East Bay. **Bristol ❺**, about 15 miles (24km) south, held the nation's first Fourth of July parade in 1785. Its patriotic celebration continues all during July. Even the center line on Main Street is red, white, and blue. At the **Blithewold Mansion, Gardens & Arboretum** (101 Ferry Road; tel: 401-253 2707; www.blithewold.org; grounds open daily; mansion open mid-Apr–mid-Oct, Wed–Sun and most Mon holidays; Dec: limited hours; charge), visitors can tour the 45-room mansion built by Pennsylvania coal magnate Augustus van Wickle in 1908 to resemble a 17th-century English country manor. (Blithewold is old English for "happy woodland.") The 33 acres (13 hectares) of landscaped grounds include rock, water, and rose gardens.

The Audubon Society's **Environmental Education Center** (1401 Hope Street/Route 114; tel: 401-934 2149; daily) has some of the best bird watching in New England. The guided tours of the grounds and overlooks of Narragansett Bay are particularly nice for those unfamiliar with the region's flora and fauna.

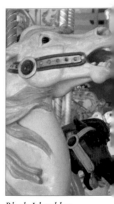

Rhode Island has several Victorian carousels, including the Crescent Park Looff Carousel in East Providence, a National Historic Landmark (open Easter–Columbus Day Thur–Sun, tel: 401-435 7518.

BELOW: Old Slater Mill, Pawtucket.

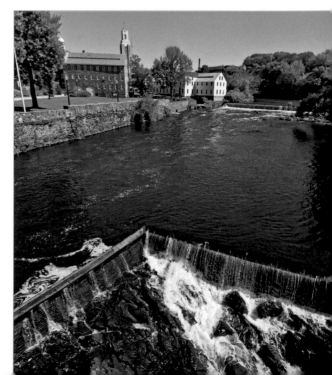

Bowen's Wharf at Christmas. In season, the Jamestown & Newport Ferry (tel: 401-423 9900) runs a passenger service between here and Jamestown Village, Rose Island, Fort Adams, and Perrotti Park. Ride-all-day passes are available.

BELOW: Green Animals Topiary Gardens.

The America's Cup Hall of Fame, more than 50 classic yachts, and over 500 scale models used by shipbuilder Capt. Nat Herreshoff, are displayed at **Herreshoff Marine and America's Cup Museum** (1 Burnside Street; tel: 401-253 5000; open May–Oct daily; charge). He's credited with designing eight consecutive defenders of the America's Cup. Visitors can step aboard many of the famous, vintage, and impeccably restored sailing and racing vessels.

Colt State Park on the west side of Bristol Harbor (Poppasquash Road off Route 114) is considered the gem of Rhode Island's state parks. The entire western boundary of the park is a panoramic vista of Narragansett Bay. The 464-acre (188-hectare) park has well-tended fruit trees, flowering plants, and putting-green-perfect lawns. There are over 100 picnic tables scattered across the grounds. The open-air **Chapel-by-the-Sea**, with a backdrop of the water, is a popular spot for weddings. The park is the location of **Coggeshall Farm Museum** (tel: 401-253 9062; Tue–Sun; charge). Southern New England's only

hands-on, multisensory living history museum, it transports visitors back to a working farm in 1799. Accurately clothed interpreters working with equally authentic tools and heirloom plants and animals recreate Rhode Island's agricultural past.

Little Compton and the eastern peninsula

A 30-minute detour to Rhode Island's less-visited eastern peninsula takes you to the state's oldest winery and one of its oldest towns. Leaving Bristol, take Route 114 N to Route 24 N. Take exit 5 (North Tiverton) on Route 138 and follow the turn onto Route 77 to head south. (This is Rhode Island. Distances are not great.)

Folks drive in from as far as Providence to get their recommended daily allowance of calcium at **Gray's Ice Cream** (tel: 401-624 4500; May–Sept Mon–Thur 6.30am–9pm, Fri–Sun 6.30am–10pm; Oct–Apr Tue–Sun noon–8pm) at the junction of Route 77 and Route 179.

The route passes through undeveloped countryside on its way to **Little Compton ❻**. The town was first settled by entrepreneurial Pilgrims eager to expand their land holdings. Many houses from the 17th to the 19th centuries surround the town common – the only communal grazing area left in the state – although you are more likely to see residents walking their Labradors than watching their Holsteins.

Just outside town is **Sakonnet Vineyards** (162 W. (162 W. Main Road; tel: 800-919-4637; tours daily at noon and 3pm; tasting room open daily). Founded in 1975, it takes advantage of soil and microclimate similar to the maritime climates of northern France to produce Vidal Blanc, Chardonnay, and Pinot Noir.

Topiary gardens

Returning to the Bristol area, just off Route 114 in **Portsmouth ❼** is **Green Animals Topiary Garden** (380 Cory's

Lane; tel: 401-847 1000; May–mid-Oct daily; charge; combined admission ticket with Newport mansions available). Eighty sculpted trees and shrubs represent everything from an ostrich to a camel.

Middletown and Aquidneck Island

The major city on Aquidneck Island is Newport, but the rest of the island should not be ignored. The environs around **Middletown** ❽ are not much changed in appearance from the earliest years of settlement. In **Paradise Valley Park** (Paradise and Prospect avenues), **Boyd's Windmill** (1801), the only eight-vaned windmill in the country, is occasionally put into operation. **Paradise School** (1875) is a classic one-room schoolhouse with displays of area history. Docents are at both locations (both open Sun July–Aug; tel: 401-849 1870; donation).

Prescott Farm (2009 West Main Street; tel: 401-849 7300; open daily dawn–dusk; free) gives a glimpse of early Aquidneck Island life through its buildings and landscape. The 1812

windmill is original to the site, while several other structures were moved from other locations. The kitchen and herb garden is noted for its plantings of heirloom varieties and use of sustainable practices. The farm offers workshops in stone wall building, beekeeping, open hearth cooking, and gardening.

Whitehall Museum House (311 Berkeley Avenue; tel: 401-846 3116; July–Aug Tue–Sun; charge) was the home of Dean (later Bishop) George Berkeley, who lived here from 1729 to 1731. He dreamed of starting a college where sons of colonists and Native Americans could study together. When funds were not forthcoming, he returned to England, but not before donating his property and library to Yale University. His gift led to the creation of the Berkeley Divinity School at Yale. A century later, when the University of California established a campus near San Francisco, they named the town where it would be built after him – Berkeley.

East of Paradise Park, **Norman Bird Sanctuary** (tel: 401-846 2577; daily 9am–5pm; charge) has over

TIP

There are interesting shops along the Thames Street Landing on Bristol's downtown waterfront. The height of elegance is the Point Pleasant Inn and Resort (tel: 401-253 0627; www.pointpleasantinn. com), a 25-acre (10-hectare) restored English mansion overlooking the bay with luxurious accommodations.

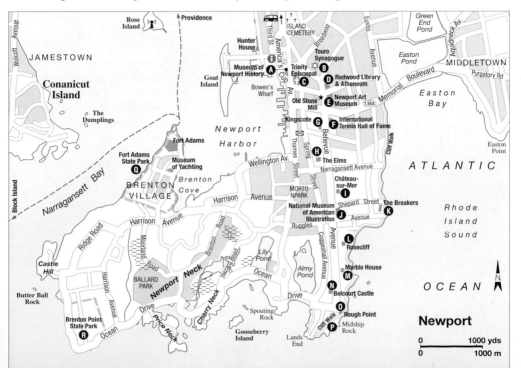

Newport

TIP

Fancy a game of tennis on courts once graced by Martina Navratilova and John McEnroe? You can rent a court from 30 minutes to 5 hours at the International Tennis Hall of Fame (tel: 401-846 0642; www.tennisfame.com) from May through September.

BELOW: a hoagie style sandwich with salami, ham, turkey, cheese, lettuce and tomato.

7 miles (11km) of trails and fabulous views of the ocean. Just beyond is **Sachuest Point National Wildlife Refuge** (tel: 401-847 5571; trails open daily dawn–dusk; visitor center daily 10am–4pm), with trails and viewing platforms. Third Beach is within the boundaries of the wildlife refuge. It is actually four separate public and semi-private beaches on Rhode Island Sound.

NEWPORT

Few places have the location, history, and ambience of **Newport ❾**. The views of sailboats and yachts in Narragansett Bay are Hollywood-perfect; the atmosphere is imbued with Revolutionary and nautical history; the elegance of the Gilded Age mansions is tempered with casual gatherings at dockside bars. Known for its music and cultural festivals, its excellent dining, and its comfortable lodgings, it's a town where visitors linger.

A good place to begin a visit is downtown at the **Visitor Information Center** (23 America's Cup Avenue;

tel: 800-976 5122/401-845 9123; www.gonewport.com). They have extensive information on the area, including maps. Be sure to pick up detailed directions to **Ocean Drive**, the stretch of Ocean Avenue that combines great Atlantic views with glimpses of Newport's grand mansions. Free 30-minute parking (have your ticket validated in the visitor center) is available in the parking lot adjacent to the center. There's also discounted parking when using public transportation.

Thames Street along the harbor is lined with shops and restaurants, many concentrated on **Bowen's Wharf**, lined with handsome craft tied up at yacht-club slips. Get your historical bearings at the award-winning **Museum of Newport History Ⓐ** (127 Thames Street; tel: 401-846 0813; daily; donation) in Washington Square, in the restored 1762 Brick Market building. Engaging displays introduce the waterfront denizens, Gilded Age millionaires, religious rebels, and ambitious immigrants who've inhabited Newport. Museum staff offer walking tours of the city.

Food in Translation

When ordering food in Rhode Island, you might need translations for some of the more unique items on the menu. A grinder in New England is known in other parts of the world as a hoagie, po'boy, or submarine sandwich. Stuffies are clam stuffing appetizers baked in a clam shell, something like clams casino. If you order chourico, you'll get a dense and spicy Portuguese sausage. A frappe (pronounced *frap*) is milk, ice cream, and flavoring mixed together. (In other places, it would be a milk shake. In Rhode Island, a milk shake is just milk and flavoring mixed together without ice cream.) A cabinet is a coffee-flavored frappe. Coffee milk is sweet coffee syrup mixed with milk. Regardless of what you order, it will almost all be delicious.

Whitehorne House (416 Thames Street; tel: 401-847 2448; May–Oct Thur–Mon; guided and self-guided tours; charge) houses the Doris Duke Collection of 18th-century Newport furniture. Some of the most outstanding examples of American furniture are displayed in the Federal mansion on the waterfront. The formal gardens behind the house recreate a period garden for an affluent, urban family. (You can purchase a combination ticket for Whitehorne House and Rough Point, Duke's mansion on Bellevue Avenue.)

The **White Horse Tavern** (26 Marlborough Street; tel: 401-849 3600) is the country's oldest operating tavern (1673). With its clapboard walls, gambrel roof, and interior beams, it is considered the very essence of 17th-century American architecture. Newport has a remarkable legacy of colonial architecture. Much of it is found around Washington Square. At 85 Touro Street, the Georgian **Touro Synagogue** ❸ is the nation's oldest Jewish house of worship (1763). The adjacent **Ambassador Loeb Visitor Center** (tel: 401-847 4794; opening hours for center and synagogue tours vary greatly during the year, so call; charge) explores Rhode Island's tradition of religious tolerance, the history of Jews in colonial and Revolutionary America, and the nation's policy of separation of Church and State. A landmark of colonial Newport is the white clapboard 1725–26 **Trinity Episcopal Church** ❻ (tel: 401-846 0660; services Sun at 8am and 10am) on Queen Anne Square. The chandeliers seem to list to the north, but it is the building which leans, the result of 300 years of resisting winds blowing from the sea.

Many of Newport's attractions, including the famous mansions, line Bellevue Avenue. The 1748–50 **Redwood Library and Atheneum** ❶ (50 Bellevue Avenue; tel: 401-847 0292; open daily; donation) is the oldest continuously used library building in the US and contains a collection of portraits of notable colonials.

The 1862 "Stick Style" **Newport Art Museum** ❺ (76 Bellevue Avenue; tel: 401-848 8200; closed Mon; charge; Sat free 10am–noon) exhibits paintings by luminaries including Winslow Homer and George Innes as well as works by regional artists.

The state-of-the-art **International Tennis Hall of Fame** ❻ (194 Bellevue Avenue; tel: 401-849 3990; open daily; charge) is the country's largest tennis museum. It's housed in the Newport Casino, which never had anything to do with gambling, but was America's most exclusive country club when it opened in 1880 and hosted the first US National Tennis Championships the following year. It displays memorabilia, trophies, art, and fashion dealing with tennis from the 12th century to the present. There's a self-guided audio tour in English, French, Spanish, and Russian.

The mansions

The Vanderbilts, Astors, and other elite of America's 19th century chose the oceanside real estate of Newport for their summer "cottages." Exercises in conspicuous consumption, they were

TIP

The Coastal Wine Trail maps out a route to the regional wineries from Newport to Cape Cod. Pick up a copy at the Newport Visitor Center or download it at www. coastalwinetrail.com.

BELOW: Trinity Episcopal Church, which has pew boxes paid for by members of the original 1726 congregation.

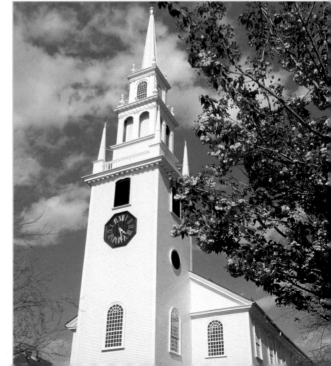

TIP

Opening times for Newport's mansions vary. Check the schedules and admission fees with Preservation Society of Newport (PSN; tel: 401-847 1000; www. newportmansions.org).

BELOW: one of the many bedrooms at Marble House.

largely abandoned as fortunes and economics changed. By the 1960s, many were deteriorating shells. Rescued by the **Preservation Society of Newport** (242 Bellevue Avenue; tel: 401-847 1000; www.newportmansions.org; seasons and hours vary greatly, call or check website; charge), many are now maintained as museums of another age. The Society sells a variety of tickets for admission to up to 11 properties. While all of the mansions have guided tours, several now have optional self-guided audio tours. The Society also sells tickets to the dockside **Hunter House** (54 Washington Street), a prosperous merchant's 1748 home, and the Topiary Gardens.

Most of the mansions are located on Bellevue Avenue. Directional signs to the area often point to "the cottages," the term the wealthy used for their summer homes. **Kingscote** was the first of the summer cottages, built in Gothic Revival "Stick Style," making playful use of asymmetry and varied textures, sprouting a wealth of pendants, lattices, and gables. It is one of the most intact historical houses in the country, containing the furnishings, art, and documents of over five generations of the King family.

The coal-rich Edward Julius Berwind commissioned **The Elms**, built in French Renaissance style, based on Château d'Asnières near Paris. It borrows from a range of styles, including Chinese, Venetian, and Louis XIV.

William S. Wetmore built **Château-sur-Mer** in 1852, a confection of Victorian lavishness, and Newport's showiest mansion when built. For a break from the mansion trek, view works by Norman Rockwell, Maxfield Parrish, and N.C. Wyeth, among others, at the **National Museum of American Illustration** (492 Bellevue Avenue; tel: 401-851 8949; general admission late May–early Sept Sat–Sun; guided tour by advance reservation Fri at 3pm; winter: Fri tours only; charge)

The Preservation Society of Newport pays the grand sum of $1 a year to rent **The Breakers**. Considered the most magnificent of the Newport "cottages," this opulent Italian Renaissance palace contains 70 rooms extravagantly adorned with marble, alabaster, gilt, mosaic, crystal, and stained glass. The kitchen alone is the size of a small house. The tour here is more in-depth than most of the others, interpreting The Breakers and the Vanderbilts with respect to their place in America's architecture, society, and culture. Self-guided audio tours are available, which reduces the wait on busy summer days.

Farther along Bellevue Avenue, Mrs Hermann Oelrichs hired Stanford White to design **Rosecliff**, an imitation of Versailles' Grand Trianon. It has a huge French-style ballroom and a heart-shaped staircase.

Marble House, another of Hunt's designs, manages to upstage The Breakers for ostentation, although it is not as large. It was built in 1892 for William K. Vanderbilt and styled after the Grand and Petit Trianons of Versailles. A Chinese teahouse stands in the grounds.

Belcourt Castle **N** (tel: 401-846 0669; 1-hour guided tours June–Aug daily, Sept Wed–Mon, Oct Thur–Mon; closed Jan) is at 657 Bellevue Avenue. Styled after a Louis XIII hunting lodge at Versailles, it is owned by Harle Hope Hanson Tinney, who may guide you on your tour. The castle has the largest collection of objets d'art of any of the mansions, including a full-size gold coronation coach.

"The Richest Little Girl in the World" spent her summers at **Rough Point O** (680 Bellevue Avenue; tel: 401-847 8344; www.newportrestoration.org; Apr–mid-May Thur–Sat, mid-May–mid-Nov Tue–Sat; charge). Doris Duke was the only child of tobacco baron James Duke. When he died in 1925, he left his 12-year-old daughter the bulk of his estate, estimated at somewhere around $80 million. The 49-room mansion was built in 1890, at the height of the Gilded Age. The landscape was created by Frederick Law Olmstead, who designed New York's Central Park. The house is as she left it, filled with French furniture, Chinese porcelains, and Turkish carpets.

(You can purchase a combination ticket for Rough Point and Whitehorne House on Newport's waterfront, which holds Duke's collection of late-18th-century furnishings.)

Strollers can examine the backyards of the Bellevue Avenue mansions from the **Cliff Walk P** (www.cliffwalk.com), a 3.5-mile (5.5km) path that overlooks Rhode Island Sound. Crusty local fishermen saved this path for public use by going to court when wealthy mansion owners tried to close it. Most of the walk is an easy, well-maintained public right-of-way, but the southern portion requires scrambling across rocks which are often slippery and subject to bracing winds. Visitors who don't wish to walk the entire length can start at the end of Narragansett Avenue and reach the water by way of the Forty Steps, partway along the route.

Music events

During the summer, Newport hosts a number of major outdoor music events, such as the Newport Folk Festival (www.newportfolkfest.net)

Rough Point was one home of the heiress and horticulturalist Doris Duke (1912–93).

BELOW: the Music Room at The Breakers.

The Cliff Walk in Newport offers views of the water and the famous mansions.

BELOW: a family farm in Little Compton

and the Newport Jazz Festival (www. newportjazzfest.net) at **Fort Adams State Park Q** (Fort Adams Drive; tel: 401-841 2400). Fortifications were first built in the early days of the Revolution; it remained the largest coastal fortification in the US until 1950 (guided tours end of May–mid-Oct daily; charge).

While there, take a look at the **Museum of Yachting** (Ocean Drive; tel: 401-847 1018; open mid-May–Oct 1, Thur–Sun; charge). Exhibits include the history of the America's Cup, which was held in Newport waters from 1930 to 1983, and the ongoing restoration of the 1885 yacht *Coronet*. You can take a water taxi across the harbor to see the work in progress. A mile out to sea, the **Rose Island Lighthouse** (tel: 401-847 4242; www. roseislandlighthouse.org; tours July 1–first weekend in Sept; charge) was abandoned after the Newport Bridge was completed in 1969, restored to its 1912 appearance and using eco-sensitive energy generation. Visitors can spend the night or become "keepers" for a week.

Ocean drive

One of the region's most magnificent drives extends for 10 miles (16km) around Narragansett Bay to the tip, where the bay meets the Atlantic Ocean, at **Brenton Point State Park R**. There are sweeping views and the rocky shores are great for exploring tidal pools and for sunset-watching.

Jamestown

Just across the Newport Bridge (toll), follow signs to historic **Jamestown ⑩**. The southern tip of Conanicut Island offers New England scenery at its most picturesque. In **Beavertail State Park** (Beavertail Road; tel: 401-423 9941), the Atlantic coast's third-oldest lighthouse is preserved at **Beavertail Lighthouse and Museum** (open Memorial Day–June 15 and Labor Day–Columbus Day weekends; June 16–Labor Day daily; charge). The tower is open periodically; call for dates.

The 275-acre (110-hectare) **Watson Farm** (445 North Road; tel: 401-423 0005; open June–mid-Oct, Tue, Thur, and Sun; charge) on Narragansett Bay has been a working farm since 1787. Visitors can take a self-guided tour and hike 2 miles (3km) of scenic trails. Just down the road is the 1787 **Jamestown Windmill** (North Main Street; tel: 401-423 0784; climb to the top and see the inner workings on weekends in July–Sept; museum open Wed–Sun).

SOUTH COUNTY

From Jamestown, continue west on Route 138 across the graceful Jamestown-Verrazano Bridge to Route 1A, and turn north to **Wickford ⑪**, whose historic waterfront, lined with galleries, shops, and restaurants, is one of the loveliest in Rhode Island. Many of the buildings in town date to the 18th century. A mile north of town is the inappropriately named **Smith's Castle** (55 Richard Smith Drive; tel: 401-294 3521; tours June–Aug

Thur–Sun, May and Oct Fri–Sun; charge). The three-story clapboard house is one of the country's oldest plantation houses. Originally built in 1678 to garrison soldiers, it now preserves four centuries of Rhode Island history, which docents in period clothing bring to life.

South along the Narragansett Bay

Backtrack 5.5 miles (9km) south on Route 1A to **Saunderstown ⑫**. One of early America's most famous portrait artists was born in 1755 at the **Gilbert Stuart Birthplace** (815 Gilbert Stuart Road; tel: 401-294 3001; open May–mid-Oct Thur–Mon; tours on the hour; charge). The property encompasses an authentically restored and furnished workingman's house of the period, the country's first snuff mill, a grist mill, a colonial herb garden, and a fish ladder that teems with frantically migrating fish in spring.

To the south on Route 1A, at the town beach in **Narragansett ⑬**, you can stroll along the pier and admire the Twin Towers – the stone structures that are the remains of a casino destroyed by fire in 1900.

Between Narragansett and Point Judith is a skein of fine, sandy state-owned beaches (parking fee).

Whale-watching tours depart from **Point Judith**. Backtrack a short distance on Route 108, past the entrance for **Captain Roger W. Wheeler State Beach** (tel: 401-789 3563; parking fee) and follow signs to **Galilee ⑭**, the departure point for the ferry to Block Island.

The **Block Island Ferry** (tel: 401-783 7996/866-783 7996; www.block-islandferry.com) offers high-speed and traditional passenger ferry service from Galilee and Newport's Fort Adams.

Southwest

Head north on Route 108 to US Route 1 and continue south along the Block Island Sound. In **South Kingston**, the **Trustom Pond National Wildlife Refuge ⑮** (1040 Matunuck Schoolhouse Road) protects the state's only undeveloped salt pond.

Jamestown Windmill ground corn from 1787 until 1895.

BELOW: Newport Bridge leads to Jamestown.

The Ocean State

Water dominates the geography of Rhode Island. Only 48 miles long and 37 miles wide (77km by 60km), it claims 400 miles (640km) of coastline. Rhode Island, in the singular, is a misnomer; there are 35 islands within the state, with names as varied as the islands are numerous: Aquidneck (also called Rhode), Block, Conanicut, and Prudence. Others include Hen, Hog, Rabbitt, Boat, Old Boy, Patience, Hope, and Despair.

Using Rhode Island as a base, pirates raided merchant ships in the North Atlantic until a clampdown in the 1720s. Later, Newport was the birthplace of the modern US Navy: President Chester Arthur developed a new fleet – built of steel, rather than wood – in Newport in the early 1880s.

Among the state's distinctions are: America's first textile mill, in Pawtucket, and America's only operational water-powered snuff mill, in Saunderstown. The state boasts the country's first synagogue, its first department store, and its oldest enclosed shopping mall.

Despite the concentrated population, parklands are plentiful. And precisely because the state is so small – it takes less than two hours to drive from one end to the other – a visitor can walk historic city streets in the morning, picnic in an idyllic grove at noon, and savor the delights of the seashore by moonlight.

Block Island sells itself as a hideaway destination, unsullied by developers and fast-food chains.

BELOW: Block Island has a population of just over 1,000.

To the southwest, in **Charlestown**, more than 250 bird species regularly visit the diverse habitat at the **Ninigret National Wildlife Refuge** (50 Bend Road; tel: 401-364 9124).

In **Westerly**, the half-mile **Misquamicut State Beach** (tel: 401-596 9097; parking fee) is one of the state's most popular; get there early on a hot summer day. The village of **Watch Hill** , with its Victorian cottage mansions, shops, and the *c.*1876 landmark **Flying Horse Carousel**, the oldest in the country, is well worth seeing.

Block Island

When Rhode Islanders want to get away from it all, they head for **Block Island** , a 3- by 7-mile (5km by 11km) island some 12 miles (19km) south of the entrance to Narragansett Bay. Whereas Newport is packed to the gills with hotels, shops, restaurants, and tourists, Block Island – named by the Nature Conservancy as one of the 12 "last great places" in the western hemisphere – remains a hideaway that holds its own, quite successfully, against developers and fast-food chains.

Narragansett Indians were the first inhabitants. They called it Manisses, which means "Island of the Little God." In 1614, Dutch explorer Adriaen Block spotted it and in an early example of shameless self-promotion, named it after himself. Captain Kidd visited occasionally, although there's no indication he deposited any of his ill-gotten treasures under the sand. Tourists sometimes arrive via planes out of Westerly RI (a 10-minute hop), but most people take the ferry.

The **Block Island Ferry** (tel: 401-783 7996/866-783 7996; www. blockislandferry.com) offers passenger-only service from Point Judith and Newport's Fort Adams. The schedule changes seasonally. Although it's possible to visit as a day trip, it is worth staying at least overnight. The ferry docks in **Old Harbor**, the island's only town, a charming, small-scale resort. Charter fishing boats line the dock near the ferry.

Ferries from Fort Adams

At Fort Adams, you can catch the Jamestown to Newport ferry (tel: 401-423 9900; www.jamestownnewportferry.com) for a peaceful trip across Newport Harbor to the historic town of Jamestown on Conanicut Island.

Some ferry boats stop off at Rose Island, where a historic lighthouse once guided ships into and around the harbor. Rose Island was once used to store live munitions for the local naval base, so parts of the island are off-limits to visitors. The lighthouse has been restored and offers excellent views of the area.

The ferries also stop at Perrotti Park and Market Square in Newport. Even if you're not traveling between locations, the ferry is a scenic route to see the harbor of Newport.

Visitors come to Block Island for fine beaches, fishing, tranquility, and the romantic allure of aging Victorian hotels with huge verandas and a sense of bygone splendor. The **Spring House** (tel: 401-466 5844; www.springhousehotel.com), on a 15-acre (6-hectare) promontory, opened its doors in 1852; and the **National House** (tel: 401-466 2901/800-225 2449), a majestic wooden ark of a building, opened in 1888 in the heart of Old Harbor. To spend time in either of these two lodgings is to be caught in a time warp.

The **Block Island Historical Society** (Old Town Road; tel: 401-466 2481; www.blockislandinfo.com), in an 1850 farmhouse, does a good job of recreating the island's farming and seafaring history. Shipwrecks were a recurring event. Many luckless captains and their ships came to misery on the submerged rocks and sandbars around "The Block." The perils of the sea are elaborated upon at the interpretive center in **North Lighthouse** (Corn Neck Road; tel: 401-466 3200 for opening hours).

The island's beaches include **Surfers Beach**, popular with surfers, as its name suggests; **State Beach** and others on the east are calmer and attract the most visitors. The westerly strands are windswept and usually deserted. The Nature Conservancy (www.nature.org) and local groups help to preserve more than 40 percent of the island. Not surprisingly, hiking is very popular. One trek not to be missed is the hike to the magnificently scenic **Mohegan Bluffs**, where the 1874 **Southeast Lighthouse** perches above the cliffs. The legend that the Mohegan tribe was driven off the cliffs by a rival tribe is a fabrication. On the island's south side, **Rodman's Hollow**, is a 230-acre (90-hectare) swath of conserved land formed more than 20,000 years ago by glacial meltwater.

When the kids have had enough ice cream and body surfing, visit **Manisses Farm** (1 Spring Street; tel: 401-466 2421), behind the Manisses Hotel. It has an exotic menagerie, including camels, llamas, emus, sheep, and donkeys.

One of Block Island's attractions is its many fine beaches. Fred Benson Town Beach and Ballard's Beach have lifeguards on duty.

BELOW: sailboats and yachts are docked in the quiet waters of Wickford on Narragansett Bay.

On the Water

The refreshing, salt-tinged air brings out the latent sailor in even the most untested landlubber. There are almost as many scenic cruises as there are seagulls in Narragansett Bay. Perhaps the most economical way to tour Narragansett Bay is on the Jamestown–Newport ferry. The boats follow a circuit across the bay, including three piers in Newport. An all-day round-trip ticket gets reduced admission to Rose Island, Fort Adams, and the Museum of Yachting. Narrated cruises tell the tales of Newport's role in merchant shipping, naval warfare, and competitive sailing. Indulge in Newport's nefarious past with a tour on a motor yacht once used by bootleggers (www.cruisenewport.com), sample the thrill of the America's Cup with a sail on a Cup contender (www.12metercharters.com), or see 10 lighthouses up close on a narrated tour (www.rhodeislandbaycruises.com). Whale watchers should contact Frances Fleet (www.francesfleet.com) for July and August tours. You can rent sail and motor boats at Wickford Boat Rentals (tel: 401-295-0050; www.wickfordboatrentals.com). Those who want to learn how to sail should consider a multiday course at the Newport Sailing School (www.newportsailing.com) or JWorld Sailing School (www.jworldschool.com).

RESTAURANTS AND BARS

Prices for a three-course dinner per person with a half-bottle of house wine:
$ = under $20
$$ = $20–45
$$$ = $45–60
$$$$ = over $60

Restaurants
Block Island

Eli's Restaurant
Chapel Street
Tel: 401-466 5230
www.elisblockisland.com
$$–$$$
A small bistro with Asian-inspired menu and good vegetarian options.

Hotel Manisses
1 Spring Street
Tel: 401-466 2421
http://blockislandresorts.com
$$$$
Sophisticated fare reflecting chef's worldwide culinary experiences.

The Beachead
Corn Neck Road
Tel: 401-466 2249
www.thebeachead.com
$$
Ahi sliders, native steamed mussels, and seafood nachos for casual meals; roasted duck and Block Island Bouillabaisse.

The Oar
221 Jobs Hill Road (at the Boat Basin)
Tel: 401-466 8820
www.blockislalndresorts.com
$$
Casual, outdoor eating with view of boat basin and Great Salt Pond. Salads, lobster rolls, seafood entrées.

Bristol

DeWolf's Tavern
Thames Street Landing
Tel: 401-254 2005
www.dewolftavern.com **$$–$$$**
Contemporary American dishes with an Indian twist in an historic, waterfront warehouse. Look for charcoal tandoor roasted chicken and creamy ricotta tortellini.

Lobster Pot
119–21 Hope Street, Route 114
Tel: 401-253 9100
www.lobsterpotri.com **$$**
This local harborfront institution has served up fresh fare since 1929. Raw bar, innovative takes on seafood (scallop and mushroom ravioli), lobster in many ways.

Persimmon
31 State Street
Tel: 401-254 7474
www.persimmonbristol.com
$–$$
Small (38-seat) bistro with fine dining, seasonal menu. Three tasting menus (one vegetarian) are worth the expense. closed Mon.

Jamestown

Slice of Heaven
32 Narragansett Avenue
Tel: 401-423 9866
www.sliceofheavenri.om **$–$$**
Euro-style bakery, restaurant, caé. Breakfast treats like Grand Marnier French toast.

Trattoria Simpatico
13 Narragansett Avenue
Tel: 401-423 3731
www.trattoriasimpatico.com

$$$–$$$$
Superb Italian fare, alfresco dining under the beech trees with live jazz in good weather.

Middletown

Johnny's Atlantic Beach Club & Pavilion
55 Purgatory Road
Tel: 401-847 2750
www.atlanticbeachclub.com
$$–$$$
Casual dining on the beach with a view of the Cliff Walk. Burgers, salads, and fish platters at lunch. Add extensive pasta list, lobsters, duck pinot noir at dinner.

Narragansett

Aunt Carrie's
1240 Ocean Road, Point Judith
Tel: 401-783 7930
www.auntcarriesr.com **$**
This classic seaside clam shack claims it invented the clam cake. Serving traditional seafood meals since 1920. BYOB.

Basil's
22 Kingstown Road
Tel: 401-789 3743
www.basilsri.com **$$–$$$**
French Continental cuisine in an elegant Victorian restaurant near the pier. Award-winning wine list. Reservations recommended.

George's of Galilee
250 Sand Hill Cove Road
Tel: 401-783 2306
www.georgesofgalilee.com
$$–$$$
Wide selection of seafood, including lobsters and seafood pot pie, sushi, chicken

with bourbon glaze.

Turtle Soup Restaurant
113 Ocean Road
Tel: 401-792 8683 **$$–$$$**
Bayfront restaurant with an eclectic menu with European and American influences. Drinks on the lawn overlooking Narragansett Bay. No reservations.

Newport

The Black Pearl
Bannister's Wharf
Tel: 401-846 5264
http://blackpearlnewpor.com
$$–$$$$
A renowned harborside tvern serving classic French and American fare, including prize-winning clam chowder. Jackets and reservations required in Commodore Room. Posh, but friendly. Waterside patio bar and tavern are more casual.

Castle Hill Inn
590 Ocean Avenue
Tel: 401-849 3800
www.castlehillinn.com **$$$–$$$$**
This magnificent 1874 summer "cottage" overlooking Narragansett Bay specializes in New England cuisine and offers several prix-fixe options. Jackets for dining.

Clarke Cooke House
Bannister's Wharf
Tel: 401-849 2900
www.hannistersnewport.com
$$$$
Formal, waterview dining in a 1790 colonial house. Candy Store bar is popular

with yachting set.

Newport Dinner Train
19 America's Cup Avenue
Tel: 401-841 8700
http://newportdinnertrain.com
$$$–$$$$
Multicourse lunches and dinners served aboard a beautifully restored train which travels 22 miles (35km) along Narragansett Bay.

Puerini's Restaurant
24 Memorial Boulevard W
Tel: 401-847 5506
www.puerinisrestaurant.com
$$–$$$
Small, family-run restaurant with an extensive menu of innovative Italian specialties. Homemade pastas, tortellini with seafood, veal specialties, and a reasonably priced wine list.

Scales and Shells
527 Thames Street
Tel: 401-848 9378
www.scalesandshells.com
$$–$$$
Open kitchen draws diners who watch as the chefs work. Menu is based on the catch of the day.

White Horse Tavern
26 Marlborough Street
Tel: 401-849 3600
www.whitehorsetavern.us **$$$**
The country's oldest continually operating tavern (est. 1687) serves classics such as grilled DeBrenton pork rib chop, grilled shrimp polenta, bouillabaisse.

Pawtucket

Modern Diner
364 East Avenue
Tel: 401-726 8390 **$–$$**
On the National Register

ofHistoric Places, an autentic diner in a 1941 railcar. Legendary breakfasts: cream cheese and blueberry-stuffed French toast, kielbasa and cheddar omelets. No credit cards.

Providence

Al Forno
577 S. Main Street
Tel: 401-273 9760
www.alforno.com **$$$–$$$$**
Arguably New Englan's preeminent temle of *nuova cucina*. Classic Northern Italian specialties with an upscale spin.

Angelo's Civita Farnese
141 Atwells Avenue
Tel: 401-621 8171
www.angelosonthehill.com
$–$$
Like being at an Italian family reunion. A friendly and boisterous place serving large portions of low-priced Italian classics since 1924. Reservations accepted.

LaLaiterie Bistro
184 Wayland Avenue
Tel: 401-274 7177
www.farmsteadinc.com **$$$**
"Haute farmhouse cuisine." One of the original restaurants embracing the concept of locally grown and sourced fine dining.

New Rivers
7 Steeple Street
Tel: 401-751 0350
www.newriversrestaurant.com **$$$**
Recently renovated and expanded, incorporating original materials into the design. Rhode Island cod and scallops, rabbit, tagliatelle. Charcuterie menu and sampler.

Rue de L'Espoir
99 Hope Street
Tel: 401-751 8890
www.therue.com **$$–$$$**
Brings originality to the bistro concept. From salads and small plates to an "eat seriously" menu.

Warwick

Iggy's Doughboys & Chowder House
889 Oakland Beach Avenue
Tel: 401-737 9459
www.iggysdoughboys.com
$–$$
Oldest clam shack in Rhode Island (1924). Family owned and run, serving clams, fish and chips, and other seafood staples. Doughboys are hush puppies, fried dough balls served with sweet toppings.

Watch Hill

Olympia Tea Room
74 Bay Street
Tel: 401-348 8211

www.olympiatearoomcom
$$–$$$
Full-service, Art Deco dining room with high-backed wooden booths and a view of Little Narragansett Bay.

Bars

Celtica Irish Public House
95 Long Wharf, Newport
Tel: 401-847 4770
www.cellcanewport.com
"Strong ale, black porter, sweet whiskey." A full menu of live music from Irish to soul, along with a limited bar menu featuring paninis and chowder.

Trinity Brewhouse Pub & Bar
186 Fountain Street, ProvidenceTel: 401-453 2337
www.trinitybrewhouse.com
Little Rhody's biggest brewery handcrafts beers, ales, porters, and stouts, and serves them up alongside everything from sweet potato fries to Reubens.

Right: in September, Providence's Food for Thought Festival showcases local chefs and vineyards.

NEWPORT'S GILDED AGE MANSIONS

Newport, a 19th-century summer playground for the rich and famous, became a showplace for America's greatest architects and designers

With the coming of the railways in the mid-19th century, vacationing became ever more popular, and the delights of Newport, set on an island with a fine summer climate, became readily accessible from New York and Boston. Wealthy and influential families began to spend their summers here. Many had made vast fortunes from industry and began to lavish unstinting funds on creating opulent summer homes, where they would entertain and impress all those who mattered.

The country's most innovative architects – names such as Stanford White and Richard Morris Hunt – were employed, creating designs that reflect the full range of styles in vogue at the time. Building materials and furnishings were often imported from Europe (for Marble House, for instance, different colored marbles were imported from Italy to be worked by Italian craftsmen in Newport). Interior decor frequently borrowed from European or Far Eastern styles; fine paintings, furnishings, and objets d'art collected from around the world filled the rooms.

Eight of these mansions are now maintained by The Preservation Society of Newport and are open to the public, as is the Astor family's Beechwood Mansion.

ABOVE: The Elms, at 367 Bellevue Avenue, replicates a two-story château near Paris, with the servants' quarters placed behind the roof balustrade and the kitchens located in a cellar. It was built in 1901 for the coal baron Edward Julius Berwind, the son of German immigrants.

LEFT: Ochre Court, a Beaux-Arts mansion built in 1892. It is now owned by the local Salve Regina University. Only The Breakers is larger.

LEGACY OF THE VANDERBILTS

The Breakers was commissioned in 1893 by Cornelius Vanderbilt II to replace an earlier house destroyed by fire. Vanderbilt, chairman of the New York Central railway and a director of 49 other railways, was the head of America's wealthiest family. His younger brother, William, had inherited equal shares in the family fortunes, some part of which he spent building Marble House, on nearby Bellevue Avenue. A serious, modest, and gentle man, Cornelius II gave free rein and an unlimited budget to Richard Morris Hunt, the architect of Marble House and of the grand Vanderbilt houses on Fifth Avenue in New York. Hunt followed the Italian Renaissance layout adopted for 16th-century palaces, where rooms were grouped symmetrically around a central courtyard. With 70 rooms, including 33 for resident staff and visitors' servants, The Breakers is Newport's largest "cottage." Vanderbilt died in 1899, aged 55, four years after the house was completed.

Above: The Breakers was designed by architect Richard Morris Hunt, who took his inspiration from the 16th-century palaces of Genoa and Turin, and employed an international team of builders.

Above: an interior room at Marble House shows the luxurious furnishings designed by Richard Morris Hunt, and inspired by the Petit Trianon at Versailles, Paris.

Above: a ball held at Beechwood

CONNECTICUT

This historic state of Connecticut offers maritime traditions along its coast, rural charm in its hillside villages, and the sites of early patriotism and social reforms

onnecticut's picturesque colonial villages, with their carefully kept, white clapboard homes and manicured lawns, evoke an image of quiet wealth, propriety, and old school ties. Its dollar-savvy Puritan founders left a legacy of sharp business acumen which has served the state well. But there is also a great pride in the place and a heartfelt sense of its history.

With Long Island Sound as its southern border, Connecticut roughly forms a rectangle measuring 90 miles (145km) from east to west and 55 miles (89km) north to south. The Connecticut River bisects the state; along with the Thames and Housatonic rivers, they were vital avenues of settlement and industrialization.

The state capital

The skyline of **Hartford** ❶, Connecticut's capital, is dominated by the towering headquarters of the nation's largest insurance companies. So many insurance firms are located here that the city calls itself the Insurance Capital of the World. Mergers and other economic factors have reduced the number in recent years; health care and education have filled the gap. Those two areas are responsible for approximately 20 percent of the jobs in the city.

Settled in 1635 and Connecticut's oldest city, Hartford has always maintained political, economic, and social pre-eminence. In 1662, a royal charter was drawn up uniting the colonies of Hartford and New Haven and guaranteeing their independence. Sir Edmund Andros, appointed governor of all New England in 1687, had the charter revoked. In defiance, colonists stole the charter and hid it in the trunk of an oak tree at the center of the town. Two years later, on the accession of William III, Andros was recalled to England, and the charter was reinstated. A plaque at

PRECEDING PAGES: white picket fences.
LEFT: the State Capitol.

Charter Oak Place, in the south end of the city, marks the spot where the magnificent oak stood until 1856, when a windstorm felled it. That's the tree featured on the Connecticut state quarter.

The **Greater Hartford Welcome Center** (1 Pearl Street; tel: 860-244 0253; daily 9am–5pm) distributes a free guide which includes a map and walking tour of the city.

Old State House

Begin at the **Old State House ⓐ**, at the intersection of Main Street and Asylum Avenue (800 Main Street; tel: 860-522 6766; July–Columbus Day Tue–Sat, Oct–June Mon–Fri; charge; guided and self-guided tours). Built in 1796, it is one of the nation's oldest state house buildings, although it has been replaced as the active center of state government by the State Capitol building. The building was the site of the 1839 *La Amistad* slaveship mutiny trial.

The interactive, multimedia presentation *History is All Around Us*, on the lower floor, is an introduction to 300 years of Connecticut history. In 1798, lawmakers shared the building with **Joseph Steward's Museum of Curiosities**. The reconstruction of the room which displayed things like a two-headed calf and the alleged mummified hand of Ramses is on the second floor. The city's oldest historic site is the **Ancient Burying Ground ⓑ** (corner Gold and Main streets; maps at the Main Street gate; guided tours noon late June–early Aug). Between 1648 and the early 1800s, it was Hartford's first and foremost graveyard. Around 6,000 people are interred here, the oldest gravestones dating from 1648.

Wadsworth Atheneum

Directly to the south, also on Main Street, is the **Wadsworth Atheneum Museum of Art ⓒ**, America's oldest continually operating public art museum (600 Main Street; tel: 860-278 2670; Wed–Sun; charge). Housed in

five buildings – themselves historically and architecturally significant – the museum has Greek and Roman antiquities, Baroque, Impressionist, modernist, and surrealist paintings, Hudson River landscapes, and American decorative arts. Sculptor Alexander Calder's 50ft (15-meter) -high red stabile, *Stegosaurus*, dominates the plaza. The **Amistad Center for Art and Culture**, located within the Atheneum, concentrates on the African-American experience from slavery through the civil rights movement.

The State Capitol

Perched on Capitol Hill, the white marble, gold-domed **Connecticut State Capitol ⓓ** (210 Capitol Avenue; tel: 860-240 0222; tours Mon–Fri; self-guided booklet available) is an 1878 Gothic wedding cake of turrets, gables, porches, and towers. Its ornate interiors of hand-painted columns, marble floors, and elaborate stained-glass windows were designed to reflect the prosperity of the community it served. The new Hall of Fame honors outstanding Connecticut locals like

A statue in the State Capitol of the Connecticut patriot Nathan Hale, who was hanged in 1776. His (debated) famous last words: "I only regret that I have but one life to lose for my country."

BELOW: a gallery in the Wadsworth Atheneum.

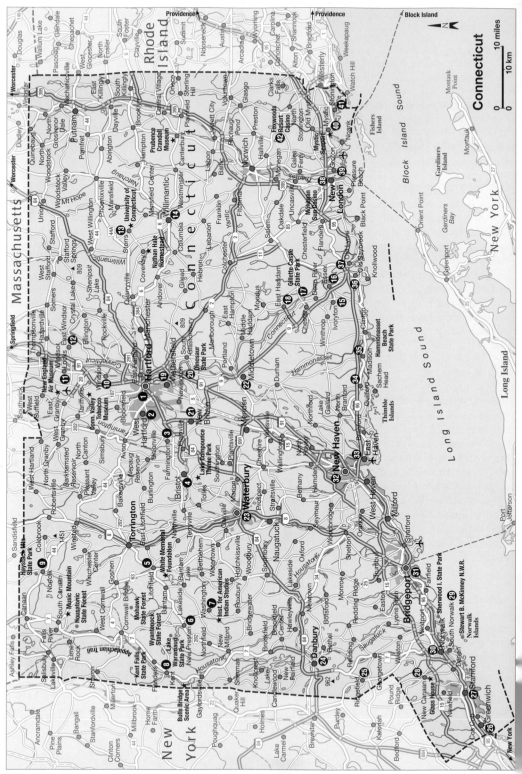

Jackie Robinson, Paul Newman, and Marian Anderson.

The Capitol overlooks 41-acre (17-hectare) **Bushnell Park**  (tel: 860-232 6710; www.bushnellpark.org), a pleasant urban oasis. The Gothic brownstone **Soldiers and Sailors Memorial Arch** (tel: 860-956 7919; tours May–Oct Thur noon; free) honors the 4,000 Connecticut residents who fought in the Civil War. A climb up the 96 steps gives a panoramic view of the park.

In the late 1800s, there were nearly 3,000 carousels gracefully spinning in parks. The hand-carved horses were considered works of art, with Solomon Stein's and Harry Goldstein's among the best. Their **1914 carousel** (tel: 860-585 5411; May–mid-Oct; charge), with 48 carved wooden steeds, carries riders accompanied by music from a Wurlitzer band organ. Free concerts are held in summer at the outdoor performance pavilion on the park's west side.

The **Bushnell Center for the Performing Arts** (166 Capitol Avenue; tel: 860-987 6000; www. bushnell.org), Connecticut's premier performing arts center, has an impressive program of concerts, ballet, opera, and theater all year. To the south of the Capitol is the **State Library** (a treasury of documents and archives for researchers) and the **Museum of Connecticut History** (231 Capitol Avenue; tel: 860-757 6535; Mon–Sat; free). Exhibits include the state's 1662 royal charter, the Mitchelson Coin Collection (with one of every coin ever minted in the US), and an extensive collection of Colt firearms.

Travelers' Tower has an observation deck giving a good view of the Hartford area (1 Tower Square; tel: 860-277 4208; Mon–Fri; free).

The **Butler-McCook House and Garden and Main Street History Center** (396 Main Street; tel: 860-522 1806; Apr, Oct–Dec Sat–Sun, May–Sept Thur–Sun; charge) was home to this family of physicians, missionaries,

and social reformers from 1782 to 1971. It is one of the best-documented homes in America and shows how life along Main Street changed from the American Revolution through the mid-20th century.

The new **Connecticut Science Center** (250 Columbus Boulevard; tel: 860-SCIENCE; open July–Aug daily, Sept–June Tue–Sun; charge) has 150 hands-on activities which concentrate on sports science and inventing tools for people with visual or hearing obstacles.

Mark Twain House

Hartford's most famous resident, Samuel Langhorne Clemens, was better known by his pen name, Mark Twain. Clemens thought Hartford was the loveliest city he'd ever seen and moved here in 1884. The **Mark Twain House and Museum** (351 Farmington Avenue; tel: 860-247 0998; guided tours Mon–Sun 9.30am–5.30pm, Sun noon–5.30pm; last tour starts at 4.30pm; closed Tue Jan–Mar; charge) is a wonderful, whimsical display of Victorian Gothic indulgence.

TIP

You can hop aboard the free downtown Hartford Star Shuttle which passes every 10–12 minutes Monday–Friday 7am–11pm, and Saturday 3pm–11pm. It stops at or within a short walk of most major attractions including Bushnell Park, the Atheneum, Convention Center, Riverwalk, Arts District, and Science Center.

BELOW:
Mark Twain House.

Bushnell Park, named after local pastor Horace Bushnell (1802–76).

Outdoor porches and balconies give the impression of a Mississippi riverboat, while the grand interiors feature design elements by Tiffany. Clemens/Twain wrote his most famous works, *The Adventures of Huckleberry Finn*, *Tom Sawyer*, *The Prince and the Pauper*, and *A Connecticut Yankee in King Arthur's Court* in the handsome billiard room. The optional tour of the servants' wing gives insights into Victorian-era manners (additional charge). Tours fill quickly, especially on weekends. They cycle generally every half-hour.

The museum features an introductory film by Ken Burns on Twain's life and influence on social issues and literature. There are displays of the family's personal items and a 12-volume set of his works in Russian. The building is the first museum in the country (and the first structure of any kind in Connecticut) to meet Leadership in Energy and Environmental Design (LEED) specifications, something Clemens, who deeply loved the natural world, would have appreciated.

Harriet Beecher Stowe Center

Clemens' neighbor was Harriet Beecher Stowe, author of *Uncle Tom's Cabin*. She lived next door in a 14-room Gothic Revival home built in 1871 by friend and abolitionist Franklin Chamberlin. She moved there in 1873 and wrote several of her later works in the house. Her restored house is a part of the **Harriet Beecher Stowe Center ⓛ** (77 Forest Street; tel: 860-522 9258; Wed–Sun; also Tue in June–Oct; charge). The tour gives a glimpse into Stowe's personal life and her preference for informal homemaking, something at odds with prevailing Victorian pretence.

The neighborhood where Clemens and Stowe lived is called "Nook Farm." It was a fashionable community of abolitionists, suffragettes, actors, and social activists. The self-guided walking tour available at the Center introduces influential characters most people have never heard of.

The **Connecticut Historical Society Museum ⓜ** (1 Elizabeth

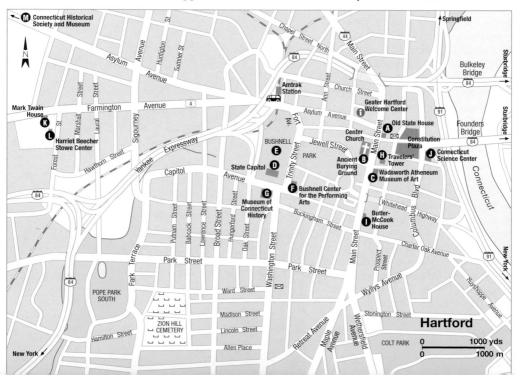

Hartford

Street; tel: 860-236 5621; Tue–Sat; charge) has a lot of interactive displays of Connecticut history from 1500 to the present. Visitors can work on a World War II assembly line, replace bobbins in a textile mill, and sew a Native American moccasin.

West Hartford

In **West Hartford ❷**, a 2.5-acre (1-hectare) rose garden with 15,000 bushes is the centerpiece of **Elizabeth Park** (915 Prospect Avenue; tel: 860-757 9970). Rambling roses cover archways over paths which meander past borders and fences covered with climbing and shrub roses. The "new" Heritage Garden has been planted with 100 old rose varieties and will be in full bloom in 2017 – the centennial of the Connecticut Valley Garden Club.

Noah Webster House

The author of the first American dictionary (1828) lived at what is now **the Noah Webster House and West Hartford Historical Society** (227 South Main Street; 860-521 5362; Thur–Mon; charge). The dictionary, now revered, was not initially a big seller, and Webster had to mortgage his home to bring out a second edition. New exhibits examine Webster's influence on government and education, creation of a national language, and his personal life. Another new exhibit looks at the development of Hartford, with stations where you can sniff the aromas of the area's varied culinary traditions and listen to local musicians.

The Children's Museum

The **Children's Museum** (950 Trout Brook Drive, exit 43 off I–84; tel: 860-231 2824; Mon–Sun; charge) has lots of creative, hands-on exhibits, live animals, and space and science shows in the digital planetarium. Outside a 60ft (18.2-meter) replica sperm whale sprays water through his blowhole on hot summer days.

WEST OF HARTFORD

Take I–84 south to exit 39 to **Farmington ❸**, 10 miles (16km) west of Hartford. Often called one of the loveliest towns in New England, its elegant 18th- and 19th-century mansions display untouched architectural detail.

A particular gem is the **Hill-Stead Museum** (35 Mountain Road; tel: 860-677 4787; guided tours Tue–Sun; charge). The 19-room, Colonial Revival home on 150 acres (60 hectares) was the retirement home of industrialist Alfred Atmore Pope, a friend of the artist Mary Cassatt and a great admirer of French Impressionism. As much an art gallery as a residence, scattered throughout the mansion are a number of familiar canvases, including paintings from Monet's *Haystack* series, Manet's *The Guitar Lady*, and Degas's *The Tub*.

The **Stanley-Whitman House** (37 High Street; tel: 860-677 9222; Wed–Sun noon–4pm; last tour begins at 3.15pm; charge) is a living-history center which invites visitors to immerse themselves in early colonial

Hartford's Riverfest, which includes concerts and parades, is held every July.

BELOW: a summer festival in the grounds of Hill-Stead Museum.

life by using everyday objects. The museum also maintains Memento Mori, the town's "ancient burying ground," with the earliest gravestone dating to 1685.

Bristol

Continue south on I–84 to exit 34 to **Bristol ❹**. The town was a 19th-century clockmaking capital, producing more than 200,000 clocks in a single year. The **American Clock and Watch Museum** (100 Maple Street; tel: 860-583 6070; late Mar–early Dec daily; charge) displays watches and clocks dating from 1595, including a two-story tower clock and the finest collection of American-manufactured timepieces in the world. The chiming and striking of the clocks on the hour is musical, synchronized audio chaos. Don't miss the sundial garden outside.

One of the most extensive collections of hand-carved, antique and contemporary carousel horses and band organs is featured at the **New England Carousel Museum** (95 Riverside Avenue; tel: 860-585 5411; Mar–Dec Mon–Sun; charge). The museum is housed in the **Bristol Center for Arts and Culture**, which is also home to the **Museum of Fire History**, displaying firehouse memorabilia, and several art galleries.

Two wooden roller coasters and an antique 1911 carousel are the classic highlights among 50 rides at **Lake Compounce Theme Park** (186 Enterprise, exit 31 off I–84; tel: 860-583 3300; www.lakecompounce.com; open daily July–Aug; limited hours off-season; charge). There are also daredevil and kiddie rides and live shows. Splash Harbor Water Park, the state's only water park, is located here.

THE LITCHFIELD HILLS

In the northwest corner of Connecticut, the wooded Litchfield Hills are dotted with quintessential New England villages, covered bridges, and the tumbling stone walls of forgotten farms. Through it runs the **Housatonic River**, crystal clear and freckled with trout, and excellent for canoeing. Hikers may want to follow the Appalachian Trail from Kent to Salisbury and Mt Frissell.

Litchfield ❺, 35 miles (56km) from Hartford, is dominated by a spacious green, graced by the tall-steepled Congregational Church. During the Revolution, it housed Loyalist prisoners and was a depot for military supplies. The town's rich history is documented at the excellent **Litchfield History Museum** (7 South Street; tel: 860-567 4501; mid-Apr–Nov Tue–Sun; charge). Admission includes entrance to the **Tapping Reeve House and Litchfield Law School**, the nation's first school of law (82 South Street, Route 63), where visitors learn about student life in the early 19th century through role-playing and interpretive exhibits.

Just east of town, off Route 118, is Connecticut's first winery, **Haight-Brown Vineyard** (29 Chestnut Hill Road; tel: 860-567 4045; open daily). They produce a wide range of wines, from a dry, barrel-fermented

Chardonnay to lateharvest Vidals and Vignoles.

Head south out of Litchfield for 3.5 miles (6km) on Route 63 to **White Flower Farm** (167 Litchfield Road, Morris; tel: 860-567 8789; Apr–Oct daily), where something is always in bloom in the 5 acres (2 hectares) of display gardens.

White Memorial Foundation, 2 miles (3.2km) west of Litchfield on Route 202/Whitehall Road (tel: 860-567 0857; museum open daily; charge for museum), the state's largest nature conservation center, encompasses 4,000 acres (1,600 hectares) and includes 35 miles (56km) of trails. The Museum uses dioramas with mounted specimens to interpret local natural history.

Lake Waramaug

Continue south on Route 202 for approximately 6 miles (10km) to **New Preston** ❻, a tiny, picturesque town, and continue north on Route 45 for 5 miles (8km) to **Lake Waramaug State Park** (30 Lake Waramaug Road; tel: 860-424 3200; charge May–Oct weekends and holidays), a tranquil hideaway with a swimming beach and canoe and kayak rentals.

Washington

To the southeast, on Route 47 is the magnificently preserved town of **Washington** ❼, home to three historic districts, a select group of fine shops, and five private schools (including The Gunnery, founded in 1850 with students from 15 countries and 20 states).

Continue onto Route 199 to the turn-off for the **Institute for American Indian Studies** (38 Curtis Road; tel: 860-868 0518; open daily; charge), dedicated to the stewardship of American Indian culture. Exhibits trace the 10,000-year history of Connecticut's American Indian population. Outside, there's a model Algonquin village, a replicated archaeological dig, and a garden with medicinal plants.

West to Kent

The Housatonic Valley has one of its most dramatic moments in the town

Lake Waramaug, named after an Indian chief of the Wyantenock tribe, has an average depth of 22ft (7 meters).

BELOW: the West Cornwall Bridge was built in 1864.

You can canoe, kayak, or raft down the Housatonic from Clarke Outdoors' headquarters on Route 7 in West Cornwall (tel: 860-672 6365). It offers 6-mile (10km) or 10-mile (16km) trips.

BELOW: serenity at Tyler Lake, Goshen.

of **Kent** ❽ at **Kent Falls State Park** (Route 7; tel: 860-927 3238; charge May–Oct weekends and holidays), where water tumbles 250ft (76 meters) down a natural stone staircase. There's also a covered bridge. In fall foliage season, the colors are extraordinary.

Dip south on Route 7, where an easy trail from the parking lot gives access to the handsome covered bridge, waterfalls, and rapids at **Bulls Bridge Scenic Area**. A hiking trail connects with the Appalachian Trail.

To the north on Route 7, in **West Cornwall**, a much photographed 1836 covered bridge spans the Housatonic.

At **Falls Village**, Music Mountain (Gordon Hall; tel: 860-824 7126; www.musicmountain.org; charge) hosts the country's oldest continuing summer chamber music festival. The 120-acre (48-hectare) property encompasses Gordon Hall, known for its excellent acoustics and a setting which allows concertgoers to enjoy the natural surroundings as well as the music. Most of the chamber music concerts are held Sunday afternoons; Saturday evenings feature jazz.

Norfolk ❾, on Route 44 almost on the border with Massachusetts, is another classic town with handsome 18th-century homes clustered around a tidy green. The **Ellen Battell Stoeckel Estate** (Routes 44 and 272; tel: 860-542 3000; www.yale.edu/norfolk; charge for concerts) hosts Yale University's renowned **Norfolk Chamber Music Festival**. Buy tickets well in advance, and bring a picnic.

On a clear day you can almost see forever – or at least to Long Island Sound and the Berkshires – from the top of the 34ft (12-meter) tower at the top of 1,716ft (523-meter) Haystack Mountain. A road in **Haystack Mountain State Park** (385 Burr Mountain Road, Route 272; tel: 860-482 1817; free) goes halfway up the mountain, and from there it's a rather rugged half-mile hike to the summit.

NORTH OF HARTFORD

In the 1920s and 1930s, more than 35,000 acres (14,000 hectares) of land along the Connecticut River Valley between Hartford and the Massachusetts border were devoted to growing shade tobacco for cigar wrappers. Today, much of the land is covered by houses, but a few farmers carry on; Connecticut wrappers are still considered the world's best.

The importance of the now-declining industry to the region is well told in **Windsor** ❿ at the **Luddy/Taylor Connecticut Valley Tobacco Museum** (Northwest Park, 135 Lang Road, Windsor; exit 38 off I–91; tel: 860-285 1888; Mar–mid-Dec Tue–Thur and Sat; charge). Nearby is "Elmwood," the beautifully preserved 1780 **Oliver Ellsworth Homestead** (778 Palisado Avenue, Route 159; tel: 860-688 8717; mid-May–mid-Oct Wed, Thur, Sat, and last Sun of the month; charge). Expelled from Yale for his "pranks," he made good, eventually becoming the third Chief Justice of the US Supreme Court. His house is furnished with beautiful antiques of the period. The grounds of the 12-acre

(5-hectare) estate are graced with stately oak, beech, and mulberry trees.

Cheek by jowl with Bradley International Airport in **Windsor Locks** ⑪ is the **New England Air Museum** (36 Perimeter Road, exit 40 off I–91; tel: 860-623 3305; daily; charge), a must for aviation buffs. The three massive hangars hold over 125 aircraft – including WWII gliders, a B-29, a replica of the pudgy Gee Bee air racer, and a Lockheed Electra that's a twin of the one Amelia Earhart flew – and thousands of aviation artifacts from posters and charts to flight suits and simulators. Just down the road at the **Connecticut Firefighters Memorial** (34 Perimeter Road), an eternal flame burns atop a granite base to commemorate those who died in the line of duty. In **East Windsor** ⑫, the history of firefighting is chronicled at the **Connecticut Fire Museum** (230 Pine Street, Manchester; tel: 860-649 9436; mid-Apr–mid-Nov Fri–Sun; donation). Appropriately housed in a 1901 firehouse, it's filled with pumpers and ladder trucks, as well as leather fire buckets and other firefighting memorabilia. A ticket to the museum also includes a visit to the **Connecticut Trolley Museum** (tel: 860-627 6540, (tel: 860-627 6540; June–Aug Wed–Mon, Apr–May, Sept–Oct hours vary; call first; charge), located next door. The highlight is riding a variety of antique trolleys on a 3-mile (5km) journey.

The Quiet Corner

The Nutmeg State's relatively unheralded northeastern region has been dubbed the "Quiet Corner." The best way to enjoy the small, scenic villages is to "shun pike" – avoid the well-traveled highways and explore the meandering byways.

For a small town, **Storrs** ⑬ has much to offer. The extensive campus of the **University of Connecticut** is located here, and it encompasses numerous museums. The **William Benton Museum of Art** (245

Glenbrook Road; tel: 860-486 4520; closed Mon; donation) hosts a wide variety of temporary exhibits during the year. The **Connecticut Museum of Natural History** (2019 Hillside Road; tel: 860-486 4460; Mon–Fri; donation) is the repository of a vast collection of Connecticut Native American, colonial, and industrial artifacts. The **Archaeology Center** uses "story stations" to integrate Connecticut's natural and social history. The **Ballard Museum of Puppetry** (6 Bourn Place, Depot Campus; tel: 860-486 4605; Fri–Sun; donation) is a magical place filled with puppets, marionettes, and shadow figures from Bali, Italy, Java, and beyond. The **Jorgensen Center for the Performing Arts** (2132 Hillside Road, UConn campus; tel: 860-486 4226; www.jorgensen.uconn. edu) has a dynamic schedule of classical and contemporary music and dance.

Dip southwest to **Coventry** and the **Nathan Hale Homestead** (2299 South Street; tel: 860-742 6917; June–Aug Wed–Sun, Sept–Oct Fri–Sun; charge), the family home of the official state

A Boeing B-29A Superfortress on show in the New England Air Museum.

BELOW: the Thread City Crossing in Willimantic is known as Frog Bridge.

The Conneticut River Museum.

BELOW: Sculpture Mile, Madison CT.

hero, hanged as a spy by the British in 1776. Adjacent is the 1730 **Strong-Porter House Museum** (2382 South Street; tel: 860-742 7474; June–Oct Sun; donation). A recently reconstructed two-story barn, carriage shed, and carpenter shop give a glimpse into rural life of the times. The museum is particularly proud of their "accurately reconstructed" privy. **Willimantic** , is home to the **Connecticut Eastern Railroad Museum** (55 Bridge Street; tel: 860-456 9999; May–Oct Sat–Sun; charge). Exhibits housed in vintage railroad buildings include locomotives, rolling stock, and a reconstructed roundhouse.

The **Windham Textile and History Museum** (411 Main Street; tel: 860-456 2178; Fri–Sun; charge) demonstrates how the experiences of craftspeople, workers, designers, and consumers influenced the technology, immigration, and culture of Connecticut.

To the east in **Canterbury**, the **Prudence Crandall Museum** (Junction Routes 14 and 169; tel: 860-546 7800; May–Oct Thur–Sun; charge) was the home of Connecticut's

Official Heroine. In 1833, she admitted an African-American woman to her boarding school. The town reacted by passing a law forbidding her to accept African-American students. She was arrested for refusing to obey the law. When her conviction was overturned, a mob attacked the building, forcing her to close the school and leave Connecticut, eventually settling in Kansas. In 1886, the Connecticut legislature awarded her a pension, while the citizens of Canterbury signed a petition apologizing for their actions.

ALONG THE RIVER VALLEY

Beginning as a mountain stream near the New Hampshire–Canada border, the Connecticut River travels 410 miles (660km) through four states and ends its journey to the sea as a broad and majestic tidal estuary. The Native Americans named it Quinnituckett, which means "the long, tidal river." Throughout history, the Connecticut River has linked valley residents with the outside world. A fertile floodplain nourishes crops, and water power has generated energy for small industries.

The Sculpture Mile

Walk along the main streets of Madison or Essex and you'll enjoy a unique outdoor art exhibit. The Sculpture Mile brings world-class sculpture by nationally recognized artists to the "living museum" of a town. You expect to see artwork along the shopping district or in front of municipal buildings, but they are also beside parking lots and on the lawns of churches. The idea is to present art to people who would not usually visit art galleries or museums. The styles and materials are as varied as the locations: traditional to abstract; bronze to steel; granite to wood. The 30 pieces are refreshed annually. Other Connecticut towns are adopting the program. For information, www.hollycroft.org.

Begin a tour of the valley in **Ivoryton** ⑮, a center of piano-making 100 years ago which takes its name from the material used to make the keys.

The historic **Ivoryton Playhouse** (103 Main Street; tel: 860-767 7318; www.ivorytonplayhouse.org) was the first self-supporting stock theatre in the country. Katherine Hepburn, Alan Alda, and Marlon Brando, among other stars, have trod the boards here. Down the road, the **Museum of Fife and Drum** (62 N. (62 North Main Street; tel: 860-767 2237; July–Labor Day Sat–Sun; charge) presents a visual and musical history of America on parade from the Revolutionary War to the present. Free concerts are presented Tuesday evenings in July–August.

Essex

Essex ⑯, founded in 1645, was an important shipbuilding center during the 18th century. The *Oliver Cromwell*, America's first warship, was launched here in 1776. Yachts and cabin cruisers still berth here, and tall masts and yards of tackle lend the town a distinctly nautical air. The **Connecticut River Museum** (67 Main Street; tel: 860-767 8269; daily; charge) highlights the importance of the Connecticut as transportation, recreation, and resource with exhibits, boats, and a replica of the *Turtle*, the nation's first submarine. A combination ticket includes a cruise on the museum's schooner, the *Mary E*. There are also eagle watch cruises in February and March.

Take an old-fashioned journey by steam locomotive and riverboat by means of the **Essex Steam Train and Riverboat Ride** (1 Railroad Avenue; tel: 860-767 0103; www.essexsteamtrain.com; open May–Dec with varied schedule; charge). You board a 1920s coach car and ride along the river through the villages of **Chester** and **Deep River**. At Deep River, passengers board a riverboat for a 90-minute cruise. The round trip takes about 2.5 hours.

Head north on Route 154 and east on Route 148 to the **Chester-Hadlyme**

Ferry (54 Ferry Road; tel: 860-443 3856; daily Apr–Nov; charge). It has been transporting people across the Connecticut River to East Haddam since 1769.

Gillette Castle

Crossing the river, you can't miss seeing the spectacularly eccentric **Gillette Castle** at **Gillette Castle State Park** ⑰ (67 River Road; tel: 860-526 2336; castle open Memorial Day–Columbus Day daily; charge; grounds open daily; free). William Gillette (1853–1937) was a much admired American actor whose stage portrayal of Sherlock Holmes brought him fame and fortune.

For his dream house, the actor selected a hilltop aerie overlooking the Connecticut River and its surrounding countryside. Work on the 122-acre (49-hectare) site with its stone-and-concrete castle began in 1914, took five years, and cost more than $1 million. The results are whimsical and bizarre. He installed hidden mirrors so that he could spy on public rooms from the master bedroom. The

William Gillette's will stated that his castle should not be sold to any "blithering saphead who has no conception of where he is or with what surrounded." In 1943 it was bought by the State of Connecticut.

BELOW:
Essex Steam Train.

park's 184 acres (75 hectares) have hiking trails and fine views of the river.

North on Route 82 is the charming Victorian town of **East Haddam** . The 1876 **Goodspeed Opera House** (tel: 860-873 8668; www.goodspeed. org), which sits majestically on the banks of the Connecticut River, was a popular stopover in the heyday of steamboat travel. Beautifully restored, it is considered the incubator for new musicals. *Man of La Mancha* and *Annie* are just two shows which premiered here. Its schedule includes revivals of Broadway musicals, as well as original productions (productions Jan–Nov; tours June–Oct Sat 11am–1pm; charge).

It's worth stopping for a quick visit at the one-room **Nathan Hale Schoolhouse** (29 Main Street; tel: 860-873 3399; May–Oct daily; donation) where Connecticut's celebrated patriot once taught.

SOUTH OF HARTFORD

Take I–91 south to exit 25S, and CT 3S to **Wethersfield** ,"Ye Most Auncient Towne" according to 1650 colonial records. The red onion, which features prominently on the town's logo, was developed in the farmland near here. More than 300 of the 17th- and 18th-century "downtown" homes have been preserved. Three can be toured at the **Webb-Deane-Stevens Museum** (211 Main Street; tel: 860-529 0612; May–Oct Wed–Mon, Nov–Apr Fri–Sun; charge). George Washington planned the Yorktown campaign in the Webb House. Silas Deane, envoy to France during the Revolution, used his home as his political headquarters. The Stevens house shows middle-class life in the 1820s and 1830s.

The **Buttolph-Williams House** (249 Broad Street; tel: 860-529 0612; May–Oct Mon and Wed–Sun, Nov–Apr weekends) gives a rare look inside the life of the Puritans. It is also the setting for the novel, *The Witch of Blackbird Pond*.

The **Wethersfield Historical Society** (200 Main Street; tel: 860-529 7161; closed Mon; charge) has displays about the lives of ordinary people who created and built the town. It also maintains the adjacent 1790 Hurlbut-Dunham House, which is furnished to show life in the early 20th century, and maritime exhibits at the Cove Warehouse (both places, June–Sept weekends; charge).

Comstock, Ferre & Co. (263 Main Street; tel: 860-571 6590; Sun–Thur), housed in a collection of buildings dating as far back as the 1700s, was established as a seed house in 1811. Its inventory of heirloom seeds for sale in the store is one of the largest in the horticultural world. During renovation of the buildings, workers uncovered a hoard of agricultural treasures hidden under the dust and debris. Plans are to create a living history museum of agriculture in a setting that company founder William Comstock would recognize.

Dinosaur State Park

Continue south on I–91 to exit 23 to Rocky Hill and **Dinosaur State Park** (400 West Street; tel: 860-529 8423; Tue–Sun; charge; grounds open daily

BELOW: Dinosaur State Park.

9am–4pm; free). Dinosaur tracks were found here in 1966 during building excavation. A massive geodesic dome protects some 500 of over 2,000 tracks found. An arboretum features plants descended from those the dinos munched.

New Britain to Middletown

In **New Britain** ㉑, works from all eras and styles by artists including Cassatt, Whistler, and Sargent are on exhibit at the **New Britain Museum of American Art** (56 Lexington Street; tel: 860-229 0257; closed Mon; charge). Free concerts, featuring everything from jazz to country to rock 'n' roll, are presented at the Davis Miller Band Shell in **Walnut Hill Park** (next to the museum) on Monday and Wednesday evenings in July–August.

Southeast of New Britain on Route 9, **Middletown** ㉒ is home to Wesleyan University and a romantic Main Street and town square.

West to Waterbury

In **Waterbury** ㉓, creative exhibits at the **Mattatuck Museum Arts and History Center** (44 West Main Street; tel: 203-753 0381; closed Mon; charge) document the industrial, social, architectural, and cultural history of the Naugatuck Valley. New exhibits include oral histories and family stories. Button-making was an important industry here; over 10,000 buttons made of cinnabar, ivory, and other materials and as diverse as those from George Washington's coat and floral bouquets made from human hair are on display. The art galleries focus on Connecticut landscapes and important figures from the 18th century to the present day.

The Renaissance Revival **Palace Theater** (100 East Main Street; tel: 203-346 2000; www.palacetheaterct. org) is the city's primary venue for performing arts.

Danbury

To the west along I–84 at **Danbury** ㉔, the **Danbury Railway Museum** (120 White Street, exit 5 off I–84; tel: 203-778 8337; Memorial Day–Labor Day daily, Sept–May Wed–Sun; charge), with its 6-acre (2.43-hectare) switchyard, has over 70 engines – from steam to diesel – and rolling stock on display. Visitors can ride on a 90ft (27-meter) turntable. For an additional fee, there's a 20-minute ride through the rail yard in the cab with the engineer.

Danbury was the center of the millinery world in the 19th century. You can glimpse that era's fashionistas' fads at the **Danbury Museum and Historical Society** (43 Main Street; tel: 203-743 5200; Thur–Sat; charge). The society also oversees the studio of the famous contralto Marian Anderson (call for openings).

To the south in **Ridgefield** ㉕, the **Aldrich Contemporary Art Museum** (258 Main Street; tel: 203-438 4519; Tue–Sun; charge, free admission on Tue) is the only museum in Connecticut devoted to contemporary art. It has no permanent collection; exhibits are by emerging and mid-level artists.

Tarrywile Mansion, a community center for Danbury in the city-owned Tarrywile Park, is a large recreation area with picnic spots and 21 miles (34km) of hiking trails.

BELOW: the wealthy Gold Coast has a big appetite for antiques.

Visitors from Long Island can cross the Sound to the Connecticut shore by ferry from Orient Point to New London. The car ferry takes 80 minutes. The passenger-only ferry takes 40 minutes.

BELOW: feeding time at South Norwalk's Maritime Aquarium.

Just down the street, at the **Keeler Tavern Museum** (132 Main Street; tel: 203-438 5485; Feb–Dec Wed and Sat–Sun; charge), costumed guides conduct tours of exhibits which cover three centuries of Ridgefield history from the late 18th century to mid-20th century. A British cannonball from a skirmish between colonials and Redcoats in 1777 is embedded in an outer wall.

THE SOUTHWESTERN SHORE

China clippers and Yankee whalers sailed from the harbors of New Haven, New London, and Stonington out to seek their fortunes. People along Connecticut's coast still retain a fondness for the sea, and most towns have at least one marina. On a clear summer's day the horizon of Long Island Sound is filled with billowing sails.

The Gold Coast

"Greenwich, Cos Cob, Stamford, Darien, and Rowayton" – to the thousands of Connecticut residents who work in New York City, this is a railroad conductor's litany. About

an hour from Manhattan by train, the Connecticut suburbs are among the nation's smartest bedroom communities.

The coastal area that parallels I-95 from Greenwich to Westport – lower Fairfield County – is sometimes referred to as the "Gold Coast" because of the many wealthy communities it encompasses.

In **Greenwich** ㉖, the **Bruce Museum** (One (1 Museum Drive; tel: 203-869 0376; closed Mon; charge) features fine and decorative arts, natural science, and anthropology. Docent-led tours are on Fridays at 12.30pm. There's a self-guided audio tour app for smartphones.

Nearby, Cos Cob's **Bush-Holley Historic Site** (39 Strickland Road; tel: 203-869 6899; Mar–Dec Wed–Sun; docent-led tours at 1, 2, and 3pm; limited hours Jan–Feb, call; charge) explores two distinct historical periods. The first looks at the development of the community from 1790 to 1825. The other focuses on Cos Cob when it became the state's first art colony to attract Impressionist painters.

In **Stamford** ㉗, take a stroll through the **Bartlett Arboretum and Gardens** (151 Brookdale Road; tel: 203-322 6971; daily; charge), a 91-acre (37-hectare) swath of wildflower meadows, wetlands, boardwalks, and trails. Nature-lovers will also want to visit **Stamford Museum and Nature Center** (39 Scofieldtown Road; tel: 203-322 1646; museum and farm: daily; charge; observatory: Friday nights; charge). Two very distinctive attractions are here. The Henri Willis Bendel Mansion was the realization of the residential dream of designer and department store owner Bendel. His elaborate house combined elements of Tudor manor homes he admired in England. It's lavishly furnished inside with the epitome of interior design of the 1920s. Outside, Italian sculpture graces the grounds. The museum, housed in the mansion, has a small but excellent collection of American

art, Native American art and cultural objects, and objects of American history from the 1600s to World War II. The Nature Center has a completely different focus. The 118 woodland acres (48 hectares) include a working farm with cows and a creamery, pig pen, ducks, maple sugar house, and organic garden.

New Canaan

Take Route 7N off I–95 to CT 123 and **New Canaan** ㉘ to visit **Philip Johnson's Glass House** (199 Elm Street; tel: 203-594 9884/866-811 4111; www.philipjohnsonglasshouse.org; tours May–Nov Wed–Mon; charge). This is the architect's minimalist masterpiece – once his private (if glass-walled) retreat – on 47 magnificently landscaped acres (19 hectares). The estate is operated to preserve and interpret modern architecture, landscape, and art. There are several different tours, which sell out quickly. Reservations are highly recommended. The **New Canaan Nature Center** (144 Oenoke Ridge; tel: 203-966 9577; Mon–Sat; donation), on

a 40-acre (16-hectare) site with an unusual variety of habitats, has walking trails, a raptor exhibit, and a 4,000-sq-ft (372-sq-meter) greenhouse; the **New Canaan Historical Society** (13 Oenoke Ridge; tel: 203-966 1776; Tue–Fri; charge) complex encompasses an 1845 pharmacy, an old schoolhouse, a sculpture studio, and a tool museum. The **Silvermine Guild Arts Center** (1037 Silvermine Road; tel: 203-966 9700; galleries open Wed–Sun) began as an artist colony in 1908 by visionary sculptor Solon Borglum (brother of Mt Rushmore sculptor Gutzon). Today, it is an association of over 300 juried artists, an award-winning school for visual arts, home to five galleries, and a venue for performing art productions.

The Norwalks

South Norwalk ㉙, with its upscale galleries and shops, has been dubbed "SoNo" for its emulation of New York's SoHo district.

The huge **Maritime Aquarium** (10 N. (10 North Water Street; tel: 203-852 0700; daily; charge) on the banks of the Norwalk River has more than 1,000

Connecticut has the oldest public library in the US in the the Scoville Memorial Library. Locals could borrow and return books on the third Monday of every third month. As today, fees were collected for damages; the most common damage was "greasing", when wax dripped from the candles onto the pages of the book as it was being read.

BELOW:
Marlon Brando, 1924–2004.

The Greatest Hits

Mention any great Broadway play or musical and chances are it was first performed at the Shubert Theater in New Haven. Since 1914, the Shubert has seen over 600 pre-Broadway tryouts, including over 300 world premiers. Richard Rodgers so loved the place that most of his musicals premiered here, including *Oklahoma* (originally called *Away We Go*) and *South Pacific*. *My Fair Lady*, *The Caine Mutiny Court Martial*, and *A Long Day's Journey into Night* are also on the roster. Young actors hoping for their big break gravitated to the Shubert. Unknowns when they arrived – Henry Fonda, James Earl Jones, Shirley MacLaine, John Travolta, and Marlon Brando, among many others – their names were familiar after opening night.

Westport's Levitt Pavilion for the Performing Arts.

BELOW: seeing the sights of Bridgeport.

marine animals and plenty of hands-on displays relating to the marine life and maritime culture of Long Island Sound. Seal feedings are at 11.45am, 1.45pm, and 3.45pm. There's also an IMAX movie theater. The aquarium's research vessel takes passengers on a 2.5-hour excursion daily in July and August, and weekends from April to June and in October.

You can hop on board the catamaran ferry at Hope Dock for a scenic cruise to **Sheffield Island** and a guided tour of an 1868, 10-room lighthouse (tel: 203-838 9444; Memorial Day–Sept daily; www.seaport.org; charge). On a clear day, you can see the New York skyline from the lighthouse. The **Stewart B. McKinney National Wildlife Refuge** is also here. In nearby **Norwalk** ⓧ, tours are offered of "America's first château," the restored, 62-room Victorian **Lockwood-Mathews Mansion Museum** (295 West Avenue, Matthews Park; tel: 203-838 9799; Apr–early Jan Wed–Sun tours, at noon, 1, 2, and 3pm; audio tours if no docent is available;

charge). Tours show off the incredibly detailed woodwork and craftsmanship in the design and construction of the mansion, as well as the elaborate furnishings. Children 10 years old and younger will enjoy the hands-on activities at **Stepping Stones Museum for Children** (303 West Avenue; Matthews Park; tel: 203-899 0606; daily 10am–5pm; charge). Expanded and renovated, it's a center for learning through play.

Westport

One of the country's most affluent communities, Westport is perhaps best known for its **Westport Country Playhouse** (25 Powers Court; box office tel: 203-227 4177/888-927 7529 (closed Mon); www.westportplayhouse.org), which mounts award-winning experimental plays as well as reinterpretations of the classics. The outdoor **Levitt Pavilion for the Performing Arts** (40 Jesup Road; tel: 203-226 7600; www.levittpavilion.com) hosts more than 50 free events throughout the summer, including bands, movies, and children's shows

Sherwood Island State Park by Long Island Sound is the location of the Connecticut Living 9/11 Memorial (Sherwood Island Connector off Route 1 in Westport; tel: 203-226 6983; open daily; charge in season. Before the attack, the Twin Towers were clearly visible from the beach. The monument and benches around it face the skyline.

Bridgeport

To the east, **Bridgeport** ⓧ is a major industrial center. The **Barnum Museum** (820 Main Street; tel: 203-331 1104) is a showcase for memorabilia connected to circus pioneer P. T. Barnum (1810–91), with a 4,000-piece miniature circus, clown props, bogus "oddities" like the Feejee Mermaid, and items relating to the diminutive Bridgeport native General Tom Thumb. The building was hit by a tornado in 2010 and is currently closed

MIDDLEBANK II
BRIDGEPORT, CT

for repairs. Museum officials hope to reopen in late 2012. Call for updates.

Highlights at Connecticut's **Beardsley Zoo** (1875 Noble Avenue; tel: 203-394 6565; daily; charge), the state's only zoo, include over 300 North and South American species and a tropical rainforest.

New Haven

New Haven 32, settled by Puritans in 1638, was an independent colony until 1662, when it merged with the Hartford settlement. At first a seafaring community, New Haven later embraced industry and pioneered such inventions as the steel fish hook, the meat grinder, the corkscrew, and the steamboat.

New Haven is best known, however, for **Yale University** (visitor center, 149 Elm Street; tel: 203-432 2300; visitor center open daly; tours Mon–Fri 10.30am and 2pm, Sat and Sun 1.30pm; self-guided tours for MP3 players in English and Spanish available). Founded in 1701 by a group of Puritan clergymen, it was originally located in nearby Saybrook. In 1716,

the school was moved to New Haven, and two years later it took the name of benefactor Elihu Yale.

Alumni include both presidents Bush, Bill and Hillary Clinton, Supreme Court justices Sonia Sotomayor and Clarence Thomas, Paul Newman, Jodie Foster, and Cole Porter. The buildings on campus evoke the British universities of Oxford and Cambridge.

Any visit to the university should include the **Beinecke Rare Book and Manuscript Library** at 121 Wall Street (tel: 203-432 2977; open Mon–Sat year-round), where an edition of the Gutenberg Bible and original Audubon bird prints are displayed.

Two blocks south, the **Yale University Art Gallery** (1111 Chapel Street; tel: 203-432 0600; open Tue–Sun; no charge) has a comprehensive collection of American, African, and ancient art, and canvases by Manet, Van Gogh, Corot, Degas, and Matisse. Across the street is the **Yale Center for British Art** (1080 Chapel Street; tel: 203-432 2800/877-BRIT-ART; Tue–Sun; no charge). It has the largest collection of British art outside

Sherwood Island State Park has facilities for shore fishing and saltwater swimming in Long Island Sound.

BELOW: Joseph Cinque, leader of the *La Amistad* slave revolt.

The Saga of La Amistad

In 1839, a group of slaves took over the *La Amistad*, the vessel carrying them to sugar plantations in Cuba. They sailed up the East Coast, eventually arriving in Long Island Sound. The ship was towed to New Haven, where the fate of "the Amistads" became one of the first legal fights over slavery. The protracted legal battles raised questions of morality and sovereignty. The Amistads insisted that as they were kidnapped, they were free. Spain, which ruled Cuba, countered that the US had no jurisdiction in the matter, as the "cargo" was loaded in Havana and destined for another Cuban port, and the mutiny occurred in international waters.

As it worked its way up the court system, each appeal found in favor of the Amistads, much to the annoyance of President Martin Van Buren, who was eager to appease Spain and keep face with the slave-holding South. But even the Supreme Court, with a majority of Southerners on the bench, decided against the Spanish claims. All people, it ruled, lived in a natural state of freedom and the Amistads were freed. It was the first antislavery decision by the Supreme Court. It took several years to raise the money to pay for their voyage home, but eventually the surviving Amistads retuned home. Ironically, "amistad" means "friendship."

A breath of fresh air for a vintage vehicle.

BELOW: students heading to class at Yale University.

the UK, donated in 1966 by industrialist Paul Mellon.

Collections at the **Peabody Museum of Natural History** (170 Whitney Avenue; 203-432 5050; open daily; charge) include dinosaur fossils, native birds, meteorites, and minerals. Guided tours are offered on weekends at 12.30 and 1.30pm. An audio tour, via wand or MP3 download, is also available.

Over 1,000 musical instruments are displayed at the **Yale Collection of Musical Instruments** (15 Hillhouse Avenue; tel: 203-432 0822; Sept–June Tue–Sun; www.yale.edu/musicalinstruments; free). It concentrates on Western art music. Concerts are given periodically throughout the year.

Adjacent to the university, New Haven Green is surrounded by a trinity of churches constructed in Gothic Revival, Georgian, and Federal styles.

New Haven's cultural offerings include Yale University's **Institute of Sacred Music** (409 Prospect Street; tel: 203-432 5180), which presents concerts, art exhibitions, and films; the award-winning **Yale Repertory Theater** (1120 Chapel Street; tel:

203-432 1234; www.yalerep.org), a professional company known for producing new plays and innovative interpretations of classics; the **Long Wharf Theater** on the downtown waterfront (222 Sargent Drive; tel: 203-787 4282); and the **Shubert Theater** (247 College Street; tel: 203-624 1825; www.shubert.com), the "Birthplace of the nation's greatest hits". The **New Haven Symphony Orchestra** (tel: 203-865 0831; www.newhavensymphony.org) performs at Woolsey Hall on the Yale campus.

The **Grove Street Cemetery** (227 Grove Street; tel: 203-389 5403; daily; free tours Sat 11am and on 1st and 3rd Sun noon), also known as the New Haven Burial Ground, was established in 1797 to replace the common mass burial ground on the village green. It was the first in the country to have family plots instead of random interments. Eli Whitney and Noah Webster are two of the notables resting here. The database of known burials has over 14,000 entries.

ALONG THE EASTERN SHORE

Just off I–95 in **East Haven** ❸, the **Shore Line Troley Museum** (17 River Street; tel: 203-467 6927; May and Sept–Dec Sat–Sun, Memorial Day–Labor Day and Dec 26–30 daily; charge) preserves some 100 trolleys, the oldest rapid transit car, and a rare parlor car. Hop aboard for a 3-mile (5km) ride on one of the vintage cars.

East on Route 146 off Route 1 in **Branford**, cruises by Thimble Islands Cruise & Charter (tel: 203-488 8905; www.thimbleislandcruise.com), Capt. Bob Milne (tel: 203-481 3345; www.thimbleislands.com), and Capt. Dave Kusterer (tel: 352-978 1502/203-397 3921; www.thimbleislander.net) sail from the town's nearby **Stony Creek** dock for hour-long narrated tours of the **Thimble Islands**, a cluster of islands – 23 of them inhabited – just offshore.

Farther east on Route 146, **Guilford** ❸ was settled in 1639 by the Reverend

Henry Whitfield. His home, the oldest stone dwelling in New England, is now the **Henry Whitfield State Museum** (248 Old Whitfield Road; tel: 203-453 2457; May–mid-Dec Wed–Sun; charge). The self-guided tour of the three-story building, whose thick stone walls served as a fort for the first colonists in the area, gives visitors a feel for how early settlers lived.

Guilford has one of the largest and prettiest town greens in New England. Nearby are several historic houses, including the 1690 **Hyland House** (84 Boston Street; tel: 203-453 9477; June–Labor Day Tue–Sun, Sept–Oct weekends; charge) and the 1774 **Thomas Griswold House** (171 Boston Street; tel: 203-453 3176; mid-June–Sept Tue–Sun, weekends in Oct; charge), with a restored blacksmith shop and colonial garden. The **Dudley Farm** (2351 Durham Road; tel: 203-457 0770; May–Oct Thur–Sun; charge) is a working 1840 farmstead and living-history museum.

Five miles (8km) east, **Madison** ㉟ has some of the state's most beautiful summer and year-round homes. The

1681 **Deacon John Grave House** (581 Boston Post Road; tel: 203-245 4798; call for hours; charge), home for seven generations of the family, has been a school, wartime infirmary, inn, tavern, and courtroom.

Hammonasset Beach State Park (1288 Boston Post Road/Route 1; tel: 203-245 2785; parking fee mid-Apr–Memorial Day and Labor Day–Oct) is the state's longest public beach, with 2 miles (3km) of sand.

At **Old Saybrook** ㊱, by the mouth of the Connecticut River, **Fort Saybrook Monument Park** (Saybrook Point/Route 154) has storyboards chronicling Saybrook Colony from 1635. The monument is a statue of English military engineer Lion Gardiner, who built the fort in 1636 to protect the settlers from the Pequot Indians. The park offers fine estuary views, with opportunities for bird watching from the boardwalk. Stop in for a Miss James Sundae at the **James Gallery & Soda Fountain** (2 Pennywise Lane; tel: 860-395 1229; open June–Aug daily, Sept–May Wed–Sun). The building has been a general

The Florence Griswold Museum has been restored to how it looked around 1910 when the local art colony was the center of Impressionism in America.

What Did Nathan Hale Really Say?

Every schoolchild in New England learns the story of Nathan Hale, the 21-year-old soldier in the Continental Army hung as a spy by the British in 1776. As he stood by the gallows, Hale said, "I only regret that I have but one life to lose for my country."

No eyewitness account mentions the quote, although one British officer's memoir has Hale saying, "I am so satisfied with the cause in which I am engaged, that my only regret is, that I have not more lives than one to offer in its service."

The much more repeatable and memorable version seems to stem from a newspaper article in 1799. In it, a British witness remembers Hale saying he regretted having only one life to lose for his country – not so much quoting Hale as paraphrasing his final words.

A graduate of Yale University, Hale was familiar with contemporary literature of his times. A play by Joseph Addison, *Cato*, was well known and contained a passage which directly applied to his situation and could have inspired him:

How beautiful is death, when earn'd by virtue
Who would not be that youth?

What pity is it that we can die but once to serve our country.

Much else about Hale's execution is equally mysterious. Three places in Manhattan vie for recognition as the site of the actual hanging; no one knows what happened to his body; and no one knows what Hale actually looked like. All of the statues of the patriot are idealized imaginings.

Hale has long been considered a hero of the American Revolutionary War, and in 1985 he was designated the official state hero of Connecticut. Although he never actually fought in battle, Hale was the only volunteer willing to travel behind enemy lines and spy on the British forces.

Not much else is known about Nathan Hale. The only contemporary source is the diary of a British officer who was present at his execution, who wrote "He behaved with great composure and resolution, saying he though it the duty of every good Officer, to obey any orders given him by his Commander-in-Chief; and desired the Spectators to be at all times to meet death in whatever shape it might appear."

store or inn since 1790. It's currently the site of a Moroccan-themed shop – still selling ice cream and soda fountain favorites (as well as Moroccan pastries) – but also spices, lotions, and beautiful Moroccan pottery. The **Katharine Hepburn Cultural Arts Center**, or "The Kate" (300 Main Street; tel: 860-510 0473; www. katharinehepburntheater.org), is a new venue dedicated to honoring Old Saybrook's most celebrated resident with cultural and artistic presentations. There's a small museum (Tue–Fri 10am–2pm and one hour prior to performances) with her awards, costumes, and movie memorabilia.

Old Lyme to New London

Old Lyme ❸ boasts a rich artistic heritage – thanks in large part to Florence Griswold. The daughter of one of the town's many sea captains, she lived a privileged life until the Civil War and the rise of steam sea power reversed the family fortunes, and she was forced to take in boarders. One of them was painter Henry Ward Roger, recently returned from Europe and eager to

start an art colony. A few years after his 1899 arrival, Old Lyme was the center for a new school of Impressionist landscape painting. It lasted for nearly three decades and included American artists like Childe Hassan, William Chadwick, and Matilda Browne. The "home" for many of them is now the **Florence Griswold Museum** (96 Lyme Street; tel: 860-434 5542; closed Mon; charge), which contains a stunning array of works by her illustrious American Impressionist boarders. Some were so moved by her hospitality that they left painted mementos on the doors, mantels, and paneled walls. The on-site café provides blankets and baskets for patrons who want to picnic in the fabulous gardens.

The **Lyme Art Association** (90 Lyme Street; tel: 860-434 7802; closed Mon) continues the support of artists started by "Miss Florence" by showcasing works by regional representational artists.

New London

New London ❸ was one of America's busiest 19th-century whaling ports. Many a vast fortune was accumulated by its merchants. Evidence of this wealth can be seen on "Whale Oil Row" on Huntington Street, with its grand mansions.

When petroleum began to replace whale oil, manufacturing became New London's chief occupation. But the city maintained its ties to the sea and today is the home of the **US Coast Guard Academy** (31 Mohegan Avenue; tel: 800-883 USCG; cadet-led tours Mon, Wed, and Fri at 1pm; call to pre-register). You will need a photo ID to enter the base and buildings. There is also a self-guided walking tour with maps available at the Coast Guard Museum and admissions office (both in Waesche Hall). The museum has 200 years' worth of Coast Guard history and memorabilia. The tall ship *Eagle*, the academy's training vessel, is open for tours when in port.

New London was also the summer boyhood home of Eugene O'Neill

BELOW:
Lyman Allyn Art Museum.

(1888–1953), the Nobel Prize-winning playwright. The O'Neill family's **Monte Cristo Cottage** (325 Pequot Avenue; tel: 860-443 5378; Memorial Day–Labor Day Thur–Sun; charge) was the setting for his autobiographical work, *Long Day's Journey into Night*, and has been restored to reflect O'Neill's set directions and sketches for the play. Nearby, **Ocean Beach Park** (98 Neptune Avenue; tel: 860-447 3031/800-510 7263; open week before Memorial Day–Labor Day daily; admission charge), on Long Island Sound, has a large sugar-sand beach, huge pool, entertainment boardwalk, kid rides, a fully equipped fitness facility (additional charge), and a full-service restaurant. The two restored **Hempstead Houses** (11 Hempstead Street; tel: 860-247 8996; May–June and Sept–Oct Sat–Sun, July–Aug Wed, Fri, Sat, and Sun; charge) are far removed from the casual beach scene. Joshua Hempstead lived his entire life in the frame house built in 1678. He was, at various times, a farmer, judge, gravestone carver, and shipwright. His grandson Nathaniel built the stone

house next door in 1759. They are furnished with period pieces tracing the evolution of colonial lifestyles.

American Impressionist paintings and 18th- to 20th-century decorative arts are highlighted at the **Lyman Allyn Art Museum** (625 Williams Street; tel: 860-443 2545; closed Mon; charge). There is no admission to the Outdoor Art Park and September 11th Memorial Gardens.

USS *Nautilus*

Across the Thames River from New London is the city of **Groton** ㊴, known as the "Submarine Capital of the World" – the manufacture of nuclear submarines is its major industry. Non-claustrophobes who wish to view the interior of a submarine may visit the USS *Nautilus* at the **US Naval Submarine Force Museum** (1 Crystal Lake Road at exit 86, off I-95; tel: 860-694 3174/800-343 0079; closed Tue, also closed first two weeks of Nov and Apr; free). The museum has the world's largest collection of submarine artifacts, photos, and documents. It chronicles the development

Mystic Aquarium.

BELOW: the USS *Nautilus* at Groton.

Connecticut's Nicknames

Like every other state, Connecticut has a nickname. Actually, it has several. Most often, it's called The Constitution State, but the Nutmeg State crops up occasionally, as do a few more colorful terms

In 1638, the Connecticut Colony Council adopted the Fundamental Orders – generally considered the first written constitution anywhere in the world. Although the men who drafted the document were loyal British subjects, the Orders make no reference to the king or sovereign (nor to any government outside of Connecticut for that matter). The Orders created a General Assembly, determined how to elect officials, set terms of office, and determined how taxes would be decided and levied. At the time, these were all radical, if not revolutionary, concepts.

The Nutmeg State, another nickname, comes from traditional folklore. Thomas Haliburton, a Canadian author who used the pen name "Sam Slick," wrote humorous essays about rural Canada and New England in the 1830s. One of his stories claimed that Connecticut traders were so shrewd that they could convince gullible customers that knobs of wood were nutmegs.

But it's "The Land of Steady Habits" that has a fanciful origin that would make Sam Slick proud. The moniker shows up in a 1951 book, *The Dictionary of Americanism on Historical Principles*. The book says it's an allusion to the strict morals of the inhabitants enforced by the Connecticut "Blue Laws." The statutes were allegedly written in 1650 by Puritan clerics, printed in London on blue paper (hence the name "Blue Laws"), and distributed to households in New Haven. It sounds very authentic, but it's a great hoax. The real story is this: in 1781, Rev. Samuel Peters – a loyalist Anglican cleric who returned to England during the Revolution – published *A General History of Connecticut*. Far from an attempt to accurately describe Connecticut (or any other part of the rebellious colonies, for that matter), Peters' book is an over-the-top effort to make the Colonials appear backwards and foolish. He invented the Blue Laws story. In his *History*, he lists all 45 of the "laws." They include such decrees as "No woman shall kiss her child on the Sabbath" and "No one shall celebrate Christmas, make minced pies, dance, play cards, or play any instrument of music except drum, trumpet, and jaw harp." Despite their absurdity, the legend of the Blue Laws took root and – as seen by its use in the 1951 *Dictionary* – is an urban legend still widely accepted as truth.

In the real world, however, there really are Blue Laws. That's the term used for laws regulating activities on Sunday (probably coming from the Blue Laws legend). Most of them deal with gambling and liquor sales. Ironically, Connecticut is one of only three states which still prohibit Sunday liquor sales, and groups regularly work to see the repeal of Connecticut's one legitimate Blue Law.

ABOVE: this 1998 statue on New London's City Pier shows playwright Eugene O'Neill as he was when he spent his boyhood summers here.
LEFT: Thomas Chandler Haliburton, 1796–1865. Lawyer, politician, judge, writer, born in Nova Scotia.

of submarine technology and warfare from the Revolutionary War *Turtle* to today's super subs.

Fort Griswold Battlefield State Park (Monument Street and Park Avenue; tel: 860-449 6877; museum and monument open Memorial Day–Labor Day Wed–Sun) is the site of a notorious incident during the Revolution. British forces led by traitor Benedict Arnold overran the fort and massacred 88 of the 165 defenders after they surrendered. The ruins of the fortifications remain and the stone house where the wounded survivors were tended is a museum.

Mystic

Five miles (8km) east, at exit 90 off I–95, is **Mystic ⓭**, an old maritime community of trim white houses, sitting at the tidal outlet of the Mystic River. For generations, Mystic was the home of mariners and fishermen and was condemned by the British during the Revolution as a "cursed little hornets' nest" of patriots. The village teemed with activity during the Gold Rush days of 1849 when shipbuilders vied to

see who could construct the fastest clipper ships to travel round Cape Horn to the boom town of San Francisco. The *Andrew Jackson*, a Mystic-built clipper launched in 1860, claimed the world's record: 89 days, 4 hours.

Beluga whales, sharks, penguins, sea lions, and sea otters are just a few of more than 3,500 creatures at the **Mystic Aquarium and Institute for Exploration** (55 Coogan Boulevard; tel: 860-572 5955; open daily; charge; additional charges for some activities and exhibits). Visitors utilize the latest deep-sea technology, including live cameras, robots, and a live Web feed to dive under the sea, visit kelp beds, and watch sea otters romp. Another exhibit displays many of the treasures brought up from the ocean floor while researching the wreck of the *Titanic*.

Mystic Seaport

Down Route 27 just a mile, **Mystic Seaport, The Museum of America and the Sea** (75 Greenmanville Avenue; tel: 888-973 2767; daily; www.mysticseaport.org; charge), is a living replica of a 19th-century waterfront community

Spinning a yarn at Mystic Seaport.

BELOW: the whaling ship *Charles W. Morgan* at Mystic Seaport.

One of the Mystic Seaport workshops.

BELOW: Dodson Boatyard, Stonington.

during the heyday of sailing ships. The site includes over 60 buildings and is so authentic that it was used as the 1839 setting for New Haven's harbor in Steven Spielberg's 1997 movie *Amistad*, about a revolt aboard a slave ship sailing from Africa (*see page* 263).

A full day and plenty of stamina are required to tour the entire seaport properly. Visitors can wander along the wharves and streets of the village and taste the old seafaring way of life. Most buildings are set up to show

their functions at the time. Others have special exhibits like a collection of carved ship figureheads or the story of women and the sea. A planetarium demonstrates how sailors used the stars for navigation.

The museum's collection of ships and boats from the age of sail and early machine power is unmatched. The **Charles W. Morgan**, the last surviving whaling ship from a fleet which once numbered over 600, and the oldest American merchant ship afloat, is berthed here. She is currently in dry dock at the museum and is being restored to seaworthy status. Plans are for her to be re-rigged and launched under sail in late 2012. In the meantime, visitors can board the tall ship **Joseph Conrad**, built in 1882 by the Danish as a training vessel. There are sloops, an island steamer, an open launch, and a Danish lighthouse tender used to smuggle Jews to Sweden during World War II.

From Memorial Day through Columbus Day, the museum offers cruises up the river on some of its historic fleet (additional fee). Visitors can also rent rowboats and sailboats. Each

June, the seaport hosts an international Sea Music Festival, when the sound of sea chanteys floats across the docks.

Stonington

Five miles (8km) farther east is the charming old whaling port of **Stonington ④**. The **ld Lighthoue Museum** (7 Water Street; tel: 860-535 1440; May–Oct daily, Apr and Nov Sat–Sun; charge) is inside an 1823 building. The light atop this sturdy stone edifice was visible 12 miles out to sea. The six rooms depict life of Stonington's residents: not just the fishermen, but boat builders, farmers, and tradesmen.

Admission to the museum includes a visit to the **Captain Nathaniel B. Palmer House** (40 Palmer Street, Route 1A; tel: 860-535 1440; May–Oct Wed–Sun; charge), built by the seal hunter and clipper ship designer who in 1820 discovered "land not yet laid down on my chart" – it turned out to be Antarctica. The house contains memorabilia of that trip as well as family portraits, artifacts, and furnishings.

Massive casinos

Ten miles (16km) north of Stonington, on the **Mashantucket Pequot Reservation**, the massive **Foxwoods Resort Casino ㊷** (Route 2; open 24 hours) welcomes gamblers by the busload. On the grounds is the **Mashantucket Pequot Museum and Research Center** (110 Pequot Trail; tel: 800-411 9671; Wed–Sun; charge). Using walk-through, life-size dioramas – starting with a descent into a sensorily-accurate glacial crevasse – visitors experience the Pequot people's history from the last ice age to the present. Interactive exhibits and videos create a comprehensive picture of the Natives of New England. The on-site restaurant serves Native American fare as well as more familiar dishes. An annual powwow, usually held in mid-September, is one of the largest on the East Coast, with dancers, drumming, validated craftspeople, demonstrations, and a rodeo.

The **Mohegan Sun casino**, a worthy rival to Foxwoods, is just to the southwest in **Uncasville**.

Ascending the lighthouse at Stonington.

BELOW: a rodeo on the Mashuntucket Pequot Reservation.

The Coming of the Casinos

Considered sovereign entities under US law, Native Americans are permitted to run casinos on their own land, even in states where gambling is not permitted

In 1972, Russell and Helen Bryan, a Chippewa couple living in a used house trailer on Indian land in rural Minnesota, received a property tax bill for $147.95. Since Indian reservations are considered lands belonging to a sovereign nation and are not subject to taxation, they refused to pay. The case eventually was heard by the Supreme Court, which issued a unanimous decision: not only could governments not tax reservation lands; they could not regulate what Native Americans do on their tribal lands.

Thus began the age of the Indian casinos. It came at an ideal time for the Native Americans. Long considered at best an anachronistic remnant of another age and denied the economic and social opportunities of the larger society, in the 1980s Indian tribes were experiencing a new sense of identity and a developing legal savvy to push their agenda of social, political, and economic advancement.

Eastern Connecticut's Mashantucket Pequots were the first New England tribe to gamble on casinos. They began developing hundreds of acres of tribal lands in Ledyard CT, creating a vast casino-and-hotel complex: Foxwoods. At 4.7 million sq ft (4.37 sq km) it is the world's largest casino complex, with gambling, entertainment, shopping, and hotels. By 1998, just six years after it opened, Foxwoods was also the world's highest-grossing casino, raking in more than $1 billion annually, more than any single casino in Las Vegas or Atlantic City.

The money was a windfall for the tribe, which numbered fewer than 1,000 members. Most of them were employees of the casino or the other businesses the tribe soon opened. The money also funded a child development center, a tribal police force, post office, and employment, education, and social services for members. One of the biggest projects was the creation of the Mashantucket-Pequot Museum and Research Center on the grounds of the casino resort. A state-of-the-art facility, it is a point of pride for the tribe.

Spurred by Foxwood's success, the Mohegan tribe opened their own casino a few miles away. It's only slightly smaller than Foxwoods and is nearly as profitable. Both casinos give 25 percent of their gross to the state of Connecticut, with a minimum of $100 million annually.

But while the Native nations are exempt from many US laws, they are not exempt from the effects of worldwide economic collapse. With less money to spend, fewer gamblers are at the tables. Foxwoods had expanded exponentially during the boom years and by 2009 was nearly $2 billion in debt. Mohegan Sun's debt is reportedly about half that. Like every other overextended and financially troubled company, both casinos are working with lenders to survive the downturn, but no one expects a change in their fortunes until the economy recovers.

ABOVE: part of the giant Foxwoods Casino complex.
LEFT: Jennifer Lopez in concert at the Mohegan Sun.

RESTAURANTS AND BARS

Prices for a three-course dinner per person with a half-bottle of house wine:
$ = under $20
$$ = $20–45
$$$ – $15–60
$$$$ = over $60

Restaurants

Avon

Ferme Restaurant
Avon Old Farms Hotel, 279 Avon Mountain Road
Tel: 860-269 0240
www.avonoldfarmshotel.com **$$$**
With the exception of some artisan cheeses for the charcuterie board, everything is sourced within 100 miles. Many vegan selections; many courses have the option of a full or small serving, which means you'll have room for the blueberry cheesecake or cherry pie ice cream.

Bristol

Applewood Restaurant and Bar
820 Farmington Avenue
Tel: 860-589 7133
www.applewood-resaurant.com **$–$$**
Good diner-style restaurant with a menu as long as I–95. Open 24/7.

Latino
417 Broad Street
Tel: 860-585 5642
www.latinorestaurantllc.com **$$**
Serving authentic Hispanic dishes, particularly from Peru and Cuba. The menu is bilingual (Spanish before English), but food is a uni-

versal language.

Fuji Japanese Steak House
1186 Farmington Avenue
Tel: 860-583 0088
www.fujisteakhousebristol.com **$$**
Enjoy the flashing knives and sizzle-at-your-table show at this hibachi restaurant; the sushi selection and quality is very good. They also have a Thai menu, which is unusual for a Japanese-centric establishment, but the dishes are well-prepared.

Danbury

Chuck's Steakhouse
20 Segar Street
Tel: 203-792 5555
www.chucksdanbury.com **$$**
Back in 1959, Chck's was one of the first places to introduce the concept of the grill and salad bar in the dining room. It was a good idea then, and it still is.

Rosy Tomorrow's
15 Old Mill Plain Road
Tel: 203-743 5845
www.rosytomorrows.com **$$**
Friendly place with an eclectic menu (and building; part of it is an old railroad caboose morphed onto a house with a glass atrium at one end). Emphasis on fresh ingredients: salads are made with fresh greens, not delivered in bulk bags.

East Lyme

Flanders Fish Market and Restaurant
22 Chesterfield Road, Route 161
Tel: 860-739 8866

www.flandersfish.com **$$–$$$**
Casual, comfortable seafood restaurant that takes advantage of being a fish market as well. "Today's catch" was swimming in the ocean last night, maybe even this morning. Snag a table on the outside deck in the summer. Kids' menu. Try the lobster potpie.

Essex

The Black Seal
15 Main Street
Tel: 860-767 0233
www.theblackseal.net **$$**
The food is well-prepared and plentiful. Along with the usual sandwiches and wraps, there's the bay scallop casserole made with spinach, shallots, and sun-dried tomatoes and a herbed breadcrust; 8-inch hot dogs with kraut, chili, and cheddar; or the house special: Whittingly, a croissant with apple butter, turkey, ham, and melted cheddar.

Glastonbury

Bricco Trattoria
124 Hebron Avenue
Tel: 860-659 0220
www.billygrant.com **$$–$$$**
Upscale Italian restaurant with heavy emphasis on making traditional country dishes in the traditional manner – hand-rolled pasta, artisan cheeses, sauces made from scratch. Try the chef's nightly special – a prix-fixe menu reflecting his mood and what's freshest in the season.

Groton

Norm's Diner
171 Bridge Street
Tel: 860-445 5026
www.whydrive.biz/normsdiner **$**
A classic 1950s diner with a display case of desserts, Formica-topped tables in the booths, jukebox, friendly waitresses, and a gang of regulars who hang out there all day. Good basic food; breakfast all day. The new owner started out as a waitress there and bought it when the original owners decided to retire after 30 years. Open 24/7.

Hartford Area

Carbone's Ristorante
588 Franklin Avenue
Tel: 860-296 9646
www.carbonesct.com **$$–$$$**
The city's premier Italian restaurant has been winning awards since it opened in 1938. It pulls off the trick of being both upscale, almost formal, but still welcoming. Tableside preparations are a specialty.

Costa Del Sol Restaurant
901 Wethersfield Road
Tel: 860-2961 1714
www.costadelsolrestaurant.net **$$$**
Expanding the culinary experiences of Hartford by bringing diners the flavors of the Galicia region of Spain. Paella is a specialty, but you can easily spend an evening sampling tapa bites and Spanish wines. Reservations suggested.

Prices for a three-course dinner per person with a half-bottle of house wine:
$ = under $20
$$ = $20–45
$$$ = $45–60
$$$$ = over $60

Hot Tomato's
1 Union Station
Tel: 860-249 5100 **$$–$$$**
With a patio overlooking the Capitol and chic decor of leather booths with stone and wrought-iron accents, this is a popular spot for business lunches. It's a trendy choice for dinner, too. New England favorites like maple-glazed pork chops are treated with honor, but the tortollini rosé will have you wishing you could lick the plate.

Restaurant Bricco
78 Lasalle Road, West Hartford
Tel: 860-233 0220
www.billygrant.com **$$–$$$**
The inspiration for this restaurant is Italian comfort food, according to owner/chef Billy Grant. That means a plate of "My Mom's Spaghetti Carbonara" is almost mandatory. But his kitchen is far from mundane, creating dishes like braised swordfish with pistachios, raisins, and broccoli rabe. New and popular, reservations are suggested. (Grant also owns Grant's Restaurant; 977 Farmington Road, West Hartford, tel: 860-236 1930, which specializes in steaks) and Bricco Trattoria.

Ivoryton

Brasserie Pip at The Copper Beech Inn
46 Main Street
Tel: 860-767 0330
www.copperbeechinn.com **$$$–$$$$**
The redesign and relaunch of the restaurant in the elegant Copper Beech Inn was an immediate success. The gleaming copper-top bar with wood accents serving French brasserie and modern American cuisine was voted the Best New Restaurant in a state-wide poll, and one of the Top 100 Restaurants in the Country. You can go à la carte or choose between a 5-course or 7-course tasting menu.

Kent

Fife 'n Drum Restaurant
53 North Main Street
Tel: 860-927 3509
www.fifendrum.com **$$$**
The French-influenced menu avoids trendiness, opting instead for superbly prepared classics like grilled lamb with mint; grilled fillet with Béarnaise sauce; roasted duck flambé.

Litchfield

Village Restaurant
25 West Street
Tel: 860-567 8307 **$$**
The sort of neighborhood pace you wish wold open up in your home town. The pub serves the usual range of chilis, wings, enhanced nachos, and big sandwiches, all made on-site. The cozy dining room serves glazed salmon and homemade ravioli. The warm apple crisp comes with a scoop of homemade ice cream.

West Street Grill
43 West Street (Route 202)
Tel: 860-567 3885
www.weststreetgrill.com **$$$**

Executive Chef James Cosgriff oversees a kitchen staff who spends a lot of time in the farmers' markets and who deliver American fare with flair. The Bistro menu is unusually authentic to its French roots.

Madison

Café Allegre
Inn at Lafayette, 725 Boston Post Road (Route 1)
Tel: 203-245 7773
www.allegrecafe.com **$$$**
Classy, but friendly, Chef Silvio Supp has a restaurant and kitchen that blend Old World tradition with modern tastes and sensibilities. Very upscale Italian preparation and presentations, but without pretensions. The seasonal prix-fixe ($$) is a good option. Nightly specials include Osso Buco and Rack of Veal, a far cry from most places' "nightlies."

Manchester

Cory's Catsup and Mustard, a Burger Bar
623 Main Street
Tel: 860-432 7755
www.catsupandmustard.com **$**
How a graduate of Johnson and Wales' culinary school makes burgers. Freshly-ground, 7oz wonders. Purists can stay with simple grilled beef, but there's also the "double-stuffed chipotle, blue cheese, and bacon" burger, the "7-napkin" burger, and the "buried under cheese" burger. Also wraps and sandwiches as big as the burgers and sweet potato fries with maple mayo. Very

Left: Apricots in Farmington offers riverside dining.

popular with families, it's brightly lit and brightly painted. The bar was voted the Best in Manchester.

Sukhothai
841 Main Street
Tel: 860-432 7405
www.sukhothaict.com **$–$$**
An unusual find: excellent Thai food in a bright restaurant on Manchester's Main Street. Family-owned and operated with a lot of pride. If you already know the cuisine, it's a treat; if you are unfamiliar, this is a great place for an introduction. The menu is semi-self-explanatory, and the staff is very accommodating in explaining what is not. Big vegetarian selection.

Mansfield

The Altnaveigh
957 Storrs Road (Route 195)
Tel: 860-429 4490
www.altnaveighinn.com **$$$**
Country charm and elegant dining in a restored 1730s house in historic Spring Hill district. Classic presentation of classic dishes: filet mignon and foie gras Wellington style, steak au poivre, pan-seared sea bass. Seasonal sides. Reservations recommended.

Mystic

Ancient Mariner
21 Main Street
Tel: 860-536 5200
www.ancientmarinermystic.com **$$**
In the midst of all Mystic's activity, it complements the desire of visitors who want the whole "New England" culinary experience. The menu is obviously heavy on

seafood, but there are also New England culinary icons like chicken potpie, lobster rolls, and Yankee pot roast. The shareable "bait bucket" appetizer serves up clams, scallops, mussels, shrimp, and calamari. Guitarists and duos entertain Wed–Sun, loud enough to be heard, but you can still have a conversation without yelling.

Anthony J's
6 Holmes Street
Tel:860-536 0448
www.anthonyjsbistro.com **$$–$$$**
Lively, young, contemporary crowd enjoys life in this jazzy Italian bistro just steps away from the Mystic drawbridge. Pizzas are cooked on hot rocks. Some entrées are cooked (by you) at the table the same way. The rest of the menu is filled with Italian favorites. International beer list. The early-bird special is a good deal.

Latitude 41° Restaurant
105 Greenmanville Road (North gate of Mystic Seaport)
Tel: 860-572 5303
www.coastalgourmetct.com **$$$**
Contemporary seafood and steak dishes in a spacious, light-filled room overlooking the Mystic River. Part of the "Farm to Chef" program which supports locally sourced ingredients; upscale – there's a suggested wine pairing with main dinner courses – but there's also a nice kids' menu. The soup of the day is always vegan. The new Shipyard Tavern, featuring beers and ales from the regional Shipyard Brewery, serves "share plates" of

appetizers, flatbread pizza, and fish 'n' chips.

S&P Oyster Co.
1 Holmes Street
Tel: 860-536 2674
www.sp-oysters.com **$$–$$$**
Quite possibly the most scenic location in Mystic. The outdoor patio is on the river, just beside the drawbridge. Enjoy fresh-shucked oysters and lobster bisque in the garden at a café table under the black umbrellas. The menu has refreshing, innovative preparations of familiar New England and Atlantic fish (lobster tacos: lobster with cotija cheese and crème and served with pico de gallo) and chicken (10-spiced, wood-grilled). Very large gluten-free menu (including crème brûlée and flourless chocolate cake with caramel sauce) and nice children's menu.

Sea Swirl
30 Williams Ave (Junction Routes 1 and 27)
Tel: 860-536 3452
www.seaswirlofmystic.com **$**
A Mystic institution, this seasonal clam shack (it started life as a Carvel's ice cream stand) fries up "whole belly" clams – not strips – along with scallops, oysters, and cod. Seating is at the picnic tables overlooking the flood tide. Finish up with a "dip cone" of soft ice cream.

Voodoo Grill
12 Water Street
Tel: 860-572 4422
www.thevoodoogrill.com **$$**
Nawlins' North – the popular, sometimes noisy, always consistently good restaurant draws its inspiration from the Big Easy;

the place has more Mardi Gras and New Orleans decorations on the walls than you'd find in a souvenir shop in the French Quarter. Every Cajun and Creole dish is on the menu, but so are BBQ, hush puppies, fried chicken, and other Southern staples. Live entertainment almost every night, and big screen TVs for sports addicts.

New Haven

Bentara Restaurant
76 Orange Street
Tel: 203-562 2511
www.bentara.com **$$–$$$**
Maylasian cuisine isa blending of Indian, Chinese, Dutch, Portuguese, and English influences. The result is flavorful and often spicy. The best authentic Malaysian dishes are found here. How authentic? Chef-owner Hasni Ghazali was requested to cook for the Malaysian prime minister during his visit to Washington and New York.

Claire's Corner Copia
1000 Chapel Street
Tel: 203-562 3888
www.clairescornercopia.com **$**
Vegetarian, vegan, organic, sustainable, Kosher, and – by the way – tasty food. Many Mexican dishes, plus pizza and veggie burgers. The greens for their salads are often grown on their deck in organic earth boxes. Very large gluten-free menu.

Frank Pepe's Pizzeria Napoletana
157 Wooster Street
Tel: 203-865 5762 **$**
www.pepespizzeria.com
Routinely rated as one of

Prices for a three-course dinner per person with a half-bottle of house wine:
$ = under $20
$$ = $20–45
$$$ = $45–60
$$$$ = over $60

Connecticut's most popular restaurants and best pizza, "Pepe's" has been satisfying appetites with Napoletana "tomato pies" since 1925. Frank reportedly invented the "white clam pie."

Ibiza Tapas Café
39 High Street
Tel: 203-865 1933
www.ibizanewhaven.com
$$–$$$
Authentic Spanish tapas elevate group grazing to an art. Dine at your table or enjoy the selection at the bar. For those unfamiliar with Spanish cuisine, the tasting menu is an affordable, excellent choice.

Union League Café
1032 Chapel Street
Tel: 203-562 4299
www.unionleaguecafe.com
$$$–$$$$
Directly across from the Yale campus, in a Beaux-Arts brownstone with an airy bar and inviting fire in the hearth, this is a temple to fine French cuisine. Imaginative, seasonal, contemporary touches to classic bistro fare, with dishes such as roasted Nova Scotia lobster, and wild mushroom risotto.

New London

Adrienne
218 Kent Road (Route 7)
Tel: 860-354 6001
www.adriennerestaurant.com
$$$
Fine fireside New American dining in a pretty, white, 19th-century farmhouse. One of the few places where game is routinely on

the menu. They also have a very large gluten-free menu, plus a nice selection of vegetarian and low-carb dishes.

Dev's on Bank Street
345 Bank Street
Tel: 860-442 3387
www.devsonbank.com $$–$$$
When you've lived in both Spain and Asia and have come to love both cuisines, what else is there to do but open a tapas restaurant that fuses the two culinary traditions? The result is an exciting menu by Candace Devenditti that's drawing enthusiastic customers to this new dining spot in downtown New London. Closed Monday.

Norwalk

Harbor Lights
82 Seaview Avenue
Tel: 203-866 3364
www.harborlights restaurant-ct.com $$–$$$
Floor-to-ceiling windows provide fabulous views at this waterside restaurant. They want you to linger and enjoy the food and the view; table seatings are scheduled on a two-hour basis. Seafood is prepared with a Mediterranean accent. The raw bar dinner is something to consider: a whole poached lobster, plus east coast oysters, cherrystone and littleneck clams, and Gulf shrimp. Reservations recommended.

Sono Brewhouse
13 Marshall Street
Tel: 203-853 9110
www.sonobrewhouse.com $$
The restored brick building

includes copper kettles used to brew beer in Alleen, Germany. Here they are for decoration only. But true to its name, the brewhouse has a lot of beers on tap and in bottles from the US and Europe, even a Porter from Finland.

Old Lyme

The Chestnut Grill at the Bee & Thistle Inn
100 Lyme Street
Tel: 860-434 1667/800-622 4946
www.beeandthistleinn.com $$$$
Award-winning American cuisine is elegantly served in romantic, historic inn, built in 1756 and retaining all of the charm that suggests. Dinners are served on the enclosed porches which overlook the sunken gardens. Wed and Fri nights, there are prix-fixe dining options. Strolling musicians add to the ambience on Fri and Sat nights.

Old Saybrook

Otter Cove
99 Essex Road
Tel: 860-388 4836
www.ottercoverestaurant.com
$$–$$$
Very comfortable, spacious dining rooms with many windows to enjoy the view, beadboard wainscoting, stone walls, and sleek wooden tables and chairs. Lots of seafood, of course, but Yankee pot roast and rigatoni with meatballs for those who've been "seafood-ed" out. Big kids menu with some "grown-up" options in kid-size portions.

LEFT: traditional fare at the Griswold Inn, Essex.

Tissa's Le Souk
2 Pennywise Lane
Tel: 860-395 1781
www.tissasmarketandcafe.com **$**
The James Pharmacy, opened in 1898, was one of the oldest soda fountains in the country. It closed in the late 1990s, but has been resurrected in a way the original owners could never have imagined. The soda fountain once again serves ice cream, but the food menu in the café is from Morocco. Saffron grilled chicken; lamb, sausage, and apricot tagine; plus Italian panini and gyros for the culinarily cautious. The shop also carries lots of spices and Mediterranean bath and body products.

Ridgefield

Luc's Café
3 Big Shop Lane
Tel: 203-894 8522
www.lucscafe.com **$$$**
A little bit of France in old ew England. Very authentic bistro, but since the owner was born and raised just outside Paris, it should be. Excellent food, which makes you understand why the French take dining so seriously.

Stonington

Dog Watch Café
194 Water Street
860-415 4510
www.dogwatchcafe.cm **$$**
One of the best views in ton, looking west over the Dodson Boatyard, so you're guaranteed great sunsets. Owned by avid sailors, it's something of a hangout for the local boaters and those who like to

talk about sailing and cruising, but it's equally popular with tourists exploring the town. Good clam chowder, seared tuna over Asian noodles. Mon–Wed, they often contribute part of the bill to local charities; ask your server.

Storrs

Sara's Pockets
125 N. Eagleville Road
Tel: 860-429 2900
www.saraspockets.com **$**
A good place to pick up light lunch to go or a no-hassle sit-down dinner, close to UConn. Middle Eastern and Mediterranean emphasis, with veggie and grilled meat pita pockets (hence the name of the place), kebab plates, and spinach and cheese pies.

Vernon

Rein's New York–Style Delicatessen
435A Hartford Turnpike, Route 30 (I–84, Exit 65)
Tel: 860-875 1344
www.reinsdeli.com **$**
The most authentic deli fare available north of Manhattan.

Westport

Open Table
27 Powers Court
Tel: 203-226 1114
www.dressingroomhome grown.com **$–$$$**
Co-founded by Paul Newma and chef/food policy activist Michael Nischan, its creative, delicious menu of American heirloom foods is at a level with Newman's best performances: not to be missed. Located adjacent

to the Westport Community Playhouse, it has early hours during the playhouse season. L Wed–Fri, D Tue–Sun, Sat/Sun brunch.

Tavern on Main
150 Main Street
203-221 7222
www.tavernonmain.com **$$$**
With creaking hardwood floors and three brick fireplaces, this is filled with rustic New England charm. The outdoor patio allows for great people-watching. Very wide-ranging menu, anything from grilled tuna club to Angus New York strip. Live jazz on Wed nights.

Woodbury

Zeeburger Sizzle & Shake
670 Main Street
203-405 6011
www.zeeburger.com **$$**
The new Zeeburger Sizzle &Shake has a lot of fun applying creative principles to casual dining, resulting in dishes like Kobe beef hot dogs. The genuine milk shakes alone are worth the trip.

Carol Peck's Good News Café
694 Main Street
203-266 4663
www.good-news-cafe.com **$$**
Carol's has a well-deserved reputation as one of the top restaurants anywhere for her exciting, creative dishes that raise the loco-source/farm-to-table/sustainable cooking concept to new heights.

Bars

The Federal Café
84 Union Place, Hartford
Tel: 860-527 0394

The only snack at one of the city's oldest watering holes is peanuts in the shell, but it remains one of the most popular spots in town for a reasonably priced pitcher of beer, some darts or pool, or to watch a game.

Rudy's Bar & Grill
1227 Chapel Street,
New Haven
Tel: 203-865 1242
When the new owners had to move to a new location, many long-time customers viewed it as the end of civilization. The "new" Rudy's is cleaner and sleeker, but has the same crowd of regulars. New Belgian owners now offer frites with dipping sauces, but they haven't changed the down-home charisma that has made this neighborhood spot a popular hangout for more than three decades. Live music many nights.

Hot Rod Café
114 Bank Street,
New London
"Wings, Beer, and Atmosphere" in a newly expanded night spot that is hugely popular with New London's under-30 set. 17 different styles of wings, along with a long list of wraps and sandwiches. DJs on weekends; reggae on Thursdays.

Ted's Bar
16 King Hill Road, Storrs
"Killing your parents' credit card bill since 1965." Very popular with UConn students, alumni, and visitors, it has bands, karaoke, and theme parties every night. 16 varieties of beer on tap.

Vermont and
New Hampshire

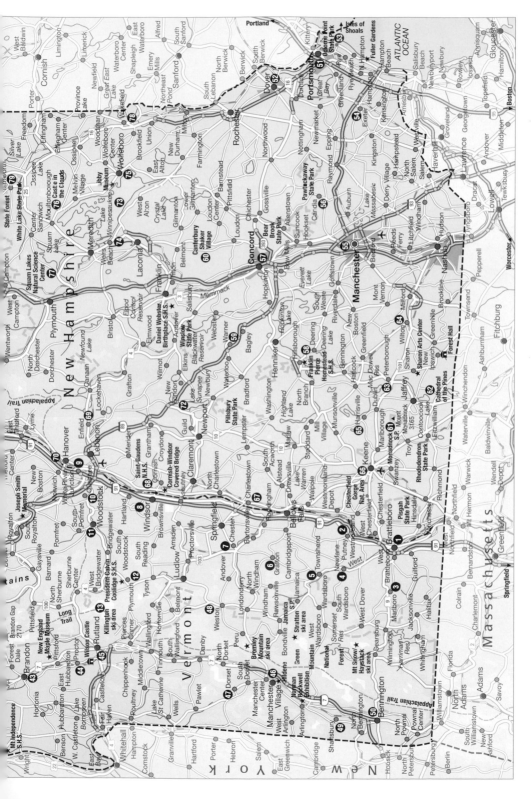

VERMONT

The Green Mountain State is alive with the sound of leaves crunching underfoot, the sight of red barns and white steeples, the smell of country lanes, and the taste of freshly-tapped maple sugar

I magine New England, and you will very likely imagine Vermont. When you round a bend to find a valley painted in a thousand shades of green, or stand atop Mount Mansfield to see a quilt of farm and forest rumpled against Lake Champlain, or drop down from the mountains into a white village framed in the glorious colors of autumn, your preconceptions become reality.

Lakeside retreats

Vermont's fresh air, fine scenery, and good fishing attracted tourists before the Civil War, but what really kicked the state's tourism industry into overdrive was the selling of winter. The ski boom began during the 1930s when the first mechanical lifts and cut trails appeared. By the early 1970s, dozens of ski areas had given rise to a burgeoning vacation-home industry and to worries over runaway development.

That same era brought an influx of new Vermonters, mostly young people looking for a simpler way of life. The cliché is that they were hippie communards, but the vast majority were tradespeople, artisans, and young professionals. What they shared was a sense that

they had found someplace special and that they wanted to keep it that way.

In alliance with progressive locals, the new Vermonters crafted a far-reaching array of environmental regulations, from a ban on highway billboards to controls on development in rural areas. All that change hasn't gone down smoothly; there is still considerable chafing between conservative locals and the "flatlanders" whom they feel have moved in and taken over the state.

Main attractions
BRATTLEBOSO
GRAFTON
QUECHEE GORGE
ROCK OF AGES QUARRY
WATERBURY
STOWE
LAKE CHAMPLAIN
SHELBURNE
BENNINGTON

PRECEDING PAGES: Waits River.
LEFT: a classic farm scene in Reading on a beautiful October day.
RIGHT: a sleigh ride near Stowe.

The lower Connecticut River Valley

The long, lazy Connecticut River forms the entire boundary between the states of Vermont and New Hampshire. Covered today by a hydro-electric dam, Vermont's first permanent settlement – Fort Dummer, founded in 1724 – has been reduced to a mere marker on the shore.

A few miles north, however, **Brattleboro** ❶, the town the fort was meant to protect, became an early resort when a local physician parlayed its pure springs into a "water cure." In the 1970s, some of the more dedicated "back-to-the-land" crowd settled here and sunk their roots deep into the community.

Some turned their talents to the arts, and the works of some 350 artisans from woodworkers to glass blowers are displayed at **Vermont Artisan Designs & Gallery** (106 Main Street; tel: 802-257 7044; daily 10am–6pm, Fri until 8pm). The 1938 Art Deco **Latchis Building** on Main Street houses a movie theatre which shows first-run and indie films. Upstairs from the theater is the 30-room,

A farmer stirs the vats of maple sugar in a sugar house.

boutique **Latchis Hotel** (802-254 6300; www.latchis.com) providing a unique experience to stay in the town. The **Brattleboro Museum and Art Center** (tel: 802-257 0124; open Thur–Mon 11am–5pm; fee) is in the Union Railroad Station. A "non-collecting" museum, it hosts changing art exhibits that offer unique views of the world by contemporary artists.

Putney to Townshend

Vermont's dairy industry owes its start to Charles Houghton, a Boston lawyer. In 1866, he started the first Hostein herd in the state on the family farm in **Putney** ❷, a few miles north on US 5.

Larger-than-life puppets, fantastic sets, and original scripts are featured at the **Sandglass Theater** (17 Kimball Hill Road; tel: 802-387 4051; www.sandglasstheater.org; no regular tours, but call to arrange a tour). Performances are in the 60-seat theater in a converted barn as well as at venues throughout the region. It hosts a 10-day international puppet festival held on "even" years. Follow US 9 (also known as the Molly Stark Trail) west

New England's Last Frontier

The Vermonter's streak of independence and the land's remoteness led to decades of self-sufficiency that define the peoples' character. Even to this day, Vermonters are known to be a hardy lot, ready to forge their own way, be it in politics or environmental policy.

Squeezed between New York, New Hampshire, and New France (as Colonial-era Canada was sometimes called), Vermont's wild territory was slow to be settled, and the people who took on the challenge were often as untameable as the terrain. The French and their Indian allies were one threat. Once those were eliminated, the Vermonters had to deal with the colonists to either side of them. Ethan Allen and his staunchly independent Green Mountain Boys, an informal militia, fought off "Yorker" surveyors in order to protect the interests of the Vermonters. In between, they dealt with repulsing the British invasion from Canada during the American Revolution.

Vermont's interest in getting rid of the British did not mean it was eager to join the new republic. It was not

one of the original colonies and it remained the Republic of Vermont, initially known as New Connecticut, from 1777 until finally becoming the 14th state of the Union in 1791. Uniquely, Vermont abolished slavery before joining the Union, and was the first state to have done so.

Things began to change in the mid-1800s. The 1849 California Gold Rush lured some young Vermonters from their farms, and the Civil War lured many more. As the nation expanded, it drew sturdy Vermonters to take on challenges far from the mountains. Between 1865 and 1960 Vermont's population declined. Today, it is rising again as the lure of the mountains and of living a simpler life closer to the land attracts people with the same strong abilities and ambitions as the first settlers.

Vermont is unique in several ways, because it is the only state in New England that does not border the Atlantic Ocean. Without a strong maritime tradition, Vermonters have been forced to seek inspiration elsewhere, in the mountains and lakes of the beautiful landscape.

to **Marlboro ❸** – the hilltop home of small, liberal arts Marlboro College, which every summer hosts the world-renowned, chamber music **Marlboro Music Festival**, founded by the late Rudolf Serkin (book early for tickets; tel: 802-254 2394 in summer; tel: 215-569 4690 rest of year; www.marlboromusic.org). Stop at the **Hogback Mountain Scenic Overlook** to savor the view and visit the **Southern Vermont Natural History Museum** (May–Oct 10am–5pm daily; weekends Nov–May; tel: 802-464 0048), where more than 600 mounted specimens of native mammals and birds are displayed in dioramas. A raptor center is home to birds which cannot be released into the wild.

A few miles farther west at Wilmington, turn north to reach **West Dover**, home to **Mount Snow/ Haystack** (tel: 802-464 3333 or 800-245 SNOW; http://mountsnow.com), a behemoth ski area and summer resort. It's a popular spot for hikers and mountain bikers; on weekends throughout the summer and daily in fall, scenic chairlift rides are available.

Route 30 northwest out of Brattleboro follows the West River, past the 1872 West Dummerston Covered Bridge to the postcard-perfect town of **Newfane ❹**. Its broad common is lined with shady elms and surrounded by stately Greek Revival public buildings and the requisite high-steepled church.

Farther up Route 30 the handsome town of **Townshend ❺** has a 2-acre common whose focal point is the 1790 Congregational Church. The **Big Black Bear Shop and Museum** (Mon–Sat 10–5, Sun 11–5; (tel: 802-365 4160; Mon–Sat 10am–5pm, Sun 11am–5pm) sells Mary Meyer Stuffed Toys, from the state's oldest toy maker. In the free museum, kids get to play with the exhibits. North on Route 30, Scott Bridge, the state's longest single-span covered bridge, was built in 1870.

Just past it is the turn for **Townshend Lake Recreation Area** (tel: 802-365 7703; open late May–early Sept daily 8am–8pm; fee). Created by a dam built in the 1960s, it's a fine spot to take a swim, picnic, or cook-out.

Making life easier for snowboarders, Mount Snow uses hundreds of fan guns that combine compressed air and water to create additional snow.

BELOW: watching for hawks on Putney Mountain.

Green New England

New Englanders cherish their environment – 33 million acres (13 million hectares) of forests; endless mountain vistas; 30,000 small family farms in pastoral valleys; and miles of wave-pummeled, rocky coasts

Lobstermen and fishermen depend on unpolluted ocean waters to provide their catch. Even major cities like Boston and Providence recognize that the nearness of such unsullied lands adds to their quality of life.

It was not always that way. The Industrial Revolution brought great economic development to the region, but at a great ecological price as huge manufacturing plants ravaged the region's rivers and landscapes. Urban development focused solely on rapid growth and quick profits, while logging operations harvested timber quickly without considering the wisdom of reforestation. The ocean was a commodity with limitless supplies of fish and a convenient disposal site for garbage.

That is changing as the undeniable effects of thoughtless practices become clear. A combination of practicality, frugality, and New England's historic mistrust of authority has fueled a region-wide ecological

movement. The goal is to maintain a high quality of life by finding a balance between the financial benefits of development and the preservation and restoration of the environment.

There are as many issues as there are trails in the White Mountains: acid rain; the use of toxic chemicals in the daily environment; development; energy generation; garbage disposal; and transportation just for starters. But there are an equal number of groups working to address them.

Many initiatives are grassroots and very local, following the historic patterns of individual community action: a town in Massachusetts holds "barn-raising"-type events to weatherize low-income housing; a village in Maine installs solar-powered street lights; a neighborhood in Boston plants vegetable gardens in vacant lots; a parent organization in Rhode Island works to remove toxic chemical cleaners from schools.

The closeness of communities – both geographically and philosophically – naturally leads to networking and ways to address the problems on a larger scale. The New England Grassroots Environmental Fund has a vast database of groups, resources, and programs throughout the region and encourages connections between them. Conferences of "green" organizations are clearinghouses of ideas, strategies, and successful actions. There are councils of environmental businesses, a think-tank that studies the finances of environmental issues, and an association of "eco-friendly" lodgings and resorts. More than a dozen New England colleges and universities offer academic majors in environmental studies and are magnets for research projects. Job training for "green" careers is offered through community colleges. There's even EarthShare New England, which oversees payroll contribution to environmental groups. On a larger scale, all six New England states are members of the Regional Greenhouse Gas Initiative, which has set goals for reducing greenhouse gas emissions.

Not all ideas are popular. Wind energy has many opponents who consider the windmills a blight on the landscape. Solar power is difficult, given the long, dark, snowy New England winters. Proposals to limit fishing and lobstering are met with fierce resistance by boat captains and crews. But no one doubts that solutions will eventually be found, especially as the private sector and governments are realizing that investing in a healthy environment is good economically, which will keep New England "green" in every sense of the word.

LEFT: a wind turbine in Searsburg, Vermont.

You can follow a trail to the 125ft (38-meter) Hamilton Falls at **Jamaica State Park** (off Route 30; tel: 802-874 4600; open early May–Columbus Day 10am–9pm; fee).

Grafton

About 10 miles (16km) north of Townshend on Route 35, **Grafton ❻** is a Greek Revival town in an 1840s time warp. Once a thriving agricultural center, it was suffering the same fate as many other small Vermont towns until the Windham Foundation took it over. Interested in doing more than just preserving the setting, it re-established the businesses which once thrived here. The **Grafton Village Cheese Company** (tel: 800-462 3866 or 802-843 2210; open daily 10–6) makes award-winning cheddar with milk from local cows; the Grafton Forge is a working blacksmithing forge. You can watch honeybees at work and dig for fossils at the small **Nature Museum** or view a miniature village made entirely from Vermont granite at the **Vermont Museum of Mining and Minerals**. The **Grafton Historical Society Museum** (on the common; Sun 2–4; tel: 802-843 1010; graftonhistoricalsociety.org; donation) is housed in a homestead built in 1845 and relates the town's fascinating history. Collections range from soapstone objects to musical instruments.

Claim a rocker on the porch of the 1801 **Old Tavern at Grafton** (92 Main Street; tel: 802-843 2231; www.old-tavern.com), whose guests have included notables from Thoreau and Kipling to Ulysses S. Grant and Teddy Roosevelt.

There are more than 2,000 acres (800 hectares) of trails suitable for year-round use at the inn's **Grafton Ponds Nordic Ski and Mountain Bike Center** (783 Townshend Road; tel: 802-843 2400; www.graftonponds.com).

Chester

Route 35 winds north about 7 miles (11km) to **Chester ❼**, which straddles three branches of the Williams River. An 1850s stone village-within-a-village features 30 homes faced in gneiss ledgestone – a type of granite – built before the Civil War. The town is a good base for cyclists and boating enthusiasts. One easy bike ride runs from the delightfully named Popple Dungeon Road to Tater Hill Golf Course.

The **Vermont Institute of Contemporary Art** (15 Depot Street; tel: 802-875 4808; www.vtica.org), has gallery exhibits, poetry readings, live performances, and cinema.

Chester is also the northern terminus for **the Green Mountain Flyer** (54 Depot Street; tel: 800-707 3530 or 802-463 3069; www.rails-vt.com; fee), a diesel-powered excursion train that journeys 13 miles (21km) to the southeast in Bellows Falls.

Upper Connecticut Valley

A center of invention during the 19th century, **Windsor ❽** became home to Vermont's machine tool industry. **The American Precision Museum** (196 Main Street/Route 12 East; tel: 802-674 5781; open late May–Oct daily

TIP

The Green Mountain Flyer has its origins in Vermont's earliest railroads, built from 1843. Rail became important for transporting freight, from milk to lumber, and in the early 20th century up to 18 passenger trains a day traveled through Bellows Falls. The current tourist operation began in 1984.

BELOW: mixed traffic in Grafton.

The Quechee Polo Club plays on Saturdays during the summer months.

BELOW: in theory, Vermont has enough land to produce food for the entire state.

10–5; fee; free for military members and families with ID) is housed in a National Historic Landmark, the 1846 Robbins and Lawrence Armory. It has a fascinating array of the machinery that made "Yankee ingenuity" a byword: machine tools, an extensive firearms collection, sewing machines, and measuring devices.

Windsor is also famed as the birthplace of Vermont, because it was here in the **Old Constitution House** (tel: 802-828 3051; open late May–mid-Oct, Sat and Sun, 11am–5pm; fee) that delegates met in 1777 to draw up a constitution for the prickly little republic, which was as wary of the other states as of the Crown.

In the early years of the 20th century, the natural beauty of the area drew artists like Maxfield Parrish and Frederic Remington. The **Cornish Colony Museum** (Old Firehouse Building, 147 Main Street; tel: 802-674 6008; open late May–Oct, Wed–Sun 11am–5pm; fee) houses an excellent collection of their works and others inspired by the Vermont and New Hampshire landscapes. Just up Main Street, the

Windsor–Cornish Covered Bridge spans Connecticut River to lovely Cornish, New Hampshire. It's the longest covered bridge in the United States. Note that the Saint-Gaudens National Historic Site is just across the bridge in New Hampshire.

North to Woodstock

Sixteen miles (26km) to the north, **White River Junction** ❾, at the intersection of Interstates 91 and 89, is dveloping into a major arts community. An old railroad town (Amtrak still stops here), the entire downtown is a registered National Historic District with buildings from the late 1800s and early 1900s. The **Main Street Museum** (58 Bridge Street; tel: 802-256 2776; Tue–Sun 1am–6pm) is quirky fun, filled with the sorts of things museums collected long ago. The **Northern Stage** (28 Gates Street; tel: 802-291 9009; www.northernstage. org) is an award-winning, professional regional theater company which performs from October to May. A few miles west on Route 4 at **Quechee** ❿, the 162ft (49-meter) -deep **Quechee Gorge**, "Vermont's Little Grand Canyon," is best viewed from the bridge which spans it, or from the 0.8-mile (1.3km) trail at the **Quechee State Park** (fee). The mile-long gorge is a legacy of the last ice age. The name is from the Abenaki language and means "Great Chasm."

The **Vermont Institute of Natural Science** (6565 Woodstock Road; tel: 802-359 5000; www.vinsweb. org; daily 10am–4pm, later in summer; fee) rehabilitates and cares for injured raptors. There's also a songbird aviary featuring local birds. The "Human–Nature" audio tour (download to MP3 player or cell phone, Apr–Oct) is designed to redefine the way people look and interact with the landscape.

Frustrated with the direction the traditional crafts were taking in Europe, Irish artisan Simon Pearce moved to Vermont in 1971. He transformed **The**

Mill at Quechee (1760 Quechee Main Street; tel: 802-295 2711; www.simon-pearce.com; open daily 10am–9pm), an abandoned flannel factory, into an inviting complex where he and his fellow artisans create distinctive glass-works and pottery. No assembly lines here; each piece is made using traditional glassblowing skills. The pottery is also individually thrown and hand-glazed. The adjacent **Glassblower Café** offers fine dining overlooking the Ottauquechee River. The sprawling, very commercial **Quechee Gorge Village** (Route 4, tel: 802-295 1550) includes the Cabot Quechee store (with lots of cheese samples), an antiques mall, and several gift shops, including the **Vermont Toy & Train Museum**, a jumbled collection of antique and more recent playthings. An antique carousel operates on summer weekends through mid-October. The **Quechee Polo Club** (Dewey's Mill Road; tel: 603-443 2000; fee) holds matches most Saturdays beginning at 2pm from mid-June through Labor Day at its field a half-mile (1km) north of Route 4.

Woodstock

Woodstock ⓫, just to the west, was one of the first Vermont towns to be discovered – and given a high polish –by outsiders.

A passion for maintaining a graceful balance between society and nature has long been the keynote to Woodstock's renown. Vermont native Frederick Billings returned from his lucrative law practice in San Francisco in the 1890s to become a pioneer in reforestation and a zealous model farmer. The slopes of Mount Tom and Mount Peg and the restored **Billings Farm and Museum** (Route 12 East; tel: 802-457 2355; http:billingsfarm.org; open May–Oct daily 10am–5pm, weekends Nov–Feb 10am–3.30pm; fee) are testaments to his love for rural Vermont. A working farm with draft horses, sheep, oxen, and a herd of milk-producing Jersey cows, it recreates life on an early 19th-century farmstead. In 1998 the Billings family mansion and its surrounding 500 acres (200 hectares) were bequeathed as the **Marsh-Billings-Rockefeller National Historical Park** (Route 12;

BELOW: the red-tailed hawk *(Buteo jamaicensis)* is a bird of prey, one of three species colloquially known as the "chickenhawk," though it rarely preys on chickens.

Vermont Institute of Natural Science

The Vermont Institute of Natural Science is New England's premier avian wildlife rehabilitation center. Veterinarians and rehabilitators treat over 400 birds each year – not just hawks and eagles, but waterfowl, song-birds, even hummingbirds that are injured or orphaned. About 40 birds that cannot be released into the wild live permanently in outdoor enclosures which are as close to their natural habitat as possible.

Daily programs cover topics as diverse as the mechanics of avian flight, conservation issues, and the mysteries of seasonal migration. The most popular programs are those which show the raptors – eagles, hawks, falcons, and owls – in action and those demonstrating rehabilitation techniques. The Adopt a Raptor program provides donors with a photo of their bird, adoption papers, and a fact sheet about that species.

VINS's greater goal is to teach people to understand the wildlife and diverse natural habitats they encounter in daily life – even in urban settings – with empathy and intelligence. The "Human–Nature" audio walking tour (for MP3 players or cell phones) along the VINS nature trails and the path to Quechee Gorge is designed to redefine how people look at the Vermont landscape, their impact on the natural world, and how to make that impact positive (or at least less damaging).

TIP

The tinkling melodies from dozens of music boxes fill the air at the Porter Music Box Museum (33 Sunset Hill Road/Route 66, Randolph; tel: 802-728 9694 or 800-811 7087; May–Oct daily 9.30am–5pm). The 30-minute guided tour starts with a video about how music boxes are made and includes music boxes from private collections as well as those made by the Porter Music Box Company.

tel: 802-457 3368; www.nps.gov/mabi; visitor center open Memorial Day–Oct daily 10am–5pm; mansion tours by advance reservation Memorial Day–Oct; fee; grounds open free year-round). This is Vermont's only national park and the only park in the system to concentrate specifically on conservation. The Queen Anne mansion houses more than 400 paintings, including a superb collection of Hudson River art.

For further glimpses of Woodstock's past, visit the **Woodstock Historical Society** headquarters (Elm Street; tel: 802-457 1822; late June–Columbus Day; fee): nine rooms of period furnishings, fine art, clothing, textiles, silver, ceramics, photographs, and early American toys in the 1807 Dana House.

The **Woodstock Inn and Resort** (tel: 802-457 1100; www.woodstockinn.com) on the green is one of the state's finest lodgings, and its Robert Trent Jones golf course and **Suicide Six** ski area (tel: 802-457 6661) offer year-round amusements. Despite its ominous-sounding name, most of the ski trails are for beginners and

intermediate skiers. On the other side of the green, a covered bridge leads to Mountain Avenue, a redoubt of old summer cottages, and a park at the base of Mount Tom.

The Coolidge homestead

The nation's 30th president was born and is buried at the **President Calvin Coolidge State Historic Site** (of Route 100A; tel: 802-672 3773; open late May–mid-Oct daily 9.30am–5pm; visitor center open year-round Mon–Fri) in **Plymouth** ⑫, 15 miles (24km) southwest of Woodstock. Coolidge (1872–1933) was a taciturn man, who became president after the sudden death of Warren Harding. Coolidge's father, a notary public, swore in his son in the middle of the night when they received the news.

One of the nation's most authentic presidential sites, the site preserves not only "Silent Cal's" home, but his entire boyhood village, including his father's general store, the dance hall which served as his summer White House, and a barn holding a superb collection of 19th-century agricultural equipment.

Killington

North and west via Routes 100 and 4, New England's largest ski area, **Killington** ⑬ (4763 Killington Road; tel: 802-422 6200 or 800-621 6867; www.killington.com), covers seven peaks and encompasses 200 trails. "The Beast of the East" also ranks top among the Northeast ski resorts for nightlife. With a 4,241ft (1,296-meter) peak reached by gondola for sightseers as well as skiers, the resort is active year-round – the skiing often lasts from October through June. In the summer, it joins with nearby Pico Peak to become an outdoor adventure center with mountain-biking trails, golf, an alpine slide, climbing walls, and lift rides.

The tiny village of **Strafford** ⑭ was the birthplace of Vermont Representative and Senator Justin Smith Morrill, author of the 1862 Morrill Acts which established

BELOW: the Justin Morrill Homestead.

America's system of land grant colleges and universities. Sales of federal lands support 105 such schools. The **Justin Morrill Homestead** (Route 132; tel: 802-765 4484; open Memorial Day–mid-Oct, Sat and Sun 11am–5pm; fee) is a 17-room pink Carpenter Gothic home, built between 1848 and 1851.

Mormon connections

Joseph Smith, a visionary who founded the Mormon religion, was born in **South Royalton** in 1805. Just off Route 14, Mormons maintain the **Joseph Smith Memorial and Birthplace** (357 LDS Road; tel: 802-763 7742; May–Oct Mon–Sat 9am–7pm; Sun 1.30am–7pm; Nov–Apr Mon–Sat 9am–5pm, Sun 1.30am–5pm), with a 38.5ft (11.5-meter) obelisk – 1ft for each year of Smith's life – made from a single block of Barre granite, and a museum.

North of South Royalton on Route 110, five covered bridges span the First Branch of the White River in **Tunbridge ⓯**. In "even" years, it welcomes historical societies, museums, and heritage groups for the Vermont History Expo. The Tunbridge World's Fair is the epitome of a country fair, with ox pulls, sheepdog trials, clog dancing, and a horse show. It's been held every September since 1867.

Brookfield

North on Route 14, the tranquil village of **Brookfield ⓰** is in the geographical center of the state. In 1812, a 320ft (98-meter) floating bridge, supported by 380 tarred barrels, was built across Sunset Lake at the center of town. Replaced eight times so far, the current incarnation has been declared unsafe and is currently closed to vehicles. State and local engineers are debating funding and construction plans to repair it. In the meantime, it is open to pedestrians and is popular for fishing. One of the last ice harvests in the East is now the occasion for an annual festival on the lake, held in late January with ice cutting, ice sculpting, and dog sledding.

Rock of Ages

About 10 miles (16km) to the north, on Route 14 between Brookfield and Barre, **Graniteville ⓱** is site of the lagest granite quarry in the world, the **Rock of Ages Quarry** (visitor center, 773 Graniteville Road; tel: 802-476 3119; www.rockofages.com; mid-May–Oct, Mon–Sat 9am–5pm; also mid-Sept–Oct, Sun). There is a large array of quarry and factory tours, a sandblasting activity, and other features. The visitor center has all the details, times, and prices.

Mining began soon after the War of 1812 and boomed with the influx of skilled immigrant stoneworkers between 1880 and 1910. Fed up with poor wages and working conditions (many died of silicosis), the granite workers elected a Socialist mayor of Barre – many decades before liberal Burlington was ready to do the same.

Barre

Many of the workers in the quarries were Italian immigrants, as evidenced by the names on the headstones at **Hope Cemetery** (off Route 14) in

A country lane near Tunbridge, where the annual agricultural event is grandly known as the "Tunbridge World's Fair."

BELOW: Coolidge State Historic Site.

TIP

The discovery of granite drove Barre's growth, increasing its population from 2,060 in 1880 to 10,000 by 1894 as immigrants arrived from Italy, Scotland, Spain, Scandinavia, Greece, Lebanon, and Canada. The Italians' militancy over labor practices helped elect a Socialist as town mayor in 1916.

BELOW: autumn comes to the area around Montpelier.

Barre (pronouned *Barry*). Quarry workers commemorated their own with touching artwork. Among the standouts: a half-scale racing car and the life-size statue of labor leader Elia Corti, shot down in 1903 at a Socialist rally.

The workers' heritage and politics are much in evidence in downtown **Barre.** The larger-than-life statue of a mustachioed Italian stonecutter at the corner of North Main Street and Maple Avenue looks toward Granite Street, site of the old Socialist headquarters, the **Old Labor Hall,** a National Historic Landmark now being renovated by the Barre Historical Society (46 Granite Street; tel: 802-476 0567).

The granite **Robert Burns Memorial** in front of the 1891 school on Washington Street was erected in 1899 by Scots who also worked in the quarries.

The **Vermont Granite Museum and Stone Arts School** (7 Jones Brothers Way; tel: 802-476-4605; www.granitemuseum.org) is an ambitious work-in-progress. Housed in a massive turn-of-the-century granite manufacturing plant, when completed it will detail the geologic, historic, technologic, and artistic impact of the state's granite industry. At the school, sculptors learn carving techniques from working professionals. There are no regular hours, but visitors are very welcome to call for personal tours.

Montpelier

Home to about 8,000 people, **Montpelier** ⓲ (pronounced *Mont-peel-yer*) is the nation's smallest state-capital. The lively little downtown is dominated by the gold-leaf dome of the **Vermont State House** (State Street; tel: 802-828–2228; tours July–mid-Oct Mon–Fri 10am–3.30pm, Sat 11am–2.30pm; self-guided and audio tours year-round Mon–Fri 7.30am–4.15pm, and July–Oct Sat 11am–3pm; no charge).

Initially, Vermont's capital rotated through the state, but with the completion of the original nine-sided building in 1808 the seat of power settled here. When an imposing stone successor was gutted by fire, the portico and

granite walls withstood the flames to form a shell for the present structure. The Senate Chamber is considered the most beautiful room in the state.

Adjacent to the State House is the **Vermont Historical Society and Museum** (109 State Street; tel: 802-828 2180; www.vermonthistory.org; Tue–Sat 10am–4pm; fee). Housed in a re-creation of an Italianate Pavilion-inspired hotel which served early legislators, the award-winning museum is a virtual time-travel experience. Visitors walk through Vermont's history from Abenaki wigwams, the tavern hangout of the Green Mountain Boys, and military training camps of World War II.

Montpelier is home to the **New England Culinary Institute**, whose students and teachers staff two excellent dining spots on Main Street. Start the day off with European-style pastries at **La Brioche** (89 Main Street; tel: 802-229 0443; Mon–Fri 6.30am–5pm, Sat 7am–5pm, Sun 8am–2pm), which also serves luncheon fare. **NECI on Main** (118 Main Street; tel: 802-223 3188) is open Tuesday to Saturday for lunch, afternoon light fare, and dinner. Its Sunday brunch buffet is justly famous.

Lost Nation Theater (tel: 802-229 0492; www.lostnationtheatre.org) is widely recognized as one of the top regional theaters in the US. Their April–October season features classic and contemporary shows for adults and youth at the **City Hall Arts Center** (39 Main Street). The **Savoy Theater** (26 Main Street; tel: 802-229 0598; www.savoytheater.com) is run by dedicated cinemaphiles. They screen a wonderful schedule of indie and world films nightly.

Tapping maple trees for their sap which is turned into syrup and sugar is an early-spring affair, but many of the "sugar works" are open year-round to demonstrate the process (and to sell you all varieties of the products). Two of them near Montpelier are the **Norse Farm Sugar Works** (1168 County Road/Main Street, 2.5 miles [4km] from town; tel: 800-223 2740;

www.morsefarm.com; open daily) and **Bragg Farm** (Route 14, north of intersection of Route 14 and Route 2; tel: 802-223 5757, 800-376 5757; www.braggfarm.com; June–Aug 8.30am–8pm, Sept–May 8.30am–6pm). Both offer free tours, tastings, activities for kids, and large gift shops.

Sugarbush to Waterbury

Some 20 miles (32km) west of Montpelier, the Green Mountain range attains heady heights that tempt skiers as well as mountain climbers and bikers. South of I-89 on Route 100 (exit 10), the Mad River Valley towns of **Waitsfield ⑳** and **Warren** support two ski areas. The challenging **Mad River Glen ski area** (www.madriverglen.com), opened in 1948, is strictly a winter destination. The more developed and extensive **Sugarbush** (www.sugarbush.com) is open year-round, with summer activities focusing on golf, hiking, and tennis. Both towns are full of inviting restaurants, cozy inns, gift shops, and galleries.

To get an unusual perspective on the countryside, consider a soaring

The folk art statue atop the State House is the Roman goddess of agriculture, Ceres. It was carved in 1938 by 87-year-old Dwight Dwinell, the building's chief usher.

BELOW: the Vermont State House.

Mount Mansfield, Vermont's highest peak, has hiking trails and ski slopes, and alpine tundra survives here from the ice ages.

BELOW: a hot-air balloon festival at Stowe VT.

excursion in a sailplane towed by **Sugarbush Soaring** (Warren-Sugarbush Airport, Route 100; tel: 802-496 2290; flights May–Oct). North on Route 100, the **Vermont Icelandic Horse Farm** (3061 North Fayston Road, Fayston; tel: 802-496 7141; www.icelandichorses.com) is home to a herd of the hardy, friendly, sure-footed pony-sized horses. You can take an hour's ride or up to a six-day trek.

For a more conventional scenic tour, head for one of the nearby "gaps" (glacially formed passes through the mountains). The road to **Lincoln Gap** begins on Route 100 south of Warren Village and climbs for 3 miles (5km) to 2,424ft (739 meters) before descending into tiny Lincoln. The road through **Appalachian Gap** begins on Route 17 and winds past Mad River Glen to the 2,365ft (721-meter) crest before its descent into the Champlain Valley. (Note: gaps can't accommodate trailers, and Lincoln Gap is closed in winter.)

Waterbury

Fourteen miles (22km) northwest of Montpelier, by either I–89 or Route 2, is **Waterbury** ㉑, where a pair of "flalander" entrepreneurs turned this famous dairy state into ice cream heaven. **The Ben & Jerry's Homemade Ice Cream Factory** offers tours and tastings daily (tel: 866-258 6877 for schedule; www.benjerry.com; fee). If you want to actually see ice cream being made, schedule a weekday visit. On weekends, there's a video of the process. Either way, the 30-minute tour ends at the tasting room.

Amtrak still stops at the restored Victorian train station in Waterbury. It is also the visitor center for **Green Mountain Coffee Company** (daily 7am–6pm). One of the first coffee companies to commit to "fair trade" principles, its free, self-guided, multi-media tour explains how coffee is grown and produced.

Continuing north on Route 100, stop for samples of the "Best Cheddar in the World" at the **Cabot Annex Store complex** (2653 Waterbury-Stowe Road; tel: 802-244 6334; daily 9am–6pm). Lake Champlain Chocolates, Vermont Teddy Bear, and Snow Farm Winery also have stores here. Watch fine-art glassblowing at **Ziemke Glassblowing** (3033 Waterbury-Stowe Road; tel: 802-244 6126; daily 10am–6pm). One mile (1.3km) farther north, watch cider being pressed, sneak a peek at the action inside a beehive, maybe watch apple jelly being made, and visit the Grand View Winery tasting room to try hard cider (if you are over 21) at the **Cold Hollow Cider Mill** (3600 Waterbury-Stowe Road; tel: 800-327 7537; daily; Nov–June 8am–6pm, July–Oct 8am–7pm).

The headquarters of the **Green Mountain Club** (4711 Waterbury Road; tel: 802-244 7037; www.green-mountainclub.org; Memorial Day–Labor Day Mon–Sat, rest of year Mon–Fri) is the best place to pick up information about the **Long Trail**, Vermont's "footpath in the wilderness," which follows the ridges of the Green Mountains for 270 miles

(430km) from the Massachusetts border to the Canadian line, as well as other hiking trails. The Appalachian Trail shares about 100 miles (160km) of the Long Trail.

Stowe

Ten miles (16km) north on Route 100 is **Stowe 22**, one of the premier winter destinations in New England. The **Ski Museum** (1 South Main Street; tel: 802-253 9911; www.vermontski museum.org; Wed–Mon noon–5pm; donation) chronicles the development of skiing in Vermont from the days of wooden skis and leather boots to the present. But even before skiing arrived in the 1930s, the town enjoyed a reputation as a stylish summer place. Summer or winter, sports opportunities abound, particularly along the **Stowe Recreation Path**. Ideally suited for skiers, cyclists, wheelchair racers, runners, walkers, and stroller pushers, the 5.3-mile (8.5km) paved path skirts the West Branch river from town to **the Topnotch Resort and Spa** (www. topnotchresort.com), passing a number of appealing inns, restaurants,

and shops en route. Another notable inn is the Austrian-style **Trapp Family Lodge** (www.trappfamily. com). Founded by the Baroness Maria Von Trapp of *Sound of Music* fame, the 2,700-acre (1,100-hectare) resort has Vermont's oldest cross-country ski trail system, part of one of the biggest networks in New England. Raising a beer stein in salute to the Austrian love of lager, the lodge has started its own on-site brewery producing European-style lagers.

Both **Eden Dog Sledding** (tel: 802-635 9070; www.edendogsledding.com) and **Peace Pups Dog Sledding** (tel: 802-888 7733; www.peacepupsdogsledding) have snow and dry-land mushing opportunities throughout the year.

On **Mount Mansfield 23** Ralph Waldo Emerson had a bracing vacation in 1823 at the Summit House, where, he recounts, his "whole party climbed to the top of the [mountain's] nose and watched the sun rise over the top of the White Mountains of New Hampshire." Hikers still favor this craggy human profile. Several trails of varying difficulty lead to the summit, including

TIP

Stowe Performing Arts (tel: 802-253 7792; www.stoweperforming arts.com) has a schedule of several outdoor concerts every week in the summer, all with a backdrop of the mountains. Several of them, including the noonday series, are free.

BELOW:
Maria Von Trapp and family at the Trapp Family Lodge in 1965.

The von Trapp Family Saga

Orphaned before she was 7, Maria Augusta Kutschera was raised by her father's cousin as a socialist, atheist, and religious cynic. While in college, she heard a sermon by a visiting priest which changed her outlook. Newly devout, she joined a convent. Worried that the restrictions of convent life were damaging her health, her doctor recommended that she become the tutor of a daughter of a retired Austrian naval officer, Georg von Trapp. In true "this will be Hollywood material some day" fashion, they fell in love and were married in 1927. "The Trapp Family Choir" formed after Georg lost his fortune in a bank collapse. Their departure from Austria was not a dramatic escape across the mountains; they simply boarded a train to Italy on their way to a US concert tour. Vermont reminded them of Austria, so they purchased land near Stowe for what became the Trapp Family Lodge.

Maria sold film rights to a memoir she had written to a wily producer for just a few thousand dollars, effectively cutting herself out of the millions of dollars of profit. Far from the strict, unfeeling character portrayed on stage, Georg (who died in 1947) was a gentle, devoted father. After working in the South Pacific as a missionary, Maria returned to Vermont where she died in 1987. She is buried in the family cemetery next to the lodge.

"Profanity Trail," which works its way along the ridgeline. A far easier ascent is to take the 4.5-mile (7.5km) **Auto Road** (fee), a century-old toll road that ends at a small visitor center. A moderate hike of 1.5 miles (2km) reaches the nose. Even easier is an eight-passenger gondola (Route 108; fee) which zips to 3,625ft (1,105 meters), close to the 4,393ft (1,338-meter) "chin," the state's highest point.

The handsome Cliff House at the upper terminus of the gondola serves an elegant lunch along with spectacular views when the lift is operating. The new **Spruce Peak Performing Arts Center** (tel: 802-760 4643; www. sprucepeakarts.org) at the resort has the ambitious goal of establishing itself as the region's outstanding cultural venue.

Other big summertime draws are the Stoweflake Hot Air Balloon Festival and a midsummer classic car rally; in mid-January, during the Stowe Winter Carnival, the whole town parties.

Over Smugglers Notch

The nearby ski area at **Smuggler's Notch Resort ㉔** (Route 108 South;

tel: 800-451 8752 or 802-644 8851; www.smuggs.com) was so named for its role during the War of 1812 when trade with Canada was forbidden. Wintertime visitors hoping to fit in a visit are in for a surprise – and a drive: the direct road from Stowe (Route 108) is closed in winter, and those who've traveled it in summer will understand why. Hundred-foot cliffs and giant boulders crowd the narrow, winding roadway.

You'll need to loop north on Route 100, west on Route 15 and south on Route 108 to get there. "Smuggs" offers downhill skiing on three peaks as well as cross-country trails and is popular with families for its well-thought-out children's programs. In summer the attractions are hiking, horseback riding, and an assortment of water slides.

The town closest to the resort, **Jeffersonville**, has a restaurant, the historic Smugglers Notch Inn (www. smuggsinn.com), with a covered hot tub for six and a well-equipped general store with a liquor outlet.

BELOW: St Johnsbury, with a population of 8,000, is known locally as St Jay.

The Northeast Kingdom

The **Northeast Kingdom** is the name given to the region north of Route 15. It's a nearly 2,000-sq-mile (over 5,000-sq-km) swath of crystal lakes and deep forests, a region sparsely populated and with little industry. *Where the Rivers Run North* is the title writer Howard Frank Mosher gave his 1978 collection of short stories in honor of a region known for its backwater quirks.

Continue south on Route 15 through Morrisville and Hardwick. Turn south on Route 215 to **Cabot** and the **Cabot Creamery Co-operative** (2878 Main Street; tel: 800-837 4261; June–Oct daily 9am–5pm, Nov–May Mon–Sat 9am–4pm, Jan Mon–Sat 10am–4pm; cheese isn't made every day, call to confirm cheese-making days; fee). Founded in 1919, the co-op draws on some 1,200 member farms for the milk that goes into its award-winning cheddar cheese.

St Johnsbury

The city of **St Johnsbury** ㉕, the largest community in the Northeast Kingdom, remains a vibrant pocket of Victoran charm. From the bank buildings downtown to the Fairbanks mansion on the Plains overlooking the valley, the stamp of architect Lambert Packard (1832–1906) and his wealthy patrons is visible everywhere. Thaddeus Fairbanks started making the world's first platform scale here in the 1830s, and he and his sons were great civic benefactors.

The handsome **St Johnsbury Athenaeum** (11/1 Main Street; tel: 802-748 8291; Mon–Fri 10am–5.30pm, Sat 9.30am–5pm; fee for gallery), built in 1871–73, houses both the city library and an art gallery. The huge skylights in the gallery were restored in 2011 and provide better lighting for the gallery, including the panorama *Domes of the Yosemite* by artist Albert Bierstadt. This is one of the oldest intact art collections in the country, with great attention paid to the Hudson River School.

The Romanesque **Fairbanks Museum and Planetarium** (corner of Main and Prospect Streets; tel: 802-748 2372; www.fairbanksmuseum.org; Apr–Oct Mon–Sat 9am–5pm, Sun

Bronze statue of Civil War General William W. Wells in Burlington's Battery Park. After the war, Wells (1837–92) moved to Burlington and became one of its most prominent businessmen.

*The library in
St Johnsbury's
Athenaeum.*

BELOW: a hayride
with a view of
Burke Mountain.

1am–5pm; Nov–Mar Tue–Sat 9am–5pm, Sun 1am–5pm; fee – planetarium show additional fee) is northern New England's Museum of Natural History. View 4,000 mounted creatures (many in dioramas of natural settings) in northern New England's only public planetarium with a new, state-of-the-art projection system, and an interactive "omniglobe" explaining geology and climate. East out of downtown St Johnsbury on Route 2, watch for the sign for **Stephen Huneck's Dog Mountain** (143 Parks Road off Spaulding Road; tel: 800-449 2580; www.dogmt.com; gallery May–Oct daily 10am–5pm; Nov–Apr Mon–Sat 10am–4pm, Sun 11am–4pm; grounds are always open), where the late artist and woodcarver created a chapel to memorialize man's best departed friends. Dogs scamper up the hiking trails and splash in the pond on the property. Sales of his woodcuts and other artwork at the on-site gallery help maintain the property and keep it open.

Nearby, visit **Maple Grove Farms** (1052 Portland Street, Route 2; tel: 802-748 5141; tours Apr–May Mon–Fri 8am–5pm; June–Dec Mon–Fri 8am–5pm, Sat–Sun 9am–5pm) for a tour of the factory to learn how syrup and maple products are made.

East Burke

About 10 miles (6km) north of St Johnsbury, in **East Burke** ㉖, **Kingdom Trails** (Route 114; tel: 802-626 0737; ww.kingdomtrails.com; fee) is a network of multi-use trails covering more than 100 miles (160km). It is consistently voted among the top trail systems for mountain biking, hiking, trail running, Nordic skiing, and snowshoeing. The welcome center is in town behind Bailey & Burke Store. **East Burke Sports** (tel: 802-626 3215), across the street from the welcome center, rents bikes.

West and north of St Johnsbury via routes 15 and 16, **Greensboro**, on Caspian Lake, is a peaceful retreat long favored by writers, academics, and professionals. **Willey's Store** – the heart of the tiny village – dispenses local information and carries an astounding inventory ranging from boots to Beaujolais to *The New York Times*.

The Craftsburys

Northwest of St Johnsbury on Route 14, the **Craftsburys** begin. There are three: East Craftsbury, Craftsbury, an the Shangri-La of Vermont villages, **Craftsbury Common** ㉗, a tidy collection of beautifully preserved, 19th-century homes surrounding a town green on a ridge overlooking the valley. The trees around the village green were planted at the death of George Washington in 1799.

Back toward I–91, in **Glover** ㉘, the **Bread & Puppet Theater Museum** (Route 122; tel: 802-525 3031; www.breadandpuppet.org; tours on Sundays at 1.30pm; donation) is home base for an amazing collection of huge and fantastical creatures created by German immigrant Peter Schumann to illustrate the horrors of war and the wonders of life. Believing that art is to the soul what bread is to the body, he

serves freshly baked bread to the audience. The company performs many Sunday afternoons throughout the summer: check their website for the schedule.

Farther north, **Brownington** ㉙, a thriving community in the early 1800s when the Boston–Montreal stage stopped here, is best known for its elegant old homes and the **Old Stone House Museum** (off Route 58; tel: 802-754 2022; open mid May–mid-Oct, Wed–Sun 11am–5pm; fee). Its collection of local miscellanea is housed in the former county grammar school, built in 1827–30 by Alexander Twilight. He became the first African-American college graduate as a member of Middlebury College's class of 1823 and was the first African-American legislator when he was elected to the Vermont General Assembly in 1836.

Newport

Straddling the US–Canada border, 30-mile (48km) -long **Lake Memphremagog** snakes between steep wooded hills. **Newport** ㉚, the "Border City" at the southern end of the lake, is noted for its easy mingle of Canadian day-trippers, locals, and sports fishermen in search of trout and landlocked salmon. There is a lovely boardwalk along the waterfront. The **MAC Center for the Arts** (158 Main Street; tel: 802-334 1966; May–Sept Mon–Sat 10am–5.30pm, Oct–Apr Mon and Wed–Sat 10am–5pm) features a bright gallery with works by area artists inspired by the landscape and light.

Several outfitters rent canoes and kayaks for exploring the lake and the large **South Bay Wildlife Management Area**. If you explore the northern part of the lake, be aware that the border with Canada bisects it at about the halfway point, and border regulations are enforced.

About 20 miles (32km) to the west of Newport, Route 242 climbs to the ski area of **Jay Peak** ㉛ (tel: 802-988 2611 or 800-451 4449 out of area; www.jaypeakresort.com). A massive renovation and expansion largely ready to open for the 2012 winter season includes two new hotels, a large

Stained glass decorates the chapel at Stephen Huneck's Dog Mountain.

BELOW: a cabinetmaker carving scrollwork.

Why Vermont Excels at Crafts

More than 1,600 residents of Vermont identify themselves as professional artisans. That's one of the highest rates per capita in the country and makes Vermont the epicenter of the crafts revival in America.

There are more than 130 galleries scattered throughout the state, including those singled out by the Vermont Crafts Council for showcasing work only by Vermont artisans. There are guilds for nearly every media, including fiber arts, painting, photography, weaving, furniture making, woodworking, and pottery.

From the first spring weekends through fall foliage, there are as many art festivals in Vermont as there are maple trees (www.vermontfairsand festivals.com). Every small town seems to hold a weekend art show, which usually features local talent. Major two-day festivals are scheduled from July through October. The largest of these is the Southern Vermont Arts & Fine Craft Festival, held for 10 days every August in Manchester (www. craftproducers.com). Major festivals routinely attract from 200 to 400 artists who must send samples of their work to be reviewed before they are invited to participate. Acceptance in these juried shows means their work has been judged by other professionals as being of a very high standard. Meeting the artists and learning about their eclectic, and often eccentric, pasts is another insight into Vermont's unique character – and characters.

Ice windsurfing on the frozen margins of Lake Champlain. In some years, the lake freezes across its entire 10-mile (16km) width at Burlington.

BELOW: farming chores in South Hero.

indoor water park, spa, indoor skating rink, upgraded snowmaking equipment, Nordic Center, and a pro shop for summer golf.

The northwestern corner

Vermont's northwestern corner is defined by the Canadian border and the jagged, picturesque shoreline of Lake Champlain. The Vermont "mainland" here is gently rolling dairy country, growing flatter and more open as t nears the border and the great alluvial plain of the St Lawrence River. The big lake is bisected by the Alburgh peninsula descending from Quebec and by a 22-mile (35km) skein of islands, linked by bridges and causeways.

This is where Samuel de Champlain (1567–1635) first ventured out upon the waters that would bear his name, where Iroquois raiders canoed north to terrorize early French settlements, and where bootleggers' speedboats barreled south to the thirsty speakeasies of Prohibition days. Such excitement is long past, and today's northwest corner is one of Vermont's most enticing watery playlands.

Lake Champlain Islands

The **Lake Champlain Islands** ㉜ are strewn with arcadian preserves, lakeshore drives, an sleepy little towns. Te only town which is not on an island is Alburgh. It's on a peninsula that's connected to the rest of the US only by a causeway. Several state parks have fine-sand swimming beaches, including **Sand Bar** (Route 2; Milton) and **Alburgh Dunes** (off Route 129 Alburgh; both open Memorial Day–Labor Day, 10am–sunset; fee).

South Hero, on an island in the middle of Lake Champlain and on roughly the same latitude as Bordeaux, France, is home to Vermont's first winery, **Snow Farm Vineyard** (190 West Shore Road; tel: 802-372 9463; www.snowfarm.com; May–Dec daily 10am–5pm). Bring a picnic or buy a salad or sandwich at the winery and enjoy a free concert under the stars at the farm's Thursday evening concert series (mid-June–late Aug). The new Skinny Pancake Café (60 Lake St., Suite 1A, Burlington; tel: 802-540 0188; www.skinnypancake.com) is open from May to September from lunch to late afternoon.

Turn onto South Street to visit **Allenholm Farms**, where you can rent a bicycle to explore the country lanes, enjoy the petting zoo, and pick your own apples in the fall. At **Hackett's Orchards** try a fresh cider doughnut at the bake shop.

Grand Isle is also home to the 1783 **Hyde Cabin** (Route 2; open late May–mid-Oct, Thur–Mon 11am–5pm; fee), the oldest log cabin in New England. The interior is arranged as a home setting of the period. Next to it is the 1814 **Corners Schoolhouse** with a small display of books and other articles.

The Vermont Shakespeare Company (tel: 877-874 1911; www.vermontshakespeare.org) performs in the Champlain Islands and Burlington during the summer. Driftwood Tours (tel: 802-373 0022) gives tours of Lake Champlain from its home base at the **North Hero House** (tel: 888-525

3644; www.northherohouse.com), one of the island's finest inns.

On **Isle La Motte** "the oldest coral reef in the world" was left behind 10,000 years ago, when the Atlantic covered the Champlain Valley; the formations are visible at the **Goodsell Ridge Fossil Preserve** (Quarry Road; June–Labor Day Wed–Sun 11am–4pm, Labor Day–Oct Sat–Sun noon–4pm). Ever since the first French trappers said the first Mass on the island in 1666, Catholics have considered Vermont under the protection of St Anne. **St Anne's Shrine** (92 Saint Anne's Road; tel: 802-928 3362; open mid-May–mid-Oct daily) attracts the faithful for pilgrimages and prayer among the pines.

Swanton

East on Route 78 in **Swanton** ㉝, more than 200 avian species, including ospreys and blue heron, have been identified at the 6,345-acre (2,568-hectare) **Missisquoi National Wildlife Refuge** (29 Tabor Road; tel: 802-868 4781; grounds open daily dawn–dusk; visitor center open mid-May–mid-Oct Mon–Fri 8am–4pm, Sat 10am–2pm). Swanton is the tribal headquarters of the Abenaki people. The **Abenaki Tribal Museum** (100 Grand Avenue; tel: 802-868 2559; irregular hours, call) displays many items for daily and ceremonial use.

St Albans

For many years **St Albans** ㉞, 10 miles (16km) south on Route 7, was headquarters of the Central Vermont Railway, and its glory days are reflected in its fine town green, imposing brick buildings, and handsome Victorian homes. St Albans was the scene of the Civil War's northernmost northernmost skirmish: in 1864 a band of Confederates infiltrated the town, robbed the banks, and hightailed it to Canada. Caught and brought to trial, their exploits were excused as "legitimate" acts of war. Billing itself as "The Maple Sugar

Capital of the World," it hosts the Vermont Maple Festival, at the end of April (www.vtmaplefestival.org).

The city's history is ably recounted in exhibits at the **St Albans Historical Museum** (corner Church and Bishop streets; tel: 802-527 7933; open May–mid-Oct, Tue–Fri 1am–4pm, Sat 10am–2pm; fee).

A few miles east on Route 36 is the village of **Fairfield**, birthplace of President Chester A. Arthur (4588 Chester Arthur Road; tel: 802-828 3051; July-mid-Oct Sat–Sun and Mon holidays; donation). The son of an impoverished Baptist minister, he was born in 1829 or 1830 (Arthur himself was fuzzy on the date) in a primitive log cabin. (A granite monument marks the likely spot where it stood.) The parishioners quickly completed a modest parsonage for the family. A reconstruction of the house contains a pictorial record of Arthur's life and political career. He became president after the assassination of President James Garfield in 1881. Like another president born in rural poverty, Arthur advocated for civil rights.

TIP

The 1954 movie *The Raid* starring Van Heflen, Anne Bancroft, Richard Boone, and Lee Marvin, is Hollywood's very romanticized and very inaccurate version of the confederate raid on St Albans during the Civil War.

BELOW: a local farmers' market.

Church Street Market-place in Burlington, showing the First Unitarian Universalist Society Church.

Burlington and environs

A picture-postcard setting, abundant recreational and cultural opportunities, five colleges and universities, and its position as Vermont's financial and industrial center make **Burlington 🕄** a lively city. With a population of only about 40,000 – half of them students – Burlington is the smallest "state's largest city" in the country.

Burlington started as a trading post and port in 1775, but it didn't boom until the mid-1800s. Between shipping on Lake Champlain and along the Champlain Canal, the lumber industry, and water-powered mills and industries on the Winooski River, Burlington was a prosperous town with all the amenities that went with it. After World War II, it slipped into the same decline seen by many other New England cities as its waterfront decayed and was abandoned. But New England ingenuity prevailed and the city is rebounding. Throughout the downtown, over 200 buildings have been restored. A growing influx of industry, notably IBM, and the new metropolitan tone mingle to keep Burlington turning up on polls as being one of the US's "most liveable cities."

Sunset over Lake Champlain and the Adirondacks from the heights above Burlington is enough to justify a visit. But along Lake and Battery streets, the old workaday waterfront has been reborn as **Waterfront and Battery parks 🅐**, with a smoke-free park, picnic tables, and a 12-mile (19km) -long bike path developed along the old railroad right-of-way. A few blocks south, Waterfront Boat Rentals (Perkins Pier, foot of Maple St.; tel: 802-864 4858, 877-964 4858; www.waterfrontboatrentals.com) is the place to get kayaks, row boats, row-boats, and Boston Whalers.

If you'd rather someone else do the driving, the *Spirit of Ethan Allen III* (tel: 802-862 8300; www.soea.com) has 90-minute scenic cruises throughout the day, many with meals and entertainment. It departs from the **Burlington Boathouse 🅑** (formerly the Community Boathouse). For an idea of what it was like "back then," the *Northern Lights* (tel: 802-864 9669;

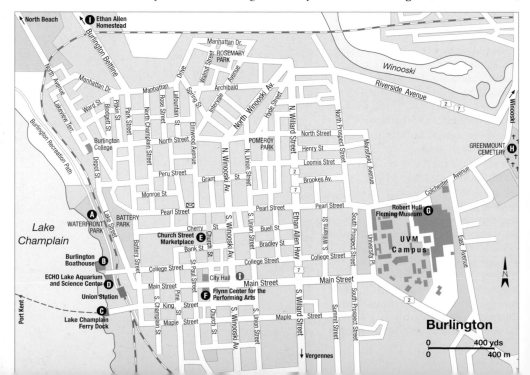

www.lakechamplaincruises.com) is a 155ft (35-meter) replica of a 19th-century steamboat ferry which also has scenic, sunset, and dinner cruises. It leaves from the **Lake Champlain Ferry Dock** Ⓒ on King Street.

Just when you think you've seen enough nature centers to last a lifetime, you enter the **ECHO Lake Aquarium and Science Center** Ⓓ (on the lake at the southern edge of Waterfront Park; tel: 877-324 6386; www.echovermont.org; daily 10am–5pm; fee). Even the most jaded adult can spend an entire day here, gazing over the waters of Lake Champlain from the observation deck if nothing else. But there is a lot of "else": hand-feeding of animals, a 3-D frog-call tracking station, exploring a submerged shipwreck via a remote control camera, learning the indigenous peoples' perspective on the lake. In the plaza outside, **the US Navy Memorial** features a statute of *The Lone Sailor*. It's a twin of the memorial statue in Washington.

The **Church Street Marketplace** Ⓔ in the center of the historic district is lined with shops, restaurants, and businesses. It's the site of events and celebrations from open-air art shows and jazz festivals to the "Festival of Fools" – a gathering of international street performers (usually in August). (From Waterfront and Battery parks, walk east on Cherry Street. You'll pass the two-story, enclosed Burlington Town Center with the usual mix of chain retail stores.)

The **Flynn Center for the Performing Arts** Ⓕ (153 Main Street; tel: 802-652 4500; www.flynncenter. org), a 1930 Art Deco movie palace, hosts an impressive line-up of dance, music, and theater. The stage has seen k.d. lang, *South Pacific*, and the Zoppé Family Italian Circus.

Many of the buildings on and surrounding the University of Vermont campus are architectural gems. Preservation Burlington (tel: 802-985 8935) has brochures for self-guided

tours of the waterfront and historic district. They can arrange for a guide. European and American paintings are displayed in UVM's **Robert Hull Fleming Museum** Ⓖ (61 Colchester Avenue; tel: 802-656 0750; May–Labor Day Tue–Fri 12am–4pm, Sat–Sun 1am–5mp; Labor Day–Apr Tue, Thurs, Fri 9am–4mp, Wed 9am–8pm, Sat–Sun 1am–5pm; closed mid-Dec–mid-Jan; fee). It includes more than 20,000 anthropological artifacts from around the world, an expanded Native American collection, and works by painters of the Hudson River School as well as Sargent, Homer, and Fragonard.

To the northeast of the campus on Colechester Avenue is **Greenmount Cemetery** Ⓗ, the final resting place of Ethan Allen. His grave is easily found under an 8ft-tall statute of Allen atop a 42ft (13-meter) granite shaft.

Five miles (8km) north of Burlington, off Route 127, is the **Ethan Allen Homestead** Ⓘ (tel: 802-865 4556; May–Oct, Thur–Mon 10am–4pm; fee). The flamboyant, belligerent, beloved backwoodsman-turned-soldier-turned-philosopher

Taking aim at the Lake Champlain Maritime Museum.

BELOW: the Ethan Allen Homestead.

The Ticonderoga on dry land.

BELOW: Shelburne Museum, Round Barn Visitor Center.

built this modest home just two years before he died. The restored 1787 farmhouse has an excellent exhibit on the state's history. There are also miles of walking trails along the Winooski River.

On Burlington's northern outskirts, near the bike path, **North Beach** (60 Institute Road; tel: 802-852 0942; fee) has a sandy beach, snack bar, and changing rooms.

In nearby **Colechester**, **Saint Michael's Playhouse** (1 Winooski Park; tel: 802-654 2281; http://academics.smcvt.edu/playhouse), on the campus of Saint Michael's College, has mounted a professional summer theater from June to August since 1951.

Farther along Route 15 in the town of **Jericho** ㊱ is the **The Old Red Mill** with the **Snowflake Bentley Exhibit** (tel: 802-899 3225; Apr–Dec Mon–Sat 10am–5pm, Sun 11.30am–4pm; Jan–Mar Wed and Sat 10am–5pm, Sun 11.30am–4pm). The lower level of the mill is devoted to the work of Wilson "Snowflake" Bentley. In the early years of the 20th century, he took thousands of microphotographs of snowflakes, proving the contention that no two snowflakes are alike. The exhibit is filled with copies of his photos of delicate ice crystals.

Southeast of Burlington on Route 2, take the turn south at Richmond and head for **Huntington** ㊲ and the **Birds of Vermont Museum** (tel: 802-434 2167; May–Oct daily 10am–4pm; Nov–Apr by appointment; fee). Amazingly detailed and realistic carvings of 500 birds by master carver Bob Spear are displayed in realistic habitat settings. Each wing of the California Condor took over 100 hours to carve.

Shelburne

Head south out of Burlington on Route 7 to **Shelburne** ㊳ and one of Vermont's major destinations, the **Shelburne Museum** (tel: 802-985 3346; www.shelburnemuseum.org; mid-May–Oct Mon–Sat 10am–5pm, Sun noon–5pm, until 7.30pm on Thurs mid-June–mid-August; fee – ticket is good for two days). This beautifully assembled 45-acre (18-hectare) complex reflects the tastes of one very passionate and well-funded collector. Electra Havemeyer Webb (1888–1960) developed an eye for Americana and folk art long before anyone else was paying attention. Her passion fills 39 galleries and buildings. Even the buildings are part of the collection, as they include barns, the Lake Champlain lighthouse, even a jail and the Lake Champlain side-wheeler *Ticonderoga*. Impressionist and American 19th- and 20th-century artists are well represented; there are displays of folk art, quilts, and carved bird decoys. One of the most popular exhibits is of two hand-carved miniature circuses, each with over 3,000 figures.

Just south of the museum, is the **Shelburne Vineyard Winery and Tasting Room** (6308 Shelburne Road, Route 7; tel: 802-734 8700; shelburnevineyard.com; tasting room open daily 11am–5pm; tasting fee; free tours of winery daily); the winter-hardy grapes are grown right at the vineyard.

Shelburne is home to a number of attractions including **Vermont Teddy Bear** (6655 Shelburne Road; tel: 802-985 3001; factory tours: July–mid-Oct daily 9.30am–5pm; mid-Oct–June daily 10am–4pm; no production on weekends, and the staff takes a 12.30–1pm lunch break). Built in 1859, the **Shelburne Country Store** (29 Falls Road; tel: 800-660 3657; daily 9am–6pm) overflows with backpacks and books, toiletries and tools, antiques and art. On Bostwick Road off Route 7, **Shelburne Orchards** (tel: 802-985 2753; mid-Aug–Oct Mon–Sat 9am–6pm, Sun 9am–5pm) has apples, peaches, and cherries in season. They've perfected their apple cider recipe and are now making apple brandy and cider vinegar.

Another Shelburne landmark is the 100-room, lakefront Queen Anne–style "cottage" of Dr William Seward and Lila Vanderbilt Webb. Its surrounding estate was designed by Frederick Law Olmsted, designer of New York City's Central Park. This 1,400-acre (570-hectare) property, **Shelburne Farms** (off Route 7; tel: 802-985 8686; www.shelburnefarms. org; May–mid-Oct daily 9am–5.30pm, mid-Oct–Apr daily 10am–5pm; fee, guided tour daily in summer for a small fee, trails open daily dawn–dusk) is a model ecological farmstead with an award-winning cheese-making facility, extensive grounds, and a children's farmyard. The mansion offers superb accommodations and dining throughout the summer.

South of Shelburne

Charlotte ㊴, 6 miles (10km) south of Shelburne, is home to the unusual **Vermont Wildflower Farm** (3488 Ethan Allen Highway; tel: 802-846 9453; gardens ope May–Oct daily 10am–4.30pm). Something colorful is always in bloom from May through October. A lovely self-guided tour meanders along a brook and pond. Charlotte is also a Lake Champlain crossing point; a ferry (www.ferries. com) to the little town of Essex NY operates from spring to late autumn.

Quakers, farmers, abolitionists, authors, and artists – four generations of the Robinson family – lived

The Vermont Fresh Network is a farm and chef partnership which works directly to source food from farms to restaurants with the connections directly strengthening the local economies and communities. Member restaurants display a green decal showing a barn bracketed by a knife and fork.

BELOW: kayaking on Lake Champlain.

Vermont's covered bridges are probably the state's most appreciated man-made landscape feature. Although lovely to look at, the design served a purely practical purpose. Putting a roof over the wooden supports extended the life of the bridge by as much as 40 years.

BELOW: the Robert Frost Cabin in Ripton VT, part of the Robert Frost Farm National Historic Landmark.

in **Ferrisburg** at what is now the **Rokeby Museum** (4337 Route 7; tel: 802-877 3406; open mid-May–mid-Oct Thur–Sun; guided tours of the house at 11am, 12.30pm, and 2pm; fee; self-guided tour of outbuildings and farmstead, no charge; audiotape tour available). The farm is one of the best-documented "stations" on the Underground Railroad. The building overflows with 200 years' worth of furniture and belongings, and the guides enjoy relating the very rich history of this remarkable family. Outside, a self-guided hike, "How a Farm Becomes a Forest," is well worth the walk.

There are maple syrup and cheese-making operations galore in Vermont, but only one where you can visit a smokehouse as well. The **Dakin Farm** (5797 Route 7, Ferrisburg; tel: 800-99 DAKIN; daily 8am–5pm) was established by Timothy Dakin in 1792. His descendants welcome visitors to see the operations (and buy the tasty results).

Maritime attractions

Lake Champlain's maritime traditions are preserved just west of **Vergennes**

at the **Lake Champlain Maritime Museum** ⑩ (4472 Basin Harbor Road; tel: 802-475 2022; www.lcmm.org; late-May–Oct daily 10am–5pm; fee). It's a fun take on the lake's history, with a replica 1776 gunboat, a nautical archaeological center researching over 300 wrecks on the lake bottom, and watercraft from early canoes to vintage steamboats on display. Divers can get information on wreck dives here.

Vermont spawned the world-famous Morgan horse, a barrel-chested steed which, as one celebrant boasted, "can outrun, outpull, and outlast any other breed, just as you would expect a Vermont horse to do." The **UVM Morgan Horse Farm**, off Route 23, in the village of **Weybridge**, is a working farm with training demonstrations and tours (74 Battell Drive, Woodbridge off Route 23; tel: 802-388 2011; May–Oct daily 9am–4pm; tours on the hour, last tour 3.30pm; fee). The foals are irresistibly cute.

Middlebury ⑪, directly down Route 7 from Vergennes, is the ideal college town, a verdant campus of grand, well-spaced 19th-century

buildings, accompanied by a lively community of pubs, shops, and restaurants. The traditional arts of Vermont are highlighted at the **Vermont Folklife Center** (88 Main Street; tel: 802-388 4964; Tue–Sat 10am–5pm). The shop features the work of artisans who carry on cultural traditions like quilting, basket weaving, and beeswax candle-making. A superb collection of late-18th- and 19th-century Vermontiana is housed in the **Henry Sheldon Museum of Vermont History** (1 Park Street; tel: 802-388 2117; open Tue–Sat 10am–5pm, also May–Sept Sun 1pm–5pm; fee). Housed in a three-story residence built in 1829, recent exhibits trace leisure in the 19th century and Vermont's role in the Civil War.

Collections at the **Middlebury College Museum of Art** (Route 30 South; tel: 802-443 5007; Tue–Fri 10am–5pm, Sat–Sun noon–5pm) explore Asian and Western art from the 4th millennium BC to the present day. The 20th-century collection has a particular emphasis on photography and prints. There's a 45-minute audio

walking tour (or brochure) of sculpture on the college campus.

A slightly different version of handcrafted artwork is at **Otter Creek Brewing** (793 Exchange Street, Middlebury; tel: 802-388 0727; daily 11am–6pm; free self-guided tours and tastings). Their first beers were brewed in a storage garage at the edge of town. They now produce a range of popular seasonal and year-round brews from a much larger and more suitable location.

In search of Robert Frost

The poet Robert Frost spent his summers writing in a log cabin 7 miles (11km) east on Route 125 in **Ripton** ㊷, in the northern section of the 400,000-acre (161,874hectare160,000-hectare) **Green Mountain National Forest**, which stretches across two-thirds of the state. The cabin is not far from **Bread Loaf Inn**, home of the prestigious 10-day Bread Loaf Writers' Conference, founded in 1926.

The mile-long **Robert Frost Interpretive Trail**, beginning at his home, the Homer Noble Farm, is marked by several of his poems which

Horse breeding is a well established tradition in Vermont.

*The Robert Frost
Stone House Museum.*

BELOW: the Haskell
Free Library and
Opera House in the
US town of Derby
Line. The black line on
the floor indicates the
US/Canadian border.

are mounted at appropriate spots along the walk. For great scenery, continue on State 125, through steep **Middlebury Gap**; you can return to Route 7 by following Route 100 for 6 miles (10km) south and heading back west on equally scenic Route 73 through Brandon Gap. The route circumnavigates the **Moosalamoo National Recreation Area**. Covering 20,000 acres (8,000 hectares), it has over 70 miles (110km) of trails for biking, hiking, horseback riding, cross-country skiing, and enjoying marvelous vistas. Many trails have interpretative panels explaining the wildlife and environmental features. A birding guide, moose-viewing drive map, and other information are available for free download (www.moosalamoo.org).

The entire core of **Brandon** ㊸ – more than 200 buildings – is listed on the National Register of Historic Places. Stephen A. Douglas was born in the white cottage next to the Baptist Church, north on Route 7; he was the Illinois senator whose famous seven debates with Abraham Lincoln, the rival for his seat in 1858, focused on the issue of slavery. His birthplace is now a small museum and visitor center (4 Grove Street; daily 8am–6pm), where you can pick up the self-guided walking tour brochure.

At **Brandon Music** (62 Country Club Road; tel: 802-465 4071; www.brandonmusicvt.com; Wed–Mon 10am–6pm) Stephen and Edna Sutton maintain an arts oasis focused on music. It's home to their classical music recording company, a CD store specializing in hard-to-find artists and "boutique" labels, a café and proper British tearoom (they're transplants from the UK), an art gallery, and an antiques shop featuring – among other things – old phonographs. There are regular concerts with local and international artists.

Two historic sites near Brandon commemorate two important contributions by Vermont to the American Revolution. On the shore of Lake Champlain, west of Orwell, the fortification at **Mount Independence State Historic Site** (497 Mt. Independence Road; tel: 802-948 2000; end May–mid-Oct daily 9.30am–5.30pm; fee)

An International Opera House

The town of Derby Line is directly on the US/Canadian border, at the northernmost end of Route 5 or Interstate 91. On the other side, the town becomes Stanstead, Quebec. The Haskell Free Library and Opera House sits astride the border; during performances, the audience is in the US while the stage is in Canada. The placement and location is quite deliberate; the building was donated by Martha Stewart Haskell with the intention of creating a center for learning and cultural enrichment for residents in both countries. The full schedule of plays, concerts, and international cultural performances supports the free library. The entrances to the building are on the American side, so you don't need your passport to see a performance.

was a massive structure designed to defend against a British invasion from Canada. Manned by 12,000 soldiers, it was one of the largest communities in North America in 1776. When the advancing British saw this fort and Fort Ticonderoga, they returned to Canada and prepared for a new invasion the following spring. The fort was evacuated in the face of the overwhelming British numbers. After Gen. Burgoyne's surrender in October 1777, the fort was no longer needed and was destroyed. Today it is one of the most valuable Revolutionary War military archaeological sites. The museum demonstrates how artifacts and modern technology explain the story of the fort.

Southwest of Brandon, the **Hubbarton Battlefield** (5696 Monument Road; tel: 802-759 2412; end May–mid-Oct Thur–Sun 9.30am–5.40pm; fee) is the site of the only Revolutionary War battle fought entirely in Vermont. In July 1777, the Green Mountain Boys held off a much larger British force intent on splitting New England from the rest of the colonies. Although the British held the field at the end of the day, their losses were so great that they retreated. By October, the Redcoats had lost the battles of Bennington and Saragota and Burgoyne had surrendered his army. The site includes a visitor center museum and walking trails on the battlefield. On most Sundays, there are interpretive programs.

In **Pittsford**, the **New England Maple Museum** (Route 7; tel: 802-483 9414; May–Oct and mid-Mar–Apr daily 8.30am–5.30pm, Nov–Dec daily 10am–4pm; closed Jan–Feb; fee) bills itself as "the world's largest maple museum." One hundred feet (30 meters) of murals and scale-model dioramas show the process from sap collection to syrup production. There's a tasting room for the different grades of syrup, and a large gift shop sells syrup, maple candy, and cookies.

Proctor

Just off routes 7 and 3, the town of **Proctor ㊹** ("Marble Center of the World") is the logical spot for the **Vermont Marble Museum** (52 Main Street; open mid-May–Oct daily 9am–4pm; fee). It offers a glimpse into the workings of the Vermont Marble Company factory which flourished here for more than 100 years, a hands-on exploration of geologic evolution, and a moving display on the history of the Tomb of the Unknown Soldier. A new nature path leads from the museum to the original Proctor Quarry overlook, a surprisingly lovely spot for a picnic.

Off Route 3 in Proctor, Dr John Johnson built a home for his wife, a wealthy English aristocrat, in 1867. **Wilson Castle** (West Proctor Road; tel: 802-773 3284; open late May–mid-Oct daily 9am–5pm; fee) is an opulent stone mansion with 32 rooms, 12 fireplaces, and 84 stained-glass windows.

Vermont's second-biggest city, **Rutland ㊺**, is filled with palatial Victorian homes, a restored Art Deco movie theatre, and an enclosed

Pittsford is the town where the first US Patent was issued in 1790, for the process of making pearl-ash.

BELOW: the Vermont Marble Museum.

The Olde Tavern, Manchester.

BELOW: the painting *Breaking Home Ties* at the Norman Rockwell Museum.

regional shopping mall (one of the largest in the state).

The **Chaffee Center for the Visual Arts** (16 South Main Street; tel: 802-775 0356; www.chaffeeartcenter.org; Tue–Sat 10am–5pm) showcases the artistic expressions of local talent. The **Paramount Theater** (30 Center Street, tel: 802-775 0903; www.paramountvt.org), with its restored Victorian opera house interior, hosts film and live performances. Just outside town, **Hathaway Farm** (741 Propsect Hill Rd.; tel: 802-775 2624; www.hathaway-farm.com) is a wonderful menagerie of barnyard animals. From late July through October, it operates the largest corn maze in Vermont: 12 acres (5 hectares) of twisting, meandering trails through head-high ripe corn.

East of Rutland on Route 4 is the **Norman Rockwell Museum** (654 Route 4 E; tel: 877-773 6095; daily 9am–4pm). The prolific illustrator is best known for the covers of *The Saturday Evening Post*, which often showed a nostalgic, romanticized Americana. He lived in nearby Arlington from 1939 to 1953. The museum has several thousand of his illustrations, including the powerful four-part series *The Four Freedoms*.

The Manchesters

Franklin Orvis gave the local tourist industry a boost in 1849 when he began taking in summer guests at his father's house, located next to the 1769 Marsh Tavern in **Manchester Village** , where Ethan Allen and his Green Mountain Boys plotted the Tories' overthrow. The hotel kept expanding until it grew into the **Equinox Resort and Spa** (3567 Main Street, Route 7A; tel: 800-362 4747; www.equinoxresort.com), a grand resort on more than 1,300 acres (530 hectares). Rooms are scattered among five buildings, including 19th-century farmhouses. Guests can indulge themselves in an array of unique outdoor experiences, like an introductory course in falconry or off-road driving on an 80-acre (32-hectare) track.

Franklin Orvis's younger brother, Charles, also had a clever idea – why not teach the leisured class to catch their supper along the banks of the abundant Battenkill River?

The store they opened to supply their students, Orvis (4180 Main Street, Route 7A; tel: 802-362 3750; Mon–Sat 9am–6pm, Sun 10am–5pm), with its core emphasis on fly-fishing, has grown into an outdoor-lifestyle powerhouse. Its huge retail store is billed as "Vermont's largest retail attraction." There are indoor and outdoor trout ponds; at the latter, patrons can test equipment.

Next door to Orvis is the **American Museum of Fly Fishing** (Route 7A; tel: 802-362 3300; www.amff.com; Tue–Sun 10am–4pm; fee). It's home to the world's largest collection of angling and angling-related items, including the fishing rods of Ernest Hemingway and Herbert Hoover. Orvis's success inspired a raft of other upscale companies such as Ralph Lauren, Brooks Brothers, Joan & David, and Giorgio Armani to open outlets in nearby **Manchester**, turning that one-time quaint town into a wall-to-wall shopping mall.

An artistic venue as expansive as the resort is the **Southern Vermont Arts Center** (West Road; tel: 802-362 3274; www.svac.org; Tue–Sat 10am–5pm, Sun noon–5pm; closed Sun Jan–Apr; fee for museum; gallery and grounds free admission). Set on a 407-acre (165-hectare) estate, there are galleries with a permanent collection of nearly 800 pieces 19th- and 20th-century art. A restored Georgian Revival mansion has 10 galleries selling works, and the grounds are an outdoor sculpture garden. A 400-seat auditorium, noted for its fine acoustics, is the site of live performances.

A contender for "most scenic drive in Vermont" is the 5-mile (8km) **Skyline Drive** toll road (Route 7A; tel: 802-362 1114; www.equinoxmountain. com; daily May–Oct, weather permitting; toll for car and each passenger). The twisting road with 20 hairpin turns follows the ridgeline of Equinox Mountain to a visitor center at the summit. There are plenty of places to pull over and savor the view. Vintage sports

cars race to the summit in an annual rally every summer. The mountain and road are owned by an order of monks who were bequeathed the property by the mountain's former owner.

Although Abraham Lincoln never visited Vermont, his wife and children did. Buoyed by fond memories of happier times, Lincoln's son, Robert Todd, returned many years later to build **Historic Hildene** (Route 7A; tel: 802-362 1788; www.hildene.org; daily 9.30am–-4.30pm; fee). The massive 8,000-sq-foot (700-sq-meter) mansion displays richly appointed Georgian Revival rooms, a 1,000-pipe organ (daily concert), observatory and telescope, and the 1928 Franklin Roadster that belonged to Robert Lincoln's daughter. The expansive grounds are open to cross-country skiers and summer strollers.

Out of Manchester

The picturesque, marble-paved village of **Dorset** ⓐ, 8.25 miles (13km) northwest of Manchester, is home to the **Dorset Playhouse** (tel: 802-867 5777; www.dorsetplayers.org). The

The Equinox Resort and Spa.

BELOW: the Hildene Mansion.

The Appalachian Trail

In 1921, Benton MacKaye proposed a trail system to "provide leisure, enjoyment, and the study of nature for people living in the urban areas of the Eastern United States"

By 1937, the Appalachian Trail was completed. Stretching from Mt Katahdin in Maine's Baxter Park to Springer Mountain GA, the 2,175-mile (3,500km) footpath crosses 14 states, including five of the six in New England (Rhode Island misses out).

Each year, about 4 million people hike part of the Appalachian Trail. Almost 2,000 of them hike its entire length, traveling from South to North. Their odyssey takes an average of 5–6 months (and about as many pairs of hiking boots). Known as "thru-hikers" and going by such colorful trail names as Paul Bunion and Itchyfeet, they leave Georgia in early April, hoping to reach Mt Katahdin by late September, before the trail closes for the winter.

New England claims 734 miles (1,120km) of the Appalachian Trail. It has both the most stunning scenery and the most rugged terrain. While some stretches are nearly impossible for even the most experienced backpacker, casual hikers can have a lot of fun, savor some memorable views, and brag about hiking the trail when they return home.

When in New England and traveling from South to North as most of the thru-hikers do, hikers first cross into Connecticut, where the trail is relatively gentle. The trail goes from Kent to Salisbury, passing through the villages of Cornwall and Lime Rock. Moderate climbs up the foothills of the Berkshire Mountains are tempered by miles of trails along river banks and open farmland. Popular with day-hikers, it's a civilized adventure.

The cascades of Sages Ravine announce the start of the Appalachian Trail in southwest Massachusetts. Moving deeper into the Berkshires, hikers face steep climbs, but panoramic vistas. In summer, the coolness of the mountains, including the summit of Mt Greylock (3,491ft, 1,064 meters), Massachusetts' highest peak, is a welcome relief from the sticky sweat of a day on the trail.

Vermont's 150 miles (241km) are probably the best for hikers looking for a bigger challenge but not ready for the fierce finale of the trail in New Hampshire and Maine. Entering Vermont near Bennington, the trail rises into the Green Mountains, joining with Vermont's Long Trail for nearly 100 miles (161km). The colors during fall foliage are unforgettable. During spring melts, known for good reason as mud season, the trail is an impassable, slippery morass. The trail brushes by Woodstock, another good base for hikers who want to explore only a small section.

The views along the trail in New Hampshire and Maine are breathtaking, and so is the effort required to reach them. Here, the Appalachian Trail is the domain of only the most seasoned, physically fit, and determined hikers. Much of New Hampshire's section is above the tree line in the White Mountains. Hikers are exposed to extreme, rapidly changing weather, with snow squalls or worse – even in summer – on Mt Washington (6,288ft, 1,917 meters). The climactic 282 miles (454km) in Maine sees hikers fording streams at the foot of steep, narrow trails, and making lung-gasping climbs through the Grafton and Mahoosuc notches – the latter a notorious mile-long scramble through a boulder-filled gorge – before the final climb to Mount Katahdin.

LEFT: an Appalachian Trail hiking sign.

community theatre group puts on productions from October to May. In the summer, it hosts a professional festival from June to August in a rustic barn with offerings as diverse as Agatha Christie and Stephen Sondheim. The **Dorset Inn** (tel: 802-867 5500; www.dorsetinn.com) on the village green has welcomed guests since 1796. It's the oldest continually operating inn in Vermont.

Just 6 miles (10km) northeast of Manchester, on Route 11, is **Bromley Mountain** (tel: 802-824 5522; www.bromley.com). A popular winter ski resort, it is a huge and hugely successful summer adventure park with thrill rides like a 5-story high, half-mile-long, 50mph zip-line; water slides; and climbing walls.

Weston

Vermont's oldest summer playhouse is about 15 miles (24km) east of Bromley via routes 11 and 100, in the hill village of **Weston 48**. The first show at **Weston Playhouse** (tel: 802-824 5288; www.westonplayhouse.org) in 1937 featured a young actor by the name of

Lloyd Bridges. The theatre building, which incorporates three old barns, has been newly renovated and updated. The Café at the Falls, overlooking the waterfall at the Playhouse, serves bistro fare on performance evenings.

The town is also home to another of the state's major attractions, the **Vermont Country Store** (657 Main Street; tel: 802-824 3184; daily 7am–5.30pm), a purveyor of cracker-barrel atmosphere and useful (and arcane) merchandise since 1946. Raggedy Ann dolls, Fuller brushes, and Bonomo's Turkish Taffy evoke instant nostalgia.

In a 1769 stone house on Main Street in **Shaftsbury 49**, poet Robert Frost wrote *Stopping by Woods on a Snowy Evening* and *New Hampshire*, which concluded, "At present I am living in Vermont." His home is now the **Robert Frost Stone House Museum** (121 Route 7A; tel: 802-447 6200; May–Nov Tue–Sun 10am–5pm, last admission to house 4.40pm; fee). Exhibits are planned so that visitors feel as though they have met Frost. The grounds are much as he saw them, with the trees, stone walls, and

The process of turning maple sap into syrup involves inserting a tube into the trunk of a maple tree (tapping) in early spring through which the warming sap can flow. It's caught in buckets hung onto the tubes. The sap is boiled down to the desired consistency, originally in big vats in sugar shacks.

BELOW: fly-fishing on the Housatonic River near Manchester.

The Vermont Country Store in Weston.

BELOW: the Bennington Battle Monument.

landscapes which inspired his work unchanged.

Bennington

Frost is buried just to the south on Route 7 in **Bennington 50**, at the Old Burying Ground. His epiph reads siply, "I had a lover's quarrel with the world." The cemetery is next to the 1805–06 **Old First Church** (tel: 802-447 1223; Mon–Sat; Sun pm; donation), with its unusual three-tiered steeple.

Bennington, home to Bennington College, looms large in Vermont's history, and a crucial 1777 skirmish is commemorated by the 306ft (93-meter) **Bennington Battle Monument** (15 Monument Circle; tel: 802-447 0550; open mid-Apr–Oct daily; fee). The battle actually took place a few miles to the west in New York State, where General John Stark and 1,800 ragtag troops forced the Redcoats back across the Walloomsac River. But it was a colonial supply dump on this site that General John Burgoyne was after, and his failure to attain it proved a turning point in the British campaign. The tallest structure

in Vermont, an elevator whisks visitors to the top for a spectacular view.

Nearby, the **Bennington Museum** (75 West Main Street, Route 9; tel: 802-447 1571; www.benningtonmuseum. org; Thur–Tue 10am–5pm, also Sept–Oct Wed; closed Jan; fee) exhibits an exceptional collection of regional history and art, including the largest public collection of works by Grandma Moses and many portraits of early and sometimes prominent Vermonters. There are fine collections of Vermont furniture and the largest collection of Bennington pottery anywhere.

Near Route 67A in **North Bennington** is the 35-room **Park-McCullough House** (1 Park Street; tel: 802-442 5441; open for guided tours mid-May–Oct daily 9am–4pm, last tour at 3pm; fee). Pre-dating the mansions of Newport by a quarter-century (1865), it's equally opulent. On the National Register of Historic Places, it is a time capsule of the family that lived here for more than 100 years. Its furniture and decorative arts are among the most outstanding in Vermont.

RESTAURANTS AND BARS

Prices for a three-course dinner per person with a half-bottle of house wine:
$ = under $20
$$ = $20–45
$$$ = $45–60
$$$$ = over $60

Restaurants
Arlington

West Mountain Inn
River Road (off Route 313)
Tel: 802-375 6516
www.westmountaininn.com **$$$**
Fixed-price, New American cuisine featuring local, fresh, organic fish and prime meat in a low-beamed paneled dining room at a romantic but family-friendly inn.

Bennington
Four Chimneys
21 West Road (Route 9)
Tel: 802-447 3500
www.fourchimneys.com **$$$–$$$$**
American and continental cuisine in the gracious dining room of a restored 1910 Colonial Revival inn. closed Tue and Thur.

Pangaea
1&3 Prospect Street, North Bennington
Tel: 802-442 7171
www.vermontfinedining.com **$$$–$$$$**
A sophisticated menu that changes with what's fresh. Flexible "create your own tasting menu" option. D Tue–Sat. Award-winning wine list. Outdoor terrace.

Lounge has lighter fare (**$$**) and global beer list.

Brandon
Café Provence
11 Center Street
Tel: 802-247 9997
www.cafeprovencevt.com **$$**
Casual, relaxing place, perfect after a day of sightseeing or outdoor activity. Outdoor café dining in summer. Bistro fare and hearth over pizza. Large gluten-free menu.

Cattails
2146 Grove Street
Tel: 802-247 9300
www.cattailsvt.com **$$–$$$**
Vermont home-style cooking. Tenderloin, fish and chips, fisherman's pasta. Apple-cinnamon pancakes, many omelets, steak and eggs. Always room at the Vermont slate bar.

Brattleboro
Peter Havens
32 Elliot Street
Tel: 802-257 3333
www.peterhavens.com **$$–$$$**
The locals' favorite New American bistro is a tiny art-filled space. Dishes include roasted duck breast with black currant and sour cherry sauce, homemade pastas with scallops and shirmp. Casual dress; reservations "encouraged."

T.J. Buckley's
132 Eliot Street
Tel: 802-257 4922
www.tjbuckleys.com **$$$**

Reservations required for this 20-seat, intimate restaurant in a tiny 1920s diner. Limited menu changes regularly. Parmesan cheese tart, seared wild King Salmon, rabbit loin. No credit cards.

The Marina
28 Spring Hill Road (Off Route 5)
Tel: 802-257 7563
www.vermontmarina.com **$$**
Rebuilt after a devastating fire, this casual dining spot is once again serving seafood and burgers at its picturesque location where the Connecticut and West rivers meet. No extra charge for the sunsets.

Burlington Area
Daily Planet
15 Center Street

Tel: 802-862 9647
www.dailyplanet15.com **$$**
Mediterranean with sian influences ina cheerful restaurant with a delightful solarium. Specialties include soups and tapas.

Pauline's Cafe and Restaurant
1834 Shelburne Road (Route 7 S), South Burlington
Tel: 802-862 1081
www.paulinescafe.com **$$–$$$**
Recently remodeled, comfortably upscale with warm wood paneling and mellow jazz in the background. Regional specialties. Summer balcony patio. Early-bird dinner for two is excellent value.

Penny Cluse Café
169 Cherry Street

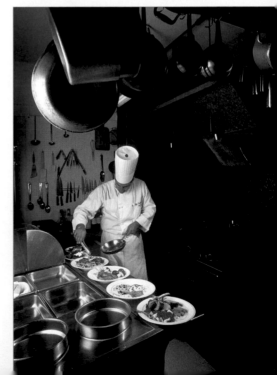

RIGHT: a chef at work in the Craftsbury Inn.

Prices for a three-course dinner per person with a half-bottle of house wine:
$ = under $20
$$ = $20–45
$$$ = $45–60
$$$$ = over $60

Tel: 802-651 8834
www.pennycluse.com **$**
The only problem here is the crowds, who pack in for creative breakfast and lunch creations such as gingerbread pancakes, and chorizo and egg tacos.
Sakura
2 Church Street
Tel: 802-863 1988
www.sakurabanavt.com **$$–$$$**
Skillfully prepared Japanese specialties include tempura and sashimi. Large Sushi bar. "Bento box" lets you sample several entrées.
Trattoria Delia
152 Street Paul Street
Tel: 802-864 5253

www.trattoriadelia.com **$$–$$$**
Award-winning Old World Italian trattoria. Authentic handmade pastas, hardwood-grilled chops, and authentic veal dishes. Cozy and casual fireplace dining on snowy nights.

Chester
Alice's on The Common
90 The Common
Tel: 802-875 3344
www.alicesrestaurantvermont.com **$$–$$$**
Italian accents, smoked salmon rosettes, personalized pizza in a Victorian house. Outdoor seating on the wraparound porch in summer. closed Mon and Tue.

Craftsbury
Craftsbury Inn
Main Street
Tel: 802-586 2848
www.craftsburyinn.com **$$$**
The nightly able d'hôte at

this 1850 Greek Revival village inn features Continental fare. Closed Mon.

Dorset
Chantecleer Restaurant
Route 7A, East Dorset
Tel: 802-362 1616
www.chantecleerrestaurant.com **$$$–$$$$**
The Swiss chef at on of the area's favorite restaurants prepares Euro-American cuisine using fresh fish and game in a handsomely renovated dairy barn. Reservations required. Closed Mon and Tue.
Dorset Inn
8 Church Street and Route 30
Tel: 802-867 5500
www.dorsetinn.com **$$–$$$**
Wine Spectator Magazine says it's one of America's best restaurants. Superb regional cooking in the oldest continually operating inn in Vermont. Tavern, garden, or dining in the 1796 hostelry.
Mio Bistro
3239 Route 30
Tel: 802-231 2530
www.miobistro.net **$$–$$$**
Comfortable, friendly restaurant with an open kitchen. Lobster mac and cheese, weekly international theme nights in winter. Reservations suggested.

East Burke
River Garden Café
427 Route 114
Tel: 802-626 3514
www.rivergardencafe.com **$$–$$$**
Artichoke dip, friedravioli, pan-roasted duck breast, butterflied rainbow trout.

Kids' menu.

Grafton
Old Tavern at Grafton
Route 121
Tel: 802-843 2231
www.old-tavern.com **$$–$$$**
Dishes with a New Englnd slant. Produce from their kitchen garden. Carriage house serves pub fare Thur to Sun from late afternoon. Live music on Sat nights.

Greensboro
Highland Lodge
1608 Craftsbury Road
Tel: 802-533 2647 **$$–$$$**
Popular resort and ski lode welcomes non-guests formealtimes. Lamb "sliders," schnitzle, portabello tart. Calling the Iskabibble dessert a brownie à la mode is like calling "Jaws" a big fish!

Killington
Choices
2820 Killington Road
Tel: 802-422 4030
www.choices-restaurant.com **$$–$$$**
Chef Claude specializes in roisserie, with entrées such as filet mignon with Saga blue cheese, and rack of lamb. Good vegetarian selections. Resident pastry chef creates memorable desserts. Lively thirty-something bar scene.
Hemingway's
4988 Route 4
Tel: 802-422 3886
www.hemingwaysrestaurant.com **$$$$**
In an 1860 country house, New American cuisine with international flavor. Hailed as among nation's best

LEFT: lobster pie at the Old Inn, at Grafton.

restaurants. Prix-fixe options.

Lake Champlain Islands

Blue Paddle Bistro
Route 2, South Hero
Tel: 802-372 4814
www.bluepaddlebistro.com
$$–$$$
Phoebe Bright and Mandy Hotchkis smile a lot as they create Gorgonzola-stuffed meatloaf, half-pound burgers with hand-cut fries, coffee-crusted pork tenderloin, and crab-stuffed ravioli. Sunday brunch features duck hash and lobster Benedict.

Lower Waterford

Rabbit Hill Inn
48 Lower Waterford Road, Route 18
Tel: 802-748 5168
www.rabbithillinn.com
$$$–$$$$
Dazzling New American cuisine from a 5-course prix-fixe menu served in an atmosphere of understated elegance in a romantic 1795 country inn. Closed Wed.

Manchester

The Equinox
Route 7A
Tel: 802-362 4700
www.equinoxresort.com
$$$–$$$$
Two dining opions at the resort New Chop House features red meat (rack of lamb, 32oz rib-eye) in a setting of a refined hunter's lodge. D Wed–Sun. Marsh Tavern predates the Revolution and features regional foods.
Ye Olde Tavern
5183 Main Street

Manchester Center
Tel: 802-362 0611
www.yeoldetavern.net **$$$**
Colonial candlelight dining in gracious 1790 inn which served the Green Mountain Boys. Traditional New England fare: cranberry fritters with maple butter, pot roast, cidered chicken.

Middlebury

Fire and Ice
26 Seymour Street
Tel: 802-388 7166/800-367 7166
www.fireandicerestaurant.com **$$**
Hand-cut steaks, lobster, homemade mashed potatoes, a huge salad bar, and lots of nooks and crannies filled with Vermontabilia. Supervised children's VCR Theater watches the kids while parents dine alone.
Two Brothers Tavern
86 Main Street
Tel: 802-388 0002
www.twobrotherstavern.com **$$**
Quintessential Vermont pub-style tavern where locals, students from Middlebury College, and tourists gather for casual food and conversation. Vermont comfort food: cheddar and onion soup, tavern sandwiches, meat loaf. 15 microbrews including locally brewed Otter Creek.
The Storm Cafe
3 Mill St.
Tel: 802-388 1013
www.thestormcafe.com **$$–$$$**
American cuisine with changing seasonal menu: pan-seared local chicken, penne carbonara, chipotle BBQ pork. Outdoor patio is a splash away from the creek.

Montpelier

Coffee Corner Diner
Corner of State and Main
Tel: 802-229 9060
www.coffeecorner.com **$**
Serving Vermont farmer comfort food since 1959. Substantial breakfasts with Vermont syrup, sausage, cheese, baked goods, and omelets with eggs produced by hardworking Vermont chickens.
NECI on Main
118 Main Street
Tel: 802-223 3188
www.necidining.com **$$–$$$**
Students of the New England Culinary Institute refine their skills at this learning kitchen. Prix-fixe, 3-course dinner, and tapas menu, plus à la carte menu.
Sarducci's
3 Main Street
Tel: 802-223 0229
www.sarduccisrestaurant.com **$$**
Mediterranean Italian fare, including pastas, pizza, and panini from a wood-burning oven. Gluten-free menu.

Newfane

Old Newfane Inn
Route 30 and the Common
Tel: 802-365 4427
www.oldnewfaneinncom
$$$–$$$$
Fine dining at this classic 189 coaching stop on the village green. Game in season, chicken, duckling, lamb.
Rick's Tavern
386 Route 30
Tel: 802-365 4310
www.rickstavern.net **$–$$**
Good pub fare with homemade soups, fresh fish daily from Boston docks, pizza, good sandwiches. Live jazz on Thur nights. Closed Tue.

Newport

The East Side Restaurant
47 Landing Street
Tel: 802-334 2340
www.eastsiderestaurant.net
$–$$
Popular lakefront restaurant serves familiar casual restaurant fare in large, cheerful dining room. Seriously substantial breakfasts and spend-all-day-grazing Sunday brunch buffet.
Lago Trattoria
95 Main Street
Tel: 802-334 8222
www.lagotrattoria.com **$$**
A genuine Italian trattoria with an open kitchen producing aromatic and tasty dishes like aioli beef carpaccio, thick- or thin-crust pizza, handcut pasta with veal medallions.

Putney

Curtis' Barbecue
7 Putney Landing Road, Putney
908 Route 103 Souh, Chester
Tel: 802-387 5474
www.curtisbbqvt.com **$–$$**
You know it's real 'Q when you smell the smoke before you get out of your car. Barbecue, slow-cooked and served up from an old school bus. Slabs of ribs, chicken, beans – all the staples. Seating is at outdoor picnic tables. The Chester location, with indoor seating, is open year-round.

Quechee

Simon Pearce Restaurant
The Mill, 1760 Main Street
Tel: 802-295 1470
www.simonpearce.com **$$–$$$**
Fine country cuisine n modern café in an old riverside mill overlooking the

Prices for a three-course
dinner per person with a
half-bottle of house wine:
$ = under $20
$$ = $20–45
$$$ = $45–60
$$$$ = over $60

waterfall on the
Ottauquechee River which
powers the restaurant and
Pearce's glassblowing and
pottery-making studios.

St. Johnsbury

Elements Food and Spirit
98 Mill Street
Tel: 802-748 8400
www.elementsfood.com **$$–$$$**
"Bold, simple flavors that-
start with fresh ingredi-
ents," served in a
150-year-old riverside mill.
New seasonal dinner
menu every month. "We
take vegetarians
seriously."

Shelburne

Café Shelburne
5573 Shelburne Rd (Route 7)
Tel: 802-985 3939
www.cafeshelbure.com **$$$**
Highly awarded restaurant
serves conemporary French
bistro fare. Across from the
Shelburne Museum.

Inn at Shelburne Farms
Harbor Road
Tel: 802-985 8498
www.shelburnefarms.com **$$$**
Gourmet dining in the ele-
gant dining room of a
Queen Anne–style manor
overlooking Lake
Champlain. Seasonal
menu with most of the
ingredients coming from
the farm itself. Sunday
brunch is a local institution.

La Villa Bistro
3762 Shelburne Road
Tel: 802-985 2596

www.lavillabistro.com **$$**
Casual 60-seat bistro, soft
lighting, jazz. Perfect place
to enjoy pizza, pasta,
tapas, paninis, and grilled
food. Families welcome.

Springfield

**Fifty-Six Main Street
Restaurant**
56 Main Street (Route 11)
Tel: 802-885 6987
www.fiftysixmainstreet.com **$$**
Cozy, comfortable, cheerful
place serving American
food with Mexican and
Italian accents. Nice vegetarian selections.

Stowe

Blue Moon Café
35 School Street
Tel: 802-253 7006
www.bluemoonstowe.com **$**
Menu changes monthly to
reflect wat's in season.
Fresh American cooking
with Mediterranean and
East Asian influences.

Great Room Grill
Stowe Resort
Tel: 802-253 4754
www.stowe.com **$$**
Bistro-grill with four exhibi-
tion cooking stations.

Harrison's
25 Main Street
Tel: 802-253 7773
www.harrisonsstowe.com **$$**
Cozy dining room, quiet
booths, barn-board walls
covered with photos of
"Old Stowe." Menu suits all
palates: ginger-blueberry
ahi tuna, grilled rib eye,
penne Florentine.

Mr Pickwick's Gastropub
433 Mountain Road
Tel: 802-253 7558
www.englandinn.com
$$$–$$$$
Old English pub and restau-
rant in popular inn. Amazing

wine cellar. Amazing menu:
pub grub with influences
from the days of the Raj in
India, plus specialties like
wild boar ribs, Kobe beef
sirloin. It's worth finding the
dates of the monthly ale-
tasting dinners.

Pie in the Sky
492 Mountain Road
Tel: 802-253 5100
www.pieintheskyvt.com **$–$$**
Casual, friendly, busy, basic
pizza (wood-fired oven) and
Italian family food stop.
Pizza buffet Mon–Fri lunch
(pizza, salad, soup). Nice
deck in summer.

Waitsfield

American Flatbread
46 Lareau Road
Tel: 802-496 8856
www.americanflatbread.com **$$**
How Vermont does pizza:
all-natural baked in a prim-
itive, wood-fired oven.
Locations in Burlington
and Middlebury as well.

Hyde Away Inn
1428 Millbrook Road
Tel: 802-496 2322
www.hydeawayinn.com **$$**
Casual restaurant in an
1824 farmstead. Dining
room, deck, tavern serves
cheddar-stuffed meat loaf,
maple BBQ ribs, lemon dill
cod, good burgers, and pub
food.

Mint
4403 Main Street
Tel: 802-496 5514
www.mintvermont.com **$$**
Natural, organic, whole
food, vegetarian menu with
many vegan and gluten-
free items. Falafel, cran-
berry greens, and tempeh.

Warren

Pitcher Inn
275 Main Street

Tel: 802-496 6350
http://pitcherinn.com **$$$**
Elegant dining in one of the
are's finest inns. Local and
regional ingredients reflect
the day's market. Private,
tasting menu for up to 6
people in the Wine Cellar.

The Common Man
Rustic, simple, romantic
dining spot in a 150-year-
old converted barn. Locally
sourced, "all made from
scratch" kitchen.

Waterbury

Cider House BBQ and Pub
1675 Route 2
Tel: 802-244 8400
www.ciderhousevt.com **$$**
Southern-style home-
cookin' in the Veront
mountains. Many vegetar-
ian and gluten-free
options. Note: apple cider
is just fine for kids; hard
cider is for grown-ups.

Hen of the Wood Restaurant
92 Stowe Street
Tel: 802-244-7300
www.henofthewood.com **$$**
An acclaimed restaurant in
a 19th-century mill, fea-
tures seasonal ingredients
from local farms and cre-
ates dishes that bring out
the flavors of the individual
ingredients. 15-item artisan
cheese list and boutique
North American wines.
Closed Sun and Mon.

Ocha Thai Restaurant
6 North Main
Tel: 802-244 7642
www.ochathairestaurant.com **$$**
Very large menu of the full
range of Thailand's deli-
cate, complex cuisine.
Staff is very willing to walk
you through the menu if
you are unfamiliar with the
food. Pad Thai is the
national dish.

West Brattleboro

Chelsea Royal Diner
487 Marlboro Road (Route 9)
Tel: 802-254 8399
www.chelsearoyaldiner.com $
"High-end home style cuisine. Original 1938 diner with large menu of well-done diner fare.

West Dover

TC's Family Restaurant
178 Route 100
Tel: 802-464 5900
www.tcsrestaurant.com $–$$
Very casual, family-friedly place that's largely a tribute to local girl Kelly Clark, a three-time Olympic champion in snowboarding. Small wonder: her parents own and operate the place. Lots of memorabilia on display, including her Olympic Gold Medal (2002).

West Townshend

Windham Hill Inn
Windham Hill Road
Tel: 802-874 4080
www.windhamhill.com $$$$
Elegant, eclectic menu with crative touches. Guests can choose between a 3-course prix-fixe menu or a separate, multi-course tasting menu (wine pairings optional and additional charge). Reservations required.

Windsor

Mariam's Restaurant
70 Main St.
Tel: 802-674 2662
www.mariamsrestaurant.com $–$
An unusual find: an African rstaurant with recipes from Tanzania. Curries and casseroles. The staff is more than happy to explain it all and make suggestions.

T.L.C. Vittles
19½ Union St.
Tel: 802-674 6776
www.tlcvittles.com $–$$
Smoker going behind the building, turning out serious BBQ from April to October. Order one of the "feasts," a combo of smoked meats and homemade sides, and sit at one of the picnic tables under the trees.

Windsor Station
Depot Avenue
Tel: 802-674 2052
www.windsorstation.com $$
Bistro fare in a family-oriented spot in a converted c.1900 railroad station.

Woodstock

Bentleys
3 Elm Street
Tel: 802-457 3232; 800-457 3232
www.bentleysresturant.com $$
Well-prepared food in a historicbuilding in Downtown: maple mustard chicken, crispy duck, Jack Daniels steak. "Victorian casual" decor: sofas, oriental rugs. L Mon–Sat; D nightly; Sun brunch lasts all day (until 4pm).

Mountain Creamery Restaurant
33 Central Street
Tel: 802-457 1715, 800-498 1715
www.mountaincreameryvt.com $
Everything from scratch, many of the ingredients coming from the nearby farm run by the owners. The ice cream is, of course, homemade.

Prince and the Pauper
24 Elm Street
Tel: 802-457 1818
www.princeandpauper.com $$$
Two menus offered nightly: a 3-course prix-fixe and a smaller, bistro à la carte menu.

Bars

Charley O's
70 Main Street, Montpelier
Tel: 802-223 6820
Small, spartan, often crowded, has pool tables and a juke box. Clientele ranges from legislators to students.

Three Penny Taproom
108 Main Street, Montpelier
Tel: 802-223 TAPS
Craft beer mecca with at least 20 global brews on tap at any given time. Menu items come with beer-pairing suggestions.

McGrath's Irish Pub
at the Inn at Long Trail
709 Route 4, Sherburne Pass, Killington
Tel: 802-775 7181
Celtic ambience. Guinness on draft, and Vermont's largest selection of Irish whiskies. Children welcome. Live Irish music on weekends.

Pickle Barrel Nightclub
1741 Killington Road, Killington
Tel: 802-422 3035
Central Vermont's most popular spot for big-name entertainment has three levels of dance floors, performance stages and bars.

Nectar's
188 Main Street, Burlington
Tel: 802-658 4771
The place for live music in Burlington. Blues, boogie, groove, and straight-up rock. Phish started here.

Rusty Nail Bar & Grille
1190 Mountain Road, Stowe
Tel: 802-253-6245
Very popular après-ski spot. Live music and dancing. DJ, jazz, blues. 20ft screen, widescreen plasmas.

NEW HAMPSHIRE

This state serves outdoor pleasures on a platter, making the most of the dramatic and rugged White Mountains, with plenty of historical sites, romantic idylls, and charming villages thrown in for fun

Tucked between the metro bustle of Boston, the vast wilderness of Maine, and the bucolic charm of Vermont, New Hampshire manages to absorb the best features of each of those states while maintaining its own sense of identity.

"Live Free or Die" is the state motto, and that sentiment permeates the attitude of its residents. The fierce streak of independence early settlers needed just to survive – much less thrive – in an unforgiving land shows up in sometimes diametrically different responses to modern issues.

A lower cost of living than in neighboring Massachusetts and no state income or sales tax encourages many people to live in New Hampshire and commute to jobs in Boston. But property taxes in the Granite State are among the highest in the country. In a traditionally liberal region, it is home to one of the most unapologetically conservative newspapers in the country, *The Manchester Union Leader*. Justly proud of its mountain scenery, it allows billboard spatter on its highways. Practical New Englanders, they fell into deep mourning at the collapse of the Old Man of the Mountain. Dedicated to preserving history and tradition, it celebrates two native-born pioneers of the space age and science. And its

tolerant nature dissolves into granite-hard resistance at the hint of the first presidential primary being held anywhere other than New Hampshire.

It's only about 175 miles from Dixville Notch in the north to Portsmouth and the Atlantic beaches. Along the way, visitors find elegant country resorts, B&Bs tucked into forest glades, and rustic lakeside cottages designed for making family memories. Hiking in the White Mountains is almost mandatory, as is reaching the top of Mt Washington in some fashion.

Main attractions

PORTSMOUTH
ISLES OF SHOALS
MCAULIFFE-SHEPARD
  DISCOVERY CENTER
CANTERBURY SHAKER VILLAGE
WHITE MOUNTAIN NATIONAL FOREST
FRANCONIA NOTCH
MOUNT WASHINGTON COG RAILWAY
BRETON WOODS

PRECEDING PAGES: Hart's Location.
LEFT: the Cornish-Windsor covered bridge.
RIGHT: Stark, a typical small town.

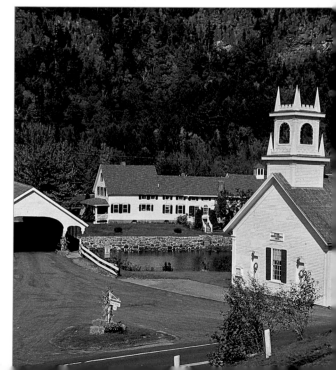

TIP

Portsmouth Harbor Trail is a guided walking tour past many of the town's important sites from its 400 years of history (tel: 603-610 5510; tours run July-early Oct Mon–Sat 10.30am, Sun 1.30pm; reservations recommended; charge).

Boaters and anglers have an array of rivers and lakes to choose from; tidy villages lie on back roads; and that short but scenic coastline is strewn with state parks. Lovers of antiques and fine architecture enjoy the gracious world of the colonial elite in Portsmouth. And remember, if you want to take one of those antiques home, there isn't any sales tax.

Portsmouth

Portsmouth 51 stands at the mouth of the Piscataqua River. Graced with a superb natural harbor, the town is the nation's third-oldest English settlement (after Plymouth and Jamestown).

The oldest continually occupied neighborhood in Portsmouth is **Strawbery Banke** A (14 Hancock Street; tel: 603-433 1100; www.strawberybanke.org; May–Oct daily; charge; tickets good for two days). A true living-history museum, it connects visitors with the past through interaction with costumed interpreters who stay in character as they recreate the lives of ordinary people from 1695 to the mid-1950s. There are 42 buildings, ranging from the humble to the grand, illustrating changes in architecture and society over time. The garden program preserves nearly four centuries of garden plants and methods. Just across from Strawbery Banke, **Prescott Park** stretches for more than 10 acres (4 hectares) along the Piscataqua River. The summer **Prescott Park Arts Festival** (tel: 603-436 2848; www.prescottpark.org) hosts family-friendly concerts, dance performances, and art shows. **Market Square** B (at Congress and Pleasant streets) is lined with cafés and chic shops housed in stately brick buildings from the 17th and 18th centuries.

Lovers of historic houses will swoon in Portsmouth. The 1763 National Historic Landmark **Moffatt-Ladd House & Garden** C (54 Market Street; tel: 603-436 8221; mid-June–mid-Oct Mon–Sun; 1pm–5pm; charge) is an imposing three-story Georgian mansion noted for choice examples of the furniture for which 18th-century Portsmouth was famous. The 1716 **Warner House** D (150 Daniel Street; tel: 603-436 5909; mid-June–mid-Oct Wed–Mon; charge) was the first of

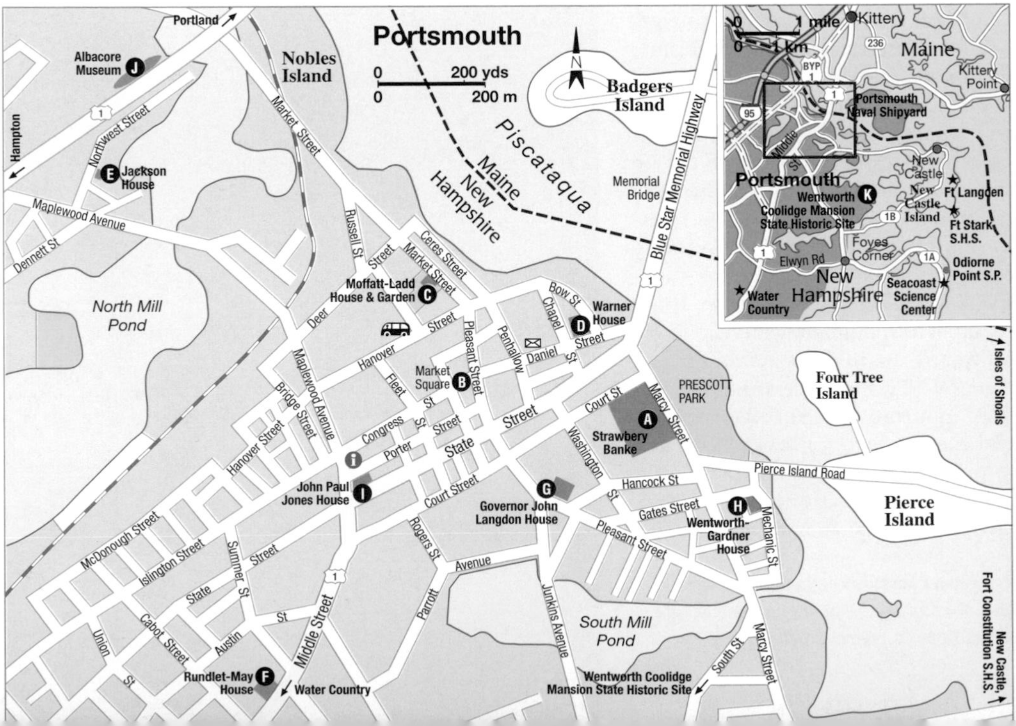

Portsmouth's many brick houses. Each room is decorated in the style of one of the six generations who lived here. The 1614 **Jackson House** Ⓔ (76 Northwest Street; 1st and 3rd Sat; charge) is the state's oldest surviving wood-frame house. The Federal-style **Rundlet-May House** Ⓕ (364 Middle Street; 1st and 3rd Sat; charge), built by a wealthy textile merchant in 1807, is filled with many of the technological advances of the day like coal-fired central heating and an indoor well. George Washington considered the 1794 **Governor John Langdon House** Ⓖ (143 Pleasant Street; tel: 603-436 3205; tours Fri–Sun; charge) the finest house in the city. The 1760 Georgian **Wentworth-Gardner House** Ⓗ (50 Mechanic Street; tel: 603-436 4400; June–mid-Oct Wed–Sun; charge) is one of the finest examples of Georgian architecture in the country. The Tobias Lear House, immediately adjacent, was home to the private secretary to President George Washington. When Washington visited, a crowd outside peeked through the parlor windows. John Paul Jones did not own the house bearing his name the **John Paul**

Jones House Ⓘ (43 Middle Street; tel: 603-436 8420; daily, Memorial Day–end of Oct; charge). The Revolutionary War naval hero once rented a room here. The 1758 Georgian home has a fascinating portrait gallery of Portsmouth's notables.

The Silent Service – as the US Navy calls it submarine fleet – is recognized at **Albacore Museum** Ⓙ (600 Market Street; tel: 603-436 3680; Memorial Day–Columbus Day daily; Columbus Day–Memorial Day Thur–Mon; charge). Built in Portsmouth, she was a seagoing testing platform for technology from 1953 to 1972. The tour gives a glimpse into the lives of the 55-man crew in their sardine-can existence.

Isles of Shoals

For a more pleasant experience on the water, consider a narrated, three-hour cruise on a replica 1900 ferryboat (Isle of Shoals Steamboat Company; tel: 603-431 5500/800-441 4620; daily in season; charge) to the **Isles of Shoals**, 9 miles (14km) offshore. The "barren piles of rock" were charted in 1614 by Captain John Smith and long haunted by pirates

The Market Square in Portsmouth, which was incorporated in 1653 and now has a population of more than 20,000.

BELOW LEFT:
an open-air theater in Prescott Park.
BELOW RIGHT:
Strawbery Banke is open for self-guided tours.

and other outcasts. Improbably enough, an arts colony blossomed here at the end of the 19th century. Kids can take a break from historic sites at New England's largest water park, **Water Country** (2300 Lafayette Road; tel: 603-427 1111; mid-June–Labor Day; charge).

New Hampshire's first royal governor, Benning Wentworth, chose a beautiful spot overlooking Little Harbor as the place to build his mansion. Two centuries later, artist and antiquarian John Templeman Coolidge restored the then-dilapidated building. The 40-room **Wentworth-Coolidge Mansion ⓚ** (tel: 603-436 6607; mid-May–mid-June and Labor Day–mid-Oct weekends; mid-June–Labor Day Wed–Sun; charge) is an outstanding example of the life of colonial-era aristocracy.

North to Dover

Dover ⓬, 10 miles (16km) north-west of Portsmouth, is the home of the **Children's Museum of New Hampshire** (6 Washington Street; tel: 603-742 2002; Tue–Sun and school holiday Mon; charge). Hands-on exhibits teach children about subjects from dinosaurs to flying machines. They can work in the museum's post office and play in a human-size kaleidoscope.

One of New Hampshire's most eclectic and eccentric museums is the **Woodman Institute Museum** (182 Central Avenue; tel: 603-742 1038; Apr–Nov Wed–Sun; charge). It's filled with antique powder horns, a saddle once used by Abraham Lincoln, a cougar killed in 1853, and many other interesting items.

South of Portsmouth

Three miles (5km) south of Portsmouth on Route 1A in **Rye**, is the 331-acre (134-hectare) **Odiorne Point State Park ⓢ** (570 Ocean Boulevard; tel: 603-436 7406; parking charge in summer). It has the largest undeveloped shoreline on the state's 16 miles (26km) of coastline.

The **Seacoast Science Center** (in the park; tel: 603-436 8043; Apr–Oct daily, Nov–Mar Sat–Mon; charge) uses interactive exhibits to teach about the coastal environment.

Continue south on Route 1A to **North Hampton and Fuller Gardens**

Below: a tugboat in Portsmouth.

(10 Willow Avenue; tel: 603-964 5414; mid-May–mid-Oct daily; charge). This magnificent turn-of-the-20th-century estate garden has more than 1,700 rose bushes, English perennial gardens, and a tropical conservatory.

There are several fine public beaches along Route 1A from Portsmouth to the Massachusetts border, including **Wallis Sands State Beach** (Rye), **North Hampton State Beach**, and **Hampton Beach State Park**.

Historic Exeter

Five miles (8km) inland, just off Route 101, the handsome town of **Exeter 54**, one of the state's earliest settlements, was founded in 1638. It's home to Phillips Exeter Academy, a prestigious college preparatory school whose alumni include Daniel Webster.

The **American Independence Museum** (One (1 Governors Lane; tel: 603-772 2622; mid-May–last Sat in Oct Wed–Sat; charge) is in a handsome 1721 building. Each room focuses on a different aspect of the Revolution and the creation of the new nation. The carefully restored **Folsom Tavern** was the center of Exeter's political scene during the Revolutionary era.

The Merrimack Valley

Flowing south from the foothills of the White Mountains, the swift Merrimack River powered one of America's earliest and most successful industrial centers. Still the state's most populous region, the Merrimack Valley is a center of government, business, and the arts.

The **Budweiser Clydesdales** are among the most recognized corporate mascots in the world. A small herd of the big horses lives at the **Anheuser-Busch Brewery** (221 Daniel Webster Highway; tel: 603-595 1202; hours vary by season, call for times) in Merrimack. The brewery tour includes a tasting for those 21 and over. A visit to the Clydesdale Hamlet (open daily) gets you close to the horses. The first Saturday of every month is Camera Day from 1pm to 3pm, when the horses pose for pictures.

Manchester

Farther north on I-93 is **Manchester 55**, which along with Nashua and several other New Hampshire cities

This 200-year-old stone chapel is on Star Island in the Isles of Shoals.

BELOW: Portsmouth sits along the Piscataqua River, the third-fastest-flowing navigable river in the world.

were centers of textile manufacturing. In the early 20th century, the massive, redbrick **Amoskeag Mills** was the world's largest textile enterprise, employing 17,000 workers in 64 buildings that stretched for 1 mile (1.6km) along the Merrimack River. As the industry declined, so did the town, but the Millyard District has become an example of adaptive reuse, with the buildings renovated as retail and office space, residences, classrooms, and high-tech incubators. The Chamber of Commerce has a self-guided walking tour of the historic millyard (54 Hanover Street; tel: 603-666 6600). If you'd rather not walk, Segway of Manchester (tel: 603-218 8150) has tours of the area, along with others focusing on the arts, cemeteries, and chocolate. The **Millyard Museum Ⓐ** (200 Bedford Street; tel: 603-622 7531; Tue–Sat; charge) recounts the natural and social history of the area from the native peoples fishing here to the industry of the 20th century. Along with a massive collection of artifacts, there's a walk-through recreation of a "night on Elm Street," with lighted

archways, store fronts with neon signs, and the State Theatre.

The **SEE Science Center** (above the museum; tel: 603-669 0400; daily; charge) is a two-story, hands-on science learning center. If nothing else, it's worth seeing the scale model of the millyard made from over 3 million Legos.

Amoskeag Fishways Visitor and Learning Center Ⓑ at Amoskeag Dam (6 Fletcher Street; tel: 603-626 3474; Mon–Sat; daily in May and June; donation) is an environmental education center. During spawning season in late spring, their fish ladder teems with herring, shad, and sea lamprey making their way upstream to spawn.

The newly expanded **Currier Museum of Art Ⓒ** (150 Ash Street; tel: 603-669 6144; closed Tue; charge, free admission Sat 10am–noon) has fine collections of European and American paintings, New England decorative arts, and contemporary crafts. It also offers modern architecture buffs access to the **Zimmerman House** (tel: 603-669 6144; Apr–Jan; no children under age 7; transportation is provided from the museum; charge; reservations

BELOW: a farming community near Manchester.

required), a 1950 design by Frank Lloyd Wright. The home, located on Manchester's outskirts and filled with the owners' modern art, pottery, and sculpture, is considered a work of art in itself. The museum offers tours.

You can catch a live performance at the **Majestic Theatre** ⓓ (281 Cartier Street; tel: 603-669 7469; www.majestictheatre.net) or at the elegantly restored 1915 **Palace Theatre** ⓔ (80 Hanover Street; tel: 603-668 5588; www.palacetheatre.org), which also presents a summer children's series.

Candia

First settled in 1742, **Candia** ㊱ (north of Route 101, east of Manchester) was originally called Charmingfare. **Candia Vineyards** (702 High Street; tel: 603-867 9751; daily, call first) is one of the smallest wineries in the northeast, but it has almost as many awards as it has wine corks.

Black bear, lynx, and porcupines as well as barnyard favorites are at **Charmingfare Farm** (774 High Street; tel: 603-483 5623; May–Oct; charge). Horse-drawn wagon tours cover the grounds; in winter, there are horse-drawn sleigh rides.

Liquid Planet Water Park (446 Route 27; tel: 603-483 2200; June–Labor Day daily; charge) is a modest water park in a beautiful setting.

Concord

Some 15 miles (24km) north of Manchester is **Concord** ㊲, New Hampshire's capital. The gold-domed 1819 **State House** (41 Green Street; tel: 603-225 8595; self-guided tours Mon–Fri 8am–4.30pm) was built of Concord granite by state prisoners and is fronted by statues of New Hampshire's political luminaries. Its Hall of Flags contains standards of over 100 New Hampshire military units from the Civil War to Vietnam.

The **Museum of New Hampshire History** (6 Eagle Square; tel: 603-228 6688; Tue–Sun; also Mon July–Oct and Dec; charge) has exhibits on the state's

history and traditions. Most impressive is an original Concord Coach, the 19th-century vehicle built here and known as "the coach that won the West," although the brightly painted and very clean coach on display doesn't look much like the battered, dust-coated stagecoaches familiar from Western movies. **The League of New Hampshire Craftsmen** gallery (36 North Main Street; tel: 603-228 8171; open daily) is one of eight in the state selling work by its members. On Saturdays from June through October, check out the Concord Arts Market (1 Bicentennial Square, near the State House; tel: 603-229 2157; June–Oct Sat 9am–3pm), a juried outdoor artisan and fine arts market.

Only one New Hampshire native has been elected president: Franklin Pierce. Elected in 1852, he tried unsuccessfully to find a compromise to the question of slavery. His administration was successful in other areas: reducing the national debt by 60 percent, establishing the office of the United States Attorney General, and opening trade with Japan. The **Pierce Manse** (14 Horseshow Pond Lane; tel: 603-225

TIP

You can traverse New Hampshire fast by driving I–95. But the state's seacoast is best discovered by meandering along the slower Route 1A, with its ocean vistas and state park beaches.

BELOW: the solidly built Concord stagecoaches, described by Mark Twain as "a cradle on wheels," were first built in 1827.

Developing industries used hydropower created by damming the Merrimack and other rivers. The dams prevented spawning fish from going upstream to their breeding areas. The solution was fish ladders. They are a series of pools, each one a foot higher than the preceding one. The pools act as steps, allowing the fish to "climb" to the top of the dam and the river above it.

BELOW: crafting a traditional broom at Canterbury Shaker Village.

4555; mid-June–Labor Day Tue–Sat, Sept–Oct Fri–Sat; charge), where Pierce and his family lived from 1842 to 1848, depicts domestic life in the pre-Civil War era.

The wonders of the universe and the dedication of those who explore it are the focus at the **McAuliffe-Shepard Discovery Center** (2 Institute Drive; tel: 603-271 7877; daily; charge), named after the first teacher in space, Christa McAuliffe, who died in the space shuttle *Challenger* disaster, and the first American in space, Alan Shepard, who was launched in May 1961. Both were natives of New Hampshire. You can plan an expedition to Mars and take a virtual walk across the sun. The observatory brings galaxies that are far, far away up close and personal. Special filters even allow you to look at sunspots. The planetarium shows (additional charge) explore black holes and celestial objects. There are special programs for younger kids.

Nature and art celebrate each other at the **Mill Brook Gallery and Sculpture Garden** (236 Hopkinton Road; tel: 603-226 2046; Apr–Oct

Tue–Sun). The gallery represents some 70 artists, with the work of sculptors set on the grounds amid blooming gardens, ponds, and woodland trails.

Near **Deering** ⑤, southwest of Concord, by Deering Lake, the **New Hampshire School of Falconry** (183 Deering Center Road; tel 603-464 6213; www.nhschooloffalconry.com) offers a two-hour Falconer's Workshop. Participants learn about the art and history of falconry and how to approach and handle a peregrine falcon. Reservations are mandatory; book well in advance. Non-participants are welcome to watch and take photos.

North of Concord

Take I–89 to **Warner** ⑤ and the **Mt Kearsarge Indian Museum** (18 Highlawn Road; tel: 603-456 2600; May Oct daily, Nov–Dec weekends; charge). Seven galleries demonstrate the culture, foodways, and ceremonies of the native nations of North America.

Head north on I–93 about 17 miles (27km) to exit 18 and follow signs to **Canterbury Shaker Village** ⑥ (288 Shaker Road; tel: 603-783 9511; mid-May–Oct daily; charge), an eloquent testament to the ingenuity and gentle faith of the Shakers. More than two dozen restored and reconstructed buildings show how the Shakers put their faith into practice. Traditional crafts like broom-making, wood-turning, and spinning are demonstrated by costumed craftspeople. There are excellent trails through the 700 acres (285 hectares) of grounds. The shop has excellent wares, particularly of goods made at the Village.

The orator and statesman Daniel Webster (1782–1852) was born in a tiny farmhouse near **Franklin**. Today the restored **Daniel Webster Birthplace** (131 North Road, off Route 127; tel: 603-934 5057; mid-June–Sept 1 daily; charge), filled with period furnishings and family memorabilia, gives visitors an idea of the rigors of 1700s farm life.

Mt Monadnock region

Mt Monadnock is a rocky 3,165ft (968-meter) peak whose 360-degree views attract record numbers of climbers. The relatively gentle ascent is surpassed in popularity only by Japan's Mount Fuji and China's Mount Tai.

Trails to the peak begin at **Monadnock State Park ❻** (116 Poole Road, off Route 12, Jaffrey; tel: 603-532 8862; charge). Hikers need to stay on the trails, wear proper shoes, and bring along enough water and bug spray.

This is a region of meandering back roads past prim white churches, innumerable antiques stores, and historic inns. **Rhododendron State Park** (Route 119W, Fitzwilliam; tel: 603-532 8862; open year-round) boasts a 16-acre (6-hectare) grove of the flowers, which bloom in mid-July. Some of the bushes are 20ft high. Other flowers start blooming as the rhododendrons fade, so there is color on the hills through autumn. To the east, the small town of Rindge is the location of the 750-seat **Cathedral of the Pines ❻** (10 Hale Hill Road; tel: 603-899 3300; May–Oct daily; donation). Sibyl and Douglas

Sloane built the open-air memorial to their son, Sandy, and all others who died in World War II. Their cathedral without walls welcomes people of all faiths in a spirit of unity and mutual respect. The view of Grand Monadnock Mountain is awe-inspiring. In the former mill town of New Ipswich, the elegant Federal *c*.1800 **Forest Hall** (the Barrett House; Main Street; tel: 860-928 4074; June–mid-Oct 1st and 3rd Sat; charge) was built by Charles Barrett Sr as a wedding gift for his son and new daughter-in-law. Its grand scale was reportedly suggested by her father. There's even a ballroom on the third floor. The house sits in 70 acres (28 hectares) of elegant lawns and gardens.

Peterborough

To the north, the handsome town of **Peterborough ❻** is home to the country's most prestigious artists' retreat, the MacDowell Colony.

The **Peterborough Historical Society** (19 Grove Street; tel: 603-924 3235; Wed–Sat; charge) exhibits early American furniture, decorative arts, and pewter. The renowned **Sharon**

Concord's 1819 State House.

BELOW: a bird-sighting competition.

Dublin's 1852 Community Church. A hurricane in 1938 snapped the steeple off the building.

BELOW: a covered bridge at Swanzey.

Arts Center (30 Grove Street; 603-924 7676; daily; charge) has two exhibition galleries featuring the artwork of regional and nationally recognized artists. A separate Fine Craft Gallery (20–40 Depot Street; tel: 603-924 2787; daily) features the work of more than 100 juried artists in a variety of media.

"When children are raised with respect and curiosity towards other cultures, the world will know more peace and less war." That philosophy is behind the **Mariposa Museum and World Culture Center** (26 Main Street; tel: 603-924-4555; mid-June–Sept 1 daily, Sept–mid-June Wed–Sun; charge). The museum is very hands-on with thousands of examples of folk art, toys, wedding gowns, and instruments from six continents.

To the east, **Frye's Measure Mill** (12 Frye Road; tel: 603-654 6581) in **Wilton ❻** is one of the country's few remaining water-powered mills and its only active measure mill. Since 1858, Frye's has been making boxes designed for accurate measurement of quantities of items such as nails. On Saturdays June–October, a 90-minute tour of the mill shows off the water-powered system and box-making machinery. Reservations are recommended.

Head west on Route 101 from Peterborough to **Dublin**, home of *Yankee Magazine* and the *Old Farmer's Almanac*, America's oldest continuously published periodical. This road is particularly scenic during the fall foliage season. The nearby village of **Harrisville ❻** is one of New Hampshire's best-preserved 19th-century mill towns.

Twelve miles (20km) to the west, **Keene ❻**, the largest city in this region, was a thriving mill town at the turn of the 19th century. Today, the town attracts visitors for its growing arts scene and natural beauty. Keene claims to have America's widest Main Street, crowned at one end by the handsome spire of the United Church of Christ. The handsome 1806 Federal home at the **Horatio Colony House Museum & Nature Preserve** (199 Main Street; tel: 603-352 0460; May–mid-Oct Wed–Sun) overflows with early-18th- to late-19th-century American and European furnishings. The **Nature Preserve** is 3.5 miles (5km) to the west off Route 9 (Daniels Hill Road). There are 3.5 miles (5km) of trails winding through the 415-acre (168-hectare) preserve. In April 1775, 29 Minutemen departed from the 1762 **Wyman Tavern** (339 Main Street; tel: 603-357 3855; June–mid-Nov Thur–Sat; charge) to join the battles in Lexington and Concord MA. The tavern reflects the 1770–1820 period. The **Historical Society of Cheshire County** (246 Main Street; tel: 603-352 1895; closed Mon; charge) concentrates on local glass, pottery, and toymaking, which were leading industries in Keene.

The city is home to **Keene State College**, whose **Thorne-Sagendorph Art Gallery** (tel: 603-358 2720; Wed–Sun) exhibits works by 19th-century artists who worked around Mt Monadnock, and more contemporary artists. The school's **Redfern Arts Center** (tel: 603-358 2168) has a lively,

innovative schedule of performing professional artists as well as shows by students and faculty.

You can experience the life of a New Hampshire dairy farmer at the 250-year-old **Keene Stonewall Farm** (242 Chesterfield Road; tel: 603-357 7278; daily dawn–dusk; donation). The morning milking is at 4.30 and you're invited to help. The rest of the day you can visit the barnyard animals and meander along the nature trails.

Just few miles to the south, **Swanzey** has the state's largest collection of covered bridges. Runners participating in the annual Covered Bridges Half-Marathon (usually in September) run through four of them.

Connecticut River Valley

Like its counterpart on the Vermont side of the river, New Hampshire's portion of the Connecticut River Valley is a realm of small towns, meandering roads, and rolling meadows but with an Ivy League college at its heart.

In colonial times, **Charlestown** ⑰, about 22 miles (35km) northwest of Keene, was a center of law and lawyers

second only to Boston. So many fine houses and buildings were constructed that the entire **Main Street** has been designated a National Historic Landmark.

The early years of the settlement were marked with vicious attacks by the French and Native Americans determined to drive the English settlers out. The **Fort at Number 4 Living History Museum** (Route 11 West; tel: 603-826 5700; May–Oct Mon–Sun; charge) recreates a 1740s settlement. Within its stockade, interpreters demonstrate such crafts as candle-dipping, weaving, and the molding of musket balls and, at certain dates, re-enact skirmishes.

Some 10 miles (16km) farther north on Route 12A in **Cornish**, the **Cornish-Windsor bridge** on the Connecticut River connects New Hampshire to Vermont and is the world's longest two-span covered bridge.

Cornish was a thriving artists' colony at the turn of the 20th century. One of the most prominent artists was Augustus Saint-Gaudens (1848–1907), the celebrated classical sculptor whose works included Boston's *Robert Gould*

Amor Caritas in the garden of Augustus Saint-Gaudens' home. The sculptor created many variations on this motif.

BELOW: the Cornish-Windsor covered bridge spans the Connecticut River between Vermont and New Hampshire.

The Saint-Gaudens National Historic Site

BELOW: the Jackson Honeymoon covered bridge, built in 1876.

Shaw Memorial. Today, his handsome home, gardens, and studios are the **Saint-Gaudens National Historic Site** ❻❽ (139 Saint-Gaudens Road, off Route 12A; tel: 603-675 2175; Memorial Day–Oct daily, Nov–May visitor center only Mon–Fri; charge). Over 100 of his works are displayed in the galleries and throughout the grounds. There is an audio tour app for smartphones.

Enfield

In Lebanon, jog east on routes 4 and 10 to **Enfield** ❻❾ and the **Enfield Shaker Museum** (447 Route 4A; tel: 603-632 4346; daily; charge), which preserves the settlement that existed here from 1793 to 1923. Far more modest than the Canterbury Shaker Village, the preserved buildings hold a collection of artifacts and displays. The six-story "Great Stone Dwelling" was designed by Ammi Burnham Young, later the architect for the US Treasury in Washington DC. The Mary Keane Chapel was built by a religious order which occupied the land after the Shakers left. It has a 26-rank Casavant pipe organ and magnificent German stained-glass windows.

Dartmouth College

Another 5 miles (8km) north along the Connecticut River is **Hanover** ❼⓿, home of Ivy League **Dartmouth College**. Dartmouth was founded in 1769, primarily for "the education and instruction of youth of the Indian tribes in this land." It is known for its business, engineering, and medical programs. One-hour, student-led campus tours show off the buildings and history and give some insight into student life.

The collections at the **Hood Museum of Art** (tel: 603-646 2808; closed Mon) run from Assyrian relief to Revere silver to Winslow Homer. If the **Hopkins Center for the Arts** (tel: 603-646 2422; www.hop.dartmouth.edu), reminds you of Lincoln Center in New York, that's probably because they were both designed by Wallace Harrison. It's an exemplary performing arts center, with over 100 live performances a year in every genre.

Just across the river in **Norwich**, VT, the wonderful **Montshire Museum of Science** (Montshire Road, Norwich VT; tel: 802-649 2200; daily; charge) has over 125 hands-on

Jackson

If you are short on time, but still want the entire "New England Experience," consider staying in Jackson. With covered bridges, white-steepled churches in quaint towns, galleries, mountain vistas, trails with requisite waterfalls, winter sleigh rides, and postcard-perfect pastures, Jackson and the surrounding area are a microcosm of New England. A big attraction is the variety of outdoor activities for non-experts. While serious devotees find excellent skiing, mountain biking, and challenging hikes, there is an equal number of beginner, intermediate, and "curious enough to try it once" activities. Great Glen Trails (Route 16, Pinkham Notch; tel: 603-466 2333) rents equipment and has all sorts of information. Their kayak tours on the Androscoggin River are a peaceful way to enjoy the region.

exhibits on natural history, physics, and astronomy. Many of them are on the nature trails.

Fifteen miles (24km) north on Route 10 in **Orford ⓱**, the entire length of Main Street is on the National Register of Historic Places. Mansions, residences, and public buildings built between 1773 and 1889 stretch along "The Ridge" in one of the state's loveliest towns. A new, 3-mile (5km) **Orford–Indian Pond Heritage Trail** is an easy walking trail with lovely scenery.

The Lakes Region

Canoes, loons, rustic family camps along wooded shores – all of the classic icons of easy days in the lake-dappled New England forest – are found in New Hampshire's "Lakes Region." It straddles the state's central section and boasts dozens of inviting lakes and ponds. One of the prettiest, **Lake Sunapee ⓲** in Newbury, has been a summer resort since the late 1800s. **Sunapee State Beach** (tel: 603-763 5561; mid-May–mid-June weekends, mid-June–Labor Day daily; charge) has a swimming beach, bathhouse,

and canoe and kayak rentals. **Mount Sunapee Resort** (Route 103; tel: 603-763 2356; www.mtsunapee.com) is a popular ski area, but is a summer destination as well. It is the venue for the nine-day **League of NH Craftsman Festival** (www.nhcrafts.org), usually held in August, which draws over 350 artisans. The chairlift ride during the fall foliage season gives a spectacular view of the colors. From the summit, a short trail makes the most of the views across to Mt Washington and other points some 75 miles (135km) distant.

About halfway between Lake Sunapee and Lake Winnipesaukee, **Tarbin Gardens** (321 Salisbury Road/Route 127 S; tel: 603-934 3518; Mother's Day–Columbus Day Tue–Sun; charge) is an oasis of tranquility from the often commercial and hectic vibe of the lake resorts. There are acres of blooming perennial English gardens which attract birds and butterflies.

Lake Winnipesaukee

To the northeast, **Lake Winnipesaukee ⓳** sprawls in convoluted splendor with 183 miles (294km) of

The Baker-Berry Library graces the campus of Dartmouth College.

BELOW: keeping cool at Lake Sunapee.

TIP

If you take the 10am cruise on the *Mount Washington* from Weirs Beach, you can stop off at one of the other lakeside towns for lunch and shopping and return by a later cruise. The vessel operates from early May through the end of October (tel: 888-843 6686 or, in NH 603-366 5531; www. cruisenh.com).

shoreline. Local folklore says there are 365 islands on the lake – one for each day of the year – but local trivia addicts can only come up with 253.

A number of towns dot the shoreline. **Weirs Beach**  (named for the weirs, or fishnets, which Indians once stretched across a narrow channel there) brings a touch of Atlantic City to Winnipesaukee's western shore, with its boardwalk, marina, and elaborate miniature golf links.

Weirs Beach is homeport for the **M/S *Mount Washington*** (tel: 603-366 5531; www.cruisenh.com), which offers day, evening dinner dance, and island cruises. For a unique tour of the lake, consider hopping aboard the mail boat *Sophie C* (tel: 603-366 5531; www.cruisenh.com) as she makes her daily rounds of five islands. A few miles to the north, the resort town of Meredith is home to the **Winnipesaukee Railroad** (154 Main Street; tel: 603-279 5253; www.winnipesaukeescenicrr.com; late May–Oct; charge), which offers a scenic ride alongside the lake to Lakeport. Trains also leave from Weirs Beach. There are several galleries and antiques shops waiting to be browsed.

Wolfeboro

One of the M/V *Mount Washington*'s ports of call is **Wolfeboro**, on the eastern shore, the oldest summer colony in the nation. In 1769, John Wentworth, the last of New Hampshire's colonial governors, built a summer home here, and comfortable old money has been following his example ever since. A stroll around reveals a wealth of architectural styles.

The **Wolfeboro Historical Society** (1164 Main Street; 603-569 4997; mid-June–Labor Day Wed–Mon; charge) maintains three buildings which look at daily life, daily work, and education, respectively. The "Ladies' Emporium" is a slice of the Victoriana fashionista's bling. The state's rich boating history is preserved at the **New Hampshire Antique and Classic Boat Museum** (397 Center Street; tel: 603-569 4554; daily Memorial Day–Columbus Day; charge). Exhibits include a magnificent collection of vintage mahogany and antique boats, canoes, and sailboats.

BELOW: a trip on Lake Winnipesaukee.

The first-rate **Wright Museum of World War II** (77 Center Street; tel: 603-569 1212; May–Oct daily, Feb–Apr Sat; charge) documents World War II with cleverly assembled exhibits. There's great emphasis on the home front.

Throughout the summer, **Great Waters Music Festival** (tel: 603-569 7710; www.greatwaters.org) presents a diverse series of entertainment. In 2011, it moved from its acoustic pavilion on the lakefront to the new, state-of-the-art Kingswood Arts Center.

Three miles (5km) north of town on Route 109, exhibits at the small, lakeside **Libby Museum** (tel: 603-569 1035; June–mid-Sept Tue–Sun; charge) are like exploring your grandmother's attic. It was voted the "Best Eclectic Little Museum" in a state poll.

Elsewhere on the lake

Looking down over the lake from the north near Moultonborough, the **Castle in the Clouds** ⓰ (off Route 171; May weekends, June–Oct daily; charge) stands as an imposing monument to one man's vision of a tranquil idyll. Built in an inventive amalgam of styles by shoe machinery magnate Thomas Gustave Plant, this 1910 mansion, which he called "Lucknow," is set in a 5,200-acre (2,100-hectare) estate with waterfalls, miles of forest trails, and magnificent views. Visitors approach the mansion via a trolley.

At **Moultonborough**, the **Old Country Store** (1011 Whittier Highway; tel: 603-476 5750; open daily), built as a stagecoach stop in 1781, makes a strong argument that it's the "Oldest Country Store" in the country. It sells just about everything, including a trove of New Hampshire–made products.

The Loon Center (183 Lee's Mill Road; tel: 603-476 LOON; May–June and Columbus Day–Dec Mon–Sat, July–Columbus Day daily, Jan–Apr Thur–Sat; donation) is devoted to the speckled birds with penetrating red eyes. The award-winning center is on one of the largest areas of natural shoreline left on the lake.

Twelve miles (19km) southwest, in **Holderness**, exhibits at the 200-acre (80-hectare) **Squam Lakes Natural Science Center** ⓱ (Route 113; tel: 603-968 7194; May–Nov 1 daily; charge) include a nature preserve for injured animals, including black bears, mountain lions, and bobcats, unable to survive in the wild. Visitors can also take a 90-minute lake cruise mid-May–mid-October.

To the east of Lake Winnipesaukee, Route 153 winds north along the Maine border toward the White Mountains, threading together a skein of tidy small towns set amidst rolling countryside.

The New Hampshire Farm Museum (1305 White Mountain Highway / Route 125 off Route 153; tel: 603-652 7840; Memorial Day–mid-Oct Wed–Sun, mid-Oct–Nov Sat) in **Milton** preserves three centuries of farm life in New Hampshire. A blacksmith and wood-shaver demonstrate essential skills; you can crack corn, feed the chickens, and sample freshly pressed apple cider. In the winter, there are horse-drawn sleigh rides.

A dock on Lake Winnipesaukee, which has more than 250 islands.

BELOW: a lakeside concert at Wolfeboro.

Above the clouds on Mount Washington.

BELOW: a rock cabin in the White Mountains.

Wakefield

More than 200 years ago **Wakefield** , "the center of New England," was the intersection of two stagecoach routes. Twenty-six of the 18th- and 19th-century buildings are listed in the National Register of Historic Places.

The **Museum of Childhood** (2784 Wakefield Road; tel: 603-522 8073; late May–early Sept daily; charge) is the overflow from Santa's workshop. It's packed with thousands of old children's toys.

Continue through the Effinghams to Effingham Falls, and turn onto Route 25, which skirts **Ossipee Lake** as it merges with Route 16 and heads northwest to the turnoff for Route 113 and **Tamworth** ⓴. Grover Cleveland, US president in 1885–89 and 1893–7, summered here. In 1931, his son founded **Barnstormers Theatre** (tel: 603-323 8500; www.barnstormerstheatre.org). It is the country's oldest professional summer theater and puts on eight well-chosen plays every season.

The **Remick Country Doctor Museum and Farm** (58 Cleveland Hill Road; tel: 603-323 7591; Mon–Fri, also Sat mid-June–Labor Day; charge) is a working farm museum which concentrates on the life of a country doctor from 1790 to the present.

The White Mountains

Continuing north on Route 16, you enter the **White Mountain National Forest**, a vast tract of almost 800,000 acres (320,000 hectares) of scenic, rugged wilderness. The Franconia and Presidential mountain ranges are both located here, as is Mt Washington, New England's highest peak. Long a forbidding wilderness, the White Mountains have evolved into an enormously popular tourist region for hikers and motorists (particularly at foliage time).

For all of their massive beauty, most of these peaks are not too demanding. Most summits can be reached within a couple of hours at a fairly leisurely pace. One of the most rewarding excursions (in terms of view obtained relative to energy expended) is the 3.2-mile (5.1km) moderate hike up **Mount Willard**. Those reaching the summit are rewarded with a magnificent panorama of **Crawford Notch** – particularly splendid at sunrise.

There are too many trails – some 1,200 miles (1,900km) all told – to attempt even a partial description here; details can be obtained from White Mountain National Forest offices (various locations in the area; tel: 603-528 8721; www.fs.fed.us/r9/forests/white_mountains) and the Appalachian Mountain Club (AMC; www.outdoors.org). The AMC maintains two lodges with comfortable accommodations and meals at the Pinkham Notch Visitors Center (361 Route 16, Gorham, at the base of Mount Washington; tel: 603-466 2721) and a new lodge at Crawford Notch (Route 302, Bretton Woods; tel: 603-278 HIKE). The AMC also maintains a network of "huts" (some fairly large) offering hikers bunk lodgings and hearty meals; it's wise to reserve (tel: 603-466 2727) well ahead for both lodges and huts. The AMC's *White Mountain Guide* is the "walker's bible."

Conway

Alternatively, you can just enjoy the scenery from the car. One of the most rewarding routes begins in **Conway** **⑳**, best known as the southern end of a stretch of shopping outlets that extends 5 miles (8km) to the bustling tourist town of North Conway, home to the **Conway Scenic Railroad** (tel: 800-232 5251/603-356 5251; www.conwayscenic.com; charge). The railroad runs daily excursions. Call for schedule and pricing information.

To the north of North Conway, at **Glen**, is **Story Land** (850 Route 16; tel: 603-383 4186; www.storylandnh. com; Memorial Day–mid-Oct; charge). There's enough here to keep children aged 2–12 occupied most of a day. Plenty of food options, some of them healthy, but who can resist Oreo funnel cake?

The Kancamagus Highway

Conway is the eastern terminus for the 34.5-mile (55km) **Kancamagus Highway** (Route 112), a designated National Scenic Byway. The "Kanc" winds alongside the Pemigewasset and Swift rivers, passing numerous trailheads offering anything from short strolls through the forest to major upland hikes. Seek out the Kancamagus, Pemi, and Hancock overlooks at the western end. Views are at their best when the fall foliage reaches its most brilliant phase, but then you may find the traffic bumper to bumper. Worthwhile short walks include the Champney Falls Trail and the Boulder Loop Trail, while pleasant roadside picnic areas are at Rocky Gorge and Sabbaday Falls.

Lincoln ㉛, at the western terminus, is home to **Loon Mountain ski area** (60 Loon Mountain Road; tel: 603-745 8111). During the summer and fall a gondola whisks visitors to the summit, where there's an artisans' village, hiking trails, and observation tower. The summit restaurant serves an all-you-can-eat Sunday morning brunch July–August.

This well-developed tourist area offers several other attractions, including one of the state's oldest attractions, **Clark's Trading Post** (Route 3; tel: 603-745 8913; mid-May–mid-Oct; charge), where black bears put on a performance; the **Whale's Tale Water Park** (Route 112;

Ice climbing in the White Mountains.

BELOW: the view from Mt Willard.

tel: 603-745 8810; mid-June–Labor Day; charge); and **Hobo Railroad** (64 Railroad Street, Lincoln; tel: 603-745 2135; www.hoborr.com), which runs excursions May–October, plus Santa Trains in November–December.

Franconia Notch

Route 3/I–93 north from **Lincoln** winds through **Franconia Notch State Park** ❷ (tel: 603-745 8391), between Kinsman and Franconia mountain ranges. A highlight of the park is **The Flume** (tel: 603-745 8391; visitor center and flume access early May–late Oct, entrance charge to flume), an 800ft (240-meter) gorge with granite walls rising 90ft (27 meters) and ending at a waterfall. It was reportedly discovered in 1803 by 93-year-old Aunt Jess Guernsey, who happened upon it while out fishing. It's no longer quite as she found it – boardwalks and viewing platforms have been added to accommodate the busloads of sightseers – but it is still an awesome sight. The Pool and Avalanche Falls – two other fine waterfalls – and a covered bridge are also in the park.

Pull into the parking lot at **Profile Lake** at the new monument to the **Old Man of the Mountain**, the rock formation that loomed just above the lake.

Directly to the north is **Cannon Mountain** (tel: 603-823 8800; www.cannonmt.com). A ski area in winter, in summer it has a lovely view of four states and Canada from the **Aerial Tramway** (tel: 603-823 8800; late May–mid-Oct daily; charge). There are walking trails and a cafeteria at the summit. At the base, the **New England Ski Museum** (11 Franconia Notch Parkway; tel: 603-823 7177; Memorial Day–early Apr daily; charge) exhibits historical paraphernalia, such as handcrafted wooden skis from the 19th century, and audio-visual exhibits.

Beyond the Notch

To the west, **Franconia** ❸ was home to poet Robert Frost in 1915–20. Here he "farmed a little, taught a little and wrote a lot." Looking out towards his favorite three New Hampshire mountains is the modest **Robert Frost Place** (158 Ridge Road, off Route 16; tel:

BELOW: the Conway Scenic Railroad has operated in the Mount Washington Valley since 1974.

603-823 5510; Wed–Mon; donation). It is maintained as the quiet refuge where the young poet found inspiration and could concentrate on his art. Among other poems, he wrote *Stopping by Woods on a Snowy Evening* here.

Route 117 from Franconia winds south to the upscale hill town of **Sugar Hill**, home to several elegant country inns, and the **Sugar Hill Historical Museum** (Main Street; tel: 603-823 5336; June–mid-Oct Fri–Sat; charge). The museum is a repository of local history, with a re-creation of a local tavern and a sleigh once owned by actress Bette Davis.

Heading north toward Mt Washington, detour to the town of **Bethlehem** and **The Rocks Estate** (Route 302; tel: 603-444 6228; hours vary with season). Originally a summer estate in the Gilded Age, it is now the Forest Society's North Country Conservation and Education Center. A self-guided walking tour includes 13 buildings on the National Register of Historic Places. Among other things, it is a sustainable Christmas tree farm. The "tree trail" explains tree farming.

Mt Washington

The **White Mountains** cover approximately one-quarter of New Hampshire and are the most rugged mountains in New England. The most difficult terrain of the 2,180-mile (3,508km) Appalachian Trail slices diagonally across them. Though hardly reaching the heights of the Rockies, the White Mountains claim 48 summits which are over 4,000ft (1,219 meters) high. Topping them all is **Mt Washington**. At 6,288ft (1,197 meters), it is the tallest summit north of the Carolinas and east of the Rockies. Its sheer bulk is impressive, at least from the bottom, but to really appreciate its height, one must tackle the peak.

There are three ways to "climb" Mt Washington: on foot, by car, or by train. The first two options are accessible from **Pinkham Notch**. A trail to the summit via **Tuckerman Ravine**, a large glacial

cirque famous for its spectacular scenery and dangerous but thrilling spring skiing, begins at the Appalachian Mountain Club's **Pinkham Notch Visitor Center ㉞** (tel: 603-466 2721). The 8-mile (13km) climb up the **Mt Washington Auto Road ㉟** (tel: 603-466 3988; opens sometime in May when the snow melts; closes in Oct when flurries start; hours vary with season; charge; includes a CD audio tour), via endless switchbacks, can be hell on radiators, the return journey tough on the best of brakes. While it is a rough trip for drivers, the views along the way – when your car is higher than the clouds – and at the summit make the effort worthwhile. You'll slap on the "This Car Climbed Mount Washington" bumper sticker with pride. For those who'd rather spare their vehicles the ordeal, a tour van departs from the base for a 90-minute tour. There's also a one-way shuttle for hikers. Be sure to bring a jacket or sweater since it can be bitterly cold in August. Sandals are not such a good idea, either.

The summit bears chilling markers commemorating those who, like 23-year-old Lizzie Bourne in

Golf and skiing at the Mount Washington Resort, Bretton Woods.

BELOW: heading up the mountain.

Farmers, Produce, and Eating Local

Farmers and eaters in New Hampshire have an unusually close relationship. About 12 percent of the harvest is sold directly to consumers, versus less than 1 percent in the rest of the country

Much of the produce and dairy, and even some meat, is sold at farmers' markets, weekly institutions which are often as important as community gatherings as they are for stocking up the larder. Also popular are Community Supported Agriculture groups (CSAs). Members pay for a "share" at the beginning of the year and receive a weekly delivery of produce from the farm. For the farmer, it provides a guaranteed income which helps their otherwise notoriously unpredictable cash flow. Members share the risk of a bad growing season or failed crops, which adds to the appreciation of what's involved in putting food on their table.

One of the pleasures of traveling New Hampshire's back roads is stopping at roadside produce stands.

Blueberries and sweet corn, plump tomatoes and slender carrots, rich red peppers and shining green beans create an organic still life. Many of the stands are unattended; there's just a table for the produce and a cigar box to hold payment. Some stands post prices, others leave it up to the customer to decide what to pay. Rarely is the food just taken and equally rarely are the contents of the honor box stolen.

Pick-your-own farms are about as "back to nature" as most urbanites can get. From May through October, these farms welcome guests to harvest berries, peaches, and apples as they come into season. Places charge either by the pound or by the basket, and they are generally liberal in their tolerance for quality control taste testing while picking. If you don't have your own container, they'll provide one.

The ease of connection with local farmers and the great variety of crops, dairy products, and meat locally available in New Hampshire have encouraged a strong locavore movement. Locavores purchase only foods grown within a self-selected radius, usually between 50 and 150 miles (80–241km). Not all are purists; many have a limited number of groceries that come from beyond that circle; coffee, tea, and spices usually head the list. In those cases, they try to buy "fair trade" items – products harvested, marketed, and sold in a way that supports the native farmers and growers.

The movement started as a dare by four California women who decided to see if they could live off local foods for a month. The challenge appeals to people who see it as a positive way to do several things: support their local farmers and, by extension, their local community and economy; to eat healthier foods, since many farms use sustainable practices with minimum application of pesticides and artificial fertilizers; to promote humane practices in raising livestock and poultry; and to reduce their carbon footprint by minimizing transportation of their food. In comparison, most produce in US groceries travels between 1,300 and 2,000 miles (2,100–3,200km) from farm to store.

Restaurants have enthusiastically embraced the concept. Chefs have arrangements with nearby growers and some maintain their own gardens. The New Hampshire Farm to Table Restaurant Connection creates partnerships between the restaurants and growers and has a list of certified restaurants. An ever-growing list of "green" restaurants is at www.nhslrp.org.

LEFT: squash for sale at a New England orchard during autumn.

September 1855, died of exposure only a few hundred yards from the top. The destination she sought, a rustic hotel called the **Tip Top House**, survives as a small museum, with the cramped dormitories where travelers bunked down on crude beds cushioned with moss.

Climatically, the summit is classified as arctic. Higher than any other mountain east of the Rockies with nothing to stop the howling winds sweeping down from Canada or across the continent, its topographic isolation results in alarmingly abrupt changes in weather, including blizzards even in summer. The highest-velocity winds ever recorded – 231mph (372kmh) – were measured here in 1934. Some buildings are chained down to keep them from blowing away.

The **Sherman Adams Summit Building** is surrounded by a deck with 70-mile (110km) views; inside is the small but fascinating **Summit Museum** (tel: 603-356 2137; mid-May–mid-Oct daily; charge). It's a comprehensive display of geology, meteorology, and ecology as it applies to the mountain.

The Cog Railway

The third way to reach the summit is almost as famous and popular as driving. The **Cog Railway** leaves from **Crawford Notch**. Turn off Route 302 onto the access road for 6 miles (10km). The 1869 **Cog Railway** (tel: 800-922 8825/603-278 5404; www.thecog.com; Apr–early Dec 8:30am–mid-afternoon; first train of the morning is powered by a steam engine; charge) is a testament to American ingenuity in the pursuit of diversion. Powered by tough little steam locomotives, the train – the world's first mountain-climbing cog railway – carts passengers 3.5 miles (5.5km) up and down the mountain, relying on a fail-safe rack-and-pinion system.

Crawford Notch

Head west on Route 302 through **Crawford Notch** ⑱, a narrow pass named for two notable early entrepreneurs. The notch was "discovered"

in 1771 (more or less accidentally) by Timothy Nash, who was tracking a moose at the time. When Nash informed Governor Wentworth of his discovery, the disbelieving governor offered him a tract of land including the notch if Nash could bring a horse through it and present the animal at Portsmouth. Nash met the challenge, incidentally opening up the White Hills (as the mountains were then called) to a steady influx of settlers and eventually tourists.

Among the first to anticipate and capitalize on the area's potential were Abel Crawford and his son, Ethan Allen Crawford. They blazed the first path to the summit of Mt Washington in 1819, advertised both it and their services as tour guides, and established inns to accommodate travelers, thereby masterminding the White Mountains' debut as a tourist attraction.

Bretton Woods

Route 302 through **Crawford Notch State Park** (tel: 603-374 2272) passes by two waterfalls you can see from your car: Silver Cascades and Flume. Nearby, the colossal **Omni Mount**

Accumulated rime ice at the weather observatory on the summit of Mt Washington.

BELOW: the Mount Washington Cog Railway.

Motorists stop to photograph a young bull moose – but collisions are not uncommon, so take care when driving.

BELOW: the Old Man of the Mountain on Cannon Mountain in the White Mountains of New Hampshire before it collapsed on May 3, 2003.

Washington Resort at Bretton Woods **87** (tel: 603-278 1000; www.omnihotels.com), which first opened in 1902, recently underwent a $60 million renovation and welcomes well-heeled visitors in a manner to which most people could easily become accustomed.

Circled by a 900ft (270-meter) veranda set with white wicker chairs and topped with red-tiled turrets, this elongated, white stucco wedding-cake contains some 200 rooms and suites, and a voluminous lobby with 23ft (7-meter) ceilings supported by nine sets of columns and illumined with crystal chandeliers.

Gorham

It's fitting that **Gorham** **88** has a **Railroad Museum** (25 Railroad Street; tel: 603-466 5338; Memorial Day–Columbus Day Tue–Sat; charge), since railroads brought the first tourists to the area. Among the displays are a 1911 steam engine and a 1920s-era railroad snow plow.

If it's moose you want to see, sign on for a trip with **Gorham Moose Tours** (at the kiosk in the town center; tel: 877-986

6673/603-466 3101; end of May–beginning of Oct Mon, Wed–Sat; also Tue in July–Aug; charge). They boast a 94 percent success rate in spotting moose, with an average of eight moose an hour.

Learn to mush at **Muddy Paw Sled Dog Kennel** (196 Main Street, Jefferson; tel; 603-545 4533; charge). Trips run from 1.5 to 3 hours, or take a three-hour sledding class. In summer, there are rolling sled dog rides and a licensed **white-water rafting** operation for all levels of experience and nerve.

The importance of the logging industry gets its due at the **Northern Forest Heritage Park** (961 Main Street; tel: 603-752 7202) in **Berlin**. There's a full-size replica of a logging camp. Guided boat tours on the Androscoggin River are offered (June–Oct Tue–Sat; charge). In October, there's a weekend lumberjack festival.

THE NORTH COUNTRY

This isolated, sparsely populated region is one of New Hampshire's better-kept secrets. The landscape is stunning: vast stretches of forest which provide its primary industry – logging.

Old Man of the Mountain

The Old Man of the Mountain was the state symbol of New Hampshire. The natural rock formation with its jutting brow, regal nose, and sharp line of the bearded chin produced not merely a likeness, but a real sense of character.

Ten thousand years of weathering finally proved too much for the Old Man. Long held together by cables and iron braces, he finally slid down the mountainside and disappeared in a pile of rubble on May 3, 2003. The cleverly designed monument at Profile Lake "recreates" the formation twice. Five granite monoliths are arranged so that the profile is seen when viewed from a platform. A similar arrangement of metal "profilers" places the face back on the mountain when viewed from the lake's shore.

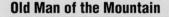

A lacework of lakes and waterways offers a delicate counterpoint to the craggy hills and mountains. The Connecticut River begins in a string of lakes just a few miles from the Canadian border, in a corner so out of the way that its allegiance was not decided, nor its boundary fixed (and then, by force), until 1840. The wilderness is a magnet for fishermen in search of salmon and trout. In winter, snowmobilers are attracted by miles of trails.

Route 3 is the road north past the Connecticut Lakes to the border. Just south of **Colebrook** ❽❾, where the Mohawk and Connecticut rivers meet, the Oblate Fathers oversee the **Shrine of Our Lady of Grace** (tel: 603-237 5511; daily; donation). More than 50 monuments are spread over the grounds. Most are traditional religious themes, but it is the location of the annual "Blessing of the Motorcycles," so the life-size granite carving called "Motorcyclists in Prayer" is perfectly at home.

From here north to Canada, it's a world of forest, water, and scattered hunting and fishing camps. Folks at **The Glen** (tel: 800-445 4536/603-538 6500; Apr–mid-Oct; www.theglennh. com; no credit cards), a handsome lakeside retreat on the western shore of the First Connecticut Lake, will be glad to provide information (as well as great home cooking), as will the **Connecticut Lakes Tourist Association** (www.nhconnlakes.com).

Route 26 east out of Colebrook follows the Mohawk River through **Dixville Notch State Park** ❾⓪ (tel: 603-538 6706; year-round). There are several yurts available for overnight camping, and the view from the top of the fire tower takes in three states and Canada. Watch for moose; the park is home to much of the state's population of these behemoths. That provides a peg for the Moose Festival (tel: 800-698 8939/603-257 8939; www.northcountrychamber. org) each August, with various events in Colebrook, Pittsburg, and across the state line in Canaan VT.

In the heart of the Notch is **The Balsams Grand Resort Hotel** (tel: 800-255 0600; www.thebalsams.com). The sprawling resort is the center of the political world every four years because it is here that the registered voters of Dixville Notch – about 30 of them – cast the first votes in every presidential election, at midnight. You can visit the Ballot Room and see the memorabilia, photos, and autographs of the politicos and reporters who've visited.

Lake Umbagog

At the junction of routes 26 and 16 in **Errol**, turn north for 5.5 miles (9km) to visit the headquarters of the 13,000-acre (5,300-hectare) **Lake Umbagog National Wildlife Refuge** ❾❶ (tel: 603-482-3415), which spreads across New Hampshire and Maine. Access is primarily by boat. Created in 1992 to conserve wetlands and protect migratory birds, its bird watching list is over 200 species long. You can also expect to spot mink, otter, and bobcat. "**Moose Alley**" is another name for Route 3. Look for low-lying marshy places beside the road or watch from a platform on Route 26 in Errol.

BELOW: the Balsams Hotel in Dixville Notch.

Pioneers and Revolutionaries

The diverse landscapes of New England were ideal for the hardy pioneers, people looking for a land willing to reward tough labor

From the seashore to the mountainous forests, New Englanders have found a way to live and work in harmony with the land, taking advantage of and protecting their greatest resource.

Like the rest of New England, New Hampshire had little to offer in the way of good soil or easy farming. The main assets of the region at the beginning of the colonial period were the deepwater port and surrounding shores of what is now Portsmouth, and the tall, straight pines, highly prized in the construction of ships. Fisheries prospered from the catches hauled from the Atlantic as far north as the Grand Banks off Newfoundland.

The impetus behind these first forays was provided by Sir Ferdinando Gorges, head of the council established by King James to govern all of New England, and Captain John Mason, an early governor of Newfoundland. They obtained grants to an ill-defined territory lining the coast and extending roughly 60 miles (100km) inland. They proposed a variety of commercial enterprises and promised healthy dividends to investors. Lack of supplies limited the scheme's progress, and the company eventually collapsed. The settlers simply divided the land up among themselves and proceeded to amass their own fortunes, without giving very much thought to the niceties of property laws.

Strong-willed settlers, gradually pushing their way up the Connecticut River from the south, laid claim first to the valleys, then to the hillsides, and finally to the mountains in the north. Despite frequent attacks by the French and their Huron, Mohegan, and Ottowa allies, settlement by British pioneers took tenuous root. John Wentworth, the first colonial governor, worked to stabilize the province by encouraging settlement and promoting commerce. When the Revolution came, New Hampshire joined early in the fight. It was the first colony to assert its independence from England (establishing its own government on January 5, 1776) and the first to suggest independence to the Continental Congress in 1775. Of the original 13 colonies, it was the only one which saw no skirmishes or battles within its boundaries.

Following the Revolution, the push inland continued, extending into the White Mountains, where the logger's axe was more useful than the plow. Even early in the 19th century, the success of rough hostelries such as the one run by Ethan Allen Crawford in Crawford Notch pointed the way for economic development: tourism. The first retreats were modest, but as railroads reached into the mountains, palatial resort hotels were built to serve wealthy clients who would arrive with servants and steamer trunks in tow. Those were followed by rustic lakeside cabins enjoyed by families and the less affluent, in keeping with New Hampshire's egalitarian approach to life and leisure. By the 1850s, "summer people" were as much a part of the mountain scenery as loons and moose.

Along the Merrimack River in the south, textile mills grew in output, creating a new economic power base, centered in Manchester and Nashua. This urban New Hampshire would become an extension of the industrial and commercial centers in Massachusetts. Between the "two" New Hampshires was a buffer of small towns and farms. That amalgam gives New Hampshire a broad economic base.

LEFT: a map of New Hampshire from 1881.

RESTAURANTS AND BARS

Prices for a three-course dinner per person with a half-bottle of house wine:
$ = under $20
$$ = $20–45
$$$ = $45–60
$$$$ = over $60

Restaurants
Bedford

Bedford Village Inn
2 Old Bedford Road
Tel: 603-472 2001
www.bedfordvillageinn.com **$$$–$$$$**
Sophisticated New England regional fare in the elegantly appointed dining room of a gracious inn. Tavern menu. Sunday brunch.

Bretton Woods

Mount Washington Hotel
Route 302
Tel: 800-258 0330
www.mtwashingtonhotel.com **$$$–$$$**
Formal dining in the renovated, updated, very upscale resort. Jackets at dinner; no jeans or sports shoes. Reservations required.

Canterbury

Greenwood's at Shaker Village
288 Shaker Road
Tel: 603-783 4238
www.shakers.org **$$**
Shaker-inspired food, which means good farmhouse cooking – cornmeal pancakes, pot roast, chicken potpie – served in the renovated blacksmith shop.

Center Sandwich

Corner House Inn
Main Street
(Routes 109 and 113)
Tel: 603-284 6219
www.cornerhousein.com **$$**
Friendly people serving good food in a delightful 1849 house. Try the chicken Oscar smothered in lobster, asparagus, and béarnaise or the hunter's meatloaf with venison and pork.

Concord

Common Man
1 Gulf Street
Tel: 603-228 3463
www.thecman.com **$$**
One of 13 different restaurants in the state created by Alex Ray, who serves up good deeds for his community along with very good food.

Granite Restaurant and Bar
96 Pleasant Street
Tel: 603-227 9000/800-360 4839
www.graniterestaurant.com **$$–$$$**
New American cuisine with Mediterranean, French, and Asian influences.

Hermanos Cocina Mexicana
11 Hills Avenue
Tel: 603-224 5669
www.hermanosmexican.com **$$**
Generally considered one of the best Mexican restaurants in all of New England. Menu is far more than the usual "burrito and combo-platter fare." Vegetarian and vegan selections. Nearly a

dozen different nacho platters; award-winning margaritas, and more types of tequila than there are cacti in the Sonoran desert.

Dixville Notch

Balsams Grand Resort Hotel
Route 26
Tel: 603-255 3400/800-255 0600
www.thebalsams.com **$$$$**
Formal dining in elegant surroundings. Jackets, "no denim." Reservations required. Wine list is beyond "extensive."

Eaton Center

Palmer House Pub
Inn at Crystal Lake, Route 153
Tel: 603-447 2120/800-43 7336

www.innatcrystallake.com **$$–$$$**
Belly up to the bar that was once in Boston's Ritz-Carlton for a bone-dry martini, then enjoy fare ranging from a bowl of chili to rack of lamb. The somewhat more formal dining room has a great view of the lake.

Franconia

Franconia Inn
1172 Easton Road
Tel: 603-823 5542/800-473 5299
www.franconiainn.com **$$–$$$**
Upscale American cuisine in a formal dining room with mountain views. Reservations recommended for breakfast as well as dinner.

RIGHT: Mount Washington Hotel, Bretton Woods.

Prices for a three-course dinner per person with a half-bottle of house wine:
$ = under $20
$$ = $20–45
$$$ = $45–60
$$$$ = over $60

Lovett's Inn by Lafayette Brook
Profile Road
Tel: 603-823 7761
www.lovettsinn.com **$$–$$$**
Owner-chef Janet Freitas serves baked Brei, pan-seared tenderloins, and "I needed that" desserts in this 18th-century inn.

Red Parka Pub
Route 302
Tel: 603-383 4344
www.redparkapub.com
$–$$
Very casual, sometimes noisy, but the steaks are aged, the prime rib prime, the fish fresh, and the salad bar items all homemade.

Hampton

Old Salt Restaurant
490 Lafayette Road (Route 1)
Tel: 603-926 8322
www.oldsaltnh.com **$$**
Traditional New England fare: lots of local seafood, plus mixed grill and pasta. Clam chowder is legendary.

Hanover

The Hanover Inn at Dartmouth College
Main Street
Tel: 603-643 4300/800-443 7024
http://hanoverinncom **$$$**
Contemporary American cuisine in "Edwardian elegance," plus outstanding wine list.

Holderness

Squam Lake Inn
28 Shepard Hill Road (Route 3)
Tel: 603-968 4417
www.squamlakeinn.com **$$**
Café that's popular with locals, summer residents, and tourists alike. Big sandwiches, lobster rolls, and salads. Dinner menu includes peach curry chicken and Parmesan-crusted halibut.

Jackson

Inn at Thorn Hill
Thorn Hill Road
Tel: 603-383 4242
www.innatthornhill.com **$$$$**
Very highly rated and reviewed restaurant serving seasonal, Continental entrées: lamb shanks, pan-roasted duck. Award-winning wine list. Reservations and jackets required.

Red Fox Bar and Grille
Route 16
Tel: 603-383 4949
www.redfoxpub.com **$$**
Specialties include wood-fired, grilled steaks and shepherd's pie.

Thompson House Eatery
193 Main Street/Route 16
Tel: 603-383 9341
www.thompsonhouseeatery.com **$$–$$$**
Grandma's chicken cutlet, shellfish sauté, Parmesan eggplant and Portabello mushroom layer in a converted 1800s barn.

Wildcat Inn and Tavern
94 Main Street/Route 16A
Tel: 603-383 6502/800-228 4245
www.wildcattavern.com **$–$$**
This popular place serves red pepper soup, Atlantic salmon, 14oz sirloins, and big burgers in a pub atmosphere.

Keene

Luca's Mediterranean Café
10 Central Square
Tel: 603-358 3335
www.lucascafe.com **$$**
Italian-born owner/chef Luca Paris takes diners on a culinary journey of Italy and the rest of the Med in his small bistro.

The Stage
30 Central Square
Tel: 603-352 9400
www.thestagerestaurant.com **$$**
American bistro serving Continental cuisine: Mesa lime chicken, Steak Morgan (with rum and shrimp sauce), good pastas.

Manchester

Cotton
75 Arms Street (in the Millyard District)
Tel: 603-622 5488
www.cottonfood.com **$$**
Sophisticated and eclectic American comfort foods in a hip, trendy atmosphere: grilled vegetarian ravioli, chicken satay, grilled meats and seafood.

Fratello's Ristorante Italiano
155 Dow Street
Tel: 603-624 2022
www.fratellos.com **$$**
Out-of-the-ordinary Italian cuisine, wood-fired pizza in a renovated textile mill. (Also in Laconia.)

Red Arrow Diner
61 Lowell Avenue
Tel: 603-626 1118
www.redarrowdiner.com **$**
A landmark 1903 lunch-eonette, open 24/7. More items on the menu than there are mountains in the Franconia Range.

The Yard Seafood and Steak House
1211 S. Mammoth Road (near the airport)
Tel: 603-623 3545
www.theyardrestaurant.com
$$–$$$

LEFT: a café in Portsmouth offers local cuisine.

Well known for their meats, especially the prime rib. Well-prepared New England fish entrées. Extensive brunch buffet. The Pub has sports TV and serves a full menu until midnight.

XO on Elm
827 Elm Street
Tel: 603-530 7998
www.xoonelm.com $$–$$$
Creative Continental cuisine served in a very contemporary setting. Large tapas menu.

Meredith

George's Diner
10 Plymouth Street (near the docks)
Tel: 603-279 8723 $
Local favorite. "Just Good Food" is the motto. What Mom would make if she opened a restaurant. Even the building looks like home.

Moultonboro

The Woodshed
128 Lee Road
Tel: 603-476 2311
www.thewoodshedrestaurant.com $$$–$$$
Special-occasion restaurant in the rustic decor of a 19th-century farmhouse and barn.

North Conway

Moat Mountain Smokehouse
3378 White Mountain Hwy/Route 16
Tel: 603-356 6381
www.moatmountain.com $–$$
The brew pub, inn, and restaurant overlooking Mt Washington specializing in great ribs, pulled pork, and wood-fired pizza. On-site brewery makes an extensive selection of year-round and seasonal brews.

Orford

Bunten Farmhouse Kitchen
1322 NH Route 10
Tel: 603-353 9252
www.buntenfarm.com $$
Small family farm serving homemade dishes from New England recipes in a cozy dining room. Homemade bread, butter churned, and cheeses made in the barn. BYOB.

Peterborough

Harlow's Pub
3 School Street
Tel: 603-924 6365
www.harlowspub.com $–$$
British pub atmosphere with live music many nights.

Twelve Pine Restaurant & Gourmet Marketplace
Depot Square
Tel: 603-924 6140
www.twelvepine.com $
Choose something tempting from the case – pork loin, roasted Asian veggies, Pacific rim fish.

Portsmouth

106 Kitchen and Bar
106 Penhallow Street
Tel: 603-319 8178
www.106kitchen.com $$
New England tradition meets New Orleans flair. Seafood gumbo, fried oyster po'boys, lobster mango cannelloni.

BG's Boat House
191 Wentworth Road
Tel: 603-431 1074
www.bgsboathouse.com $$
Lobster, fish, seafood well-prepared at a casual, family-friendly restaurant on Sagamore Creek.

Blue Mermaid Island Grill
409 The Hill
Tel: 603-427 2583
www.bluemermaid.com $$
Young, lively crowd enjoying dishes with a Caribbean flair.

Dolphin Striker
15 Bow Street
Tel: 603-431 5222
www.dolphinstriker.com $$$
This upscale riverfront tavern in an 18th-century warehouse serves "New England Comfort Cuisine." Live music nightly; all genres.

Portsmouth Brewery
56 Market Street
Tel: 603-431 1115
www.portsmouthbrewery.com $–$$
New Hampshire's original microbrewery. Unusually good menu of pub grub done with flair: hangar steak, fish and chips. Brewery tours Thur, Fri, Sat at 3pm.

Sugar Hill

Polly's Pancake Parlor
672 Sugar Hill Road/Route 117
Tel: 603-823-8849
www.pollyspancakeparlor.com $
Pancakes, waffles, all of the great breakfast favorites, even an all-you-can-eat waffle or pancake option. Gluten-free pancakes available.

Temple

Birchwood Tavern
340 Route 45
Tel: 603-878 3285
www.thebirchwoodinn.com $$
The English menu at his historic inn includes steak and ale pie, bangers and mash, and, for dessert, spotted dick and custard. Plenty of English ales on tap. Closed Mon and Tue.

Wolfeboro

Wolfetrap Grill and Raw Bar
19 Bay Street
Tel: 603-569 1047
www.wolfetrapgrillandrawbar.com $
A coastal clam shack on Lake Winnipesaukee. Patio dining with fire-grilled or steamed lobster, bouillabaisse, fried seafood platters.

Bars

Coat of Arms Pub
174 Fleet Street, Portsmouth
Tel: 603-431 0407
Cozy pub/restaurant offers "a taste of Britain." 14 draught lines, 3 cask-conditioned ales. Menu is traditional pub grub. Has the seacoast's only snooker table.

Tony's C'side Bar
73 Ocean Boulevard, Hampton Beach
Tel: 603-926 5050
Adjacent to the popular La Bec Rouge Restaurant, this attracts the party crowd with DJs, karaoke nights, and live music Thur–Sat.

Library Lounge
401 State Street, Portsmouth
Tel: 603-431 5202
"Gentlemen's retreat" feel to this book-lined, fireplaced martini and spirits bar. It has the largest vodka inventory north of Boston, with over 100 labels.

Milly's Tavern
500 Commercial Street, Manchester
Tel: 603-625 4444
Saving Manchester from commercial beers. Town's only brewery has 18 beers on tap, all hand-crafted on the premises.

Strange Brew Tavern
88 Market Street, Manchester
Tel: 603-666 4292
Live music six nights a week, Large selection of drafts, with regional and craft brews.

FLORA AND FAUNA

New England's wilderness areas are one of its big draws, attracting campers, hunters, fishermen, photographers, and nature lovers

Trees cover more than three-quarters of New England, cloaking the mountains of New Hampshire, Maine, and Vermont. These woods and mountains ring with birdsong and are carpeted with wild flowers; particularly enthralling are the alpine flowers on Mt Washington.

The most exciting animals to see in the forests are moose. Desperately ungainly, and sporting hairy dewlaps beneath large snouts, they can often be spotted in northern New England, especially in and around lakes and marshes – or licking the salt that runs off the roads in winter. A bull can grow to well over 6ft (2 meters) tall, with huge antlers, and can weigh half a ton – give him a wide berth. You may see moose as you drive around, particularly at dawn or dusk; if not, join one of many moose-watching trips organized locally.

Black bears are shy denizens of the deep forests. They seldom attack humans, but don't feed them or leave food scraps on the ground. Keep food in sealed containers and never approach cubs – their mothers are fiercely protective.

In the lakes and streams that lace the forests, beavers fell trees with their teeth, building dams and creating ponds. Their lodges built of mud and sticks may be up to 6ft (2 meters) tall. Also look out for raccoons, chipmunks, squirrels, porcupines, and skunks.

ABOVE: signs along Route 3 from Pittsburg, New Hampshire, to the Canadian border read: "Brake for Moose. It Could Save Your Life. Hundreds of Collisions." They're not kidding: attracted by salt on the road, dozens of the state's 10,000 moose can be seen just before dusk strolling along "Moose Alley." These docile beasts, said to outnumber humans in parts of Vermont's Northeast Kingdom, have spread as far south as Connecticut.

ABOVE: the fact that a Massachusetts company called Beaver Solutions dedicated itself to "resolving human/beaver conflicts and flooding-related beaver problems" indicate how North America's largest rodent wreaks havoc. Slow-moving, they take refuge in the ponds they create by building intricate dams.

LEFT: black bears are most common in Maine, which has about 23,000. Hunters in the state shoot ("harvest") an average of 3,600 a year.

ALPINE ATTRACTIONS

This cairn on Mt Washington, in New Hampshire, marks an alpine hike across this rugged arctic zone. The treeline occurs as low as 1,400ft (420 meters). The area supports mammals such as voles and shrews, living in deep crevices, and 100 species of alpine plants, many of which grow only here, on Mt Katahdin in Maine's Baxter State Park, and in Labrador and the Arctic. They have adapted to desiccation (dryness resulting from the removal or lack of water) caused by biting winds, poor soil, minimal sunlight, and a short growing season. Some take 25 years to flower. These exquisite plants, growing in and around the lichen-covered rocks with sedges and dwarfed balsam firs, include gold thread, fireweed, alpine bearberry, starflower, arnica, mountain cranberry, wren's egg cranberry, skunk currant, and the dwarf cinquefoil Potentilla robbinsiana, unique to Mt Washington. Their vibrant colors are best seen from mid-June to August. The Alpine Gardens Research Natural Area on Mt Washington is a 100-acre (40.5-hectare) protected area reserved for study of the sensitive, generally hard-to-reach environment.

ABOVE: almost four in five of New England's red foxes were wiped out in the 1990s, hit by rabies and distemper and outflanked by coyotes. But, to the alarm of chicken farmers, they have been making a comeback. They can most easily be seen in summer when they hunt food for their young.

BELOW: the loon is the state bird of New Hampshire. Some believe is the oldest bird on earth, though scientists say this is a case of mistaken identity. They are known in Europe as "divers," and their American name derives from the aquatic birds' yodel-like cry. They can live for up to 30 years.

RIGHT: waders include the American egret (pictured) and black-crowned night heron. Forest birds include pine siskin, blue jay, golden crowned kinglet, and the chickadee.

MAINE

Maine is a land of jagged coastlines and vast pine woods, of remote peninsulas and fresh lobster, inimitably captured in the soft canvases of Winslow Homer

Beyond its heavily trafficked southern coast, Maine remains a vast wilderness. Larger in area than the other five New England states combined, the "Pine Tree State" – nine-tenths covered with forest and with a savage beauty – bears little resemblance to its comfortably settled neighbors. Residents pride themselves on their rugged independence and turn a bemused eye on the strange habits of "summer people" – or, in the still-used 19th-century term, "rusticators."

The two Maines

Maine's geography dictated its economic development. Coastal Mainers made ample use of the fine natural harbors, and virtually all commerce within Maine and between Maine and the outside world was conducted by sea.

Along with trading and boatbuilding, the seaside communities of Maine depended heavily upon the fishing industry and eventually became home to New England's biggest lobster fleet. Inland Maine, where settlement was thin, became a timber empire. The "paper plantations" have kept much of northern Maine a wild paradise for campers, canoeists, hunters, and anglers, although the industry is turning more land over to potential development and shuttering mills in towns

PRECEDING PAGES: Pemaquid Point Lighthouse.
LEFT: the Marshall Point Lighthouse.
RIGHT: a tribute to a fishing heritage.

such as East Millinocket, where the overpowering aroma of paper manufacture has long been the perfume of prosperity.

THE SOUTH COAST

The best way to see Maine is to start at the southern tip and head northeast along the old coastal hghway, US 1. Although geographically the coast represents only a tiny fraction of the state, 45 percent of Maine residents call it home, and the overwhelming majority of visitors are also headed for the shore.

Main attractions

KENNEBUNKPORT
PORTLAND
BRUNSWICK
BATH IRON WORKS
WISCASSET
BOOTHBAY HARBOR
PEMAQUID POINT
MOUNT DESERT ISLAND
BAR HARBOR

Eastport, Maine

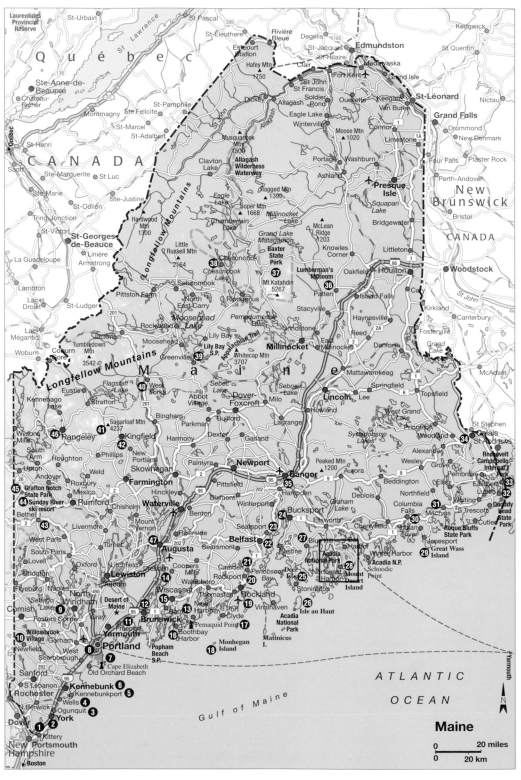

Maine

0 _____ 20 miles

0 _____ 20 km

The southernmost segment, extending from Kittery to Freeport, attracted the earliest settlers and to this day is the most heavily traveled, blending historic enclaves with built-up beaches and discount shopping malls. Just across the New Hampshire border from Portsmouth is **Kittery ❶**, home to Kittery Outlets (exit 3 off I–95; tel: 888-548 8379), one of the state's largest concentrations of outlet malls. More than 120 stores are clustered around the **Kittery Trading Post** (tel: 888-587 6246; open daily), a shopping destination for outdoor equipment and clothing since 1926.

The town is also home to **Portsmouth Naval Yard**, the nation's first, founded in 1806. **Kittery Historical and Naval Museum** (200 Rogers Road Extension; tel: 207-439 3080; open daily June–Oct; charge) documents the shipyard's history, from the construction of *Ranger* (the first ship ever to fly the Stars and Stripes, under the command of John Paul Jones in 1777) to today's submarines.

Nearby **Fort McClary State Historic Site** (off Route 103, 28 Oldsfield Road, Kittery Point; tel: 207-384 5160; open Memorial Day–late Sept; charge) was first fortified in 1715 and rebuilt repeatedly right up until the 1898 Spanish–American War. All that remains is the 1846 hexagonal wooden blockhouse, a powder magazine and the granite seawall with a scenic view of Portsmouth Harbor and Whaleback Light at the mouth of the Piscataqua River.

Fishing off the Maine Coast in 1882.

York

A few miles to the north, **York ❷**, one of Maine's first settlements, was a center of dissent during he Revolutionary era. The local chapter of the Sons of Liberty decided to hold their own tea party when a British ship carrying tea anchored in **York Harbor**. Being practical Mainers, however, they "liberated" the tea rather than throw it in the harbor.

The **Old York Historical Society** (tel: 203-363 4974) maintains nine historic sites, including the **John Hancock Warehouse** (June–mid-Oct Tue–Sun; charge), the 1750 **Jefferds Tavern**, and the **Old Gaol**,

BELOW: the calm waters of Maine.

Maine's Harbors

The "rock-bound coast of Maine" extends only 400 miles (640km) as the gull flies, but 3,500 miles (5,600km) if all the coves, inlets, and peninsulas were magically ironed out. Geologists refer to Maine's shoreline as a "drowned" coastline. The original coast sank thousands of years ago; its valleys became Maine's harbors, its mountains the islands lying offshore. As the coastline sank, receding glaciers exposed vast expanses of granite, which not only gave Maine's mountains their peculiar pink coloration, but also provided settlers with valuable building material.

The first known residents were paleolithic hunters and fishers who lived along the coast 11,000 years ago. Archaeologists debate evidence that Norse explorers visited. The earliest European explorers, in the 15th and 16th centuries, were greeted by the Abenaki tribe, whose name means "easterners" or "people of the dawn." John Cabot visited Maine in 1497–99, and his explorations established all future British claims to the land, but it wasn't until after Captain John Smith sounded "about 25 excellent harbors" in 1614 that the "Father of Maine," Sir Ferdinando Gorges, was granted a charter to establish British colonies. Rival French explorers also claimed parts of Maine and Canada, and territorial disputes that were resolved only by the French and Indian Wars of the 18th century.

TIP

Route 1 from Ogunquit through Wells is studded with antiques shops, from multi-shop flea markets to upscale galleries. There are also several excellent used-book stores, including the sprawling Douglas N. Harding Rare Books (2152 Post Road, Route 1), which also sells old maps and prints.

BELOW: the Rachel Carson National Wildlife Refuge was established in 1966 to protect salt marshes and estuaries for migratory birds.

built in 1719 (gaol June–mid-Oct Mon–Sat; charge) and restored to its 1790s appearance, complete with dungeon. It provides an interesting window on penal attitudes of yore. The **Elizabeth Perkins House** is a prime example of Colonial revivalism.

York Beach is a narrow, mile-long strip of fine sand, lined with every imaginable type of fast-seafood shack and family-entertainment facility. The **Cliff Walk** off York Harbor's boardwalk affords beautiful views of the coastline, and of Cape Neddick's 1879 **Nubble Light** (Lighthouse and grounds closed to public).

Ogunquit and Wells

Take scenic **Shore Road** north from York's Main Street to **Ogunquit ❸** ("beautiful place by the sea" in the Abenaki language). Artist and teacher Charles Woodbury arrived in 1898 and was soon followed by other artists drawn to the dramatic landscape. The **Ogunquit Museum of American Art** (543 Shore Road; tel: 207-646 4909; daily May–Oct; charge) is devoted

exclusively to 20th-century American paintings, sculpture, photography, and graphics, including Maine-inspired Edward Hopper.

Today, tourists crowd the galleries, shops, and eateries that have taken over the fishing shacks and frolic in the surf at the 3-mile (5km) **town beach** (parking charge). In summer the town is so packed with visitors that reproduction trolleys are the easiest way to get around. Ethel Barrymore, Sally Struthers, and Lorenzo Lamas all trod the boards at the **Ogunquit Playhouse**, a highly regarded summer theater founded in 1933 (Route 1; tel: 207-646 5511; www.ogunquitplayhouse.org; mid-May–Oct).

Turn right just past the museum to Perkins Cove in Ogunquit, the southern terminus for Marginal Way, a spectacular, 1-mile (1.6km) seaside walk along the cliffs.

A few miles north on Route 1, in **Wells ❹**, the **Wells Auto Museum** (1181 Post Road; tel: 207-646 9064; open Memorial Day–Sept daily 10am–5pm; charge) exhibits more than 80 antique and classic cars, including a

1949 Cadillac Fleetwood and a 1907 Stanley Steamer.

Watch for the turnoff to the **National Estuarine Research Reserve at Laudholm Farm** (342 Laudholm Road; tel: 207-646 1555; www.wellsreserve.org; visitor center open Memorial Day–Columbus Day, Mon–Sat 10am–4pm, Sun noon–4pm; charge). Exhibits explore estuarine environments and developing coastal management. The preserve has 7 miles (11km) of hiking trails along coastal marsh, uplands, and pristine beach.

The Kennebunks

East of Wells on Route 9, **Kennebunkport ❺**, once the shipbuilding center of York County, has embrace tourism; upscale shops, galleries, and restaurants are clustered around downtown **Dock Square**. The **Kennebunkport Historical Society** (125 North Street; tel: 207-967 2751; www.kporthistory.org; hours vary, call or check the website) maintains several properties. The buildings at the North Street location include a blacksmith shop, school, and exhibit gallery. In town, at 8 Maine Street, the Nott House (Sat June–Oct; fee), an 1853 Greek Revival, is a time capsule of seacoast life from the late 1700s to the mid-1900s.

From Dock Square head up North Street (which becomes Log Cabin Road) 3.25 miles (5km) to the **Seashore Trolley Museum** (195 Log Cabin Road; tel: 207-967 2712; Memorial Day–mid-Oct daily, May and late-Oct weekends; charge). One of the world's largest collections of antique trolley cars, it offers a 1.5-mile (2.4km) ride on vintage streetcars.

From town, take a drive along Ocean Avenue, past Walker's Point, the summer home of the first President Bush. After the road converges with Route 9, continue on to visit the charming fishing village of **Cape Porpoise**, site of the region's first settlement. Route 9, which passes the turnoff for **Goose Rocks Beach**, is a scenic – and

less crowded – route to Old Orchard Beach. **Kennebunk ❻**, 4.25 miles (7km) northwest of Kennebunkport, has a rich shipbuilding heritage. This is the focus of the **Brick Store Museum** (117 Main Street; tel: 207-985 4802; Tue–Sat; fee). There's a cell phone–based audio tour of the exhibits. The museum (May–Oct) also offers tours of the architecturally diverse downtown Historic District. At 105 Summer Street (Route 9A/35) look for the unmistakable 1826 **Wedding Cake House**, festooned with elaborate carved wooden scrollwork. Legend has it that a sea-bound captain who married in haste had it built to compensate his wife for the lack of a cake at their rushed ceremony. In reality, it was a way to unify disparate designs of several buildings.

North to Portland

Farther up the coast is **Old Orchard Beach**, a seaside resort popular among French Canadians. The 7-mile (11km) beach is flanked with motels and condos and, at the Ocean Pier, an old-style amusement park.

The Wedding Cake House at Kennebunk. It is said that the Gothic tastes of its creator, shipbuilder George Washington Bourne (1801–56), were inspired by Milan's cathedral.

BELOW: the harbor at Kennebunkport.

A Statue to the poet Henry Wadsworth Longfellow (1807–82) in Portland's Longfellow Square.

BELOW: the Flat Iron Building, Portland.

Eastward, just south of Portland on **Cape Elizabeth ❼**, is the oldest lighthouse on the eastern seaboard, and quite possibly the most photographed, the Portland Head Light (1791). The history of lighthouses is documented at the **Museum at Portland Head Light** (1000 Shore Road, Fort Williams Park; tel: 207-799 2661; open Memorial Day–mid-Oct daily; mid-Oct–Dec and mid-Apr–Memorial Day weekends; fee).

Portland

With a population of 230,000 in its greater area, **Portland ❽** is home to almost one-fourth of the state's population. Founded as Casco in the middle of the 17th century, the city has the advantage of being 100 miles (160km) closer to Europe than any other major US seaport and is blessed with a sheltered, deep-water harbor.

Three times the city was burned completely to the ground – by Indians in 1675, by the British in 1775, and by accident in 1866. After the last fire, it was reconfigured. Streets were widened, and an elaborate network of municipal parks instituted. The **Portland Trolley** (tel: 207-774 0808; www.portlanddiscovery.com; May–Oct; charge) provides a 90-minute tour of the city's highlights.

The atmospheric **Old Port ❍** district, a salty warren of old brick buildings and cobbled streets, is packed with sophisticated shops and restaurants. Several whale-watch and cruise ships depart from the docks along Commercial Street. Spread out beyond the harbor are the Calendar Islands – so named because John Smith reported that there were 365 of them. **Eagle Island Tours** (Long Wharf; tel: 207-774 0808; www.portlanddiscovery.com; late June–Labor Day; charge) runs visitors out to Eagle Island to tour the summer home of Admiral Robert Peary, who planted the American flag on the North Pole in 1909 (tel: 207-624 6080; late June–Labor Day 10am–5pm; charge) .

Portland remains a thriving cultural crossroads. Congress Street is the main thoroughfare of the Arts District, with museums and theaters, art galleries and studios, and plenty of chic shops and

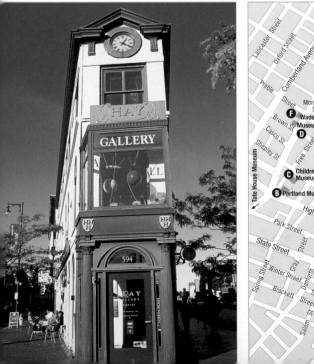

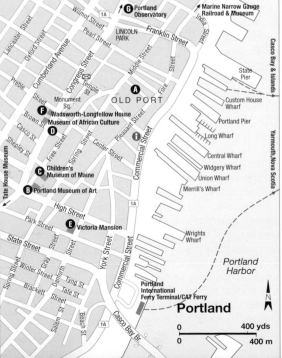

cafés. The I.M. Pei-designed **Portland Museum of Art** ❸ (7 Congress Square; tel: 207-775 6148; portlandmuseum.org; Memorial Day–Columbus Day daily, Tue–Sun rest of year; charge) is strong on locally inspired artists such as Winslow Homer, Edward Hopper, and Andrew Wyeth. Among the well-represented European masters are Van Gogh, Degas, Mary Cassatt, and Picasso.

Next door is the imaginative **Children's Museum of Maine** ❸ (142 Free Street; tel: 207-828 1234; www.childrensmuseumofme.org; daily; charge). Kids can climb inside a humpback whale, play in a dress-up theatre, and crew on a kid-size lobster boat.

The **Institute of Contemporary Art** (522 Congress Street; tel: 207-699 5029; Wed–Sun 11am–5pm; donation) presents cutting-edge works by regional and international artists. The **Museum of African Culture** ❹ (13 Brown Street; tel: 207-871–7188; www.museumafricanculture.org; Tue–Sat 10:30am–4pm, Sat noon–4pm; charge) is the only museum in northern New England dedicated to the art and culture of the sub-Sahara.

The **State Theatre** (609 Congress Street; tel: 207-956–6000; www.statetheatreportland.com) has a rich schedule of musical performances; **Portland Stage Company** (27A Forest Avenue; 207-774 0465; www.portlandstage.org) is the town's professional theatre troupe. **Merrill Auditorium** (Myrtle Street; tel: 207-842 0800; www.porttix.com) is the city's premier performing arts center. Concerts on the 5,000-pipe Kotzschmar organ are performed periodically during the year.

Several Portland neighborhoods warrant strolling – especially the Western Promenade, a parade of 19th-century architectural styles. By far the most elaborate dwelling in town is the 1859–63 brownstone Italianate villa **Victoria Mansion** ❸ (109 Danforth Street; tel: 207-772 4841; www.victoriamansion.org; May–Oct Mon–Sun; fee). Also known as the Morse-Libby House, it is considered one of the country's premier examples of pre–Civil War opulence.

In contrast is the somewhat restrained 1785–86 **Wadsworth-Longfellow House** ❶ (489 Congress Street; tel: 207-774 1822; www.hwlong

Lobsters are big business in Portland, both on the water and on the menu.

BELOW: Maine has a 400-year history of boatbuilding.

Down East

The phrase "Down East" is often used to refer to Maine, particularly coastal Maine. That's somewhat confusing, since a glance at any map shows that Maine is the eastern-most state in New England and heading "down" from any point on the coastline means heading south and southwest.

The term comes from the days of sail, when shipping was heavy between Maine ports and Boston. Ships moving up the coast towards Portland or Bath were headed east/northeast with the wind at their backs. They were, therefore, headed downwind. Downwind + eastern course = down east.

Of course, when those ships returned to Boston, they were sailing into the wind – upwind. Hence, they were going "up to Boston," even though the city is approximately 50 miles (80km) south of Maine's southern border.

The Androscoggin River rapids at Brunswick.

fellow.org; May–Oct Mon–Sun; charge), built by Longfellow's grandfather, a Revolutionary War officer. Inside are the parlor where the poet's parents were married and the room where he wrote *The Rainy Day*. Next door, exhibits at the **Maine Historical Society** (www.mainehistory.org; same hours; charge) span more than five centuries of Maine life.

Built in 1807 as a maritime signal tower, the 86ft (26-meter) -high **Portland Observatory** (138 Congress Street; tel: 207-774 5561; portlandlandmarks.org/observatory; daily Memorial Day weekend–Columbus Day; guided tours daily, sunset guided tours Thurs in July–Aug; charge) offers one of the most magnificent views in town.

Hop aboard one of the 2ft-gauge trains that once connected rural Maine to the rest of the world at the **Marine Narrow Gauge Railroad and Museum** (55 Fore Street; tel: 207-828 0814; www.mainenarrowgauge.org; May–Oct daily, Mar–Apr weekends; separate fees for train ride and museum). The train ride rumbles

BELOW: a vintage locomotive in Yarmouth Station.

along the shore of Casco Bay in an antique rail car pulled by a steam or diesel engine.

Overlooking the Fore River is the **Tate House Museum** (1267 Westbrook Street; tel: 207-774–6177; June–Oct Wed–Sun; tours on the hour; charge). Built in 1755 for George Tate, the senior mast agent for the Royal Navy who was in charge of cutting and shipping white pines to England, it's the only pre-Revolutionary house in Portland that's open to the public.

The Lakes Region

With its easy access from Portland via Route 302, **Sebago Lake** is the state's second-largest lake and the most popular of the Western Lakes, offering swimming, boating, camping, and fishing in 1,400-acre (160-hectare) **Sebago Lake State Park** (State Park Road, between Naples and South Casco; tel: 207-693 6613; open year round; entrance charge May–mid-Oct).

The *Songo River Queen II* (Route 302; tel: 207-693 6861; www.songoriverqueen.net), a replica Mississippi River paddle-wheeler, provides one-hour tours on Long Lake. Several marinas rent canoes, powerboats, pontoon boats, and Jet Skis.

Near the New Hampshire border off Route 11 not far from Newfield, 19th Century **Willowbrook Village** (70 Elm Street; tel: 207-793 2784; www.willowbrookmuseum.org; Memorial Day weekend–Columbus Day, Thur–Mon; charge) is a reconstituted late-19th-century museum village of 37 buildings, which captures aspects of this gentler time, from horse-drawn sleighs to bicycles built for two, from a classic ice-cream parlor to a century-old "riding gallery" – a working carousel.

To the north of Portland via Route 1 or I–95 in **Yarmouth**, Delorme Company, one of the leaders in cartographic technology, has a huge **Map Store** (2 Delorme Drive; tel: 800-642 0970 or 207-846 7100; daily). The centerpiece is

the astoundingly detailed "Eartha," the world's largest rotating globe.

Freeport

The little town of **Freeport⑪** is known worldwide, thanks to the legendary **L.L.Bean** outdoor equipmen store (95 Main Street; tel: 877-755 2326), open 24 hours, 365 days a year. A middle-of-the-night browse is worth the lost sleep. Their Outdoor Discovery program (tel: 888-552 3261) has courses and outings for biking, fly-fishing, kayaking, sporting clays, stand-up paddling, cross-country skiing, and snowshoeing. Many of them have same-day, walk-in registration at the store. The village of Freeport (http://freeportusa.com) is crammed with about 200 outlets, shops, galleries, and cafés. Local zoning ordinances are surprisingly effective at maintaining a small-town appearance. Even the McDonald's looks like an old house.

Atlantic Seal Cruises (25 Main Street; tel: 207-865 6112 or 877-285 7325; daily Memorial Day–late Oct) has several options: to Admiral Peary's summer home on Eagle Island, seal and osprey watch cruises, and a day-long excursion to Seguin Island Lighthouse.

Ten minutes from the heart of town, **Wolfe's Neck Woods State Park** (426 Wolfe Neck Road; tel: 207-865 4465; day-use charge) has hiking trails through copses of pine and hemlock, the saltwater estuary, and the shoreline along Casco Bay and the Harraseeket River. It's a good place for whale sightings, too.

THE MID-COAST

Brunswick ⑫ is best known as the home of **Bowdoin College** (tel: 207-725 3100 for tour information; www.bowdoin.edu). Founded in 1794, Bowdoin was originally slated to be built in Portland, but the college's benefactors found that that city offered too many "temptations to dissipation, extravagance, vanity and various vices of seaport towns." Nathaniel Hawthorne and Henry Wadsworth Longfellow were alumni, class of 1825.

On campus, the **Bowdoin Museum of Art** (Walker Art Building; tel: 207-725 3275; www.bowdoin.edu/art-museum; Tue–Sun; donations)

TIP

The Bowdoin International Music Festival (tel: 207-373 1400; www.bowdoin-festival.org), from late June through July, features chamber music concerts at sites throughout Brunswick.

BELOW: bull moose roam freely in the North Woods. Young males sometimes wander hundreds of miles from their home in search of females.

Moose Spotting

The moose is as much a symbol of Maine as lighthouses and lobster. Standing at about 6ft (1.8 meters) at the shoulder and weighing up to 1,000lbs (455kg), the bull moose in a majestic creature. Spotting one of the behemoths is a highlight of the trip for many visitors.

In the Moosehead Lake area, Route 15 near Rockwood, Route 201 from Forks to the Canadian border, and Lazy Tom Bog near Kokadjo north of Greenville are all prime moose habitat. Keep an eye out for them in the bogs. In the summer, they are most active in the early morning and late afternoon. Keep your camera close, but do not approach them. Generally placid, they will charge if they feel threatened.

Bath claims to have a slower pace and a friendly pedestrian atmosphere.

BELOW: there are more than 3 milliion lobster traps in Maine waters.

houses paintings by Stuart, Copley, and Winslow Homer; the Warren Collection of classical antiquities; and works by European masters.

Also on campus, the fascinating **Peary-MacMillan Arctic Museum** (Hubbard Hall; tel: 207-725 3416; Tue–Sun; donation) heralds the accomplishments of North Pole explorers Robert E. Peary and Donald MacMillan, who achieved their objective in 1909.

The **Pejepscot Historical Society** (159 Park Row; tel: 207-729 6606; Tue–Sat; donation) has a fine collection of material dealing with the area's history.

The Pejepscot Society oversees **the Skolfield-Whittier House** (next door to the museum; Thur–Sat; guded tours only at 11am and 2pm; charge). The house is a time capsule of three generations of a Brunswick family that was prominent in seafaring, medicine, and education. The **Joshua L. Chamberlain Museum** (226 Maine Street; tel: 207-725 6958; Tue–Sat, tours on the hour; charge) exhibits memorabilia of Chamberlain, a hero at the Battle of Gettysburg, who later served four

one-year terms as Maine's 32nd governor and became Bowdoin's president.

Bath

East of Brunswick on US 1, **Bath** ⓭ was once the nation's fifth-largest seaport and still builds ships. For a time in the 19th century, Maine's shipyards were responsible for one-third to one-half of all ships on the high seas. When the days of wooden ships ended, the old yards gave way to the **Bath Iron Works**, today a busy producer of Navy ships.

Visitors can tour the Iron Works aboard a trolley run by the **Maine Maritime Museum** (243 Washington Street; tel: 207-443 1316; daily; fee; ticket is good for two days). The 20-acre (8-hectare) campus on the Kennebac River preserves the history of shipbuilding in Bath, and Maine's relationship with the sea. Exhibits on nautical tools and gadgets capture the flavor of seafaring days, while a working boatyard demonstrates shipbuilding techniques. The museum also offers history- and nature-themed cruises.

Bath's **historic district** has fine examples of Greek Revival, Georgian,

and Italianate architecture among its mansions, cozy inns, and restaurants. **Sagadahoc Preservation** (880 Washington Street; tel: 207-443 2174; Mon–Thur) has a self-guided walking tour and podcast tours of the historic district (map available at Main Street Bath office, 4 Centre Street). Fourteen miles (22km) south of Bath on Route 209 on the **Phippsburg Peninsula** is **Popham Beach State Park** (tel: 207-389 1335; entrance charge in season), a 4.5-mile (7km) stretch of sand that is one of the prettiest and most popular beaches in the state.

Just across the Kennebec River from Bath, in **Woolwich**, visitors have several options: turn north on Route 128 for approximately 10 miles (16km) to the **Pownalborough Courthouse** (23 Courthouse Road; tel: 207-737 2504; Memorial Day–Columbus Day weekends, also July–August Tue–Fri; charge) in **Dresden** ⓮. The state's only remaining pre-Revolutionary courthouse is a handsomely restored and magnificently detailed three-floor riverfront building with a fascinating period cemetery on the grounds. (Note: if continuing north, to avoid backtracking, continue north past the courthouse for 2.5 miles [4km] to Route 27 and head south about 9 miles [14km] to Wiscasset.)

Wiscasset

Wiscasset ⓯ claims, with some justification, to be the "prettiest village in Maine." Two handsome houses reflect the style of life of successful sea captains: the Federal-era **Nickels-Sortwell House** (121 Main Street; tel: 207-882 7169; June–mid-Oct Fri–Sun; tours on the half-hour; charge) and the 1807 **Castle Tucker** (2 Lee Street; tel: 207-882 7169; June–mid-Oct Wed–Sun; tours on the half-hour; charge). Built in 1807, its furnishings are an intact vision of Victorian life.

Another offbeat tourist attraction is the **Old Lincoln County Jail and Museum** (133 Federal Street; tel: 207-882 6817; July–Aug Tue–Sun, June

and Sept weekends; charge). This is an 1811 hoosegow with granite walls up to 41ins (over 1 meter) thick. Considered a model of humane treatment in its day because prisoners were afforded individual cells, this grim repository was used until 1953 and has the graffiti to prove it.

The **Musical Wonder House** (18 High Street; tel: 207-882 7163; www.musicalwonderhouse.com; Memorial Day–Oct daily) has more than 5,000 restored musical boxes, player grand pianos and organs, spring-powered phonographs, musical birds, and the like. Off-season, the shop is open with lots of music boxes and CDs on offer.

Boothbay Harbor

North on Route 1, just over the Sheepscot River, turn onto Davis Island to visit **Fort Edgecomb State Historic Site**, an octagonal fort completed in 1809 with commanding views of the river and beyond. It's a particularly nice place to picnic and spot harbor seals and osprey (tel: 207-882 7777; daily Memorial Day–Labor Day; fee).

The Nickels-Sortwell House, Wiscasset, built in 1807 by Captain William Nickels, a ship owner and trader.

BELOW: the past is for sale in Wiscasset, which was first settled in 1663.

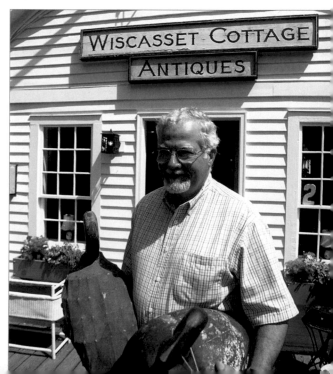

The Pemaquid Point Lighthouse.

BELOW: Boothbay Harbor is a popular yachting destination.

Although certainly subdued compared to the commercial excesses of the south coast, **Boothbay Harbor ⓰**, to the south on Route 27, is decidedly touristy. In summer, tens of thousands of visitors throng the streets of this former fishing village to inspect the shops, sample seafood delicacies, charter boats to explore offshore islands with names such as the Cuckolds and the Hypocrites, and book passage on whale watches and deep-sea fishing trips. There are yacht and golf clubs, flower shows, auctions, and clambakes.

At **Boothbay Railway Village** (Route 27, 586 Wiscasset Road, Boothbay; tel: 207-633 4727; daily Memorial Day weekend–Oct, trains operate 10am–4pm; charge), the main attraction is a narrow-gauge, coal-fired railroad, encircling a range of reconstructed buildings of yesteryear, including a barbershop, bank, and country store.

In **West Boothbay Harbor**, the **Maine State Aquarium** (194 McKown Point Road; tel: 207-633 9674; daily Memorial Day weekend–Labor Day, daily; Sept Wed–Sun) has an 850-gallon fish tank and a gallery echoing the rocky Maine coast. Kids can pet live sharks and meet a giant blue lobster.

Pemaquid Point

Farther to the north off Route 1, Route 130 cuts south through Damariscotta to **Pemaquid Point ⓱**. Turn onto Route 130 the **Colonial Pemaquid State Historic Site** (tel: 207-677 2423; Memorial Day–Labor Day; charge). Ongoing archeological digs are turning up Native American pottery, a 1600s-era building foundation, and lots of pottery shards and clay pipe stems. Guides give interpretive tours around the site.

Admission also includes **Fort William Henry**, a 1907 replica on the site of several failed Colonial stockades. The view from the roof of the fort is fabulous. At the tip of this peninsula on Route 130, in **Lighthouse Park** (parking charge) stands the **Pemaquid Point Lighthouse**, commissioned in 1827 by John Quincy Adams. Visitors can climb the tower and visit the 1857 keeper's house, now a **Fishermen's Museum** filled with a hodgepodge of nets, traps, tools, hull models, and other fishing paraphernalia (tel: 207-563 2739; daily Memorial Day–Columbus Day; donation). With powerful surf constantly breaking on the rocks, the point is a favorite spot for painters and photographers, as well as families who enjoy poking around the tide pools. The lighthouse is shown on the Maine quarter coin.

The large white mansion on the hill overlooking the St George River at the junction of routes 1 and 131 in **Thomaston** is the **General Henry Knox Museum** (tel: 207-354 8062; Memorial Day–Columbus Day Tue–Sat; fee). It's a replica of Montpelier, the home built by the Revolutionary War hero after the war. Architecturally, it compares to Monticello and Mount Vernon. Historically, it teaches about the gentleman farmer and instinctively talented artillery commander

who was vital to America's struggle for independence.

Monhegan Island

Lured by tales of marvelous people and cities in the New World, a group of Germans settled **Waldoboro** in 1748. A plaque at the center of town attests, "the promise and expectation of finding a prosperous city, instead of which they found nothing but wilderness."

One tale which was accurate, however, was the description of an island that looked like a whale. The cliffs of **Monhegan Island** ⑱, 12 miles (19km) south of Port Clyde, do indeed lend the island the appearance of a whale. An otherworldly air still pervades this 700-acre (280-hectare) isle, little changed in the past century. There are no cars or paved roads, and not all dwellings have electricity. Most of the 65 or so year-round residents make their living from the sea as fishermen or lobstermen. It's a favorite for artists in the summer. The most famous summer resident is the painter Jamie Wyeth,

son of Andrew Wyeth. There are 12 miles (19km) of steep, strenuous trails circling the island. Monhegan is served by several ferries that leave from **Port Clyde** (tel: 207-372 8848; www.monheganboat.com), Boothbay Harbor (tel: 207-633 2284; www. balmydaycruises.com), New Harbor (tel: 207-677 2026; www.hardyboat. com), and Muscongus (tel: 207-380 5460; www.sailmuscongus.com). Although it's possible to make the round-trip in one day, an overnight is advised for those who wish to ease back into a less stressful age.

West of Penobscot Bay

On the west end of Penobscot Bay is the town of **Rockland** ⑲, once a great limestone producer and now the world's largest distributor of lobsters, as well as the "Schooner Capital of Maine." These two- or three-masted schooners are a wonderful way to discover the coast as the earliest explorers encountered it. Weekend and week-long excursions may be booked aboard more than a dozen vessels, some vintage and others quite new. The Maine

TIP

Rockland's annual Maine Lobster Festival (tel: 207-596 0376; mainelobsterfestival. com), held in late July–early August, is one of the state's most popular events.

BELOW: rowing teams in training.

Rockland holds the Maine Lobster Festival at the end of July with parades, a Maine Sea Goddess contest, and cooking competitions. Details: www.mainelobster festival.com.

Windjammer Association is the central directory of the ships (tel: 800-807 WIND; www.sailmainecoast.com). The **Maine State Ferry Service** (tel: 207-596 5400; www.state.me.us/mdot/msfs) transports passengers and vehicles to **Matinicus**, a small, quiet island populated primarily by lobstermen and their families; **Vinalhaven**, where old granite quarries make fine swimming holes and the paved roads are ideal for day-tripping bicyclists; and **North Haven**, mainly given over to vacation homes. The main village has several shops, restaurants, and galleries. It's usually easy to board as a foot passenger; but taking a car means advance planning and often a wait in line.

Thanks to the 1935 bequest of "Aunt" Lucy Farnsworth, a frugal spinster who lived in but three rooms of her family mansion and left the town $1.3 million to start a museum, Rockland has a world-class collection of art. The **Farnsworth Art Museum and Wyeth Center** (16 Museum Street; tel: 207-596 6457; daily Memorial Day–mid-Oct; Wed free admission 5–8pm; Nov–end May Wed–Sun; charge) has many noted 19th- and 20th-century works, including paintings by Winslow Homer and John Marin, and sculpture by Louise Nevelson, who grew up in a Bath lumberyard.

Paintings by all three Wyeths (N. C., Andrew, and Jamie) are exhibited in a former church across from the **Farnsworth Homestead**, an 1850 Greek Revival home next to the museum. The Center is undergoing renovation and restoration and may be closed at times. Call the Museum for updates. The museum's **Olson House** (Hathorne Point Road; tel: 207-354 0102; June Wed–Sun, July–Oct Tue–Sun; charge), 14.5 miles (23km) from Rockland in Cushing, was home to Christina Olson, immortalized in Andrew Wyeth's painting, *Christina's World*.

The traditions and history of lighthouses, life saving, lifesaving services, and the US Coast Guard are lovingly preserved at the **Maine Lighthouse Museum at the Maine Discovery Center** (One (1 Park Drive; tel: 207-594 3301; Memorial Day–Columbus Day daily, Nov–May Thur–Sat; charge).

The Life of a Growing Crustacean

The colorful lobster buoys dotting the coast of Maine highlight a $130 million business. In 2010, lobstermen caught 90 million lbs (40.8 million kg) of the crustaceans. Most lobsters are caught by independent fishermen in small boats.

The hardy fishermen head out long before dawn, when the waters are calmer and before the wind has picked up, and return in the late afternoon after a hard day on the nets. Called "highliners," these lobstermen have 1,000 to 1,500 traps which need to be checked at least once a week. Although proximity to shore makes lobstering safer than other commercial fishing, it is still a dangerous profession, and is particularly grueling in the bitter Maine winter.

Lobsters are crustaceans whose external skeletons do not grow. They go through the process of molting, or shedding their old shells and growing into new, larger ones. This process happens in late June or early July. Conveniently for highliners, molting brings the lobsters closer to shore, making them easier to catch.

Without shells, the soft lobsters are vulnerable to predators such as codfish and sharks, so they migrate to shallow waters for safety. Here, they hide, expanding 15 to 20 percent in size. Over four to six weeks, the lobsters produce new shells, then return to deep water. The lobsters are now known as "soft-shell," as opposed to the "hard-shell" they have just before molting. A hard-shell lobster's meat can be up to 33 percent of its body weight, while a soft-shell's is only 25 percent, so hard-shell lobster tends to be more expensive. The taste is slightly different, and each Maine connoisseur has a preference. Some say soft-shell is sweeter, some prefer hard-shell for its stronger taste.

The New England Aquarium is studying ways of harvesting lobsters through aquaculture, but as of yet have not found a reliable method of raising lobster in a contained environment. Lobsters are cannibalistic, and will eat each other if given the opportunity. They are also incredibly slow growing, meaning that the investment has a long return, when most fishermen need a quick turnaround of their cash.

The **Owl's Head Transportation Museum** is housed in a spiffed-up hangar at the Owl's Head airport south of Rockland (117 Museum Street, Owls Head, off Route 73; tel: 207-594 4418; daily; fee). It displays a splendid collection of vehicles: 50 cars, 28 planes, plus bikes and motorcycles – ranging from an 1885 Benz to a 1939 Packard to a Model F plane, a Wright Brothers prototype. On summer weekends, some displays are taken off their blocks and sent for a spin – a worthwhile departure from usual museum practice.

Works by some of the state's finest contemporary artists are in the **Center for Maine Contemporary Art** (162 Russell Avenue; tel: 207-236 2875; Tue–Sun; fee), 6 miles (10km) up the coast in the quiet village of **Rockport ⓴**.

Camden

Camden, ㉑ "Where the Mountains Meet the Sea," has enjoyed a long reign as the ultimate in genteel summering spots. Its picturesque harbor is lined with shops and restaurants; many

ofthe finely preserved, gracious homes of 19th-century ship captains have been converted into upscale B&Bs.

Numerous excursion boats and windjammers (www.sailmainecoast. com) sail from the harbor from late May to mid-October. Rockland native Edna St. Vincent Millay penned one of her verses after climbing to the summit of 800ft (240-meter) Mt Battie in the **Camden Hills State Park** (north of town off Route 1, tel. 207-236 3109; mid-May–mid-Oct; fee). The summit is accessible on foot or via a toll road; the view of Penobscot Bay and the distant islands is one of Maine's loveliest.

Belfast and Searsport

The 19th-century captains and shipbuilders of **Belfast ㉒** built their stately mansions in a variety o architectural styles that makes the town at the mouth of the Passagassawaukeag River a fascinating place to take a stroll.

A few miles north on Route 1, **Searsport ㉓**, lined with dazzling-white sea captains' homes, calls itself "the antiques capital of Maine."

Camden's Chestnut Street Baptist Church.

BELOW: Camden from Mount Battie. Movies filmed or set in the pretty resort town include *Carousel* (1956), *Peyton Place* (1957), and *In the Bedroom* (2001).

Totems for sale in Belfast.

Below: recruits from the Maine Maritime Academy, Castine.

Between 1770 and 1920, this one town produced more than 3,000 vessels, and evidence of its rich history, along with China Trade treasures, can be found on Route 1 in **Penobscot Marine Museum** (5 Church Street; tel: 207-548 2529; daily Memorial Day–Oct; charge). The sprawling complex has a fine collection of marine and folk art, ship models, nautical paintings, and watercraft.

Farther along the coastal road, the outskirts of **Bucksport** ❷ are dominated by the **Penobscot Narrows Bridge** (tel: 207-469 6553; May–Oct daily 9am–5pm, until midnight near full moon; charge for observatory includes admission to Fort Knox). Visitors can ride an elevator to the world's tallest bridge observatory, 420ft (128 meters) above sea level, and view sweeping panoramas. The only way to reach the observatory is from the vast **Fort Knox State Park** (Route 174 off Route 1; tel: 207-469-7719; open May–Nov; fee). It was built in 1844–69; troops were stationed there during the Civil War through the Spanish–American War.

East of Penobscot Bay

Intent on getting to the justly famed Mount Desert Island, many tourists never veer from US 1 and miss one of the most scenic areas in Maine. The peninsulas along the eastern side of Penobscot Bay warrant some poking around, but be forewarned: the roads can be confusing, even with a road map and GPS.

From Route 1 in Bucksport, wind your way down routes 175 and 166 (or 166A) to **Castine**. Established as a trading post by the Plymouth Pilgrims, the tiny town became one of the most hotly contested chunks of property in New England. Changing hands nine times, it was taken from the Native Americans by the French, Dutch, British, and, eventually, Americans. Plaques around town, as well as a free walking-tour brochure available at most local merchants, fill in the details, but it's enough to wander around, beneath a canopy of elms, taking in the array of fine white houses.

Some of these houses belong to the **Maine Maritime Academy**, founded in 1941 and one of five such schools nationwide that train merchant mariners. The academy's 1952 ship, the decommissioned T/S *State of Maine*, serves as a floating classroom (tel: 800-464 6565; hourly tours Mon–Fri when school is in session at 11am and 1pm; call one week prior).

Take a detour off this detour to make a circuit of **Deer Isle** ❷, where the principal occupations are lobstering and fishing. On the eastern side of the isle is the prestigious Haystack Mountain School of Crafts (88 Haystack School Drive; tel: 207-348 2306), housed in a cluster of small modern buildings perched precipitously on a piney bank overlooking Jericho Bay. The school periodically puts on exhibits. On the southern coast of the island, the **Stonington Opera House** (tel: 207-367 2788; www.operahousearts.org), on the commercial fishing pier, is nationally recognized as a community performing arts center. For

a true getaway, take the **Isle-au-Haut Company mailboat** (tel: 207-367 5193; www.isleauhaut.com; bicycle rentals available) from the picturesque port of **Stonington** to the sparsely inhabited 5,800-acre (2,300-hectare) **Isle-au-Haut ㉖**, 6 miles (10km) out to sea. The company also offers lobster fishing and lighthouse cruises, and a cruise to Seal Island with its colony of nesting puffins.

Half of Isle-au-Haut is privately owned and occupied primarily by lobstermen and their families; the other half is part of **Acadia National Park**. Heading northeast to hook up with US 1 again, you'll pass through **Blue Hill ㉗**, long the choice of blueblood "rusticators" – summer vacationers – who didn't care for the showy social season in Bar Harbor. It's still well-heeled, with many galleries, antiques shops, and studios. The shipbuilding town is also renowned for its pottery, finished with glazes made from nearby copper mines and quarries. **Rackliffe Pottery** (Ellsworth Road, Route 172; tel: 207-374 2297) welcomes visitors.

Mount Desert Island

Spotting the 17 exposed pink granite peaks of **Mount Desert Island** in 1604, Samuel de Champlain described the place as "*l'île des monts déserts*" – and the French pronunciation still holds, more or less, so accentuate the final syllable, as in "dessert."

The reason there's so much territory to explore on **Mount Desert Island ㉘** is that 41,409 acres (16,765 hectares) of the 16- by 13-mile (26km by 34km) island belong to **Acadia National Park** (tel: 207-288 3338; www.nps.gov/acad; park open daily year-round; park headquarters: mid-Apr–Oct Mon–Fri, Nov–mid-Apr daily; Hull Cove visitor center (A) mid-Apr–Oct daily; Thompson Island visitor center mid-May–mid-Oct, hours vary), which draws more than 5 million visitors a year.

Stop at the **Mount Desert Island Information Center** (18 Harbor Drive, in the Yachtsmen's Building; tel: 207-276 5040; www.mountdesert-chamber.org; May–Sept daily) to get general information for the entire island. The park visitor centers have park maps and a schedule of naturalist

TIP

Windjammer cruises, lasting a day to a week, depart from Rockland and nearby Camden. For information, contact the Maine Windjammer Association (tel: 207-374 2993; www.sailmainecoast.com).

BELOW: the beach on Mount Desert Island.

The Making of Acadia

Society notables discovered this remote spot in the mid-19th century, and by the time the stock market crashed in 1929, millionaires had constructed more than 200 extravagant "cottages." (Only a few survive, some as institutions or inns: many were destroyed in 1947's devastating fire.) Harvard University president Charles W. Eliot had the foresight to initiate the park in 1916, and many of his peers contributed parcels. John D. Rockefeller Jr threw in 11,000 acres (4,400 hectares) crisscrossed with 50 miles (80km) of bridle paths he built to protest against the admission of horseless carriages onto the island in 1905. The trail network encourages mountain-biking, cross-country skiing, and just plain walking. And Frenchman Bay, to the northeast, is great for sailing.

activities here; there are excellent hiking maps on sale.

Most visitors will want to experience the view from Cadillac Mountain, whose form dominates the park, and to drive or cycle the Park Loop Road, but there are many other possibilities, including horse and -and-carriage tours from **Wildwood Riding Stables** and kayaking, sailing, and hiking in the less frequented areas. Even the shorter trails tend to be over uneven rock, so suitable footwear is essential.

Car traffic is kept under control by a permit system covering the mostly one-way 27-mile (43km) **Park Loop Road**, a toll road which makes a clockwise circuit of all the more scenic spots along the eastern coast; the reasonably priced permits are good for a week (major portions closed Dec–mid-Apr; may be closed other times in inclement weather). Another excellent option is the Island Explorer Shuttle (tel: 207-667 5796; late June–Columbus Day). This free bus service has eight intersecting routes through the island. Maps and schedules are available at the visitor centers and elsewhere.

BELOW: riding out on Mount Desert Island

Sieur de Monts Spring is a lovely spot dubbed "The Sweet Waters of Acadia" by the park's first superintendent. There are three attractions worth visiting clustered here. The **Wild Gardens of Acadia** (open year-round), which shows nearly 300 labeled flora arranged in several display areas; the adjacent **Nature Center** (mid-June–late Sept); with exhibits on Acadia's cultural and natural history; and a branch of the **Abbe Museum** (late May–mid-Oct daily; charge). The museum is devoted to Maine's Native American heritage. The Bar Harbor location of the museum is open year-round.

Sweeping views follow, from the Champlain Mountain Overlook across Frenchman Bay to the distant Gouldsboro Hills. The road passes the start of the **Precipice Trail**, which has iron rungs and ladders for the steep sections, and farther on are Sand Beach – edged by low cliffs and Acadia's one sandy beach – and the **Beehive Trail**, which has superb panoramas but involves some potentially dizzying sections. Thunder Hole

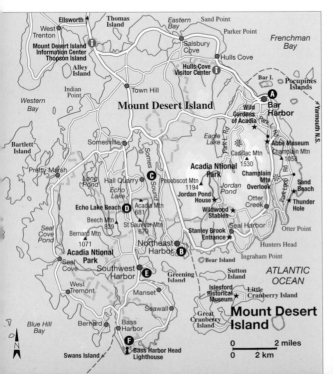

needs a wind to stir things up; in the right conditions, the spray blasts up through this chink on the coastline. Otter Point provides another memorable coastal outlook before the road heads inland, past Jordan Pond with walks along the lakeside, or on the short trail past Bubble Rock, a huge boulder transported and dumped by glacier, to South Bubble Summit. The Jordan Pond House on the shore is the only full-service restaurant in the park. A tea break with the restaurant's popovers is a park tradition.

Reached by the toll road or on foot, the tallest peak, 1,530ft (466-meter) **Cadillac Mountain**, is the highest point along the Atlantic coast north of Rio de Janeiro. The glorious 360-degree views stretch inland as far as Mt Katahdin, Maine's highest summit, and seaward to encompass myriad smaller islands – a particularly lovely vista when bathed in the glow of sunrise (a surprisingly large number of people arrive at this early hour) or sunset.

Bar Harbor

Bar Harbor Ⓐ is Mount Desert Island's main town – a bit over-commercialized, but with a pretty towngreen, a marvelous Art Deco cinema, a lovely ocean walk, some exceptional crafts stores, appealing restaurants, and a good choice of accommodations. **The Bar Harbor Historical Society** (33 Ledgelawn Avenue; tel: 207-288 3807; www.barharborhistorical.org; June–Oct Mon–Sat; donation), in the former St Edwards Convent, does a fine job of chronicling the resort town's rich history.

Numerous whale watches, cruise boats, and sailing charters set sail from the town's wharf. **Abbe Museum Downtown** (26 Mount Desert Street; tel: 207-288 3519; late May–early Nov daily, early Nov–late May Thur–Sat; closed Jan; charge) displays an extensive collection of Indian artifacts from the Wabanaki, the state's native people.

Elsewhere on the island

The "quiet side" of the island is just as lovely, but a lot less traveled. Head out of Bar Harbor on Route 3 to **Northeast Harbor** Ⓑ, known for its scenic, yacht-filled, protected harbor. Visit the spectacular seaview **Asticou Azalea Garden** (tel: 207-276 3727; May–Oct, daylight hours) and **Thuya Garden and Lodge** (Garden, tel: 207-276 3727; late May–mid-Oct daily; donation; Lodge, late May–mid-Sept; donation), the 215-acre (87-hectare) garden and home of landscape artist Joseph Henry Curtis. The **Asticou Terraces Trail** is a moderate climb with scenic overlooks ending at the gardens.

The *Sea Princess* (tel: 207-276 5352; www.barharborcruises.com) offers nature cruises around the park and through **Somes Sound** Ⓒ, the only fjord on the East Coast. The sunset dinner cruise travels to a waterside restaurant on **Little Cranberry Island**, a scenic, 400-acre (160-hectare) island 20 miles (32km) offshore.

Head south on Route 102 to **Echo Lake Beach** Ⓓ, part of Acadia

Maine's private and state-run ferries provide a vital link to many island communities.

BELOW: the dockmaster's shed at Bar Harbor.

National Park, one of the best spots for freshwater swimming. There's a hiking trail up 839ft (256-meter) -high **Beech Mountain**.

The charming little town of **Southwest Harbor** at the entrance to Somes Sound has art galleries and restaurants, plus the **Wendell Gilley Museum of Bird Carving** (4 Herrick Road; tel: 207-244 7555; June–Oct Tue–Sun, May and Nov–mid-Dec Fri–Sun; charge). It exhibits the magnificent works of the world-renowned bird carver. The "Brass Era" of automotive history – the earliest years from the 1880s to 1920 – is documented in the **Seal Cove Auto Museum** (1414 Tremont Road; tel: 207-244 9242; May–Oct daily; charge). Nearly 100 rare and exquisitely preserved autos, motorcycles, and pumpers are on display.

Cranberry Cove Boating (Upper Town Dock; tel: 207-244 5882; www. cranberryisles.com) operates a ferry to the Cranberry Isles, Isleford, and the Sutton Islands. If you'd rather be captain, rent a power boat at Manset Yacht Services (113 Shore Road, Manset; tel: 207-244 4040).

Isleford, also known as Little Cranberry Island, has restaurants, lodgings, and a few crafts shops. The **Isleford Historical Museum** (mid-June–Sept daily; donation) documents the lives of the hardy inhabitants with everything from harpoon guns and sextants to store ledgers and storage barrels. Capt. Stefanie Alley takes up to six passengers out on her working lobster boat as she checks her traps among the outer islands. The 90-minute trips run June–Sept (tel: 207-244 7466).

Bass Harbor Head Lighthouse presents a classic Maine cameo. The view from the trails is magnificent.

To the Canadian border

Back on the mainland, continue north on Route 1 and turn south onto Route 186 to the small, unspoiled fishing village of **Winter Harbor**, so named because it does not freeze in the winter, and home to a fleet of lobster boats, and nearby **Schoodic Point**, a little-visited portion of Acadia National Park with fine views of Cadillac Mountain across the bay.

North on Route 1, Washington County is also known as "Sunrise County" for its easterly location. Tourism takes a back seat to lobstering, blueberry cultivation, and Christmas trees.

Head south off Route 1 on Route 187 about 12 miles (19km), continue through the fishing villages of Jonesport and Beals to the 1,540-acre (623-hectare) **Great Wass Island** ㉙. The Nature Conservancy property, with several somewhat difficult but very rewarding trails through the woods and along the coast, is one of the state's natural treasures.

Just off Route 1 in **Columbia Falls** ㉚, tour the elegant 1818 **Ruggles House** (146 Main Street; tel: 207-483 4637; www.ruggleshouse.org; June–mid-Oct daily; fee), which has a magnificent flying staircase and intricately carved woodwork. A few miles north, turn south onto Roque Bluffs Road

BELOW: puffins on Machias Seal Island.

for about 5 miles (8km) to **Roque Bluffs State Park** (tel: 207-255 3475; mid-May–mid-Oct daily; fee) for fabulous views, a beach (with incredibly cold water), and a much warmer freshwater pond. Bird watching is particularly good here.

Machias ㉛, on Route 1, was the site of the first naval battle of the Revolutionary War. In June 1775, a month after the Battle of Lexington, the British vessel *Margaretta* anchored off Machias to stand guard over a freight ship collecting wood with which to build British barracks in Boston. After debating their course of action at **Burnham Tavern** (Main and Free streets; tel: 207-255 6930; www.burnhamtavern.com; mid-June–Sept Mon–Sat; charge), the townspeople successfully attacked and captured the *Margaretta*. A re-enactment is held every June.

Approximately 90 percent of the world's blueberry crop is harvested in the area around Machias. "The Wild Blueberry Capital of the World" celebrates with a four-day blueberry festival every August.

North on Route 1 and east on Route 189 about 18 miles (29km), **Lubec** ㉜ is the easternmost town in the United States. **Tours of Lubec and Cobscook** (135 Maine Street; tel: 888-347 9302, 207-733 2997; www.toursoflubecandcobscook.com) offers interpretive history, farm, art, and nature tours with guides who are particularly knowledgeable. Some of the tours go into New Brunswick, Canada. You will need a passport to participate in those. The easternmost American soil is **West Quoddy Point**, a dramatic landscape of rocky cliffs and crashing surf graced with a candycane-striped 1858 lighthouse. The lighthouse is closed to the public. The **visitor center** is in the lighthouse keeper's house (tel: 207-733 2180; Memorial Day–mid-Oct daily; donation).

The lighthouse is part of 600-acre (240-hectare) **Quoddy Head State Park** (tel: 207-733 0911; mid-May–mid-Oct; entrance charge). Hiking trails wander past a peat bog and through stands of wild roses and day lilies. Whales are often spotted offshore, and you can look across the Quoddy Channel to Canada.

Campobello Park

From Lubec, you can cross over the Franklin D. Roosevelt Memorial Bridge to **Roosevelt Campobello International Park** ㉝ in Canada (tel: 506-752 2922; www.fdr.net; visitor center and cottage open daily late May–Columbus Day; trails open year-round). Franklin Delano Roosevelt summered on New Brunswick's Campobello Island from 1905 to 1921, when the island was a fashionable summer resort for well-off Americans and Canadians. He returned here only briefly during his presidency. After a self-guided tour of the 34-room Roosevelt house (audio tour can be downloaded to MP3 players), which remains as the family left it, visitors can enjoy 16 miles (26km) of walking trails, including a 2-mile (3km) stroll

TIP

Visitors crossing between Maine and Canada must show a passport or certified birth certificate and photo ID at the border. Single parents, grandparents, or guardians traveling with children may need proof of custody or notarized letters from the other parent authorizing travel.

BELOW: a pie-eating contest at the Machias Wild Blueberry Festival.

BELOW: a lumberjack statue of Paul Bunyon stands approximately 30ft (9 meters) high in a Bangor park.

along the ocean. (Note: You will pass through Canadian and US passport control stations. You will need a passport or passport card. Also note that New Brunswick is one hour ahead of Maine's time zone.)

Calais

Farther north on Route 1, **Calais** ③④ has three border crossings into Canada. It is the site of **St Crox Island International Historic Site**, the only such joint site (Route 1, 8 miles [13km] south of Calais; tel: 207-454 3871; daily sunrise–sunset; ranger station manned daily Memorial Day–mid-Oct). It commemorates the ill-fated French settlement of Pierre Dugua on the island in 1604. The bitter winter claimed the lives of nearly half of the 79 colonists. The mainland site has an interpretive trail peopled by bronze statues representing the settlers and the Passamaquoddy tribespeople who tried to help them. A model of the settlement overlooks the island. Access to the island itself is limited and discouraged.

The **Moosehorn National Wildlife Refuge** is the easternmost wildlife refuge on the Atlantic flyway, the primary avian migration route. There are two sections: the 1,700-acre (690-hectare) Baring Division just southwest of Calais on Route 1 and the 7,200-acre (2,900-hectare) Edmunds Division on Route 1 between Dennysville and Whiting, bordering the tidal waters of Cobscook Bay. Between them, there are over 50 miles (80km) of trails with observation decks for better viewing of waterfowl, shorebirds, upland game birds, and raptors. Fishing is good for smallmouth bass and yellow perch. Some areas are open for deer hunting. In the summer, there are ranger-led programs at both locations. Refuge Headquarters (tel: 207-454 7161; Mon–Fri 8am–4pm) is at the Calais location. The refuge itself is open daily from a half-hour before sunrise to a half-hour after sunset.

Bangor

In the 1830s, **Bangor** ③⑤, Maine's third-largest city, was the lumber capital of the world, wih more han 300 sawmills. Today little remains of those glory days except for the huge houses built by lumber barons that line its wide avenues, and a 31ft (9.4-meter) statue of legendary lumberjack Paul Bunyan on the outskirts of town.

As the retail, cultural and service center for northeastern Maine and the Maine highlands, Bangor has a busy downtown which takes advantage of the Penobscot River waterfront. The quality and variety of its performing arts and museums rival those in larger cities, while the shopping is a delightful mix of sophisticated fashion and outdoor practicality. Restaurants take advantage of Maine's seafood and local brewing.

The **Bangor Museum and Center for History** (159 Union Street; tel: 207-942 5766; www.bangormuseum. com; June–Sept Tue–Fri; charge) is a repository for more than 10,000 early photographs and daguerreotypes, plus an exhaustive collection of 19th-century clothing – gowns, walking-suits, day and evening dresses, shoes, hats, and accessories. The center's Civil War Museum displays a sword owned by Joshua Chamberlain and soldiers' diaries and letters.

A legendary modern author makes his home in the city. Stephen King's house on West Broadway is easy to spot – it's the handsome 1856 Italianate mansion surrounded by a wrought-iron fence decorated with bats and spiders. The **Maine Discovery Museum** (74 Main Street, tel: 207-262 7200; www.mainediscoverymuseum.org; Tue–Sun; also Mon late June–August; charge) is the largest children's museum north of Boston. It has three floors packed with hands-on activities.

The Hudson Museum (second floor of the Collins Center for the Arts; tel: 207-581 1901; Mon–Sat), at the Orono campus of the University of Maine, focuses on ethnographic and archaeological collections, with a huge inventory of Pre-Columbian ceramics and gold pre-dating the arrival of the Spanish. Its Native American and Native Alaskan collection is one of the most comprehensive in the country. The gleaming **Collins Center for the Arts** (tel: 207-581 1755; www. collinscenterforthearts.com) is home to the Bangor Symphony and hosts a continuing, wide-ranging schedule of visiting performers.

THE NORTH WOODS

Much of the northernmost part of Maine consists of millions of acres of softwood foest. For an overiew of the logging boom that swept the area in the mid-19th century, visit the **Lumberman's Museum** ㊱ (61 Shin Pond Road, Patten; tel: 207-528 2650; Memorial Day–June Fri–Sun, July–mid-Oct Tue–Sun). Nine buildings of exhibits include a reconstructed 1860s cabin and a blacksmith shop.

Continue west on Route 159 to **Baxter State Park** ㊲ (tel: 207-723 5140), the legacy of Percival Baxter, governor from 1920 to 1925. When the state legislature refused to purchase and protect this land, he bought a total of 201,018 acres (81,211 hectares)

Geographically, Maine is larger than all the other New England states combined. In fact, Arostook County in Maine is larger than the combined size of Connecticut and Rhode Island.

BELOW: viewing Mount Katahdin in Baxter State Park.

Maine's Lighthouses

The craggy coast of Maine is only 250 miles (402km) long as the seagull flies, but when you straighten out the coves, harbors, inlets, and estuaries, it adds up to an impressive 3,478 miles (5,597km)

It's no surprise that 63 lighthouses pepper the treacherously rocky shoreline from Whaleback Light, guarding the Piscatagua River on the Maine–New Hampshire border in the south, to Whitlocks Mill on the St Croix River to the north and the East Quoddy Lighthouse on Campobello Island in Canada.

Although many of the lighthouses have been replaced by ocean buoys and other modern aids to navigation, the iconic image of the tall sentinels bravely sending out beacons of protection as they stand atop granite cliff pummeled by angry waves remains both dramatic and romantic. While their purpose was uniform – to guard ships through dangerous waters – each has a unique story. Portland Head Light, the oldest in Maine, was authorized by President George Washington in 1791. East Quoddy Lighthouse protected legitimate shipping,

but cramped the style of smugglers operating between the US and Canada. It's accessible at low tide by those willing to scramble over the rocks and seaweed to reach it. Owls Head Light near Rockland is reputedly haunted by a lighthouse keeper still watching over his station.

The coastline along Bar Harbor, Bristol, and Machias is dotted with lights on shore and the nearby islands. Only a handful of lighthouses allow visitors inside, although several have museums. One which provides both is Pemaquid Point near Bristol. If it looks familiar, that's because it's the light used on the Maine quarter. The tower and small fishermen's museum are open from May to October.

Rockland Breakwater Light is another good stop. The breakwater was built to protect the town's harbor from storm damage, but it became a hazard to navigation so the lighthouse was built to guide ships safely into the harbor. It's also open for tours in the summer and is the location of the Maine Lighthouse Museum (open daily; charge). Just down the coast in Port Clyde, the keeper's house at Marshall Point has another small display about lighthouse life.

It's possible to stay at some lighthouses. Goose Rocks Light (tel: 207-867 4747; www.beacon preservation.org) in the waters of the Fox Islands, and reachable only by boat, can take up to six people for an overnight stay. The light is free-standing, without an island or anywhere to go except the light itself.

There's a one-bedroom apartment in the keeper's house at Pemaquid Point (tel: 207-563 6500; www.mainecoastcottages.com) that's available for weekly rental. You bring your own linens and food when you stay at Little River Light (tel: 207-259 3833; www.littleriverlight.org) near the unspoiled fishing village of Cutler. You'll be ferried out to the island; after that, you're on your own to cook out, read a book, and savor the stars at night.

It's not a keeper's house or a lighthouse itself, but the Coast Guard Life Saving Station at Popham Beach (tel: 207-389 2409; www.pophambeach-bandb.com) has been converted into a B&B. From the rooms and the lookout tower, there are fine views of the ocean, the Kennebec River, and the Pond Island and Seguin Island lighthouses.

Left: Owl's Head Lighthouse, from 1826, stands guard at the entrance of Rockland Harbor on Western Penobscot Bay.

and deeded them to the state, requiring only that the tract remain "forever wild." The northern terminus of the 2,175-mile (3,500km) Appalachian Trail is the 5,267ft (1,605-meter) Mt Katahdin. Dozens of trails, from easy meanders to tough technical climbs, lace the park.

Running northward from the northwest corner of Baxter State Park, the **Allagash Wilderness Waterway** provides 92 miles (150km) of America's most scenic canoeing; the trip takes a week to 10 days. South of the park, the Penobscot River's West Branch offers hair-raising white-water rafting, through granite-walled **Ripogenus Gorge**. Katahdin Outfitters (tel: 800-862 2663; www.katahdinoutfitters.com) and Penobscot Adventures (tel: 877-356 0386; www.penobscotadventures. com) both offer a variety of canoeing and white-water trips.

To the west of the park, accessible only by boat or float plane, is the preserved 19th-century logging town of **Chesuncook** ⑱. The **Chesuncook Lake House** (tel: 207-745 5330) in

this lovely little village welcomes outdoors-oriented guests eager to leave the 21st century behind.

Several dozen such "camps," unchanged for decades, are tucked away in this region pocked with lakes and ponds, where fish are plentiful and moose outnumber people. Many cluster around **Moosehead Lake**, the largest body of fresh water entirely in New England, with 320 miles (510km) of shoreline.

Although tiny **Greenville** ⑲, at the southern end of the lake, has grown into a year-round vacation destination with several fine B&Bs, fishing resorts, and restaurants, it still retains its air of a wilderness hideaway. Three- and four-hour cruises on the lake and to Mt Kineo are offered aboard the National Historic Landmark *Katahdin* (tel: 207-695 2716; www.katahdin-cruises.com), a restored 1914 lake steamboat, the last of a fleet of over 50 vessels that once steamed up the lake carrying passengers, mail, and supplies. The **Moosehead Marine Museum** (tel: 207-695 2716; Memorial Day–Columbus Day Mon–Sat; donation),

The Allagash Historical Museum.

BELOW: Moosehead Lake.

The American Civil War Memorial in the town of Bethel.

BELOW: antique cars out for a spin in Bethel.

next to the boat dock, holds steamboat memorabilia and early photographs of the Greenville area.

Another great way to get a full grasp of this mammoth lake is to take a float-plane tour; try Currier's Flying Service (Greenville Junction; tel: 207-695 2778).

Lily Bay State Park (tel: 207-695 2700; mid-May–mid-Oct; charge), 8 miles (13km) north of Greenville, has a fine sandy beach and a 2-mile (3.2km) lakeside walking trail.

Whitewater rafting

About 20 miles (32km) southwest of Greenville as the crow flies (or thrice that distance by car), **West Forks** 🐵 attracts thousands of adventurers eager to try whitewater rafting along the Kennebec and Dead rivers. Suitable for anyone over 10 and in reasonably good health, these thrilling descents take only a day and alternate roiling rapids with placid floats.

Several outfitters organize trips and provide lodging and meals. Among them: North Country Rivers (Bingham; tel: 800-348 8871; www.

ncrivers.com), Magic Falls Rafting (West Forks; tel: 207-663 2200; www.magicfalls.com), and Dead River Expeditions (West Forks; tel: 877-301 2040; www.deadriverexpeditions.com).

Western lakes and mountains

In the heart of Carrabassett Valley, the ski area at **Sugarloaf** 🐵 (Route 27; tel: 207-237 2000, 00-THE LOAF; www.sugarloaf.com), on Maine's second-highest peak, has a treeless top offering superb views (including Mt Katahdin and Mt Washington) and boasts a greater vertical descent (2,820ft/860 meters) than any other winter resort in New England. The area is a year-round resort; its 18-hole golf course is considered the best in Maine. It also has fly-fishing, and hiking and mountain-biking trails.

A useful base for Sugarloaf is **Kingfield** 🐵, 18 miles (29km) to the south, which has been a magnet for sporting types since the mid-19th century. It's been called the most beautifully preserved ski town east of Aspen, with all of the requisite cafés, shops, and sports-massage therapists. The town fostered a family of home-grown geniuses, whose accomplishments are showcased in the **Stanley Museum** (40 School Street; tel: 207-265 2729; June–Oct Tue–Sun, Nov–May Tue–Fri; charge). The twins, F.O. and F.E., invented the Stanley Steamer, which wowed enthusiasts at the first New England auto show in 1898 and set a land-speed record of 127mph (203kmh) in 1906. Three restored, working samples are garaged in this Georgian-style schoolhouse, which the family built for the town in 1903.

Grafton Notch

Some of Maine's prettiest and least visited scenery is near the New Hampshire border. **Bethel** 🐵 take its name, which means "House of God," from the Book of Genesis. It gained prominence as a spa town when

Dr John Gehring attracted to his clinic many Harvard academicians suffering from nervous disorders. The hotel he built in 1913 on the pretty town green, the **Bethel Inn** (tel: 800-654–0125; www.bethelinn.com), is an elegant, upscale, all-season resort.

Also in town is the National Historic Register **Moses Mason House** (10–14 Broad Street; tel: 207-824 2908; www.bethelhistorical.org; July–Aug Tue–Sun; charge). This 1813 Federal manse is a treasure house of American primitive painting; the itinerant muralist Rufus Porter decorated the entryway and second-floor landing with, respectively, a seascape and a forest tableau. The 1821 **O'Neil Robinson House** (adjacent; Tue–Fri, also Sat–Sun in July–Aug) has on-going, developing displays about the area's history.

North of town, in **Newry**, the **Sunday River ski resort** ❹❹ (Sunday River Road; tel: 207-824 3000 or 800-543 2754; www.sundayriver.com) covers seven mountains and has the largest snow-making system in New England. Off-season, chairlifts

(weekends late June–mid-Oct) carry visitors to the top for an exhilarating ride and spectacular views. The nearby 1872 **Artists' Covered Bridge** (closed to traffic) is a delightful spot for a swim or a picnic. It's named for its popularity among painters and photographers.

Head north on Route 26, which climbs into the fabulously scenic **Grafton Notch State Park** ❹❺ (tel: 207-824 2912), known for its rugged-back country hiking trails. Less strenuous trails lead to impressive waterfalls and gorges. The cascades are most impressive during the spring snow melt.

Rangeley Lakes region

Although both routes 4 and 17 leading to the town of **Rangeley** ❹❻, overlooking the 9-mile (14km) Rangeley Lake, are designated National Scenic Byways, Route 17 has the more spectacular scenery. The **Rangeley Lakes region** is actually a collection of 112 lakes and ponds, and has been popular with outdoors enthusiasts for more than a century. Not surprisingly, fishing and paddle sports are the big

Old Fort Western in Augusta is the oldest log fort in the United States, and was built in 1754 to promote settlement in the area.

BELOW: the State House and the Governor's residence, Blaine House.

In 1912, the 40-year-old Maine-born Leon Leonwood Bean decided to build a better hunting boot. He offered the waterproof boot with a money-back guarantee. Legend has it that 90 out of the first 100 pairs fell apart. True to his word, Bean replaced the defective boots and – after absorbing the loss – began building the legendary L.L.Bean empire.

BELOW: Augusta waterfront at sunrise.

draws here, but hikers find plenty to do and, in winter, **Saddleback Ski Area** (www.saddlebackmaine.com) welcomes downhill and cross-country skiers.

The capital city

Augusta ㊼, Maine's modest-sized capital (population 22,000), stands on the Kennebec River and began its days in 1628 as a trading post. Its gold-domed State House (State and Capitol streets; tel: 207-287 1400; weekdays) was designed by Charles Bulfinch in 1832. Renovations in recent years include a granite mural with text in English, French, and the Penobscot, Passamaquoddy, and Abenaki languages.

The superb **Maine State Museum** in the **State House** complex (tel: 207-287 2301; closed Mon) is the repository for artifacts and documents from prehistory to the present – from bark canoes and silver spoons to a three-story, water-powered working mill. You can easily spend a full day exploring the extensive galleries and exhibits.

The **Children's Discovery Museum** (171 Capital Street; tel: 207-622 2209; http://childrensdiscoverymuseum.org; Tue–Sat; charge) has a bank, grocery store, and restaurant designed to teach children how to cope with such places in later life, and there's a rainforest play area for toddlers.

The city's other major sight is **Old Fort Western**, built on the shore of the Kennebec River in 1754 and America's oldest wooden fort (16 Cory Street; tel: 207-626 2385; Memorial Day–Labor Day daily, Labor Day–Columbus Day weekends; Nov–Jan, first Sunday of month; charge). The stockade and blockhouses have been evocatively recreated, complete with replica cannons.

The only active Shaker community in the world is the **Sabbathday Lake Shaker Community** (Route 26, 12 miles/19km west of Exit 12 off the Maine Turnpike, 70 Shaker Road; museum Memorial Day–Columbus Day Mon–Sat; guided tours every hour on the half-hour only; charge). The museum is in several buildings on the grounds; the daily life of the Shakers continues around them.

RESTAURANTS AND BARS

Prices for a three-course dinner per person with a half-bottle of house wine:
$ = under $20
$$ = $20–45
$$$ = $45–60
$$$$ = over $60

Restaurants

Acadia

Jordan Pond House
Acadia National Park
Tel: 207-276 3610
www.thejordanpondhouse.com **$$**
The only full-service restaurant in Acadia Park, it has lobster stew, sandwiches, salads, and fish for lunch.

Augusta

Cloud 9
Senator Inn & Spa, 284 Western Avenue
Tel: 207-622 0320
www.senatorinn.com **$$–$$$**
Eclectic menu includes brick-oven pizzas with creative toppings like roasted pear, walnut, and Gorgonzola, and filet mignon, lobster ravioli, and chicken potpie.

Riverfront Barbeque & Grille
300 Water Street
Tel: 207-622 8899
www.rvierfrontbbq.com **$–$$**
One of the capital city's nicest surprises: respectable Memphis-style barbecue.

Bangor

Market/Bistro
56 Main Street
Tel: 207-941 9594
www.marketbistrobangor.com
$–$$
Energetic, enthusiastic kithen with a fresh food, "farm-to-table" philosophy. Flatbread pizza; grilled rib eye with a coffee-chocolate rub.

Sea Dog Brewing Company
26 Front Street
Tel: 207-947 8009
www.seadogbrewing.com **$–$$**
Award-winning hand-crafted ales and solid pub fare. Big sandwiches, burgers. (Also in South Portland and Topsham.)

Thistles
175 Exchange Street
Tel: 207-945 5480
www.thistlesrestaurant.com **$$$**
Classic international fine dining with Latin touches. Argentinian-style steak with chimichurri sauce, paella, crab cakes.

Bar Harbor

Galyn's
17 Main Street
Tel: 207-288 9706
www.gaylnsbarharbor.com **$$**
Comfortable restarant popular with he locals in 1890s house which has been a sailor's boarding house and a speakeasy. Great views. Lobster bisque, lobster linguini, quiches, stuffed portobellos.

Mother's Kitchen
1502 State Hwy. 102,
Salisbury Cove
Tel: 207-288 4403
www.motherskitchenfoods.com **$**
Good place to get sandwiches for picnics at Acadia Park, with an emphasis on locally sourced ingredients. Even have PB&J for kids.

Portside Grill
38 Cottage Street
Tel: 207-288 4086
www.portsidegrill.com **$$**
Celebrating Maine's seafood, prepared by chefs who love it. Non-seafood lovers also have great choices of well-prepared food.

Bath

Kennebec Tavern
119 Commercial Street
Tel: 207-442 9636
www.kennebectaven.com **$$**

Varied menu from casual sandwices to prime rib and "shore dinner" (steamed lobster, clam chowder, steamed clams, corn on the cob, and slaw). "Senior" menu – smaller portions of main menu items. Great old post-and-beam building.

Mae's Café and Bakery
160 Centre Street (Route 209)
Tel: 207-442 8577
www.maescafeandbakery.com **$–$$**
A popular spot for light, eclectic fare, microbrews, and pecan sticky buns.

Solo Bistro
128 Front Street
Tel: 207-443 3373
www.solobistro.com **$$–$$$**
Award-winning innovative

RIGHT: lobster roll and fries, the classic Maine fast food.

cuisine and excellent service. Garlic sesame pork tenderloin; grilled swordfish brochette. Three-course prix-fixe option.

Bethel

Cho Sun
141 Main Street
Tel: 207-824 7370
www.chosunrestaurant.com **$$**
Japanese and Korean cuisine sered by a chef and staff eager to share the love of their food and to introduce newcomers to the flavors.

The Jolly Drayman Pub
150 Mayville Road
Tel: 207-824 4717
www.briarleainn.com **$$**

True British pub grub: ploughman's, bangers and mash, all-you-can-eat fish and chips (Thurs and Fri); also some Indian dishes (beef vindaloo, chicken korma).

22 Broad Street
22 Broad Street
Tel: 207-824 3496
www.22broadstreet.com
$$–$$$
Authentic Italian cuisine and Martini bar in a gracious 1848 Greek Revival house overlooking the town common. All homemade with local, fresh ingredients.

Blue Hill

Arborvine Restaurant
33 Tenney Hill
Tel: 207-374 2119
www.arborvine.com **$$–$$$**
Traditional American fare and candlelight dining in an 1823 Cape Cod–style house. Lighter dishes and

live entertainment next door in The Vinery. Deepwater Brewing Company is their own microbrew.

Boothbay Harbor Area

Boathouse Bistro Tapas House & Restaurant
12 By-Way
Tel: 207-633 0400
www.boathousebistro.com **$$**
Unhurried, casual coastal summer dining with a menu that's an alternative to the typical coastal fare. Long tapas menu from ceviche to Maine maple scallops; risotto, paella, grilled meats.

McSeagulls
14 Wharf St., at Pier 1
Tel: 207-633 5900
www.mcseagullsonline.com **$$**
A menu as long as the Maine coastline. Specializing in fish and lobster (prepared in an astonishing number of ways), they boast about visiting the docks several times a day. Large gluten-free menu; good vegetarian selections. First floor is pub-like setting; second floor is much quieter with a great view of the harbor. Outside terrace in the summer. Live music nightly.

Robinson's Wharf
20 Hendricks Hill Road
Tel: 207-633 3830
www.robinsons-wharf.com **$–$$**
Traditional lobster pound also offers chowders, fried fish, and homemade desserts. Seasonal.

Brooklin Inn
Route 175, Brooklin, Maine
Tel: 207-359 2777
www.brooklininn.com **$$$**

"Real food, classically prepared" in the dining room of this rural inn. Lighter menu in the upstairs pub. Emphasis on organically raised produce and meats, plus fresh Maine seafood. *Wine Spectator*–awarded wine list.

Brunswick

The Great Impasta
42 Maine Street
Tel: 207-729 5858
www.thegreatimpasta.com **$–$$**
Italian cucina as comortable as Grandmama's kitchen. Familiar dishes as well as regional fare from Umbria. Gluten-free and vegetarian/vegan menus. Certified "green" restaurant for its facilities, operations, and kitchen.

Camden

Atlantica Seafood Bistro
1 Bayview Landing
Tel: 207-236 6011
www.atlanticarestaurant.com
$$–$$$
This upscale harborfront bistro has a lovely deck and menu emphasizing creative fish preparations.

Cappy's Chowder House
1 Main Street
Tel: 207-236 2254
www.cappyschowder.com **$$**
Owned by folks whose families have lived here for generations, so they know seafood. Homemade chowders; lobster, clam, and crab rolls; non-seafoodies can try ribs (with Maine maple BBQ sauce), turkey hot pot pie.

Castine

The Pentagoet Inn

LEFT: Cappy's Chowder House in Camden.

26 Main Street
Tel: 207-326 8616
www.pentagoet.com **$$$**
New England specialties
an sumptuous desserts
served in the intimate, can-
dlelit dining room and
intriguing pub of a turreted
Victorian inn. Tasting menu
is a good option.

Deer Isle Village

Whale's Rib Tavern
Pilgrim's Inn, 20 Main Street
Tel: 207-348 6615; 888-778
705
www.pilgrimsinn.com **$$–$$$**
A casual, cozy spot whose
menu features fresh local
and made-in-Maine ingre-
dients. That includes the
microbrews.

Freeport

Corsican Restaurant
9 Mechanic Street
Tel: 207-865 9421
www.corsicanrestaurant.com
$–$$
Good place to take a break
frm shopping or to recover
when you're done. Casual
setting with wide range of
chowders, salads, pastas,
wraps, and very nice
desserts.

Harraseeket Inn
162 Main Street
Tel: 207-865 9377; 800-865
9377
www.harraseeketinn.com
$$–$$$$
Inn dining room has big
breakfast buffet daily and
lunch buffet Mon–Fri;
Broad Arrow Tavern Dining
Room has open kitchen,
wood-fired oven and grill.
Maine lobster Sunday
brunch buffet was voted
best buffet in Maine.

Georgetown (near Bath)

Robinhood Free Meetinghouse
Robinhood Road off Route 127
Tel: 207-371 2188
www.robinhood-
meetinghouse.com **$$–$$$$**
Five-star dining in an 1855
meetinghouse set amid
towering pines. Eclectic
menu features regional
New England, plus Cajun
and Asian flavors. Signature
dishes include 72-layer
cream-cheese biscuits.

Greenville

Auntie M's
13 Lily Bay Road
Tel: 207-695 2238 **$**
The place for breakfast,
hich is served al day.
Opens 5am for nglers,
hunters, hikers, and
insomniacs. Good lunch
fare, sandwiches, hearty
stews. Will pack lunches
for daytrippers. Daily 5am–
3pm. Cash only.

The Black Frog
17 Pritham Avenue (Route 15)
Tel: 207-695 1100
www.theblackfrog.com **$–$$**
Very casual, fun place in
the heart of town. Popular
with locals, outdoor types,
and snowmobilers in win-
ter. Only thin-crust pizza in
town, plus good sand-
wiches, soups, and salads.
Friendly bar.

The Rod-N-Reel
44 Pritham Avenue
Tel: 207-695 0388
www.rodnreel.com **$$**
Casual, family-friendly res-
taurant featuring all made-
from-scratch food: chili is a
cookoff winner, long-sim-
mered French onion soup

and haddock chowder, hand-
cut NY sirloin and prime rib.

Harpswell

Dolphin Marina & Restaurant
Basin Point Road
Tel: 207-833 6000
www.dolphinmarinaand
restaurant.com **$$**
Specializing in Maine
coastal fare, which means
lobster, clams, and fish.
Chowders, lobster stew,
blueberry muffins. Limited
choices for non-seafood
eaters. On the water's edge
overlooking Casco Bay.

Kennebunkport
Arundel Wharf
43 Ocean Avenue
Tel: 207-967 3444
www.arundelwharf.com **$$–$$$**
Casual waterfront dning in a
former sip's chandlery.
Lobster stew, prime rib,
game, vegetarian lasagna.
Good "small plate" menu,
burgers, fried clams. Deck in
summer; fireplace in winter.

Bandaloop
2 Dock Square
Tel: 207-967 4994
www.bandaloop.biz **$$**
Organic, local, lots of vege-
tarian and vegan choices.
Meats are free from feed-
lots and chemicals.
Innovative and tasty.

Cape Arundel Inn
Ocean Avenue
Tel: 207-967 2125
www.capearundelinn.com **$$$$**
Perhaps the finest dining
and the finest view in
Maine. Elegant, exquisitely
prepared dishes served in
a formal setting with unre-
stricted ocean views.

Grissini Italian Bistro
27 Western Avenue (Route 9)
Tel: 207-967 2211
www.restaurantgrissini.com
$$–$$$
When you can't bear the
thought of another lobster
roll. A stylish Italian restau-
rant featuring Northern
Italian cuisine. The "grotto"

RIGHT: an alternative to seafood in Portland.

menu in the bar is lighter, but equally nice.

One Dock
1 Dock Square at Kennebunkport Inn
Tel: 207-967 2621
www.onedock.com **$$$**
Native Maine cuisine with fusion flare using fresh local seafood and produce. Make a meal off the "small plate" menu.

Kingfield

Orange Cat Cafe
329 Main Street
Tel: 207-265 2860
www.orangecatcafe.com **$**
Good place for local gossi and atmosphere. Breakfast served all day. Excellent

lunch sandwiches. Low-carb preparations available.

Kittery

Anneke Jans
60 Wallingford Square
Tel: 207-439 0001
www.annekejans.net **$–$$$**
Hot new restaurant on the Kittery cene. Neighborhood bistro style ambience; menu reflects seasonal availability: mussels with bacon, shallots, white wine, and cream; salmon with pea puree and black trumpet mushrooms; vanilla bread pudding with spiced rum caramel and cinnamon whipped cream.

Bob's Clam Hut
315 Route 1
Tel: 207-439 4233
www.bobsclamhut.com **$**
This 50+-year-old local institution, next to the Kittery Trading Post, knows

how to fry fish.

Machias

Helen's Restaurant
111 Main Street (Route 1)
Tel: 207-255 8423
www.helensrestaurant machias.co **$–$$**
Down-home, family cooking in a down-home, locals-heavy restaurant. Desserts are incredible.

Northeast Harbor

Peabody at the Asticou Inn
15 Peabody Drive
Tel: 207-276 3344; 800-258 3373
www.asticou.com **$$$$**
Maine standards given the "haute cuisine" treatment in a grand dining room overlooking the sea. Jackets at dinner. Reservations essential.

Ogunquit

Clay Hill
220 Clay Hill Road
Tel: 207-362 2272
www.clayhillfarm.com **$$–$$$$**
Special-occasion restaurant seton the grounds of a wildlife and bird sanctuary. Piano music Tue–Sat.

MC Perkins Cove
111 Perkins Cove Road
Tel: 207-646 6263
www.mcperkinscove.com **$$–$$$**
Contemporary American cuisine with view of the ocean: oyster bar; white pizza, tea-smoked duck breast, pan-fried cod. "Dressy casual."

The Front Porch
9 Shore Drive
Tel: 207-646 4005
www.thefrontporch.net **$$**

Relaxed atmosphere, food inspired by local favorites with a contemporary tweak. Baked haddock pie, Delmonico steak, blackened burgers, flat breads, baked lobster fondue.

Portland

555
555 Congress Street
Tel: 207-761 0555
www.fivefifty-five.com **$$$**
Sophisticated, innovative, creativ dishes conjured by the Maine Restaurant Association's "Chef of the Year." Lamb with hand-rolled fettuccini, Casco Bay lemon sole with curry-lime butter, cheese plates, strawberry-hibiscus soup.

Back Bay Grill
65 Portland Street
Tel: 207-772 8833
www.backbaygrill.com **$$**
Sophisticated fare with an international flare, creating seasonal dishes such as truffled beef tartare or salmon with orange and goat cheese risotto.

Bintliff's American Grill
98 Portland Street
Tel: 207-774 0005
www.bintliffsamericancafe.com **$**
Open daily for brunch 7am–2pm, serving internationally influenced American cuisine like open-faced brie and tomato sandwiches and curry tofu sauté, as well as classic favorites such as eggs Benedict.

Fore Street and Company
33 Wharf Street
Tel: 207-775 0887
www.forestreet.biz **$$–$$$**
Hardwood- and apple-wood-grilled

LEFT: outdoor eating by Casco Bay, Portland.

meats, seafood, game, and vegetables. Menu changes nightly to reflect freshest ingredients.

Grace
15 Chestnut Street
Tel: 207-828 4422
www.restaurantgrace.com
$$–$$$
New hotspot in historic old church building. Contemporary American cuisine with Asian touches: butterfish with lemongrass-tomato puree, vegan stir-fry, oyster sampler.

Rangeley

Farmhouse Inn
2057 Main Street
Tel: 207-864 5805
www.rangeleyfarmhouseinn.com **$$**
Southwest cuisine in the dining room of the 1865 farmhouse or on the terrace overlooking the lake. Wildberry-chipotle BBQ ribs, mussels, and chorizo.

Rockland

Cafe Miranda
15 Oak Street
Tel: 207-594 2034
www.cafemiranda.com **$$**
Cozy bistro with bi menu that has funwith many ethnic accents. Fresh housemade pasta, wood-oven pizza.

Primo Restaurant
2 South Main Street
Tel: 207-596 0770
www.primorestaurant.com
$$–$$$
Three dining areas. Downstairs is special-event dining; jackets and reservations required. Upstairs, the "Counter Room" has a traditional trattoria feel; meats and farmstead cheeses are on

display; and the open-kitchen concept allows diners to sit and watch as chefs prepare the food. The "Bar Room" has both bar and table seating and a relaxed atmosphere.

Sargentville

El El Frijole
41 Caterpillar Hill Road
Tel: 207-359 2486
www.elelfrijoles.com **$–$$**
A cut above the "Mexican pltter" restaurant. "From scratch" kitchen. Carnitas, polla asado, grilled veggies Mexican-style, and, of course, a Mexican take on lobster.

Southwest Harbor

Beal's Lobster Pier
182 Clark Point Road
Tel: 207-244 7178
www.bealslobster.com **$$**
Classic wharfside lobstershack.

Café Drydock & Inn
357 Main Street
Tel: 207-244 5842
www.cafedrydockinn.com
$$–$$$
Chicken Boursin, scallops Mornay, and home-made soups and chowders in this popular inn. Good wine list.

Fiddler's Green
411 Main Street
Tel: 207-244 9416
www.fiddlersgreenrestaurant.com **$$$**
Seasonal, organic produce, farm-raised meats, fresh fish, creative menu. Lots of steak, farm-to-table roasted pig, Asian stir-fry. Restaurant also has great ocean view.

Wiscasset

Red's Eats
Water Street (Route 1)
Tel: 207-882 6128 **$**

This tiny take-outbooth just south of thebridge serves what sme say is the state's best lobster roll. No credit cards.

Sarah's Cafe
Route 1 and Water Street
Tel: 207-882 7504
www.sarahscafe.com **$–$$**
Large menu of homemade treats. Lobsters come from her dad's and brother's lobster boat. "Soup Bar." Fresh-baked breads, stuffed peppers, "rolled" stuffed pizza.

The Squire Tarbox Inn
1181 Main Road, Route 144
Tel: 207-882 7693
www.squiretarboxinn.com **$$$**
The Swiss chef at this 18th-century farmhouse inn prepares specialties such as Scandinavian dill-cured salmon and rosemary-roasted rack of lamb.

York

Ruby's Genuine Brick Oven
433 Route 1
Tel: 207-363 7980
www.rubysbrickoven.com **$**
Brick-oven pizza, pasta, ribs fajitas, burgers. Open-concept kitchen; outdoor patio. Sports TV in bar.

The Restaurant at Dockside Guest Quarters
22 Harris Island Road
Tel: 207-363 2868
www.docksidegq.com **$$–$$$**
Classic Maine, yacht-club feel without the pretense. From fried clams and steamed lobsters to classic bouillabaisse, all with a harbor view.

The Stolen Menu Cafe
127 Long Sands Road
Tel: 207-363 0298
www.thestolenmenucafe.com **$**
Breakfast and lunch stop with great omelets and

breakfast sandwiches; the lunch board is extensive.

Bars

Asylum Complex
121 Center Street, Portland
Tel: 207-772 8374
Non-stop TV action in sports bar; music downstairs; nightclub with state-of-the-art sound system and room for 700 revelers.

Carmen Verandah
119 Main Street, Bar Harbor
Tel: 207-288 2766
Pool, darts, and largest dance floor in Bar Harbor. Music nightly; live music on weekends draws throngs to this lively spot overlooking the village green.

Gin Mill
30 Water Street, Augusta
Tel: 207-622 8899
Classy lounge with 35ft-long bar, 100 beers, single malt Scotch and single batch Bourbon. Live entertainment. Thur–Sat.

The Great Lost Bear
540 Forest Street, Portland
Tel: 207-772 0300
One of Maine's great "beer bars" serves more than 60 labels, including 15 Maine microbrews. Menu includes more than 20 hamburgers.

Gritty McDuff's Brewpub
187 Lower Main Street, Freeport
Tel: 207-865 4321
One of Maine's original brew pubs. Ales and seasonal beers brewed on-site. Full pub menu. (Other locations in Auburn and Portland.)

Rooster's Road House
159 Mayville Road, Bethel
Tel: 207-824 0309
Four TVs, Wi-Fi, great sound system. Very popular with the ski crowd.

☀ INSIGHT GUIDE   **TRAVEL TIPS**
NEW ENGLAND

TRANSPORTATION

GETTING THERE AND GETTING AROUND

GETTING THERE

Flying is by far the easiest way to get to New England from abroad. If you come overland from elsewhere in the US, cars are the preferred mode of travel. Trains are less frequent than flights, and although buses connect most cities and several major towns, they are not much cheaper than a discount airfare, take significantly longer, and are less comfortable.

By Air

Virtually all international flights arrive at Boston's Logan Airport. Most major European locations have non-stop flights to Boston. If coming from Australia or Asia, you will probably land in Los Angeles or New York. There are shuttle flights from New York with Delta, JetBlue, US Airways, Air Canada, United, and Continental. You may find it easier and more economical to rent a car and drive.

Most major US carriers service the New England states. A variety of discount fares and special deals are offered, and many of the lowest are available on their own websites.

Smaller airports are in Hartford CT, Portland and Bangor ME, Manchester NH, Burlington VT, and Providence RI.

During holidays it may be difficult to find a flight, especially at Thanksgiving, when most of the US seems to be on the move.

Clearing customs can take a very long time, depending on how many flights have arrived at the same time and the current level of security enforcement. If you have a connecting flight, the more time between flights, the better. Sometimes, you can jump the

queue if you can prove to the security people that you are on a tight schedule, but there's no guarantee of that.

Airlines

Major airlines include:
Aer Lingus: tel: 800-474 7424; www.aerlingus.com
Air Canada: tel: 800-247 2262; www.aircanada.com
Air France: tel: 800-237 2747; www.airfrance.com
American Airlines: tel: 800-433 7300; www.aa.com
British Airways: tel: 800-247 9297; www.britishairways.com
Continental: tel: 800-525 0280; www.continental.ocm
Cape Air: tel: 800-352 0714; www.flycapeair.com
Delta: tel: 800-221 1212; www.delta.com
Jet Blue: tel: 800-538 2583; www.jetblue.com
Southwest Airlines: tel: 800-435 9792; www.southwest.com
United Airlines: tel: 800-864-8331; www.united.com
US Airways: tel: 800-428 4322; www.usairways.com
Virgin Atlantic: tel: 800-862 8621; www.virgin-atlantic.com

By Train

Amtrak (tel: 800-872 7245; www.amtrak.com) provides rail services to New England from Washington DC, Philadelphia, and New York, routing through coastal Connecticut and Rhode Island and terminating in Boston. The Acela Express, which travels at speeds of up to 150mph (240kmh), costs more than regular trains but is much quicker. Another route extends from Washington and New York to New Haven CT,

Springfield MA, and St Albans VT. Amtrak's Downeaster (tel: 207-780 1000; www.amtrakdowneaster.com) runs between Boston and Portland ME. Commuter trains link Boston with smaller towns in Massachusetts and Rhode Island.

International travelers (but not Canadians) planning to travel extensively on Amtrak can purchase a USA Rail Pass, good for 15 or 30 days. Rates are reduced; children ages 2–15 are half-price (under 2, free). Pass holders cannot use the Acela, and advance tickets and reservations are needed.

By Boat

The new Cruiseport Boston in South Boston, which opened in 2011, is the port for transatlantic passenger ships as well as cruise vessels for the Norwegian Cruise Line, Holland America, and Royal Caribbean.

GETTING AROUND

Boston

To and From the Airport

Boston's Logan Airport, 3 miles (5km) from downtown, is easily accessible by public transportation. A free shuttle marked "Massport" transports passengers from all airline terminals to the MBTA Airport station (Blue Line); it's also reached by the Silver Line buses, which stop at every terminal, and the water shuttle dock, where the Harbor Express water shuttle (tel: 617-222 6999; www.harborexpress.com) runs to Long Wharf and Quincy; City Water Taxi (tel: 617-422 0392;

www.citywatertaxi.com) stops at 20 locations in the Boston Harbor. The 1.6-mile (2.6km) Ted Williams Tunnel (toll payable) starts close to the car rental area and connects the airport easily with downtown and the Massachusetts Turnpike (also toll). Scheduled van services include Boston-Logan Super Shuttle (tel: 617-567 8900; www. bostonloganairportshuttle.com) and Star Shuttle (tel: 877-970 7827; www.starshuttleboston.com). Taxis from the airport to central Boston cost about $25 per person.

By Bike

Boston launched Hubway in 2011, a program of bike rentals in the downtown. More than 600 bikes are available at 61 sidewalk kiosks at a cost of $5/day. Most of the rental racks are near MBTA stops. The city has 38 miles (61km) of bike lanes.

By Car

Boston is not particularly car-friendly. Its narrow streets are congested and parking is often hard to find and expensive. The city center is compact enough that walking is a good idea.

By Public Transportation

Boston's public transportation system, universally called the "T," provides excellent coverage of the city and surrounding suburbs. A map is posted at many locations, particularly near tourist areas. Fees vary with time and distance. The "Charlie Card" pass is a pre-paid, rechargeable card useable on all "T" services. Information on the "T," including route maps and schedules, is available at www.mbta.com.

New England

By Air

Flying makes sense only if time is essential.

Cape Air (tel: 800-352 0714; www. flycapeair.cmo) and AirTran (tel: 800-247 8726; www.airtran.com) are both regional carriers.

The following New England locations have airports with scheduled regional services:
Massachusetts: Hyannis, Martha's Vineyard, Nantucket, New Bedford, Worcester
Maine: Bangor, Portland, Bar Harbor
Connecticut: Bradley Airport (near Hartford), Bridgeport, Groton, New Haven
Vermont: Burlington, Rutland
New Hampshire: Lebanon-Hanover, Manchester
Rhode Island: Providence

By Bus

Peter Pan (www.peterpanbus.com) operates the most extensive New England service. Many bus services coordinate connections with AMTRAK RAIL schedules.

C&J Trailways (tel: 800-258 7111; www.ridecj.com). Northeastern Massachusetts, New Hampshire, southern Maine, Boston's South Station and Logan Airport.

Concord Trailways (tel: 800-639 3317; www.concordcoachlines.com). Maine, New Hampshire, Newburyport MA, Boston's South Station and Logan Airport.

Greyhound (tel: 800 231 2222; www.greyhound.com). From New York to larger cities only.

Plymouth & Brockton (tel: 508-746 0378; www.p-bo.com). Cape Cod and Massachusetts' South Shore to Boston and Logan Airport.

By Train

Amtrak (tel: 800-872 7245; www. amtrak.com) services New England (see "Getting There" section).

Connecticut is served by **Metro-North** (tel: 800-638 7646), with trains between New York City's Grand Central Station and New Haven, New Canaan, Danbury, and Waterbury.

Boston has numerous commuter lines operated by the Massachusetts Bay Transport Authority (MBTA; www.mbta. com), from Boston to outlying towns.

By Car

Although the network of airplanes, buses, trains, ferries, and taxis is reliable, having your own car is the easiest way to get around (except in the congested heart of Boston), and it also offers the greatest opportunity for getting off the beaten path.

Highways

Interstate highways make distance traveling easy. You can travel from Boston to Burlington VT, a distance of 216 miles (348km) in about 4 hours.

Secondary Roads

Travel on secondary roads is much more scenic, if slower. However, beware of dirt roads – usually represented by a broken line – in mud season (typically, March into late April), when melting snow turns them into rutted and slippery quagmires. Mountain roads may be closed in winter.

Car Rental

All the major US car-rental firms are at airports and frequently in town at major cities. It's best to book ahead and take advantage of deals. Often

ABOVE: parking regulations are posted.

they tie in with hotel discounts.
Alamo: tel: 800-327 9633; www. alamo.com
Avis: tel: 800-331 1212; www.avis.com
Budget: tel: 800-527 0700; www. budget.com
Enterprise: tel: 800-261 7331; www. enterprise.com. Rents cars to those 21 years of age and older.
Hertz: tel: 800-654 3131; www. hertz.com
Thrifty: tel: 800-367 2277; www. thrifty.com

Legal requirements

Most car-rental agencies require drivers to be at least 25 and to hold a major credit card and a driver's license that is current and has been valid for at least a year; some will accept a cash deposit, sometimes as high as $500, in lieu of a credit card.

Foreign travelers will need to show an international driver's license or a license from their own country.

Insurance

Liability is not included in the terms of your lease, so advertised rates usually do not include additional fees for insurance. Collision Damage Waiver (CDW) is recommended, as it covers you if someone else damages your car. Check your own car insurance coverage; sometimes it covers rental cars. Some credit cards offer coverage on rental cars, something the car-rental firms do not tell you.

Rules of the Road

States and municipalities have specific laws and regulations regarding parking, speed limits, and the like; most are clearly posted. Speed limits on some country roads may not be well posted, and can range from 20 to 50mph (32–80kmh): be sure to find out what the local regulations are.

The speed limit on interstate highways is mostly 65mph (100kmh),

ABOVE: ferry boats in Portland, Maine.

although portions in built-up areas may be limited to 55 mph (90kmh) or lower. Enforcement, though sporadic, can be strict, with high penalties. Drunk-driving penalties are very severe in all states.

Roads with solid lines down the middle are "no passing" zones. But in Vermont passing is legal at any time except where explicitly posted as "no passing" (this is a nod to the state's rural character, where tractors and farm vehicles often travel at slow speeds).

Moose and deer are particularly active at dawn and dusk, and are a hazard to drivers on country roads, particularly in northern New England. If a deer runs in front of your car, slow down or stop – they often travel in groups and a second or third one may not be far behind. Moose, however, don't usually run. Generally weighing between 800 and 1,200lbs, they don't need to. Give them the right of way, too.

Seatbelts

These are obligatory for all occupants. In some states the police may stop vehicles and ticket unbelted passengers. Children under 6 must be buckled into safety seats or a proper child restraint, and in some states children must sit in the back seat. Many rental firms supply child seats for a small extra cost.

Fuel

Fuel is lead-free and stations are plentiful, and often open 24 hours a day near major highways (otherwise, usually 5 or 6am until 10 or 11pm). Many pumps can be activated by credit cards. British travelers should note that the US gallon is 17 percent smaller than the English equivalent. Metric users note that 1 gallon equals 3.8 liters.

Special Considerations

Unless otherwise posted, a right-hand turn at a red light is permitted. On sighting a school bus that has stopped to load or unload children, drivers in both directions must stop

completely before reaching the bus and may not proceed until the flashing red warning signals on the school bus have been switched off.

Ambulances, fire engines, and police cars with emergency lights on have right of way. Pull over, and wait until they've passed before proceeding.

Rotaries (roundabouts), especially in Boston, require caution. The official rule is that the cars already in the circle have the right of way in exiting, but this rule is often ignored in practice. It's best to proceed carefully, whether entering or exiting.

Hitchhiking and Car-Jacking

Hitchhiking is discouraged; so is picking up hitchhikers. Car-jackings are rare, but not unheard of. When you pick up your rental vehicle, ask the clerk which areas to avoid.

Breakdown

Some highways have emergency phones every few miles. You can also call tel: 911 on your cell phone for help. Otherwise, park with the hood raised and a police patrol car will stop. The **American Automobile Association** (tel: 800-222 4357; www.aaa.com) offers reciprocal breakdown services with some affiliated firms in other countries, and provides members with excellent information on road conditions.

Parking

You must park in the direction of traffic, and never by a fire hydrant. A yellow or red line on the curb means no parking is allowed. In some towns a white line along the curb shows where you can park.

Traffic/Road Conditions

For all New England States, visit www.usroadconditions.com.

Boston: For up-to-the-minute traffic information, tel: 617-374 1234; www.mass.gov/eot. WBZ radio provides traffic updates at 10:30am and at www.wbztv.com.

By Water

Ferries can save travelers hours of driving time, and, in Massachusetts and Maine, provide transportation to many of the islands. Some ferries service both passengers and vehicles; others are passenger-only. Reservations are highly recommended at all times and mandatory during peak tourist season when you're planning to transport a vehicle. During off-season, ferries may have limited schedules or may suspend operations.

Popular ferry routes

It is fairly easy to travel around New England by ferry, if you don't mind taking the scenic route. Some of the most popular routes take you from Boston out to Cape, or from Long Island back to the mainland.

Boston's Logan Airport to downtown Boston, including stops along Boston Harbor and at Long Wharf (MBTA; tel: 800-392 6100/617-222 3200; www.mbta.com). A free bus shuttle (Route 66 bus) runs between all airport terminals and the airport dock. Other MBTA ferry routes include Long Wharf to Charlestown Navy Yard; and Hull to Long Wharf and Logan Airport.

Boston to Provincetown (Cape Cod). Ferries include the passenger-only **Provincetown Fast Ferry** from Long Wharf (tel: 877-733 9425; www.provincetown.com) and **Bay State Cruise Ferry** (tel: 877-783 3779; www.baystatecruisecompany.com), which is accessed by the MBTA's Silver Line.

Woods Hole (Falmouth, Cape Cod) to Martha's Vineyard: **Steamship Authority** (tel: 508-477 8600; www.steamshipauthority.com).

Hyannis (Cape Cod) to Nantucket: **Steamship Authority** (tel: 508-495 3278; www.steamshipauthority.com).

Hyannis to Martha's Vineyard: passenger-only **Hy-Line Fast Ferry** (tel: 508-778 2600; www.hy-linecruises.com).

New Bedford MA to Martha's Vineyard: **New England Fast Ferry** (tel: 866-683 3779; www.nefastferry.com); the company also offers a less expensive, slower ferry.

Orient Point, Long Island NY to New London CT: **Cross Sound Ferry** (tel: 860-443 5281; www.longislandferry.com).

Montauk, Long Island NY to Block Island RI (passengers only): **Viking Fleet** (tel: 631-668 5700; www.viking fleet.com).

Quonset Point RI to Martha's Vineyard (shuttle from Amtrak and Providence Airport): **Vineyard Fast Ferry** (tel: 401-295 4040; www.vineyardfastferry.com).

Port Jefferson, Long Island to Bridgeport CT: **Bridgeport & Port Jefferson Ferry Company** (tel: 888-443 3779; www.bpjferry.com).

Maine State Ferries (tel: 207-596 5400; www.state.me.us/mdot/opt/ferry/maine-ferry-service.php).

Lake **Champlain Ferries** from Charlotte, Burlington, and Grand Isle VT to Essex, Port Kent, and Plattsburg NY (tel: 802-864 9804; www.lake champlainferries.com).

ACCOMMODATIONS

HOTELS, YOUTH HOSTELS, BED AND BREAKFAST

CHOOSING LODGINGS

Many lodgings close for at least part of the winter, unless they're in ski territory. Some close for "mud season," generally mid-March through April, and in November between autumn foliage and ski seasons.

Rates quoted are the range from low to high season. In general, the least expensive time to travel is November–April, although December–early March is a peak time for lodgings at or near ski areas. High seasons are during summer months and during foliage season, generally late September–mid- to late October. During these times many lodgings add a premium to their rates and may require a minimum stay of two or three nights.

Taxes

Each state has a lodging tax ranging from 6 percent to 15 percent; and some cities, including Boston and Cambridge, tack on an additional tax. Most city hotels charge $25–35 a night for parking.

Smoking

Most lodgings ban smoking on the premises or reserve just a few rooms for smokers. Some areas, like the city of Boston, ban smoking in public lodgings.

Country Inns and B&Bs

If you are tired of motels and hotels, these lodgings are a wonderful option. They range from weathered farmhouses with huge fireplaces and homemade muffins at breakfast to grand elegance. Some require sharing a bathroom and others "require" you to relax by not providing TVs or in-room phones. Most are warm and welcoming, though a few can seem slightly pretentious.

Inns and Resorts of New England (www.innsandresortsofnewengland.com) has a site specially designed for visitors from the UK and Germany.

Other resources include **Bed & Breakfast Agency of Boston** (tel: 800-248 9262, in UK: 0800-895 128; www.boston-bnbagency.com), **Host Homes of Boston** (tel: 800-600 1308/617-244 1308; www.hosthomesofboston.com), and **Bed and Breakfast Associates Bay Colony** (tel: 888-486 6018 in US and Canada, 01-617-720 0522 outside US; www.bnbboston.com), for reservations in Boston, eastern Massachusetts, and Cape Cod.

Holiday Homes

If you're planning to stay a week or longer in one location, it may be more affordable to rent a home or condominium. Popular websites for this service include www.vrbo.com, and www.homeaway.com.

Hostels and Other Budget Lodgings

Although most prevalent in the Boston area, several cities and towns throughout New England also offer budget accommodations at hostels, YMCAs, and YWCAs. Facilities might include shared common spaces and baths and/or dormitory-style rooms, but are generally clean and relatively inexpensive. Many of the YMCA/YWCA lodgings do not charge lodging or room taxes. HostelWorld.com (**www.hostelworld.com**) makes reservations for YMCAs, budget lodgings, and hostels throughout New England.

Boston International Youth Hostel
12 Hemenway Street, Boston MA 02115. Tel: 617-536 9455. www.bostonhostel.org

Hostelling International
8401 Colesville Road, Suite 600, Silver Spring MD 20910. Tel: 301-495 1240. www.hiusa.org
HI has information about facilities throughout New England.

Budget Lodgings in the Mountains

The **Appalachian Mountain Club** operates six roadside lodges with a variety of sleeping and meal options in Maine and New Hampshire.

Appalachian Mountain Club
5 Joy Street, Boston MA 02108. Tel: 617-523 0655. www.outdoors.org

Hotel Chains

Best Western Tel: 800-780 7234; www.bestwestern.com
Comfort Inn/Choice Hotels Tel: 800-424 6423; www.comfortinn.com
Days Inn Tel: 888-445 2021; www.daysinn.com
Hilton Tel: 800-445 8667; www.hilton.com
Holiday Inn Tel: 877-424 2449; www.basshotels.com
Hyatt Tel: 888-591 1234; www.hyatt.com
Marriott Tel: 888-236 2427; toll-free UK 00800-1927 1927; www.marriott.com
Quality Inn Tel: 877-424 6423; www.qualityinn.com
Radisson Tel: 800-967 9033; www.radisson.com
Sheraton Tel: 800-325 3535; www.sheraton.com

BOSTON

ABOVE: the colorful entrance to the Boston Harbor Hotel.

Boston Harbor Hotel
70 Rowes Wharf, 02110
Tel: 617-439 7000/800-752 7077
www.bhh.com
This 16-story modern beauty with old-world charm stands as a harbor gateway to the city. There are 230 standard rooms and one- and two-bedroom suites. The public spaces exhibit some fine artworks and nautical charts. $$$$

Boston Omni Parker House
60 School Street, 02108
Tel: 617-227 8600/800-843 6664
www.omnihotels.com
America's oldest continuously operated hotel, this 1855 hotel sparkles. The 551 rooms range from economy singles to spacious, grandly furnished one-bedroom suites. Parker House rolls and Boston Cream Pie were first introduced in the restaurant. $$$–$$$$

Bulfinch Hotel
107 Merrimac Street, 02114
Tel: 617-624 0202/877-267 1776
www.bulfinchhotel.com
80 rooms and suites in a nine-story hotel in the historic Flatiron Building in the West End. Close to

subway. $$$$
82 Chandler Street
82 Chandler Street, 02116
Tel: 617-482 0408
www.82chandler.com
A five-room B&B in a 19th-century brownstone with bay windows and fireplaces in the revitalized South End neighborhood. $$

Constitution Inn
150 Third Avenue, 02129
Tel: 617-241 8400/800-495 9622
www.constitutioninn.org
Under the auspices of the YMCA, this eight-story, recently refurbished hotel in the Charlestown Navy Yard has 147 pleasant rooms with refrigerators, microwaves, and a/c. Facilities include a large fitness center with indoor pool, and free Internet access. No tax on lodging. $$

Copley Square Hotel
47 Huntington Avenue, 02116
Tel: 617-536 9000/800-225 7062
www.copleysquarehotel.com
This older, centrally located, European-style hotel with 143 rooms offers a complimentary "Wine down" hour each night from 5 to 6pm. $$$$

Golden Slipper, Boston's B&B Afloat
Lewis Wharf, 02055

Tel: 781-545 2845
Lodging is a traditional 40ft Catalina Chris-Craft yacht. The boat is moored at a secure, locked marina and can be used for sunset cruises and elegant dinners aboard. Can be rented nightly or weekly. $$–$$$$

Gryphon House
9 Bay State Road, 02215
Tel: 617-375 9003/877-375 003
www.innboston.com
Near Kenmore Square and Boston University, this bowfront brownstone converted to an eight-room luxury hotel is just steps from the subway. $$$–$$$$

Hotel 140
149 Clarendon Street, 20116
Tel: 677-585 5600/800-714 0140
www.hotel140.com
Perfectly situated near the subway and train station, this is a destination unto itself, the Lyric Stage professional theatre company's home residence is at the hotel, and it has performances almost nightly. Many guests come just for the shows. $$–$$$

John Jeffries House
14 David G. Mugar Way, 02114
Tel: 617-367 1866
www.johnjeffrieshouse.com
Many of the 46 small, simply appointed rooms in this redbrick inn at the foot of Beacon Hill have kitchens or sitting areas. There's a lovely garden oasis. $$–$$$

Mid-Town Hotel
220 Huntington Avenue, 02115
Tel: 617-369 6240/800-343 1177
www.midtownhotel.com
One of the better deals, a traditional motel with 159 rooms and an outdoor pool, near the Prudential Center and Christian Science HQ. Parking included in rate. $–$$$$

Newbury Guest House
261 Newbury Street, 02116
Tel: 617-437 7666/800-437 7668
www.newburyguesthouse.com
A trio of 1882 town houses converted into a Victorian-style inn with 32 guest

rooms offers excellent value for the location, so book well in advance. $$$

Taj Boston
15 Arlington Street, 02116
Tel: 617-536 5700/877-482 5267
www.tajhotels.com
Overlooking the Public Gardens and ice-skating on Frog Pond, the public areas of this 1927 landmark are filled with art and antiques. Some rooms have wood-burning fireplaces. As the name suggests, the restaurant has many Indian influences. $$$$

Westin Boston Waterfront
425 Summer Street, 02110
Tel: 617-532 4600
www.westin.com/Boston
One of the city's newest hotels, connected to the Boston Convention and Exhibition Center, has 793 plush rooms and suites. $$$$

Brookline

The Bertram Inn B&B
92 Sewall Avenue, 02446
Tel: 617-566 2234/800-295 3822
www.bertraminn.com
Comfortably elegant 1907 Victorian B&B situated on a quiet street and convenient to the Green Line MBTA trolleys to downtown Boston. $–$$$

Cambridge

A Cambridge House B&B
2218 Massachusetts Avenue, 02140
Tel: 617-491 6300/800-232 9989
www.acambridgehouse.com
B&B with 15 rooms in a quiet, lavishly restored 1892 Victorian. Located about 1 mile north of Harvard Square, but only four blocks from a subway stop. Free parking. $$–$$$$

The Charles Hotel
1 Bennett Street, 02138
Tel: 617-864 1200/800-882 1818
www.charleshotel.com
This Harvard Square hotel overlooking the Charles River has 293 traditional-style rooms with unique

features like TVs in the bathroom mirrors. Really. Home to the popular Regattabar, which draws nationally known jazz performers. **$$$$**

The Inn at Harvard
1201 Massachusetts Avenue, 02138
Tel: 617-491 2222/800-458 5886

www.hotelsinharvard square.com
Graham Gund designed this intimate four-story, 111-room inn encircling a peaceful atrium. **$$$-$$$$**

Irving House
24 Irving Street (off Cambridge Street), 02138
Tel: 617-547 4600/877-547 4600

www.irvinghouse.com
Basic but comfortable 44-room B&B with some shared baths. Operation follows the Green Innkeeping philosophy. Just a short walk from Harvard Square. **$-$$$**

Mary Prentiss Inn
6 Prentiss Street, 02140
Tel: 617-661 2929

www.maryprentissinn.com
Tastefully appointed three-floor, 20-room Greek Revival B&B with a spacious deck. Situated between Harvard and Porter squares. Free parking. **$$-$$$$**

CAPE COD AND THE ISLANDS

Barnstable

Beechwood Inn
2839 Main Street (Route 6A)
Tel: 508-362 6618800-609 6618
www.beechwoodinn.com
Six charming rooms in an 1853 Queen Ann Victorian, some with fireplaces and/or water views. Three-course candlelight breakfasts. The owners breed and raise AKC golden retrievers. Open year-round. **$$-$$$**

Brewster

Bramble Inn & Restaurant
2019 Route 6A, 02631
Tel: 508-896 7644
www.brambleinn.com
Where the book *How to Own and Operate a Country Inn* was written. Historic country inn in two buildings (1792–1861) offers eight rooms with queen canopy or sleigh beds, and a fine restaurant. Seasonal. Call early for reservations. **$$$**

Captain Freeman Inn
15 Breakwater Road, 02631
Tel: 508-896 7481/800-843 4664
www.captainfreemaninn.com
Eleven antique-filled, spacious rooms, some with whirlpool tubs and private porches, in a luxurious 1860 shipbuilder's home with a heated outdoor pool. Cooking classes offered on-site. **$$-$$$**

Chatham

Captain's House Inn of Chatham
371 Old Harbor Road, 02633
Tel: 508-945 0127/800-315 0728
www.captainshouseinn.com

The 16 rooms of this elegant 1839 B&B and outbuildings are named after the Captain's daughters or the ships he commanded. Luxurious traditional decor; silver-service tea is served in the garden room, as are full breakfasts. Croquet equipment ready for use. **$$-$$$$**

Chatham Bars Inn
297 Shore Road, 02633
Tel: 508-945 0096/800-332 1577
www.chathambarsinn.com
This 1914 oceanfront private hunting lodge–turned–grand hotel/resort has rooms in the inn, private cottages, homes perched on a bluff, and in the spa building. A private boat fleet takes guests whale watching, sport fishing, on sunset cruises or day trips to the out islands. Schedule of children's activities. **$$$$**

The Cranberry Inn
359 Main Street, 02633
Tel: 508-945 9232/800-332 4667
www.cranberryinn.com
This 1830 inn is at the quiet end of Main Street. Many of the 18 rooms have fireplaces and/or private balconies. The comfortable tavern is a good end-of-day stop. Open year-round. **$$-$$$**

Dennis Area

Isaiah Hall B&B Inn
152 Whig Street, Dennis, 02638
Tel: 508-385 9928/800-736 0160
www.isaiahhallinn.com
Performers from the Cape Playhouse favor this lovely 1857 farmhouse, with its

10 rooms and two suites furnished with country antiques, on a residential street. Open all year. **$-$$$**

Lighthouse Inn
1 Lighthouse Road
West Dennis, 02670
Tel: 508-398 2244
www.lighthouseinn.com
An old-fashioned, nine-acre seaside resort B&B with 61 rooms in cottages and a 1855 lighthouse-turned-inn. Supervised activities for children in July and August. **$$$-$$$$**

Eastham

Inn at the Oaks B&B
3085 Route 6, 02642
Tel: 508-225 1886/877-255 1886
www.innattheoaks.com
Scottish, family-friendly hospitality in a colorful 1869 Victorian 11-room B&B near the Salt Pond Visitor Center. Offers many writers' retreat weekends and workshops. **$$-$$$$**

Whalewalk Inn
220 Bridge Road, 02642
Tel: 508-255 0617/800-440 1281
www.whalewalkinn.com
This elegant 1830s Greek Revival B&B, built as a whaling master's house, has 16 luxurious rooms in the main house and five buildings in spacious grounds. Romantic atmosphere: many rooms have fireplaces and oversize whirlpool/soaking tubs. Spa. **$$$-$$$$**

Falmouth Area

Captain Tom Lawrence Inn
75 Locust Street, Falmouth, 02540
Tel: 508-548 9178/800-266

8139
www.captaintomlawrence. com
Breakfasts are known for creations using Cape Cod cranberries and other seasonal fruit syrups poured over Belgian waffles. Afternoon snacks are equally decadent. They also work hard to accommodate special dietary needs. **$-$$**

Inn on the Sound
313 Grand Avenue S, Falmouth Heights, 02540
Tel: 508-457 9666/800-564 9668
www.innonthesound.com
A B&B in an 1880 shingled cottage on a bluff overlooking Vineyard Sound. A large porch offers great water views, as do four of the 10 rooms that have private decks. Open year-round. **$$-$$$$**

The Palmer House Inn
81 Palmer Avenue, Falmouth, 02540
Tel: 508-548 1230/800-472 2632
www.palmerhouseinn.com
Romantic Queen Anne-style B&B with stained-glass windows and rich woodwork. Breakfasts are garnished with items picked from the on-site organic herb garden, which is also a good place for meditation. Open year-round. **$$-$$$**

PRICE CATEGORIES

An approximate guide to rates for a standard double room per night:
$$$$ = more than $300
$$$ = $200–300
$$ = $125–200
$ = under $125

Harwich Port Area

Commodore Inn
30 Earle Road, West
Harwich, 02671
Tel: 508-432 1180/800-368
1180
www.commodoreinn.com
A seaside motel just yards
from the sandy beaches
and warm waters of
Nantucket Sound has 27
rooms furnished in pleas-
ing country decor.
Excellent Scottish scones.
Private patios. Open year-
round. $-$$$$

**Winstead Inn and
Beach Resort**
4 Braddock Lane, 02646
Tel: 508-432 4444/800-870
4405
www.winsteadinn.com
Fourteen rooms with all
the comforts of home, but
none are handicapped-
accessible. Great location,
right on the beach. Heated
salt pool. $$-$$$$

Hyannis

Anchor In Cape Cod Hotel
One South Street, 02601
Tel: 508-775 0357
www.anchorin.com
The town's only waterfront
hotel; some 43 rooms at
this hotel overlook Lewis
Bay and have private
decks and Jacuzzis. Close
to downtown and ferries.
Heated outdoor pool.
Open year-round. $-$$$$

Hyannis Inn Motel
473 Main Street, 02601
Tel: 508-775 0255/800-922
8993
www.hyannisinn.com
A family-run inn in the
center of town, with 77
rooms ranging from stand-
ard to deluxe, and a
heated indoor pool and
saunas. Open April–
October. $-$$$

SeaCoast Inn
33 Ocean Street, 02601
Tel: 508-755 3828/800-466
4100
www.seacoastcapecod.com
Simple, clean rooms in
central location.
Continental breakfast. $-$$

Provincetown

Cape Inn Resorts
698 Commercial Street, 02657
Tel: 508-487 1711/800-422
4224

www.capeinn.com
Motel in the East End a mile
from town center with 78
comfortable rooms and
ample parking. Some rooms
have harbor views. $$-$$$

**Gabriel's at The
Ashbrooke Inn**
102 Bradford Street, 02657
Tel: 508-487 3232
www.gabriels.com
Several buildings with
age- or situation-spe-
cific amenities. "Senior"
rooms have free-stand-
ing Jacuzzis and comfort
height toilets. "Family"
rooms have cribs and
toddler beds. Many
units have washer/
dryer. $$-$$$$

Gallery Inn
3 Johnson Street, 20657
Tel: 508-487 3010/800-676
3010
www.galleryinnptown.com
Efficiency apartments with
private entrances, or tradi-
tional rooms, both found
in this centrally located
inn. Continental breakfast
on the sundeck. $-$$$

**Harbor Hotel,
Provincetown**
698 Commercial Street, 02657
Tel: 508-487 1711/800-422
4224
www.harborhotelptown.com
A mile east from the city
center, near the hiking
trails. 119 rooms, 10
suites. Firepit is a good
place to watch the sunset
in the fall. $$-$$$$

Sandwich

Dan'l Webster Inn and Spa
149 Main Street, 02563
Tel: 508-888 3622/800-444
3566
www.danlwebsterinn.com
Some rooms at this
48-room luxury hotel in
the center of Sandwich
Village have fireplaces,
balconies, and whirlpool
tubs. Coffeehouse-style
entertainment most week-
ends. $$-$$$$

Inn at Sandwich Center
118 Tupper Road, 02563
Tel: 508-888 6958/800-249
6949
www.innatsandwich.com
Five bright bedrooms in a
1750s saltbox across from
the Sandwich Glass
Museum. Will pack

take-away lunches for early
risers going to Nantucket.
$$-$$$

Wingscorton Farm
11 Wing Boulevard, East
Sandwich, 02537
Tel: 508-888 0534
A working farm/B&B, once
a stop along the
Underground Railroad,
has rooms in the 1763
main house, a carriage
house, and a cottage five
minutes' walk from the
beach. $$-$$$$

Woods Hole

Nautilus Motor Inn
539 Woods Hole Road, 02543
Tel: 508-548 1525
www.nautilusinn.com
Two-story waterfront motel
has 54 one-bedroom
units, and a swimming
pool surrounded by gar-
dens. Seasonal. $-$$$$

**Woods Hole Passage Bed
& Breakfast Inn**
186 Woods Hole Road, 02540
Tel: 508-548 9575/800-790
8976
www.woodsholepassage.com
An 1890s carriage house
and barn converted into
an eco-friendly, romantic,
five-room B&B. Adjacent
to Woods Hole
Oceanographic Institute.
Open year-round. $$

Yarmouth Port

One Centre Street Inn
One Centre Street, 02675
Tel: 508-362 9951/866-362
9951
www.onecenterstreetinn.com
Restored, three-story
1824 Colonial inn has five
guest rooms and a one-
bedroom suite. Breakfast
is on the screened three-
season porch (or indoor
dining room when the
weather is bad). Open
year-round. Entire house is
available for rental. $$-$$$

Martha's Vineyard

Edgartown

**Harbor View Hotel and
Resort**
131 North Water Street, 02539
Tel: 508-627 7000/800-225
6005
www.harbor-view.com
A lavishly renovated waterfront 1891 shingled grad
hotel with 124 rooms and

heated pool near
Lighthouse Beach. Open
year-round. Children's day
program. Provides boat-
ing, kayaking trips. $-$$$$

**Vineyard Square Hotel
and Suites**
38 N. Water Street, 02539
Tel: 508-627 4711/800-627
4701
www.vineyardsquarehotel.
com
Centrally located, this
1911 shingled hotel has
traditional rooms and
suits. Rooftop veranda with
spectacular views. No ele-
vator in main hotel. $-$$$$

Menemsha

Menemsha Inn and Cottages
12 Menemsha Road, Off
North Road, 02552
Tel: 508-645 2521
www.menemshainn.com
Peaceful simplicity in a
1923 inn with 27 rooms
and cottages on 14 acres
with water views. Tennis
court, gym, ping pong
room. Resident herd of
alpaca welcome petting.
BYOB – the town is "dry"
and no alcohol is sold in
restaurants. $$-$$$$

Oak Bluffs

The Oak Bluffs Inn
64 Circuit Avenue, 02557
Tel: 508-693 7171/800-955
6235
www.oakbluffsinn.com
Nine rooms and one
apartment. Sits directly
across the street from two
restaurants known for the
famous faces who dine
there. Five-minute walk to
the beach. Continental
breakfast. Children wel-
come. Open spring
through fall. $-$$$$

Vineyard Haven

Thorncroft Inn
460 Main Street, 20568
Tel: 508-693 3333
www.thorncroft.com
This 1918 estate was built
for lavish entertaining and
guests who stayed a
while. Premier romantic
getaway; no children.
Many rooms offer in-room
hot tubs for two or wood-
burning fireplaces. Full
country breakfast served
in the dining room or

breakfast in bed. **$$-$$$$**

Martin House Inn
61 Centre Street, 02554
Tel: 508-228 0678
www.martinhouseinn.net
Reasonably priced, this
year-round, 13-room 1803

mariner's home is one of
the prettiest and most
congenial in town. Some
rooms have shared bath;
some have fireplaces.
Afternoon tea and snacks
on the Widow's Walk or in
their gardens. **$-$$$$**
The Wauwinet Inn

120 Wauwinet Road,
Wauwinet, 02584
Tel: 508-228 0145/800-426
8718
www.wauwinet.com
A fabulously refurbished
1850 waterfront Relais &
Châteaux hotel with 35
rooms. Luxurious,

secluded, and expensive.
Spa. Cruises on 26-seat
launch. Classes offered in
cooking, lobstering, and
other diversions.
Seasonal. **$$$$**

MASSACHUSETTS

Amherst

**The Allen House
Victorian Inn**
599 Main Street, 01002
Tel: 413-253 5000
www.allenhouse.com
Meticulously restored, this
inn has six bedchambers
with touches like antique-
style radios. Emily
Dickinson Homestead is
adjacent. Five-course full
breakfast. **$-$$**
The Lord Jeffery Inn
30 Boltwood Avenue, 01002
Tel: 413-253 8200/800-742
0358
www.lordjefferyinn.com
A traditional Colonial
Revival–style inn with 48
rooms and several restau-
rants situated on the town
green near Amherst
College. **$$$**

Concord

Concord's Colonial Inn
48 Monument Square, 01742
Tel: 978-369 9200/800-370
9200
www.concordscolonialinn.
com
A 1716 inn that witnessed
the Battle of Concord. 56
rooms on Concord's town
common. Music
Wednesday–Saturday
nights in the period tav-
ern. **$$-$$$$**
Hawthorne Inn
462 Lexington Road, 01742
Tel: 978-369 5610
www.concordmass.com
B&B with seven rooms
(some with gas fireplaces)
in the historic district,
opposite Hawthorne's
Wayside. Children wel-
come. **$$-$$$$**
Longfellow's Wayside Inn
Wayside Inn Road
South Sudbury, 01776
Tel: 978-443 1776/800-339
1776

www.wayside.org
Ten updated rooms in a
mid-18th-century tavern
close to Lexington and
Concord that's been wel-
coming guests for almost
300 years. The 125-acre
property is often the site
for historical re-enact-
ments. The restaurant
serves Yankee fare. Book
well in advance. **$-$$$**

Deerfield

Deerfield Inn
81 Old Main Street, 01342
Tel: 413-774 5587/800-926
3865
www.deerfieldinn.com
Impeccably preserved
1884 inn on the historic
main street has 24 large
rooms, including one
handicapped-accessible
room, furnished with
antiques and period repro-
ductions. Local beer on tap
in its tavern, which also
has the "101 Martinis"
menu and a Sunday jazz
brunch. **$$-$$$**

Great Barrington

Windflower Inn
684 S. Egremont Road, 01230
Tel: 413-528 2720/800-992
1993
www.windflowerinn.com
A B&B in an early-20th-
century, 10-acre country
estate with gardens and a
pool. The 13 rooms have
four-poster beds and are
decorated with antiques;
some have fireplaces.
Children welcome. **$-$$$**

Gloucester

Bass Rocks Ocean Inn
107 Atlantic Road, 01930
Tel: 978-283 7600/888-802
7666
www.bassrocksoceaninn.com
Units at this complex

overlooking the ocean are
in three buildings: the
48-unit Georgian colonial-
style motel, the 1899
Stacy House, and the sum-
mer cottage. Breakfast is
served on the sun porch.
Outdoor pool. Open May–
October. **$$-$$$**
Harborview Inn
71 Western Avenue, 01930
Tel: 978-283 2277/800-299
6696
www.harborviewinn.com
A comfortable house-
turned-B&B near the
Fishermen Memorial
statue. Six rooms, some
with ocean views, some
with fireplaces; all with pri-
vate baths. Continental
breakfast. Open year-
round. **$-$$$**

Greenfield

Brandt House Country Inn
29 Highland Avenue, 01301
Tel: 413-774 3329/800-235
3329
www.brandthouse.com
An 1890s Victorian B&B
with nine comfortable
rooms and huge porches.
All rooms have feather
beds. Cozy location for
weddings, civil unions.
Prefer children over age
12. Pets welcome. **$$-$$$**

Hadley

Ivory Creek B&B
31 Chmura Road, 01035
Tel: 413-587 3115/866-331
3115
www.ivorycreek.com
A large, comfortable, family-
friendly house with antique-
filled guest rooms, decks,
balconies, and porches on
24 wooded acres.
Handicapped-accessible
room. Lovely pool with
waterfall. Aviary with many
local birds. **$$-$$$$**

Lenox

Apple Tree Inn
10 Richmond Mountain
Road, 01240
Tel: 413-637 1477
www.appletree-inn.com
A 22-acre hilltop estate
within earshot of
Tanglewood has 15 rooms
in the 1885 main house
and 24 in the newer lodge.
$$$-$$$$
Blantyre
16 Blantyre Road (off
Route 20), 01240
Tel: 413-637 3556
www.blantyre.com
An opulent mock-Tudor
castle on 100 manicured
acres with a heated pool,
sauna, tennis courts, cro-
quet lawns, and gourmet
dining. Many rooms in the
main house have fire-
places; also units in car-
riage house, and very
private cottages. Open
year-round. **$$$$**
Garden Gables
135 Main Street, 01240
Tel: 413-637 0193/888-243
0193
www.gardengablesinn.com
Country charm in this B&B/
winery close to Tanglewood.
Rooms in the 1780 house
and cottages on 5 acres.
Most rooms have fireplaces
and private porches. Heated
pool, spa. **$$$$**
Rookwood Inn
11 Old Stockbridge Road,
01240
Tel: 413-637 9750/800-223
9750

PRICE CATEGORIES

An approximate guide to
rates for a standard double
room per night:
$$$$ = more than $300
$$$ = $200–300
$$ = $125–200
$ = under $125

www.rookwoodinn.com
Nineteen rooms in a comfortably elegant 19th-century "painted lady" at the center of town. Owner is a Justice of the Peace and able to perform wedding ceremonies on property or off. Open year-round. **$$$–$$$$**

Walker House
64 Walker Street, 01240
Tel: 413-637 1271/800-235 3098
www.walkerhouse.com
The hosts of this 1804 Federal, eight-room B&B provide nightly movies on a 12ft (3.5-meter) screen, as well as recitals on the grand piano. Children over age 12 welcome. Continental breakfast. **$–$$$**

Marblehead

Marblehead Inn
264 Pleasant Street, 01945
Tel: 781-639 9999/800-399 5843
www.marbleheadinn.com
A stately 1872 Victorian with six two-bedroom suites and five rooms; all suites have kitchenettes. All available for monthly rental. One handicapped unit. Continental breakfast. No children under age 10. **$$–$$$**

New Marlborough

Gedney Farm
34 Hartsville-New Marlborough Road, 01239
Tel: 413-229 3131/800-286 3139
www.gedneyfarm.com
Former Percheron stallion and Jersey cattle farm has been transformed into elegant lodging with 16 rooms and plenty of inside lounging and outside wandering space. On-site spa has classes; ask about packages. Continental breakfast. **$$$–$$$$**

Newburyport

Garrison Inn Boutique Hotel
11 Brown Square, 01950
Tel: 978-499 8500
www.garrisoninn.com
1809 former residence of abolitionist William Lloyd Garrison, has 24 rooms and six suites. Ultra-chic boudoirs are spacious and

richly appointed. Continental breakfast. On side street one block from the main downtown district. **$$–$$$$**

North Adams

The Porches Inn at MASS MoCA
231 River Street, 01247
Tel: 413-664 0400
www.porches.com
This lodging, in a renovated building that once housed mill workers, bills itself as "ultra savvy": all of the 47 rooms are furnished in contemporary-retro decor and fully wired for computer use; some two-room suites have spiral staircases to loft sleeping areas. Heated year-round outdoor pool; heated deck, sauna, and fire pit. Child-friendly. Breakfast included. **$$–$$$**

Northampton

Hotel Northampton
36 King Street, 01060
Tel: 413-584 3100
www.hotelnorthampton.com
Handsomely appointed, antique-crammed historic inn in the center of town has 106 rooms, and suites with whirlpool baths. Two on-site restaurants, including one moved from its original location in New Hampshire. **$$$**

Northfield

Centennial House B&B
94 Main Street, 01360
Tel: 413-498 5921/877-977 5950
www.thecentennialhouse.com
Handsome in-town 1811 Colonial with four antique-filled guest rooms (some share baths) and a third-floor suite that sleeps four. Two landscaped acres with great mountain views. Full breakfast. Children over 8 welcome. Location is near the New Hampshire and Vermont lines. **$–$$$**

Plymouth

Bradford Inn & Suites
98 Water Street, 02360
Tel: 508-746 6200/800-332 1620

www.governorbradford.com
A motel with 87 rooms right on the harbor. Child-friendly; kids under 17 stay free with adult. Free parking. Fitness center and pool. **$–$$**

John Carver Inn and Spa
25 Summer Street, 02360
Tel: 508-746 7100/800-274 1620
www.johncarverinn.com
Good place for kids. Near major attractions, this immaculate modern hotel, with 85 rooms and suites (some with fireplaces) has an indoor pool with water slide and a lap pool. All rooms have Nintendos. Kids under 18 stay free with an adult. **$$–$$$**

Pilgrim Sands Motel
150 Warren Avenue, 02360
Tel: 508-747 0900/800-729 7263
www.pilgrimsands.com
Oceanfront motel with standard units and apartments directly across from Plimoth Plantation. Handicapped-accessible rooms. Up to two children under age 6 stay free in room with adult. Senior discount, Continental breakfast. Private beach. **$–$$$$**

Rockport

Addison Choate Inn
49 Broadway, 01966
Tel: 978-546 7543
www.addisonchoateinn.com
Lovely summery decor and a quiet in-town setting for this Greek Revival inn with five rooms. Breakfast in the fireplaced dining room or porch. **$$**

Linden Tree Inn
26 King Street, 01966
Tel: 978-546 2494/800-865 2122

www.lindentreeinn.com
A one-time captain's home 800ft from the beach, with 12 well-priced B&B rooms, a carriage house with efficiency units, and an innkeeper who bakes marvelous scones. **$–$$$**

Seacrest Manor
99 Marmion Way, 01966
Tel: 978-546 2211
www.seacrestmanor.com
This 1911 clapboard mansion has eight comfortable rooms (some with shared baths), well-tended gardens, sea views, and some private decks. Some rooms can be expanded into suites. Open April–November. House is available for winter rentals. **$$–$$$**

Seaward Inn
44 Marmion Way, 01966
Tel: 978-546 3471/877-473 9273
www.seawardinn.com
A welcoming summer house-turned-B&B on a beautifully landscaped seaside ledge. Rooms in the main inn, two nearby houses, and adjacent cottages. Children under age 6 stay free. **$$$–$$$$**

The Tuck Inn B&B
17 High Street, 01966
Tel: 978-546 7260/800-789 7260
www.tuckinn.com
Comfortable in-town 1790 Colonial home. Some of the 12 rooms have separate entrances and/or decks. There's also an apartment with full kitchen. Breakfast (5–8am) features made-from-scratch breads, muffins, and scones. **$$–$$$**

BELOW: Rockport keeps its maritime heritage on display.

Salem

The Amelia Payson House Bed & Breakfast
16 Winter Street, 01970
Tel: 978-744 8304
www.ameliapaysonhouse.com
1845 Greek Revival B&B with four bright, airy rooms; convenient for museums and historic sites. Owners are great sources for area history and legends. Open May–October. **$$**

Hawthorne Hotel
18 Washington Square West, 01970
Tel: 978-744 4080/800-729 7829
www.hawthornehotel.com
A 1920s hotel with 93 rooms and seven suites, and harbor views from the top floors. Many packages which include admission to sites and theatre tickets. The restaurant serves a popular Sunday jazz brunch buffet. **$-$$$$**

Sheffield

Birch Hill B&B
254 S. Undermountain Road, 01257
Tel: 413-229 2143/800-359 3969
www.birchhillbb.com
Casual, sprawling, simply furnished 1780 country inn with pool, set in 20 acres on the Appalachian Trail. Some of the seven rooms have fireplaces. Some shared baths. Children over 9 welcome. **$$-$$$**

Stockbridge

The Red Lion Inn
30 Main Street, Stockbridge, 01262
Tel: 413-298-5545
www.redlioninn.com
A classic old inn (est. 1773) at the center of a Norman Rockwell town. Some of the 108 rooms in the main inn are quite small and share baths; those in the adjacent buildings are a bit larger and offer private entrances and driveways. Heated outdoor pool. Resident massage therapist available after a day of hiking. **$-$$$$**

Williamsville Inn
Route 41, West Stockbridge, 01266
Tel: 413-274 6118
www.williamsvilleinn.com
Sixteen rooms in a restored 1790s farmhouse, barn, and cottages on 10 acres of landscaped grounds and gardens. Summer sculpture garden. Taste of Germany Restaurant. Culinary school in the restaurant; guests can take classes. **$$-$$$**

Sturbridge

Publick House Historic Resort
277 Main Street
Route 131, The Common, 01566
Tel: 508-347 3313/800-782 5425
www.publickhouse.com
A cluster of historic houses, plus a modern motel-style annex, offering 115 rooms in all. Good situation near Old Sturbridge Village. Murder-mystery dinners and seasonal packages. **$-$$$**

Williamstown

The Guest House at Field Farm
554 Sloan Road (off Route 43), 01267
Tel: 413-458 3135
www.thetrustees.org
This 1948 American Modern mansion B&B, set on over 300 acres of conservation land, has six large rooms with modern furnishings. Amenities include a pool, tennis courts, pond (fishing rods available), and hiking trails, but no TVs. Children over 12 welcome. **$$-$$$**

The Orchards
222 Adams Road (Route 2), 01267
Tel: 413-458 9611/800-225 1517
www.orchardshotel.com
A peaceful, elegant oasis despite its location on an unappealing commercial strip of Route 2. The 49 modern rooms have antique furnishings. Sauna. Area is a popular wedding destination; LGBT-friendly. **$$$-$$$$**

River Bend Farm
643 Simonds Road, 01267
Tel: 413-458 3121
www.windsorsofstonington.com/RBF
A painstakingly restored 1770 Colonial house. Furnishings are simple, even rustic, as befits the Colonial period in this four-room B&B. No private baths; two bathrooms are shared by all guests. Children welcome. Big breakfasts. No credit cards. **$-$$**

Worcester

The Beechwood Hotel
363 Plantation Street, 01605
Tel: 508-754 5789/800-344 2589
www.beechwoodhotel.com
A handsome, modern 73-room luxury boutique hotel overlooking the lake. **$$-$$$$**

Grafton Inn
25 Grafton Common, 01519
Tel: 508-839 5931
www.grafton-inn.com
Seven comfortable, affordable rooms. Casual, child-friendly dining on-site. Casual bar. **$-$$$**

Sleigh Maker Inn B&B
87 West Main Street, 01581
Tel: 508-836 5546/877-836 5545
www.sleighmakerinn.com
Eastlake Victorian building decorated with items relating to sleigh-making, which was the structure's original use. Full breakfast. **$-$$**

RHODE ISLAND

Block Island

The Barrington Inn
584 Beach Avenue, 02807
Tel: 877- 324 4667
www.theinnatblockisInd.com
Century-old Victorian farmhouse has six rooms and two apartments on a hilltop overlooking New Harbor. Open May–October. **$$-$$$$**

Spring House Hotel
Spring Street, Old Harbor, 02807
Tel: 401-466 5844/800-234 9263
www.springhousehotel.com
A classic 49-room hotel (built in 1852) with Victorian furnishings, a cupola-topped mansard roof, and a wraparound porch. Set on 15 acres above the ocean. No a/c, but ocean breezes take care of that. **$-$$$$**

Victorian Inns by the Sea (formerly Block Island Inns)
Tel: 800-992 7290
www.blockislandinns.com
A consortium of inns, cottages, and houses throughout the island, including the romantic, award-winning, 11-room Blue Dorey Inn. **$$-$$$$**

Bristol

Bristol Harbor Inn
259 Thames Street, 02809
Tel: 401-254 1444/866-254 1444
www.bristolharborinn.com
The East Bay's only waterfront lodging, in downtown Bristol, has 40 well-appointed rooms, many with views of Narragansett Bay. Penthouse apartments available. **$$-$$$**

Bristol House Bed & Breakfast
14 Aaron Avenue, 02809
Tel: 401-396 9066
www.bristolhousebnb.com
Three beautifully decorated rooms, two share a bath. Cozy gathering spaces, outdoor patio, backyard garden. **$-$$$**

Jamestown

East Bay Bed & Breakfast
14 Union Street, 02835

PRICE CATEGORIES

An approximate guide to rates for a standard double room per night:
$$$$ = more than $300
$$$ = $200–300
$$ = $125–200
$ = under $125

Tel: 401-423 0330/800-243 1107
www.eastbaybnb.com
Located in the heart of historic area, each of the four guestrooms has a private bath. Children over 12 welcome. **$–$$**

Little Compton

The Edith Pearl Bed and Breakfast
250 W. Main Road, 02837
Tel: 401-592 0053
www.edithpearl.com
Renovated 1840s Colonial on 240 acres of preserved and working farmland. Bikes, croquet equipment, board games. The Rice family will teach you how to make apple cider. **$$–$$$$**

Harmony Home Farm Bed and Breakfast
456 Long Highway, 02837
Tel: 401-635 2283
www.harmonyhomefarm.com
Two rooms in a country oasis. Continental breakfast. **$$**

Narragansett

The Anchor Motel
825 Ocean Road, 02882
Tel: 401-792 8550
www.theanchormotel.com
Thirteen basic but clean rooms just across from Scarborough State Beach and close to the Block Island Ferry. Open year-round. **$–$$$**

Blueberry Cove Inn
75 Kingstown Road, 02882
Tel: 800-478 1426
www.blueberrycoveinn.com
Five-minute walk to town center. Seven rooms and two whirlpool suites, with upscale amenities like Egyptian cotton linens and plush robes. Big breakfasts. Open year-round. **$$–$$$$**

Newport

Castle Hill Inn
590 Ocean Drive, 02840
Tel: 401-849 3800/888-466 1355
www.castlehillinn.com

Scientist and explorer Alexander Agassiz' 1874 estate is now a first-rate resort which encompasses his mansion along with several other lodgings. The 40-acre property has one of the area's most magnificent views. **$$$$**

Cliffside Inn
2 Seaview Avenue, 02840
Tel: 401-847 1811/800-845 1811
www.cliffsideinn.com
Near the Cliff Walk, an 1880 Victorian villa carved into grand, dramatic quarters. The 15 rooms in this B&B are light and airy, and some have working fireplaces and whirlpool tubs. **$$$$**

The Hotel Viking
1 Bellevue Avenue, 02840
Tel: 401-847 3300/800-556 7126
www.hotelviking.com
This 1926, five-story hotel in the Historic Hill neighborhood has kept its Old World charm while upgrading for modern times. All 209 rooms and 20 suites are well appointed and comfortable. Indoor pool, fitness center, spa, and restaurant. **$$$–$$$$**

The Inns of Newport
Tel: 401-848 5300/800-524 1386
www.innsofnewport.com
A group of five historic downtown inns: The Clarkeston, Admiral Farragut, The Wynstone, Elm Street Inn, and Cleveland House. All have a colonial ambience and offer breakfast. **$$–$$$$**

Rose Island Lighthouse
Newport
Tel: 401-847 4242
www.roseislandlighthouse.org
Live the dream of being a lighthouse keeper. Stay for a night or a week in an operating lighthouse a mile offshore. Must be able to physically carry

your own gear and climb the steps. Open year-round. **$–$$$$**

Newport Beach Hotel & Suites
One Wave Avenue, 02842
Tel: 401-846 0310/800-655 1778
www.newportbeachhoteland suites.com
Newport's only beachfront hotel has two buildings with regular rooms, plus one- and two- bedroom suites with refrigerator and microwave. All standard resort amenities. Family-friendly, and steps from the beach. **$$$–$$$$**

Victorian Ladies Inn
63 Memorial Boulevard, 02840
Tel: 401-849 9960/888-849 9960
www.victorianladies.com
A pair of c.1850s vintage lovelies, in period style, offering 11 B&B rooms and elaborate gardens. Near First Beach and the Cliff Walk. Children over 10 welcome. **$$$–$$$$**

Providence

Christopher Dodge House
11 We. Park Street, 02908
Tel: 401-351 6111
www.providence-inn.com
The 1858 three-story mansion is small but right in the heart of all the action. Some of the rooms still have their original 11ft-high tin ceilings. Full breakfast. Close to the State House, RSDI, and Brown. **$$**

Hotel Providence
311 Westminster Street, 02903
Tel: 401-861 8000/800-861-8990
www.thehotelprovidence.com
Eighty elegantly appointed rooms and suites with European decor in a restored turn-of-the-19th-century building in downtown's Historic District. Writing, painting, creative computer skills, and cooking weekend workshops

offered during the year. **$$$$**

The Old Court B&B
144 Benefit Street, 02903
Tel: 401-751 2002
www.oldcourt.com
Near the Rhode Island School of Design, an 1863 rectory retrofitted as an elegant Victorian-style inn. Ten spacious rooms with high ceilings, private baths, chandeliers. **$$–$$$$**

Westerly

Andrea Hotel
89 Atlantic Avenue, Misquamicut Beach, 02891
Tel: 401-348 8788/888-318 5707
www.andreahotel.com
Old-fashioned hotel sits directly on the beach; offers 24 rooms with private balconies and fabulous water views. Hotel has staff lifeguard on the beach in season. In-season nightly entertainment and restaurant. **$–$$$**

Grandview Bed and Breakfast
212 Shore Road, 02891
Tel: 401-596 6384/800-447 6384
www.grandviewbandb.com
A comfortable turn-of-the-20th-century house with nine cozy guest rooms (some with ocean views), gardens, and a stone wraparound porch. Short drive to Mystic, Newport, or Watch Hill. **$–$$$**

Shelter Harbor Inn
10 Wagner Road (Route 1), 02891
Tel: 401-322 8883/800-468 8883
www.shelterharborinn.com
Once a working farm, now a luxury 24-room getaway near Weekapaug Beach. Croquet and bocce ball are afternoon favorites. The roof deck has a barbecue grill and a hot tub. **$$–$$$$**

CONNECTICUT

Branford

By the Sea Inn & Spa
107 Montowese Street, 06405
203-483 3333

www.bytheseainnspa.co
Three comfortable, country-casual rooms n a renovated farmhouse in quiet

area of a shoreline town. Wicker chairs in reading nooks. Adjacent full-service spa is the largest day-

spa in the county. **$$–$$$**

Thimble Islands B&B
28 West Point Road, 06405
Tel: 203-488 3693

www.thimbleislandsbb.com Ideally located in the secluded village of Stoney Creek, this two-room B&B is about as private as it gets. Waterside location with views of the Thimble Islands you can see without getting out of bed. Only 12 miles from New Haven. **$$$**

Bristol

Chimney Crest Manor
5 Founders Drive, 06010
Tel: 000-502 4219
Thirty-two elegantly appointed rooms in a Tudor-style, castle-like mansion in the historic district overlooking the Farmington Valley just 20 minutes west of Hartford. **$$-$$$**

Coventry

The Daniel Rust House
2011 Main Street, 06238
Tel: 860-742 0032
www.thedanielrusthouse.com
Originally licensed as The Bird in Hand in 1800, the house has three rooms (one with whirlpool) and a suite with kitchenette. The "hidden closet" in one room is thought to have been used by the Underground Railroad. Very close to UConn and Sturbridge. **$$**

Essex

Griswold Inn
36 Main Street, 06426
Tel: 860-767 1776
www.griswoldinn.com
In operation since 1776, historical appointments in the 31-room inn include ancient firearms, antiques, and Currier & Ives prints. Eight of the 14 suites have fireplaces. The "family cottage" across the street is ideal for larger groups; the annex rooms are small and basic, but a good deal if you don't spend a lot of time in your room. **$-$$$$**
Ivoryton Inn
115 Main Street, 06442
860-581 0991
www.ivorytoninn.com
Newly refurbished, the 22 rooms are very basic but clean, comfortable, and reasonably priced. Across the street from the

Ivoryton Playhouse, the inn was a residence of many actors before they were "names," like Marlon Brando and Gloria Swanson. No children under age 12. **$-$$**

Fairfield

The Inn at Fairfield Beach
1160 Reef Road, 06824
Tel: 203-255 6806
www.innatfairfieldbeach.com
Only beachfront accommodation in town. Designed for those planning to stay a few days, there are eight suites and six studios, all with kitchenettes. Each room has a theme: the usual nautical and colonial accents, as well as a "safari" and a "Bermuda" room. **$$-$$$**

Glastonbury

Butternut Farm
1654 Main Street, 06033
Tel: 860-633 7197
www.butternutfarmbandb.com
Painstakingly and lovingly restored colonial farmhouse with several rooms and a private apartment. Except for the modern bathrooms and electricity, you think you've stepped back in time. Harriett the Goose runs the barnyard; the three Abyssinian cats run the house. **$-$$**

Hartford

Hilton Hartford
315 Trumbull Street, 06103
Tel: 860-728 5151
www.hilton.com
Downtown hotel for upscale travelers and business travelers; connected to the Hartford Civic Center. Indoor pool and fitness center. Frequent packages for getaways and families. **$$$-$$$$**
Ramada Plaza Downtown
50 Morgan Street, 06120
Tel: 860-549 2400
www.ramadahartford.com
At the intersection of I-84 and I-91, the hotel is close to all of the downtown attractions and businesses. 350 rooms and suites; pet- and family-friendly. Some special packages combine rooms with breakfast and attractions. **$$-$$$$**

Ivorytown

Copper Beech Inn
46 Main Street, 06442
Tel: 860-767 0330/888-809 2056
www.copperbeechinn.com
Romantic, luxurious inn with rooms in an 1890 Victorian home, carriage house, and European-style annex on 7 acres (3 hectares). Period antiques, Oriental rugs. No children under 16. **$$$-$$$$**

Kingsfield

Kingsfield Bed and Breakfast
827 North Street, 06078
Tel: 860-668 5050
www.kingsfieldbandb.com
Spacious, comfortable, and historically accurate. A carefully maintained 1722 New England saltbox with all the period accents and all the modern amenities. Continental breakfast; afternoon tea and sherry. Halfway between Hartford and Springfield. Four rooms: one reflects the Shaker influence from the area; another has a secret room used by the Underground Railroad. **$$**

Ledyard

Stonecroft
515 Pumpkin Hill Road, 06339
Tel: 800-772 0774
www.stonecroft.com
Actually two properties: the original 1807 colonial farmhouse with rooms reflecting period atmosphere and The Grange, the newly finished conversion of the post-and-beam barn with large "country modern" decor. Grounds have been landscaped with gardens, pond, and waterfall. **$$$-$$$$**

Litchfield

Litchfield Inn
432 Bantam Road (Route 202), 06759
Tel: 860-567 4503/800-499 3444
www.litchfieldinnct.com
Central location is a plus at this sophisticated inn, with its 32 rooms decorated in the Colonial style. The parlor has a baby grand piano

and fireplace. **$$$-$$$$**
Tollgate Hill Inn & Restaurant
571 Torrington Road (Route 202), 06759
Tel: 860-567 4545/866-567 1233
www.tollgatehill.com
Three buildings with hunt country and farmhouse appointments. Rooms in a 1745 tavern, an "old" farmhouse (built in 1992), and a historic schoolhouse with adjoining rooms that work well for families. **$-$$$**

Madison

Madison Beach Hotel
94 West Wharf Road, 06443
Tel: 203-245 1404
www.madisonbeachhotel.com
Re-opening in spring 2012 after an 18-month renovation. The plans will keep the nautical, sea-swept feel and maximize the great views of the Sound. **$$-$$$**
Tidewater Inn B&B
949 Boston Post Road (Route 1), 06443
Tel: 203-245 8457
www.thetidewater.com
A former shorefront stagecoach stop turned cozy, antique-filled B&B with nine rooms (some with fireplaces). Walking distance to Madison village. Many, many packages, especially in the off-season. **$-$$$**

Mystic Area

Harbour Inne & Cottage
15 Edgemont Street, Mystic, 06355
Tel: 860-572 9253
www.harbourinne-cottage.com
A family-friendly, pine-paneled 1950s bungalow with six nautical-themed rooms and a three-room cottage on the Mystic River. In quiet area, walking distance to the seaport and boat dock. **$$-$$$**

PRICE CATEGORIES

An approximate guide to rates for a standard double room per night:
$$$$ = more than $300
$$$ = $200-300
$$ = $125-200
$ = under $125

Inn at Mystic
Routes 1 and 27, Mystic, 06355
Tel: 860-536 9604/800-237 2415
www.innatmystic.com
Choose from motel units, guesthouses, or the National Historic Register Colonial Revival mansion at this 15-acre (6-hectare) property overlooking Mystic Harbor. Outdoor pool, tennis, boating, and kayaking. $$$–$$$$

Steamboat Inn
73 Steamboat Wharf, Mystic, 06355
Tel: 860-536 8300
www.steamboatinnmystic.com
Only waterfront inn in Mystic. Eleven rooms with a variety of decor and atmospheres, from the expected nautical and colonial to island pastels or Old World elegance. Most rooms have fireplaces or whirlpools; some have kitchens. $$–$$$$

Whaler's Inn
20 E. Main Street (Route 1), Mystic, 06355
Tel: 860-536 1506/800-243 2588
www.whalersinnmystic.com
The inn is downtown Mystic's largest lodging, with 41 comfortable, homey guest rooms. Easy walking to all of the town's attractions and the river. Families welcome. Continental breakfast. $$–$$$

New Haven

New Haven Hotel
229 George Street, 06510
Tel: 203-498 3100/800-644 6835
www.newhavenhotel.com
Completely renovated and rejuvenated. Contemporary furnishings; state-of-the-art entertainment system in all rooms. Excellent location in the heart of Yale country. $$$–$$$$

The Study at Yale
1157 Chapel Street, 06511
Tel: 203-599 4111
www.studyhotels.com
Completely renovated. "Study" theme with reading areas in each room, along with workspace, free Wi-Fi, glass shower stalls. 124 guestrooms, including eight "studies" (suites). Take-away inspired room service. In the heart of Yale's arts campus. $$$–$$$$

Touch of Ireland Guest House
670 Whitney Avenue, 06511
Tel: 203-787 7997/866-787 7990
www.touchofirelandguesthouse.com
Four comfortable rooms and a family suite in a nicely situated 1920s Colonial B&B less than a mile from the Yale campus. Private baths for all rooms, but some are across the hall. No children under 10. $$

New Preston

Hopkins Inn
22 Hopkins Road, 06777
Tel: 860-868 7295
www.thehopkinsinn.com
1847 Federal-style country inn perched high above Lake Waramaug has 11 comfortable, simply furnished rooms with wicker rockers, and two apartments. Apartments have washer/dryer and can be rented for longer stays. $$–$$$

Norfolk

Mountain View Inn
67 Litchfield Road, 06058
Tel: 860-542 6991/866-792 7812
www.mvinn.com
Across the street from the venue for the Yale Summer Music Concerts on 3 acres with mountain views. Decor is heavily Gilded Age with four-poster beds and many antiques. Good location for area touring. $$–$$$

Norwalk

Silvermine Tavern
194 Perry Avenue, 06850
Tel: 203-847 4558
www.silverminetavern.com
A 1785 country inn set by a waterfall has 11 antique-filled bedrooms; some have fireplaces. There's a jar of cracked corn in each room to feed the ever-hungry ducks and geese on the property. $–$$$$

Old Lyme

Bee & Thistle Inn
100 Lyme Street, 06371
Tel: 860-434 1667/800-622 4946
www.beeandthistleinn.com
A 1756 Colonial home with 11 rooms and a cottage, set peacefully beside a river. The elegant dining room serves prix-fixe dinners by advance reservation. $$$–$$$$

Old Saybrook

Deacon Timothy Pratt Bed & Breakfast
325 Main Street, 06475
Tel: 860-395 1229
www.pratthouse.com
Located in the quintessential New England village with gas-lit streets and sea captains' mansions, this 1746 house is filled with historical charm, like fireplaces in each room, with the modern amenities. Homemade Continental breakfast during the week; full breakfast on weekends. Garden has two-person hammock in the shade. Old fashion ice-cream parlor next door. $–$$

Ridgefield

Green ROCKS Inn
415 Danbury Road, 06877
Tel: 203-894 8944
www.greenrocksinn.com
Eco-friendly in every respect, from the organic bedding and food to the water filtration and sleep systems. Tucked in the woods, guests enjoy deer and wild turkeys foraging outside the inn. Four spacious, peaceful suites. One of the owners is a Justice of the Peace, and the inn is a popular place for weddings for GLBT couples. $$$–$$$$

Salisbury

Ragamont House
8 Main Street, 06068
Tel: 860-596 0555/866-424 7095
Elegant, sophisticated country retreat in the northwest corner of the state. Guests are encouraged to use the main rooms in order to appreciate the restoration of the building and the pleasant furnishings. $$$

Springfield

Hilton Garden Inn
800 Hall of Fame Avenue, 01105
Tel: 413-886 8000
www.hiltongardeninn.com
Located on the grounds of the Basketball Hall of Fame and close to Six Flags and other attractions, this is a popular spot for families. Five restaurants on the grounds. Used by business travelers, it has all the technology amenities in the rooms. Many packages for quick getaways and combos with attractions. $$–$$$

Springfield Marriott
2 Boland Way, 01115
Tel: 413-781 7111
www.marriott.com
In the heart of Springfield, within walking distance of most things; close to the free shuttle. Well-appointed rooms, upscale business technology amenities. $$–$$$

Stonington

Inn at Stonington
60 Water Street, 06378
Tel: 860-535 2000
www.innatstonington.com
Overlooking Stonington Borough harbor, home of Connecticut's last surviving commercial fishing fleet of lobstermen and a largely untouched, undeveloped village, this contemporary inn has 18 rooms and suites with fireplaces; 10 have Jacuzzis. $$$–$$$$

Suffield

The Lily House
13 Bridge Street, 06078
Tel: 860-668 7931
www.thelilyhouse.com
Four nicely appointed rooms in a rambling Victorian (complete with wraparound porch) in a New England farm town. Four pleasantly decorated rooms. Guests are encouraged to use the common room with games and an antique Victrola and 100 records. Owner is eager to accommodate guests with special dietary needs or food allergies. $$

Spencer-on-Main
264 S. Main Street, 06078
Tel: 860-668 5862

www.spenceronmain.com
Wonderful 1871 Second
Empire house on the last
non-commercial Main
Street in Connecticut. One
of the owners is a
descendant of the found-
ers of the town, so there's
a lot of love and care going
into the place. Two suites
and one bedroom, all with
marble fireplaces. On 8
landscaped and wooded
acres and with a summer
swimming pool. Children
over 12 welcome. **$$–$$$**

Wallingford

The Wallingford Victorian
245 N. Main Street, 06492
Tel: 203-269 4492
www.bedandbreakfast
wallingford.com

Very grand "painted lady"
two blocks from the heart
of the town center. Fresh,
clean, comfortable rooms
with a variety of decor
without a lot of frills and
antiques. Several of the
rooms can connect; the
suite at the top of the
house includes the turret
sitting room. **$$**

West Springfield

Comfort Inn and Suites
100 Capital Drive, 06492
Tel: 413-736 5000
www.comfortinn.com
Well-located, clean, rea-
sonably priced hotel with
full breakfast buffet,
indoor pool and hot tub,
and microwave and fridge
in all rooms. Often has

weekend packages and
combos with local attrac-
tions. **$–$$**

Wethersfield

Chester Bulkley House B&B
184 Main Street, 06109
Tel: 860-563 4236
Five-room B&B (three with
private bath) in an elegant
1830 Greek Revival home
located in an historic town
5 miles (8km) from
Hartford. Lots of special
touches, fresh flowers,
mints on the pillow. Full
breakfast every day. **$–$$**

Woodbury

Longwood Country Inn
1204 Main Street S, 06798
Tel: 203-266 0800
www.longwoodcountryinn.com

Very romantic inn on
acres of wooded land-
scape; four rooms and
three suites. The rooms
are very nice; the suites
are pure luxury. **$$$–$$$$**

Woodstock

Elias Child House
50 Perrin Road, 06281
Tel: 860-974 9836/877-974
9836
www.eliaschildhouse.com
Guests experience "home
and hearth," sometimes
literally when the innkeep-
ers demonstrate hearth
cooking in the 1714
house. On 47 acres of
pasture and woodlands,
it's very quiet and restful.
Two rooms and one suite.
Kids welcome. **$–$$**

VERMONT

Many Vermont inns take a
break between foliage and
the Christmas holidays,
and again during the
March–April "mud
season."

Arlington

West Mountain Inn
River Road (off Route
313), 05250
Tel: 802-375 6516
www.westmountaininn.com
Originally built as a farmhouse in 1849 and now
an 18-room inn with
mountain views on 150
country acres (60 hec-
tares). Mill house has several apartments suitable
for longer stays. Miles of
snowshoeing and hiking
trails, children's games

room, and an on-site
llama ranch. **$$$–$$$$**

Bennington

**Four Chimneys Inn and
Restaurant**
21 West Road (Route 9), 05201
Tel: 802-447 3500
www.fourchimneys.com
New owners have revitalized
this large but intimate, gra-
cious manor. The innkeepers
love the place so much they
were married here, years
before they left their corpo-
rate jobs for their new careers
as innkeepers. Eleven taste-
fully elegant, totally comforta-
ble rooms. **$$–$$$$**

Bolton Valley

The Black Bear
Bolton Access Road, 05477

Tel: 802-434 2126/800-395
6335
www.blkbearinn.com
Lodge located adjacent to
the Bolton Valley Ski
Resort trails. Discount lift
tickets available at front
desk. Twenty-four rooms,
but it feels much more
intimate. Some of the
rooms have balconies, hot
tubs, and fire stoves. Hotel
has been given "green"
status by the State. **$$–$$$**
Forty Putney Road B&B
192 Putney Road (Route 5),
05301
Tel: 802-254 6268/800-941
2413
www.fortyputneyroad.com
The six rooms on land-
scaped grounds overlook-
ing the West River are
pleasantly decorated and
the ambience is welcom-
ing and personal. The owners are two former
executives who ditched
the fast track for a more
satisfying lifestyle. The pub
has over 30 craft beers;
there's a beer tasting on
Saturday nights. **$$–$$$**
Latchis Hotel
50 Main Street, 05301
Tel: 802-254 6300/800-798
6301
www.latchis.com
A 1938 Art Deco boutique
hotel, right in the heart of

downtown. New manager
has upgraded the decor
and added special pack-
ages: weekend retreats
with in-room spa services;
theatre packages. The
hotel is attached to the
Latchis Theater, one of
Brattleboro's cultural
mainstays. The suites are
a particularly good deal.
$–$$

Bridgewater Corners

October Country Inn
362 Upper Road, 05035
Tel: 802-672 3412/800-648
8421
www.octobercountryinn.com
A cozy, 19th-century farmhouse with 10 rooms on
two of Vermont's scenic
byways, midway between
Killington and Woodstock.
Part of the Vermont "farm-
to-table" project, the
meals feature locally
grown and harvested
ingredients. Their occa-
sional ethnic dinners are
great fun. **$$–$$$**

PRICE CATEGORIES

An approximate guide to
rates for a standard double
room per night:
$$$$ = more than $300
$$$ = $200–300
$$ = $125–200
$ = under $125

BELOW: Vermont lodges are popular with leaf-peepers in the fall.

Brookfield

Green Trails Inn
Main Street, 05036
Tel: 802-276 3412
www.greentrailsinn.com
The sprawling 13-room
B&B just outside
Montpelier, built around
1790, and 1830 farm-
houses already had a rep-
utation as a laid-back
alternative to ski resorts.
New owner, cookbook
author Jane Doefer,
enhanced that with
remodeling and refurbish-
ing of all the public areas
and bedrooms. She also
offers cooking and yoga
classes. **$–$$$**

Burlington

Lang House on Main Street
360 Main Street, 05401
Tel: 877-919 9799
www.langhouse.com
A lovingly and precisely
restored 11-room, 1881
Victorian in one of the
more lovely residential
areas of town. Convenient
to the UVM campus and
downtown, the innkeeper
is assisted by enthusias-
tic, energetic UVM stu-
dents. **$$–$$$**

Willard Street Inn
349 S. Willard Street, 05401
Tel: 802-651 8710/800-577
8712
www.willardstreetinn.com
Fourteen antique-filled
rooms in an imposing
brick Victorian mansion
with all of the rich accents
– wood paneling in the
foyer, "grand entrance"
staircase, and exterior
marble staircase leading
to the formal gardens.
Wonderful views of Lake
Champlain. **$$–$$$$**

Chittenden

Mountain Top Inn
Mountain Top Road, 05737
Tel: 802-483 2311
www.mountaintopinn.com
This large, comfortable,
fully contained, year-
round family resort deep
in the countryside north
of Rutland is an active
destination. Everything
from clay shooting to hiking, horseback riding,
and boating on the
Chittenden Reservoir in

the summer; excellent
Nordic skiing, dog-sled-
ding, and sleigh rides in
the winter. Full breakfast
included. **$$$–$$$$**

Craftsbury Common

Craftsbury Inn
Main Street (Route 14),
Craftsbury, 05826
Tel: 802-586 2848/800-336
2848
www.craftsburyinn.com
Country comfort in an
1850 Greek Revival inn.
Ten rooms with wrapa-
round verandas overlook-
ing lavish gardens. Several
of them share a bath:
plush robes are provided.
One room is specifically
for kids with bunk beds
and lots of toys. **$–$$**

Dorset

Dorset Inn
Church and Main Streets, 05251
Tel: 802-867 5500
www.dorsetinn.com
One of the state's oldest
(1796) – and reliably com-
mendable – inns, with 31
updated rooms (one ADA-
compliant), half with fireplaces and whirlpools, all
with views of the green or
the gardens. "Older" chil-
dren welcome. **$$$–$$$$**

East Burke

Inn at Mountain View Farm
Darling Hill Road, 05832
Tel: 800-572 4509
www.innmtnview.com
A reason to visit the
Northeast Kingdom.
Fourteen casually elegant
guest rooms with private
baths and antiques in a
1890 Georgian inn on the
grounds of a one-time
creamery. Popular for wed-
dings and civil unions.
With 440 acres, there are
miles of cross-country,
hiking, and mountain bik-
ing trails. Open mid-May–
October. **$$$–$$$$**

Village Inn
606 Route 114, 05832
Tel: 802-626 3161
www.villageinnofeastburke.com
Six simple, clean, some-
what smallish rooms with
private baths in a homey
B&B close to several ski
areas and Kingdom Trails
mountain biking. Public

areas are bright, open,
and comfortable. They
have their own herb,
flower, and vegetable gar-
den, plus a 100-hive api-
ary. Huge country
breakfasts. **$–$$**

East Middlebury

Waybury Inn
457 E. Main Street, 05740
Tel: 800-348 1810
www.wayburyinn.com
A gracious country inn
that's popular with the
local residents, who stop
by for afternoon libation or
dinner (Robert Frost was a
frequent diner) or to linger
in the lower-level pub with
its vast selection of international brews. There are
worse ways to spend an
afternoon than sitting on a
rocking chair on the
veranda. **$$–$$$**

Essex Junction

Inn at Essex
70 Essex Way (off Route 15),
05452
Tel: 802-878 1100/800-727
4295
www.vtculinaryresort.com
Run by the New England
Culinary Institute, this is
an elegant country resort
inn with a full-service spa
and cooking school
among its amenities.
Other goodies include an
indoor lap pool, fly-fishing
in the stocked pond, hot-
air ballooning, and tennis.
120 casually elegant
rooms, many with fire-
places, and some one-
and two-bedroom suites
with kitchenettes for
longer stays. There are
many packages available,
including cooking classes
for guests. **$$$–$$$$**

Fair Haven

Maplewood Inn
1108 Route 22A South, 05473
Tel: 800-253 7729
www.maplewoodinn.net
A warm and comfortable
inn a little bit off the beaten
track, which is part of its
appeal. A five-room B&B
with fanciful decor and
hearty breakfasts in an
1843 Greek Revival home.
Fair Haven has a beautiful
collection of Victorian

architecture, worth stroll-
ing through. **$–$$**

Grafton

Old Tavern at Grafton
Route 121, 05146
Tel: 802-843 2231/800-843
1801
www.old-tavern.com
One of New England's old-
est inns, built in 1801 as a
stagecoach stop in the
picture-perfect village of
Grafton. The village is run
by the Windham
Foundation with a goal of
preserving Vermont's rural
traditions. Eleven rooms in
the inn plus 11 additional
properties scattered
around the grounds, all
reflecting the historic character and construction of
the buildings, but with all
the modern touches, hid-
den when possible (a cell-
phone tower is in the
chimney). Swimming
pond, tennis courts, ice-
skating, and cross-country
ski trails. **$$–$$$$**

Jay

**Jay Peak Ski and
Summer Resort**
Route 242, 05859
Tel: 802-988 2611/800-451
4449
www.jaypeakresort.com
Completely rebuilt and
expanded in 2011, it now
has all of the upscale ski
resort amenities, plus a
vast range of après-ski and
family vacation attractions,
including a huge indoor
water park. All new rooms,
from relatively basic "I'm
here to ski" lodging to mul-
tiroom luxury suites and
condos. **$$–$$$**

Jericho

Sinclair Inn B&B
389 Route 15, 05465
Tel: 802-899 2334/800-433
4658
www.sinclairinnbb.com
An elegant 1890s
"painted lady" just 25 min-
utes from Burlington has
six spacious, guest rooms
with lots of windows and
elaborate perennial gar-
dens. The huge porch is
perfect for enjoying the
views of Mt Mansfield.
Near Smuggler's Notch

and Stowe. Breakfast is served in the Victorian dining room. **$$**

Killington

Cascades Lodge
58 Old Mill Road, 05751
Tel: 800-345 0113/802-422 3731
www.cascadeslodge.com
This modern lodge with 45 rooms and suites stands at the base of Killington Mountain, steps from golf and ski lifts. Amenities include an indoor pool and sauna, and there's a restaurant and pub on the premises. They host a number of weekend events and have good packages in the off-season and during fall foliage. Breakfast included. **$$–$$$**

Inn at Long Trail
Route 4, 05751
Tel: 802-775 7181/800-325 2540
www.innatlongtrail.com
A 1938 rustic 19-room ski inn was the first lodge built for skiers. Very close to Killington's Pico base lodge. It's also popular with hikers on the Appalachian Trail. McGrath's Irish Pub has a huge selection of Irish whiskies and live Irish music on weekends. **$–$$**

BELOW: lodges at Killington, New England's largest ski resort.

Mountain Meadows Lodge
Thundering Brook Road, 05751
Tel: 802-775 1010
www.mtmeadowslodge.com
This large, family-oriented, serene lakeside farmhouse with 18 guest rooms has an extensive network of hiking/cross-country trails. The farmyard is run by Alice, a potbellied pig who loves people, especially if they sneak her some treats from breakfast. Expanded Continental breakfast during the week; full hot meal on weekends. **$–$$**

Lake Champlain Islands

Henry's Sportsman's Cottages Inc.
218 Poor Farm Road, Alburg, 05440
Tel: 802-796 3616
www.henryscottagesvermont.com
Fifteen lakefront, one-, two-, and three-bedroom rustic, fully furnished housekeeping cottages with screened porches for a family or sportsman's vacation. Private beach; boat and motor rentals. **$–$$**

North Hero House Inn and Restaurant
Route 2, North Hero, 05474

Tel: 802-372 4732/888-525 3644
www.northherohouse.com
Situated on the water on North Hero Island on Lake Champlain, this historic lakefront inn was recently restored to its 1891 appearance, while bringing it totally up-to-date with amenities and functionality. Twenty-six rooms in the main building and three guesthouses, all of which have second-floor balconies and some private porches where you can savor the lake and mountain views. Full breakfast included. **$$–$$$**

Shore Acres Inn and Restaurant
237 Shoreacres Drive North Hero, 05474
Tel: 802-372-8722
www.shoreacres.com
A comfortable 23-room lakeside motel with a vast veranda and wide lawn affording splendid views. Very laid-back atmosphere: croquet and horseshoes; tennis court and swimming. Boat dock and night mooring. Restaurant serves dinner nightly in season; closed in winter. **$$–$$$**

Lower Waterford

Rabbit Hill Inn
Route 18, 05848
Tel: 802-748 5168/800-762 8669
www.rabbithillinn.com
Very romantic, very luxurious, very beautiful inn located in the heart of the Northeast Kingdom. Twenty elegant rooms, many with fireplaces, oversize whirlpool tubs, and other plush touches in a romantic, Greek Revival inn on 15 wooded acres. There's a superb restaurant, and lots of pampering personal touches. ADA-compliant. Non-smoking. Trails for walking or cross-country skiing; canoes can also be arranged. **$$$$**

Lyndonville

Wildflower Inn
Darling Hill Road, 05851
Tel: 802-626 8310/800-627 8310

www.wildflowerinn.com
Great country "resort" on 570 sprawling acres; 23 rooms and suites in five houses and converted farm buildings. Especially good for families, there's a barn that's a giant indoor kids' center with mazes, slides, and other high-energy activities. The petting barn has horses, goats, a calf, and the requisite barn cats. It's also home to the Vermont Children's Theater which stages performances in season. The property is designed so that there's plenty of non-kid privacy and activities, too, but it's more for the active guests than those looking for a quiet, romantic escape. Many packages for all age groups and interests. The restaurant can accommodate gluten-free and other dietary needs. **$$–$$$$**

Manchester

The Equinox and the Charles Orvis Inn
Route 7A, 05254
Tel: 802-362 4700/800-362 4747
www.equinoxresort.com
One of Vermont's premier historic hotels has 183 rooms and suites in the main inn, nine suites in the Charles Orvis Inn, and fireplaced rooms in the 1811 House. Amazing array of activities (mostly add-ons). **$$$$**

Wilburton Inn
River Road (off Route 7A), 05254
Tel: 802-362 2500/800-648 4944
www.wilburton.com
A railroad baron's 100+-year-old brick mansion plus villas and cottages set on 20 acres (8 hectares). There's an outdoor sculpture garden (part of the Museum of the Creative Process) and a

PRICE CATEGORIES

An approximate guide to rates for a standard double room per night:
$$$$ = more than $300
$$$ = $200–300
$$ = $125–200
$ = under $125

greenhouse where much of the inn's produce is grown. The rooms have a country-home feel, but the amenities and services are of a full-scale, full-service fine hotel. **$$–$$$$**

Middlebury

Inn on the Green
71 Pleasant Street
Tel: 802-388 7512/888-244 7512
www.innonthegreen.com
Clean, contemporary decor is a refreshing change from the over-abundance of antiques and Victorian garnishes in many inns. Perfectly sited in the heart of this bustling, riverside college and arts town. Eleven rooms, half of which can sleep up to four people. Continental breakfast is delivered to your room each morning. **$$–$$$**

Middlebury Inn
14 Court House Square, 05753
Tel: 802-388 4961/800-842 4666
middleburyinn.com
An 1827 inn, 1825 mansion, and more modern annex overlooking the village green combine modern conveniences with classic historic charm as befits the setting. Rooms reflect the "high society" style of the period. The town is centrally located; inn is a good place to use as a base for exploring most of Vermont. **$$–$$$$**

Montgomery

English Rose Inn
Route 242, Montgomery Center, 05471
Tel: 802-326 3232/888-303 3232
www.theenglishroseinn.com
1850s farmhouse just 3.5 miles (6km) from Jay Peak has 14 very Victorian guestrooms and suites. Rates include full breakfast and afternoon tea. Offers wedding/civil union packages. **$–$$$**

Inn on Trout River
Main Street, 05471
Tel: 802-326 4391/800-338 7049
www.troutinn.com

The owners of this Victorian country farmhouse say they specialize in "stress management." Ten rooms furnished in English and Victorian country styles with down quilts and flannel sheets (in winter). Big fireplaces in the main dining room and parlor. Close to hiking, skiing, and golf in both the US and Canada; bring your passport. The town has seven covered bridges and other scenic joys. **$–$$**

Montgomery Center

Phineas Swann Country Inn
195 Main Street, 05471
Tel: 802-326 4306
www.phineasswann.com
Close to Jay Peak, this is a very romantic inn, and a very – very – dog-friendly place, as well. Dogs roam and play on the grounds; there's a dog spa package, and staff care for pets while guests are doing "no pets allowed" activities. The restaurant is equipped to provide meals for all dietary conditions. The outside gazebo is popular for small weddings and civil unions. **$$–$$$$**

Montpelier

Capitol Plaza Hotel and Conference Center
100 State Street, 05602
Tel: 802-223 5252/800-274 5252
www.capitolplaza.com
Full-service hotel adjacent to the State House with a "country inn" attitude and 62 rooms with views of the Winooski River. On-site steak house was recently renovated. **$$–$$$**

Inn at Montpelier
147 Main Street, 05602
Tel: 802-223 2727
www.innatmontpelier.com
A pair of adjoining Federal mansions with 27 rooms make a convenient in-town retreat. The main inn has a wraparound porch to take in the views of the Winooski and North Branch rivers. Inside, there are 10 fireplaces, a

grand staircase, and other touches evoking the era of Grand Living. Extensive Continental breakfast from students at the New England Culinary Institute's in-town bakery. Children under 6 stay free; cash and checks preferred. **$$–$$$**

Newfane Area

Four Columns Inn
21 West Street, Newfane, 05345
Tel: 802-365 7713/800-787 6633
www.fourcolumnsinn.com
Very elegant, very upscale "country" decor in this majestic Greek Revival inn on 150 acres on the picturesque village green. Very popular for "escape" weekends (lots of packages). The stream on the property is a popular setting for weddings and civil unions. **$$$–$$$$**

River Bend Lodge
Route 30, 05345
Tel: 802-365 7952
www.riverbendlodgevt.com
Twenty recently redecorated rooms, very simple but comfortable, in a sprawling lodge on 30 acres with mountain views and private trails. On the banks of the West River on the edge of Newfane, a town so historic that the entire place is on the National Register of Historic Places. Near Stratton Mountain and Mt Snow. **$**

Quechee

Quechee Inn at Marshland Farm
Clubhouse Road, 05059
Tel: 802-295 3133/800-235 3133
www.quecheeinn.com
"Classic country lodging" on a historic 1793 farmstead with 24 rooms in a bucolic riverside setting. Resident outdoor guide available for guided hikes, fly-fishing instruction, and other outdoor activities. Guests can use the nearby Quechee Club for golf, fitness center, indoor pool, and sauna. **$–$$$**

Shelburne

Inn at Shelburne Farms
Harbor Road, 05482
Tel: 802-985 8498
www.shelburnefarms.org
Lila Vanderbilt's turn-of-the-20th-century lakefront Tudor-style mansion, set amid the working farm, offers 24 guest rooms (some with shared bath), and four cottages, including the three-bedroom Glass House. Open mid-May–mid-October. **$$$–$$$$**

Shoreham

Shoreham Inn
51 Inn Street, 05770
Tel: 802-897 5081/800-255 5081
www.shorehaminn.com
Ten antique-filled B&B rooms with private baths in an historic 18th-century inn that's been welcoming travelers since 1790. Recently achieved "Green Hotel" status from the State for its eco-friendly operations. The gastropub serves excellent comfort food and pub grub and a good selection of local brews. **$$–$$$**

Stowe

Alpenrose Motel
2619 Mountain Road, 05672
Tel: 802-253 7277/800-962 7002
www.gostowe.com/saa/alpenrose
Small motel halfway between the village and Mt Mansfield offers standard rooms and efficiencies with all the amenities, plus an outdoor pool. **$–$$**

Green Mountain Inn
Route 100, 05672
Tel: 802-253 7301/800- 253 7302
www.greenmountaininn.com
A total of 104 units in an 1833 in-town inn, suites, and adjacent town houses. Rooms blend classic New England charm with up-to-date technology. Facilities include a year-round outdoor heated pool, and a health club with a masseuse for après-ski or -hiking therapy. **$$–$$$**

**Topnotch at Stowe
Resort and Spa**
Mountain Road, 05672
Tel: 800-451 8686
www.topnotch-resort.com
Very upscale, intimate,
luxury inn with ski-lodge
charm. 68 rooms and 40
chalets. A top-rated spa
and many activities.
Programs for kids from
toddlers to teens.
$$$–$$$$

Trapp Family Lodge
700 Trapp Hill Road, 05672
Tel: 802-253 8511/800-826
7000
www.trappfamily.com
On 2,800 acres (1,100
hectares), this European-
style lodge has 96 rooms,
100 chalets, and several
villas to create an
Austrian village. A full
resort, not just a lodge.
There's a fitness center,
several fine restaurants,
and a first-rate cross-
country ski facility.
$$$–$$$$

Basin Harbor Club
Basin Harbor Road, 05491
Tel: 802-475 2311/800-622
4000
www.basinharbor.com
A classic, 700-acre
(300-hectare) lakeside
summer colony built
around an old farmhouse
and full of timeless pleas-
ures. Most of the 138
accommodations are in
newer cottages, many
with fireplaces and refrig-
erators. Amenities
include a beach, swim-
ming pool, golf course,
tennis courts, and a play-
ground. Extensive chil-
dren's and teen activities.
Open mid-May–October.
$$$$

The Inn at Lareau Farms
Route 100, 05673
Tel: 802-496 4949
www.lareaufarminn.com
This 13-room B&B on 67
acres of woods and pas-
tures near the Mad River
has an authentic farm-
house atmosphere with
country-style rooms.
American Flatbread
makes pizza here Friday

and Saturday nights.
$–$$

Round Barn Farm
1161 E. Warren Road, 05673
Tel: 802-496 2276/800-721
8029
www.theroundbarn.com
Luxuriously retrofitted
farmhouse B&B on 245
acres with 12 plush
guest rooms with
canopy beds, some with
whirlpool baths. The
unusual "round"
Shaker-style barn is
used for summer con-
certs and parties.
Designated a "Green
Hotel" by the State, the
owners were among the
founding members of
the Vermont Fresh
Network, which con-
nects farmers and chefs.
$$–$$$$

Pitcher Inn
275 Main Street, 05674
Tel: 802-496 6350
www.pitcherinn.com
Each of the 11 elegant
rooms and suites at this
white clapboard Relais &
Châteaux property has a
different decorating theme:
"school" has a blackboard
as the bed's headboard;
"mallard" has a goose
decoy suspended from the
ceiling and "camouflage"
bedding. All have Jacuzzis,
and many have steam
showers and fireplaces.
$$$$

The Old Stagecoach Inn
18 N. Main Street, 05676
Tel: 802-244 5056/800-262
2206
www.oldstagecoach.com
Classic Vermont bed-and-
breakfast: beautifully
restored 19th-century
stagecoach stop has eight
comfortable guest rooms
and three efficiency
suites. Several rooms
have fireplaces and sitting
areas; some share bath.
Nice location for day trips.
$–$$

Inn at Sawmill Farm
7 Crosstown Road, Route
100, 05356

Tel: 802-464 8131/800-493
1133
www.theinnatsawmillfarm.
com
Twenty-one guest rooms
and Nonna's, a first-rate
Italian restaurant, in an
old farmstead jazzed up
with bold decorative
touches. The grounds
include a pond, pool, and
walking trails. This is
country elegance at its
best. Convenient to Mt
Snow and Haystack
Mountain ski areas.
$$–$$$

Windham Hill Inn
311 Lawrence Drive, 05359
Tel: 802-874 4080/800-944
4080
www.windhamhill.com
Recently appointed a
member of the ultra-ele-
gant, ultra-exclusive
Relais & Châteaux
collection of lodgings.
Richly appointed rooms,
fine dining in elegant
settings, exclusive spa.
Located 10 miles (16km)
north of Newfane and 10
miles (16km) east of
Stratton Mountain ski
area. **$$$–$$$$**

Applebutter Inn
Happy Valley Road,
Woodstock, 05091
Tel: 802-457 4158
www.applebutterinn.com
Six-room B&B in an
1854 Federal house full
of fluffy comforters;
three fireplaced sitting
rooms. Quiet and unpre-
tentious, very warm inn-
keepers. Nicely situated
for visiting Dartmouth,
30 minutes from
Killington and Pico; 10
minutes from Suicide Six.
$$–$$$

**Jackson House Inn and
Restaurant**
37 Route 4 W, Woodstock,
05091
Tel: 802-457 2065/800-448
1890
www.jacksonhouse.com
Just outside Woodstock,
it's close enough to make
use of all the town's facili-
ties and activities while
being away from the

hustle. Refined elegance
is the hallmark of this
lovingly restored 1890s
clapboard house, now a
15-room B&B. The
restaurant, with an
outstanding wine list,
also serves five-course
breakfasts, which are
included in the room
rate. The view from the
bright, airy dining room
invites lingering over
your morning coffee.
$$$–$$$$

Kedron Valley Inn
Route 106, South
Woodstock, 05071
Tel: 802-457 1473/800-836
1193
www.kedronvalleyinn.com
You've seen the inn
many times; it's the
snow-covered inn the
Budweiser Clydesdales
are passing in the
"Christmas card" commer-
cial. Five miles south of
Woodstock, heirloom
quilts dress up the 28
tastefully decorated
rooms. Most have fire-
places; a few also have
Jacuzzis. The restaurant
has a fine-dining
menu, but invites
customers to dress
casually. **$$–$$$$**

**Woodstock Inn and
Resort**
14 The Green (Route 4)
Woodstock, 05091
Tel: 802-457 1100/800-448
7900
www.woodstockinn.com
An elegant in-town estate
facing the village green.
The 142 rooms are deco-
rated with an upscale
Vermont country concept:
natural wood-beam
bedframes, furniture by
Vermont crafters. The
bedding and toiletries
are plush and exclusive.
The new spa offers a
range of pampering as
befits the setting.
$$$–$$$$

An approximate guide to
rates for a standard double
room per night:
$$$$ = more than $300
$$$ = $200–300
$$ = $125–200
$ = under $125

NEW HAMPSHIRE

Bedford

Bedford Village Inn
2 Village Inn Lane, 03110
Tel: 603-472 2001/800-852 1166
www.bedfordvillageinn.com
Boutique hotel with opulent touches in the 14 luxury suites with four-poster beds and marble bathrooms at an inn carved out of a three-story barn south of Manchester. $$$–$$$$

Bethlehem

Adair Inn
80 Guider Lane (at Route 302), 03574
Tel: 603-444 2600/888-444 2600
www.adairinn.com
Set on 200 acres, this 1927 Georgian Colonial mansion is now a nine-room, upscale B&B; the rooms have four-posted beds and wing chairs in the sitting area, but it's far

from pretentious – there's a casual tap room and vintage pool table. Rooms have either garden or mountain views. $$$–$$$$

Mulburn Inn
2370 Main Street, 03574
Tel: 603-869 3389/800-457 9440
www.mulburninn.com
Originally a summer home for a branch of the Woolworth family, it welcomed Marilyn Monroe, Cary Grant, Barbara Hutton, and Thomas Edison, among other notables. Chances are you'll stay in a room one of them used. Architectural touches include stained-glass windows, rich wood paneling, ornately carved mantles, and imported fireplace tiles. $$–$$$

Bretton Woods

Mount Washington Hotel and Resort
Route 302, 03575

Tel: 603-278 1000
www.omnihotels.com
Built in 1902, this National Historic Landmark grand hotel is finishing a $50 million renovation, restoration, refurbishment, and redevelopment project designed to position it as a premier destination resort in New England. The long list of both summer and winter activities and amenities includes skiing, spa services, retail shopping, kids' program, fine and casual dining, tennis, golf, zip-line touring, and eco-tours. Rooms are very spacious and luxurious. $$$–$$$$

Concord

Centennial Hotel
96 Pleasant Street, 03301
Tel: 603-227 9000/800-360 4839
www.thecentennialhotel.com
A landmark in town, this four-story Queen Anne Victorian hotel. Restored to keep the architectural details, but with a cool, contemporary interior decor. Each of the 32 guest rooms is individually decorated, with upscale bedding and furnishings. Large-hotel services with small-hotel attention. $$–$$$

Dixville Notch

Balsams Grand Resort Hotel
Route 26, 03576
Tel: 800-255 0600
www.thebalsams.com
A sprawling, 19th-century, 215-room resort hotel, set in its own natural preserve. Activities include dancing and entertainment nightly, pool, tennis courts, skiing, fishing, and children's programs. Upscale traditional country room decor. Jackets required in public areas after 6pm. (If "Dixville Notch" sounds familiar, that's because this is where the first voting for presidential primaries and general elections is held.) $$$–$$$$

Eaton Center

Inn at Crystal Lake
Route 153, 03832
Tel: 603-447 2120/800-343 7336
www.innatcrystallake.com
Warm, friendly, comfortable 1884 Victorian B&B in a sleepy lakeside village just minutes from Conway. CD collection available for use is heavy on opera and the classics, since the owner was a classical voice major in college. Walk to the beach. Palmer House Pub serves great chili. $–$$$

Franconia

Franconia Inn
1300 Easton Valley Road, 03583
Tel: 603-823 5542/800-473 5299
www.franconiainn.com
This rambling, 19th-century resort with 29 rooms and three suites in the main building and adjacent restored cottage has 107 acres to explore. The main house has two verandas with fantastic views of the White Mountains. $$–$$$

Glen

The Bernerhof
Route 302, 03838
Tel: 877-389 4852
www.bernerhofinn.com
Top-to-bottom renovation makes this a romantic, boutique lodging. Rooms have double whirlpool baths, eco-friendly fireplaces, and plush bedding. The ADA- compliant rooms are equally well-appointed. The inn's private, European-style pub serves afternoon tea and hors d'oeuvres and has a respectable selection of Vermont craft beers. $$–$$$$

Covered Bridge House B&B
Route 302, 03838
Tel: 603-383 9109/800-232 9109
www.coveredbridgehouse.com

BELOW: inns come in a variety of styles, some rustic, some sophisticated.

The name comes from the covered bridge on the property which crosses the Saco River. Built in 1850, it was closed to traffic many years ago and now houses a gift shop. The inn has six comfortable B&B rooms with quilts, braided rugs, and rocking chairs. Full breakfast each morning in a sunny dining room. **$–$$**

Hampton Beach

Ashworth by the Sea
295 Ocean Boulevard, 03842
Tel: 603-926 6762/800-345 6736 (outside NH)
www.ashworthhotel.com
Built in 1912, this landmark oceanfront hotel has 105 spacious, contemporary rooms with ocean views, some with balconies. Indoor heated pool, fine and casual dining. **$–$$$$**

Hanover

Hanover Inn at Dartmouth College
Main Street, 03755
Tel: 603-643 4300/800-443 7024
www.hanoverinn.com
An integral part of the Dartmouth campus, this four-story, traditionally decorated Georgian brick building with 92 rooms began as a tavern and became a hotel in 1813. Relax in a rocker on the gracious porch overlooking the common. The restaurants are almost as revered as the college. **$$$–$$$$**

Henniker

Colby Hill Inn
3 The Oaks, 03242
Tel: 603-428 3281/800-531 0330
www.colbyhillinn.com
More of a small country hotel than a traditional B&B, the 14 rooms are furnished with antiques and Colonial reproductions; four rooms have fireplaces. The restaurant routinely wins accolades from wine and cuisine experts. West of Concord, near Pat's Peak ski area. **$–$$$**

Holderness

The Manor on Golden Pond
Route 3 and Shepard Hill Road, 03245
Tel: 603-968 3348/800-545 2141
www.manorongoldenpond.com
Luxury hideaway intimate hotel overlooking Squam Lake (the Golden Pond of the movie). A 1903 English manor–style stone mansion and annox with 19 rooms; some with fireplaces, all with lavish private baths (some with steam showers and whirlpools). The on-site spa and dining rooms are equally distinctive and pampering. **$$$$**

Jackson

Inn at Thorn Hill
Thorn Hill Road, 03846
Tel: 603-383 4242/800-289 8990
www.innatthornhill.com
Ranked as one of the top inns in the country. Luxury with a view; this elegant estate overlooks Mt Washington and has 25 romantically decorated rooms, suites, and cottages. Full day-spa with extensive list of therapies to relax and refresh. The restaurant is equally highly rated. **$$$–$$$$**

Whitney Inn at Jackson
Route 16B, 03846
Tel: 603-383 8916/800-677 5737
www.whitneysinn.com
Rooms in this 1840 inn include 16 in the main building, eight two-bedroom suites in the lodge, and two two-bedroom cottages, all with rustic lodge appointments. Situated on nine acres at the base of Black Mountain ski area, it has both downhill and cross-country trail access. Full (very full) country breakfast each morning. The pub serves Yankee favorites in an old stone barn. **$–$$$**

Wildcat Inn & Tavern
Route 16A, 03846
Tel: 603-356 8700/800-228 4245
www.wildcattavern.com

A 12-room B&B in the social center of town with delightful, albeit tiny, suites and an extremely popular restaurant. The rooms adjacent to the kitchen or above the tavern can be noisy. **$–$$$**

Keene

Carriage Barn
358 Main Street, 03431
Tel: 603-357 3812
www.carriagebarn.com
A thoroughly renovated Civil War–era barn with four rooms simply furnished with antiques and handmade quilts. Great breakfasts in a sunny room overlooking meadows. Across from Keene State College. **$**

E.F. Lane Hotel
30 Main Street, Central Square, 03431
Tel: 603-357 7070/888-300 5056
www.thelanehotel.com
In a beautifully maintained, century-old building, this full-service, boutique hotel was completely renovated in 2011. The 40 rooms and suites (some two-level) make the most of the original exposed brick walls and oversize windows. The lobby has a brand new bar and welcoming fireplace. **$$–$$$**

Lincoln

Profile Motel and Cottages
391 Route 3, 03251
Tel: 603-745 2759/800-282 0092
www.profilemotel.com
Clean, homey motel units with microwaves, refrigerators, TV, and free Wi-Fi, as well as one- to five-bedroom cottages. The 5-acre property has a heated outdoor pool, fire pit, and family games. **$–$$**

Littleton

Beal House Inn
2 W. Main Street, 03561
Tel: 603-444 2661/888-616 2325
Jose Luis from Argentina and Catherine from the Netherlands met while working on a cruise ship.

Of course, they would decide that opening a B&B in New Hampshire was the natural thing to do. Their restored 1833 Federal inn close to town has eight cozy, antique-filled rooms and suites with four-poster beds; some fireplaces. Between the two of them, they speak French, German, Spanish, Dutch, and Portuguese, as well as American and British English. Open seasonally. **$$–$$$**

Thayer's Inn
111 Main Street, 03561
Tel: 603-444 6469/800-634 8179
www.thayersinn.com
One of the Top Historic Places to Stay, this white-columned Greek Revival inn in the center of town started life as a railroad hotel in 1843. One of New Hampshire's oldest hostelries, the 36 rooms range from small and simple to quite plush, but are all comfortable and reasonably priced. **$–$$**

Manchester

Ash Street Inn
118 Ash Street, 03104
Tel: 603-668 9908
www.ashstreetinn.com
The Queen City's premier in-town B&B, a three-story 1885 Victorian, has many of its original 19th-century accents, including magnificent stained-glass windows. The antique-filled guest rooms have thick quilts, Egyptian cotton sheets, and down pillows. Breakfast is included; proper afternoon tea is available for a modest fee. **$$–$$$**

New Castle

Wentworth by the Sea Hotel and Spa
Wentworth Road, 03854
Tel: 888-252 6888

PRICE CATEGORIES

An approximate guide to rates for a standard double room per night:
$$$$ = more than $300
$$$ = $200–300
$$ = $125–200
$ = under $125

TRANSPORTATION

ACCOMMODATIONS

ACTIVITIES

A – Z

www.wentworth.com
One of the seacoast's premier destination inns, a Victorian confection owned by Marriott, offers first-class accommodations. Most of the 161 rooms and suites have water views; there's a full-service spa and a fine restaurant. It is to hotels what the Newport mansions are to summer cottages. **$$$–$$$$**

New London

Inn at Pleasant Lake
Pleasant Street, 03257
Tel: 603-526 6271/800-626 4907
www.innatpleasantlake.com
Overlooking Pristine Lake and Mt Kearsarge in the Lake Sunapee region, this 1790 inn has 10 guest rooms on 5 acres. The five-course prix-fixe menu Chef Brian MacKenzie creates in the restaurant should not be missed. Canoes, kayaks, and row-boats for guests. **$$–$$$**
Maple Hill Farm
1200 Newport Road, 03257
Tel: 603-526 2248/800-231 8637
www.maplehillfarm.com
A family-friendly, comfortably furnished 1824 farmhouse near Little Lake Sunapee has 10 basic guest rooms (four with shared baths) with antiques and handmade quilts, plus several resident dogs and cats. Good meals, welcoming attitude. Kind of like a good visit at Grandma's. **$–$$**

North Conway

The 1785 Inn
Route 16, 03860
Tel: 603-356 9025/800-421 1785
www.the1785inn.com
This colonial inn at the Scenic Vista, one of the most photographed and painted spots in the White Mountains, is comfortably furnished with colonial, Victorian, and country-style pieces. The restaurant has a highly acclaimed wine list. **$–$$**
Farm by the River B&B
2555 West Side Road, 03860

(Off Route 16/302, 1 mile (1.6km) from Echo Lake State Park)
Tel: 603-356 2694
www.farmbytheriver.com
The property has been in the same family since 1771. Nestled on 70 acres, this 1785 classic country farmhouse with nine guest rooms has a beach on the Saco River. The rooms have modern features, like gas fireplaces and soaking tubs, but maintain the historic country feel. An on-site stable has horses for trail rides and sleigh rides in the winter. **$$–$$$**
Stonehurst Manor
Route 16, 03860
Tel: 603-356 3113/800-525 9100
www.stonehurstmanor.com
Once part of the summer estate of carpet baron Erastus Bigelow, this 100-year-old mansion amidst 33 acres of pine forest has 25 upscale country rooms (seven with fireplaces), an outdoor pool, hot tub, and tennis court. Great mountain views from the gardens or near the fireplace on snowy afternoons. **$$–$$$**

North Sutton

Follansbee Inn on Kezar Lake
Route 114, 03260
Tel: 603-927 4221/800-626 4221
www.follansbeeinn.com
A cozy, 1840s inn on Kazar Lake (just south of Lake Sunapee/Dartmouth) caters to adults and older teens looking for an active, eco-tourism vacation. Kayaks, canoes, bikes, and snowshoes are available for guest use. There are 17 guest rooms and a cabin. **$$**

North Woodstock

Woodstock Inn
Main Street (Route 3), 03262
Tel: 603-745 3951/800-321 3985
www.woodstockinnnh.com
Five Victorian and country houses in the bustling tourist town. The rooms vary from romantic to

family-friendly and are good value. Guests have access to the nearby Mountain Club Resort's amenities like pool and health club. Rates include a full breakfast at the Clement Room Grille. **$–$$**

Pittsburg

The Glen
118 Glen Road, 03592
Tel: 603-538 6500/800-445 4536
www.theglen.org
The Connecticut lakes region's premier (and state's northernmost) resort, a mile down a private road, offers six rooms in the main lodge, two one-bedroom hillside cottages, and seven lakefront cottages that sleep up to eight. Hiking, boats, motors, and guides. Open May–October. **$$**
Tall Timber
609 Beach Road, 03592
Tel: 603-835 6343
www.talltimber.com
Since 1946, the sporting lodge has been a destination for anglers and nature lovers. Accommodations range from simple rooms with shared or private bath in the main lodge to private, luxury cottages. Kids 16 and under stay free with adult. **$$–$$$$**

Portsmouth

Inn at Strawbery Banke
314 Court Street, 03801
Tel: 603-436 7242/800-428 3933
www.innatstrawberybanke.com
1800 sea captain's house adjoining the historic preserve has seven handsome guest rooms. Breakfast room overlooks (what else?) a strawberry patch. Inn is well-suited for parking the car and walking to attractions. **$$**
Martin Hill Inn
404 Islington Street, 03801
Tel: 603-436 2287
www.martinhillinn.com
An 1812 Colonial main house and a country-style 1850 guesthouse set amid beautifully designed and always blooming perennial gardens. Lavish

breakfasts. Seven rooms. **$–$$$**
Sise Inn
40 Court Street, 03801
Tel: 603-433 1200/877-747 3466
www.siseinn.com
A small hotel in an elegant 1881 Queen Anne Victorian "painted lady" on Haymarket Square, then, as now, one of the more desirable locations in town. Some of the 34 rooms have fireplaces, whirlpool baths, and stereos. **$$$**

Snowville

Snowville Inn
92 Stuart Road, Off Route 153, 03832
Tel: 603-447 2818/800-447 4345
www.snowvillageinn.com
New owners completely refurbished and refreshed the aging inn, formerly the Snowvillage Inn, bringing it back to its former glory. Comfortable and spacious rooms are in three buildings. Some have gas fireplaces; most have great views of the Presidential Range. Big breakfast is included in the rates. **$$–$$$**

Sugar Hill

Hilltop Inn
Route 117, 03585
Tel: 603-823 5695/800-770 5695
www.hilltopinn.com
This homey 1895 Victorian inn in the village is a classic B&B, with six cozy rooms (all with private baths), a crackling hearth, and terrific country-style breakfasts. **$$–$$$**
Sugar Hill Inn
Route 117, 03580
Tel: 603-823 5621/800-548 4748
www.sugarhillinn.com
Classic lodging at this 18th-century farmhouse inn with 13 guest rooms includes the Bette Davis Luxury Suite, where the actress often stayed, and a plush and very private cottage. Some rooms/suites have fireplaces and whirlpool tubs. No need to leave the

grounds for dinner: the restaurant is excellent. **$$$–$$$$**

Sunset Hill House
Sunset Hill Road, 03586
Tel: 603-823 5521/800-786 4455
www.sunsethillhouse.com
This sprawling, 28-room inn is perched on a 1,700ft (520-meter) ridge overlooking the Presidential Range in Franconia Notch. Moose occasionally wander by to check out the tourists. Accommodations range from small rooms with twin beds to two-room suites, but all have mountain views. Facilities include a restaurant, tavern, pool, golf course, and hiking trails. The innkeepers are very proud of their eco-active operation. **$$–$$$**

Sunapee

Dexter's Inn
258 Stage Coach Road, 03782
Tel: 603-763 5571/800-232 5571
A secluded, yellow clapboard 1801 house with 17 rooms, tennis courts, hiking trails, cross-country and snowshoeing outfitter, and an outdoor pool. **$$–$$$**

Burkehaven Lodge
179 Burkehaven Road, 03782
Tel: 603-763 2788/800-567 2788
www.burkehaven.com
Totally updated, home-like setting and ambience. Close to the lake, but not in the middle of the action. Eleven pleasant units and a two-bedroom penthouse suite, all with electric fireplaces, overlooking Sunapee Harbor. It's on the new 3-mile walking "loop" around town. Pool; Continental breakfast. **$–$$**

Temple

Birchwood Inn
Route 45, 03084
Tel: 603-878 3285
www.thebirchwoodinn.com
British hospitality New Hampshire style in a c.1800 B&B with seven guest rooms (two with shared bath). The London Tavern, open Wednesday–Sunday, serves proper English pub grub (although it's hard to explain away the nachos) and ale. Breakfast included. **$–$$**

Waterville Valley

Waterville Valley Resort
Waterville Valley, 03223
Tel: 800-468 2553
www.waterville.com

A resort complex with more than 700 rooms, cupped in a high valley, with skiing in winter, hiking, tennis, and other sports the rest of the year. **$–$$$$**

West Chesterfield

Chesterfield Inn
20 Cross Road, 03466
Tel: 603-256 3211/800-365 5515
www.chesterfieldinn.com
Originally a tavern, this 1798 building has been converted into a luxurious 15-room inn. Spacious, well-appointed rooms. The inn invites a lot of lazing and lounging in the gardens or by the in-room fireplace. Breakfasts cooked to order. **$$$–$$$$**

Whitfield

Mountain View Grand
Mountain View Road, 03598
Tel: 603-837 2100/8866-484 3843
www.mountainviewgrand.com
One of the classic "Grand Hotels" from the Golden Age. The 1865 hostelry has been faithfully restored, but with all the modern amenities and features for first-class comfort and casual elegance. High level of service and many activities,

including a Ralph Barton–designed 18-hole golf course. The mountain setting alone is worth the trip. On-site spa with broad range of services, many keyed to the season. **$$$–$$$$**

Spalding Inn
199 Mountain View Road, 03598
Tel: 603-837 2572/800-368 8439
www.spaldinginn.com
A quiet but full-scale family resort on 200 acres, operating since 1926, with golf course, tennis courts, and heated pool. Accommodations in the main inn, a lodge, and separate cottages. 45 rooms. **$$–$$$**

Wolfeboro

Wolfeboro Inn
90 N. Main Street, 03894
Tel: 603-569 3016/800-451 2389
www.wolfeboroinn.com
The village inn, with spectacular views of Lake Winnipesaukee, has been a hostelry since 1812. It has 44 rooms and suites, a private beach, and fishing. Its upscale Wolfe's Tavern has several dining rooms, some with fireplaces. A 70ft replica paddle boat offers lake cruises. **$$–$$$$**

MAINE

Note that many of Maine's hotels and inns are open only in summer. When known, that's noted in the listing.

Acadia National Park Area

Bar Harbor Inn & Spa
Newport Drive, 04609
Tel: 207-288 3351/800-248 3351
www.barharborinn.com
Overlooking Frenchman Bay, this has been a vacation destination for more than 125 years. 153 rooms in three buildings in town. Most rooms have fireplaces and views; some have private decks.

$$–$$$$
Manor House Inn
106 West Street, 04609
Tel: 207-288 3759/800-437 0088
www.barharbormanorhouse.com
An 1887 Victorian inn with 14 one- and two-bedroom units and a carriage house, both surrounded by gardens. No children under 12. The owners are both Bar Harbor natives, so they have all the scoop on what to see and do and the best way to accomplish that. **$–$$**

Edgewater Motel & Cottages
Salisbury Cove

Tel: 207-288 3491/888-310 9920
www.edgewaterbarharbor.com
Economical oceanfront lodging, with an eight-unit two-story motel (four with fully equipped kitchens and fireplaces), 11 cottages, and four suites. All rooms have a sliding glass door opening to a balcony which faces Frenchman's Bay. Private pebble beach. **$–$$**

Ellsworth

Acadia Birches Knights Inn
20 Thorsen Road, 04605
Tel: 207-667 3621/800-435 1287

www.acadiabirchesmotel.com
This well-situated motel offers 67 basic but comfortable motel rooms, along with its nine-hole, par-34 golf course and inexpensive restaurant. Children under 16 stay free with adult. **$–$$**

Twilite Motel
147 Bucksport Road (Routes 1 and 3), 04605

PRICE CATEGORIES

An approximate guide to rates for a standard double room per night:
$$$$ = more than $300
$$$ = $200–300
$$ = $125–200
$ = under $125

ABOVE: Boothbay Harbor, a former fishing village, attracts thousands of visitors in summer.

Tel: 207-667 8165/800-395 5097
www.twilitemotel.com
Clean rooms and friendly service are hallmarks of this small, 22-room motel on six acres and 18 miles from Acadia National Park. Complimentary breakfast in season. **$–$$**

Trenton
Open Hearth Inn
1147 Bar Harbor Road, 04605
Tel: 207-667 2930/800-655 0234
www.openhearthinn.com
Just 8 miles from Acadia National Park, this inn offers numerous affordable options, including non-housekeeping cottages, B&B suites, a motel, and apartments. Clean and comfortable, this is a good option if you are spending more time sightseeing and doing things than lounging in the room. Continental breakfast. **$–$$**

Addison
Pleasant Bay B&B
386 West Side Road, P.O. Box 222, 04606
Tel: 207-483 4490
www.pleasantbay.com
On the shores of Pleasant River, this 110-acre

working llama farm has four guest rooms with shared or private baths and splendid views. You can take a llama for a morning guided walk on the mountain trails. **$–$$**

Bailey Island
Log Cabin, An Island Inn
P.O. Box 410, 04003
Tel: 207-833 5546
www.logcabin-maine.com
Although the island is attached to the mainland by a bridge, guests will feel they're at sea in this handsome log B&B with nine elegant, nautically themed, waterfront guest rooms. Wonderful views without getting out of bed. The rustic restaurant ($$–$$$) serves dinner nightly. **$$$–$$$$**

Bath
The Galen C. Moses House
1009 Washington Street, 04530
Tel: 207-442 8771
www.galenmoses.com
Staying here is like stepping back into the history of Bath, when it was the center of shipbuilding and displayed all the wealth that came along with that. Most of the architectural features and furnishings

of the period remain in this National Register of Historic Houses 1874 pink Victorian mansion with five antique-filled guest rooms; one has a marble fireplace and bay windows. **$$–$$$$**
Inn at Bath
969 Washington Street, 04530
Tel: 207-443 4294/800-423 0964
www.innatbath.com
An elegant, antique-filled, romantic, luxurious mid-1800s B&B in the Historic District. Eight guest rooms include two with wood-burning fireplaces and whirlpool baths. ADA-compliant. **$$–$$$**

Bethel
Austin's Holidae House B&B
85 Main Street, 04217
Tel: 207-824 3400/877-224 3400
www.holidae-house.com
Seven charming rooms in an in-town Victorian. German spoken. The innkeepers will take you on for three days in their "Innkeeper 101" class. Free shuttle to nearby ski resort in season. **$$**
Bethel Inn and Resort
Village Common, 04217
Tel: 207-824 2175/800-654 0125
www.bethelinn.com
Three colonial buildings with rooms and suites, plus town house accommodations overlooking the golf course and mountains. Tennis, golf, and a lake for water sports for those who want their adventures close at hand. **$$$–$$$$**

Blue Hill
Blue Hill Farm Country Inn
Route 15, 04614
Tel: 207-374 5126
www.bluehillfarminn.com
A 14-room B&B (seven rooms in the farmhouse, seven in a renovated barn) in a rural retreat 5 miles (8km) from Blue Hill village on the Penobscot Peninsula. On 48 acres of woods, the walking trail goes along a brook;

guests often see otter, moose, and the occasional coyote. Local acoustic musicians jam in the dining room on some evenings. **$**

Boothbay Harbor Area
Five Gables Inn
Murray Hill Road
East Boothbay, 04544
Tel: 207-633 4551/800-451 5048
www.fivegablesinn.com
Each of the 16 rooms in this spiffed-up 1865 summer hotel has views of Lineken Bay and the ocean from the broad veranda (complete with hammock). Open mid-May to mid-October. Full breakfast and afternoon refreshments on the lawn watching the fishing boats and pleasure craft return to port. Children over 12 welcome. **$$–$$$**
Linekin Bay Resort
92 Wall Point Road
Boothbay Harbor, 04538
Tel: 207-633 2494/866-847 2103
www.linekinbayresort.com
One mile outside Boothbay Harbor, this is an all-inclusive sailing resort. Five classic Maine lodges are along the waterfront; another 35 cabins are scattered on the rocky coastline, hidden in the pines. There's sailing (with instruction), kayaking, fishing, and swimming (in the heated pool). No telephones or TVs in the room; movies are shown nightly in the lodge. **$$$$**
Spruce Point Inn Resort & Spa
Grandview Avenue, Boothbay Harbor, 04538
Tel: 207-633 4152/800-553 0289
www.sprucepointinn.com
A historic inn on a 57-acre peninsula has rooms in the main house, luxury lodges, and cottages. Facilities include a swimming pool, tennis court, fitness room, croquet, badminton, and a putting green; and both a formal restaurant and a bistro.

One of the best family resorts around. **$$$–$$$$**

Brooksville

Oakland House Seaside Resort
435 Herrick Road, 0461
Tel: 207-359 8521
www.oaklandhouse.com
A casual 1889 complex with waterside cottages offering 33 rooms set on 50 acres near Blue Hill on Penobscot Bay. Nature trails; tidal pools; local outfitters will deliver kayaks. Cabins are rented by the week only. **$$$$**

Brunswick

Brunswick Inn
165 Park Row, 04011
Tel: 207-729 4914/800-299 4914
www.brunswickbnb.com
This charming historic house within walking distance of the Bowdoin College campus has 15 guest rooms and suites decorated with handsome handmade quilts and other comforting touches. All of the amenities of a large hotel – like plush robes and resident concierge – but with the attention and personal service of a B&B. **$$–$$$**

Captain Daniel Stone Inn
10 Water Street, 04011
Tel: 207-725 9898/877-373 2374
www.captaindanielstoneinn.com
Reopened in the fall of 2011 after months of renovation, there are now 24 guest rooms and suites with custom furnishings and fine linens. Many of the rooms have views of the Androscoggin River. **$$$–$$$$**

Camden

Camden Harbor Inn
83 Bayview Street, 04843
Tel: 207-236 4200/800-236 4266
www.camdenharborinn.com
A broad porch circles both the ground and first levels of this 1874 B&B with 18 rooms that's just a five-minute stroll from the heart of Camden. The indulgently

appointed rooms are nice to start with, but the staff invite you to ask for other touches – flowers, artwork, wine – that will make your stay more memorable. **$$$–$$$$**

Lodge at Camden Hills
P.O. Box 794, Camden, 04843 (Route 1)
Tel: 207-236 8478/800-832 7058
www.thelodgeatcamdenhills.com
Family-owned getaway on a 9-acre wooded property a short stroll from town. Fourteen recently renovated and upgraded units from rooms to bi-level suites and cottages. All have panoramic water views. **$$–$$$**

Lord Camden Inn
24 Main Street, 04843
Tel: 207-236 4325
www.lordcamdeninn.com
Four-story boutique hotel in a restored 1893 Masonic Hall in the heart of town. In-room spa and wine services for the 36 luxury rooms and suites with balconies overlooking the harbor. Full buffet breakfast in season; expanded Continental breakfast in winter. ADA-compliant. **$$–$$$**

Maine Stay Inn
22 High Street (Route 1), 04853
Tel: 207-236 9636
www.camdenmainestay.com
When the house was built in 1802, the property was a family farm. Camden has developed since then, but the house on the outskirts of the town center welcomes guests as though they were family. Many of the rooms and common areas still have the original flooring and architectural details. The gardens are particularly beautiful. The big country kitchen is a hangout for the guests as they raid the pantry and chat. Two parlors have wood-burning fireplaces; a glass-enclosed porch overlooks the gardens. Eight rooms. **$$–$$$$**

Cape Elizabeth

Inn by the Sea
40 Bowery Beach Road (Route 77), 04107
Tel: 207-799 3134/ 800-888 4287 (outside Maine)
www.innbythesea.com
Luxury beachfront accommodations in a recently fully renovated inn and cottages. Garden suites are all on one level, with oversize soaker tubs; traditional guest rooms have gas fireplaces; cottages have balconies with ocean and garden views. Pets are as pampered as their owners. **$$$$**

Cape Newagen

Newagen Seaside Inn
Route 27, 04552
Tel: 207-633 5242/800-654 5242
www.newagenseasideinn.com
Old-fashioned full-service resort at the tip of Southport Island, 6 miles (10km) from Boothbay Harbor. Completely refurnished and refurbished, the rooms are casual coastal retreats with quilts, coastal colors, and hardwood floors, but no TVs. All have ocean views. Many stress-free activities, like biking, rowing, nature trails, or just relaxing and enjoying the view and the ocean breezes. **$$–$$$**

Castine

Pentagoet Inn
Main Street at Perkins Street, 04421
Tel: 207-326 8616/800-845 1701
www.pentagoet.com
Castine's oldest, original "summer hotel" in one of the original summer vacation towns. A turreted, 1894 Queen Anne Victorian beauty houses this luxury boutique hotel close to the harbor. The town seems as though it was created to showcase the inn. Antique-filled rooms, blooming perennial garden, candlelight dining. The pub is straight out of a Rudyard

Kipling story, with treasures from India and Tajikistan. **$$–$$$$**

Chebeague Island

Chebeague Island Inn
Box 492, 04017
Tel: 207-846 5155
www.chebeagueinn.com
On one of the Portland harbor islands, the inn is accessible only by ferry. The classic, three-story inn looks out over the ocean as it has for over a century. Restored to the original level of elegance, the public areas and each of the 21 guest rooms were decorated by Maine designers using Maine crafts and products. Low-key; the most stressful decision of the day is which pastry to have with your morning coffee. **$$$–$$$$**

Chesuncook

Chesuncook Lake House
Box 656, Route 76, 04441
Tel: 207-745 5330
www.chesuncooklakehouse.com
A newly completed road means you can now reach the lodge by car; until then it was accessible only by boat, air, or snowmobile. The ultimate "off-the-grid" getaway, this 1864 farmhouse is in the middle of an abandoned lumber camp 50 miles north of the Moosehead Lake Region and is on the Federal Historical Register. It has four guest rooms with shared bath. Three new housekeeping cabins are heated by wood stoves. The owners raise their own food, including meats, and bake their own breads. If you want to try "back to the land" living, this is the place to do it. **$$–$$$$**

PRICE CATEGORIES

An approximate guide to rates for a standard double room per night:
$$$$ = more than $300
$$$ = $200–300
$$ = $125–200
$ = under $125

Deer Isle

Pilgrim's Inn
20 Main Street (Route 15A), 04622
Tel: 207-348 6615/888-778 7505
www.pilgrimsinn.com
Four-story, National Register of Historic Places 1793 inn overlooking Northwest Harbor has 12 relaxing rooms and three seaside cottages. The restaurant ($$) serves American fare. Inn is open May to October; restaurant has limited hours in winter. $$–$$$

Eastport

The Milliken House
29 Washington Street, 04631
Tel: 207-853 2955/888-507 9370
www.eastport-inn.com
Benjamin Milliken was a shipwright, supplying oceangoing merchant ships with their needs and receiving treasures from the world and hefty profits in return. He furnished his house with the pick of Victorian furnishings and accents, most of which remained after his death. This 1846, antique-filled Victorian near the town's Historic District has five second- and third-floor guest rooms with private baths. Well-behaved children and pets welcome. Open all-year. The breakfasts are excellent. $

Freeport

Harraseeket Inn
162 Main Street, 04032
Tel: 207-865 9377/800-342 6423
www.harraseeketinn.com
Luxury in a town of bargains. An 1850 Greek Revival home with modern appointments, an indoor pool, and elegant gardens. Many of the 84 rooms have fireplaces. The chef works with local farmers to design menus with seasonal ingredients. If you decide to see what L.L. Bean is like at 3am (the store is open 24/7), it's only a short walk to the store. $$–$$$
Kendall Tavern Inn B&B
213 Main Street, 04032

Tel: 207-865 1338/800-341 9572
www.kendalltavern.com
Surprisingly quaint and peaceful setting, close enough to the outlets that you can carry your purchases back to the inn. This centrally located early 1800s farmhouse has seven cozy, air-conditioned rooms with private baths on the second and third floors. The spacious front porch is the perfect place to sip an iced tea (or other libation) and reflect on the day's shopping. $$–$$$

Georgetown Island

The Grey Havens Inn
Seguinland Road, 04548
Tel: 207-371 2616/800-431 2316
www.greyhavens.com
New owners have finished restoring one of the last of the East Coast's classic shingle-style inns. The grand, oceanfront, hillside 1904 building has 14 guest rooms including four turret rooms with remarkable views. The Sunday brunch buffet in the summer is a great way to start the week. $$$–$$$$

Greenville

Chalet Moosehead Lakefront Motel
Route 15, Greenville Junction, 04442
Tel: 207-695 2950/800-290 3645
www.mooseheadlodging.com
Two properties: the Chalet Lakefront Motel is directly on Moosehead Lake. It has regular and deluxe motel rooms, plus efficiency units. Guests can use kayaks, canoes, outdoor grills, and paddleboats. The motel ($–$$) is open from May to October. In town, the Indian Hill Motel is open year-round with 15 basic, clean rooms. It has convenient access to snowmobile trails. One unit is ADA-compliant. $
Lodge at Moosehead Lake
Lily Bay Road, 04441
Tel: 207-695 4400/800-825 6977

www.lodgeatmoosehead lake.com
An eminently civilized wilderness retreat built in 1917 with five bedrooms in the main lodge and four suites in the carriage house. Not your average hunting lodge: rooms have four-poster beds and whirlpool baths; some have private decks and spectacular lake views. Full North Woods breakfast in a dining room with floor to ceiling windows. $$$$

Isle au Haut

The Inn at Isle au Haut
P.O. Box 78, 04645
Tel: 207-335-5141
www.innatisleauhaut.com
Four simple rooms in a gracious home overlooking the water on an island 6 miles out to sea. The first-floor room has its own bath and ocean views; three on the second floor share a bath. All meals, including a picnic lunch, included in rate. No TV or phone or children. $$$$

Kennebunk

The Lodge at Kennebunk
95 Alewive Road, Route 35N, 04043
Tel: 207-985-9010/877-918-3701
www.lodgeatkennebunk.com
Simple, clean, affordable family- and pet-friendly resort on 8 wooded acres; one, two-, and three-room suites; heated pool, game room, BBQ grills. $–$$

Kennebunkport

Bufflehead Cove
Bufflehead Cove Road, 04046
Tel: 207-967 3879
www.buffleheadcove.com
A rambling, early 20th-century Victorian B&B on 6 acres overlooking the Kennebunk River offers five beautifully furnished and luxuriously updated rooms and a sumptuous cottage. Rooms have glassed-in balconies, gas fireplaces, original artwork, and plenty of serenity. $$$–$$$$
Captain Jefferds Inn
Pearl Street, 04046

Tel: 207-967 2311/800-839 6844
www.captainjefferdsinn.com
Wonderfully appointed rooms in an 1804 Federal mansion and carriage house. Upscale and elegant, the rooms' decor varies from "grand mansion" elegance to refreshing beach cottage casual to rustic cabins – if the cabin was owned by a Rockefeller. $$$–$$$$
The Colony Hotel
140 Ocean Avenue, 04046
Tel: 207-967 3331/800-552 2363
www.thecolonyhotel.com
A gracious survivor of the Golden Age of massive oceanfront resort hotels. On a rocky promontory overlooking the Atlantic, many of the 123 antique-filled rooms at this coastal grand hotel built in 1914 have splendid ocean views. Private beach and heated saltwater pool. Breakfast buffet included. Open mid-May–October. $$–$$$$
White Barn Inn
37 Beach Avenue, 04046
Tel: 207-967 2321
www.whitebarninn.com
Relais & Château–level luxury in 1820 farmhouse and adjoining complex between town and beach. Romantic, elegant rooms, attentive service, and opulent amenities – plush robes, housekeeping twice daily, concierge service. $$$$

Kingfield

The Herbert Grand Hotel
246 Main Street, P.O. Box 67, 04947
Tel: 207-265 2000/888-656 9922
www.herbertgrandhotel.com
"The Ritz of Carrabassett Valley," an eccentric but charming downtown hotel heralded upon its 1918 debut as "A Palace in the Wilderness." Rooms are small but clean and well-appointed with antiques, and reflect the feel of the hotel's golden age. $
Three Stanley Avenue
3 Stanley Avenue, 04947
Tel: 207-265 5541

www.stanleyavenue.com/bed-and-breakfast
Six comfy rooms (three with private bath) in a Victorian home designed by one of the Stanley brothers of Stanley Steamer fame. The house still feels like their private residence, with rooms decorated like a Victorian middle-class dwelling. The gazebo in the garden was once the town bandstand. Open year-round. The restaurant next door is equally Victorian and serves "classic Maine cuisine." It's open for ski season. **$**

Kittery

Coachman Inn
380 US Route 1, 03904
Tel: 207-439 4434/800-824 6183
www.coachmaninn.net
Motel directly across the highway from Kittery's outlet malls. 43 clean, unusually spacious and well-appointed rooms. Continental breakfast buffet in sunny room; heated outdoor pool. **$$**

Portsmouth Harbor Inn and Spa
6 Water Street, 03904
Tel: 207-439 4040
www.innatportsmouth.com
An 1889 brick Victorian B&B close to the town green and overlooking the harbor and the Piscataqua River has five nicely furnished rooms; some clawfoot tubs good for soaking after a day of hiking around town. **$$–$$$**

Lubec

Home Port Inn and Restaurant
45 Main Street, P.O. Box 50, 04652
Tel: 207-733 2077/800-457 2077 (outside Maine)
www.homeportinn.com
You may find your bedroom was once the library or even the dining room of this charmingly converted 1880s family home. Transplanted Southerners Dave and Suzannah Gale serve up a full Maine breakfast, with the occasional nod to their roots,

like stone-ground grits. Seven cheerful, spacious guest rooms with private baths. Open May–October. **$**

Monhegan Island

The Island Inn
Ocean View Terrace, 04852
Tel: 207-596 0371
www.islandinnmonhegan.com
Turn-of-the-20th-century summer hotel on a bluff with a postcard-perfect view of the harbor. Original architecture and antiques, but down duvets and crisp linens in the rooms. No phones or TVs in the rooms. Bring a jacket; it can get chilly even in the summer and it will be cold in the fall. Big breakfast buffet. Open May–October. **$$$–$$$$**

The Monhegan House
1 Main Street, 04852
Tel: 207-594 7983
www.monheganhouse.com
Renovated and updated (in particular by improving and adding bathrooms), the four-story, 1870s B&B has 29 small, basic, but cheerful single and double rooms (some still share baths). All have ocean or meadow views. Open May–October. **$$–$$$**

Northeast Harbor

Asticou Inn
15 Peabody Drive, 04662
Tel: 207-276 3344/800-258 3373
www.asticou.com
A cultured carryover from Bar Harbor's heyday as Society's summer playground. Gentile, turn-of-the-century, elegant, 1885 Victorian-style inn and three annexes overlooking Great Harbor. 47 rooms. Open May–October. **$$$–$$$$**

Ogunquit

Anchorage by the Sea
125 Shore Road, 03907
Tel: 207-646 9384
www.anchoragebythesea.com
A modern oceanfront resort on the Marginal Way footpath looks and

feels more like a hotel at a major beach destination than a country inn on the coast of Maine. The rooms in the main buildings all have private balconies; many have ocean views. 245 rooms (some with Jacuzzis); indoor and outdoor pools, hot tubs, a poolside café, and gazebos. **$–$$$$**

Cliff House Resort and Spa
Shore Road (off Route 1), 03907
Tel: 207 361 1000
www.cliffhousemaine.com
The Weare family opened the first seaside hotel here in 1872, and they've been welcoming guests ever since. High atop the craggy, rocky cliffs facing the ocean, the large, modern resort with five three-story buildings has comfortable rooms with ocean views and the usual array of vacation-resort amenities and activities. **$$–$$$$**

The Dunes on the Waterfront
518 Main Street, Route 1, 03907
Tel: 207-646 2612
www.dunesonthewaterfront.com
One of the original 1930s cottage colony resorts on 12 acres with 19 updated, charming New England cottages and 17 guest rooms in the main building. On the tidal Ogunquit River, 200 yards from Ogunquit Beach. Swimming dock, with rowboats; outdoor pool. **$–$$$$**

Gorges Grant Hotel
449 Main Street, Route 1, 03907
Tel: 207-646 7003/800-646 5001
www.ogunquit.com/gorgesgrant
A sleek contemporary hotel just north of the town center. A base of operations, not a destination. Trolley stops at hotel to shuttle guests to the beach or other locations. 81 rooms, indoor and outdoor pools, a Jacuzzi, and fitness center. **$–$$**

Portland

Eastland Park Hotel
157 High Street, 04101
Tel: 207-775 5411/888-671 8008
www.eastlandparkhotel.com
Landmark, 12-story, 1927 hotel has comfortable sophistication and a fantastic view from the rooftop lounge. 204 rooms with all of the modern amenities; staff provides attentive service. **$$–$$$**

Pomegranate Inn
49 Neal Street, 04102
Tel: 207-772 1006/800-356 0408
www.pomegranateinn.com
One of the city's most elegant inns is an art- and antique-filled home in the upscale West End. The eight rooms are sophisticated, comfortable, luxurious fun; five have gas fireplaces. The owner is also a cookbook author, so the breakfasts are wonderful. **$$–$$$$**

Portland Regency Hotel
20 Milk Street, 04101
Tel: 207-774 4200/800-727 3436
ww.theregency.com
A snazzily refurbished, five-floor, boutique hotel in a converted 19th-century armory in the Old Port. Many of the 95 spacious rooms have huge windows with great views of the downtown and the port. **$$$–$$$$**

Prouts Neck

Black Point Inn Resort
510 Black Point Road, 04074
Tel: 207-883 2500
www.blackpointinn.com
Winslow Homer loved the view so much that he set up a studio here. Classic gray-shingle hotel from the 1870s, updated with pools and fitness center, but keeping the "back then" charm. Fifteen minutes

PRICE CATEGORIES

An approximate guide to rates for a standard double room per night:
$$$$ = more than $300
$$$ = $200–300
$$ = $125–200
$ = under $125

from downtown Portland.
$$$–$$$$

Rangeley

Country Club Inn
56 Country Club Road, 04970
Tel: 207-864 3831
www.
countryclubinnrangeley.com
An all-season 1920s inn,
plus 1950s-era motel
units. The inn's grand liv-
ing room has two fire-
places, a cathedral ceiling,
and lovely views of the
lake. The rooms are basic,
but the views and activi-
ties more than compen-
sate. **$$**

Rockland

**Captain Lindsey House
Inn**
5 Lindsey Street, 04841
Tel: 207-596 7950/800-523
2145
www.lindseyhouse.com
Former windjammer
schooner captains Ken
and Ellen Barnes dropped
anchor to take over this
tidy and well-appointed
three-story, 1835 antique-
filled inn. It has all the
attributes of a boutique
hotel with the intimacy of a
B&B. The parlor with over-
stuffed chairs and fire-
place is a refuge in winter.
Nine spacious guest
rooms. **$$–$$$$**
LimeRock Inn
96 Limerock Avenue, 04841
Tel: 207-594 2257/800-546
3762
www.limerockinn.com
Cheerful lodging in a
Queen Anne Victorian,
very "painted lady" on a
residential street near the
Farnsworth Museums.
Wraparound porch and
private gardens. Some of
the rooms have whirlpool
or clawfoot soaker tubs
and private decks.
$$–$$$$

Rockwood

Maynards-in-Maine
Rockwood, 04478
Tel: 207-534 7703/866-699
0857
www.maynardsinmaine.com
A classic year-round hunting camp, founded in
1919 with cedar paneling,
wide plank floors, and

antler trophies mounted
on the walls of the lodge's
porch. Rooms in the main
lodge, one- to three-bed-
room cabins, and four effi-
ciencies. **$**

South Casco

**Migis Lodge on Sebago
Lake**
P.O. Box 40, 04077
Tel: 207-655 4524
www.migis.com
A tranquil, old-fashioned
100-acre (40-hectare)
resort with six lodge
rooms and 31 rustic cot-
tages scattered across the
wooden waterfront.
Facilities include sailing,
canoeing, waterskiing,
and tennis courts. The
dining room serves tradi-
tional New England fare.
$$–$$$$

Southwest Harbor

The Claremont Hotel
P.O. Box 137, 04679
Tel: 207-244 5036/800-244
5036
www.theclaremonthotel.com
Mount Desert Island's 1884
grand hotel has maintained
its elegant charm. On the
less-visited side of the
island, it has all the views
without the bustle. Rooms
in the main inn, two guest
houses, and 14 cottages.
Waterfront location for
swimming, boating. Also
tennis and croquet.
$$$–$$$$
Inn at Southwest
371 Main Street, 04679
Tel: 207-244 3835
www.innatsouthwest.com
Seven second- and third-
floor elegant, romantic
rooms and suites with
antique furnishings in an
1884 Victorian home
overlooking the harbor.
$$–$$$

Spruce Head

**Craignair Inn &
Restaurant**
5 Third Street, 04859
Tel: 207-594 7644/800-320
9997
www.craignair.com
A basic, cheerful shore-
front B&B inn near a
nature preserve between
Rockland and Tenant's
Harbor. Originally built in

1928 to house workers
from the nearby quarries.
The second-story porch
looks out over the well-
tended lawn and rocky
shoreline. Many of the
rooms share a bath. **$–$$**

Stonington

Inn on the Harbor
Main Street, 04681
Tel: 207-367 2420/800-942
2420
www.innontheharbor.com
Most of the rooms in this
waterside inn on Deer Isle
look out on the dock where
the windjammers and fish-
ing fleet dock. The 1880s
house captures the
essence of Downeast
Maine. 13 comfortable
rooms; some have fire-
places. Open year-round.
$–$$$

Vinalhaven

**Tidewater Motel and
Gathering Place**
Main Street, 04863
Tel: 207-863 4618
www.tidewatermotel.com
The island's only water-
front lodging is on a
bridge. Most of the
bright rooms with a
beach house theme
overlook Carver's Pond
and the town. All have
private decks; dangle
your feet in the water at
high tide. Some have full
kitchens. Open year-
round. **$$–$$$**

Wiscasset

Marston House
Main Street, 04578
Tel: 207-882 6010
www.marstonhouse.com
A small private carriage
house/antiques shop with
just two spacious, second-
floor rooms with fireplaces
and Wi-Fi. The town has
over 20 antiques shops;
the innkeepers know them
all. Continental breakfast
is delivered to your room.
$$

York Area

Dockside Guest Quarters
Harris Island Road (Off Route
103), York, 03909
Tel: 207-363 2868/888-860
7428
www.docksidegq.com

Distinctive lodging in a
seacoast manor or 12 cot-
tages carefully placed to
take advantage of the
location at the mouth of
York Harbor. Very upscale
decor: spacious rooms,
high-end furniture and linens. Breakfast buffet.
$$$–$$$$
Stage Neck Inn
8 Stage Neck Road off Route
1 A, York Harbor, 03911
Tel: 207-363 3850/800-340
1130
www.stageneck.com
A small boutique resort
at seaside, emphasizing
low-key luxury. Only 60
rooms, but all of the
services and amenities
of a full-scale resort:
pools, spa, tennis, golf,
oceanfront dining.
Queen Anne–style
rooms with refrigera-
tors; many with ocean
views. Restaurant **($$$)**.
$$$–$$$$
The Union Bluff Hotel
8 Beach Street
York Beach, 03910
Tel: 207-363 1333/800-833
0721
www.unionbluff.com
A classic, five-story ocean-
front hotel built in 1873.
Sixty-three large but basic
guest rooms, some with
whirlpools, decks, and
ocean views. **$–$$$**
York Harbor Inn
Route 1A, York Harbor, 03911
Tel: 207-363 5119/800-343
3869
www.yorkharborinn.com
A seaside inn on the north
side of York Harbor made
up of several classic
Maine manors in the style
of sea captains' man-
sions. Some of the 54
upscale Colonial-style
rooms have fireplaces,
Jacuzzi spa tubs, and
ocean views with decks.
Moose occasionally stroll
through the grounds.
$$–$$$$

PRICE CATEGORIES

An approximate guide to
rates for a standard double
room per night:
$$$$ = more than $300
$$$ = $200–300
$$ = $125–200
$ = under $125

ACTIVITIES

FESTIVALS, THE ARTS, NIGHTLIFE, SHOPPING AND SPECTATOR SPORTS

FESTIVALS

Ethnicity and history; agriculture and the arts – New England has a unique cultural depth. And it celebrates it all with festivals. Throughout the year, every weekend sees some exciting, entertaining, or delicious salute to what makes New England special. These are just a very few of the annual events:

Patriot's Day, Boston, Lexington, Concord: Held the Monday closest to April 19. www.bostoncentral.com.

Newport Flower Show: The largest flower show in New England. June. www.newpotrmansions.org.

Boston Harborfest: Week-long, city-wide festival culminating on the Fourth of July. www.bostoncentral.com.

New Hampshire Craftsman's Fair: 10 days in August. www.nhcrafts.org

Feast of the Blessed Sacrament, New Bedford: Largest Portuguese festival in the country. August. www.portuguesefest.com.

Newport Folkfest: Prestigious folk festival. www.newportfolkfest.net

Maine Lobsterfest, Rockland: 20,000oz (9,072kg) of lobster. August. www.mainelobsterfestival.com.

Mashpee Wampanoag Pow Wow, Mashpee MA: One of the largest in the country. August. www.mashpeewampanoagtribe.com.

Madawaska Acadien Festival, Madawaska ME: Celebration of French Canadian and American roots. Some events are in Canada; bring your passport. August. www.acadienfestival.com.

The Big "E", West Springfield MA: 17-day-long agricultural festival.

Mid-September through early October. www.thebige.com.

Connecticut Renaissance Faire, Hebron CT: The largest Renfest in New England. Weekends late September–mid-October. www.ctfaire.com.

Haunted Happenings, Salem MA: If it's ghostly, haunted, or can appear so, it will happen here during October. www.hauntedhappenings.org.

Thanksgiving in Plymouth: A celebration of Pilgrim life and early relations with the Algonquins. Held the week before Thanksgiving. www.usathanksgiving.com.

THE ARTS

The Puritans may have found performing arts objectionable, but from Colonial times forward, theater, music, dance, and film have found enthusiastic audiences. Connecticut's proximity to New York makes it a focus of new theater, while music festivals are held throughout the region.

Cinema

Massachusetts

Harvard Film Archive (24 Quincy Street, Cambridge; tel: 617-495 4700) shows classic, foreign, nostalgia, and art films. The Art Deco **Kendall Square Cinema** (1 Kendall Square; tel: 617-499 1996/617-621 1202, www.landmarktheaters.com) offers frothy cappuccino with its foreign and art movies.

Pleasant Street Theater (27 Pleasant Street, Northampton; tel: 413-586 0935) runs independent, foreign, and art films.

Connecticut

Cinestudio (300 Summit Street, Trinity College, Hartford; tel: 860-297 2463) shows first-run and art films.

Rhode Island

Providence Place Cinema's six-story-high **Feinstein IMAX Theater** (tel: 401-453 4446) shows the latest films.

Vermont

Catamount Arts (60 Eastern Avenue, St Johnsbury; tel: 802-748 2600) offers a little bit of everything: art films, dance, classical music.

Downtown Montpelier's historic **Savoy Theatre** (26 Main Street, tel: 802-229 0509) offers an old-fashioned theater experience.

New Hampshire

Hopkins Center for the Arts (Dartmouth College, Hanover; tel: 603-646 2422) shows classic and experimental films (but only while Dartmouth is in term).

Maine

To experience the old-time theater experience, catch a movie or concert at the restored **Strand Theater** (345 Main Street, Rockland; tel: 207-594 0070), built in 1923. There's even a balcony.

Classical Music

Massachusetts

Boston Symphony Orchestra and **Boston Pops** are heard at the acoustic and aesthetic **Symphony Hall** (301 Massachusetts Avenue; tel: 617-266 1492/888-266 1200).

New England Conservatory's Jordan Hall (30 Gainsborough Street; tel: 617-585 1271) hosts its own classical concerts.

Berklee College of Music Performance Center (136 Massachusetts Avenue, Boston; tel: 617-747 2261 for tickets) excels in jazz performances by faculty and students, many international.

The **Great House** at Ipswich's Castle Hill (290 Argilla Road; tel: 978-356 4351) presents a season of classical, pop, and folk music.

The **Springfield Symphony Orchestra** (34 Court Street; tel: 413-733 2291; www.springfieldsymphony.org) performs both classical and pops concerts, including a popular Friday lunchtime series, in Symphony Hall.

Rhode Island

Rhode Island Philharmonic (222 Richmond Street, Providence; tel: 401-248 7000; www.ri-philharmonic.org) performs all year.

The 1928 **Providence Performing Arts Center** (220 Weybosset Street; tel: 401-421 2787) has concerts, Broadway shows, and other events.

Theatre-by-the-Sea (Cards Pond Road off Route 1, South Kingston; tel: 401-782 8587) hosts musicals and plays in a National Register of Historic Places building.

Connecticut

Hartford Symphony performs at The Bushnell (166 Capitol Avenue; tel: 860-246 8742; www.hartfordsymphony.org).

New Haven Symphony Orchestra, the fourth oldest in the States, holds a concert series at Yale University's Woolsey Hall (33 Whitney Avenue; tel: 203-865 0831; www.havensymphony.org).

The renowned **Norfolk Chamber Music Festival** (Routes 44 and 272, Norfolk; tel: 860-542 3000) includes chamber music and choral concert.

Vermont

Marlboro Music Festival (Marlboro Music Center; tel: 802-254 2394) has one of the most renowned summer line-ups in New England.

The **Vermont Symphony Orchestra** (tel: 802-876 9293 ext. 10; www.vso.org), under the musical direction of Jaime Laredo, performs concerts in more than 20 communities throughout the state.

New Hampshire

In Portsmouth, **The Music Hall** (28 Chestnut Street; tel: 603-436 2400) features international classical musicians, while **Music in Market Square** is a classical summer series (North Church; tel: 603-436 9109).

North Country Chamber Players (tel: 603-444 0309) perform world-class chamber music throughout the area from mid-July to mid-August.

Maine

Portland Symphony Orchestra (20 Myrtle Street, Portland; tel: 207-773 6128; www.portlandsymphony.org) performs year-round except during September.

Collins Center for the Arts (tel: 207-581 1755; www.collinscenterforthearts.com) at the University of Maine in Orono hosts classical concerts, dance performances, and children's theater.

The Pierre Monteux School for Conductors and Orchestra Musicians (tel: 207-460 0313; www.monteuxschool.org) in Hancock presents faculty and student concerts in their concert hall in June and July.

Bowdoin Summer Music Festival (Brunswick; tel: 207-725 3895) hosts renowned six-week concert series.

Kneisel Hall Chamber Music Festival (Route 15, Blue Hill; tel: 207-374 2811), dating back to 1902, has a developed a fine reputation for its summer concerts.

Dance

Massachusetts

The world-renowned **Boston Ballet** (tel: 617-695 6950; www.bostonbllet.org) performs regularly at the Wang Theatre, 270 Tremont Street.

The **Dance Complex** (536 Massachusetts Avenue, Central Square, Cambridge; tel: 617-547 9363 ext. 12; www.dancecomplex.org) hosts workshops and performances.

Jacob's Pillow Dance Festival (tel: 413-243 9919; www.jacobspillow.org) runs every June–August in the Berkshire Hills near Becket, with over 50 dance troupes and artists, and over 200 performances. Tickets go on sale in February.

Connecticut

The **Connecticut Ballet** (tel: 203-964 1211; www.connecticutballet.com) stages performances all over the state. Their cutting edge **Zig Zag Ballet** troupe is headquartered at the Stamford Center for the Arts.

The **Hartford City Ballet** (166 Capitol Avenue; tel: 860-233 8552; www.hartfordcityballet.org) stages both classical and modern dance productions.

Free Concerts

Summer and fall in New England are times for festivals and county fairs, and many include free musical performances. On the Fourth of July many towns and cities celebrate with free fireworks and music. College campuses are lively spots for free entertainment. And many small towns offer free band concerts on their town greens in summer. Local papers are good sources of information.

Massachusetts

In summer Boston offers many free outdoor concert series – including a huge July 4th fireworks celebration at the **Hatch Shell** on the Charles River Esplanade. Also check for performances at the waterfront **Bank of America Pavilion** (290 Northern Avenue; tel: 617-728 1600; www.bankofamericapavilion.com) and the Jordan Hall of the **New England Conservatory of Music** (290 Huntington Avenue; tel: 617-585 1260; www.newenglandconservatory.edu); lunchtime concerts at Copley Plaza and City Hall Plaza; and free Shakespeare on Boston Common – and in Springfield – presented by the **Citi Performing Arts Center** (tel: 617-532 1252; www.citicenter.org).

Connecticut

Both Foxwoods (tel: 800-369 9663; www.foxwoods.com) and Mohegan Sun casinos (tel: 888-266 7711; www.mohegansun.com) offer free concerts. Check their websites or local newspapers.

The town of Trumbell hosts outdoors concerts at the Town Hall Gazebo Tuesday evenings from mid-June through mid-September (tel: 203-452 5060).

There are free concerts throughout the summer at Westport's riverfront Levitt Pavilion for the Performing Arts (tel: 203-221 2153).

New Hampshire

In July and August there are free concerts in Portsmouth's Prescott Park (tel: 603-436 2848; www.prescottpark.org) and at Hampton Beach (tel: 603-926 8717; www.hamptonbeach.org).

Maine

Free concert series include L.L. Bean's Summer Concert Series in Freeport (http://freeportevents.com).

Opera

Massachusetts

Boston Lyric Opera Company (114 State Street; tel: 617-542 4912; www.blo.org) produces three operas each season at the Shubert Theater.

Connecticut

The **Connecticut Opera Guild** (www.ctoperaguild.org) mounts full-scale performances in Hartford's Bushnell Performing Arts Center. **Goodspeed Opera House** (Goodspeed Landing, East Haddam; tel: 860-873 8668; goodspeed.org) showcases operas, musicals, and revivals from April to December.

Vermont

The Green Mountain Opera Festival (tel: 802-496 7722; www.greenmountainoperafestival.org) mounts full-scale productions at the Barre Opera House in June, and offers free open rehearsals and master classes.

New Hampshire

Each August **Opera North** (Hanover; tel: 603-448 0400; www.lebanonoperahouse.org) mounts fully staged productions at the Lebanon Opera House, and offers informal concerts throughout the area.

Theater

Many theaters present special children's productions throughout the season. That information will be on the theater website.

Massachusetts

Boston's theater district, at the intersection of Tremont and Stuart streets, has many first-rate and historic theaters, including the **Wang Center**, **Schubert**, **Colonial**, and **Wilbur**. High-quality drama is found across the city, however, with performances on show at the **Boston Center for the Arts** (539 Tremont Street; tel: 617-426 5000) and Boston University's **Huntington Theater** (264 Huntington Avenue; tel: 617-266 0800), with the city's largest professional company in residence.

American Repertory Theater Company (64 Brattle Street, Harvard Square, Cambridge; tel: 617-495 2668), a highly acclaimed award winner, has two stages at the Loeb Drama Center.

On the north shore, the **Firehouse Center for the Performing Arts** (Market Square, Newburyport; tel: 978-462 7336; www.firehouse.org) produces year-round plays, and specializes in children's theater. **Merrimack Repertory Theater** (50 East Merrimack Street, Lowell; tel: 978-654 4678; www.merrimackrep.org) stages professional productions.

Cape Playhouse (off Route 6A, Dennis; tel: 508-385 3911; www.capeplayhouse.com) offers some of the best

summer stock on the Cape; check local listings for other current shows.

The **Center for Arts in Northampton** (17 New South Street; tel: 413-584 7327; www.nohoarts.org) presents theater, dance, music, and art.

The **Barrington Stage Company** (60 Union Street; tel: 413-236 8888; www.barringtonstageco.org) presents familiar and classic works as well as a separate schedule of new plays and a musical theater lab.

Rhode Island

Providence's Tony-award-winning group at **Trinity Square Repertory Company** (201 Washington Street, Providence; tel: 401-351 4242; www.trinityrep.com) puts on innovative productions. **Brown University** (Leeds Theater, 77 Waterman Street; tel: 401-863 2838; www.leedscenter.com) stages contemporary to classical and everything in between. **Sandra Feinstein-Gamm Theatre** (31 Elbow Street; tel: 401-723 4266; www.gammtheatre.org) presents classic and contemporary plays in its 75-seat hall.

Connecticut

In Hartford, the **Hartford Stage Company** (50 Church Street; tel: 860-527 5151; www.hartfordstage.org), an award-winning ensemble, produces new plays, as well as classics. **Theaterworks** (233 Pearl Street; tel: 860-527 7838; www.theaterworkshartford.org) features more experimental theater. The **Bushnell Center for the Performing Arts** (166 Capitol Avenue; tel: 860-987 5900; www.bushnell.org) is one of the city's premier performing arts centers, presenting Broadway and off-Broadway shows, films, and music.

The **Little Theater** (177 Hartford Road, Manchester; tel: 860-645 6743; www.cheneyhall.org), Connecticut's oldest theater, presents local talent.

Two Tony-award-winning theater companies reside in New Haven. The **Long Wharf Theater** (222 Sargent Drive; tel: 203-787 4282; www.longwharf.org) premiered Arthur Miller's *The Crucible* and still produces many prize-winning shows. **Yale Repertory Theater** (222 York Street; tel: 203-432 1234; yalerep.org) shows experimental work by Yale students.

Westport Country Playhouse (25 Powers Court; tel: 203-227 4177; westportplayhouse.org) launches six productions every summer in a renovated barn.

Vermont

In Colchester **Saint Michael's**

Playhouse (1 Winooski Park; tel: 802-654 2281; www.saintmichaelsplayhouse.org) is Vermont's oldest equity playhouse. **Flynn Theater for the Performing Arts** (153 Main Street; tel: 802-863 8778; www.flynncenter.org) is the venue for big-name and big-audience productions.

Weston Playhouse Theater Company (tel: 802-824 5288; westonplayhouse.org) is home to Vermont's oldest summer theater.

Dorset Playhouse (Dorset; tel: 802-867 5777 ext. 1; www.dorsettheatrefestival.org) stages professional performances in the summer, but in the winter a fine consortium of community folks takes to the stage.

The new 150-seat **Waterbury Festival Playhouse** (2933 Waterbury-Stowe Road, Waterbury Center; tel: 802-498 3755; www.waterburyfestivalplayhouse.com) launches plays for both adults and children.

New Hamsphire

Seacoast Repertory Theater (125 Bow Street, Portsmouth; tel: 603-433 4472/800-639 7650; www.seacoastrep.org) features both adult and children's productions year-round.

Colonial Theater (95 Main Street, Keene; tel: 603-352 2033 ext. 2; www.thecolonial.org) showcases live performances and films.

Palace Theater (80 Hanover Street, Manchester; tel: 603-668 5588) puts on six productions a year, including dinner theater by its resident company, **Stage One Productions**.

Hopkins Center for the Arts (Dartmouth College, Hanover; tel: 603-646 2422; www.hop.dartmouth.edu) stages multiple musicals and various other theater productions.

New London Barn Playhouse (290 Main Street; tel: 603-526 4631; www.nlbarnplayhouse.org), the state's oldest continuously operating theater, presents plays and musicians in a renovated barn in the summer.

Maine

Portland Performing Arts Center (25a Forest Avenue, Portland; tel: 207-773 3150; www.portlandovations.org) is a multipurpose venue offering space for music, dance, and theater. Also in Portland, check the local newspapers for anything mounted by the **Portland Stage Company** (tel: 207-774 0465; www.portlandstage.org).

Ogunquit Playhouse (Route 1,

Ogunquit; tel: 207-646 5511; www.ogunquitplayhouse.org) stages musicals, theater, and plays during the summer at one of the oldest playhouses in the US.

Arundel Barn Playhouse (53 Old Post Road; tel: 207-985 5552; www.arundelbarnplayhouse.com) in Arundel presents professional classic summer theater June–late August.

Hackmatack Playhouse (Route 9, Beaver Dam, Berwick; tel: 207-698 1807; www.hatmatack.org) launches plays with local performers.

NIGHTLIFE

The nightlife scene in New England is very varied. Urban areas and those with colleges have lively music and dance scenes, while the underpopulated rural areas are devoid of much besides the occasional town tavern. This changes in ski season, when the resorts attract thousands of vacationers eager to indulge in après-ski fun. The gay and lesbian communities are also mostly in larger cities or in their immediate suburbs.

Massachusetts

Boston is the hub of nightlife in Massachusetts. Along with Cambridge, it has the most sophisticated music, dance, and club scene in the state. Most nightclubs – including Axis, with a dance floor holding 1,000 people – are found along Lansdowne Street. Although clubs are open until 2:30am, remember that the "T" shuts down at 12:30am. Home to the Berklee College of Music, which is dedicated to jazz and rock music, the students hang out and jam at Wally's Café. If you think that folk music has gone the way of love beads and lava lamps, the legendary Club Passim, where Joan Baez and Bob Dylan played, is still hosting acoustic artists in Cambridge. And while the spirits of unamused Boston Brahmin and sour-spirited Puritans may frown, several comedy clubs in both Boston and Cambridge keep audiences laughing with their takes on life, relationships, and politics. If your idea of a good night out is sipping beer while watching and debating the Red Sox and Patriots, you'll find plenty of opportunities at any sports bar. McGreevey's on Boylston Street claims to have invented the concept. Just steps away from Fenway Park, it's dedicated to Boston sports history, specifically to the Red Sox. If you find yourself on

the losing side of an argument, say something like, "All that really matters is that the Yankees lose." The house will probably buy you a beer.

Elsewhere in Massachusetts, **Springfield** has a Club Quarter. Centered around Stearns Square, it has about 75 clubs, dance venues, and restaurants, from sports bars, bistros, and swanky lounges to places where *Animal House* seems like a meditation at a monastery. Some of the best blues in the country is found at Theodore's on Worthington Street, which promises (and delivers) "Booze, Blues, and BBQ."

Rhode Island

The revitalized river walk area and its proximity to Brown and RSDI make **Providence** the destination for nightlife. Most of the activity is along Washington Street, but for a total sensory overload, visit Monet Lounge on Harris Street. It's a vast, upscale, incredibly trendy nightclub with a light and sound system that cost more than the total tuition of the entire freshman class at Brown and RDSI combined. The *Providence Phoenix*, a free paper (www.thephoenix.com/providence), is a good source for local action.

In Newport, Thames Street is where it's happening. Bars and clubs have live music nightly. On Block Island, the place for rock is Captain Nick's; McGovern's Yellow Kittens Tavern has reggae and blues in the music mix.

Connecticut

"SoNo," as **South Norwalk** is called, and Hartford vie for the best nightlife. SoNo may edge out the state capitol, just because it's smaller and everything is closer together. Washington Street and the immediate area is the place to look for dancing, with Liquid and its two floors of dancing and Ego on South Main with its state-of-the-art sound and dance system equally popular. The Loft on Washington Street has a hip martini bar. In **Hartford**, the downtown stays lively after work, particularly along Allyn Street. The Brickyard Café has three dance levels; Sully's Pub on Park Street requires bands to keep the sound volume to non-deafening levels. The best sports bars in town are the Arch Street Tavern and Coach's on Allyn, with 38 TVs.

Vermont

Not a lot of nightlife in the land of early-rising dairy farmers, but in **Burlington** the quality iS good, if the quantity is meager. The Church Street

Marketplace is the city's central retail and entertainment district. You'll find the town's two jazz clubs there. The Club Metronome is the only live music venue of any size in town, although some bars feature local bands. Perhaps not surprisingly, folk music has a home in this town, at Radio Bean Coffeehouse. The entertainment scene becomes much more lively during ski season, with resorts and the towns surrounding them opening seasonal bars and clubs.

New Hampshire

Manchester has a smattering of clubs in the downtown. The Grand on Canal Street has DJs and live music, plus a racquetball court and a swanky bar. Another place worth visiting is Milly's Tavern, which is saving the city from drowning in commercial beers by brewing its own in its brewpub in the Mill District. Its nightclub has live music on weekends and a DJ during the week. As with Vermont, most of the action is at the ski resorts in the winter.

Maine

The Downeasters know how to party, at least during the tourist season. All of the popular tourist towns along the coast have bars, lounges, even a few comedy clubs. While there is dancing, the big dance clubs are not to be found; there just isn't enough traffic to support them. You'll find local bands in local bars. As most are seasonal and subject to the fluctuations of the economy, the best option is to ask around or check out the scene when you arrive. Most towns are small enough that the stroll you were going to make down the main street anyway will let you locate the action. The exception to this is Portland, where the downtown theater district is the hub for year-round clubs and entertainment. Styxx on Spring Street is the hot, newly renovated dance emporium. Microbrew aficionados gravitate to Gritty McDuff's, where beer is brewed on premises.

Gay and Lesbian Venues

New England is very welcoming to the LGBT community. **Provincetown** on Cape Cod has long been known as a gay-friendly vacation and year-round residential area, as are **Cambridge** MA and **Providence** RI. With its influx of professional expatriates from New York seeking a simpler life, **Portland** ME has also become a new gay magnet. **Burlington** VT has a history of progressive attitudes and a small, but strong, gay community. Perhaps

ABOVE: Boston offers a surprising variety of street performances.

the most unlikely place is **Springfield** MA in the bucolic Berkshires. The most up-to-the-minute entertainment listings throughout New England are found at www.edgenewengland.com. **Boston**-centric news is at www.edgeboston.com. The most chic venue in Boston remains the Club Café and Lounge on Columbus Avenue. Another good source is www.baywindows.com. The scene is always changing in **Provincetown**, although the Boatslip on Commercial Street is a reliable gathering place. **Danbury** CT's Triangles hosts special nights for men, women, and transgenders.

SHOPPING

Best Buys

The Choice

Although shopping isn't usually the prime reason people visit New England, he region offers a large and diverse number of options ranging from giant malls to tiny shops selling homemade specialty foods including chocolates, maple syrup, salsas, and artisanal cheeses. Some retail giants, such as Maine's L.L. Bean and the Vermont Country Store, have become tourist destinations in their own right. Several states, including Connecticut with its Wine Trail (www.ctwine.com) and Vermont with its Cheese Trail (www.vtcheese.com), have developed touring routes for visitors.

Boston, home to Pilgrims and, later, Boston's upper-crust Brahmins,

has never been famous for high fashion. But retailers such as Saks Fifth Avenue, Neiman Marcus, Barney's New York, and Lord & Taylor have established outposts in the city, offering shoppers a wide range of upscale merchandise. New England's factory outlets are well known to bargain hunters. Once places where manufacturers sold discounted wares to employees, today the towns of Kittery and Freeport in Maine and Manchester Center VT have converted themselves into giant outlet centers, vying to offer shoppers discounts on big names such as Reebok, Armani, Anne Klein, and Crate & Barrel.

Other sprawling outlet complexes have opened up throughout the region, including in Manchester and North Conway NH, where the absence of a state sales tax makes the deals even sweeter.

Taxes

All states except New Hampshire have a sales tax of 5 to 7 percent. Some cities such as Vermont's Burlington and Williston, add an additional 1 percent on top of the state tax.

Antiques

New England's towns and roadways are dotted with antiques shops, some run by one owner, others a collection of "stalls" stocked by individuals and operated by a joint management. While you can "go antiquing" almost anywhere, here are a few areas which have a larger concentration of shops:

Cape Cod: Dennis, Ipswich
Connecticut: Woodbury, Old Saybrook, Putnam
Maine: Wells, Jonesport
Massachusetts: Boston, Sturbridge, Sheffield
New Hampshire: Manchester, Concord
Rhode Island: Newport
Vermont: Waterbury, Quechee, East Middlebury

Arts and Crafts Galleries

Painters, sculptors, potters, weavers, woodworkers – New England is home to many fine artists. Crafts fairs, such as the League of New Hampshire Craftsmen's show (www.nhcrafts.org) each August at Mount Sunapee, and Vermont's Stowe Foliage Art and Craft Festival (www.craftproducers.com) in August are a fine way to see the wares of local craftspeople.

Massachusetts

Many of Boston's largest galleries are on Newbury Street and in the Fort Point Channel area near South Station. Also try Tremont Street in the South End. The **Society of Arts and Crafts** (175 Newbury Street; tel: 617-266 1810; www.societyofcrafts.org) sells high-quality crafts.

The **Worcester Center for Crafts** (25 Sagamore Road, Worcester; tel: 508-753 8183; www.worcestercraftcenter.org) houses one of America's oldest crafts complexes.

The north shore town of Rockport has more than two dozen art galleries, as does Northampton in western Massachusetts.

Rhode Island

OOP! (339 Ives Street and 220 Westminster Street; tel: 401-374 3739; www.oopstuff.com) features a whimsical collection of crafts and jewelry.

Newport, too, has many fine galleries. **MacDowell Pottery** (220 Spring Street; tel: 401-846 6313) displays New England potters' work; and **Newport Scrimshanders** (14 Bowen's Wharf; tel: 800-635 5234; www.scrimshanders.com) sells Nantucket lightship baskets.

Connecticut

SoNo (South Norwalk) has revitalized itself with art galleries, chichi cafés, and shops. Kent also has more than a dozen galleries.

In Hartford, **The Artists' Collective** (1200 Albany Avenue; tel: 860-527 3205; www.artistscollective.org) exhibits the arts and culture of the African diaspora.

Dozens of pottery and crafts shops are located in the Litchfield Hills. On Route 128 in West Cornwall, visit **Cornwall Bridge Pottery and Store** (tel: 860-672 6545; www.cbpots. com). **O'Reilly's Irish Gifts** (248 Main Street, Farmington; tel: 860-677 6958; www.gotirish.com/oreillys. aspx) is the largest purveyor of Irish goods in the US.

Vermont

Many artists exhibit their works in collectives and communal galleries, including Montpelier's **Artisans Hand** (89 Main Street; tel: 802-229 9492; www.artisanshand.com). **Frog Hollow State Craft Center** (Church Street Marketplace, Burlington) shows works by leading artists and craftspeople.

Bennington Potters (324 County Street and 127 College Street, Burlington; tel: 802-447 7531; www. benningtonpotters.org/vermont) sells both quality items and bargain-priced seconds.

New Hampshire

In Portsmouth, **Three Graces Gallery** (105 Market Street; tel: 603-436 1988; www.threegracesgallery.com) offers New Hampshire and Maine coastal landscapes.

The **Dorr Mill Store** (Hale Street; tel: 800-846 3677; www. dorrmillstore.com) in Guild is a national craft center for hand hooking, braiding, and wool quilting.

Maine

Students and teachers at the nearby **Haystack Mountain School for Crafts** show their work at 22 Church Street, Deer Isle (tel: 207-348 2306; www.haystack-mtn.org).

Eclipse Gallery (12 Mount Desert Street; tel: 207-288 9088; www. eclipsegallery.us) in Bar Harbor exhibits contemporary handblown glass, ceramics, and furniture.

There are galleries in Rockland along Northeast Harbor's Main Street, clustered around the Farnsworth Museum, and in downtown Ogunquit.

China and Glass

Massachusetts

In the Berkshires, **Fellerman & Raabe Glassworks** (Main Street, Sheffield; tel: 413-478 0489; www.stephenfellerman.com) sells handmade glass.

At **Pairpoint Crystal** (Route 6A, Sagamore; tel: 800-899 0953; www. pairpoint.com), glassmakers use a variety of techniques developed in

nearby Sandwich, world-renowned in the 1800s for innovative glassmaking.

Rhode Island

Watch glassblowers at work at **Thames Glass** (688 Thames Street, Newport; tel: 401-846 0576; www. thamesglass.com); make your own paperweight or Christmas ornament.

Vermont

The renowned **Simon Pearce** (Main Street, Quechee, and Industrial Park, Windsor; tel: 802-295 2711; www. simonpearce.com) makes and sells first- and second-quality glassware and other fragile items; there is a fine restaurant in the Quechee complex.

Maine

Stained-glass artist **Richard MacDonald** welcomes visitors to his studio at 7 Wall Point Road in Bar Harbor (tel: 207-633 4815; www. macdonaldglass.com).

Destination Retailers

Massachusetts

At **Yankee Candle Flagship Store** (25 Greenfield Road, South Deerfield; tel: 877-636 7707; www. yankeecandle.com/flagship), it's always Christmas – one of the region's most imaginative stores.

Vermont

Vermont Country Store (flagship store 657 Main Street, Weston; tel: 802-824 3184; www. vermontcountrystore.com) offers local goods at a good prices.

Maine

Kittery Trading Post (301 US Route 1, Kittery; tel: 888-587 6246) have been outdoor outfitters since 1938.

The legendary **L.L. Bean Flagship Store** (95 Main Street, Freeport; tel: 800-441 5713), open 24 hours, is a paradise for outdoor enthusiasts.

Malls/Retail Stores

Massachusetts

In Boston, **Copley Place** (100 Huntington Avenue; tel: 617-369–5000) has almost 100 upscale stores and restaurants. **Faneuil Hall Marketplace** (North End; tel: 617-523 1300), one of the city's major tourist attractions, has more than 150 small shops and food stands, and sells everything from funky sportswear to Red Sox souvenirs.

Elsewhere in the state, the Holyoke Mall, just off I–91 in Holyoke,

is one of the biggest in western Massachusetts.

Rhode Island

The **Warwick Mall** (400 Bald Hill Road, Warwick; tel: 401-739 7500) houses many national chains.

Connecticut

The **Danbury Fair Mall** (Backus Avenue, off I–84, Danbury; tel: 203-743 3247) has 240 shops, including five department stores.

Vermont

The state's largest malls are in Burlington. One is the **Burlington Town Center Mall** (tel: 802-658 2545; www.burlingtontowncenter.com).

New Hampshire

Shops fill Portsmouth's revitalized waterfront area near Market, Bow and Ceres streets.

The 19th-century **Colony Mill Marketplace** (222 West Street, Keene; tel: 781-273 5555; www.colonymillnh. com) encompasses 33 stores.

Maine

The Dock Square area (27 Dock Square; tel: 207-967 9099) in Kennebunkport is lined with upscale shops.

Portland's **Old Port**, a dense few blocks along Fore and Exchange Streets, is a great place for browsing and buying.

Outlet Shopping

Discount men's, women's, and children's clothing chains with branches throughout New England include **Marshall's**, **T.J. Maxx**, and **Filene's Basement**.

Massachusetts

Filene's Basement closed its doors on Washington Street and reopened at 497 Boylston Street, Boston (tel: 617-424 5520; www. filenesbasement.com).

Connecticut

Clinton Crossing Premium Outlets (Route 81, Clinton; tel: 860-664 0700; www.premiumoutlets.com/clinton).

Vermont

The **Outlets of Manchester** (tel: 800-955 7467; www. manchesterdesigneroutlets.com), including stores such as Armani, Gap, and Bose are together, close to town.

New Hampshire

Seventy **State of New Hampshire Liquor Outlets** (tel: 800-543 4664;

www.liquorandwineoutlets.com) sell tax-free wines and liquors, many at bargain prices.

Maine

Major outlet shopping includes **Freeport** and **Kittery**.

Specialty Foods

Massachusetts

Cardullo's (8 Brattle Street, Cambridge; tel: 617-491 8888; ww.cardullos.com) displays New England's largest selection of chocolates and teas.

Rhode Island

Gray's Ice Cream (16 East Road, Tiverton; www.garysicecream.com) has been a popular stop for homemade ice cream for more than 80 years. Close by, **Milk and Honey Bazaar** (3838 Main Road, Tiverton; tel: 401-624 1974) sells more than 100 artisanal cheeses.

In Providence, homemade almond and hazelnut biscotti are specialties at **Scialo Brothers** (257 Atwells Avenue; tel: 401-421 0986). **Gasbarro's** (361 Atwells Avenue; tel: 401-421 4170) has one of – if not the – largest wine selections in the state. **Costantino's Venda Ravioli** (275 Atwells Avenue; tel: 401-421 9105) sells more than 50 varieties of freshly made pasta.

Connecticut

Pick your own fruit and purchase freshly baked pies at **Lyman Orchards** (Routes 147 and 157, Middlefield; tel: 860-349 6015; www.lymanorchards.com).

Vermont

Ben & Jerry's Ice Cream Factory (Route 100, Waterbury) has daily tours and tastings.

One of Vermont's premier cooperative cheese companies lets visitors sample their fine wares at the **Cabot Annex Store** (2653 Waterbury-Stowe Road, Waterbury Center; tel: 802-244 6334).

Sugarbush Farm in Woodstock (tel: 800-281 1757) is a sugarhouse open for tours. They also make cheeses and homemade mustards. Call for directions.

New Hampshire

Littleton Grist Mill (18 Mill Street; tel: 603-259 3205), in a restored, waterwheel-powered 1798 working grist mill, sells fine crafts, gifts, and organically grown whole grains and stone-ground flour.

Maine

Pick your own apples, wander through the corn maze, and watch cider being pressed at **Ricker Hill Orchards** (11 Ricker Hill Road, Turner; tel: 207-225 5552; www.rickerhill.com).

SPECTATOR SPORTS

Generally, the New England states are represented by Boston's teams: basketball's **Boston Celtics** (Fleet Center, Sept–May, tel: 617-624 1000), baseball's Boston **Red Sox** (Fenway Park, Apr – Oct; tel: 617 267 1700), and hockey's **Boston Bruins** (Fleet Center, Oct–Mar; tel: 617-624 1000 for tickets).

The **New England Patriots** (Aug–Dec; tel: 508-543 1776/800-543 1776; www.gillettestadium.com for tickets, Aug–Dec) and the city's professional soccer team, **New England Revolution** (tel: 508-543 8200; www.revolutionsoccer.net) play at Gillette Stadium in the southern suburb of Foxboro.

Minor-league baseball is a New England tradition, and admission is inexpensive (in comparison to major-league contests). The games are family-oriented, and most teams go to great lengths to keep the children amused. Among the teams, the AA affiliate of the Boston Red Sox, the **Portland Sea Dogs**, plays in downtown Portland (Hadlock Field; tel: 800-936 3647). In Rhode Island the Red Sox's AAA affiliate, the **Pawtucket Red Sox**, plays 72 home baseball games each season at the McCoy Stadium (1 Ben Mondor Way, Pawtucket; tel: 401-724 7300). Vermont's **Lake Monsters**, a Class A affiliate of the Washington Nationals, play home games at Centennial Field in downtown Burlington (tel: 802-655 4200).

For up-to-date information on schedules and locations, check the sports section of any local daily newspaper.

OUTDOOR ACTIVITIES

New England has the most physically fit population in the US. That's not surprising, since the area begs to be explored by hiking, kayaking, boating, riding, biking, and camping – for starters. There's no way to include every resource or outfitter in the region. Nor can all information be totally up-to-date. Fortunately, most changes are positive, as more bikeways open, more outfitters offer

canoe trips, more trails are expanded. The best advice when traveling to someplace new is to ask about conditions and changes at outdoor stores, the tourism office or Chamber of Commerce, or the locals at the general store or diner.

Biking

The eastern and southern parts of New England are welcoming to casual bikers, since they are largely flat. If there's no designated biking trail, most of the secondary and back roads are lightly traveled and most drivers are polite to bikers. In the mountains, it's a different story, at least as far as physical exertion is concerned. "Mountains" sums it up. Biking here is of the "mountain bike" variety, which is off-road and demanding. Bike rentals are generally available at all towns which cater to tourists.

Massachusetts

In eastern Massachusetts, mountain bikers can explore the trails of **Blue Hills Reservation** (tel: 617-698 1802) in Milton, just south of Boston, or in **Maudslay State Park** in Newburyport on the North Shore. In the western part of the state, **Mount Greylock State Reservation** (tel: 413-499 4262; www.mass.gov/dcr/parks/mtGreylock/) near Williamstown has a number of mountain biking trails.

Bikers also flock to the **Cape Cod Rail Trail**, a scenic 30-mile (48km) paved path along the former Penn Central Railway route from South Dennis to South Wellfleet. In Provincetown, the paved **Province Lands Trail** winds for 7.25 miles (11.5km) through the dunes.

A classic urban bike path is Boston's **Dr Paul Dudley White Bikeway**, an 18-mile (29km) loop that follows both sides of the Charles River. **The Norwattuck Rail Trail** (tel: 413-586 8706) extends 10 miles (16km) from Northampton to Belchertown. Boston is striving to encourage more biking as an alternative to auto use. The new Hubway (tel: 855-448 2929; www.thehubway.com) is a rent-as-you-go system where you can rent a bike by the hour, picking it up and leaving it at many kiosks and bike stands in town. The city now has over 30 miles (50km) of designated bike lanes.

Rhode Island

The 14.5-mile (23km) **East Bay Bicycle Path** follows Narragansett Bay and winds through several towns between East Providence and Bristol.

On Block Island and in Tiverton and Little Compton, the relatively quiet roads are popular with bikers.

Bikers can also follow Newport's **Bellevue Avenue** and **Ocean Drive** for about 15 miles (24km) past the mansions and along the shore.

For a free *Guide to Cycling in the Ocean State*, visit www.dot.state. ri.us/bikeri. Rhode Island Greenways (www.rigreenways.org) is an excellent source for up-to-date information about all trails in the state, not just for bikers but for skaters, runners, wheelchair users, and equestrians.

Connecticut

Winding Trails Recreation Area off Route 4 in Farmington (tel: 860-677 8458; www.windingtrails.org) and **Woodbury Ski Area** (tel: 203-263 2203; www.woodburyskiarea.com) are big with Connecticut mountain bikers.

For a free Connecticut Bicycle Map, visit www.ctbikemap.org.

Vermont

Several downhill ski areas are converted into mountain-biking centers after the winter season ends. This list is constantly expanding as resorts seek to expand their business in the off-season. You might do well to check ski resorts along your itinerary on-line.

Mount Snow (tel: 802-464 3333; www.mountsnow.com), home to the first American mountain-bike school, has 45 miles (72km) of bike terrain and runs one-day coaching programs, leads mountain tours, and hosts family bike weekends.

At **Killington** (tel: 802-422 6232; www.killington.com), mountain bikers can cruise 50 miles (80km) of trails. Vermont is popular for upscale inn-to-inn tours.

Bike Vermont (tel: 800-257 2226; www.bike-vermont.com) puts together tours in all six states.

Stowe's 5.5-mile (9km) paved bike path winds from downtown to the base of Mt Mansfield.

The Northeast Kingdom's **Kingdom Trails** (tel: 802-626 0737; www.kingdomtrails.com) network, which begins in East Burke, offers a diverse mountain-biking terrain.

New Hampshire

Several ski areas offer summer and fall mountain biking. **Loon Mountain** attracts novice through advanced riders to 21 miles (34km) of trails, where lifts serve the steepest biking routes. Nearby, the self-guided **Franconia Notch Bike Tour** starts at Echo Lake, passes the Old Man of the Mountain site, and

ends at the Loon Mountain ski area.

Near Mt Washington, **Great Glen Trails** (tel: 603-466 2333; www. greatglentrails.com) offers learn-to-mountain-bike courses, ranging from a short introductory class to more in-depth skill-building.

New England Hiking Holidays (tel: 800-869 0949; www.nehikingholidays. com) packages inn-to-inn and biking tours in New Hampshire.

Maine

When the snow melts, the Sunday River Ski area turns into the **Sunday River Mountain Bike Park** (tel: 207-824 3000; www.sundayriver.com), where bikers can ride the lifts up and then bike down 60 miles (100km) of trails.

Back Roads (tel: 800-462 2848; www.backroads.com/trips/BMNI) is one of several companies offering bicycle tours in the state of Maine.

Camping

Camping is a popular way of enjoying the outdoors; you can be "primitive" and sleep in a tent under the stars or stay in a motor home with all the amenities of a hotel. RV (recreational vehicle/caravan) camping is extremely popular since it allows you to set your own itinerary, fix your own meals, and not worry about checkout times. There are several companies which rent RVs by the week or longer. Among the best known are www.cruiseamerica. com (tel: 800-671 8042) and www. gorving.com. Rental is not cheap; a standard RV which sleeps 5 will cost about $150–$200/night (plus a mileage charge of about 30¢ a mile). There are few places which rent equipment for backpackers or tent campers. Campgrounds are plentiful; state parks usually have camping facilities, while commercial campgrounds frequently have activities as well as spots to park and hook up your camper. In high season and leaf-peeper season, reservations are absolutely necessary. KOA Campgrounds are vetted for their quality. Woodalls (www.woodalls. com) is a company which produces an annual campground directory which is very thorough. If you choose to rent an RV, you would do well to join the Good Sam Club (www.goodsamclub.com). A yearly membership is about $20, and it provides roadside travel assistance in case of a breakdown or accident, plus discounts at many campgrounds and other facilities.

All states produce campground

directories, all of which can be viewed on-line if not actually downloaded: Connecticut: www.campconn.com Maine: www.campmaine.com. Massachusetts: www.campmass.com (with interactive map) New Hampshire: www.ucampnh.com Rhode Island: campground directory is part of the state's travel booklet (www.visitrhodeisland.com) Vermont: www.campvermont.com

Canoeing, Kayaking, and Rafting

As with biking, New England offers both extremes of paddling adventures. There are placid streams and gently flowing rivers and throat-tightening rapids, and the challenge of paddling in bays or the ocean. Most outfitters offer instruction and guided trips, which are particularly handy if you are unfamiliar with the area.

Massachusetts

In Boston and the nearby suburb of Newton, **Charles River Canoe and Kayak Center** (tel: 617-965 5110; www.paddleboston.com) rents canoes and kayaks on the Charles River for an hour or more. **Community Boating** (21 David Mugar Way; tel: 617-523 1038; www.community-boating.com) also rents kayaks (a two-day membership fee is required) and gives lessons.

South Bridge Boat House in Concord (tel: 978-369 9438; www. canoeconcord.com) has canoes for rent on the lazy Sudbury and Concord rivers.

At Nickerson State Park on Cape Cod, **Jack's Boat Rentals** (tel: 508-349 9808; www.jacksboatrental.com) rents canoes, kayaks, sunfish, pedal boats, sailboards, and seacycles.

Sportsmen's Marina Boat Rental Company in Hadley (Route 9; tel: 413-586 2426) rents canoes and kayaks, as does the **Northfield Mountain Recreation and Environmental Center** (tel: 800-859 2960). In western Massachusetts, **Zoar Outdoor** (tel: 800-532 7483; www.zoaroutdoor.com), based along the Mohawk Trail in Charlemont, runs whitewater rafting expeditions for all levels on the Deerfield River, and two- or three-day learn-to-kayak and canoe clinics.

Rhode Island

Coastal sea kayaking is popular and the **Kayak Centre** (tel: 401-295 4400; www.kayakcentre. com) in Wickford leads a variety of excursions, including a Newport tour with ocean glimpses of mansions; the company also runs a multi-day trip

ABOVE: a baseball game at Boston's Fenway Park.

to Block Island. At their Charlestown location (tel: 401-364 8000; www. kayakcentre.com), they offer kayaking on Ninigret Pond.

Telephone **Blackstone Valley Tourism Council** (tel: 800-454 2882; www.tourblackstone.com) for free information about canoeing the 45-mile (72km) -long Blackstone River. They have the latest information about where to rent along the river.

Sakonnet Boathouse in Tiverton (www.sakkonetboathouse.com) has kayak rentals and lessons on Narragansett Bay.

Connecticut

For whitewater rafting or canoeing, head for the Housatonic River. **North American Whitewater Expeditions** (tel: 800-727 4379; www.nawhitewater.com) organizes Housatonic rafting trips.

At 170 Main Street in New Hartford, **Main Stream Canoe and Kayaks** (tel: 860-693 6791; www. mainstreamconoe.com) rents canoes and kayaks and conducts day trips on the Farmington River.

Canoes can be rented at several state parks, including Burr Pond in Torrington and Lake Waramaug in New Preston. Rentals are on a first-come, first-served basis. For information, call **Clarke Outdoors** (tel: 860-672 6365; www. clarkeoutdoors.com). For general information, check www.ct.gov.com.

Vermont

True North Kayak Tours (tel: 802-238 7695; www.vermontkayak.com) runs kayak tours in Vermont.

In Stowe, **Umiak Outdoor Outfitters** (849 South Main Street;

tel: 802-253 2317; www.umiak.com) offers tours and rentals.

New Hampshire

Saco Bound River Outfitters (tel: 603-447 2177; www.sacobound. com) runs a river kayaking school and leads canoeing expeditions, guided kayak trips, and whitewater rafting trips at several New Hampshire and Maine locations.

North Star Canoe Livery (tel: 603-542 6929; www.kayak-conoe.com), based in Cornish, conducts canoe trips on the Connecticut River.

Appalachian Mountain Club's New Hampshire chapter (tel: 603-466 2725; www.amc-nh.org) offers organized trips, courses, and instruction on waterways throughout New England.

Maine

With more than 2,000 coastal islands and their protected waters, Maine has become a center for sea kayaking. The **Maine Island Kayak Company** (tel: 207-766 2373; www. maineislandkayak.com), based at Peaks Island near Portland, runs a range of sea-kayaking trips and instructional courses. **Old Quarry Ocean Adventures** (Oceanville Road; tel: 207-367 8977; www.oldquarry. com) in Stonington rents kayaks, canoes, and sailboats and organizes boat trips.

H2Outfitters (tel: 207-833 5257; www.h2outfitters.com), on Orr's Island near Brunswick, offers one-day sea-kayaking classes, as well as multi-day trips.

The Kennebec, Dead, and Penobscot rivers offer challenging whitewater rafting. **North American**

Whitewater Expeditions (tel: 800-727 4379; www.nawhitewater.com) runs Maine river-rafting trips for novices through experts.

The **Allagash Wilderness Waterway**, a 92-mile (150km) corridor of lakes and rivers from Baxter State Park to the Canadian border, is a well-known canoeing and rafting destination. Outfitters in this area include **Allagash Canoe Trips** in Greenville (tel: 207-280 0191; www.allagashconoetrips.com) and **Mahoosuc Guide Service**, based in Newry (tel. 207-824 2073; www. mahoosuc.com).

For more sedate paddling, the **Maine Audubon Society** (tel: 207-781 2330; www.maineaudubon.com) offers guided canoe trips and rentals in Scarborough Marsh, the state's largest salt marsh.

On Mount Desert Island, **National Park Canoe and Kayak Rentals** (tel: 207-244 5854; www. nationalparkconoerental.com) has canoes for hire on Long Pond.

Dog Sledding

The **Vermont Outdoor Guide Association** (tel: 800-425 8747; www.voga.org) has a roster of trainers and outfitters who give rides and instruction in dog sledding. Many of them have adapted equipment so it can be used in the summer. You can take a short ride, a one-day course, or a longer overnight adventure.

Fishing

Fly-fishing, ice fishing, kayak fishing, shark fishing, deep-sea angling: there's a remarkable choice of ways to catch your supper, all year round.

Massachusetts

Numerous charters go out of Boston Harbor or nearby Winthrop Harbor. Among them are: **C.J. Victoria** (tel: 617-283 5801; www.cjvictoria.com); and **Good Time Charters** (tel: 617-435 4126; www.goodtimecharter.com).

For saltwater fly-fishing, check with **Orvis Saltwater School** (Chatham; tel: 800-235 9763) on Cape Cod. They run a course that teaches basic saltwater techniques. Also on the Cape, **Patriot Party Boats** (tel: 508-548 2626; www.patriotpartyboats. com), operating out of Falmouth Harbor, offers deep-sea fishing trips.

The Orleans-based **Rock Harbor Charter Fleet** (tel: 508-255 9757; www.rockharborcharters.com) also runs fishing excursions.

On Cape Ann, **Yankee Deep**

ABOVE: fly fishing on the Contoocoock River, New Hampshire.

Sea Fishing (75 Essex Avenue, Gloucester; tel: 978-283 0313/800-942 5464; www.yankeefleet.com) journeys out to Stellwagen Bank and Jeffrey's Ledge.

Rhode Island

Saltwater Edge (Newport; tel: 401-842 0062; www.saltwateredge.com) offers fly-fishing lessons as well as guided saltwater fishing outings. You can also find many independent charter boats by simply walking the docks in Narraganset marinas. There are some leaving Newport, but that wharf is more geared towards yachts and pleasure craft.

Numerous fishing charter boats line the harbor near the ferry terminal on Block Island.

Connecticut

All along the Connecticut coast, charter boats run half-day or full-day fishing expeditions. The best thing to do is get a list of operators from the **Connecticut State Tourism Office** (tel: 800-282 6863; www.ctvisit.com) or head to the harbor where you want to go out and talk to the captains directly. There's lots of info at www.ctfisherman.com.

Catch-and-release fly-fishing is popular on the Housatonic River.

Vermont

With 7,000 miles (11,000km) of river and more than 800 lakes and ponds, Vermont is a fishing paradise. Vermont Fish and Wildlife has a good website: www.vtfishandwildlife.com.

Anglers flock to the trout-laden Battenkill River near Manchester, where **Orvis** (tel: 802-362 3622) runs a program of fly-fishing classes for all levels of skill.

Battenkill Anglers (6204 Main Street, Manchester; tel: 802-379 1444; www.battenkillanger.com) provides a fly-fishing guide service in both Vermont and the Catskills.

The **Fly Rod Shop and Fly Fish Vermont** (2703 Waterbury Road, Route 100, Stowe; tel: 803-253 7346) is an outfitter and provides a guide service.

New Hampshire

Great Glen Trails (tel: 603-466 2333; www.greatglentrails.com) offers introductory fishing classes and arranges guided fly-fishing trips.

For ocean fishing, several charter companies operate on the seacoast, including **Atlantic Fishing Fleet** (Rye; tel: 603-964 5220; www.atlanticwhalewatch.com) and **Al Gauron Deep Sea Fishing** (Hampton Beach; tel: 603-926 2469; www.algauron.com).

Maine

The Rangeley area is a popular destination for those who fly-fish.

For ocean fishing excursions, **Devils Den** (tel: 207-773 7632; www.dimillos.com/marina) runs half- and full-day trips from DiMillo's Marina in Portland.

In Kennebunkport, **Tidewater Fishing Charters** (tel: 207-229 0201; www.tidewaterfishing.com) operates fly-fishing and light-tackle charters from the Nonatum Resort (95 Ocean Avenue).

Four-hour fishing trips on Frenchman's Bay depart from the **Bar Harbor Inn Pier** at 8am and 1pm.

In the Boothbay region, **Sweet Action Charters** sails daily from June to September from Kaler's Crab and Lobster House (tel: 207-633 4741; www.sweetactioncharters.com).

Hiking

"Hiking" can have many different definitions. For some people, a stroll from their B&B to the antiques store down the street qualifies; others don't consider it "hiking" unless you're wearing heavy-duty footgear and are groaning under a backpack. Most people like a happy medium: enough exertion to feel virtuous, without needing Ben-Gay ointment to ease aching muscles that night. There are probably as many hiking trails in New England as there are leaf-peepers in the fall. Outfitters, outdoor stores, and local residents – many of whom are hikers themselves – are good sources for local information.

Massachusetts

Close to Boston, hikers can explore the 150 miles (240km) of trails **at Blue Hills Reservation** (see Biking). More ambitious hikers head west to **Mount Tom State Reservation** in Holyoke **or Mount Greylock State Reservation** (see Biking), which includes a stretch of the Appalachian Trail.

Rhode Island

Rhode Island Audubon Society (tel: 401-949 5454) leads nature hikes. On Block Island, contact the **Nature Conservancy** (Ocean Avenue; tel: 401-466 2129) for the best hikes.

Connecticut

The **Appalachian Trail**, a 2,000-mile (3,200km) trail linking Maine and Georgia, traverses about 50 miles (80km) of western Connecticut, and the Appalachian Mountain Club (Boston; tel: 617-523 0636; www.amcmaine.com) provides detailed trail information. This is one of the "easier" stretches of the Trail through New England.

At **Talcott Mountain State Park** in Simsbury, hikers who reach the peak of the 1.5-mile (2.5km) walk get panoramic vistas of the Farmington River Valley. On clear days, visibility can be up to 50 miles (80km).

Macedonia Brook State Park in Kent and **Sleeping Giant State Park** in Hamden run scenic day hikes. Contact the **Connecticut State Bureau of Parks and Recreation** (tel: 860-424 3200; www.ct.gov/dep/stateparks) for details.

Vermont

Vermont's topography offers everything from easy day hikes to multi-day mountain jaunts. Long-distance hikers gravitate to the

Appalachian Trail, which cuts across southern Vermont, and to the **Long Trail**, a 270-mile (435km) traverse across Vermont's highest peaks between the Massachusetts state line and the Canadian border.

Green Mountain Club (4711 Waterbury-Stowe Road, Waterbury Center; tel: 802-244 7037, ext. 10; www.greenmountainclub.org) has specific trail information and publishes the *Day Hiker's Guide to Vermont*.

To mix serious hiking with country-inn comforts, contact **Country Inns Along the Trail** (tel: 802-247 3300; www.inntoinn.com), which organizes inn-to-inn tours. **New England Hiking Holidays** (tel: 800-869 0949; www. nehikingholidays.com) also packages inn-to-inn hiking (and biking) tours in Vermont, New Hampshire, and Maine.

New Hampshire

The 86 major peaks of the White Mountains provide plenty of hiking challenges. The most strenuous stretches of the Appalachian Trail are in New Hampshire.

The **Appalachian Mountain Club** (tel: 603-466 2725, ext. 4; www.outdoors.org) has detailed trail information about the Trail and other paths in New Hampshire; this group maintains a network of huts in the White Mountains providing overnight accommodations (for hut reservations, call tel: 603-466 2727). Hikers who want to reach the summit of Mt Washington by foot can take a shuttle partway up the mountain.

For inn-to-inn hiking tours, contact **New England Hiking Holidays** (tel: 800-869 0949) in North Conway.

Maine

The website www.maineoutdoors. com/hiking has reliable information.

Baxter State Park (tel: 207-723 5140; www.baxterstateparkauthority. com) in Maine's North Woods draws thousands of hikers who tackle the day-long climb to the summit of **Mt Katahdin**, the state's highest peak (5,267ft [1,755 meters]). Eighteen mountains in the park are taller than 3,000ft (900 meters).

Horseback Riding

Most resort areas have at least one stable which offers trail rides through the mountains. The horses are well trained, although many of them make a game out of seeing how much they can eat along the way and how thoroughly they can ignore your efforts to make them stop. **Lucky 7 Stables** (Londonderry NH; www.lucky7stables.

com) is one of the few which operates year-round; riding in the snow is an incredible experience.

Ice-Skating

Many municipal ponds are open for skating when conditions warrant. Some are even lit at night. Only a few have skate rental. Boston, Portland, Providence, and Newport have downtown skating rinks.

Sailing

Billowing sails are a familiar sight along the New England coastline, but even landlocked Vermont has Lake Champlain. Novices can sign up for a day-long tutorial and learn to operate a Sailfish; experienced sailors can rent a boat and explore the coastline on their own.

Massachusetts

Boston's **Community Boating** (tel: 617-523 1038; www.community-boating.org), America's oldest public sailing program, sells two-day (and longer) memberships for Charles River sailing. Experience is required.

In Marblehead, **Atlantic Charters** (tel: 978-590 4318; www.atlantic-charters. com) offers lessons and charters.

Rhode Island

Newport, "the Sailing Capital of the World," is a good base for short harbor excursions and learn-to-sail vacations. **Sightsailing of Newport** (tel: 401-849 3333; www.sightsailing. com) offers harbor sails, rentals, and instruction. **Newport Sailing School** (tel: 401-848 2266; www. newportsailing.com) runs narrated one- and two-hour sailing tours plus classes. **Sail Newport** (tel: 401-846 1983; www.sailnewport.org) in Newport's Fort Adams State Park rents sailboats by the hour.

Block Island Club (tel: 401-466 5939; www.blockislandclub.org) offers full sailing instruction and one-week family memberships.

Connecticut

Mystic is a center for sailing activity on Long Island Sound. The **Offshore Sailing School** (tel: 800-221 4326; www.offshoresailing.com) conducts five-day learn-to-sail courses in town. **Mystic Seaport** (tel: 888-973 2767; www.mysticseaport.org) rents sailboats to ticket holders.

Vermont

Lake Champlain and **Lake Memphremagog** are the principal sailing lakes.

Winds of Ireland (Burlington Boathouse; www.windsofireland.net) runs day and sunset sailing cruises. On Lake Memphremagog, you can rent pontoon boats at **Newport Marine** (tel: 802-334 5911; www. newportmarinerv.com).

New Hampshire

Marinas abound on Lake Winnipesaukee, the state's largest lake. Although it's a popular powerboating spot, some marinas rent sailboats, including **Fay's Boat Yard** (Gulford, tel. 003-293 8000, www.faysboatyard.com), whose fleet has 16ft daysailers and 26ft sloops.

Maine

The Rockport–Camden area is Maine's center for windjammer cruising. The **Maine Windjammer Association** (tel: 800-807 9463; www.sailmainecoast. com), headquartered in Blue Hill, represents a number of windjammers that offer multi-day excursions. **Maine Windjammer Cruises** (tel: 888-692 7245; www. mainewindjammercruises.com) is also a good bet.

Do-it-yourself sailors can contact **Manset Yacht Service** (tel: 207-244 4040; www.mansetyachtservice. com), near Acadia National Park, to arrange sailboat rentals. **Sebago Sailing** on Sebago Lake rents sailboats by the week and offers lessons (tel: 207-647 4400; www. sebagosailing.com).

Sightseeing Cruises

Massachusetts

Not everyone was meant to be a sailor, but that doesn't man you can't enjoy the water. Sightseeing cruises can be informational and historic, educational, or simply relaxing. Most boats are stable enough that even the queasiest passenger will have no discomfort and enjoy the trip.

Numerous tour boats cruise Boston Harbor, including the *Spirit of Boston* (tel: 866-856 3463; www. spiritofboston.com), which offers lunch and dinner sailings; and **Boston Harbor Cruises** (tel: 617-227 4321; www.bostonharborcruises.com), which also runs whale watches.

The schooner *Bay Lady II* (tel: 508-487 9308; www.sailcapecod. com) makes two-hour sails from Provincetown into Cape Cod Bay.

Cape Ann Whale Watch (415 Main Street, Gloucester; tel: 800-877 5110; www.caww.com) guarantees sightings.

Rhode Island

In Newport, **America's Cup Charters**, with a fleet of Cup winners (tel: 401-846 9886; www.americascupcharters. com) runs evening sails and half- or full-day sailboat charters. Other charters include *Flyer* (tel: 401-848 2100), a 57ft catamaran; *Spirit of Newport* (tel: 401-849 3575); the 72ft schooner *Madeline*; and the 58ft classic speedboat *Rum Runner II* (tel: 401-847 0298).

Connecticut

Deep River Navigation Company (Saybrook Point; tel: 860-526 4954) offers narrated cruises along the Connecticut River shoreline. Among companies that offer cruises along the Thimble Islands are *Volsunga IV* (tel: 203-481 3345; www.thimbleislands. com) and *Sea Mist II* (tel: 203-488 8905; www.thimbleislandcruise), which also operates dinner cruises and seal watches. **Captain John's Sports Fishing Center** (tel: 860-443 7259; www.sunbeamfleet.com) in Waterford gives lighthouse, seal, and bald eagle cruises.

At **Argia Cruises** (tel: 860-536 0416; www.argiamystic.com) in Mystic, sail aboard the tall ships *Argia* or *Mystic*; there are also two- to six-day cruising adventures. The tall ship *Mystic Whaler* (tel: 800-697 8420; www.mysticwhalercruises. com) hosts day, overnight, and lobster dinner cruises. **Mystic Seaport** (tel: 888-973 2767; www.mysticseaport. org) offers cruises aboard a variety of craft, including the 1908 coal-fired steamboat *Sabrino*, and the 20ft Crosby cat boat *Breck Marshall*.

Maine

The **Beal & Bunker** (tel: 207-244 3575; www.cranberryisles.com/ ferry_b_and_b.html) sets sail from Northeast Harbor to Little Cranberry Island. **Island Cruises** (tel: 207-244 5785; www.bassharborcruises.com) in Bass Harbor cruises to nearby islands.

Near the Bar Harbor Town Pier, hop aboard the *Acadian* for two-hour narrated tours of Frenchman Bay (tel: 888-533 9253; www. barharborwhales.com). Nearby, *The Katherine* (tel: 207-288 3322) runs lobstering and seal-watching cruises.

Songo River Queen II, a replica of a Mississippi stern paddle wheeler, sails from Naples (tel: 207-935 2369; www.songoriverqueen.net).

Skiing

Although tourists began visiting New England in the summer to escape

ABOVE: Boston's Franklin Park Zoo has more than 220 species of animals.

the heat farther south and inland, skiing is what really established New England's tourism industry. Only flat Rhode Island lacks a ski center. Most ski resorts have a variety of trails with varying difficulty. They all offer classes. While downhill skiing dominates, cross-country skiing is popular, particularly among those whose knees can no longer cooperate with going downhill. www.alpinezone. com updates conditions throughout New England twice daily in season.

Massachusetts

Massachusetts' best downhill skiing is in the Berkshires. One major area is **Jiminy Peak** in Hancock (tel: 413-738 5500; www.jiminypeak.com).

In the eastern part of the state, the largest area is **Wachusett Mountain** in Princeton, about an hour west of Boston (tel: 978-464 2300/800-754 1234; www.wachusett.com).

The Berkshires are the most reliable for cross-country skiing. **Northfield Mountain Recreation and Environmental Center** (99 Miller's Falls Road; tel: 800-859 2960) has 26 miles (42km) of trails.

Closer to Boston, two smaller areas are **Weston Ski Track** (tel: 781-891 6575) and, in Carlisle, **Great Brook Farm** (tel: 978-369 7486; www.greatbrookski.com).

Connecticut

There are several small downhill areas in the Litchfield Hills region: **White Memorial Foundation** (tel: 860-678 9582) in Litchfield, **Mohawk Mountain** (tel: 860-672 6100) in Cornwall, and **Mount Southington** (tel: 860-628 0954) in Southington.

For cross-country skiing, try the **Woodbury Ski and Racquet Area** (tel: 860-567 0857; www.

whitememorialcc.org) or Farmington's **Winding Trails Cross Country Ski Center** (tel: 860-678 9582; www. windingtrails.org).

Vermont

For many, Vermont is synonymous with New England skiing. In the south, the largest downhill mountains are: **Stratton** (Jamaica; tel: 802-297 4000/800-787 2886; www.stratton. com), **Okemo** (Ludlow; tel: 802-228 4041/800-786 5366; www.okemo. com), and **Mount Snow** (tel: 800-245 7669; www.mountsnow.com). **Killington** (Rutland; tel: 802-422 3261; www.killington.com) – the Beast of the East – is monumental.

In the north, check out: **Stowe** (tel: 802-253 3600; www.stowe. com), **Sugarbush** (Warren; tel: 802-583 2381/800-537 8427; www. sugarbush.com), **Jay Peak** (Jay; tel: 802-988 2611; www.jaypeakresort. com), and **Smugglers' Notch** (tel: 800-419 4615; www.smuggs.com).

One of Vermont's largest cross-country skiing areas is **Craftsbury Nordic Center** (tel: 800-729 7751; www.craftsbury.com), but Stowe also has several excellent centers, including **Edson Hill** (tel: 802-253 8954; www.edsonhillmanor.com), **Topnotch** (tel: 802-253 8585; www. topnotchresort.com) and **Trapp Family Lodge** (tel: 802-253 8511; www.trappfamily.com).

Serious Nordic skiers ski the 300-mile (480km) **Catamount Trail**, which runs nearly the length of the state; contact the Catamount Trail Association (Burlington; 802-864 5794; www.catamounttrail.org).

New Hampshire

Major areas include: **Waterville Valley** (tel: 603-236 8311; waterville. com), **Loon Mountain** (Lincoln; 603-

745 8111; www.loonmtn.com), and **Cannon Mountain** (Franconia; 603-823 5563; www.cannonmt.com).

Smaller areas include: **Attitash Bear Peak** (Bartlett; tel: 603-374 2368/800-223 7669; www.attitash.com), **Bretton Woods** (tel: 603-278 5000; www.brettonwoods.com), and **Wildcat** (tel: 603-466 3326; www.skiwildcat.com), in Jackson.

The state's largest cross-country ski centers are **Jackson Ski Touring Foundation** (tel: 800-927 6697; www.jacksonxc.com) and **Mt Washington Valley Ski Touring** (off Route 16, Intervale; tel: 603-356 9920; www.mwskitouring.org).

South of the White Mountains, you'll find the **Nordic Center** (Waterville Valley; tel: 603-236 4666) and **Franconia Village Cross Country Center** at the Franconia Inn (tel: 603-823 5542/800-473 5299; www.franconiainn.com).

Maine

The largest areas for downhill skiing are: **Sunday River** in Bethel (tel: 207-824 3000/800-543 2754; www.sundayriver.com), **Sugarloaf/USA** in Kingfield (tel: 207-237 2000/800-843 5623; www.sugarloaf.com), and **Saddleback** in Rangley (tel: 207-864 5671; www.saddlebackmaine.com). Bethel is also home to several cross-country ski centers, including: **The Bethel Inn Ski Center** (tel: 800-654 0125; www.bethelinn.com) and **Carter's Cross Country Ski Centers** in Bethel and Oxford (tel: 207-539 4848; www.cartersxcski.com).

Other Nordic skiing spots include the **Harris Farm Cross Country Ski Center** in Dayton (tel: 207-499 2678; www.harrisfarm.com).

CHILDREN'S ACTIVITIES

Although the historic sites and cultural venues can bore kids to distraction, many have programs and activities specifically to entertain them. (If they learn a little in the process, so much the better.)

Carousels

Massachusetts

Downtown Holyoke's **Heritage State Park** (tel: 41-538 9838; www.holyokemerrygoround.org) carousel dates back to 1929; rides are still $1.

Rhode Island

The **Flying Horse Carousel** (Bay Street, Watch Hill) with beautiful hand-carved horses, lays claim as the oldest merry-go-round in the country.

Connecticut

The Carousel (Bushnell Park, Hartford; tel: 860-246 7739; www.bushnellpark.org) is a 1914 merry-go-round with hand-carved horses.

Museums

These are generally the ones with the most hands-on activities.

Massachusetts

In Boston, the **Children's Museum** (Museum Wharf, 300 Congress Street, Boston; tel: 617-426 8855; www.bostonchildrensmuseum.org) provides hours of hands-on fun for kids of all ages. There are hundreds of hands-on exhibits to spark the excitement of children aged 3 and up, and an Omni Theater, at The **Museum of Science** (Science Park at the Charles River Dam; tel: 617-723 2500; www.mos.org). The **New England Aquarium** (Central Wharf; tel: 617-973 5200; www.neaq.org) is a world-class facility that supports serious marine research.

In Sandwich, on Cape Cod, the **Thornton W. Burgess Museum** (4 Water Street; tel: 508-888 6870; www.thorntonburgess.org) is dedicated to the creator of *Peter Rabbit* and other children's books.

Connecticut

The brand-new **Connecticut Science Museum** (250 Columbus Boulevard, Hartford; tel: 860-SCIENCE; www.ctsciencecenter.org) has 150 hands-on activities and a 3-D digital theater.

Children 10 and under will delight in the hands-on exhibits at **Stepping Stones Museum for Children** (303 West Avenue, Mathews Park, Norwalk; tel: 203-899 0606; www.steppingstonesmuseum.org).

Children of all ages will enjoy the live animals and digital space and science show at the **Children's Museum** in West Hartford (950 Trout Brook Drive; tel: 860-231 2824; www.sciencecenterct.org).

Vermont

ECHO Lake Aquarium and Science Center (1 College Street, Burlington; tel: 802-864 1848; www.echovermont.org) teaches youngsters and "oldsters" about the lake's history and ecology. This is one of the best science centers anywhere.

New Hampshire

Montshire Museum of Science (Montshire Road, Norwich; tel: 802-649 2200; www.montshire.org) is small in scale, but there's a lot to explore and discover in the natural and manmade worlds.

Maine

The highly interactive **Children's Museum of Maine** (142 Free Street, Portland; tel: 207-828 1234; www.childrensmuseumofme.org) will keep even the most boisterous youngsters occupied for hours – hauling in traps on a lobster boat, broadcasting the news, making stained glass, and more.

Bangor's new **Maine Discovery Museum** (74 Main Street; tel: 207-262 7200; www.mainediscoverymuseum.org) has three floors of interactive, fun exhibits for kids.

Theme Parks

Massachusetts

Six Flags (1623 Main Street, Agawam; tel: 413-786 9300; www.sixflags.com) is New England's largest theme park, with more than 35 rides just for kids.

Connecticut

Lake Compounce (822 Lake Avenue, Bristol; tel: 860-583 3631; www.lakecompounce.com) is America's oldest amusement park.

New Hampshire

Children can explore caves carved by the last ice age at **Lost River Gorge and Boulder Caves** (Route 112; tel: 603-745 8031; www.findlostriver.com) in North Woodstock. **Clark's Trading Post and the White Mountain Central Railroad** (Route 3, Lincoln; tel: 603-745 8913; www.whitemountaincentralrr.com) has live bear shows, a family circus, and train excursions.

Christmas is alive all summer at **Santa's Village** (Route 2, Jefferson; tel: 603-586 4445; www.santasvillage.com), with rides and live reindeer. Next door, bumper boats, waterslides, and go-karts are just part of the fun at **Six Gun City and Fort Splash Water Park** (tel: 603-586 4592; www.sixguncity.com). Theme rides, shows, and storybook characters are all part of the fun at **Story Land** (Route 16, Glen; tel: 603-383 4186; www.storylandnh.com).

Maine

Palace Playland (Old Orchard Street, Old Orchard Beach; tel: 207-934 2001; www.palaceplayland.com) features an old carousel and Ferris wheel and lots of other rides.

Seacoast Fun Park (Windham;

tel: 207-892 5952; www. seacoastfunparks.com) has a 100ft (30-meter) free-fall ride, driving range, bumper boats, go-karts, and mini-golf.

A wooden roller coaster is one of the main attractions at **Funtown/Splashtown** (Route 1, Saco; tel: 800-878 2900; www. funtownsplashtownusa.com). There's also a water park with slides, a tube river run, and a play area.

Train Journeys

Most of these are seasonal, running all week during the summer, with limited hours in spring and fall. Many of them have Christmas excursions, with Santa on board.

Massachusetts
Berkshire Scenic Railway Museum (10 Willow Creek Road, Lenox; tel: 413-637 2210; www. berkshirescenicrailroad.org) has train rides from May through October.

Connecticut
Naugatuck Railroad of New England (83 Bank Street, Waterbury; tel: 203-575 1931; www.rmne.org) offers a historic ride through Black Rock State Park.

Essex Steam Train (Railroad Avenue, Essex; tel: 860-767 0103; www.essexsteamtrain.com) runs an old-fashioned service that can be combined with a riverboat ride.

New Hampshire
Winnipesaukee Railroad (South Main Street, Weirs Beach; tel: 603-279 5253; www.hoborr.com) runs historic coaches around the lake.

Conway Scenic Railroad (North Conway; tel: 603-356 5251/800-232 5251; www.conwayscenic.com) offers excursions from the 1874 station.

Buying Tickets

BosTix (tel: 617-262 8632; www.bostix.org), with booths in Copley Square and Faneuil Hall Marketplace, is a major entertainment information center. Half-price tickets go on sale at 11am on the day of the event. Cash and travelers' checks only.

TickCo (tel: 800-279 4444; www.tickco.com) dispenses tickets for sporting events (including the Red Sox), theaters, and nightclubs.

At most other venues throughout New England, tickets can be purchased by calling the theater in advance.

What's On

Massachusetts
Boston
The Phoenix (weekly; club line, tel: 617-859 3300; www.thephoenix. com) contains a large Arts and Entertainment section, as does *The Boston Globe*'s (www.boston.com/ bostonglobe) Thursday Calendar.
Western Massachusetts
For cultural events, consult the Five College Calendar of Events, published monthly, *The Valley Advocate* (www.valleyadvocate. com), a free weekly paper; or the *Springfield Republican*'s Weekend section, published in the paper on Thursdays, or their website: www. masslive.com/entertainment.

Rhode Island
Rhode Island Monthly is a good source for what's happening throughout the state, as is their website: www.rimonthly.com.

Connecticut
Pick up a copy of *Connecticut*

Mount Washington Cog Railway (tel: 603-278 5404; www.thecog. com) has the second-steepest railway track in the world. This is one of the most popular ways to get to the top of Mt Washington. The first trip every morning uses a steam locomotive.

Maine
Seashore Trolley Museum (Log Cabin Road, Kennebunkport; tel: 207-967 2800; www.trolleymuseum.org) offers 4-mile (6km) trolley trips.
Maine Eastern Railroad (tel: 866-637 2457; www. maineeasternrailroad.com) tours the Mid-Coast with restored vintage cars.
Boothbay Railway Village (Route 27, Boothbay; tel: 207-633 4727; www.railwayvillage.org) offers a short train ride through a recreated New England village; its museum houses an excellent collection of antique vehicles.

Dozens of antique steam locomotives, coaches, and cars are housed in a historic waterfront building at **Maine Narrow Gauge Railroad** in Portland (58 Fore Street; tel: 207-828 0814; mainenarrowguage.org); there's also a 3-mile (5km) ride on a 2ft narrow-gauge train along Casco Bay.

Zoos

Massachusetts
In Boston, **Franklin Park Zoo**

Magazine at the newsstand, or check www.connecticutmag. com. The state's website, ctvisit. com, lists current information. The free *Hartford Advocate* and *New Haven Advocate*, found in many restaurants, have sharp listings.

Vermont
The free weekly publication *Seven Days* (www.7dvt.com) lists events throughout the state. The weekly Calendar in *Burlington Free Press*'s (www.burlingtonfreepress. com) Thursday edition covers events throughout northern Vermont.

New Hampshire
Each month the magazine *To Do* (www.nhtodo.com) lists events throughout the state.

Maine
The monthly *Down East* (www. downeast.com) magazine is an excellent resource.

(Blue Hill Avenue at Columbia oad; tel: 617-541 5466) has a free-flight aviary and African Tropical Rain Forest exhibit, along with animals including giraffes, gorillas, kangaroos, and zebras.

Rhode Island
Roger Williams Park Zoo (Elmwood Avenue, Providence; tel: 401-785 3510; www.rogerwilliamsparkzoo. org) is outstanding. The rest of the park has so much that you can spend the entire day there: a 400-plus-acre (160-hectare) park with an antique carousel, tiny train, and lots of animals to keep the children entertained.

Connecticut
Beardsley Zoo (1875 Noble Avenue, Beardsley Park, Bridgeport; tel: 203-394 6565; www.beardsleyzoo.org) features North and South American animals, a carousel, and a New England farmyard petting zoo.

Maine
In Gray, rescue and rehabilitation are the focus at **Maine Wildlife Park** (tel: 207-657 4977; www. mainewildlifepark.com), with more than 30 Maine species.

Acadia Zoological Park (Route 3, Trenton; tel: 207-667 3244) is small (just 15 acres/6 hectares), but it will occupy the kids.

A – Z

A HANDY SUMMARY OF PRACTICAL INFORMATION, ARRANGED ALPHABETICALLY

A

Age Restrictions

The legal age for both the purchase and consumption of alcoholic drinks is 21. Liquor stores are state-owned or franchised in Vermont, New Hampshire, and Maine; privately owned in southern New England. Laws on Sunday purchase vary between states.

Some restaurants have a license restricting them to serve only beer and wine. Restaurants without a liquor license usually permit customers to bring their own beer or wine (BYOB); some may charge a "corkage" or "set-up" fee. When driving, keep bottles of alcohol unopened and out of sight in the car.

B

Budgeting for Your Trip

Industry research estimates that the average visitor spends about $300–$400/day. This breaks down to:
Double room per night in a three-star hotel in high season: $160–$260; in a city, parking may be an additional $30–$40 per night.
Simple lunch for two (without alcohol, with tax and 15 percent gratuity) is approximately $30–$35.
Three-course dinner for two (without alcohol, with tax and 20 percent gratuity): $80–$120.
Car hire per week (excluding taxes and fees): $200.
Admission charges for two: about

$50 per day.
Miscellaneous (drinks, taxis, etc): $75–$100 per day.

There are many discount plans available: family passes, and reduced admission for students and senior citizens. These are sometimes offered by a destination and sometimes by a group of attractions. Their availability changes annually, if not seasonally, but if you can browse the tourism websites and those of attractions of interest, you can probably find some very nice options. Some of those include accommodation, meals, and entrance charges. They are always posted at the admission booth of attractions, which will usually also post information about combination passes with other attractions.

Passes: In Boston, CityPass (tel: 888-330 5008; www.citypass.com) is good for nine consecutive days, and saves 50 percent at six popular attractions: the Museum of Science, New England Aquarium, Skywalk Observatory, Museum of Fine Arts, Harvard Museum of Natural History, and John F. Kennedy Library & Museum. Passes are sold at all six venues.

The **GoBoston Card** (tel: 800-887 9103; www.gobostoncard.com), available for one to seven days, and gives visitors unlimited access to more than 60 attractions as well as restaurant and shopping discounts, and excursions outside the city.

Many other cities with multiple attractions also offer combination rates: be sure to ask in advance of ticket purchase. Mystic CT has a pass with reduced admissions to several attractions and meal deals. Newport RI has discounts to the mansions.
Disabled persons: US citizens and permanent residents with disabilities

can apply for a free lifetime pass (documentation required) to all US National Parks (www.nps.gov).
Accommodations: Discounted lodgings and airfare are available on numerous websites including hotwire. com, travelocity.com, sidestep.com, priceline.com, and roomsaver.com. Discount hotel and motel coupons and books with last-minute hotel reservations are distributed free of charge at most Interstate rest stops and tourist information centers.
Seniors: Many businesses and attractions offer discounts of 10–15 percent to senior citizens; the qualifying age can range from 60 to 65, although ID is seldom requested.
Students: Both the Student Advantage Card (tel: 800-333 2920; www.studentadvantage.com) and the STA Travel Discount Card (tel: 800-781 4040; www.statravel.com) provides students with substantial discounts while travelling in the US.

C

Children

It's quite easy to travel in New England with children. There are hands-on museums, theme parks, and toy and book stores throughout the region. With proper planning, driving distances between destinations can be kept quite short. Almost all attractions which charge admission have a discounted rate for children, and many change nothing at all for very young kids, often 5 and under.

Many restaurants offer children's menus, but some – particularly the more expensive – may not welcome young children at dinner. Lodgings generally welcome children and do not charge for those under 18, although they may add on $10 or $15 for a cot or crib. It is quite common for bed-and-breakfasts to have age restrictions, so be sure to check in advance.

Many hotel concierges will provide lists of local agencies which provide sitters; this can be quite costly, as the agencies charge a referral fee plus an hourly fee, but the sitters are carefully screened. Two agencies in Boston include **Parents in a Pinch** (45 Bartlett Crescent, Brookline; tel: 617-739 5437; parentsinapinch.com) and **Boston's Best Baby Sitters** (513 East Broadway, Boston; tel: 617-268 7148; bbbabysitters.com).

Laws in each state are quite specific about driving with children in a car. If you are renting, be sure to tell the agency in advance how old your children are so that they will have the proper size car seats available, and check with them about state requirements.

Climate

New England's climate is as varied as its landscape, with large variations from state to state and from season to season. Massachusetts and Connecticut have very similar temperature patterns. In the west, the summer temperatures will be around 80°F (27°C), 85°F(32°C) in Boston, and about 81°F(27°C) on Cape Cod and the islands and along the Connecticut coast. The winters can be quite cold; temps in the mountains are frequently 20°F (−7°C) or colder. They will be warmer in Boston; 32°F (0°C) is about the norm. Along the water, the air temperature may be either side of freezing, but the "wind chill" makes it seem much colder.

Rhode Island: Temperatures are similar to those in Boston and Cape Cod. Block Island has an average January temperature of about 31°F (−1°C) and an average July temperature of about 70°F (21°C).

Vermont and New Hampshire have considerable variations in temperature depending on proximity to the mountains. In general, winter temperatures in the mountains are 17°F (−8°C) and average July temperatures are 70°F (21°C). In the central areas of both states, the mean January temperature is 22°F (−6°C) with a mean July temperature of 70°F (21°C).

Atop Mt Washington, which has its own weather pattern, the average July temperature is 50°F (10°C) and the mean January temperature 6°F (−14°C). In April 1934, winds of

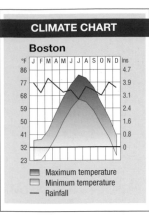

CLIMATE CHART

Boston

- ■ Maximum temperature
- □ Minimum temperature
- — Rainfall

231mph (372kmh) were recorded on the summit of Mt Washington.

Maine: The coastal part of the state has a maritime climate. Winter temperatures are much milder than those inland; summer temperatures are cooler. Northern Maine, however, is extremely cold with a high snowfall. In 1925, Maine's lowest recorded temperature of −48°F(−44.4°C) was observed. The south is the warmest part of the state.

What to Wear

Clothing styles in New England vary from state to state, as well as from region to region. In rural areas, people tend to dress in casual clothes geared towards outdoor life, whereas attire in cities in Massachusetts, Connecticut, and Rhode Island is more traditional. A few formal restaurants may require a jacket and tie for men. "Business casual" is an often-quoted dress code. For men, that means a short-sleeved shirt or polo shirt and khaki or twill trousers. Women's attire should have a similar accent. Denim jeans are usually permitted if they are not obviously faded, worn, or patched.

While "relaxed" is the norm, some bars and nightclubs ban jeans and T-shirts.

Some warm clothing, such as jumpers, jackets, and windbreakers, should be packed even during the summer, when evening temperatures tend to dip in the mountains and on the coast. Winters generally necessitate heavy outerwear, including hats, scarves, gloves, and boots. The best advice for winter dressing is to dress in layers in order to adapt to immediate situations. Keep in mind that denim, once wet, becomes very heavy, provides no insulation, and is nearly impossible to dry.

When to Visit

Generally, the tourist season runs from early June through the first weekend in September. It's particularly crowded along the coastline of Maine, Cape Cod, Martha's Vineyard, Nantucket, and Newport. Make reservations as early as possible. The other very busy time is fall foliage season, from mid-September through October. Reservations are required everywhere, even in areas which otherwise see few tourists.

In the summer, humidity, even in the mountains, can be draining, and there will often be afternoon thunderstorms, which can often cause downpours. While New England rarely is affected by hurricanes, the storms can strike, as Hurricane Irene did in August 2011, causing massive flooding. Hurricane season runs from June through November, with August and September the most active months. Coastal areas may be evacuated ahead of an approaching storm.

Winter blizzards are much more likely. New England is generally ready for them, but massive storms can shut down the region and cause power outages. Most resorts and hotels have their own generators which kick in if the power grid turns off. If driving, make sure you have plenty of gas, carry a blanket in case you are stuck and cannot be reached immediately, and keep your cell phone charged.

Early spring, from March through April, is often called "mud season", and for good reason. The melting snow turns many unpaved roads into morasses that challenge even four-wheel drive vehicles. Many of the seasonal tourist attractions are still closed, although those in cities are usually open, if with limited hours.

Customs Regulations

Visitors aged 21 or over may bring the following to the US, providing they are staying in the country for at least 72 hours and have not declared the same amounts within the past six months:
- 1 liter of duty-free alcohol
- 1,200 duty-free cigarettes, or 2kg tobacco, or 100 cigars (non-Cuban)
- Gifts worth $100 if non-US citizens or $800 if US citizens
- Up to $10,000 in US or foreign cash, or travelers' checks; any more must be declared.
- Import of meat, seeds, plants, and fruit is forbidden.

For more information, contact US Customs (tel. 202-927 1770; www.customs.ustreas.gov).

When returning to your country from the US:

Australian citizens: Australian Customs Service (tel: 1300/363-263; outside Australia, tel: 02 6275 6793; www.customs.gov.au).

Canadian citizens: the Canada Border Services Agency (tel: 866-335 3237 in Canada [24-hour computer information; live operators Mon–Fri 8am–6pm], or outside Canada, tel: 204-983 3500 or check their website: www.cbsa-asfc.gc.ca).

UK citizens: HM Revenue and Customs (tel: 0845-010-9000 in the UK [8am–8pm Mon–Fri], or, outside the UK, tel: 44-2920-501-261; www.hmce.gov.uk).

D

Disabled Access

The Americans with Disabilities Act requires handicapped access for most buildings used by the public, but there are exceptions. Most attractions, restaurants, and lodgings comply, but it's a good idea to check in advance, particularly when visiting older historic sites which may be physically unable to provide access.

Resources include **Society for Accessible Travel and Hospitality** (tel: 212-447 7284; www.sath.org); **Accessable Travel Source** (tel: 303-232 2979; www.accessable.com), which recommends travel agents who specialize in bookings for the disabled; and the comprehensive information website at **MossRehab** (www.mossresourcenet.org).

For access on public transportation throughout Boston, contact the **Massachusetts Bay Transportation Authority's Office for Transportation Access** (tel: 617-222 5976/800-543 8287; www. mbta.com).

E

Electricity

Most wall outlets have 110-volt, 60-cycle, alternating current plug bays. If using European-made appliances, step down the voltage with a transformer and bring a plug adaptor as sockets are two-prong. These can be purchased at stores in airports and some office supply stores (Staples and Office Depot) and at AAA stores, but are otherwise not easy to find.

Embassies and Consulates

For a listing of embassies in the US, log onto: embassy.org/embassies. Many countries have a consulate office in New England, usually in Boston. For a complete list: www.state.gov/s/cpr/rls/fco/index.htm.

Australia: No consultate. Embassy: 1610 Massachusetts Avenue, Washington DC; tel: 202-797 3000.

Canada: Two consulates: 1 Canal Plaza, Portland ME; tel: 207-775 1547; and 3 Copley Place, Boston; tel: 617-262 3760.

India: No consulate. Embassy: 2107 Massachusetts Avenue, Washington DC; tel: 202-939 7000.

Ireland: 535 Boylston Street, Boston; tel: 617-267 9330. Embassy: 2234 Massachusetts Avenue, Washington DC; tel: 202-232 5993.

Israel: 20 Park Plaza, Boston; tel: 617-542 0041. Embassy: 3514 International Drive NW, Washington DC; tel: 202-364 5412.

United Kingdom: 1 Broadway, Cambridge MA; tel: 617-245 4500. Embassy: 3100 Massachusetts Avenue, Washington, DC; tel: 202-588 7870.

G

Gays and Lesbians

Boston has a vibrant gay community, as do Cambridge, Springfield, and Northampton MA and Portland ME. Provincetown on Cape Cod is the country's best-known gay summer vacation spot. Most college towns have some kind of gay community,.

Information concerning gay-oriented activities and businesses can be found in alternative weeklies such as northern Vermont's *Seven Days*; western Massachusetts' and Connecticut's *The Advocate*; and Boston's *Bay Windows*; and in the Boston and regional editions of *The Phoenix*. "One in Ten," broadcast Sundays 8–10pm on Boston's WFNX Radio (92.1 FM), is also a source of information for the gay and lesbian communities.

A good in-town networking source, for those visiting Boston, is Calamus Books (92B South Street; tel: 617-338 1931; calamusbooks.com).

H

Health and Medical Care

Most visitors to New England have

Emergencies

For all emergencies, dial tel: 911. If you can be very clear about your location, it will help responders reach you more quickly.

no health problems during their stay; sunburn is the main nuisance for the majority. Even so, non-Americans should never leave home without travel insurance to cover themselves and their belongings. It's not cheap to get sick in the United States. Your own insurance company or travel agent can advise you on policies, but shop around, as rates vary. Make sure you are covered for accidental death, emergency medical care, cancellation of trip, and baggage or document loss.

Pharmacies stock most standard medication (though some painkillers that are available over the counter in other countries may be prescription-only in the US).

Hospitals are signposted on highways with a white H on a blue background. Major hospitals have 24-hour emergency rooms – you may have a long wait before you get to see the doctor, but the care and treatment are thorough and professional.

Walk-in clinics are commonplace in cities, where you can consult a nurse or doctor for a minor ailment without an appointment. If cost is a concern, turn first to clinics offering free or pro-rated care (look under "Clinics" in the Yellow Pages).

A couple of serious health hazards exist in the region:

• Lyme disease (borne by deer ticks hiding in high grass) is a potentially dangerous chronic condition. Starting with a rash, it develops into flu-like symptoms and joint inflammation, and possible long-term complications such as meningitis and heart failure. When hiking, wear light-colored pants tucked into socks, and spray the clothing with an insecticide. Inspect your skin afterwards: if a tick has attached itself, it should be removed very carefully, using tweezers. Place the tweezers as low on the tick's body as possible, and remove slowly and deliberately; tick mouth parts left in the skin can still deliver the infection. Disinfect the area with alcohol, and visit a doctor or clinic if a red rash begins to appear.

• Poison ivy causes only temporary discomfort, but this can be avoided by keeping an eye out for the shiny three-leaf clusters and washing immediately upon accidental contact. Calamine lotion is good for soothing the skin.

Tap water is safe to drink, but avoid stream water as it can cause giardia, an intestinal disorder spread by wild animal wastes. Use a filter or purification tablets, or boil water, when hiking or camping.

Bear, moose, and other wildlife are unpredictable and can be very dangerous. Never try to approach any wild animal. They can charge at you without warning, particularly if you disturb a female with young (who may be hidden nearby) or a male in rutting season. Before hiking, ask about sightings.

If an animal acts particularly friendly – raccoon or fox, for example – it may have rabies. Do not touch it. If you do, get to a medical facility immediately and report the contact. The animal does not have to be having convulsions or foaming at the mouth to be contagious, and the bacteria is extremely virulent.

There are both rattlesnakes and copperheads in the woods, although they try to avoid us as much as we try to avoid them. If bitten, put a firm binding around the bite – do not use a tourniquet – keep the bitten limb below the level of the heart, and get to a medical facility as soon as possible.

Internet

Wi-Fi access is nearly universal. Restaurants, visitor centers, even gas stations often have access, usually at no charge. In small towns, access may be limited. Most lodgings have service, although in more rural areas the connection may be weak. Larger hotels often have in-room connections, but many of them charge a fee, which can be as much as $20/day. Others have business centers, which are generally free of charge. Most public libraries will let you use their computers for free or a small fee.

M

Media

Newspapers and Magazines

As well as the US nationals such as *USA Tody* and the financial *Wall Street Journal* and *The New York Times*, New England has many local newspapers. Larger cities have their own dailies. Boston's free, weekly *Phoenix* covers New England's entertainment

venues (also at www.thephoenix. com). In western Massachusetts the free, weekly *Valley Advocate* (valleyadvocate.com) is an excellent resource for the Pioneer Valley. Alternative papers, often with excellent events and entertainment listings, thrive in college towns. Foreign magazines and papers are sold on newsstands in the larger cities.

Radio Stations

AM radio is geared toward talk, news, and information programming. (Saturday and Sunday mornings are often when local stations in small towns broadcast local news – including obituaries and anniversaries – and on-air "flea markets" with people selling everything from non-functioning snowmobiles and dining room sets to dairy cows.) FM stations tend to offer specific music formats, such as country or classic rock. Red Sox games are broadcast on 68 stations throughout New England, anchored in Boston by WRKO (680 AM) and WEEI (850 AM). New England Patriot games are aired on WBCN (104.1 FM).

National Public Radio, known for in-depth news coverage, classical music, and special programming, has affiliates throughout New England. Among them: 88.5 FM in western Massachusetts, 89.5 FM

BELOW: rural mailboxes: a classic design.

in southern Vermont, 89.7 FM in the Boston area, and 89.1 FM in Concord, NH. WBUR (90.9 FM) is NPR's news source in Boston.

Station formats can change to reflect listener ratings. What was classic rock today can be Top 40 tomorrow. The easiest way to find what you are listening for is to use the "scan" button on your radio setting.

Television Stations

Cable and satellite television is ubiquitous, although how many channels you receive depends on the plan your accommodation pays for. At the very least, you will get "local" stations – although in rural areas, that can mean a city 50 miles away – which carry the major networks (ABC, NBC, CBS), The Weather Channel, CNN, Fox, ESPN (sports), at least one movie channel, most likely HBO, and probably a Public Broadcasting System (PBS) channel, which is advertisement-free and has some of the better-quality programs.

Money

Paper money is issued in $1, $2 (very rare), $5, $10, $20, $50, and $100 denominations.

Coins come in seven denominations: 1¢ (a penny); 5¢ (a nickel); 10¢ (a dime); 25¢ (a quarter);

50¢ (a half dollar; infrequently seen); gold-colored coins worth $1 (which are nearly the same size and hue as the quarter and are universally despised and rarely used); and the rarely-seen silver dollar.

ATMs are ubiquitous in all but the smallest of towns throughout New England, and, although they charge a fee, they are an extremely convenient way to get cash as you need it. They will convert your transaction automatically at a generally good rate. Unlike Europe, most places in the US are not equipped to handle currency exchange, even in major cities.

Credit cards are almost universally accepted, except in some very small towns and a few eateries. Some are more welcome than others. Visa and MasterCard are taken almost everywhere, but American Express is occasionally not accepted. Discover is another card with relatively wide acceptance. Most cards charge a fee of 3 percent for international transactions and do not convert at a favorable rate. Almost all retailers accept debit card purchases and pre-paid debit cards.

If your credit card is lost or stolen, report it to the company immediately. Visa's US emergency number: tel: 800-847 2911. For American Express cardholders: tel: 800-992 3404. American Express traveler's check holders: tel: 800-221 7282. For MasterCard: tel: 800-307 7309. Discover: tel: 800-DISCOVER. To find phone numbers for other credit cards, call the toll-free directory at tel: 800-555 1212.

International visitors can exchange funds at exchange booths at Logan Airport: Sovereign Bank BCE Travelex Foreign Exchange (tel: 800-287 7362; travelex.com) booths are open daily at terminals B and E, and they have an office open daily at 745 Boylston Street in downtown Boston. There is a Bank of America Exchange at terminal C. All exchanges charge a processing, service, and/or administration fee.

Up-to-the-minute exchange rates are posted on x-rates.com and finance.yahoo.com/currency.

Banks are generally open Monday through Friday from 9am until 5pm. Some may remain open later on Thursdays and Fridays, and others may open Saturday mornings (but don't count on it).

Though they are becoming less and less popular, travelers' checks are accepted by many businesses, although smaller establishments may be hesitant to accept, and make change for, larger denominations.

When exchanging checks for cash, you will get the best rate at banks: hotels generally give a poor rate. Most financial establishments will charge a commission fee when cashing travelers' checks.

Tipping

Tip appropriately (unless the service is poor) or it will be interpreted as an insult. For meals, hairdressers, bartenders, and taxi drivers, around 15 percent is the norm (20 percent for exceptional waiter service or if the bill is $100 or more). Don't tip on the tax portion of the bill.

Give a few dollars to the doorman if he performs a service such as hailing a cab, $1 per bag to the bellhop, and $1 to the parking attendant each time you use valet parking; housekeepers should get $2 per day.

O

Opening Hours

Government, and most business, offices are open weekdays from 9am to 5pm. Most large retail stores open at 9am and stay open at least until 5pm; many stay open until 6pm, and often later on Thursday and Friday nights. Stores in malls generally open at 10am and close at 9pm Monday through Saturday, although many stay open later in the evening; on Sundays malls generally open at noon and close at 8pm.

Smaller shops throughout New England, particularly in tourist areas, are usually open in the summer from 10am until at least 5 or 6pm. But these hours vary tremendously with location and season.

Many museums are open daily from 10am to 5pm in the summer, but others are closed on Monday or Tuesday. Off-season hours will vary a great deal, particularly in smaller towns.

In larger cities many gas stations and convenience stores remain open 24 hours, as do those close to Interstate exits.

P

Pets

In recent years, travel with pets has become increasingly popular in New England, and some lodgings are now setting aside "pet-friendly" units. Many charge a cleaning fee ranging from $25 to $35 a night;

Postal Services

There are post offices in most New England villages and towns. They are generally open daily Monday through Friday, and Saturday mornings.

If you do not know where you will be staying in a particular town, you can receive mail simply by having it addressed to you, care of General Delivery, at the main office in that town – but you must pick up such mail personally (within 30 days). Check with postal officials about charges and the variety of mail-delivery services available.

Stamps may be purchased at hotel desks. There are occasionally vending machines in shops and airports. Many grocery stores also sell stamps. For domestic and international rates, log onto www.usps.com and click on "calculate postage."

To facilitate quick delivery within the US, include the five-digit zip code when addressing communications. Zip code information may be obtained from any post office or on: usps.com.

and some will request a damage deposit, returnable at the end of a stay provided the pet did no permanent harm. Pets are not permitted in restaurants, but are generally welcome at establishments with outdoor seating, providing the pet does not have to go through the restaurant to get in.

Some stores will permit pets. Burlington VT is particularly pet-friendly, and stores welcoming them have signs posted in their windows.

Car interiors can heat up rapidly in summer. Do not leave your pet unattended in a car on a warm day, even with windows ajar. The heat can quickly cause brain damage or death, and at the least may cause a concerned passerby to break your window to rescue your pet. Many states and local governments have made such negligence a crime; you can be fined and, if the situation is extreme, jailed.

Public Holidays

During the holidays listed below, some or all state, local, and federal agencies are closed. Local banks and businesses may also close on the following days:
• New Year's Day
• Third Monday in January: Martin Luther King's Birthday

- Third Monday in February: Presidents Day, marking Lincoln's and Washington's birthdays
- Third Monday in April: Patriots' Day (Massachusetts only)
- Last Monday in May: Memorial Day
- July 4: Independence Day
- First Monday in September: Labor Day
- Second Monday in October: Columbus Day
- November 11: Veterans Day
- Fourth Thursday in November: Thanksgiving
- December 25: Christmas Day

S

Smoking

The legal age in New England to buy tobacco is 18. Although the laws vary somewhat between states, in general smoking is banned in most indoor public places, restaurants, workplaces, and on transport. Hotels have non-smoking rooms; many inns and B&Bs ban smoking.

T

Tax

All states levy taxes on meals and accommodation, and all but New Hampshire on all sales. When restaurants and hotels quote prices, these taxes are not normally included – they can bump up the cost by up to 12 percent. Ticket prices for transport have tax included.

Telephones

Although scarce, public telephones can still be found in some hotel lobbies, restaurants, garages, and convenience stores. Local calls require a deposit of 50¢–$1 (coins only) before you dial the number. If your call lasts longer than three

Weights and Measures

32°F = 0°C; 60°F = 15.5°C;
80°F = 26.7°C; 100°F = 37.8°C
1 US gallon = 0.85 Imperialgallon or 3.79 liters
1 mile = 1.6km
1 inch – 2.54cm
1ft = 0.3048 meter
65mph = 105kmh
1 acre = 0.4 hectares
1lb = 0.45kg

minutes, the operator will require an additional deposit to continue the call.
- For **emergencies**, dial tel: 911; coins are not needed.

The charge for using a phone in your hotel room can vary greatly from one lodging to another: some will charge an access and per-minute fee even if you use a calling card; some may charge for local calls; and others will offer the service at no charge. This information is usually posted in your room.

If you are visiting from outside the US and your cell (mobile) phone plan does not cover international calls, consider renting a phone when you arrive. The cost is generally under $50 a week for unlimited incoming and outgoing calls. Providers in the US include **All Cell Rentals** (tel: 877-724 2355; allcellrentals.com) and **Travel Cell** (tel: 877-235 5746; travelcell.com).
- All 800, 877, 866, and 888 numbers are toll-free.

Directory assistance for any location from any location: tel: 411.
- To dial a long-distance number, dial 1, then the area code, then the number.

Tourist Information

Larger cities have tourist information centers; in smaller towns, the Chamber of Commerce or town hall fills that role. State tourist agencies all have their tourism brochures available on their websites.
Connecticut
(tel: 888-288 4748; ctvisit.com)
Maine
(tel: 888-624 6345; visitmaine.com)
Massachusetts
(tel: 800-227 6277; massvacation.com)
New Hampshire
(tel: 800-386 4664; www.visitnh.gov)
Rhode Island
(tel: 800-556 2484; visitrhodeisland.com)
Vermont
(tel: 802-828 3237/800-837 6668; www.travel-vermont.com)
Discover New England
(discovernewengland.org) supplies telephone numbers and accommodation, plus maps of each state except Connecticut.
There is a Massachusetts Office of Travel and Tourism in the UK at: c/o First Public Relations, Molasses House, Clove Hitch Quay, Plantation Wharf, York Place, London SW11 3TN; tel: 020 7978 7429.

V

Visas and Passports

Immigration and visitation procedures

can change rapidly depending on real and perceived threats to security.

To enter the United States, foreign visitors need a passport and many also need a visa. You may be asked to provide evidence that you intend to leave the United States after your visit is over (usually in the form of a return or onward ticket).

You may not need a visa if you are a resident of one of 27 countries that participate in the Visa Waiver Program (VWP) and are planning to stay in the US for less than 90 days. You must, however, log onto the Electronic System for Travel Authorization's unmemorably named website, esta.cbp.dhs.gov at least 48 hours before traveling and provide personal information and travel details; either your application will be accepted (and will be valid for multiple visits over two years) or you will be told to apply for a visa. If you don't have Internet access, you'll need to find someone who does.

Anyone wishing to stay longer than 90 days must apply for a visa in any case. This can be done by mail to the nearest US Embassy or Consulate. Visa extensions can be obtained in the US from United States Immigration and Naturalization Service offices. Applications can be downloaded at www.travel.state.gov.

Canadian citizens traveling to the US by air or across the land border need a passport to enter the country.

The US Department of Homeland Security maintains a website at: www.dhs.gov/xtrvlsec.
Immunization Requirements
Log onto travel.state.gov for a complete list of immunization requirements by country.

W

Websites

The following sites provide general information on visiting the region.
www.visitingnewengland.com
www.gonewengland.about.com
www.discovernewengland.org
www.visitnewengland.com
www.visitingnewengland.com – Hotel, B&B, inns, motels, and resort reservations throughout the region.
www.511maine.com – Road conditions (including travel advisories) in Maine, Vermont, and New Hampshire.
www.newenglandweather.com – Real-time weather reports.

FURTHER READING

TRANSPORTATION

History and Culture

Builders of the Bay Colony, by Samuel Eliot Morison. New England's most celebrated historian tells the story of the men – and one woman – who gave New England its intellectual underpinnings.

A Week on the Concord and Merrimack Rivers, Walden, The Maine Woods, and **Cape Cod**, by Henry David Thoreau. Thoreau's four greatest works describe his travels on foot and by canoe – and his sojourn at Walden Pond; detailed descriptions of mid-19th-century landscape and people combine with the blunt, often ornery musings of an archetypal New England intellect.

Paul Revere's Ride, by David Hackett Fischer. Historian Fischer explains what really happened on that April night, which is a lot juicier and more interesting than what's generally taught in school.

The Encyclopedia of New England, edited by Burt Feintuch and David H. Watters. A magisterial compendium of New England persons, places, and accomplishments (in the same vein, look for New England University Press's **The Vermont Encyclopedia** (2003, edited by Duffy, Hand, and Orth, a very readable Green Mountain gather-all).

The Proper Bostonians, by Cleveland Amory. Not satire or skewering, but a lighthearted yet near-anthropological study of a Brahmin elite with "grandfather on the brain."

The Prince of Providence, by Mike Stanton. The story of very colorful Providence mayor Buddy Cianci, who oversaw the rebirth of his city and was convicted of corruption while still in office.

The Enduring Shore: A History of Cape Cod, Martha's Vineyard, and Nantucket, by Paul Schneider. Natural and social history, with an emphasis on human impact on a fragile, ultimately ephemeral environment.

The Outermost House: A Year of Life on the Great Beach of Cape Cod, by Henry Beston. Beston's classic rivals Thoreau's Walden as an account of a year of blissful solitude in the loveliest of natural surroundings.

String Too Short to Be Saved: Recollections of Summers on a New England Farm, by Donald Hall. A poet's warm, elegiac recollections of life on his grandfather's small New England farm in the 1940s.

The Survival of the Bark Canoe, by John McPhee. An account of a Maine river trip in a modern bark canoe, interwoven with the story of an uncompromising New Englander who builds the timeless craft.

The Lobster Chronicles: Life on a Very Small Island, by Linda Greenlaw. New England's iconic fishery, seen from the inside by one of the first women captains to break a famously rigid gender barrier.

All Souls, by Michael Patrick MacDonald. A searing memoir of an anguished childhood growing up in Boston's Irish housing projects.

Send Us Your Thoughts

We do our best to ensure the information in our books is as accurate and up-to-date as possible. The books are updated on a regular basis using local contacts, who painstakingly add, amend and correct as required. However, some details (such as telephone numbers and opening times) are liable to change, and we are ultimately reliant on our readers to put us in the picture.

We welcome your feedback, especially your experience of using the book "on the road". Maybe we recommended a hotel that you liked (or another that you didn't), or you came across a great bar or new attraction we missed.

We will acknowledge all contributions, and we'll offer an Insight Guide to the best letters received.

Please write to us at:
Insight Guides
PO Box 7910
London SE1 1WE
Or email us at:
insight@apaguide.co.uk

Mayflower, by Nathaniel Philbrick. A well-researched, entertainingly written, unvarnished, and unromantic account of the Pilgrims.

A Civil Action, by Jonathan Harr. Story of Woburn MA and its suits against two large firms held responsible for polluting the town's water source and causing illness and death.

Hackers, by Steven Levy. Largely focusing on MIT, it explores how hackers are responsible for the increasing sophistication of computer technology.

Landscape, Natural History

A Guide to New England's Landscape, by Neil Jorgensen. Written in layperson's English, a comprehensive look at how today's mountains, lakes, farmland, and coastline evolved in deep and recent geologic time.

Hands on the Land: A History of the Vermont Landscape, by Jan Albers. The story of human interaction with the land the glaciers left – a never-easy process that yielded a remarkably beautiful balance between the natural and built environments.

In Season: A Natural History of the New England Year, by Nona Bell Estrin. In a region with some of the world's sharpest seasonal divisions, the drama of life's winter ebb and summer flow.

Cod, by Mark Kurlansky. Surprisingly fascinating account of how codfish and the fishing industry impacted New England and the rest of the world.

The Secret Life of Lobsters, by Trevor Corson. Told from the perspectives of lobstermen and marine biologists, it explores the near-collapse of the lobster industry in the 1980s and unravels the mysteries of a lobster's life cycle, living arrangements, and mating habits, often in hysterical detail.

Not Without Peril, by Nicholas Howe. Stories of climbers in New Hampshire's Presidential range from 1849 to 1994.

Architecture

Houses of Boston's Back Bay: An Architectural History, 1840–1917,

ACCOMMODATIONS
ACTIVITIES
A–Z

by Bainbridge Bunting. A social as well as an architectural history, this amply illustrated book describes the evolution – and living style – of Boston's fist planned neighborhood.
New England's Architecture, by Wallace Nutting. A fine collection of sketches and photographs drawn from books on the architecture of individual New England states by the late antiquarian Nutting, who pioneered the preservation of the region's vintage homes and furnishings.
Spenser's Boston, by Robert Parker. A photographic journey in and around the city with the author of the popular mystery series as your guide. Quite a few settings from the novels, of course, but it's really a love letter from Parker to his city.

Fiction

Writing New England: An Anthology from the Puritans to the Present, edited by Andrew Delbanco. This carefully chosen collection of New England authors represents nearly four centuries of the region's intellectual development.
The Late George Apley, by John P. Marquand. A deft and wry portrayal of a Brahmin trapped within his class, as its grip on Boston weakens.
The Last Hurrah, by Edwin O'Connor. The ethnic-based machine politics of 20th-century Boston shape the career of a protagonist based on Boston's roguish Mayor James Michael Curley.
Northern Borders, by Howard Frank Mosher. A coming-of-age tale, set among Mosher's vanishing breed of back-country Vermonters equally at home with sawmills and Shakespeare.
Empire Falls, by Richard Russo. The Pulitzer Prize–winning novel of a mill town's deterioration.
Blues, by John Hersey. An old fisherman and a youth explore Cape Cod, life, and the New England outdoors.
An Arsonist's Guide to Writers' Homes in New England, by Brock Clarke. A wonderful send-up of memoirs, mystery fiction, and the adulation of New England's literary icons.

Movies Set in New England

Revolutionary Road (2008), based on the Richard Yates novel, depicts the disaffections of striving Connecticut suburbanites in the 1950s.
The Departed (2006) is Martin Scorcese's Oscar-winning take on the Boston underworld. Jack Nicholson's character was allegedly based on

fugitive gangster Whitey Bulger.
Little Children (2006) stars Kate Winslett as the matriarch of a family surviving a tumultuous summer in a Boston suburb.
Mystic River (2003), director Clint Eastwood's retelling of the Dennis Lehane novel, examines lives tightly intertwined in a working-class Irish Boston neighborhood.
The Perfect Storm (2000), starring George Clooney and based on the real-life **Andrea Gail** tragedy, is a paean to the 10,000 Gloucester men who have lost their lives in the North Atlantic fishery.
A Stranger in the Kingdom (1998), a retelling of an early Howard Frank Mosher novel, examines a racial incident in a small Vermont town.
Affliction (1997), from the Russell Banks novel, is the story of a small-town sheriff in New Hampshire who crosses his ethical lines.
Where the Rivers Flow North (1994) features Rip Torn in a Howard Frank Mosher tale of fierce Yankee independence run to ground in 1920s Vermont.
Dead Poets Society (1989), set in a New England prep school, centers on Robin Williams's performance as an inspiring English teacher.
The Bostonians (1984), an elegant Merchant-Ivory production, screens Henry James's tale of propriety's clash with social activism in the 19th-century Hub.
On Golden Pond (1981), filmed at New Hampshire's Squam Lake, was Henry Fonda's final role, as crusty Yankee professor Norman Thayer.

The Last Hurrah (1958), a political drama based on the career of Boston Mayor James M. Curley, features Spencer Tracy as a master of machine politics.
Northwest Passage (1940) features Spencer Tracy as French-and-Indian War hero Major Robert Rogers, in one of cinema's better New England historical dramas; they even got the geography right.

Other Insight Guides

Insight Guide titles cover every major travel destination in North America, from Alaska to Arizona. City titles include Boston, New York, Chicago, and San Francisco. Regional and state titles include New England, USA: On the Road, Arizona and the Grand Canyon, Florida, California, and Alaska.

These are complemented by a comprehensive range of easy-fold **Insight FlexiMaps**, laminated to make them durable and waterproof, and containing useful travel details. Local titles include Florida, Orlando, New York, and San Francisco.

Two compact series cover a range of US destinations:

Insight Step by Step Guides provide precise itineraries and recommendations from a local, expert writer for dining, lodgings, and sightseeing; titles include San Francsico, New York City, and Boston.

Insight Smart Guides are packed with information, arranged in a unique and easy accessible A–Z format. Titles include New York, Orlando, and San Francisco.

BELOW: Mark Wahlberg and George Clooney in *The Perfect Storm*.

ART AND PHOTO CREDITS

INDEX

Main attractions are in bold type

Boston Subway Ⓣ

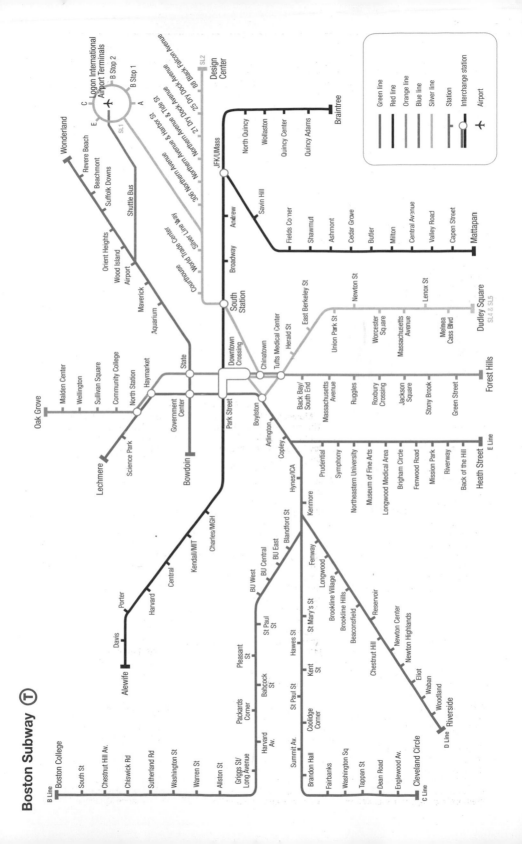